THE LAW OF
BANKING
IN SCOTLAND

Lorne D Crerar, LLB
Partner, Harper Macleod
Lecturer in Law, University of Glasgow

Butterworths
Edinburgh
1997

United Kingdom	Butterworths, a Division of Reed Elsevier (UK) Ltd, 4 Hill Street, EDINBURGH EH2 3JZ and Halsbury House, 35 Chancery Lane, LONDON WC2A 1EL
Australia	Butterworths, SYDNEY, MELBOURNE, BRISBANE, ADELAIDE, PERTH, CANBERRA and HOBART
Canada	Butterworths Canada Ltd, TORONTO and VANCOUVER
Ireland	Butterworth (Ireland) Ltd, DUBLIN
Malaysia	Malayan Law Journal Sdn Bhd, KUALA LUMPUR
New Zealand	Butterworths of New Zealand Ltd, WELLINGTON and AUCKLAND
Singapore	Reed Elsevier (Singapore) Pte Ltd, SINGAPORE
South Africa	Butterworth Publishers (Pty) Ltd, DURBAN
USA	Michie, CHARLOTTESVILLE, VIRGINIA

The moral right of the author has been asserted. A CIP Catalogue record for this book is available from the British Library.

ISBN 0 406 05458 4

Typeset by Phoenix Photosetting, Chatham, Kent
Printed and bound in Great Britain by
Mackays of Chatham PLC, Chatham, Kent

Preface

When I set out to write this text I had intended to provide a guide to banking law in Scotland for my students in the Law School of the University of Glasgow. However, over time my self-imposed remit has rather extended and I have endeavoured to examine the banker/customer relationship and the essential matters which flow from it in a modern and practically relevant fashion. It is my hope that the book is of value to students, practitioners and bankers alike.

The banking market continues to change at pace as do the relationships which emanate from it. I have taken the view that it is important to understand the criticisms which are made with regard to some key elements of the subject together with the consequent proposals for change. It is principally for that reason that there is regular reference to the Jack Committee Report, Law Commission proposals, the banks' codes of practice and the views of the Banking Ombudsman. Some more traditional areas of the subject are not dealt with in substantive detail and may be better found elsewhere. The more testing areas of unjust enrichment and the law relating to floating charges are dealt with in very brief form, but reference is made to the excellent texts which are available. I have, however, endeavoured to cover those matters which I most commonly encounter in banking practice.

I am very grateful to all of those who have assisted me in my research and preparation of the text. In particular, thanks are due to William J Stewart of MacMillans, David A Steel of Dundas & Wilson and Roderick McKenzie of Harper Macleod who have made valuable suggestions for the improvement of the text. As a novice to the world of publishing I am also very appreciative of the assistance of Butterworths.

The full responsibility for all of the shortcomings of the book are mine alone and I have tried to state the law as at the end of January 1997.

Lorne D Crerar
Glasgow
May 1997

Contents

Table of Statutes

Table of Orders, Rules and Regulations

Table of Cases

D

H

M

N

S

PAGE

W

Bibliography

Bank of Scotland — *Bank of Scotland 1695–1995, A Very Singular Institution*

Bell (G J) — *Commentaries on the Law of Scotland and on the Principles of Mercantile Jurisprudence* (7th edn, 1870) (T & T Clark)

Principles of the Law of Scotland (10th edn, 1899) (T & T Clark)

Checkland (S G) — *Scottish Banking: A History 1695–1973* (1975)

Cusine (D J) — *Standard Securities* (1991) (Butterworths)

Ellinger and Lomnicka — *Modern Banking Law* (2nd edn, 1994)

Erskine — *An Institute of the Law of Scotland* (2 vols) (8th edn, 1871)

Gloag and Henderson — *The Law of Scotland* (10th edn, 1995 by W A Wilson, A D M Forte, A F Rodger, Ann Paton and Laura Dunlop) (Greens)

Gloag and Irvine — *The Law of Rights in Security and Cautionary Obligations* (1897)

Gordon (J J) and Mitchell (W A) — *Scottish Banking Practice* (6th edn, 1989) vol 10

Graham Stewart (J) — *The Law of Diligence* (1898) (Greens)

Gretton (G L) — *The Law of Inhibition and Adjudication* (2nd edn, 1996) (Butterworths)

Halliday (J M) — *Conveyancing Law and Practice in Scotland* vols I, 3 (1985) (Greens)

Conveyancing and Feudal Reform (Scotland) Act 1970 (2nd edn, 1977)

Hume — *Lectures* vol IV (Stair Soc vol 17, 1955 ed GCH Paton)

Paget — *Law of Banking* (11th edn, 1996 by M Hapgood QC) (Butterworths)

Stair — *The Institutions of the Law of Scotland* (5th edn, 1832) (reprinted 1981: Edinburgh University Press and Glasgow University Press)

Stair Memorial Encyclopaedia — *The Laws of Scotland: Stair Memorial Encyclopaedia* (vol 2, 1988), (vol 3, 1994), (vol 4, 1991), (vol 12, 1992), (vol 18, 1993), (vol 20, 1992) (Butterworths)

Walker (D M) — *Principles of Scottish Private Law* (4th edn, 1988) vol 3

Wallace and McNeil — *Banking Law* (10th edn, 1991 by D B Caskie) (Greens)

Wilson (W A) — *The Scottish Law of Debt* (2nd edn, 1991) (Greens)

Abbreviations

AC	Law Reports, Appeal Cases (House of Lords and Privy Council) 1890–
ALR	Argus Law Reports (Australia) 1895–1973 and Australian Law Reports 1973–
Ad & El	Adolphus and Ellis's Reports (King's Bench and Queen's Bench) (England) 1834–42
All ER	All England Law Reports 1936–
App Cas	Law Reports, Appeal Cases (House of Lords) 1875–90
B & Ad	Barnewall and Adolphus's Reports (King's Bench) (England) 1830–34
B & C	Barnewall and Cresswell's Reports (King's Bench) (England) 1822–30
B & S	Best and Smith's Reports (Queen's Bench) (England) 1861–70
BCC	British Company Cases 1983–
BCLC	Butterworth's Company Law Cases 1983–
Bell App	S S Bell's Scotch Appeals (House of Lords) 1842–50
Bing NC	Bingham's New Cases (Common Pleas) (England) 1834–40
Bro CC	W Brown's Chancery Reports (England), 4 vols, 1778–94
CA	Court of Appeal
CB	Common Bench (England) 1845–56
CBNS	Common Bench, New Series (England) 1856–65
CLC	CCH Commercial Law Cases
CLR	Commonwealth Law Reports (Australia) 1903–
CLY	Current Law Yearbook 1947–
CMLR	Common Market Law Reports 1962–
COD	Crown Office Digest
CPD	Cape Provincial Division Reports, 1910–46
Camp	Campbell's Reports (Nisi Prius) (England) 1807–16
Ch	Law Reports, Chancery Division (England) 1890–
Ch App	Law Reports, Chancery Appeals (England) 1865–75
Ch D	Law Reports, Chancery Division (England) 1875–90
Cl & Fin	Clark and Finnelly's Reports (House of Lords) 1831–46
Cm	Command Papers 1986–
Cmnd	Command Papers 1956–1986
Com Cas	Commercial Cases 1895–1941
Com LR	Commercial Law Reports 1981–
Cr App Rep	Criminal Appeal Reports (England) 1908–
Crim LR	Criminal Law Review (England) 1954–
D	Dunlop's Session Cases 1838–62
DLR	Dominion Law Reports (Canada) 1912–55; 2d, 1956–67; 3d, 1968–83; 4th 1984–
Dow	Dow's Reports (House of Lords) 1812–18
Drew	Drewry's Reports, Chancery (England) , 4 vols, 1852–59
E & B	Ellis and Blackburn's Reports (Queen's Bench) (England) 1852–58
E & E	Ellis and Ellis's Reports (Queen's Bench) (England) 1858–61
ECR	European Court of Justice Reports 1954–
ER	English Reports 1220–1865

Esp	Espinasse's Nisi Prius Reports (England) 1793–1807
Ex D	Law Reports, Exchequer Division (England) 1875–80
Exch	Exchequer Reports (England) 1847–56
F	Fraser's Session Cases 1898–1906
FC	Faculty Collection (Court of Session) 1752–1825
FCR	Family Court Reporter
FTLR	Financial Times Law Reports
F Supp	Federal Supplement (USA) 1932–
Fam Law	Family Law
GWD	Green's Weekly Digest 1986–
H & C	Hurlstone and Coltman's Reports (Exchequer) (England) 1862–66
HL	House of Lords
HL Cas	House of Lords Cases 1847–66
HLR	Housing Law Reports 1981–
Hare	Hare's Reports, Chancery (England), 11 vols, 1841–53
Hume	Hume's Decisions (Court of Session) 1781–1822
ICLR	International Construction Law Review
IH	Inner House (Court of Session)
ILT	Irish Law Times 1867–
IR	Irish Reports 1893–
JC	Justiciary Cases 1917–
JIB	Journal of the Institute of Bankers
JP	Justice of the Peace Reports (England) 1837–
John & H	Johnson and Hemming's Reports, Chancery (England), 2 vols, 1859–62
KB	Law Reports, King's Bench Division (England) 1900–52
LDAB	Legal Decisions Affecting Bankers
LJ Ex	Law Journal, Exchequer (England) 1831–75
LJ Ch	Law Journal, Chancery (England) 1831–1946
LJCP	Law Journal, Common Pleas (England) 1831–75
LJKB	Law Journal, King's Bench (England) 1900–52
LJQB	Law Journal, Queen's Bench (England) 1831–1900
LQR	Law Quarterly Review 1885–
LR CP	Law Reports, Common Pleas (England) 1865–75
LR Eq	Law Reports, Equity (England) 1865–75
LR Exch	Law Reports, Exchequer (England) 1865–75
LR HL	Law Reports, House of Lords (England and Ireland) 1866–75
LR PC	Law Reports, Privy Council 1865–75
LR QB	Law Reports, Queen's Bench (England) 1865–75
LT	Law Times Reports (England) 1859–1947
Lloyd's Rep	Lloyd's List Law Reports 1951–67; Lloyd's Law Reports 1968–
M	Macpherson's Session Cases 1862–73
M & W	Meeson and Welsby's Reports (England) 1836–73
MPR	Maritime Provinces Reports (Canada), 53 vols, 1930–67
Macl & R	Maclean and Robinson's Scotch Appeals (House of Lords) 1839
Macq	Macqueen's House of Lords Reports 1851–65
Man & G	Manning and Granger's Reports, Common Pleas, 7 vols, 1840–45

Mer	Merivale's Reports (Chancery) (England) 1815–17
Mood & R	Moody and Robinson's Reports, Nisi Prius (England), 2 vols, 1830–44
Mor	Morison's Dictionary of Decisions (Court of Session) 1540–1808
Morr	Morrell's Reports, Bankruptcy, 10 vols, 1884–93
NBR (2d)	New Brunswick Reports, 1949–
NLJ	New Law Journal, 1965–
NSWLR	New South Wales Law Reports, 1971–
OH	Outer House (Court of Session)
OWN	Ontario Weekly Notes, 71 vols, 1909–62
P & CR	Planning and Compensation Reports 1949–67; Property and Compensation Reports 1968– (England)
Pat	Paton's House of Lords Appeal Cases 1726–1821
QB	Law Reports, Queen's Bench Division (England) 1891–1901, 1952–
QBD	Law Reports, Queen's Bench Division (England) 1875–1890
R	Rettie's Session Cases 1873–98
Robin	Robinson's Scotch Appeals (House of Lords) 1840–41
Russ & Ry	Russel and Ryan's Crown Cases Reserved (England), 1 vol, 1800–23
Ry & M	Ryan and Moody's Reports, Nisi Prius (England), 1 vol, 1823–26
S	P Shaw's Session Cases 1821–38
SC	Session Cses 1907–
SCLR	Scottish Civil Law Reports 1987
SLR	Scottish Law Reporter 1865–1925
SJ	Scottish Jurist 1829–73
STC	Simon's Tax Cases 1973–
Sh Ct	Sheriff Court
Sh Ct Rep	Sheriff Court Reports in Scottish Law Review 1885–1963
Sol Jo	Solicitor's Journal (England) 1856–
Sw & Tr	Swabey and Tristram's Reports, Probate and Divorce (England), 4 vols, 1858–65
TLR	Times Law Reports
Taunt	Taunton's Reports (Common Pleas) (England) 1807–19
Term Rep	Term Reports (England) 1785–1800
VLR	Victorian Law Reports (Australia) 1875–96
VR	Victorian Reports (Australia) 1870–72, and 1957–
Ves	Vesey Junior's Reports (Chancery) (England) 1789–1817
W & S	Wilson and Shaw's House of Lords Cases 1825–34
WLR	Weekly Law Reports 1953
WN(NSW)	Weekly Notes (New South Wales), 1884–
WR	Weekly Reporter (England) 1852–1906
WWR	Western Weekly Reports (Canada) 1911–50, and 1955–

Chapter 1

Historical Development of Banking in Scotland

1. THE EARLY YEARS

At the beginning of the seventeenth century the Scottish economy was still at a very formative stage. Being so small, Scotland was considerably affected by larger and more developed economies. Although the influence of France and the Low Countries was important, the proximity of England and the Union of the Crowns had a greater bearing upon the development of the Scottish economy and it was from England that Scotland took its direction.

By the mid-seventeenth century the merchants of London had established a practice of placing their gold and silver in the keeping of the City Goldsmiths for safe keeping. The goldsmiths issued deposit receipts which effectively came to be treated as transferable notes and at the same time began lending moneys on a large scale both to individuals and businesses. It was in this way that an embryonic system of banking developed. In Scotland, by contrast, there were only a few such merchants and development of a banking system was very slow. Nevertheless in Edinburgh at least, the merchants and goldsmiths participated in forms of commercial activity that could be described as very basic banking.

By 1660, bills of exchange as well as forms of security bonds were in existence in Scotland. However, credit instruments were used only by the wealthy, and the remainder of mercantile society, unenlightened as to the value of such documents, would accept payment only in coin and kind, which preserved the simplistic economy and led to vulnerability when there was a shortage of coin. Such shortages were only too evident at the end of the seventeenth century and were to the considerable detriment of the Scottish economy whose difficulties were compounded by the tendency of many Scottish merchants to export precious metals to pay their foreign creditors. Such a practice was particularly prevalent in times of deficient crops when payment for foreign corn required to be immediate.

At this time England was at war with Louis XIV of France and in order to raise the required finance the Bank of England was founded in 1694, promoted by a Scotsman, William Paterson, who lived in London. The sponsors raised capital of £1,200,000 sterling which was to be loaned to the Government in perpetuity at 8 per cent annual interest. The bank was invested with legal personality and awarded a virtual monopoly of the banking market but was prohibited from engaging in general trade. In order to raise the required capital for war with France the bank was authorised to make loans and to deal in bullion and bills of exchange. It was due to the requirement to fund the war with France that the money market in London developed and the English system of banking became established.

By contrast, Scotland although not at war, was experiencing unprosperous times. When England superseded Holland as Europe's great money market, Scotland, through trade and migration, was indirectly affected by the move of power away from its traditional ally to London. Furthermore, the Scots' Parliament was particularly eager to support enterprises which encouraged manufacturing and foreign trade. This general concern for the promotion of economic growth led to the Scottish economy embarking upon two major projects. The first was an attempt to create a Scottish trading entity to rival the East India Company. Such a company was created in 1695, being promoted by an Act of Parliament and was sponsored by the same William Paterson who had promoted the Bank of England. It was known as the 'Darien Company' and is an important milestone in Scottish mercantile evolution. The second major project was the establishment of a public bank in Edinburgh — the Bank of Scotland.

2.   CREATION OF THE BANK OF SCOTLAND

Whilst it was a Scotsman who promoted the Bank of England, perhaps ironically, it is an Englishman who is credited with the foundation of the Bank of Scotland. This Englishman was John Holland, a merchant and employee of the East India Company. He, along with most of the other promoters involved, had a similar background of being trained in the Dutch accounting methods in Holland. They also had a common political interest in the success of the Protestant Settlement under William III (William of Orange) and Queen Mary, who held the thrones of England and Scotland which together with the re-establishment of the Presbyterian Church would, it was believed, bring peace and result in an increase of trade.

Holland formulated a strategy for the creation of the bank. The plan involved the drawing up of a Bill to lay before the Scottish Parliament. The Darien Company and Paterson were hostile to the proposals and attempted to incite opposition. They were, however, unsuccessful in their protests and on 17 July 1695 the Bill was passed and the Bank of Scotland was founded. Holland's formulation has been shown to stand the test of time, for the bank, as well as being the only institution created by the Scottish Parliament to survive to the present day, still trades under its founding document. This is summarised in a history of the bank —

'The nominal capital of the bank was to be £1,200,000 Scots (£100,000 sterling), of which one-third was to be raised in London and the rest in Edinburgh. A Foundation Committee of twelve was authorised, five in Edinburgh and seven in London. The Act specified the books which the Company should maintain for so long as it had a corporate existence but it also included three specific and unique privileges. First, the Company was granted a banking monopoly in Scotland for a period of twenty one years. Second, the Adventurers[1], were granted limited liability; that is to say that, in the event of Company failure, they were liable to lose only the value of their subscription, a benefit not available to most business organisations until the 1856 and 1862 Companies Acts. Third — and in view of the subsequent history of Scotland, a peculiarity — up until 1920 anyone becoming a Proprietor of the Bank could claim Scottish nationality. The likeliest reason for this clause is that it protected English shareholders from prosecution for attempting to break the Bank of England's monopoly, which would have been petty treason'[2].

The strong London banking connection was due to a number of factors, the principal of which was that London was the centre of international trade and without the benefit of English intermediaries, Scottish merchants were in a weak trading position. Furthermore, the Scots currency lacked strength and was subject to extreme fluctuations, due partly to the collapse of the Scottish mint in 1681. By this time moreover, Scottish merchants preferred to make their settlements in sterling, and the growth of paper currency in the form of bills of exchange expressed in sterling provided the security and certainty that Scots coinage could not offer. In addition the Scots economy was further weakened by the dramatic deterioration of climate that occurred from 1695 onwards. Although affecting all of Europe north of the Alps, Scotland was already relatively weak and could ill-afford the crop failures, grain price increases and the near famine that ensued.

The system of dual government between Edinburgh and London was to prove inconvenient and inefficient. It was argued by John Holland, then Governor of the Bank of Scotland, that there required to be a single, effective, control centre in Edinburgh. He persuaded the English partners to consent to the whole number of directors of the bank being chosen out of persons residing in Scotland. In order to acquire such consent, concessions required to be made. The English partners were authorised to set up

'a kind of London court, a business sub-committee and a Thesary sub-committee, thus paralleling the Edinburgh arrangements. The two bodies were to have full and regular exchange of information, with reciprocal arrangements for attendance, though not for voting. In this way the London trustees intended to constitute, in effect, a London office of the bank. The needs to be served in London were numerous: help in the provision of capital operating on the Edinburgh–London exchanges, provision of reports on

1 Ie the original subscribers.
2 *Bank of Scotland 1695–1995, A Very Singular Institution* (1995) p 14.

personal credit-worthiness or on general economic conditions (including government intentions and the business politics of the City of London), and generally acting as correspondents'[1].

In the initial years the bank was concerned largely with the development of effective credit systems — loans were made upon the basis of securing land, making personal pledges and the provision of caution. The bank also extended its lending capacity by accepting deposits, but these were quickly repaid, without the payment of interest. Real progress was made when the bank began to issue its own notes. Paper currency, was not a novel idea, negotiable goldsmiths' notes having been deployed as currency in England, Amsterdam and Northern Italy. The issuing of such Scots notes would allow credit to expand and facilitate repayment. From the beginning the bank determined that it would be prudent to use sterling units in preference to the unreliable Scots pound. The notes were put into circulation by the bank making payment in them to their borrowers.

Two types of bank note were issued; one was negotiable only at the point of issue and bore the name of the payee, thus the bearer could demand payment in cash on sight. The other note could pass from one bearer to another and thus was the direct forerunner of our modern day bank notes. Denominations of £100, £50, £10 and £5 were used. The popularity of such notes was immediate, as apart from being more stable in value than coinage, they were more practical to pass on to others, being lighter and safer than the use of silver or gold. Almost as a direct result, the Adventurers attained high profits and the economy prospered. To facilitate the increase in the use of such notes, as well as to expand the Bank's business, local offices were established in Glasgow, Aberdeen, Dundee and Montrose.

This period of uninterrupted growth was short-lived, for in February 1696 William Paterson returned to Scotland with the Darien Company. His return was not a glorious one. The activities of the Darien Company had infringed the monopolies of the Bank of England and the East India Company in London, whilst Paterson himself was considered by the directors of the Bank of England to have betrayed them. Despite its clouded history, the Darien Company retained a large amount of disposable capital at hand. Due to John Holland's connections with their rivals, the East India Company, the Darien Company treated the Bank of Scotland as little more than a front for their competitors.

These combined factors provided Paterson with the incentive to revive his original intention that the Darien Company should become, in essence, a Scottish bank. The Darien Company began to lend from its excess funds, to charge interest on the loans and to issue notes. In recognition of the potential damage to the Bank of Scotland, its customers presented large quantities of their notes demanding payment in coin. Worse still for the bank, the Darien Company began to buy up vast quantities of the bank's notes in order that they could be accumulated and returned to the bank together with a demand for cash. By August 1696 the bank was facing a liquidity crisis. The possibility of taking legal action against Darien for

1 S G Checkland *Scottish Banking: A History 1695–1973* (1975) pp 29–30.

infringing its banking monopoly was considered by the bank's directors, but was rejected due to fears of an expensive, and probably fruitless, legal action.

To meet the demands for payment, the bank ceased lending and in total called in 30 per cent of its nominal capital. The Adventurers in Edinburgh produced their money promptly but it was not so with their English counterparts, for at this juncture England, for once, was experiencing financial difficulties, the Bank of England partially having suspended its payments and calling up some of its subscribed capital. It transpired, however, that the call for capital by the Bank of Scotland was sufficient to extinguish the demands being made upon the bank but the bank's branch network was closed down in this period of attrition.

The bank had been fortunate that at this time the Darien Company was facing difficulties of its own. Their English supporters had withdrawn after the company had been attacked in both the Houses of Commons and Lords as being harmful to the East India Company and the Kingdom itself. In addition, Paterson had lost control of the company, there were apparent shortfalls in the subscriptions and there were strong rumours of embezzlement. The Darien Company's venture into Scottish banking had been an unsuccessful and unprofitable one and it was for these reasons that it turned its attention to trade and colonisation. By early 1698 the bank succeeded in repaying to its proprietors the last of the called-in capital, leaving the original £100,000 for trading. By 1697 John Holland had returned to England and a new Governor had been appointed. The bank had survived and won the first of Scotland's bank wars but it was not the last that the bank was to face.

The bank made an important and innovative decision in 1704. Until then, the notes issued by the bank were confined to large denominations, the smallest being £5. In this year the Bank began to issue a £1 note which led to a reduction in the use of coinage in smaller transactions. This development was partly the cause of the bank's over-extension of trading which when coupled with the large export of coin south of the border to assist with the financial and political problems there, led to the bank facing its second liquidity crisis. As a result the bank was unable to make payments for six months. However the bank managed to sustain itself through this difficult period and was in a stronger position to face the political and economic merger of Scotland and England which took place with the Act of Union of 1707.

3. THE ACT OF UNION 1707 AND THE EIGHTEENTH CENTURY

Initially, the economy of Scotland was dramatically bolstered by the Union with England. Much of the national debt was to be cleared and those who had lost in the failed attempt at colonisation by the Darien Company were to be compensated. Perhaps most importantly for banking, there was to be reimbursement for the costs and losses incurred in the recoinage of the Scots coin. In addition, sanctions and restrictions imposed upon Scottish merchants, in order to protect their English rivals, were removed. It was generally agreed that the net result of these actions would be a huge flow of coin from England to Scotland. Such a result greatly concerned the directors of the Bank of England, who instead of sending all of the promised sum in coin, sent the majority of it in Exchequer bills. 'Effectively a new paper currency was to be launched in Scotland which was designed, quite deliberately, to challenge the Bank of Scotland's monopoly and extend the Bank of England's operations in Scotland'[1].

The result was that sending coinage to Scotland was delayed. Further, such was the Scots desperation for moneys that they were prepared to accept the English bills, then accept payment on them at a discount, which in reality meant that the Exchequer was sending less value than that agreed upon by the Act of Union. When this became publicly known and it was revealed that the Scottish Privy Council had been abolished, riots broke out and further English bills were refused. The Scottish Commissioners demanded more coinage to settle the most pressing obligations. Concessions were made by both sides but eventually the agreed obligations were fulfilled by the English.

The years which followed were mixed and unsettled politically. This mix was reflected in the new British economy, but the bank prospered comparatively. It was with the onset of the Jacobite rebellion in 1715, in favour of the Old Pretender, that the bank faced its third crisis of liquidity. There was such a demand for cash in this time of uncertainty, that the bank was required to suspend payments for a period of eight months. The bank took several years to recover fully and many years passed before it could match its earlier profits. It is fair to say that the rebellion was to have far greater and longer lasting effects on the bank because in 1716 the bank's monopoly in Scotland came to an end and no renewal was made. Refusal to renew the monopoly was justified by the new British government upon the basis that the bank was a supporter of the Jacobite cause. Such a suggestion was in fact an unsubstantiated and probably groundless allegation[2]. This development was to have dramatic consequences for the future of Scottish banking generally and the Bank of Scotland in particular.

In 1727, a second public bank came into existence in Scotland. Its background and evolution lay partly in the isolation of the Bank of Scotland due to its alleged past Jacobite support. At the same time the new Whig Prime Minister, in order to rally support amongst Scots, wished to be seen to be promoting positive influences in the Scottish economy. It was considered that the creation of a second Scottish public bank might have the desired political effect. It was in this way and working through the medium of an equivalent company (a society of debenture holders, which had the intention of practising banking, had been incorporated by an Act of Parliament in 1724) that a campaign was started with the aim of creating a further bank.

1 *Bank of Scotland 1695–1995* p 33.
2 *Bank of Scotland 1695–1995* p 37.

Despite the objections of the Bank of Scotland, a charter was granted to the new Royal Bank on 31 May 1727. The new bank had an authorised capital of £111,347 sterling with the power to increase this sum by £40,000, a total far greater than the £100,000 authorised for the Bank of Scotland. The new bank was given authority and liberty to exercise all the powers of banking in Scotland. Meanwhile in England the monopoly of the Bank of England was maintained.

The Royal Bank began an immediate attack on the Bank of Scotland. It commenced issuing its own notes of £100, £50, £20, £10, £5 and £1. It also began gathering large amounts of the Bank of Scotland's notes in exchange for its own. These notes were presented in vast and unexpected quantities in order to embarrass the Bank of Scotland should it be unable to pay and thus undermine its solvency. The Royal Bank's strategy was successful and in March 1728 the Bank of Scotland suspended payments and closed its doors to business. However, such action was expensive for the new Royal Bank and in order to avoid collapse, it became aware that an amalgamation might be preferable and cheaper than a head-on battle. In the end merger proposals proved to be unsuccessful, but the temporary retreat had provided the Bank of Scotland with the opportunity to recover and prepare itself for the subsequent banking war that took place whilst the dual system subsisted until 1746.

As damaging as this battle may have been for the banks, it did lead to many developments in banking generally. The Royal Bank took the lead in the competition and began to develop more sophisticated forms of lending. Instead of being reliant upon the then cumbersome heritable bonds, it further refined the system of personal security. It promised customers, on the provision of cautioners, loans on demand up to an agreed limit, rather than by lending purely lump sums. In so doing, they were formulating a basic system of overdraft. Although more risky and complex than the 'traditional' forms of lending it provided far greater flexibility and proved to be very popular and attractive to customers. It was not long before the Bank of Scotland began to emulate this system of lending.

It was at this time that the Bank of Scotland was also providing innovation in the banking market place. On several occasions general bank payments had been stopped and the bank realised their vulnerability and the need to develop some form of self protection. It was this recognition which led to the insertion of an 'optional clause' in their bank notes. Under this clause the bank could pay on their notes on demand, or they could opt to defer payment for six months, paying interest at a stated date. Furthermore, they began accepting deposits, on which they paid an agreed rate of interest and which were repayable at the fixed future date. Both of these innovations were followed at a later date by the Royal Bank.

In the ensuing years the Royal Bank appears to have taken a lead over the Bank of Scotland in its forging of strong connections in London and in Glasgow where wealth and power were gathering due principally to the burgeoning tobacco trade. The Bank of Scotland did not manage to formulate such wide-spread connections and failed in its attempt to re-establish a branch network. Both banks, however, suffered severe losses amidst the political unrest of the second Jacobite rebellion when Prince Charles Edward Stuart challenged the Hanoverians. Recovery was eventually made and progress continued, culminating in 1751 when both banks agreed to accept each other's notes.

In the fifty years since the creation of the Bank of Scotland, the economy of Scotland had changed dramatically. No longer was there such dependence upon coin as there had been previously and banking, although still relatively primitive, was becoming a profitable business venture. It was at this juncture that Scotland moved from dualism to become a multiple banking system with the British Linen Company offering banking services. In addition a large number of private banks were set up in Glasgow, Dundee, Perth and Aberdeen, as well as in Edinburgh. Checkland observes that:

> 'For a brief period [the private banks] relegated the public banks to a secondary role, doing so without the protection of limited liability. The use of bills of exchange was greatly extended in Scotland, a development made possible by the discounting facilities provided by the banks. The cash credit system underwent striking growth. By 1772, by these means, the banking system of Scotland was perhaps the most developed in Europe, ready to respond to the demands of rapid industrialisation'[1].

However, in 1772 the banking community in Scotland sustained a severe setback when the Ayr Bank collapsed as a result of its extensive practice of long-term lending and covering its exposure with short-term borrowing. Many other private banks suffered a similar fate shortly afterwards. In the resulting crisis, Scottish paper was heavily discounted, particularly since the Bank of England refused to negotiate it. Considerable public panic ensued due in no small measure to the fact that in 1772 the Ayr Bank's notes accounted for two-thirds of the notes in circulation in Scotland[2].

It was incumbent upon the two chartered banks, the Bank of Scotland and the Royal Bank to create order and settle panic. They decided to accept the Ayr Bank's notes to the extent of the good security they could provide. In so doing they were relying upon the revenues of the landed estates of the principal proprietors. This state of affairs could not be sustained for long and money was borrowed from the London money market and an Act of Parliament was promulgated, authorising these proprietors to issue redeemable annuities, pledged against the revenues of their estates. In this way the funds necessary to discharge much of the Ayr Bank's debt were realised[3]. Given the unlimited liability of the Ayr Bank, it is estimated that 114 of the 226 partners in the bank became bankrupt as a result of the bank's failure. The consequence was the changing of hands of a great deal of property in Ayrshire and the adjacent counties.

The Scottish banking system survived this arduous time and once again the two chartered banks dominated the market place. The Ayr Bank experience is said to have taught the banks two important lessons.

> 'First, that despite their comparatively limited resources the two Edinburgh chartered banks acting together could in practice operate as a quasi-reserve bank for the whole Scottish system, and therefore could discipline the more aggressive new banks. Second, each realised that it was undercapitalised for

---

1 *Checkland* pp 91–92.
2 *Bank of Scotland 1695–1995* p 63.
3 *Checkland* pp 132.

Scotland's requirements. In 1744 an Act of Parliament permitted Bank of Scotland to double its authorised capital to £200,000. This was called up and available by the beginning of 1775. For one observer of the Ayr Bank disaster the years between 1772 and 1775 were spent reflecting and writing about what he had observed. Adam Smith's The Wealth of Nations appeared in 1776'[1].

4.   GROWTH AND THE GOLDEN AGE OF THE NINETEENTH CENTURY

The nineteenth century proved to be the golden age in the development of banking in Scotland. Between 1776 and 1810 there was steady growth in the banking world. However, after the initial productive reaction to the 1772 calamity, the two chartered banks fell into a period which lacked any great innovation or development. The British Linen Company was lagging behind the two leaders and was becoming more concerned with competing rather than promoting change or progression. Through private banking, Glasgow had become the UK's most important provincial banking centre, but the outbreak of the war of the American Revolution in 1776 all but ended its tobacco connections with the result that banking initiatives were not considered to be the foremost priority.

This period of stagnancy came to an abrupt end in 1810 with the formation of the Commercial Bank of Scotland in Edinburgh. The Commercial Bank was the first joint stock bank in Scotland. As well as having greater capital, larger stockholders and far more branch activity, it was run by men of considerable expertise. The National Bank of Scotland was formed fifteen years later upon the same principles as the Commercial Bank. These new entities jeopardised the dominance of the established banks and were accompanied by a drive in Glasgow to open a series of such joint stock banks, notably the Union (1830), the Western (1832) and the Clydesdale Bank (1838). In addition, the British Linen Company attained a charter in 1813.

In 1810 the first savings bank was opened in the Parish of Ruthwell in Dumfriesshire. Others soon opened throughout the country. The other banks at that time were generally disinclined to accept deposits of less than £10. Scotland was the first country in the world to instigate such a scheme and was the pioneer of the savings movement. As early as 1818 there were 182 independent savings banks in Scotland.

By the mid-nineteenth century the Scottish system stood at the height of its prestige having survived a series of financial disasters and setbacks. The public and joint banks were large by British standards, which was no minor achievement given the relatively small size of the country and population. With the dawn of the savings banks movement, access to banks was no longer limited to the wealthy and those in business and commerce and now became available to a large proportion of the population.

1 *Bank of Scotland 1695–1995* p 65.

Further, the banks played an integral role in the progression of the industrial revolution in the nineteenth century through their financing and lending. The second half of that century witnessed the vast expansion of industrialisation and the growth of urbanisation, with the economy becoming increasingly dependent upon foreign trade. Scotland was now very different from what she has been at the turn of the century, and banking had to develop to meet the new demands placed upon it.

In the past, the growth of banking had primarily involved an increase in the number of institutions offering banking services. At this juncture however, there was far less emphasis placed upon the quantity of banks, with a movement away from regional operations to national ones, in order to fulfil the changing demands placed on them. Amalgamations took place in order to attain scale and stability. Those who could not compete failed — for example, the Western Bank in 1857 and the City of Glasgow Bank in 1878. The net result of these developments was that the overall number of separate banking institutions reduced considerably to ten by 1878.

The failure that year of the City of Glasgow Bank led to yet another banking crisis. It was discovered that for some time, in order to hide the dramatic losses suffered, the directors of the bank had been disclosing false accounts. There followed charges and convictions for fraud against some of the directors. The Scottish banking system was brought into disrepute and the Scottish courts were faced with an enormous volume of litigation as shareholders attempted to avoid liability following the collapse. Furthermore, the public began to distrust bankers generally. As a result, the remaining banks issued statements in an attempt to reassure their customers of their strong position and their honest approach. In recognition of their own weaknesses, they began to exercise a more conservative form of banking. For example, after the incidents of 1878, the banks voluntarily introduced a system of independent auditing of their accounts and balance sheets.

It was apparent to investors, that it was the shareholders of the City of Glasgow Bank who had suffered the greatest loss. The private banks thus faced the dilemma of protecting their shareholders by adopting limited liability (available under the Companies Acts) or preserving public confidence by maintaining unlimited liability. (The three oldest Scottish banks had of course always enjoyed limited liability.) The problem was resolved by the government passing the Companies Act 1879 which introduced the concept of 'reserve liability' whereby subscriptions for additional capital could be acquired without actually being called, except in instances of illiquidity or failure. The remaining private banks, seven in number, adopted the provisions of the Act and added 'limited' to their titles.

It was at this time that some of the Scottish banks opened London offices in order to deal with their English business and thus avoid the inconvenience and expense of requiring to deal through English correspondents. By 1883, seven of the Scottish banks had such London offices and were gathering a number of non-Scottish customers.

There followed two decades of stability in banking. There was little in the way of innovation and competition between the banks seemed to decline. Notable developments during this period included the Caledonian Bank being taken over by the Bank of Scotland in 1907 and the amalgamation of the Town and Country Bank with the North of Scotland

Bank, thus reducing the three northern banks to one. By 1914 the Bank of Scotland was still the leader amongst the Scottish banks, but by the end of this period, the Edinburgh dominance was slightly reduced as Glasgow's relative share of business steadily increased. The Clydesdale Bank had begun to grow in strength, whilst the British Linen Bank fell from its relatively powerful position to being the weakest of the Scottish banks.

5. THE WAR YEARS AND MODERN DEVELOPMENTS OF THE TWENTIETH CENTURY

To meet the feeling of panic sweeping the country during the 1914–18 war, the banks formed a unified front. In order to appease the government, they stayed closed beyond the bank holiday immediately following the declaration of war so that mass withdrawals, made in panic, could be avoided. Distribution of gold was suspended in order to preserve the commodity. Initially loans of 10 per cent of all UK banks' deposits were to be made available to the government for the war effort. This level was increased by July 1915 to 25 per cent of all deposits and by June 1916, the Scottish banks held some £60,000,000 in war loans.

At this time, all staff within the banks were male. Large numbers were called up for military duty which inevitably led to understaffing and overwork. As a response the banks cautiously proceeded to enlist women to work within the system. The move was seen as a temporary one and the woman's role was restricted to the lowest level; thus for positions of greater authority, the banks were dependent upon older men ineligible for military duty.

By the end of the war in 1918 banking had changed considerably. Never before had the commitment to government securities been so high, the Bank of Scotland had weakened, the Royal Bank of Scotland had moved into pole position and the Clydesdale Bank's position had strengthened in the west.

After the economic slump of 1931,

> 'the ability of the banks to lend was drastically curtailed, both by lack of business confidence and by the efforts, especially of the large companies in industry and commerce, to economise on the 5 per cent rate of interest payable on overdrafts by turning to internal finance and providing for their new developments out of accumulated reserves. Moreover, rival forms of finance continued to expand, including the very popular hire-purchase facilities. However, the banks were still the country's most important financial intermediaries and the providers of medium and short-term credit'[1].

This part of the twentieth century witnessed a deceleration in banking growth in comparison to its expansion in the nineteenth century. Nevertheless, facing the social and economic problems of the inter-war depression, the banks showed initiative. The Scottish banks entered into

1 *Checkland* p 569.

discussion with government bodies. Arising from these deliberations, proposals relating to the financing of Scottish agriculture and industry were formulated. However, whilst the government's intentions were to boost the flagging economy, the banks, fearing further losses by lending to companies which would default or fail, were disinclined to promote such schemes positively, preferring instead to limit their involvement to advice and guidance.

This era came to an end on 3 September 1939 with the onset of the Second World War. War had been impending for some time, and few were surprised at its outbreak. Furthermore, as the experience of 1914–18 was in the minds of many, the banks were better prepared than they had been at the outbreak of the First World War. Many of the same problems had to be faced, for example, vastly diminished numbers of staff. This issue was dealt with as before — by the employment of women. However, there were many aspects to this war which had not existed before and in particular there was a continuing fear that Britain might be invaded, and thus contingency plans for the evacuation of the banks were made.

To some extent, staff relations were vastly improved through the war period. For example, those on national service received the same salary they would have earned had they been at work, and, like all employers, the banks were bound by law to guarantee that servicemens' jobs would still be available to them upon their return. (This meant that many of the war-time recruits, being largely women, had temporary positions only.) Bonuses were given to the staff of some banks to meet the increased cost of living and allowances were paid to those members of staff who had lost their homes and possessions as a result of air-raids.

In order to finance the war effort, the banks again required to lend to the government and there was a commensurate reduction in lending to private borrowers. The public began to regard the banks with cynicism, perceiving them as channelling all funds to the state. In response, a Banking Information Service was set up to deal with public relations matters. By the end of the war in 1945 the Royal Bank of Scotland maintained its position as the new leader, whilst the Bank of Scotland fell to third place, behind the Commercial Bank.

In 1945 the banks held large amounts of government debt, as they had at the end of the 1914–18 war. Inflation was running high and the economy was growing. In 1946 the Bank of England was nationalised, with the result that, through this institution, the Treasury could control all banking, including that within Scotland. Thereafter, the Governor and the Board of Directors of the Bank of England were Crown appointments.

In Scotland between the years of 1946 and 1958 the banks were largely concerned with post-war reconstruction. Lending, sometimes on a relatively high-risk basis, was encouraged and practised in an attempt to boost the economy. Indeed, the government and banks co-operated to found the Industrial and Commercial Finance Corporation and the Finance Corporation for Industry. These organisations were set up in order to provide longer term finance for small to medium size businesses. The 1950s witnessed a number of amalgamations between the Scottish banks (following the English initiative). In 1950 the Clydesdale Bank and the North of Scotland Bank merged, as did the Bank of Scotland with the Union Bank in 1953, and the National with the Commercial Bank in 1958.

In 1952, with expenses mounting, due to increasing salaries, pensions, property maintenance and amenities, the banks all reached a decision to introduce a system of bank charges like that of England.

Notwithstanding these developments further and more dramatic change was required. The government decided to instigate a comprehensive examination of the working of the UK's monetary system. The Radcliffe Committee was appointed in 1957 with one of its two economist members being Professor A K Cairncross of the University of Glasgow.

The combined effect of the Radcliffe Report, sustained economic growth and massive social change led to an acceleration in banking development. Joint stock banking was subjected to extensive government controls and as the relative wealth of the population increased, so too did the demand for banking facilities. These factors led to the gap in the 'banking' market being filled by the secondary banking sector. Checkland says:

> 'Perhaps the most important element in the secondary sector were the merchant banks. They greatly extended their lending and promotional services, often attracting deposits that might have gone to the joint-stock banks, taking these on a time basis at a somewhat higher rate of interest and relending them in a highly flexible manner, also at a higher rate and on various terms. The merchant banks thus supplied advances for many businesses which the banks, under official constraints were obliged to decline. The merchant banks performed a second range of functions, especially in company formation and in carrying through mergers and take-overs. This brought them into very intimate contact with industry and commerce and its financial needs; they were both marriage brokers and midwives. This second group of activities when combined with banking functions of borrowing and lending placed the merchant bankers in a strong position'[1].

However, no Scottish merchant banks were opened, although in the late 1960s and early 1970s, some of the London based merchant banks did open branch offices in Scotland. Their introduction coincided with the Scottish oil boom and the merchant banks had the advantage of size, international relations and consortium structure which enabled them to deal with the oil industry more effectively than the joint-stock banks. Inevitably, however, the transactions involved were so vast that they required inter-bank collaboration, which lead to communication and inter-action between the merchant banks and the joint-stock banks.

Further competition arrived from various sources, for example the Post Office, building societies and insurance companies. It became clear that the banks had to react quickly in order to keep their customers and attract new ones. This they did by extending the services which were available within the bank in order to meet many of the 'novel' services offered to the public by the rival institutions; for example unsecured personal loans. Perhaps more importantly and certainly more effectively, many of the banks began to act through specialist subsidiary companies. In this way the banks were then able to offer all the facilities of the merchant banks as well as those of the finance and hire-purchase companies.

This era also marked a further reduction in the number of Scottish banks. In 1969 the Royal Bank of Scotland and the National Commercial

1 *Checkland* p 660.

Bank merged, with the Bank of Scotland and the British Linen Bank merging in 1971. The amalgamations were in recognition of the need for less costly larger-scale units in order that the Scottish banks could feasibly stand aside their English contemporaries as well as compete with the rival institutions. The result was that Scotland was left with three clearing banks: the Royal Bank of Scotland, the Bank of Scotland and Clydesdale Bank. The Trustee Savings Bank joined their ranks some time later, following upon re-organisation under the Trustee Savings Banks Act 1985 which provided for the transfer of assets and liabilities of the individual trustee savings banks into a new entity — Trustee Savings Bank Scotland plc.

The late 1970s and 1980s witnessed considerable growth in statutory regulation of the provision of banking services — the Banking Acts of 1979 and 1987 and the Building Societies Act 1986. All of these statutes were reflective of a perceived need to enhance the supervision of banks, improve the law relating to securities and investments and better protect depositors and investors. A mood was developing that the technological changes in banking systems were so great that further consideration of the law relating to banking services should be considered.

In this age of consumerism there was pressure to examine the body of statute law and precedent which covered the actual mechanics of banking and the relationships which flow from it (for example the Bankers' Books Evidence Act 1879, the Bills of Exchange Act 1882 and the Cheques Act 1957) but did not concern itself with regulation and supervision. The government in appointing an independent review of banking services law in January 1987 took the view that although UK banking law had withstood the test of time, the nature of banking had changed beyond recognition since the foundation statutes were drafted and that it would be valuable to have a full and coherent review of the law relating to banking mechanisms and practices.

The Treasury subsequently declared the terms of reference of the independent review body to be:

> '... [the examination of] the statute and common law relating to the provision of banking and business customers, including payment and remittance services; but excluding taxation, company law and parts of the law whose relevance is to trading or to the provision of services in general rather than particularly to banking'[1].

It is revealing that at the very outset the review committee made it clear that the inquiry into banking services law did not arise from any deep public disquiet but rather from the impetus of a general concern of banks and their customers that the present framework of banking law was inadequate to meet the problems posed by technological and general banking developments. In February 1989 the committee, chaired by Professor Robert Jack of Glasgow University, presented its report which was very wide ranging in its recommendations.

---

1 *Report of the Review Committee on Banking Services: Law and Practice* (the Jack Report) (Cm 622) (1989) para 1.01.

The committee's report is generally credited with many of the recent improvements in the provision of banking services to personal and business customers. One of the most important recommendations was the promulgation of the Good Banking Code which was a voluntary code of practice to be observed by banks, building societies and card issuers when dealing with customers. The code appeared in its first form in December 1991 and was prepared by the British Bankers' Association in conjunction with the Association for Payment Clearing Services and the Building Societies Association[1]. The principal objective of the code was to promote good banking practice in relations with personal customers and came into effect on 16 March 1992. The code was reviewed and the second edition came into force on 28 March 1994[2]. The third revision of the code is due to be completed by March 1997. The Scottish clearing banks have also issued their own codes of practice which are based upon the principles of the 'good practice code'[3].

A further and very important development in the supervision of banking services was the establishment on 1 January 1986 of the Banking Ombudsman Scheme. This was established upon the initiative of the clearing banks and was established 'to facilitate the satisfaction, settlement or withdrawal of complaints about banking services'. The scheme is, however, entirely voluntary and has no statutory basis although all the main clearers, the Bank of England and other banks with personal customers are members. Member banks agree to be bound by decisions of the Ombudsman although the complainer retains the right to pursue legal action if dissatisfied with the outcome. The scheme is confined to private borrowers or small companies with a turnover of less than £1million a year[4].

It is no surprise that there has been such an extension of statutory and voluntary regulation due to the enormous pace of change in the numbers using the banking system and the extension of customers' expectation of services. The Jack Committee noted:

> 'Of changes that have already taken place, or are at least largely complete, by far the most important, underlying all the rest, has been the vast increase in the banking population, from around 30 per cent of the adult population holding accounts with financial institutions in 1959 to around 87 per cent in 1984. This growth, now generally believed to be at, or approaching its limit,

---

1 In relation to modern clearing controls and supervision, see ch 8 below.
2 The major differences between the first and second editions of the Good Banking Code were:
   - requirement to provide customers with regular statements of account (para 4.6)
   - pre-notification of charges (para 5.3)
   - provision of information about credit interest to customers (para 6)
   - provision with regard to disclosure to Credit Reference Agencies (para 8.3)
   - definition of status enquiries (para 9)
   - requirement to advise whether a guarantee or third party security is limited or unlimited (para 14.1 (ii)).
3 For examples of Codes of Practice, see Appendix 1 below.
4 For a further description of the scheme, see ch 2, pp 40 and 41 below.

can be seen as a symptom of rising living standards under the policies of successive post-war governments. For much of this time, certainly, rising inflation was a contributory cause, but the banks themselves were acting in trying to push the banking habit down the social spectrum. Many of the newly banked turned initially to the trustee savings banks whose development and eventual merger to form the TSB group of today illustrates the growing public demand for a wider range of more sophisticated banking services'[1].

With the growth of numbers of users of the banking system, expectation as to the nature and extent of service has also expanded which has led to its own difficulties. The Jack Committee's view of expectation of customers and delivery of banking services was:

'Where, to conclude our survey, does all this leave the banking–customer relationship? Under constant scrutiny from Stock Market analysts, banks have inevitably become more sharply commercial in their outlook towards customers. The bank manager has moved away from his role as trusted financial adviser, the "man of business" to that of a salesman of a whole range of products and services. Automation has further depersonalised the relationship putting it upon a more formal basis of contract. While high standards of service are generally maintained — despite occasional complaints of failing standards in certain areas — customers could be said to have found a new, less patient, attitude taking over from the "friendly paternalism" of the past; increasingly they have become parties to a business relationship little different from any other. For the private customer, the halcyon simplicity of the pre-war era may be thought to have gone forever — a lost Eden'[2].

An understanding of the historical development of banking in Scotland leads to the conclusion that the law and the relationships which flow from it are constantly changing. It is sensible to assume that the forces of change into the next century are likely to radically alter banking services and methods of delivery. The important judgment of Salmon J In *Woods v Martins Bank Ltd*[3] should serve as a constant reminder that change in the banker–customer relationship will be the rule rather than the exception.

1 Jack Report, para 2.20.
2 Jack Report, para 2.31.
3 [1959] 1 QB 55, [1958] 3 All ER 166. For full discussion, see p 43 below.

Chapter 2

The Legal Framework of Banking and its Supervision

1. INTRODUCTION

The legal framework of banking is composed of a mixture of elements:

> 'Statute law relating to banking services is limited, and mostly of venerable age; what exists is largely of a technical character, concerned with the usage of cheques and bills of exchange. Thus, the banker–customer relationship has been largely left to implied contract, whose terms have been elucidated by a patchwork of judicial decisions. Much of this case law is again some-what ancient, and has changed remarkably little over time. Until fairly recently, there had been scant use of express contractual terms agreed between the parties concerned'[1].

1 *Report of the Review Committee on Banking Services: Law and Practice* (the Jack Report) (Cm 622) (1989) para 2.07.

Three components emerge from this description. The first is statute law. The Bills of Exchange Act 1882 was a codification of the law relating to bills of exchange and remains the main statutory authority for most forms of negotiable instrument and cheque usage. The rapid post-war growth in cheque circulation led to the creation of the Cheques Act 1957, an important statute enacted as a result of considerable lobbying by the banking community and which resulted in the removal of the general need for cheque indorsement, as well as extending the protection of collecting bankers in circumstances where they had acted in good faith and without negligence. Statutes less integral to the law of banking, but nonetheless important, include: the Bankers' Books Evidence Act 1879; the Building Societies Act 1986; the Banking Acts 1979 and 1987; and the Cheques Act 1992[1].

The second component of the legal framework is implied contract which has arisen by way of course of trade and practice and has been elucidated in court decisions[2]. Perhaps the best example is the fundamental principle of the banker's duty of confidentiality to his customer which derives from our general body of common law and has been declared in modern case law[3].

The third component, express contract, is a more modern phenomenon and is symptomatic of the move towards a more arms-length relationship between banker and customer. It is not uncommon for banks to determine express terms, for example, in instances where the bank issues a cheque card or credit card or opens a special credit facility. Further, until banks began circulating their own codes of practice, the use of any express terms by them was the exception rather than the rule in banking contracts.

The codes[4], however, are evidence of a move to lay down in express written form the respective rights and duties of the parties to the banking contract[5]. It is also necessary to ensure compliance with the standard of best practice, which requires a bank in any communication with its customer relative to the terms of the contract, to ensure he is given a fair and balanced view of those terms, and of the rights and obligations which exist on each side[6].

---

1 See *HM Advocate v Burns* 1967 JC 15, 1967 SLT 170; the Bank Notes (Scotland) Act 1845; the Currency and Bank Notes Act 1954; and the Coinage Act 1971.
2 Eg *Joachimson v Swiss Bank Corpn* [1921] 3 KB 110, CA; *Royal Bank of Scotland v Skinner* 1931 SN 66, 1931 SLT 382, OH; *Macdonald v North of Scotland Bank* 1942 SC 369, 1942 SLT 196.
3 *Tournier v National Provincial and Union Bank of England* [1924] 1 KB 461, CA.
4 See examples in Appendix 1 below.
5 In instances where banks do choose to set out their terms and conditions in express contracts, care must be taken to ensure that they comply with the Unfair Contract Terms Act 1977 and EC Council Directive 93/13 (OJ L95, 21.4.93, p 29) on unfair terms in consumer contracts.
6 Jack Report, para 6.25; Code of Banking Practice *Good Banking* (2nd edn) para 4.1.

2. WHAT CONSTITUTES 'A BANK'

The diversity of banking institutions in the UK is such that it has never been considered necessary to clearly distinguish banks from other financial institutions. It is not a requirement for authorised institutions under the Banking Act 1987 (the 1987 Act)[1] to be 'banks' and perhaps strangely, no useful definitions of 'bank' have emerged from the numerous statutory provisions relating, and directly ancillary, to the law of banking[2].

It is generally agreed that there are three cardinal principles laid down by the courts in deciding the common law definition of 'a bank'. Broadly, these three principles are:

(1) The meaning of 'bank' and 'banking business' may change from time to time. What was 'banking business' in 1918 is not necessarily the same in 1958, which was the analogy used in *Woods v Martins Bank Ltd*[3].

(2) What is considered to be a 'bank' or 'banking business' in one jurisdiction may not be considered so in another. The most commonly quoted examples are the jurisdictions of Ireland[4] and Australia[5] where an organisation which accepts money from the public to relend it, still carries on a banking business even though it does not operate current account cheque drawing facilities.

(3) A number of cases also stress the importance of reputation in assessing whether or not to consider an institution a 'bank'.

The leading case upon the status of what is or is not a 'bank' is *United Dominions Trust Ltd v Kirkwood*[6] in which the plaintiffs claimed that as bankers they were exempt from the provisions of the Moneylenders Acts. The Court of Appeal defined three characteristics usually found in a banker's business:

(a) accepting money from and collecting cheques for customers and paying the cheques to the customers' credit;

(b) honouring cheques or orders drawn on them by their customers when presented for payment and debiting their customers' accounts accordingly; and

(c) keeping current accounts, or something of that nature, in their books in which the credits and debits are entered[7].

Beyond considering its business activities, the crucial element in determining whether or not an institution is a bank is the reputation of the institution concerned[8].

---

1 See the 1987 Act, s 3.
2 See eg the Bills of Exchange Act 1882, s 2; the Cheques Act 1957, s 1; the Solicitors (Scotland) Act 1980, s 35(2); the Banking Act 1987, Sch 6, para 1; and the Income and Corporation Taxes Act 1970, ss 107, 159(1)(b).
3 See [1959] 1 QB 55 at 70, per Salmon J.
4 *Commercial Banking Co Ltd v Hartigan* (1952) 86 ILT 109.
5 *Melbourne Corpn v Commonwealth of Australia* (1947) 74 CLR 31.
6 [1966] 2 QB 431, [1966] 1 All ER 968, CA.
7 See [1966] 1 All ER 968 at 975, CA, per Lord Denning, MR.
8 [1966] 1 All ER 968 at 980, CA, per Lord Denning, MR, though cf Harman LJ at 983.

This Court of Appeal decision does not remove the confusion of the numerous considerations as to the criteria of qualification of a bank for different purposes. The problem of definition was greatly ameliorated however by the Banking Acts of 1979 and 1987. The principal purpose of both Acts was the regulation of the taking of banking deposits, which is only one of the bankers' functions. However, the Acts contain a prohibition upon the use of the words 'bank' or 'banking' or the carrying on of 'banking business' by anyone except 'an authorised institution' and go a long way to meet the danger of such words being used to mislead the public as to the standing of the organisation[1].

The modern position is not entirely satisfactory. The Banking Acts provide for some exceptions to the general rules and in particular some overseas financial institutions may in certain circumstances use the names by which they are known in their own countries notwithstanding that they would not qualify to do so in the UK. Questions may still arise as to the scope of the important terms of 'banks' or 'banking' but it is clear that the courts will have in mind the three cardinal principles as described together with the wider criteria of the Banking Acts, where appropriate.

The discussion of the ambit of the terms 'bank' and 'banking' is important because there exist several statutes which use these terms without positive direction as to their definition. Further, there are rights under common law and statute which are available to a person by virtue of being a bank or banker, which include the banker's lien, the banker's right of set-off and the defences available to banks for cheques drawn upon them in terms of the Bills of Exchange Act 1882, as supplemented by the Cheques Act 1957. Statute also makes provision for investment of funds on behalf of third parties with banks only (for example, Solicitors (Scotland) Accounts Rules); and the Bankers' Books Evidence Act 1879, provides privileges to banks in relation to the supply of banks' ledgers or record books which include information which is required in legal proceedings.

Ellinger and Lomnicka in *Modern Banking Law*[2], state their view:

> 'It is believed that, where a statute fails to define a "bank" in clear terms, it is safest to examine, on the basis of the spirit of the Act as a whole, whether the word is to be understood in the narrow or in a wide sense. Where an Act exempts "banks" from onerous provisions applicable in the case of particularly sensitive transactions, it stands to reason that the provision applies to a restricted group of outstanding bodies such as institutions entitled to be called or described as banks. Where the Act regulates a widely defined transaction, it is safe to construe the term "bank" in its broader sense. To avoid ambiguity, it is desirable that Parliament clarify the position by adding suitable definitions to any Act with a lacuna'.

It is generally accepted, however, that major reform is practically unattainable and the word 'bank' has been, and will continue to be, used to describe wide-ranging groups of businesses which are not necessarily united by a common thread. It is sensible that the law recognises the existing and developing diversifications and in times of constant change, definition of the term 'a bank' would be more obstructive than constructive. It

---

1 See pp 25 and 26 below.
2 Ellinger and Lomnicka *Modern Banking Law* (2nd edn, 1994) p 83.

is difficult to envisage with certainty the extent of the range of services which will be provided by banks in the year 2000.

3.   BANKING INSTITUTIONS IN THE UK

(1)   THE BANK OF ENGLAND

The Bank of England is the pre-eminent bank in the UK. Founded in 1694, the Bank of England was originally established for the purpose of financing a war against France[1]. Thereafter, the bank established itself as a successful joint stock company until the Bank of England Act 1946, by which it became a nationalised government institution. Despite its name, the Bank of England is the central bank of the UK and it has powers for the sole issue of bank notes in England and Wales. Since the Banking Act 1979, the Bank of England has been at the head of a system designed to regulate deposit taking businesses[2].

(2)   CLEARING BANKS

A clearing bank is a bank which is a member of the British Banker's Clearing House and clears cheques for its customers. There are four main English clearing banks: National Westminster, Lloyds, Midland and Barclays Bank. There are a number of smaller clearing banks now operating in England and Wales which include: Abbey National, Girobank, Standard Chartered Bank, Co-operative Bank and TSB Bank (the group of TSB banks now being a subsidiary of Lloyds Bank). The Scottish clearing banks (Bank of Scotland, Clydesdale Bank, Royal Bank of Scotland and TSB Bank Scotland) carry out the same functions of clearing cheques and have close relations with the English banks. Unlike their English counterparts, the Scottish banks (with the exception of TSB Bank Scotland) retain the right to issue bank notes[3].

(3)   TRUSTEE SAVINGS BANKS

The first savings bank in the UK was established in 1810[4]. A savings bank was defined as

---

1   See ch 1, p 2 above.
2   See pp 25 ff below.
3   For development and structure of Scottish clearing banks, see ch 1, pp 2 ff above. The issue and circulation of bank notes in Scotland are governed by the Bank Notes (Scotland) Act 1845, the Currency and Bank Notes Act 1954 and the Coinage Act 1971 as amended.
4   See ch 1, p 9 above.

'a society formed in the UK, the Isle of Man or any of the Channel Islands for the purpose of establishing and maintaining an institution in the nature of a Bank — (i) to accept deposits of money for the benefit of the persons making the deposits and deposits of money for a trustee, and (ii) to accumulate the produce of the deposits (so far as not withdrawn) at compound interest, and (iii) to return the deposits and produce to the depositors after deducting any necessary expenses of management but without deriving any benefit from the deposits or produce'[1].

Under the Trustee Savings Banks Act 1985, a scheme was implemented to restructure the existing savings banks into one public limited company with four subsidiaries, one each for England and Wales, Scotland, Northern Ireland and the Channel Islands[2]. The relationship between the Trustee Savings Bank and its depositors was the subject of two important House of Lords cases, namely *Ross v Lord Advocate*[3] and *Trustee Savings Banks Central Board v Vincent*[4] in which it was held that TSB depositors had no interest in the surplus and were only entitled to their deposit with interest.

(4)   MERCHANT BANKS

A merchant bank is difficult to define but is loosely known as any deposit-taking or lending institution which does not fit neatly into any other category of bank[5]. The majority of merchant banks operate upon a single office system rather than through a network of branches and are situated mostly in the City of London but some have offices in the main provincial cities[6]. Although in practice there is much overlap, merchant banks are known either as accepting houses or issuing houses. Accepting houses are members of the Accepting Houses Committee and their business activities are wide, including foreign exchange dealings, money and investment management, financing capital ventures, capital issues, stockbroking and bullion transactions. Issuing houses are members of the Issuing Houses Association and are concerned mainly with offering financial expertise to large industrial companies, advising on matters such as raising finance, mergers, takeovers and capital reorganization. Under the Banking Act 1987, it is an offence for an organisation to use the term 'merchant bank' or 'merchant banking' unless the institution is exempted from the prohibition against deposit-taking[7].

---

1 Trustee Savings Banks Act 1981, s 1(3)(a).
2 See ch 1, p 14 above.
3 1986 SC (HL) 70, 1986 SLT 602.
4 [1986] 3 All ER 79, [1986] 1 WLR 1077, HL.
5 The largest and best known being Brown Shipley & Co and NM Rothschild & Sons.
6 For an account of development of merchant banking, see JJ Clay and BS Wheble *Modern Merchant Banking* (3rd edn, 1990).
7 Banking Act 1987, s 4.

(5)   FOREIGN AND OVERSEAS BANKS

The foreign banks are largely situated in London, reflecting that city's importance as a centre of international banking. Most major world banks have offices in the City of London. Banks in this category are members of one of four organisations: (1) the Foreign Banks and Securities Houses Association[1]; (2) the British Overseas and Commonwealth Banks Association; (3) the American Bankers Association of London; or (4) the Japanese Banks Association. Many overseas banks have branches in Scotland.

(6)   THE NATIONAL SAVINGS BANK

The National Savings Bank, formerly called the Post Office Savings Bank, was established by the Post Office Act 1969[2]. It accepts deposits through the Post Office and allows withdrawals of not more than £50 on demand at any Post Office branch. The National Savings Bank is part of the National Savings Movement and its deposits are passed on to the National Debt Commissioners, who in turn invest the money in government securities. Its business is to accept deposits from the public which can be as little as £1 (or £5 in the case of investment deposit) but cannot exceed £10,000. The bank is regulated by the National Savings Bank Act 1971 and is outside the ambit of the regulatory provisions of the Banking Act 1987.

(7)   GIROBANK

The Girobank, previously known as the National Girobank, was established by virtue of the Post Office Act 1969. It was established to simplify and modernise the transmission of money through the Post Office and restricted its original activities to offering money transfer facilities. The services offered include money transfer, standing orders, personal loans, cheque cards, deposit accounts and travel facilities. Although most of its customers are individuals there is a vehicle for the corporate business of National Girobank, namely Girobank plc, founded in 1985. In view of its history, Girobank's branches were located in Post Offices, but the close connection with the Post Office network was considerably diluted when the ownership of Girobank was acquired by the Alliance and Leicester Building Society on 2 July 1990. Girobank is an 'authorised institution' within the terms of the Banking Act 1987.

---

1   This association superseded the Foreign Banks Association and has the largest membership of any of the financial houses in the city (in excess of 150 members and over 30 associate members). All foreign banks and security houses which operate in the UK under their own name for an office located here are entitled to full membership. Foreign banks not carrying on business in the UK but having a representative office are entitled to associate membership.
2   Post Office Act 1969, s 94(1).

(8)   DISCOUNT HOUSES

The discount houses specialise in discounting bills of exchange, treasury bills and the placing of money on the short-term market. Their funds are obtained by borrowing, mainly from the commercial banks, at a slightly lower rate of interest than they can charge for discounting bills. A high proportion of the bills are short-term Treasury bills by which the government raises short-term finance. Eight discount houses operate in the City of London and they are members of the London Discount Market Association[1]. They are authorised institutions within the terms of the Banking Act 1987 and all have the status of recognised banks under the Banking Act 1979.

(9)   THE BRITISH BANKERS' ASSOCIATION

The principal objective of the British Bankers' Association is to facilitate a forum for discussion of matters of interest to the UK banks and to make representations on their behalf. The association focuses areas of concern for the banking community and effects representations on its behalf to the Bank of England, government opinion formers and other interested parties. The association represents the UK in the European Banking Federation, and has close working relationships with similar overseas associations and regulators as a means to promote the interests of its members. Full membership is available to all banks with their head office in the UK and also to a UK branch or subsidiary of a bank with a head office in another European Union country. All banks authorised under the Banking Act 1987 which do not qualify for full member status are entitled to associate membership. The association represents over three hundred banks from more than sixty countries. It is the principal trade association for the banking and financial services industry. It is evidence of the character of London as the world's leading international banking centre that in 1996 17 per cent of the Association's members had their corporate headquarters in the UK. More than 60 per cent of the Association's members have their head offices outside the European Union. The size of the members of the Association greatly vary. However over 50 per cent of the membership have less than one hundred staff in the UK. Approximately 15 per cent of the membership offers a retail or personal customer banking business in the UK[2].

4.   THE SUPERVISION OF BANKING

There are several tiers of supervision of the institutions generally termed 'banks'.

---

1   The largest and most prominent discount house is Gerrad & National Ltd.
2   Full information about the association may be obtained from British Bankers' Association, Pinners Hall, 105-108 Old Broad Street, London, EC2N 1EX.

(1) STATUTORY REGULATION OF DEPOSIT-TAKING BUSINESS

Authorisation of institutions

The banking supervision system is contained in the Banking Act 1987 which superseded the Banking Act 1979[1]. The 1987 Act is primarily concerned with regulating the acceptance of deposits in the course of a deposit-taking business. The Bank of England ('the Bank') has the regulatory powers conferred upon it by the Act and has the duty to supervise the institutions authorised by it in the exercise of those powers[2]. This duty exists over and above its other specific regulatory functions and powers. It is also the duty of the Bank to keep under review the operation of the Act and developments in banking which appear to it to be relevant to the exercise of its powers and the discharge of its duties[3].

The legislation required the Bank to establish as soon as possible after 1 October 1987, a committee to be known as the Board of Banking Supervision. The Board consists of three ex officio members (the Bank's Governor, the Deputy Governor and the Executive Director of the Bank responsible for the supervision of institutions authorised under the Act) and six independent members[4]. It is the duty of the independent members to give such advice as they think fit to the ex officio members regarding the exercise by the Bank of its statutory functions under the Act and on any matter relating to or arising out of the exercise of those functions[5]. It is likewise the duty of the ex officio members to report to the Chancellor of the Exchequer in those instances where it is decided by the Bank that the advice of the independent members should not be followed. To this duty is added the explicit right for the independent members to approach the Chancellor giving reasons for their advice[6].

The provision which is the cornerstone to the supervisory system is section 3 of the Act. This section places an absolute prohibition on the acceptance of deposits by a person carrying on a business which, for the purposes of the Act, is a deposit-taking business, unless that person is an institution for the time being so authorised by the Bank. A 'deposit' means

'a sum of money paid on terms — (a) under which it will be repaid with or without interest or a premium, and either on demand or at a time or in circumstances agreed by or on behalf of the person making the payment and the person receiving it; and (b) which are not referable to the provision of property or services or the giving of security'[7].

In *SCF Finance Co Ltd v Masri (No 2)*[8] the Court of Appeal held that money paid to the plaintiffs in connection with dealings in the commodity futures

---

1 The 1979 Act was enacted to deal with the uncertainty of the market following the secondary banking crisis and to implement the First Banking Co-ordination Directive (ie EC Council Directive 77/780 (OJ L322, 17.12.77, p 30) which aimed at harmonising controls and procedure for authorising credit taking institutions throughout Europe.
2 1987 Act, s 1(1).
3 s 1(2).
4 s 2(2).
5 s 2(3).
6 s 2(5).
7 ss 5(1) and 5(2).
8 [1987] QB 1007, [1987] 1 All ER 175, CA.

market was not accepting of deposits under the Act as it related to the provision of services by the plaintiffs. A business is a 'deposit-taking business' if '(a) in the course of business money received by way of deposit is
lent to others; or (b) any other activity of the business is financed, wholly
or to any material extent, out of the capital of or the interest on money
received by way of deposit'[1].

The Bank cannot grant an application for authorisation unless satisfied
that the criteria specified in Schedule 3 to the Act are fulfilled with respect
to the applicant[2]. These criteria broadly provide as follows. Firstly, every
director, controller or manager of the institution must be a fit and proper
person to hold that particular position. Regard is had to the person's probity, competence, judgment, diligence, honesty, propriety and previous
conduct. Consideration is also given as to whether the interest of depositors are, or are likely to be, threatened by his or her tenure. Secondly, at
least two individuals must effectively direct the business (the so-called
'four eyes' rule) and thirdly, in the case of an institution incorporated in
the UK, the directors must include such number of directors without
executive responsibility for the management of its business as the Bank
considers appropriate having regard to the circumstances of the institution and the nature and scale of its operations.

The criteria for authorisation are relevant in two important situations.
Firstly, the Bank must decide at the outset whether to authorise an institution to carry on the business of accepting deposits. Secondly, if, following authorisation, it appears to the Bank that the criteria have not been or
are not being fulfilled, the Bank has two courses of action available. The
first course is to revoke the institution's authorisation. The Bank has
power to revoke authorisation in a very wide range of circumstances
broadly related to the taking of deposits. The primary object is to seek to
protect the institution's depositors[3]. The power of revocation is also exercisable in other circumstances relating to the non-acceptance of deposits[4]
and includes for example, instances where there has been the revocation
of an authorisation granted under the Financial Services Act 1986[5]; the
making of compositions or arrangements with creditors[6], the appointment
of a receiver or manager[7], the taking possession of property subject to a
charge in favour of debenture holders[8], and the making of an administration order under the Insolvency Act 1986[9]. The Bank must revoke the
authorisation of an institution, wherever incorporated, where it appears
to the Bank that a winding-up order has been made against it in the UK or
a resolution for its voluntary winding up in the UK has been passed[10].

1   1987 Act, s 6(1).
2   s 9(2).
3   s 11(1).
4   s 11(2).
5   s 11(4).
6   s 11(7)(a).
7   s 11(7)(b).
8   s 11(7)(c).
9   s 11(8).
10 s 11(6).

The second course of action is to restrict the authorisation. Where it appears to the Bank that there are grounds on which the Bank's power to revoke an institution's authorisation are exercisable, but the circumstances are not such as to justify revocation, the Bank may restrict the authorisation instead of revoking it[1]. An authorisation may be restricted by limiting its duration and/or by imposing such conditions as the Bank thinks desirable for the protection of the institution's depositors or potential depositors[2]. The Bank could, for example, require the institution to take certain steps or to refrain from adopting or pursuing a particular course of action or to restrict the scope of its business in a particular way or impose limitations on the acceptance of deposits, the granting of credit or the making of investments.

The Bank was required as soon as practicable after 1 October 1987 to publish a statement of principles in accordance with which it will act (1) in interpreting the criteria specified in Schedule 3 and the grounds of revocation specified in section 11, and (2) in exercising its power to grant, revoke or restrict an authorisation[3]. In May 1988, the Bank issued its first statement of principles and its general approach to section 11 was set out in paragraph 4.2:

> 'In general, the Bank's powers become exercisable when there is a threat to the interests of depositors and potential depositors. The threat may be relatively slight or remote or it may be both immediate and serious. The Act recognises that the immediacy and severity of such threats may vary but, as a general rule, the Bank is given discretion to decide whether to revoke, impose restrictions or take some other action'.

If the Bank makes a material change in these principles it must incorporate a statement of the change in the annual report made under section 1(3) of the Act[4].

The Act provides a notification procedure in section 13 for instances where the Bank proposes to revoke or restrict an authorisation or to vary the restrictions imposed on an authorisation otherwise than with the institution's agreement. The Bank must give a notice specifying the proposed restrictions or variation, stating the grounds upon which the Bank proposes to act, and giving particulars of the institution's right to make representations[5]. Where a ground for a proposed revocation or for a proposal to impose or vary a restriction is that it appears to the Bank that a person who is or is to be a director, controller or manager of the institution is not a fit and proper person to hold the particular position which he holds or is to hold[6] the Bank must give that person a copy of the notice, together with a statement of his right to make representations to the Bank[7]. The Bank must give the institution and any person upon whom the notice was served, written notice of its decision within the period of twenty-eight

1 1987 Act, s 12(1).
2 s 12(2).
3 s 16(1).
4 s 16(2).
5 ss 13(2) and (3).
6 In terms of Sch 3, para 1.
7 s 13(4).

days beginning with the day on which the original notice was given, failing which the Bank will be treated as having at the end of that period given a notice that no further action is to be taken[1]. Except where the Bank's decision is to take no further action, the decision notice must state the reasons for the decision, give particulars, and in the case of a decision to restrict or to vary otherwise than as stated in the original notice, of the right to make further representations, and in all cases, of the right of appeal[2]. In *R v Bank of England, ex parte Mellstrom*, the High Court refused an application for judicial review brought by a director of a banking company who had been deemed by the Bank not be a fit and proper person to be allowed to accept deposits[3]. The correct procedure would have been for the director to exercise his statutory right of appeal under section 27 of the Act[4].

The Bank has a power to give an institution directions in the broad circumstances specified by section 19. It is empowered to give directions to an institution at the time of, or after giving notice of a revocation; after expiry of a restricted authorisation; after surrender or after service of a disqualification notice under section 183 of the Financial Services Act 1986[5]; *and* to protect the interests of depositors or potential depositors and to safeguard the institution's assets or otherwise[6].

An institution aggrieved by a decision of the Bank may appeal against that decision in terms of section 27 of the 1987 Act. Appeal lies at first instance to a banking appeal tribunal consisting of a chairman appointed by the Lord Chancellor in consultation with the Lord Advocate and two other members appointed by the Chancellor of the Exchequer[7]. In instances where:

(1) a ground for the decision to refuse, revoke, restrict or vary an authorisation is that a person who is, or is to be, a director, controller or manager of the institution is not a fit and proper person to hold the particular position which he holds or is to hold, or
(2) the effect of a decision is to restrict or vary an authorisation, or
(3) to give or vary a direction requires the removal of a person as director, controller or manager,

the person to whom the ground relates or whose removal is required also has a right of appeal against the finding of such a ground or, as the case may be, the decision to require his removal[8]. In Scotland a further appeal on any question of law lies from the tribunal to the Court of Session at the instance of an institution or other person who has appealed to a banking appeal tribunal or at the instance of the Bank[9].

---

1 1987 Act, s 13(10).
2 s 13(7).
3 [1995] COD 161, QBD.
4 For discussion of broad supervisory powers of the Bank, see *R v Smith (Wallace)* [1994] 1 WLR 1396, CA.
5 1987 Act, s 19(1).
6 s 19(2).
7 s 28(2).
8 s 27(2).
9 s 31; *R v Smith (Wallace)* [1994] 1 WLR 1396, CA. For illustration of litigation dealing with action against the authoriser or regulator, see *Yuen Kun Yeu v Attorney General of Hong Kong* [1988] 1 AC 175, [1987] 2 All ER 705, PC.

Controllers of authorised institutions

There are detailed provisions in the 1987 Act concerning the controllers of authorised institutions. No person may become a minority, 10 per cent, 20 per cent, 33 per cent, majority or principal shareholder, parent or an indirect controller of an authorised institution incorporated in the UK[1] unless he has served on the Bank a written notice stating that he intends to become such a controller of the institution[2]; and either the Bank has, before the end of the period of three months beginning with the date of service of that notice, notified him in writing that there is no objection to his becoming such a controller of the institution or that period has elapsed without the Bank having served on him under section 22 or 23 a written notice of objections[3].

The Bank may serve a notice of objection unless it is satisfied as to three matters: firstly that the person concerned is a fit and proper person to become a controller of the institution; secondly that the interests of depositors and potential depositors of the institution would not be in any manner threatened by that person becoming a controller; and thirdly that the criteria in Schedule 3 would continue to be fulfilled or if not, that that person is likely to undertake adequate remedial action[4]. Before serving a notice of objection, the Bank is obliged to serve the person concerned with a preliminary written notice, which must specify the matters about which the Bank is not satisfied, the reasons for not being satisfied and the rights of that person under section 27 to make written representations to the Bank[5]. The Bank has similar powers of objection towards existing shareholder controllers[6].

Regulation of advertisements for deposits

The 1987 Act also regulates the issue, form and content of advertisements for deposits. A 'deposit advertisement' means any advertisement containing an invitation to make a deposit or information which is intended or might reasonably be presumed to be intended to lead directly or indirectly to the making of a deposit[7]. The Treasury may, after consultation with the Bank and the Building Societies Commission, make regulations concerning deposit advertisements[8] and the making of unsolicited calls on persons in the UK or from the UK to persons elsewhere[9]. If the Bank considers that any deposit advertisement issued or proposed to be issued by or on behalf of an authorised institution is misleading, it may in terms of section 33(1) and (2), serve a notice in writing giving the institution a direction to cease or alter such advertisements[10].

1   1987 Act, s 21(1).
2   s 21(1)(a).
3   s 21(1)(b).
4   s 22(1)(c).
5   s 22(2) and (4).
6   s 23.
7   s 32(5).
8   s 32(1).
9   s 34(1).
10   s 33(2).

Duty of disclosure of authorised institution

The 1987 Act importantly imposes duties of disclosure in relation to authorised institutions. An authorised institution must give written notice to the Bank of the fact that any person has become or ceased to be a director, controller or manager of the institution[1]. A person who becomes a significant shareholder (that is, one who holds, alone or with associates, control of 5 per cent or more of the voting power at the institution's general meeting or of another institution of which it is a subsidiary in relation to an authorised institution incorporated in the UK) must, within seven days, give written notice of that fact to the Bank[2]. An authorised institution, other than one whose principal place of business is outside the UK, must make a report to the Bank if

(1) it has entered into a transaction relating to any one person as a result of which it is exposed to the risk of incurring losses in excess of 10 per cent of its available capital resources; or

(2) it proposes to enter into a transaction or transactions relating to any one person which, either alone or together with a previous transaction or previous transactions entered into by it in relation to that person, would result in its being exposed to the risk of incurring losses in excess of 25 per cent of those resources[3].

An authorised institution incorporated in the UK must immediately give written notice to the Bank if the institution proposes to give special notice to its shareholders of an ordinary resolution removing an auditor before expiration of his term of office or gives notice replacing an auditor at the expiration of his term of office with a different auditor[4].

General regulatory powers

The Bank has general supervisory powers in connection with the regulation of deposit-taking institutions. Some of the most important powers are to obtain information and documents. As regards information, the Bank may require an institution to provide the Bank with such information as it may reasonably require for the performance of its functions under the 1987 Act and supply a report by an accountant or other person with relevant professional skill on any matter about which the Bank has required the institution to provide information[5]. In the case of documents, which includes information recorded in any form[6], the Bank may, by written notice, require an authorised institution to produce such document or documents of such description as may be specified in the notice, as the Bank may reasonably require for the performance of its functions under the Act[7]. As regards both information and documents, the Bank may

---

1   1987 Act, s 36(1).
2   s 37(1).
3   s 38(1).
4   s 46(1).
5   s 39(1).
6   s 106(1).
7   s 39(3)(a).

authorise an officer, servant or agent of the Bank, on producing evidence of his authority, to require an authorised institution to provide him forthwith with such documents, as he may specify, being such information or documents as the Bank may reasonably require for the performance of its functions under the Act[1].

Obtaining information and documents

The Bank also has extensive rights of entry to obtain a wide range of information and documents[2]. If considered necessary by the Bank, the Bank may appoint an investigator to investigate the business of any body corporate which is or has been at any relevant time, a holding company, subsidiary or related company of the institution under investigation or other related bodies within any of the prescribed classes[3]. The 1987 Act confers upon a person so appointed a right to enter premises[4] and imposes a duty upon every person who is or was a director, controller, employee, agent, banker, solicitor, or significant shareholder of a body under investigation to produce documents, to attend before the person so appointed, and otherwise to give that person reasonable assistance in connection with the investigation[5].

The Bank is given important powers under section 42 of the 1987 Act to investigate suspected contravention of section 3 (the restriction on deposit-taking) and section 35 (fraudulent inducements to make a deposit) of that Act. In *Bank of England v Riley*[6] the defendants' lawyer having been arrested and charged with fifty-three offences of theft and obtaining money by deception, the Bank brought injunctions restraining the defendant from contravening section 3 of the Act. It was held that section 42 requires a person suspected of contravening the Act to provide specific information and documents pursuant to the order and such a person is not entitled to rely on the privilege against self-incrimination.

Accounts and auditors

Auditors may be involved in the regulatory process when the Bank exercises powers under sections 41 and 42 of the 1987 Act[7]. An authorised institution is obliged at each of its offices in the UK at which it holds itself out as accepting deposits, to keep a copy of its most recent audited accounts and during normal business hours make that copy available for inspection by any person on request[8]. A significant measure is section 47, which relaxes the auditor's and reporting accountant's duty of confidentiality, or of loyalty or trust relating to any information or opinion on a

1 1987 Act, s 39(3)(b).
2 s 40(1) and (2).
3 s 41(2).
4 s 41(7).
5 s 41(5).
6 [1992] Ch 475, [1992] 1 All ER 769, CA.
7 See p 30 above.
8 s 45(1).

matter to which the section applies and is relevant to any function of the bank under the Act[1].

(2)   DEPOSIT PROTECTION

The Banking Act 1987 continued the existence of the Deposit Protection Scheme which had been established under the 1979 Act. A Deposit Protection Board[2] continued its tasks of managing the scheme. The object of the scheme is to ensure that in the event of the insolvency of an authorised institution there is paid out of the Deposit Protection Fund a sum to depositors[3]. The Fund is a standing fund where contributions are levied at the outset upon authorised institutions in the form of initial contributions[4]. Further contributions may be levied where the amounts standing to the credit of the Fund drop below £3 million[5] or they may be levied in the form of special contributions where payments out are likely to exhaust the Fund[6]. The minimum initial contribution required from each authorised institution was £10,000 and further contributions not exceeding £300,000. The total of contributions paid or to be paid (less certain repayments) must not exceed 0.3 per cent of a contributory institution's 'deposit base'[7]. A depositor who has a 'protected deposit' with an authorised institution which becomes insolvent[8], or in relation to which an administration order is made under the Insolvency Act 1986, may receive a compensation payment of up to three-quarters of his protected deposit[9]. A 'protected deposit' is the total liability of that institution to that depositor limited to £20,000 in respect of the principal amount of and accrued interest on sterling deposits made within the UK offices of the institution. These figures and proportions may be amended by order[10].

(3)   BANKING NAMES AND DESCRIPTIONS

The 1987 Act contains important detailed provisions controlling the use of banking names used by institutions carrying on business in the UK. A banking name is any name which indicates or may reasonably be understood to indicate that a person is a bank or banker or is carrying on banking business[11]. Subject to certain exemptions, no person carrying on business in the UK may use any banking name unless it is an authorised institution which, in terms of section 67(2) must be:

1 See *Report of Inquiry into the Supervision of The Bank of Credit and Commerce International* (the Bingham Report) (Cm 198) (1992).
2 1987 Act, s 50, Sch 4.
3 s 51.
4 s 53.
5 s 54.
6 s 55.
7 ss 56-57.
8 s 59.
9 s 58(1).
10 s 60 (1) and (5).
11 s 67(1).

(a) a company incorporated in the UK which has (1) an issued share capital[1] in respect of which the amount paid up is not less than £5million (or an amount in equivalent value denominated wholly or partly otherwise than in sterling), or (2) undistributable reserves falling within section 264(3)(a), (b), or (d) of the Companies Act 1985 of not less than that sum (or such an equivalent amount), or (3) such undistributable reserves of an amount which, together with the amount paid up in respect of its issued share capital equals not less than that sum (or such an equivalent amount); or

(b) is a partnership formed under the law of any part of the UK in respect of which one or more designated fixed capital accounts[2] are maintained to which there has been credited not less than £5million (or such an equivalent amount).

The exemptions from these regulatory procedures fall into two categories. Firstly, there are certain institutions to which the provisions do not apply such as the Bank of England, other European Union central banks, and various other international economic and development banks[3]. Secondly, certain uses of names are outwith the remit of section 67 of the 1987 Act. These include the use by an authorised institution which is a company incorporated under the law of a country or territory outside the UK, or is formed under the law of a member state other than the UK[4], of a name under which it carries on business in that country, territory or state (or an approximate translation in English of that name)[5].

There are also restrictions on the use of banking descriptions. Subject to certain exemptions, no person carrying on business in the UK may so describe himself or hold himself out as to indicate or reasonably be understood to indicate, that he is a bank or banker or is carrying on a banking business unless he is an authorised institution[6]. An authorised institution to which the prohibition on the use of banking names applies may not use a banking description which is in such immediate conjunction with the name of the institution that the description might reasonably be thought to be part of it[7]. There is an exemption in favour of the Bank of England, the central bank of any member state and certain international economic and development banks[8]. The restriction does not prohibit a person from using the expression 'bank' or 'banker' or a similar expression where it is necessary for him to do so in order to be able to assert that he is complying with, or entitled to the advantage of any enactment, statutory instrument, international agreement, rule of law or commercial usage or practice which applies to a person by virtue of his being a bank or banker[9].

---

1 1987 Act, s 67(3), (5) and (6).
2 s 67(4).
3 s 68(6).
4 See the Banking Coordination (Second Council Directive) Regulations 1992, SI 1992/3218, reg 2 ('another member state').
5 1987 Act, s 68(3).
6 s 69(1).
7 s 69(2).
8 s 69(6).
9 s 69(4).

The Bank is empowered to object to a name it considers misleading or otherwise undesirable by giving written notice of the objection[1]. An authorised institution may appeal to the court within three weeks of service of the notice of objection[2]. There are also provisions linked to the Companies Act 1985 in respect of the registration of substitute corporate names by overseas companies where the Bank has notified its objections[3]. A contravention of these provisions is a criminal offence[4].

(4) REGULATION OF OVERSEAS INSTITUTIONS WITH REPRESENTATIVE OFFICES

A number of overseas institutions have established representative offices in the UK for purposes which do include the acceptance of deposits. There are provisions governing the regulation of names used, or to be used, by overseas institutions in relation to their activities in the UK. A 'representative office' is defined as premises from which the deposit-taking, lending or other financial or banking activities of the overseas institution are promoted or assisted in any way. 'Establishment' in relation to such an office includes the making of any arrangements by virtue of which such activities are promoted or assisted from it[5]. 'Overseas institution' for these purposes means a person, (other than an authorised institution or exempted person) who is a body incorporated in a country or territory outside the UK or a partnership or other unincorporated association formed under the law of such a country or territory or which has its principal place of business in such a country or territory[6].

An overseas institution must not establish a representative office in the UK unless it has given not less than two months' notice to the Bank, and such notice must specify any name the institution proposes to use in relation to activities conducted by it in the UK after the establishment of that office[7]. Institutions which established a representative office before 1 October 1987 and had not given notice of that fact to the Bank under section 40 of the Banking Act 1979, were required to give written notice to the Bank of the continued existence of that office by 1 December 1987[8].

The Bank has power to object in certain instances to a name used or proposed to be used by an overseas institution if considered to be misleading to the public or otherwise undesirable. Prior notice must be given and the Bank may object to any name proposed to be used or to any change in a name already being used[9] subject to a right of appeal to the court[10]. As in terms of section 72, there are provisions covering the registration of sub-

---

1   1987 Act, s 70(1).
2   s 71.
3   1987 Act, s 72.
4   s 73.
5   s 74(3).
6   s 74(1).
7   s 75(1)(a).
8   s 75(2).
9   s 76.
10 s 77.

stitute corporate names by overseas institutions[1]. There also exists the obligation of an overseas institution with a representative office in the UK, by notice to provide information and documents to the Bank as the Bank may require[2]. Although the Act does not confer on the Bank the same powers as under sections 39 and 40 in relation to obtaining information and documents from authorised institutions, provision is made for the Treasury to order that those sections shall apply to overseas institutions[3].

(5)   OTHER RELEVANT MEASURES

The Banking Act 1987 contains a series of miscellaneous provisions which are of significance to the supervisory system as a whole. The court, having jurisdiction under the Insolvency Act 1986, may wind up an authorised institution in terms of section 92 of the 1987 Act upon a petition presented by the Bank if the institution is unable to pay its debts in terms of sections 123 or 221 of the 1986 Act, or the court is of the opinion that it is just and equitable that the institution be wound up. An institution which defaults in an obligation to pay any sum due and payable in respect of a deposit is deemed to be unable to pay its debts[4].

A number of additional criminal offences are created by virtue of section 96 of the 1987 Act. Where any such offence committed by a body corporate is proved to have been committed with the consent or connivance of, or to be attributable to any neglect on the part of any director, manager or secretary or other similar officer of that body corporate or any person who was purporting to act in any such capacity, he, as well as the body corporate, is guilty of that offence and liable to be prosecuted accordingly[5]. Where the officers of a body corporate are managed by its members, this applies in relation to the acts and defaults of a member in connection with his management functions as if he were a director[6]. It is a defence for the person charged to prove that he took all reasonable precautions and exercised due diligence to avoid the commission of the offence by him or any other person under his control[7].

The Treasury has powers under the Act to make orders and regulations and to give directions. These include the power to amend Schedule 2 (exempted persons)[8], to amend the meaning of 'deposit' and 'deposit taking business'[9] and to direct the Bank to serve a section 22 notice of objection[10]. The powers of the Treasury to make orders and regulations under the Act are exercisable by statutory instrument[11].

1 1987 Act, s 78.
2 s 79.
3 s 79(7).
4 1987 Act, s 92(1).
5 s 96(1).
6 s 96(2).
7 s 96(4).
8 s 4(3).
9 s 7(1).
10 s 23(1).
11 s 102.

(6)   NEED FOR REFORM

The effectiveness of the banking supervision system has been questioned in recent years. The Bank of Credit and Commerce International (BCCI) began operating in the UK in the late 1970s, which was the period during which the Bank of England was first given effective statutory powers of supervision. The collapse of BCCI signalled by the appointment of a provisional liquidator in July 1991, left some local authorities and other ordinary depositors with substantial and much-publicised losses. Criticisms of the Bank of England's role as supervisor emerged from the inquiry into the supervision of BCCI conducted by Bingham LJ[1] and in particular two fundamental complaints were raised. Firstly, that the Bank failed to use the provisions of the then Banking Act 1979 to proper effect. It was, however, argued in mitigation of the Bank's actings that these statutory provisions were, at least in the early 1980s, untried and untested. Nonetheless, the Bank was accused particularly of misapplying the criteria laid out in Schedule 3 of the 1979 Act[2]. The second criticism was that the Bank did not pursue the truth about BCCI with the rigour which the BCCI's market reputation deserved. It was suggested that in the later stages immediately prior to BCCI's collapse, the Bank placed an unwarranted and excessive reliance upon the auditors of BCCI despite the fact that the duty to supervise was a duty which could not be delegated[3]. Being in possession of information casting doubt on the financial probity of the BCCI's activities, it was cogently argued that the Bank failed in general terms to act positively to prevent BCCI from defrauding its depositors.

It is not clear whether reforms are intended to be made to the system. In favour of reform is the argument that under the present law, depositors are in an invidious position. In instances similar to the BCCI affair, where depositors lost large sums of money as a result of undetected fraud, deposit protection offers only limited assistance. Although it is competent for depositors to obtain compensation from the majority of shareholders of deposit-taking institutions, there is no guarantee that such shareholders will be willing or indeed capable of providing compensation. Moreover, depositors are not able to rely upon the law of negligence since legal principle and policy considerations preclude establishing a duty of care on the Bank itself or on the members of the Board[4], unless it can be shown that the act or omission was in bad faith, or on the auditors of the defaulting institution[5]. However, it can be satisfactorily argued that the Bank's traditional practices based on trust, frankness and a willingness to co-operate are successful in the overwhelming majority of cases. The Bank itself has steadfastly refused to accept any need for major change, preferring to submit proposals to increase its powers under the 1987 Act and develop a better investigation capacity[6]. The problems of supervisory patrol are also being

1   *Report of Inquiry into the Supervision of The Bank of Credit and Commerce International* (the Bingham Report) (Cm 198) (1992).
2   Bingham Report, paras 2.23–2.31.
3   Bingham Report, para 2.484.
4   1987 Act, s 2(7).
5   *Caparo Industries plc v Dickman* [1990] 2 AC 605, [1990] 1 All ER 568, HL; *Yuen Kun Yeu v Attorney General of Hong Kong* [1988] 1 AC 175, [1987] 2 All ER 705, PC.
6   Bingham Report, paras 3.9–3.16.

compounded by the prevalent worldwide tendency to ease local supervision of foreign banks. It is hoped that a fresh banking crisis will be averted although its occurrence is at best unlikely rather than impossible. The scandals and near collapse of Baring's Bank in 1995 have polarised anxiety and further supervisory regulation is more likely than previously[1].

(7) INTERNATIONAL DEVELOPMENTS

International developments have had an effect upon the supervisory system of banks. The Basle Committee on Banking Regulations and Supervisory Practices, was established in 1974 by the governors of the central banks of the Group of ten (now twelve) industrial nations. The Committee's 1975 concordant aimed to provide that no bank established in a foreign country should be able to escape supervision and to that effect, responsibility for the supervision of such banks being allocated between 'host' and 'parent' authorities. In the wake of the failure of the BCCI, new standards announced by the Committee were indorsed by the central bank governors. The four main features are:

(1) any international banking group should be supervised on a 'consolidated basis', taking account of its operations anywhere in the world, by a single home authority;
(2) if a bank intends to establish branches in a jurisdiction outwith its home country, it will require the consent of both the home country and the regulatory body in the host country;
(3) the home country supervisor will have the right, in co-operation with the host regulator, to receive information on the international operations of banks under the host's supervision; and
(4) if a country is not satisfied as to the supervision of a bank whose domicile is elsewhere, it may impose restrictive measures on branches of that bank in its territory, including, if necessary, a prohibition on operating branches in that country.

(8) THE EUROPEAN UNION

Legislative initiatives from the European Union in the banking sector have been significant. The First Banking Co-ordination Directive[2] was instrumental in leading to the Banking Act 1979[3]. This implemented the common basic licensing criteria and the common definition of a 'credit institution' as 'an undertaking whose business is to receive deposits or repayable funds from the public and to grant credits for its own account'. The European Commission's Large Exposures Directive[4] discourages an

---

1 Ellinger and Lomnicka *Modern Banking Law* (2nd edn, 1994) pp 60, 61.
2 EC Council Directive 77/780 (OJ L322, 17.12.77, p 30) (as amended).
3 See pp 25 ff above ('Authorisation of Institutions'). The Banking Act 1979 was entirely replaced by the Banking Act 1987.
4 EC Council Directive 92/121 (OJ L29, 5.2.93, p 1) on the monitoring and control of large exposures of credit institutions.

excessive concentration of loan exposure to a single customer or customer group, by introducing reporting requirements for large exposures. Another crucially important directive concerns the prevention of the use of the financial system for the purpose of money laundering[1]. The Second Banking Co-ordination Directive[2] made it mandatory for supervisory authorities to supervise banking groups in the European Union. This requirement applies to financial institutions[3] and credit institutions[4] and seeks to ensure that no such body escapes supervision, which should take place at least once per year by the designated authorities in the institution's home country. The adoption in December 1989 of the Second Banking Co-ordination Directive is of considerable significance. Its three main features are: (1) a single licence for credit institutions (which includes all banks) known as the 'home passport' or 'single licence' concept based on the premise that the home country will be responsible for the authorisation of branches; (2) a list of activities to be permitted under the licence; and (3) the provision of common supervisory rules.

The Second Consolidated Supervision Directive[5] was adopted in April 1992 and provided that there should be consolidated supervision where a parent company is a non-bank financial institution and the parent of a bank and non-bank subsidiaries must provide the regulators with the information they seek.

'Single licence' — 'home passport'

The single banking licence reflects the principle of freedom of establishment in the European Union. An institution must be 'established' in a member state, which requires it to have a real and continuous link with the economy of that country. Once established in its 'home' country, the institution may open branches[6] in other countries, known as host countries. This may be subject to notification requirements, but requires no further authorisation from the institution's home country[7]. The process allows banks and other credit institutions to expand throughout the community, either through branches[8] or by offering cross-border services[9]. Some host states have minimum standards which must be met, but they

---

1 EC Council Directive 91/308 (OJ L166, 28.6.91, p 77).
2 EC Council Directive 89/646 (OJ L386, 30.12.89, p 1) given effect by the Banking Coordination (Second Council Directive) Regulations 1992, SI 1992/3218 which came into force on 1 January 1993. See also EC Council Directive 92/5030 (OJ L110, 28.4.92, p 52) on the supervision of credit institutions on a consolidated basis.
3 As defined in EC Council Directive 77/780.
4 This includes subsidiaries which are 90 per cent owned by one or more credit institutions and comply with other conditions: see EC Council Directive 77/780, arts 1(6) and 18(2).
5 Ie EC Council Directive 92/5030.
6 Notably this only refers to branches and not subsidiaries which require their own authorisation: see EC Council Directive 77/780, arts 18 and 20.
7 See EC Council Directive 77/780, art 6.
8 See EC Council Directive 77/780, arts 18 and 20.
9 This was not expressly provided for in the First Banking Directive but the acceptability of cross-border services was established in Case 205/84 *EC Commission v Germany* [1986] ECR 3755, [1987] 2 CMLR 69, ECJ (the German Insurance Case).

play a purely 'complimentary' role[1] as the home county is primarily responsible for the supervision of the institution.

A credit institution must comply with certain rules in order to obtain a single licence. These broadly are the maintenance of adequate minimum funds of 5 million ECU[2]; that its business must be directed by at least two persons of good repute; an obligation to inform the competent authority of the identity of the owners or controllers of the institutions; and to submit a list of the types of business the applicant intends to carry on together with details of its structural organisation.

Permitted activities

Once the bank has obtained a licence from its home country it may carry on in any member state a list of permitted activities without the need for further 'local' authorisation. The list of activities permitted under the licence is not exhaustive and further activities may be added as required. The activities presently permitted[3] are acceptance of deposits and repayable funds from the public; lending, including consumer credit; mortgage credit; factoring and other financing of commercial transactions; financial leasing; money transmission services; issuing and administering means of payments (for example cheques); guarantees and commitments; trading for own account or for the account of customers in money market instruments (for example cheques); foreign exchange; financial futures and options; exchange and interest rate instruments and transferrable securities; participation in share issues and the provision of services related to issues; advice to undertakings on capital structure, industrial strategy and related questions, including questions relating to mergers and the purchase of undertakings; money broking; portfolio management and advice; safekeeping and administration of securities; credit reference services; and safe custody services.

Common supervisory rules

The modifications to the Draft Second Directive were introduced by the European Commission in 1989 to simplify the procedures for applications from individual institutions in non-European Union countries. These rules make it clear that in return for banking access to the European market, reciprocal facilities must be offered to European Union banks aiming to establish branches in non-member states. The Banking Coordination (Second Council Directive) Regulations 1992 implemented the Second Banking Co-ordination Directive and consequently amended the Banking Act 1987, the Financial Services Act 1986 and the Consumer Credit Act 1974 to allow banks from other European Union states to carry on 'passported' activities in the UK without the need for UK authorisation.

---

1 *Completing the Internal Market*, White Paper from the Commission to the European Council, COM (85) 310.
2 As at 1 October 1996 this was equivalent to £4,038,772.
3 See SI 1992/3218, Sch 1.

5.   THE BANKING OMBUDSMAN SCHEME

The Banking Ombudsman Scheme was founded on 1 January 1986 and is sponsored voluntarily by the banking sector with the object of receiving unresolved complaints about the provision of banking services and aiming 'to facilitate the satisfaction, settlement or withdrawal of such complaints'[1]. The stated objective of the scheme is the resolution of complaints 'by agreement, by making representations or awards, or by such other means as seem expedient'[2]. The service is provided free. Although the applicant must exhaust the bank's complaints procedure first, the emphasis is upon non-adversarial conciliation. The complainer's application will not be accepted if other proceedings have already been taken against the bank on the same matter[3].

The scheme is administered by a board of directors (appointed by the banks from among their own full time executives) which appoints the eight members of the Council of the Banking Ombudsman. The Banking Ombudsman and his Secretariat are appointed by and accountable to the Council. The terms of reference of the Ombudsman have been regularly extended, the most recent being 10 May 1995. This recent extension of powers provided that the Ombudsman is entitled to deal with three additional areas of complaint which had previously been outside the ambit of his remit :

(1)   a retailer who is not the bank's customer and accepts a cheque drawn in his favour against a cheque guarantee card is entitled to complain against the bank which issued the card if the guarantee is not met;

(2)   the 'true owner' of a cheque or the person entitled to possession of it, despite being a non-customer, may complain against the bank into which a stolen cheque was paid by someone not legally entitled to it; and

(3)   a non-customer receiving a banker's reference or status opinion may complain against the bank which provided it.

The complainant must be an individual customer, small trader, partnership, club or other unincorporated business. Small companies are now included in the scheme but only for events occurring after 26 January 1993 and if their turnover is under £1million per annum. A dispute is referred to the Ombudsman by an individual customer or a group of customers after the bank's internal complaints procedure has been exhausted and provided the complaint falls within the terms of reference of the Ombudsman. The scheme only covers claims not exceeding £100,000 and matters relating to 'banking services'[4]. Banking services broadly cover all business normally carried out through bank branches including credit

1   See the Banking Ombudsman Scheme *Terms of Reference* (set out in Appendix 2 below).
2   *Terms of Reference*, para 1.
3   Full information and an annual report may be obtained from the Office of the Banking Ombudsman, 70 Gray's Inn Road, London, WC1X 8NB; Tel: 0171 404 9944.
4   *Terms of Reference*, para 29(a).

card services. It does not, however, cover complaints about the bank's commercial judgment in lending or their general commercial policies (including interest rate policies).

In 1996 the Ombudsman received 17,606 specific complaints by telephone and 8,044 preliminary complaints in writing. Of these complaints, 736 complaints were accepted as eligible for full investigation and in these instances the bank's own internal complaints procedure had been exhausted and there did not appear to be any realistic opportunity by the Ombudsman to effect a fair settlement between the parties prior to full investigation. The total of full investigation complaints had increased 2.6 per cent upon the comparable figure for 1995[1].

The Ombudsman may seek to facilitate a settlement between the applicant and the bank or he may recommend a withdrawal of the complaint. Where the recommendation of the Ombudsman is accepted within one month by the applicant but not the bank, he may make an award against the bank which does not exceed £100,000. The award is binding, on the applicant and the bank if accepted by the applicant within one month. The scheme is entirely voluntary and has no statutory basis. While membership is voluntary, all of the main clearing banks are members, as are other banks with personal customers and the Bank of England. The scheme is funded entirely by the member banks and awards are not binding upon the applicant unless accepted. Importantly the Ombudsman in exercising decision making powers must be guided by 'what is in his opinion fair in all the circumstances'[2]. The Ombudsman is also expressly required to have regard to 'general principles of good banking practice and any relevant code of practice'[3] and may consider 'any maladministration or other inequitable treatment'[4] as a breach by a bank of its duties to its customers. It follows that the Ombudsman has a very wide discretion to uphold complaints which do not in fact involve infringements of legal obligations. Notwithstanding that the general remit of the Ombudsman is somewhat narrow and directed towards the resolution of the individual complaints of banking customers against their banks he has already been successful in influencing banking law and practice. The Ombudsman issues persuasive annual reports which make general observations and recommendations as to changes and improvements to current banking practice. The Jack Report[5] indorsed the scheme and made recommendations for extension of the Ombudsman's remit which were promptly actioned. The Jack Committee's proposal that the scheme should have a statutory basis was, however, rejected upon the basis that it would undermine the Ombudsman's ability to make mandatory awards binding on the banks. It is worth considering whether the Ombudsman would have reached a different decision from the courts in *Mumford v Bank of Scotland and Smith v Bank of Scotland*[6].

---

1 The Banking Ombudsman Scheme, Annual Report 1995–96.
2 *Terms of Reference*, para 14.
3 *Terms of Reference*, para 14(b).
4 *Terms of Reference*, para 14(c).
5 Jack Report, Appendix H.
6 1994 SCLR 856, 1994 SLT 1288, OH; 1995 SCLR 839, 1st Div.

Chapter 3

Customers of a Bank

1. THE CUSTOMER — AN INTRODUCTION

Surprisingly the term ' a customer' of a bank has never been defined by statute and little assistance is given by the primary banking law statutes, the Bills of Exchange Act 1882 and Cheques Act 1957. An examination of some of the earlier cases details the requirements that to be a customer, a person has to have an account with the banker and be able to display some course of dealings or transactions[1]. This generalist principle has, however, been superseded by the view that the account itself is the most important element rather than its duration or transaction occurrence:

> 'I do not think it is necessary that he should have drawn any money or even that he should be in a position to draw money. I think such a person becomes a customer the moment the bank receives the money or cheque and agrees to open an account'[2].

It is now accepted that agreement by the manager or other appropriate official of the branch of the bank to accept an instruction to open an account is of itself sufficient to establish the banker–customer relationship. In *Woods v Martins Bank Ltd*[3] an inexperienced young man, Woods, who had inherited a substantial sum of money, was given careless advice regarding an investment by one of Martins Bank's branch managers. At the time of the advice, Woods did not have an account with the bank but he decided to act upon the advice of the branch manager and he arranged for moneys to be uplifted by the bank from another institution and paid into a new account at Martin's for utilisation of the transaction. It was held that the banker–customer relationship had come into existence at the point when the branch manager agreed to accept the instruction to open an account in Woods' name. It was also shown that the negligent investment advice was reiterated to Woods at that time and the bank was found

---

1 *Matthews v Brown & Co* (1894) 63 LJQB 494, 10 TLR 386; *Great Western Rly Co v London and County Banking Co Ltd* [1901] AC 414, 70 LJKB 915, HL.
2 *Ladbroke & Co v Todd* (1914) 19 Com Cas 256 at 261, per Bailhache J.
3 [1959] 1 QB 55, [1958] 3 All ER 166.

to have failed to observe the duty of care it owed to its customer under the auspices of the banker–customer relationship.

A mere 'course of dealing' not distinctly relating to banking business is not sufficient to establish the banker–customer relationship. In *Great Western Railway v London and County Banking Co Ltd*[1] a rate collector habitually exchanged crossed cheques for cash at a bank where he had no account and which charged him nothing for the service. It was held by the House of Lords that he was not a customer.

There are two principal conclusions arising from an analysis of 'who is a customer?' Firstly, the banker–customer relationship comes into existence at the point the bank agrees to open an account in the customer's name. A habitual relationship is not necessary. Secondly, by becoming a customer, the bank agrees to act as the customer's agent and to exercise skill and care in the carrying out of his transactions.

2. NATURAL PERSONS

(1) PERSONS AGED UNDER SIXTEEN AND UNDER EIGHTEEN

For many centuries the law of Scotland followed its Roman law roots and made a distinction between pupils and minors. Pupils (girls under twelve and boys under fourteen) generally had no legal capacity and their representatives, called tutors, acted on their behalf. Accordingly, any contract between a bank and a pupil was null and of no legal effect[2]. Once a young person entered minority at twelve or fourteen he or she had a limited legal capacity, which was a clear compromise between the law's recognition of an adult's full contractual powers and the desire to protect the weak from a bad or oppressive bargain[3]. Minors could act on their own behalf and incur liability, yet rules existed for the reduction of a minor's contracts on the grounds of what was termed 'minority and lesion'[4]. The role of the representative of a minor (called a curator) was mainly advisory, although a curator required to consent to a minor opening a bank account, unless the minor was in business on his own account or had held himself out to be of full age and capacity[5].

The rules have been replaced by the Age of Legal Capacity (Scotland) Act 1991[6]. Norrie says that:

> 'Although the primary motivation of this short Act was to codify and simplify the law on contractual capacity of young persons, its import is much wider and its effect significantly more far reaching, the alterations made to the law of Scotland must not be underrated'[7].

1 [1901] AC 414, 70 LJKB 915, HL. See also *Taxation Comrs v English, Scottish and Australian Bank Ltd* [1920] AC 683, 89 LJPC 181, PC.
2 *Hill v City of Glasgow Bank* (1879) 7 R 68 at 74; *Erskine* I,7,33.
3 *Stair* I,6,44; *Erskine* I,7,34.
4 See eg *O'Donnell v Brownieside Coal Co Ltd* 1934 SC 534, 1934 SLT 493.
5 *Erskine* I,7,36.
6 Which came into force on 25 September 1991.
7 Norrie 'The Age of Legal Capacity (Scotland) Act 1991' (1991) 36 JLSS 434. See also Barr and Edwards 'Age of Legal Capacity: Further Pitfalls' 1992 SLT (News) 77, 91.

Pupillarity and minority are not abolished but the distinction is legally irrelevant as far as contractual capacity is concerned, because one age of legal capacity exists which, as a general rule, is sixteen[1]. Children under sixteen do not have the capacity, as a general rule, to enter into transactions having legal effect[2]. A statutory challenge procedure to prejudicial transactions entered into by persons over the age of sixteen and under eighteen has been introduced[3] and the status of 'guardian' supersedes the distinction which was previously drawn between tutors and curators[4].

There are, however, exceptions to the general rule that the age of legal capacity is sixteen and these are detailed in section 2 of the Act. Of practical relevance to bankers is section 2(1) which provides:

'A person under the age of 16 years shall have legal capacity to enter into a transaction — (a) of a kind commonly entered into by persons of his age and circumstances, and (b) on terms which are not unreasonable'.

There is a degree of uncertainty as to which transactions are subject to the exception. Arguments have been put forward that courts might interpret section 2(1), and in particular 'commonly', as implying the need for frequency rather than looking to the nature of the transaction itself. It would therefore follow that the fifteen-year-old buying sweets would be deemed capable of contracting, whereas the fifteen-year-old seeking legal representation for the first time may not be capable of contracting[5]. Further, the absence of judicial authority interpreting the terms of the 1991 Act makes conclusive predictions of any kind difficult to make. The aim of the Act is to provide clarity and certainty but the effect may be to cause some confusion in certain cases. Under the old law, it was clear that pupils had no legal capacity whatsoever, minors having capacity of a limited nature. The new provisions in sections 1 and 2 of the Act retain a two-tier system which is potentially unclear in operation. From the wording of section 2(1) it is questionable whether or not banks are entitled to honour the young person's cheques. A person's capacity to bind himself on a bill is co-extensive with capacity to contract[6]. Where a bill is drawn or indorsed by an 'infant' or 'minor' the drawing or indorsement entitles the holder to receive payment on the bill and to enforce against any other party thereto save for the 'infant' or 'minor' drawer[7]. A cheque drawn by such a person possesses all the characteristics of a cheque drawn by a person of full age and capacity except that it would be competent to argue on occasion that the young person is not ultimately liable as drawer.

The nature of the banking contract offered to young persons must be on terms which are not unreasonable and banks should be careful in the manner in which complicated services are offered to persons under the age of sixteen. Many young persons do hold bank accounts and will fall within

1 1991 Act, s 1(1).
2 1991 Act, ss 1(1)(a) and 9.
3 1991 Act, s 3.
4 1991 Act, s 5.
5 Thomson 'Legal Capacity of Young Persons — an Exercise in Bad Law Reform?' (1992) SLG 55 at 58.
6 Bills of Exchange Act 1882, s 22(1).
7 1882 Act, s 22(2).

the category of a common transaction within the terming of section 2(1) much to the comfort of all institutions involved in the making available of such facilities.

As regards lending money to young persons, the risks are such that a bank would find difficulty in enforcing the obligation under the Act, against the average person under sixteen-years-old. The loan of money to a young person would be a high risk transaction fraught with difficult recovery problems.

Reduction of prejudicial transactions

The law traditionally provides, in certain circumstances, redress to persons who, on attaining majority, seek to reduce a transaction entered into during years of minority[1]. The 1991 Act largely reflects this arrangement in providing a challenge procedure for eighteen to twenty-one-year-olds in respect of contracts entered into, when between the ages of sixteen and eighteen[2]. There are substantial differences from the former law and the procedure is no longer viewed in the context of minority. Although the age of majority remains eighteen[3] the challenge procedure is no longer available for young persons entering contracts while *under* the age of sixteen. By the old law, a minor could challenge a contract entered into during minority, on attaining majority and until the age of twenty-two, under the *quadriennium utile*, upon proof of lesion. Section 1(5) of the 1991 Act abolishes actions of reduction on grounds of minority and lesion, the Act providing that a person under the age of twenty-one may apply to the court to set aside a prejudicial transaction entered into only when the applicant was sixteen or over but under the age of eighteen[4].

A notable and important change concerns the substantive grounds of challenge and in terms of section 3(2) of the 1991 Act a 'prejudicial transaction' is one which '(a) an adult, exercising reasonable prudence, would not have entered into in the circumstances of the applicant at the time of entering into the transaction, and (b) has caused or is likely to cause substantial prejudice to the applicant'.

It is sensible to accept that the old cases dealing with minority and lesion apply equally to contracts entered into after commencement of the Act[5]. Certainly the new provisions, despite the changes in terminology, do not restrict the scope of challenge for prospective applicants. A useful procedure of ratifying proposed transactions has been introduced, by which application is made by the young person and the other contracting party to the sheriff court[6]. The result is the provision of safeguards[7] against possible challenge and reduction of the contract at a later date, which may on

---

1 *Stair* I,6,44; *Erskine* I, 7,34; Bell *Principles* s 2098.
2 1991 Act, s 3.
3 Age of Majority (Scotland) Act 1969, s 1.
4 1991 Act, s 3.
5 *Stevenson v Adair* (1872) 10 M 919; *Hill v City of Glasgow Bank* (1879) 7 R 68; *McFeetridge v Stewarts and Lloyds Ltd* 1913 SC 773, 1913 1 SLT 325; *O'Donnell v Brownieside Coal Co Ltd* 1934 SC 534, 1934 SLT 493; *Forbes v House of Clydesdale Ltd* 1988 SCLR 410, 1988 SLT 594.
6 1991 Act, s 4.
7 1991 Act, s 4(2).

occasion be useful to a bank seeking comfort for the enforceability of a facility made available to a young person. Only proposed transactions may be ratified judicially. If the transaction has been completed the banker would require to approach the young adult after he or she had reached majority to ascertain whether he or she would ratify it[1].

(2) GUARDIANS

The legal guardian acts on behalf of the young person (a person under sixteen) and has legal control over his person and property[2]. Under the 'old' law, the guardian of a pupil was known as a tutor while the guardian of a minor was known as the curator. The 1991 Act abolishes the status of curatory[3] and accordingly the guardian of a person under sixteen has in relation to that young person and his estate the powers and duties which, immediately before the commencement of the 1991 Act, a tutor had in relation to his pupil[4]. Thus, the guardian has the authority to consent only on behalf of persons under sixteen, while young persons on or over the age of sixteen have general legal capacity[5] within the limitations previously discussed. Since persons under sixteen may no longer entertain an action of reduction on grounds of minority and lesion[6], there is no ground to reduce any contract made by the guardian on the ward's behalf[7].

Bank accounts are commonly opened in the name of persons under sixteen and often by relatives wishing to lodge moneys on their behalf. It is incumbent upon banks to establish a procedure allowing themselves to be satisfied as to the identity of a new customer[8]. The effect, is that banks should identify the young person to their own satisfaction when guardians open accounts in the young person's name[9]. A young person is only considered to be a customer of the bank when he or his representative attends the bank with money or a cheque and this is accepted or deposited in an account. Although authority suggests that generally speaking, a banker–customer relationship is established on the mere opening of an account[10], as far as a child is concerned the mere act of the guardian in opening an account per se is likely to be insufficient to establish the relationship in the full sense. The creation of the banker–customer relationship is likely to confer upon the person under sixteen substantial advantage. Considerable care must be taken where cheque signing or investment powers are involved in the operation of the account. In such

1 1991 Act, s 3(3)(h).
2 1991 Act, s 5(1).
3 1991 Act, s 5(3).
4 1991 Act, s 5(1).
5 1991 Act, s 1(1).
6 1991 Act, s 1(5).
7 The only recourse against the guardian is an accounting upon grounds of breach of trust since a guardian is a trustee within the meaning of the Trusts (Scotland) Acts 1921 and 1961.
8 See the Cheques Act 1957, s 4; *Lloyds Bank Ltd v EB Savory & Co* [1933] AC 201, 102 LJKB 224, HL; *Marfani & Co Ltd v Midland Bank Ltd* [1968] 2 All ER 573, [1968] 1 WLR 956, CA.
9 See Ann Arora 'Banking Law review since the Jack Committee Report on banking services' (1991) 12 Co Law 182.
10 See eg *Woods v Martins Bank Ltd* [1959] 1 QB 55, [1958] 3 All ER 166.

circumstances it would be prudent to assume the child's presence at the bank is required.

The National Savings Bank Regulations contain special provisions which permit a 'minor' who has attained the age of seven to withdraw money deposited by him or lodged in his name[1]. The Director of Savings is also empowered to the effect that if a deposit belonging to a 'minor' under seven years of age is urgently required for his education, maintenance or benefit or other appropriate reason, he may allow withdrawal by another appropriate person (for example, a parent)[2].

Guarantee (cautionary) obligations

A person under sixteen does not have legal capacity to enter into a cautionary obligation. However, a cautioner of a minor's obligation to his banker will be liable notwithstanding that the principal creditor/debtor contract is void due to lack of capacity[3]. The cautioner who undertakes an obligation for a principal debtor who is not legally bound impliedly undertakes to make good any resulting loss[4]. In England, however, it was decided that the guarantors of an infant's overdraft, where all parties knew the facts, were not liable to the bank[5].

(3) MARRIED WOMEN

It may seem strange to the modern reader that 'married women' are considered in a separate banking capacity. However, it is only in comparatively recent times that the distinction has become redundant. At common law, a woman, whether a minor or an adult, upon marriage, lost title and interest to make and enforce contracts by passing into the legal curatory of her husband[6]. However, in a series of statutes culminating in the Family Law (Scotland) Act 1985, the limitations upon married women's contractual capacity were removed[7]. Accordingly, as may be obvious, female customers, married or not, may now be treated in the same way as any other person of full age and capacity.

(4) PERSONS OF UNSOUND MIND

In the case of persons unable to manage their own affairs, as a result of senility or mental disorder, the court may on application by the next of

---

1 National Savings Bank Regulations 1972, SI 1972/764, reg 25.
2 Ibid, reg 6(4).
3 *Stevenson v Adair* (1872) 10 M 919.
4 (1872) 10 M 919 at 922, per Lord Ardmillan.
5 *Coutts & Co v Browne-Lecky* [1947] KB 104, [1946] 2 All ER 207; 2 *Stair Memorial Encyclopaedia* para 1234.
6 *Stair* I,4,10; *Erskine* I,6,20.
7 Conjugal Rights (Scotland) Amendment Act 1861, ss 5-6; Married Women's Property (Scotland) Act 1877; Married Women's Property (Scotland) Act 1881, ss 1–2; Married Women's Property (Scotland) Act 1920, s 1; Law Reform (Husband and Wife) (Scotland) Act 1984, s 3(1); Family Law (Scotland) Act 1985, s 24(1).

kin, supported by two medical certificates, appoint a curator bonis to act for such persons. Once the curator bonis has been appointed, the incapax has no contractual capacity or power to act upon his own behalf[1]. The curator bonis has a duty to manage the estate of the incapax and he is entitled to uplift any sum standing to the credit of the incapax on production to the bank of a certified copy of the court interlocutor appointing him. Where questions with third parties arise, the person for whom the curator bonis has been appointed is deemed incapable of consenting even when he is in fact capable or appears to be capable of consent. The position of a curator bonis has been criticised:

> 'A curator bonis takes over the management of the adult's whole estate. The curator's powers are not tailored to the needs and abilities of the adult. There is uncertainty as to the correct balance between conserving the estate and spending it for the adult's benefit, and as a result many curators adopt a conservative approach. Curatory, which is an appointment that lasts until recalled, may be imposed on adults whose needs could be met by a short-term order limited to a particular area of need. Curatory is expensive and the problem of high initial and running costs is particularly acute with small estates'[2].

The banker does, however, have certain responsibilities towards incapax customers. The curator bonis is an Officer of Court and as such is under the supervision of the Accountant of Court. Before entering upon his duties he must find caution for his intromissions. The banker should establish the authority of the curator in the form of an extract of his Act and Warrant before allowing the curator to operate upon the account[3]. In instances where no curator bonis has been appointed, the person's contracts are void if, at the material time, the person did not have the mental capacity to consent and understand the obligations he was undertaking[4]. The capacity of the individual is a question of fact and the non-appointment of the curator bonis is not conclusive of capacity[5]. It follows that a contract entered into during a lucid interval will be valid and enforceable against the incapax[6].

For existing customers temporary mental incapacity does not terminate the contract between banker and customer, and bankers are entitled to charge for work done while the customer was mentally incapable[7]. Drunkenness may be so disabling to render a person temporarily incapax[8], and if a person was thereby rendered incapable of transacting the kind of business in question the transaction is voidable. However, in such

---

1 *Mitchell and Baxter v Cheyne* (1891) 19 R 324.
2 *Report on Incapable Adults* (Scot Law Com no 151) (1995) para 1.19.
3 On the curator bonis, see generally *Inland Revenue v McMillan's Curator Bonis* 1956 SC 142, 1956 SLT 67. The curator must act within the terms of the rules laid down in the Judicial Factors Acts and Trusts Acts.
4 *Stair* I,10,3; *Erskine* III,1,16; *Gall v Bird* (1855) 17 D 1027.
5 However note older cases such as *Alexander v Kinneir* (1632) Mor 6278; *Christie v Gib* (1700) Mor 6283.
6 Bell *Commentaries* I,132. See also *Ballantyne v Evans* (1886) 13 R 652.
7 *Wink v Mortimer* (1849) 11 D 995; *King v British Linen Co* (1899) 1 F 928, 7 SLT 58.
8 *Stair* I,10,13; *Erskine* III,1,16.

an instance, the party cannot be relieved from the obligations under the contract unless he repudiates the contract as soon as he recovers his senses and realises what he has done[1].

(5)   EXECUTORS

Executors are persons nominated by a testator (the person making a will) or entitled by law, and confirmed in office by the court, to wind up a deceased's affairs and distribute his estate according to law or as directed by his will[2] . The executor is the representative of the deceased, but with limited liability to the extent of the estate. The office is gratuitous and an executor is not entitled to a fee for his services, except that an institution, such as a bank which acts in that capacity may take reasonable fees for its services. In circumstances where an account is opened in the name of a deceased person, and there are only two executors, cheques on the account must be signed by both. If there are more than two, the signature of the majority is sufficient[3]. It is competent to have one executor and that signature alone is sufficient. The bank has no obligation further than ascertaining that an executor has a prima facie title to manage the deceased's estate. The executor has no authority to deal with the deceased's estate until he has obtained confirmation from the court.

An executor nominate (a person or persons nominated by a will, expressly or impliedly) has, unless precluded by terms of the will, the power of trustees to borrow on the security of the estate[4]. Usually any borrowing is of a temporary nature and by way of an overdraft from the bank, instructed by a minute from the executors.

An executor dative is appointed where there is no executor-nominate or the deceased dies intestate, and that on application to the sheriff court. After making an inventory of the estate, the executor dative must find caution, usually from an insurance company. The consent of the cautioner and, prudently, the consent of the principal beneficiaries may be required to allow general borrowing, although in more straightforward matters it is common for banks to proceed upon their knowledge of, and reliance upon the executors who in many cases are solicitors who have a course of dealing with the bank. Occasionally, banks do release funds held in the accounts of deceased customers to those entitled under a will or the rules of intestacy without insisting that confirmation is obtained. If the executors borrow in the course of administering the trust estate, they are personally liable unless it has been agreed with the bank that it is only the

---

1   *Taylor v Provan* (1864) 2 M 1226; *Pollok v Burns* (1875) 2 R 497; *Harvey v Smith* (1904) 6 F 511.
2   *Manson v Hutcheon* (1874) 1 R 371.
3   The court will protect such a majority of co-executors unless it is shown that their action will be injurious to the estate or prejudice the interests of beneficiaries: *Mackenzie v Mackenzie* (1886) 13 R 507. See also *Erskine* III,9,40.
4   Under s 4 of the Trusts (Scotland) Act 1921.

estate which is liable[1]. A discharge and indemnity is taken from the person or persons receiving the funds[2].

(6) TRUSTEES

The powers and duties of trustees are regulated primarily by the trust deed or the codicil by which they are appointed. Where not at variance with the terms and purposes of the trust, trustees are given full powers including the specific power to borrow money on the security of the trust estate or any part of it, heritable as well as moveable[3]. The bank's principal concern is with the power to borrow and any limitations upon that power rather than the actings of the trustees in applying the moneys of the estate[4]. The trust nature of the account should be clearly recorded by the bank and in instances where cheques do not require signature by a majority and quorum of trustees, the operation of the account should be instructed by a minute, containing, if necessary, the power to overdraw. Trustees borrowing money in the course of administering the trust fund are personally liable unless it has been agreed with the bank that the estate alone is liable for the sums borrowed[5].

A power to borrow may however, on occasion, be implied from the terms of the trust deed[6], even in instances where the deed did not expressly specify a borrowing power. Where the deed confers full and extensive powers of management and administration, a power to borrow is usually implied[7]. Under English law there is authority for the view that a loan advanced to a trustee is recoverable from the trust estate as distinct from the trustee personally[8].

An area of concern is whether a bank may be held liable for unwittingly having assisted the customer, the trustee, in carrying out an inappropriate transaction. In *Thomson v Clydesdale Bank Ltd*[9], the owners of shares ordered their broker to sell the shares and the broker paid the money into his own overdrawn account. The broker later became insolvent and it was established that at the time of the transaction the bank knew that the cheque represented the proceeds of the sale of shares but did not know and had not asked if the money was held by the broker as agent or in his own right. The question before the House of Lords was whether the bank had sufficient notice of the transaction to be imputed with knowledge of the stockbroker's breach of trust. The bank was excused from liability

1 *Gordon v Campbell* (1842) 1 Bell App 428, HL.
2 See Wallace and McNeil's *Banking Law* (10th edn, 1991 by D B Caskie) p 36; and *Scottish Banking Practice* (5th edn, 1987 by Vivian Davey) ch 5, pp 46–48.
3 Trusts (Scotland) Act 1921, s 4, especially s 4(1)(d) (amended by the Trusts (Scotland) Act 1961, s 4).
4 *Buchanan v Glasgow University Court* 1909 SC 47.
5 *Gordon v Campbell* (1842) 1 Bell App 428, HL
6 As in *Christie's Trustees* 1946 SLT 309, OH.
7 See *Re Bellinger* [1898] 2 Ch 534.
8 *De Vigier v Inland Revenue Comrs* [1964] 2 All ER 907, [1964] 1 WLR 1073, HL.
9 (1893) 20 R (HL) 59, [1893] AC 282.

because it did not know the account was a trust account, a general principle which is supported by later authority[1]. The consequence of this principle is that the bank's liability will depend generally upon its knowledge of the nature of the account, how explicitly the trust relationship exists from the information available to the bank, and whether specific circumstances exist so as to impute the knowledge of the relationship of trust to the bank[2]. The tests laid down by Lord Moncreiff in *Jopp v Johnston's Trustee*[3] provide clear guidance:

(1) where a trustee sells trust property and lodges the proceeds in a bank account in his own name, the money which is lodged in the bank may be followed by the truster, provided it can be traced with reasonable certainty;

(2) the proposition operates, not only between truster and trustee, but between the truster and the trustee's trustee in bankruptcy;

(3) it does not matter that the moneys have been mixed with other moneys belonging to the trustee; and

(4) if after the proceeds of the trust property are lodged and mixed with the trustee's own funds, the trustee draws out part of the mixed fund, he will be held to have drawn out his own funds and not those of the trust property[4].

The bank will, in appropriate circumstances, be liable to the beneficiaries of trust property in a breach of the trust provisions by the trustee[5].

The trustee has duties and powers of investment if the trust is a continuing one and investment is authorised by the trust deed. In these circumstances trustees may be found personally liable for loss of interest on funds which could and should have been invested[6], or for the loss sustained by leaving money for an unreasonable time on deposit receipt[7]. Trustees may invest the trust fund only in those investments authorised by the Trustee Investments Act 1961[8] and accordingly bankers organising such investments on behalf of the trustee must be alert to the customer's obligations.

(7) BANKRUPT CUSTOMERS

The bankruptcy process in Scotland is known as sequestration whereby a bankrupt is judicially divested of his property which is vested in a trustee for the benefit of his creditors. A detailed set of rules is laid down in the

1 *Union Bank of Australia Ltd v Murray-Aynsley* [1898] AC 693; *Bank of New South Wales v Goulburn Valley Butter Co Pty Ltd* [1902] AC 543, PC.

2 *Re Gross, ex parte Kingston* [1871] LR 6 Ch App 632 at 640, per Mellish LJ.

3 (1904) 6 F 1028 at 1036.

4 2 *Stair Memorial Encyclopaedia* para 1237.

5 *Gray v Johnston* (1868) LR 3 HL 1. See also *Selangor United Rubber Estates Ltd v Cradock (No 3)* [1968] 2 All ER 1073, [1968] 1 WLR 1555; *Karak Rubber Co Ltd v Burden (No 2)* [1972] 1 All ER 1210, [1972] 1 WLR 602.

6 *Melville v Noble's Trustees* (1896) 24 R 243; *Clarke v Clarke's Trustees* 1925 SC 693, 1925 SLT 498.

7 *Melville* above; *Manners v Strong's Judicial Factor* (1902) 4 F 829.

8 And in any manner specified in Pt I or Pt II of Sch 1 of the 1961 Act.

Bankruptcy (Scotland) Act 1985 (as amended) which places the process under the supervision of the Accountant of Court, also known as the Accountant in Bankruptcy[1]. A petition procedure is provided for[2] whereby an interim trustee is appointed[3], and subsequently a permanent trustee is elected and appointed[4]. Commissioners represent the interests of the creditors[5]. The task of the trustee is to recover, manage and realise the estate and to distribute it in the manner prescribed in the Act[6].

One of the effects of sequestration is to prevent the customer from operating on any account held by him with the bank at the date of sequestration. Sequestration terminates the bank's mandatory authority to pay cheques drawn upon the account, unless the cheques have been drawn in the ordinary course of business between the bank and the customer and the bank was unaware of the sequestration and had no reason to believe the customer has been sequestrated[7]. The bank has a duty to surrender the funds to the permanent trustee by virtue of the act and warrant issued upon confirmation of his appointment[8]. The bankrupt may be entitled to obtain employment and with the consent of the court retain such sums from his earnings as are necessary for himself and his family[9]. It is accordingly possible for a bankrupt to open a bank account to enable him to pay for living expenses, subject to the provision, however, that he may not obtain credit of £250 or more without declaring that he is an undischarged bankrupt[10].

The estates of bankrupt persons may be wound up by means other than resorting to sequestration. The method often selected is a voluntary trust deed for creditors whereby the trustee obtains a specific right of property in the estate conveyed to him by the insolvent. The trustee is entitled to uplift any credit balance on an account belonging to the bankrupt person on exhibiting the trust deed in his favour or an extract registered copy of the deed[11].

Questions often arise as to the juncture at which a bank should begin to refuse to honour the bankrupt's cheques. As soon as the bank becomes aware that a petition has been presented to sequestrate the customer, or a trust deed granted, the bank should immediately cease to honour its bankrupt customer's cheques. Care must be taken where intimation is made orally to the bank that the customer is bankrupt and verification should immediately be sought. To continue to honour cheques after due intimation would result in the bank being exposed to reimbursement to the trustee from their own funds.

1 Bankruptcy (Scotland) Act 1985, s 1.
2 s 5.
3 s 13.
4 ss 24–29.
5 s 30.
6 s 3(1)(a).
7 s 32(9)(b)(iii).
8 s 31(1).
9 s 32(1) and (2).
10 s 67(9).
11 *Wallace and McNeil* p 38.

3.   UNINCORPORATED ASSOCIATIONS

(1)   INTRODUCTION

The nature of an association has been summarised as follows:

> 'An association may be defined as a group of persons bound together by
> agreement for a particular purpose. A club constitutes one example of an
> association. An association is distinct from a company registered under the
> Companies Acts in that it is not legally incorporated, and from a partnership
> in that its primary purpose is not profit making; in addition it differs from
> both a company and a partnership in not being treated in Scots law as a dis-
> tinct person'[1].

Unincorporated associations have no legal existence apart from the members of whom it is composed[2]. They do not have separate personality as
distinct from the members and are regulated by the rules which the members adopt which govern and form part of the contract of membership
between members. Examples of unincorporated associations are social or
sporting clubs, religious or political organisations, charities (except where
a company has been formed) and scientific associations.

Upon joining an unincorporated association a member becomes related
by contract to all of the other members in a type of multipartite agreement[3]. In *Murray v Johnstone*[4], a dispute arose as to the ownership of a
sporting trophy, presented to the respondent, J. Under the rules, the trophy cup became the property of the club after the club won it two years in
succession. The majority decision to present it to J was disputed by a
minority of members and the question was resolved in the Inner House to
the satisfaction of the appellants. The basis of the decision is that every
member of the club had an interest in the object which was the joint property of all members. The majority were acting ultra vires in seeking to bind
the minority to a decision to which they did not consent. The relationship
between the members is therefore regulated by the rules of the club or the
constitution[5]. This includes questions as to terms of admission[6] and of
expulsion, which must be exercised within the terms of the rules[7].

The powers of management of the affairs of the club are normally delegated to a committee elected by the members. The committee is, in
essence, the agent of the members. The property of the club is usually
vested in individuals who hold it as trustees for the club (who are often
separate from the members of the committee). The rules and constitution
of the club will lay down the powers and duties which are delegated to the
committee and the extent to which they may competently commit club
funds by entering into everyday contracts. Unless expressly or implicitly
agreed, the committee has no right to be indemnified by the individual

1   2 *Stair Memorial Encyclopaedia* para 801.
2   *Steele v Gourley and Davis* (1886) 3 TLR 118 at 119, per Day J.
3   *Evans v Hooper* (1875) 1 QBD 45, CA.
4   (1896) 23 R 981, 1896 4 SLT 81.
5   *Baker v Jones* [1954] 2 All ER 553, [1954] 1 WLR 1005.
6   *Martin v Scottish Transport and General Workers' Union* 1952 SC (HL) 1, 1952 SLT 224.
7   *Young v Ladies' Imperial Club* [1920] 2 KB 523, CA.

members for obligations incurred by it in its actings. In practice, the particular legal status of unincorporated bodies causes no difficulty where the account is in credit and the bank is accepting and honouring cheques in the normal course of business. However, where credit is sought, it is necessary that the committee members have the required capacity and power to enter into the transaction, either expressly by a resolution of the members or by necessary implication by consideration and interpretation of the rules[1]. The general rule is that the club debt attaches to those who have accepted responsibility for the transaction[2].

The objects of unincorporated associations are primarily non-commercial and ordinarily their main source of funds are the subscriptions of the members. Nevertheless, the relationship between the association and the bank is important and legally significant in a number of ways. Firstly, the liability of the members of the body may be limited to the amount of their subscriptions, as in the case of social clubs or political organisations[3]. Secondly, a bank must be aware that an unincorporated association does not have an independent legal personality. In the Court of Session the club is usually sued by calling the club and its officials or a representative selection of members[4]. Actions are instituted against the committee acting on behalf of the unincorporated association to recover the amounts claimed from the association's funds, and members of the committee may on occasion be held personally liable for the debts to the bank[5]. A club may sue and be sued in the sheriff court without the addition of the names of members or officials[6]. Thirdly, the committee of the association is not entitled to exceed the powers conferred on it by its own constitution. In *Flemyng v Hector*[7], the committee of the club was entitled to delegate to an agent its power to draw and indorse bills of exchange, the decision being reached on a construction of the club's constitution.

In the consideration of making available an account or borrowing facilities to a club or other unincorporated association a copy of the rules or constitution should be obtained to ascertain the powers of the committee and its office bearers. If the club or association seeks to borrow and such a power is not contained within the rules, the association should be invited to amend its constitution accordingly. The same principle applies to powers allowing the granting of security over the association's property. An extract from the minutes of the association or committee, including a specific resolution on the authorisation of the opening of the account and the powers of the persons authorised to operate the account should be obtained. The minutes themselves should be certified by the president (chairman) and the secretary.

---

1 *Thomson v Shanks* (1840) 2 D 699.
2 *Spowart v Transport and General Workers' Union* 1926 SLT 245, OH; *Cromarty Leasing Ltd v Turnbull* 1988 SLT (Sh Ct) 62; *Lennox v Scottish Branch of the British Show Jumping Association* 1994 GWD 10-581, OH.
3 *Wise v Perpetual Trustee Co* [1903] AC 139.
4 *Pagan and Osborne v Haig* 1910 SC 341, 1910 1 SLT 122; *Whitecraigs Golf Club v Ker* 1923 SLT (Sh Ct) 23.
5 *Coutts & Co v Irish Exhibition in London* (1891) 7 TLR 313, CA.
6 *Borland v Lochwinnoch Golf Club* 1986 SLT (Sh Ct) 13.
7 (1836) 6 LJ Ex 43, 2 M & W 172.

Once the account is established, and in the event of there being a change in identity of the operators of the account, a certified minute should be retained by the bank narrating these changes. It is unusual in practice for banks to offer loan facilities to clubs without either security over the club's assets or the personal guarantee of the members or officials as individuals. However, the most important criterion is to ensure the provision of the banking facilities is in strict accordance with the rules of the association. Since 1985 it has been possible to sequestrate an unincorporated association[1].

(2)   TRADE UNIONS

A trade union is in law an unincorporated association, consisting of a number of individual members described by one convenient label. It is an organisation 'which consists wholly or mainly of workers of one or more descriptions and whose principal purposes include the regulation of relations between workers of that description or those descriptions and employers or employers' associations'[2]. Trade unions are, however, capable of making contracts, capable of suing and being sued in their own name, whether in proceedings relating to property or founded on contract, delict or on any cause of action whatsoever.

The Trade Union Act 1871 provided that the purposes of a trade union would not be illegal on the common law ground of being an illegal association[3], and in 1901 it was established that a trade union could have a registered name[4]. From 1901 to 1971, although not bodies corporate, they were regarded as quasi-corporations capable of suing and being sued. The Industrial Relations Act of 1971 enacted a new regime providing preferential treatment to organisations registered under its provisions and trade unions were accorded corporate status[5]. That Act was, however, repealed by the Trade Union and Labour Relations Act 1974 and the governing statute, the Trade Union and Labour Relations (Consolidation) Act 1992, now provides that trade unions are once again unincorporated but with specified legal rights and duties[6]. The law as it now stands leads to the result that the general guidelines for unincorporated associations apply to trade unions. In addition, sections 10 to 23 of the 1992 Act consolidate the law on the status and property of trade unions, and sections 24 to 45 lay down the rules on trade union administration. Particular care must be taken, as even if the title to the property of the union is transferred to the trustees automatically in terms of section 13, the transfer of such property must be effected precisely in terms of section 14 of the Act. The banker must ensure that he is advised as to the power and authority of the office

---

1   Bankruptcy (Scotland) Act 1985, s 6(6).
2   Trade Union and Labour Relations (Consolidation) Act 1992, s 1.
3   Trade Union Act 1871, ss 2–3.
4   *Taff Vale Rly Co v Amalgamated Society of Railways Servants* [1901] AC 426, HL.
5   Industrial Relations Act 1971, s 74.
6   The 1974 Act was subsequently amended by the Employment Protection (Consolidation) Act 1978 and the Employment Acts of 1980, 1982, 1988, 1989 and 1990. The law has now been consolidated in the Trade Union and Labour Relations (Consolidation) Act 1992.

bearers and minutes of assumption or resignation should be examined and retained.

4. CHARITIES

Charities in Scotland constitute public trusts but they do not, unlike those in England, form a separate category of trust. Scottish charities are those bodies which are recognised by the Inland Revenue for the purposes of relief under section 505 of the Income and Corporation Taxes Act 1988[1].

As well as enjoying special tax advantages, there are certain specialities relating to charities. Part I of the Law Reform (Miscellaneous Provisions) (Scotland) Act 1990 provides rules of administration and imposes detailed duties upon those 'concerned in the management or control' of the recognised Scottish charities, the definition of which includes trustees and employees. These obligations include the duty to keep accounting records (section 4) and to prepare annual accounts and a report (section 5). Sections 6 to 8 deal with the supervision of charities, namely, the powers of the Lord Advocate to investigate charities and to suspend trustees (section 6); the powers of the Court of Session to deal with the management of charities (section 7) and the disqualification of trustees and other persons involved in the management or control of a charity (section 8).

Sections 9 to 11 are concerned with the administration of charities and in particular with the provision of mechanisms to enhance the effective use of funds held in trust. The criteria for the application of the *cy-près* doctrine are broadened in order that the Court of Session may approve the application of *cy-près* funds from any public trust obsolete or lacking in usefulness[2]. The problems of small funds are addressed by enabling trustees with funds with an annual income of less than £5,000 to reform their objects or to transfer their assets to other trusts without recourse to the court[3]. Where the annual income of the charity is less than £1,000, trustees are empowered to spend capital where such annual income is too small to enable the objects of the trust to be achieved[4].

Perhaps of greatest interest from a bank's perspective, is section 12 of the 1990 Act which deals with dormant charities. Where the bank account of a charity is dormant and the balance does not exceed £5,000 then the Scottish charities nominee is empowered to transfer the balance to another recognised body unless there is still someone concerned in the management of the charity or other circumstances which make it inappropriate to make the transfer (section 12(3)). Where the balance exceeds £5,000 (or section 12(3) in general does not apply), the Lord Advocate may appoint new trustees or apply to the Court of Session for the appointment of an

1 For further information relating to the tax aspects of charities, see Tolley's *Tax Planning*; Butterworth's *UK Tax Guide*; Whitehouse *Revenue Law Principles and Practice*.
2 Law Reform (Miscellaneous Provisions) (Scotland) Act 1990, s 9.
3 Ibid, s 10.
4 Ibid, s 11.

interim judicial factor or, as an alternative to the foregoing, apply subsection (3) as if the balance was less than £5,000 and neither paragraph (a) nor (b) of that subsection applied. The receipt of the nominee when an account is closed is a full and valid discharge to the bank holding the account (section 12(7))'[1].

In relation to persons acting on behalf of a charity, attention should be paid to the terms of the trust deed and the Trusts (Scotland) Act 1921, section 4 of which enables trustees to sell, lease and borrow on security where such acts are not at variance with the terms or purposes of the trust. Where such activity would be at variance with the terms or purposes of the trust, then any security which a trustee granted would be ultra vires and could be reduced at the instance of the beneficiaries, except in so far as the money lent had been applied to the benefit of the beneficiaries[2].

5.   PARTNERSHIPS

(1)   INTRODUCTION

A partnership in Scotland may be said to have a quasi-personality and is regulated by the Partnership Act 1890. It is a separate legal person distinct from the individual partners and is capable of entering into obligations and contracts, the partners contracting as agents for the firm. It may sue or be sued[3]. The firm may own moveable property in its own name and the property is held and applied exclusively for partnership purposes rather than by the partners as their own personal property[4]. The funds of the partnership belong not to the partners but to the firm itself and debts due must be constituted against the firm. The firm is the primary debtor, the partners cautioners for the firm. The firm may be sequestrated without any of the partners becoming bankrupt and conversely, individual partners can become bankrupt while the firm remains solvent. The partnership may stand in the relation of a debtor or creditor to any of its partners and may sue a partner or be sued by a partner[5]. However, unlike a corporate body, a partnership is essentially a creature of contract, rather than charter, Act of Parliament or other legislation. Accordingly, it may be formed and dissolved by the mere agreement of its members, and the death or bankruptcy of any one partner dissolves the partnership.

(2)   THE DEFINITION OF PARTNERSHIP

Partnership is defined as 'the relation which subsists between persons carrying on a business in common with a view of profit'[6]. The first require-

1 *Wallace and McNeil* p 59.
2 See discussion on trustees at pp 51–52 below.
3 *Gordon v British and Foreign Metaline Co* (1886) 14 R 75; *Mair v Wood* 1948 SC 83, 1948 SLT 326.
4 Partnership Act 1890, s 20(1).
5 *Hutcheon & Partners v Hutcheon* 1979 SLT (Sh Ct) 61.
6 1890 Act, s 1(1).

ment is that there be two or more persons, but no more than twenty unless exempted under the legislation which includes professional partnerships[1]. Provisions have been issued allowing unrestricted partnerships[2] for solicitors, accountants, stockbrokers, surveyors, auctioneers, estate agents, valuers, engineers, loss adjusters and others and within each case, a defined proportion being members of their governing professional body[3]. The business prerequisite of the definition of partnership was satisfied in *Glasgow Heritable Trust v Inland Revenue*[4] where the sale of parts of the partnership property over a number of years to shareholders in order to pay off the firm's capital debts was deemed to be business activity. At common law, where there is no written partnership agreement between the parties, the intention must be ascertained from the words and actings of the parties[5]. If no motive of profit is established, no partnership is constituted[6]. Before 1890 the profit itself had to be subject to a 'sharing' agreement but this was omitted from the 1890 definition, although it is still a relevant factor in determining whether a partnership exists[7]. It is no longer the law that profit sharing is conclusive of the existence of partnership — two or more persons may share profits and not necessarily be partners[8].

A partnership may be constituted by written agreement or oral agreement[9] or by facts and circumstances. It may take very little for the relationship of partnership to be established at law and indeed it is possible for persons to be deemed partners even after expressly providing against the possibility[10].

(3) JOINT AND SEVERAL LIABILITY

Every partner and his respective estate is jointly and severally liable for all debts of the firm and the estate of a deceased partner is also liable[11]. The debt must be constituted against the firm[12] and a partner who has paid the firm's debts is entitled to pro rata relief from the other partners[13]. A person admitted as a partner into an existing firm does not become liable to the creditors of the firm for anything contracted before he became a partner[14]. Retiring partners do not cease to be liable for debts and obligations incurred whilst a partner[15] and retired partners should make arrange-

1 Companies Act 1985, s 716.
2 1985 Act, s 716(3) as substituted by the Companies Act 1989, s 145, Sch 19, para 15(1) and (3).
3 See the 1985 Act, s 716.
4 1954 SC 266, 1954 SLT 97.
5 *Badeley v Consolidated Bank* (1888) 38 Ch D 238, CA.
6 *Thomson v Shanks* (1840) 2 D 699.
7 1890 Act, s 24.
8 *Cox v Hickman* (1860) 8 HL Cas 268.
9 *Walters v Bingham* [1988] 1 FTLR 260.
10 *Stewart v Buchanan* (1903) 6 F 15.
11 1890 Act, s 9.
12 *Highland Engineering Ltd v Anderson* 1979 SLT 122, OH.
13 1890 Act, s 4.
14 1890 Act, s 17(1).
15 1890 Act, s 17(2).

ments with the newly constituted firm *and* the creditors of it to avoid ongoing and historical liability[1]. The fact that the remaining partners have agreed to indemnify the retiring partner does not relieve the retired partner from liability to third party creditors[2]. All creditors of the firm, including a bank, may seek to recover all sums due to the firm from one partner only, leaving that partner to demand indemnification from the remaining partners.

(4)   POWERS AND LIABILITIES OF PARTNERS

Every partner is an agent for the firm and of the other partners for the purpose of the business of the partnership[3] and the authority of any partner in a question between the partners themselves will be regulated by the 1890 Act or the partnership deed. It follows that the partner's actings in carrying out the usual business of the partnership[4] and his signature of the firm name bind the firm unless he has no authority and the person with whom he deals knows he does not have power or does not know or believe he is a partner[5].

The extent of the partner's authority to act as an agent of the firm depends upon the nature of the firm's business[6] but normally extends to receiving payments and granting discharges[7], borrowing money[8], undertaking financial transactions[9] and buying and selling generally[10]. Drawing cheques is within the authority of the partners if in the usual course of the partnership business[11]. A partner in a commercial or trading partnership may bind the firm by contracting debts on its account and by pledging partnership goods or securities for the purpose of the partnership business. In non-trading partnerships, partners will only have such powers if expressly agreed upon by the partners, requiring the bank to obtain an undertaking signed by all the partners expressing their consent to the partner's mandate.

The most important consideration is to ascertain the extent of a partner's authority. Beyond what is expressly provided for in any partnership deed, it is the nature of a partnership that the partners have implied authority to bind the firm. It is generally accepted that a partner's implied authority does not extend to executing deeds in relation to heritable property; giving a guarantee in the firm name without establishing trade custom; accepting property in lieu of money in satisfaction of a partnership

---

1   1890 Act, s 17(3).
2   *Welsh v Knarston* 1972 SLT 96, OH.
3   1890 Act, s 5.
4   See *Mercantile Credit v Garrod* [1962] 3 All ER 1103; *Mann v D'Arcy* [1968] 2 All ER 172, [1968] 1 WLR 893.
5   1890 Act, ss 5–6.
6   *Ciceri v Hunter & Co* (1904) 12 SLT 293, OH.
7   *Nicoll v Reid* (1878) 6 R 216.
8   *Bryan v Butters Bros & Co* (1892) 19 R 490.
9   *Fortune v Young* 1918 SC 1.
10   *Nicoll v Reid* (1878) 6 R 216.
11   *Backhouse v Charleton* (1878) 8 Ch D 444.

debt; authorising a third party to use the firm name in legal or other proceedings and the submitting of disputes to arbitration[1].

The 1890 Act contains rules governing the power and authority of partners. Where one partner pledges the credit of the firm for a purpose not apparently connected with the firm's ordinary course of business the firm is not bound unless that partner is in fact specially authorised by the other partners[2]. In the event of there being a limitation or restriction on the power of one or more partners to bind the firm, it binds those third parties who have notice of the limited authority[3]. Reference may require to be had to the contract of co-partnery for guidance. If a wrongful act or omission of one partner, acting in the ordinary course of the business of the firm or with the authority of the other partners, causes loss or injury to any person who is not a partner, or any penalty is incurred, then the firm is liable to the same extent as the partner who is guilty of the act or omission[4]. Where one partner acting within the scope of his apparent authority receives money or property of a third person and misapplies it, or where a firm in the course of its business receives money or property of a third person and it is misapplied by one or more of them as partners while in the custody of the firm, the firm is liable to make good the loss[5]. The position is different in the instance where one partner is a trustee in a trust and improperly employs trust property in the business or on the account of the partnership. No other partner is liable for the trust property to the beneficiaries of the trust[6]. Consequences arise by virtue of each partner being an agent of the firm. An admission or representation made by any partner concerning the partnership affairs in the ordinary course of business is evidence against the firm[7] and notice to a partner who habitually acts in the partnership business of any matter relating to partnership affairs operates as notice to the firm, unless the firm is a victim of a fraud committed by that partner[8].

(5) THE FIRM AS CUSTOMER

General rules

The signature of a partner in matters relating to the ordinary business of the firm is sufficient to bind the firm and the other partners[9]. It follows that with regard to the ordinary business of the firm, the partner may operate the firm's account and is entitled to close it. However, a partner does not have the power to open a bank account in his own name so as to make the other partners liable for the debit balance[10].

1 Reeday *The Law Relating to Banking* (5th edn, 1985) pp 93–94.
2 1890 Act, s 7; *Paterson Bros v Gladstone* (1891) 18 R 403.
3 1890 Act, s 8.
4 1890 Act, s 10; *Kirkintilloch Equitable Co-operative Society Ltd v Livingstone* 1972 SC 111, 1972 SLT 154.
5 1890 Act, s 11; *Arbuckle v Taylor* (1815) 3 Dow 160; *New Mining and Exploring Syndicate v Chalmers and Hunter* 1912 SC 126.
6 1890 Act, s 13.
7 1890 Act, s 15.
8 1890 Act, s 16.
9 1890 Act, s 6.
10 *Alliance Bank Ltd v Kearsley* (1871) LR 6 CP 433.

Unless contrary evidence has been exhibited to the bank, any partner has authority to draw upon the firm's bank account in the firm name and has implied authority to bind the firm by cheque[1]. It has on occasion been argued that there is a qualification to the effect that the power of the partner to bind the firm by cheque holds only so long as the cheque is not post-dated. In *Forster v Mackreth*[2], it was held that issuing post-dated cheques was outwith the partner's authority despite the cheques having being drawn in order to raise temporary finance for the firm by means of their discount. Ellinger and Lomnicka[3] believe *Forster* is unlikely to stand the test of time, and point to supporting authority (although limited) for this proposition[4]. English law inclines to the view that a post-dated cheque is valid in all regards based on section 13(2) of the Bills of Exchange Act 1882 which provides that a bill is not invalid by reason of being post-dated, ante-dated or undated. Indeed, as between holder and drawer, a post-dated cheque is regarded as valid and as regular from its genuine date of issue. It is clear from the *Guildford Trust* case that the holder of a post-dated cheque is entitled to enforce payment of it[5]. The position is the same in Scotland.

A partner has no authority to authorise an employee of the firm or a third party to operate on the partnership account. A mandate would require to be signed by all the partners to provide appropriate authority to such a third party or employee. Where an account is opened in the name of the firm, the bank is, in the absence of any other agreement, only bound to honour cheques signed in that name[6]. The mere existence of a trade partnership does not imply that a partner has power to open an account in his own name for the purposes of the firm so as to make his co-partners liable for any debit balance. The leading case is *Alliance Bank Ltd v Kearsley*[7] in which two brothers, W and J were in partnership carrying on a business of coach builders. J opened an account with the plaintiffs in Manchester explaining that although the account was a partnership account, he was the only partner resident in Manchester and it was appropriate to open an account in his own name. The court held that the bank could not recover from W as the account was essentially J's own private account. In circumstances where the partner does open an account in his own name, he must prove that in doing so he was not acting on his own behalf but as an agent of the firm. The prudent practice for a bank is to obtain a mandate or guarantee from the partners on the opening of a partnership account.

The bank is obliged to honour the cheque of any partner drawn on an account in the name of the firm and signed in the appropriate firm name. The bank is not obliged, however, to honour a cheque drawn by anyone purporting to be a partner but who is not known to the bank as such and

1 *Backhouse v Charleton* (1878) 8 Ch D 444.
2 (1867) LR 2 Exch 163 at 166.
3 Ellinger and Lomnicka *Modern Banking Law* (2nd edn, 1994) p 234.
4 See eg *Guildford Trust Ltd v Goss* (1927) 136 LT 725.
5 *Guildford Trust Ltd* above. See also *Hitchcock v Edwards* (1889) 60 LT 636 and *Royal Bank of Scotland v Tottenham* [1894] 2 QB 715, CA.
6 *Forster v Mackreth* (1867) LR 2 Exch 163.
7 (1871) LR 6 CP 433.

with whose signature they are not acquainted[1]. Any partner has power to countermand payment of a cheque drawn in the firm name by another partner[2].

Mandates for partnership accounts

It is prudent practice for any bank operating a partnership account to ensure that *all* partners of the firm sign the mandate establishing an account. That mandate should state the name and principal address of the firm and specify the full names of the partners who are authorised to sign cheques and orders or issue instructions authorising payment on behalf of the firm. In this context, any authorised employee or third party should be named in the mandate, and the extent of the partners' authority should be specified. The signature of all the partners will authorise the named parties to operate on the partnership account; authorise the bank to deliver up any items held in safe custody and to act on the instructions of the named signatory; and contain the agreement of the partners that they will be jointly and severally liable for any debts owing to the bank[3]. The traditional view is that the bank should be satisfied as to the existence of the partnership and should obtain references or inquire as to the financial standing of the partners to satisfy itself as to the reputation of the individual partners.

Partnership property

Partnership property comprises all property, rights and interests in property originally brought into the partnership or acquired, whether by purchase or otherwise, on account of the firm or for the purposes of the partnership and in accordance with the partnership agreement[4]. Partnership property must be held and applied by the partners exclusively for the purposes of the partnership and in accordance with the partnership agreement. The title to and interest in any heritable estate which belongs to the partnership devolves according to the general rules of law, but in trust for the persons in the partnership beneficially interested in the heritable estate[5]. Persons may be co-owners of heritable property or be partners as to the profits made by the use of that property without the property being partnership property. Unless the contrary intention appears, property bought with money belonging to the firm is deemed to have been bought on account of the firm[6].

The interest of each partner to the partnership property is a *pro indiviso* share of the firm's assets. As a consequence, the partner's interest is moveable in his succession, though the property actually held may be

1 *Cooke v Seeley* (1848) 2 Exch 746.
2 *Gaunt v Taylor* (1843) 2 Hare 413.
3 Lewis *Law of Banking Services* (1991) p 78.
4 1890 Act, s 20(1); *Pillans Bros v Pillans* (1908) 16 SLT 611, OH.
5 1890 Act, s 20(2); *Morrison v Miller* (1818) Hume 720; *Cameron v Lightheart* 1995 SCLR 443, 1996 SLT 1038. See also Gretton 'Who owns partnership property?' 1987 JR 163.
6 1890 Act, s 21.

heritable[1]. The proper diligence to attach a partner's interest is arrestment in the hands of the firm, and not adjudication or poinding of the particular assets[2]. The property of a partnership is held in the name of the firm or in the name of a partner. The exception is land held by feudal tenure[3] which must be taken in the name of the partners as trustees for the firm.

Dissolution of partnership

A partnership may be dissolved in a number of ways.

(a) By expiry of a fixed term[4]. Where the partners continue to carry on the business of the partnership after the expiry date and without further express agreement the partnership is deemed to continue on the same terms and conditions by the process of tacit relocation[5], so long as the business is carried on for a period long enough to justify the inference. The continuing relationship is known as a partnership at will[6].

(b) By achievement of its object, if entered into for a single adventure or undertaking[7].

(c) By agreement, termination in terms of the partnership agreement.

(d) By notice — where the partnership is in existence for an undefined time, or is continued by tacit relocation, any partner may give notice of his intention to dissolve the partnership[7].

(e) By the death or bankruptcy of any partner[8]. The partnership is dissolved on the death or bankruptcy of any partner, in the absence of agreement to the contrary. If the bank wishes to hold a retiring partner or the representatives of a deceased partner liable for the outstanding obligations of the firm, the bank must, upon receiving notice of death or retiral, cease the operations of the account and continue the facilities of the remaining partner by way of a new account. Failure to do so applies the rule in *Clayton's* case leading to the reduction of the indebtedness as credit entries are applied to the account[9].

(f) By application of the other partners, if any partner suffers his share of the partnership property to be charged under the Act for his separate debt[10].

(g) By the happening of any event which makes it unlawful for the business of the firm to be carried on or for the members of the firm to carry it on in partnership[11].

(h) By the court. The Act[12] provides that the court may dissolve, on application by a partner, on the grounds that: a partner is of permanently

1 1890 Act, s 22; Bell *Commentaries* II,501; *Minto v Kirkpatrick* (1833) 11 S 632.
2 *Erskine* III,3,24; *Parnell v Walter* (1889) 16 R 917.
3 Bell *Principles* s 357.
4 1890 Act, s 32(a).
5 *Wallace v Wallace's Trustees* (1906) 8 F 558, 13 SLT 844.
6 1890 Act, s 27.
7 *Gracie v Prentice* (1904) 12 SLT 15, 42 SLR 9, OH.
8 1890 Act, s 33(1); *William S Gordon & Co v Mrs Mary Thomson Partnership* 1985 SLT 122.
9 *Devaynes v Noble, Clayton's Case* (1816) 1 Mer 529 at 572.
10 1890 Act, s 33(2).
11 1890 Act, s 34; *Hugh Stevenson & Sons v Aktiengesellschaft für Cartonnagen-Industrie* [1918] AC 239, HL.
12 1890 Act, s 35.

unsound mind; a partner is permanently incapable of performing his part under the partnership contract; a partner has been guilty of such conduct as having regard to the nature of the business, is calculated prejudicially to effect the carrying on of the business[1]; a partner, other than the partner suing, wilfully or persistently commits a breach of the partnership agreement, or otherwise so conducts himself in matters relating to the partnership business that it is not reasonably practicable for the partners to carry on the business in partnership with him; the business of the partnership can only be carried on at a loss and in any case, circumstances have arisen which render it just and equitable that the partnership be dissolved[2].

Effects of dissolution

The general effect of dissolution is to end the authority of the partners to bind the firm. After dissolution, 'the authority of each partner to bind the firm, and the other rights and obligations of the partners, continue notwithstanding the dissolution so far as may be necessary to wind up the affairs of the partnership and to complete transactions begun but unfinished at the time of the dissolution'[3]. However, the continued authority does not apply to a partner who is bankrupt. A bank was justified in accepting the signature of the firm name by one of the partners eight years after the firm was dissolved since the uplifting of the money was the completion of such an unfinished transaction[4]. English authorities suggest that a bank has no obligation to scrutinise carefully the actions of the surviving partners in such cases. The views expressed by the court in *Backhouse v Charleton*[5] and *Re Bourne*[6] indicate that the imposition of liability on banks for an improper scrutiny of individual partners would make too uncertain and impractical the relations between the bank and its partnership customer.

Where a partnership has been prematurely dissolved, the court may order repayment in whole or in part of any premium paid by one partner to another on entering into a partnership, unless the dissolution is wholly or chiefly due to the misconduct of the partner who paid the premium, or the partnership has been dissolved by an agreement containing no provision for return of any part of the premium[7]. Where any member of a firm has died or has otherwise ceased to be a partner and the remaining partners carry on business without any final settlement of accounts, then, unless there is agreement to the contrary, the outgoing partner's estate is entitled at their option to such a share of the profits made since dissolution as the court finds attributable to the use of his share of the partnership

1 Eg *Carmichael v Evans* [1904] 1 Ch 486.
2 *Roxburgh v Dinardo* 1981 SLT 291.
3 1890 Act, s 38.
4 *Dickson v National Bank of Scotland Ltd* 1917 SC (HL) 50, 1917 1 SLT 318. See also *Inland Revenue Comrs v Graham's Trustees* 1971 SC (HL) 1, 1971 SLT 46; *Welsh v Knarston* 1972 SLT 96, OH; *Jardine-Paterson v Fraser* 1974 SLT 93, OH.
5 (1878) 8 Ch D 444.
6 [1906] 2 Ch 427, CA.
7 1890 Act, s 41.

assets, or to the interest on the amount of his share at 5 per cent[1]. However, where the survivors have an option to purchase his share and exercise that right, the outgoing partner is not entitled to any further or other share of the profits unless there is material non-compliance with the terms of the option[2]. The term 'profits' means the profits accruing in the ordinary course of the business of the partnership pending realisation and not an increase in the value of the partnership assets[3].

Winding up

The winding up of the firm is designed to collect and realise the firm's assets and distribute the money to those entitled to it. On dissolution, any partner may apply to the Court of Session to wind up the business and affairs of the firm[4]. Under the *nobile officium*, the court has an inherent power to appoint judicial factors and the court's practice in winding up cases of partnerships is to appoint judicial factors[5]. The court will not readily proceed, at the request of a partner to appoint a judicial factor simply on averments that differences have arisen between the partners[6].

6.   SOLICITORS

The Solicitors (Scotland) Accounts Rules 1996 require solicitors to maintain a client account or accounts, and pay into the account without delay any sum exceeding £50 which is held for a client[7]. 'Client account' means a current or deposit or savings account or a deposit receipt at a branch of a bank in the UK in the name of the solicitor or incorporated practice, in the title of which the word 'client' or 'trustee' or some other indication of a fiduciary relationship appears[8]. It is the duty of the solicitor to ensure that the sum at the credit of the client account or accounts is not less than the total of the client's money held by the solicitor[9]. A solicitor or incorporated practice may not overdraw clients' accounts, but may overdraw on an account standing in the name of a client where the client has given authority in writing[10]. The rules contain detailed provisions as to what sums may be withdrawn from the client account[11].

---

1   1890 Act, s 42(1); *Vyse v Foster* (1874) LR 7 HL 318; but see *Roxburgh Dinardo & Partners' Judicial Factor v Dinardo* 1992 SC 188, 1993 SLT 16 where a commercial rate of interest was applied as considered appropriate.
2   1890 Act, s 42(2).
3   *Barclays Bank Trust Co Ltd v Bluff* [1982] Ch 172, [1981] 3 All ER 232.
4   *Pollock v Campbell* 1962 SLT (Sh Ct) 89.
5   See s 39 of the 1890 Act. See eg *McCulloch v McCulloch* 1953 SC 189, 1953 SLT 117; *Roxburgh Dinardo & Partners' Judicial Factor v Dinardo* 1992 SC 188, 1993 SLT 16.
6   See eg *Elliot v Charles W Cassils & Co* (1907) 15 SLT 190, OH.
7   Solicitors (Scotland) Account Rules, r 4(1)(b). (These rules came into effect on 1 August 1996.)
8   Ibid, r 2(1).
9   Ibid, r 4(1)(a).
10   Ibid, r 4(3)(c).
11   Ibid, r 6.

It is important to note that although the bank is under no duty to ensure that the solicitor's ' client's account' is not overdrawn, the bank has no right of set-off against any other liability of the solicitor to the bank[1]. In instances where a solicitor holds money for a client and having regard to the amount of the money, the length of time for which it is likely to be held and that it is reasonable that interest should be earned for the client, the solicitor is obliged to place such money in an interest-bearing account, and to account to the client for any interest earned thereon[2]. The bank does not incur any liability in respect of a client account which it would not incur in respect of a personal account, and is not obliged to make inquiries of, nor is deemed to have any knowledge of, the right of any person to any money paid into or credited to the account[3].

Where the Council of the Law Society is satisfied that a sole solicitor is incapacitated by illness or accident to such an extent that he cannot operate on his client account, the right to operate the account rests on the Council of the Law Society if no other arrangements acceptable to the Council have been made[4]. Similar provisions cover the death of sole solicitors and where solicitors have been struck off or suspended from practice[5]. Where a solicitor is struck off the roll or is suspended from practice, or the recognition of an incorporated practice is revoked, the Council of the Law Society of Scotland must be satisfied, within twenty-one days of the material date, that suitable arrangements have been made to enable clients or other solicitors or incorporated practices to obtain access to papers and all sums due to clients which are held on their behalf[6]. If the Council is not satisfied it may apply to the Court of Session for an order preventing any bank, building society or other body named in the order from making any payments out of an account in the name of the solicitor or his firm or incorporated practice without leave from the court[7]. There is no rule of law that a solicitor, opening an account in his own name for a named client, is personally responsible for any debit balance becoming due on the account[8]. A solicitor cannot obtain an overdraft in his own name for a client unless he has given the bank details of the client, the arrangements for repayment and that he has no personal liability for repayment[9].

1 Solicitors (Scotland) Act 1980, s 61(3) (amended by the Law Reform (Miscellaneous Provisions) (Scotland) Act 1985, s 56, Sch 1, Pt I, para 31 and the Solicitors (Scotland) Act 1988, s 6, Sch 1, para 19).
2 Solicitors (Scotland) Account Rules, r 15(1).
3 1980 Act, s 61(1) (amended by the 1985 Act, Sch 1, Pt I, para 31). See generally Crerar 'Making Money Work for You and Your Clients' (1995) 40 JLSS 108.
4 1980 Act, s 46.
5 1980 Act, s 45 (amended by the 1985 Act, Sch 1, Pt I, para 23).
6 1980 Act, s 45(1), (2), (2A), (5) (as so amended).
7 1980 Act, ss 38(1)(c), 45(3) (amended by the 1985 Act, Sch 1, Pt I, paras 16 and 23).
8 See *Royal Bank of Scotland v Skinner* 1931 SLT 382, OH.
9 Solicitors (Scotland) Account Rules, r 8.

7. STOCKBROKERS

Stockbrokers are not required to maintain a separate account for the receipt of clients' funds. A stockbroker may negotiate loans with a bank to enable his clients to buy shares and for the shares to be taken by the bank in security for such advances. There should be standing arrangements between the stockbroker and the bank whereby the bank is allowed to treat the stockbroker as its customer. A stockbroker is not entitled, without his client's consent, to pledge the securities of his client, but often such an implied right exists from a course of dealing between the parties. In such circumstances a stockbroker may pledge the securities of his client without his authority, or even against his express instructions, so as to give the bank a valid title to retain them against the specific advances made upon their security. The bank will only obtain a valid title to the securities if it has acted in good faith and with reasonable inquiry[1]. Despite the fact that the bank assumes or is entitled to assume that a broker pledging shares does so on behalf of a client, the bank need not assume that the proceeds from a sale of shares are not the broker's own money. Therefore, as the proceeds of such a sale are paid into the broker's own account the bank is entitled to use the moneys to reduce the broker's overdraft account and there is no duty to inquire as to the true ownership of the funds. As may seem obvious, if the bank has actual knowledge that the funds have been paid into the account fraudulently, the bank cannot retain the moneys in reduction of the sums due by its overdrawn stockbroker customer[2].

8. ACCOUNTANTS

Accountants are not required to maintain a separate account for the receipt of clients' funds and accordingly, there is no duty upon the bank to be alert as to whether the funds are those of clients or the accountant's own funds.

9. INSURANCE BROKERS

The Insurance Brokers (Registration) Act 1977 established a regulatory system to supervise the conduct of insurance broking businesses. Rules made under the Act[3], provide that an account requires to be set up by each

---

1 *London Joint Stock Bank v Simmons* [1892] AC 201, HL.
2 *London Joint Stock Bank* above; *National Bank of Scotland v Dickie's Trustee* (1895) 22 R 740.
3 The accounts rules made under the Act apply only to insurance brokers registered with the Insurance Brokers Registration Council and not to Lloyds Insurance Brokers, who are governed by regulations laid down by the Committee of Lloyds: Insurance Brokers Registration Council (Accounts and Business Requirements) Rules Approval Order 1979, SI 1979/489, r 14.

customer broker to isolate all receipts and payments arising directly from the insurance broking business, and it must be designated as an 'insurance broking account'[1]. Brokers are required to pay into that account money received from all sources relating to insurance transactions in connection with the business[2]. The account should not be overdrawn and it cannot be used to set off against any indebtedness due by the broker personally to the bank[3]. However, under the rules, brokers may use credit balances from an insurance broking account to purchase 'approved short-term assets,' as long as they are in the name of the broker[4].

10. BUILDING SOCIETIES

(1) GENERAL

The statutory provisions which regulate building societies are contained in the Building Societies Act 1986 and all societies formed since the Building Societies Act 1874 are deemed to be incorporated under the Act of 1986. The main effect of the 1986 Act is to relax the definition of the function of a building society. The Act greatly reduces the differences between building societies and banks by extending the powers of building societies enabling them to provide banking services, including cheque accounts and money transfer services. The previous legislation declared that building societies existed for the purpose of raising, by the subscriptions of members, a fund for making advances to members out of the funds of the society on the security of lands or buildings[5]. Section 5(1) of the 1986 Act contains a similar definition and provides that 'a society may be established if its purpose or principal purpose is that of raising, primarily by the subscriptions of the members, a stock or fund for making to them advances secured on land for their residential use'. However, a building society may now exercise subsidiary functions of a character listed in Parts I to III of Schedule 8 of the Act which greatly extends the facilities and operations afforded to customers[6]. Furthermore, the society may now raise funds otherwise than by the subscription of the members.

(2) REGULATION

The 1986 Act provides for a new system of regulation of building societies by the Building Societies Commission[7]. The Commission has a membership of four to ten persons, one of whom is the Chairman and known as

1 SI 1979/489, r 6(1).
2 r 6(3).
3 See r 6(2).
4 r 6(6).
5 Building Societies Act 1962, s 1(1).
6 Building Societies Act 1986, Sch 8, Pt II (amended by the Building Societies (Provision of Services) Order 1992, SI 1992/509).
7 1986 Act, ss 1–7 and ss 36–57.

the 'First Commissioner'[1]. Membership is either full-time or part-time[2] and in either case members are paid[3]. In an effort to avoid duplication, building societies are not regulated by the Banking Act 1987. The general functions of the Commission are listed in section 1(4) of the Building Societies Act 1986 and are very wide ranging. Section 1(5) provides that 'the Commission shall have the power to do anything which is calculated to facilitate the discharge of its functions, or is incidental or conducive to their discharge'. Societies or persons aggrieved by a determination of the Commission in the exercise of its regulatory powers have a right of appeal to a tribunal[4] and section 48 provides for a further appeal to the courts on a point of law. The Act contains no provisions conferring immunity from liability in damages on the Commission which is in contrast with the Banking Act 1987 and the Financial Services Act 1986. The absence of such provisions means that unlike the Bank of England and the Council of the Stock Exchange, the Building Societies Commission, its members and its staff could be held liable in negligence[5].

(3)   RAISING FUNDS AND BORROWING

The Building Societies Act 1986 contains detailed provisions regulating the raising of funds and borrowing[6]. By section 7(1) a building society may (a) raise funds by the issue of shares to members or (b) borrow money and receive deposits 'from any person' — a term which does not restrict building societies in respect of those from whom they may borrow. Funds raised by either method must be applied for the purposes of the society. A further distinction is drawn between retail funds and deposits; and non-retail funds and deposits[7]. The principle is that a society's liabilities in respect of its non-retail funds and deposits are restricted to an upper limit, which is expressed as a specified percentage of its total liabilities in respect of all shares and deposits. The initial specified percentage was 20 per cent, but 40 per cent is now prescribed as the maximum percentage of a building society's share and deposit liabilities which may be represented by non-retail funds and deposits[8]. The figure may be varied by order of the Commission with the consent of the Treasury.

There are two categories of non-retail funds and deposits. The first is wholesale funds and deposits which has two further sub-categories. Funds borrowed by way of 'transferable instruments'[9] are defined under section 7(19) as instruments which embody 'a right, transferable by delivery of the instrument, to receive an amount referable to a deposit with the

1 1986 Act, s 1(2).
2 1986 Act, s 1(3).
3 1986 Act, Sch 1, paras 5–6.
4 1986 Act, s 47.
5 The Bank of England and the Council incur liability only where the act or omission complained of involves bad faith.
6 1986 Act, ss 7–9.
7 1986 Act, s 7(3).
8 See the Building Societies (Limit on Non-Retail Funds and Deposits) Order 1987, SI 1987/2131.
9 1986 Act, s 7(4)(a).

society'. Funds received through 'qualifying time deposits' are defined in the same subsection as deposits in sterling subject to the following conditions: the amount of the deposit is or exceeds £50,000; the deposit is repayable at the end of a specified period of less than twelve months from the date on which the deposit is made; and the right to repayment is not assignable.

The second category of non-retail funds and deposits is funds raised otherwise than from individuals. Funds falling within this category may be raised either by the issue of shares or by the taking of deposits. Section 7(4) specifically refers to sums received by or on behalf of bodies corporate, friendly societies, charities and pension funds. Wholesale funds are excluded from this category[1].

The limits imposed by the Act on the proportion of a society's funds that may be acquired from non-retail sources have the consequence that retail funds, whether in the form of deposits or subscriptions for shares, will constitute the primary form of finance for societies. However, a society is not entirely free from restrictions: sections 7(6) and 7(16) limit the amount a society may acquire through the issue of shares or borrow, or a combination of both, from individuals to £50,000.

Not less than half of the funds of a building society should have been subscribed by members in the form of shares[2]. Section 7(2) provides that the shares may be of one or more denominations, either paid up in full or to be paid by periodical or other subscriptions and with or without accumulating interest. Whatever the type of share which has been issued, the funds so received may be repaid when they are no longer required for the purposes of the society.

The essence of the difference between shares of a building society and those of a limited liability company were described by Lord President Dunedin thus:

'A share in a limited liability company is part of the capital, and is something which cannot be got rid of. It may be transferred to someone else, but it cannot be put out of existence. Comparing it with the so-called shares of [a] Building Society the difference is apparent. A share in [the] Building Society [does not represent] a proportionate quota of the company's capital. There might be as many shares in this Society as people are inclined to apply for. The share [represents] no more than an earmarked application for a contribution .... The share might never come to maturity. It might be withdrawn long before it matured. It might either be paid back or it might be wiped out in advance. Accordingly, though the word is the same, there is nothing more than a faint analogy between it and a share in a joint stock company'[3].

1 1986 Act, s 7(4) (amended by the Building Societies (Non-Retail Funds and Deposits) Order 1990, SI 1990/2363, art 3).
2 1986 Act, s 8.
3 *Irvine and Fullarton Property Investment and Building Society's Liquidator v Cuthbertson* (1905) 8 F 1 at 6, 43 SLR 17 at 20, per Lord President Dunedin.

(4) BORROWING AND ULTRA VIRES

The contractual powers of a building society are determined by the 1986 Act and by the rules of the particular society. The rules form a contract between the society and its members and by extension prescribe the society's powers in relation to third parties. The power to borrow is one of the most important powers of a building society. Many of the powers contained in the Act for building societies must be specifically adopted and are not available to all societies. It therefore follows that to discover which powers a society has adopted reference must be made to the memorandum which is adopted by the society in terms of paragraph 2 of Schedule 2 of the Act and kept in the public file maintained in terms of section 106.

Auld v Glasgow Working-Men's Provident Building Society[1] describes clearly the contractual relationship between the members inter se and the members in relation to a building society:

> '[The] contract between the parties is a contract to be judged of by the ordinary rules, and the society or association which has made this contract with one of its members is precisely in the same contractual relation with its member as if it was with a stranger. ... Associations of this character have been under the consideration of your Lordships' House before ... The result of those simple propositions is this, that the pursuer here had a right to enforce the contract between himself and the association of which he was a member'.

The crucial issue with regard to borrowing funds is that the ultra vires rule applies to a building society's powers. Thus, as regards its capacity to borrow funds, any acquisition of funds by the society through excessive or otherwise unauthorised borrowing is beyond its powers[2]. The judgment in *Sinclair v Brougham*[3] sets out the general rules and the power to borrow must be limited to borrowing for the proper objects of the society.

Depositors, in a case where the building society is wound up and in a competition with creditors, are not entitled to recover moneys paid by them on an ultra vires contract of loan on the grounds that the money was received for the society for their use[4]. The assets remaining after payment of the outside creditors must be taken to represent, in part, funds which the depositors could follow as having been invalidly borrowed and in part, funds which the society could follow as having been wrongfully employed by its agents in the banking business. The money should be distributed *pari passu* between the depositors and the unadvanced shareholders according to the amounts respectively credited to them in the books of the society at the commencement of the winding up. This principle is subject to an application by any individual depositor or shareholder with a view to tracing his own money into any particular asset and subject to the costs of the liquidation[5].

1 (1887) 14 R (HL) 27 at 30.
2 *Shiell's Trustees v Scottish Property Investment Company Building Society (in liquidation)* (1884) 12 R (HL) 14.
3 [1914] AC 398, HL.
4 This principle was distinguished in *Re Phoenix Life Assurance Co, Burgess and Stock's Case* (1862) 2 John & H 441 and *Flood v Irish Provident Assurance Co Ltd and Hibernian Bank Ltd* [1912] 2 Ch 597, CA.
5 Applying In *Re Hallett's Estate, Knatchbull v Hallett* (1880) 13 Ch D 696, CA.

The ultra vires doctrine traditionally operated to the detriment of depositors because debts created by the deposits were not enforceable against the society[1]. However, section 7(18) of the 1986 Act provides that where a building society exceeds the statutory limits regarding its non-retail funding the validity of transactions effected in excess of the limit will not be affected. Where a society receives deposits in contravention of the shares/deposits ratio the validity of these deposits is not affected by the contravention[2]. Burgess suggests that these changes only appear to operate to save transactions which would have been rendered invalid or unenforceable due to technical infractions and the acquisition of funds which is outside the powers of a society for reasons other than excess are still subject to the ultra vires rule and therefore not capable of creating obligations binding on the society[3].

(5) USE OF FUNDS

The 1986 Act permits building societies to use funds lawfully acquired 'for the purposes of the society'[4]. Specifically, a building society may employ its funds; in the making of advances to members secured on land; in the making of loans, whether secured or unsecured, to members and others; and in the acquisition of other authorised assets. Assets of the society comprise fixed assets, liquid assets and commercial assets and there are certain rules which exist in this context. A building society is empowered to keep up to one-third of its total assets in the form of 'authorised liquid assets'[5]. A building society's fixed assets comprise land and buildings and equipment and plant used by it for the purposes of its operations. The principal items in this category will be its various offices[6]. The essentials of a building society's operations are to acquire funds for onward lending, primarily on long-term securities and given that the bulk of its funds are short-term it is important that there be maintenance of an adequate liquidity ratio. In practice, the principal types of liquid assets are cash, short dated government stocks and Treasury Bills. A building society's 'commercial assets' comprise those of its lawfully held assets which are neither fixed assets nor liquid assets and they are classified according to risk[7], Class 1 being the lowest level of risk, Class 3 the highest[8].

1 *Cross v Fisher* [1892] 1 QB 467, CA.
2 1986 Act, s 8(6).
3 See Burgess *Law of Borrowing* p 1040, para 1.53 and *Re Companies Acts, ex parte Watson* (1888) 21 QBD 301.
4 1986 Act, s 7(1).
5 1986 Act, s 21
6 1986 Act, s 6
7 1986 Act, s 20
8 See also the 1986 Act, ss 10–12 and 15.

11.   LOCAL AUTHORITIES

(1)   GENERAL

The re-organisation of the structure of local government in Scotland was effected by the Local Government etc (Scotland) Act 1994. The nine regional authorities, fifty-three district authorities and three islands authorities which were created by the Local Government (Scotland) Act 1973 were abolished and were replaced by thirty-two new local authority areas[1]. The 1994 Act came into effect on 1 April 1996 and although effecting a complete re-organisation, large parts of the 1973 Act and the Local Government (Scotland) Act 1975 remain intact. Water supply and sewerage services which were the responsibility of the regional and islands authorities[2] are now the responsibility of new water and sewerage authorities which were created by the 1994 Act.

Section 2 of the 1994 Act provides that every local government area is to have a council consisting of a convener and council[3]. Each council is a body corporate by the name 'The Council' with the addition of the name of the particular area and has a common seal[4]. Any banker that has a local authority as a customer must ensure that he has received proper instructions from a person or persons authorised by the council to give them.

Chapter 5 of the Act provides for the transitional provisions with respect to finance for the new authorities prior to 1 April 1996, and section 25 provides:

'(1) The Secretary of State may with the consent of the Treasury make grants of such amounts, and subject to such conditions, to local authorities as he considers appropriate.

(2) A local authority may with the consent of the Secretary of State (who shall in turn seek the consent of the Treasury) borrow by way of temporary loan or overdraft from a bank or otherwise any sums which they may temporarily require for the purpose of defraying expenses (including the payment of sums due by them to meet the expenses of other authorities) pending the receipt of revenues receivable by them after 1 April 1996'.

Local authorities have capacity and power to contract for the performance of their statutory functions and these numerous powers are specified in the Local Government (Scotland) Act 1973[5]. These powers include the making of standing orders with regard to contracts made by them or on their behalf[6]. Such contracts are for the supply of goods or materials or for the execution of works which would include provision for securing

---

1 The new 'unitary' authorities are named in the Local Government etc (Scotland) Act 1994 Act, Sch 1, Pt I.
2 The new water and sewerage authorities are the East of Scotland Water Authority, the West of Scotland Water Authority and the North of Scotland Water Authority (with corresponding sewerage areas): 1994 Act, s 62(1), Sch 8.
3 1994 Act, s 2(1).
4 1994 Act, s 2(3).
5 1973 Act, s 81.
6 1973 Act, s 81(1).

competition for such contracts and for regulating the manner in which tenders are invited[1]. A person contracting with a local authority is not bound to inquire whether standing orders have been complied with and non-compliance does not invalidate the contract made by or on behalf of the authority[2].

(2) LOCAL AUTHORITIES: BORROWING AND LENDING MONEY

Section 69 of the Local Government (Scotland) Act 1973 confers the subsidiary powers upon local authorities to borrow or lend money:

> 'a local authority shall have the power to do any thing (whether or not involving the expenditure, borrowing or lending of money or the acquisition or disposal of any property or rights) which is calculated to facilitate, or is conducive or incidental to, the discharge of any of their functions'.

The detailed rules are contained in section 16 and Schedule 3 of the Local Government (Scotland) Act 1975 and provide that 'without prejudice to section 69' of the 1973 Act a local authority may borrow for a number of prescribed purposes[3].

Section 165 of the 1994 Act is intended to give the Secretary of State wide powers to make regulations governing the powers of authorities to borrow and lend money which amend and extend the existing rules.

However, Schedule 3 of the 1975 Act still remains the fundamental basis for the understanding of the regulation of borrowing of local authorities. An authority may borrow such sums as may be required for: acquiring any land; erecting any building; for the execution of any permanent work; the provision of any plant or the doing of any other thing which the authority have the power to execute provide or do and which involves expenses of a capital nature; for the lending to a relevant authority or community council or any other purpose for which the authority are authorised under any enactment to borrow[3]. It is further provided that a local authority may borrow such sums as are necessary in order to provide working capital or to meet any other expenses not being expenses of a capital nature, required for the purposes of any public utility undertaking carried on by the authority provided that the sums borrowed do not, except with the consent of the Secretary of State, exceed the amount representing one half of the gross revenue of the undertaking for the immediately preceding financial year and that the sum be repaid as soon as reasonably practicable up to a maximum of two years from the date of borrowing, subject to an extension of this period by the Secretary of State[4].

The local authority may raise the money: by mortgage; by overdraft from a bank; by the issue of stock; by the issue of bonds; by the issue of bills; by an agreement entered into with the Public Works Loan Commissioners under section 2 of the Public Works Loans Act 1965; or by

1 1973 Act, s 81(2), (3).
2 1973 Act, s 81(4).
3 1975 Act, Sch 3, para 1(1).
4 Sch 3, para 1(3).

any other means approved by the Secretary of State with the consent of the Treasury[1].

The local authority may borrow by way of temporary loan or overdraft from a bank or otherwise any sums which they may require for the purposes of defraying expenses including the payment of sums due by them to meet the expenses of other authorities pending the receipt of revenues receivable by them in respect of the year in which the expenses are chargeable[2]. The authority may borrow in a similar manner for the purposes of the raising of a loan in the exercise of any statutory borrowing power[3]. A local authority may also borrow by the issue of bills, payable within twelve months from the date of issue, provided the aggregate of the amount outstanding on the bills does not exceed one-fifth of the authority's estimated gross income from the regional, general or district rate, whichever is prescribed by an order made by the Treasury[4].

All money borrowed under any statutory borrowing power by a local authority is to be secured on the whole funds, rates and reserves of the authority and all money borrowed by an authority by whatever method is deemed to have the same charge and ranks *pari passu*[5]. The interest and dividends for the time being payable in respect of money so borrowed by a local authority are to be the first charge on the rates and revenues comprising the security for the borrowed moneys[6].

Two or more local authorities may combine to exercise their powers of borrowing under Schedule 3 of the 1975 Act jointly and where they do so any limit on the amount that each authority may borrow shall apply to the amount which each authority received from the joint loan[7]. A bank or other person lending money to a local authority is not bound to inquire whether the borrowing of the money is regular or whether the money raised was properly applied and is not prejudiced by any illegality or by the misapplication or non-application of any of that money[8]. A local authority may lend to other authorities or any other authority approved by the Secretary of State[9]. The loan may be on such terms as is agreed between them, and for such a sum as that other authority may require for any purpose for which that other authority is authorised to borrow under any enactment. The local authority may establish a 'loans fund' which is applicable to 'all money borrowed by the authority and the redemption or repayment thereof and the payment of interest or dividends thereon and shall be part of the general fund of the authority'[10]. This loans fund is to be administered in accordance with paragraphs 13 to 21 of Schedule 3.

In relation to any securities created by a local authority, if at any time any sums due by way of principal or interest on such a security remains unpaid for a period of two months after a demand in writing, the person

---

1   1975 Act, Sch 3, para 2.
2   Sch 3, para 3(a)
3   Sch 3, para 3(b).
4   Sch 3, para 6.
5   Sch 3, para 8(1).
6   Sch 3, para 8 (2).
7   Sch 3, para 9.
8   Sch 3, para 26.
9   Sch 3, para 10.
10   Sch 3, para 12.

entitled thereto being the holder of such a security to the amount of not less than £1,000 or the persons entitled thereto, being the holders of such securities amounting together to not less than £2,000 may present a petition to the Court of Session for the appointment of a judicial factor[1]. The appointed factor is entitled to exercise all the powers of the local authority to levy rates and collect and receive sums due to the authority, together with such other power the court thinks fit to give him[2]. Clearly a highly unlikely and unmanageable remedy.

When opening an account for a local authority,

'... a certified excerpt from a minute of a meeting of the council should be obtained. The excerpt minute must be from a meeting of the council and not from a meeting of the finance committee. The bank should also be provided with a certificate from the authority stating that the borrowing is within the authorised statutory limit and that the consent of the Secretary of State has been obtained and showing the total amounts of money borrowed by the local authority for capital purposes and the periods to maturity of the loans outstanding'[3].

The changes made by the 1994 Act compound the difficulties of clear understanding of the applicable rules — 'The area cries out for consolidation'[4].

(3) WATER AND SEWERAGE AUTHORITIES: BORROWING AND LENDING MONEY

Part II of the 1994 Act makes provision for the creation of new water and sewerage authorities separate from local authorities. Section 84 provides for the financing of and borrowing by such authorities and contains the principal powers available to the Secretary of State to give different forms of financial assistance to the new water and sewerage authorities. The Secretary of State may fund authorities by way of grants[5]. For the purpose of the exercise of any of their functions, the authorities may, subject to conditions and obtaining the necessary consents, borrow money from (1) the Secretary of State and (2) any other person or body, whether in the UK or elsewhere[6]. The aggregate amount outstanding, otherwise than by way of interest, in respect of (a) all such lending to the new water and sewerage authorities and (b) all amounts borrowed which those authorities are liable to repay by virtue of section 91(1) of the 1994 Act, must not exceed £3,000 million, or such greater sum not exceeding £4,500 million as the Secretary of State may, with the consent of the Treasury, by order specify[7].

Section 85 supplements section 84 by enabling the Secretary of State to guarantee loans made to the new water or sewerage authorities. Section

1 1975 Act, Sch 3, para 20(1).
2 Sch 3, para 20(2).
3 *Wallace and McNeil* p 74.
4 See CMG Himsworth's introduction to the annotated Local Government etc (Scotland) Act 1994 in Current Law Statutes at p 39-11.
5 1994 Act, s 84(1).
6 1994 Act, s 84(2).
7 1994 Act, 84(7).

86 of the Act gives a very general power to the Secretary of State to require, after consultation, that surplus funds of a new water or sewerage authority are either paid to him or invested in a manner specified by him[1].

12.   INDUSTRIAL AND PROVIDENT SOCIETIES

Industrial and provident societies are incorporated under the Industrial and Provident Societies Act 1965. An industrial and provident society is a corporate body with a share capital and a minimum membership requirement. There must be a minimum membership of seven people. A society carrying on any business or trade, wholesale or retail may become registered if it is a bona fide co-operative society or is being conducted for the benefit of the community or there are special reasons why they should be registered under the Act rather than as a limited company. Examples of bodies registered under the Act include housing associations, womens' institutes, co-operative societies and other societies which exist for the benefit of the community[2]. The society is a limited company and although it is not necessarily a non-profit making body, its profits must be applied in accordance with the rules of the society. The 1965 Act[3] provides the registration procedure whereby the following must be lodged by a Scottish registered society with the Assistant Registrar of Friendly Societies for Scotland: the application for registration of a society signed by seven members and the secretary, who may also be one of the subscribing members; two printed copies of the rules signed by the members and the secretary; and the prescribed registration fee. By virtue of registration a society is a body corporate and may sue and be sued by its registered name.

The 1965 Act lists fourteen items which must be provided for within the rules of the society[4]. Care must be taken by bankers to ensure that the borrowing powers, being one of the essential fourteen items listed by the Act, cover both the borrowing of funds and deposit taking[5]. Borrowing powers should be carefully checked and deposits may be accepted from non-members of the society subject to strict limits preventing the society carrying on a business as bankers[6]. Importantly, the rules will provide how

1 For examples of interpretation of the ultra vires principle, see and consider *Attorney-General v Great Eastern Rly Co* (1880) 5 App Cas 473, HL; *Anisminic Ltd v Foreign Compensation Commission* [1969] 2 AC 147, [1969] 1 All ER 208, HL; *Wandsworth London Borough Council v Winder* [1985] AC 461, [1984] 3 All ER 976, HL; *R v Tower Hamlets London Borough Council, ex parte Chetnik Developments Ltd* [1988] AC 858, [1988] 1 All ER 961, HL; *Hazell v Hammersmith and Fulham London Borough Council* [1992] 2 AC 1, [1991] 1 All ER 545, HL; *R v Richmond upon Thames London Borough Council, ex parte McCarthy & Stone (Developments) Ltd* [1992] 2 AC 48, [1991] 4 All ER 897, HL.
2 See the Registrar of Friendly Society *Notes of Guidance for the Registration of Societies*, Form F 617.
3 1965 Act, s 73(1)(c)(ii) and s 2.
4 See the 1965 Act, Sch 1.
5 *Re Airedale Co-operative Worsted Manufacturing Society Ltd* [1933] Ch 639.
6 Friendly and Industrial and Provident Societies Act 1968, ss 4–10.

any surplus funds are distributed which will normally include a provision preventing a distribution to its members. The 1965 Act requires that there are established rules for the appointment and powers of a committee of management together with officers or managers.

A society must have a committee and a secretary. Bankers should take care to ensure that they are cognisant with the appointment, resignation and election of new office bearers together with those entrusted with cheque-signing powers. The Friendly and Industrial and Provident Societies Act 1968 lays down in detail the requirement of societies in the keeping of books of accounts including a revenue account, balance sheet and annual return which must give a true and fair view of the affairs of the society.

With the growth of housing sssociation lending, industrial and provident societies are important borrowing mediums and the banker must know that the proffered borrowing powers of the society fall intra vires the rules. An account opening with the bank or loan acceptance should be authorised by specific resolution of the committee of management, a copy of which should be retained by the banker. Details of the relevant resolutions authorising cheque signing powers should also be retained. It is competent for a society to grant a floating charge in favour of its bankers and a similar registration process to that of a limited company applies. Within twenty-one days of the creation of a floating charge, a copy of it must be delivered to the Registrar. If not delivered timeously it is void against everyone except the society[1]. However, it is not possible to appoint a receiver to the undertaking of the society.

The Credit Unions Act 1979 enabled Credit Unions to register under the Industrial and Provident Societies Act 1965. A credit union is essentially a self-help savings and loan society where the members pool their savings to provide a fund as a means to enable them to provide a source of low cost credit to its members[2].

13. FRIENDLY SOCIETIES

Historically some associations or societies were entitled to be registered as friendly societies under the Friendly Societies Act 1974. Such associations had as their purpose the provision by voluntary subscriptions of its membership with or without the aid of donations (1) for the relief or maintenance of members of the society and their families during sickness, or in old age or widowhood or if orphaned, (2) insurance of all sorts up to certain limits, and (3) the relief or maintenance of members in distress. Membership results in the establishment of a multipartite contractual relationship with all of the other members on the terms of the constitution and rules of the society[3]. The 1974 Act lays out the permitted classes of

1 Industrial and Provident Societies Act 1967, s 4(1) (as amended).
2 See the Credit Unions Act 1979, s 1(3)(a), (b).
3 *Blue v West Kilbride Free Gardeners Society Trustees* (1866) 4 M 1042.

friendly society which include cattle insurance societies, benevolent societies, working mens clubs, old peoples home societies and specially authorised societies[1]. The enabling Act provides that every registered society and branch of it has to have one or more trustees. There are detailed provisions regarding the keeping of annual accounts and their auditing. The society must have rules providing for the appointment of a committee of management and of trustees. Such friendly societies were not, however, incorporated bodies and contract by way of their appointed officers and trustees. The bank must take care to ensure that borrowing powers are not exceeded and acceptance of a facility is recorded by minute of the committee of management and that cheque-signing powers are appropriately declared. Lending to such a friendly society follows the principles of lending to any other unincorporated associations and unsecured facilities to such a friendly society are unusual. Most facilities are secured by the granting of fixed charges over heritage, the heritable property of the society being held by its trustees. Friendly societies are exempt from the registration requirement imposed on sellers of insurance and insurance related products by the Financial Services Act 1986[2]. After 8 June 1992, the commencement of the Friendly Societies Act 1992, no new societies may be registered[3] but an existing registered society or new society may incorporate under the Act. Where a friendly society converts under section 91 of the 1992 Act to a registered company its powers and capacity will be those of a registered company.

14.   COMPANIES

(1)   REGISTRATION AND INCORPORATION

A company is normally incorporated by registration with the Registrar of Companies under the Companies Act 1985 as amended by the Companies Act of 1989. It is competent but exceptional for companies to be incorporated by royal charter or by private Act of Parliament. By far the largest number of companies have been incorporated by the companies' legislation prior to 1985. The 1985 Act provides that:

> 'Any two or more persons associated for a lawful purpose may, by subscribing their names to a memorandum of association and otherwise complying with the requirements of this Act in respect of registration, form an incorporated company, with or without limited liability'[4].

This formula has subsisted in Scotland since the Joint Stock Companies Act 1856, although one person may now form a private company limited by shares or by guarantee[5].

1 See the Friendly Societies Act 1974, s 7.
2 See the Financial Services Act 1986, s 23(1). See generally 12 *Stair Memorial Encyclopaedia* paras 601–741.
3 1992 Act, s 93.
4 Companies Act 1985, s 1(1).
5 1985 Act, s 1(3A) (added by the Companies (Single Member Private Limited Companies) Regulations 1992, SI 1992/1699, Schedule, para 1).

Detailed procedural rules exist for the incorporation of companies. A company limited by guarantee and an unlimited company must present for registration, articles signed by the subscribers to the memorandum[1]. A company limited by shares may register a memorandum alone but is then deemed to have articles in the form of 'Table A' as it stands at the date of registration. With regard to companies incorporated on or after 1 July 1985, the contents of Table A are prescribed by regulation[2]. In practice, companies limited by shares almost invariably register articles which adopt and amend Table A. Both memorandum and articles of association must be attested by at least one witness and in Scotland, as well as England, this gives the documents the effect of attested deeds[3].

Registration of a company is effected by presenting the Registrar of Companies in Companies House with: (1) the memorandum and articles (if any) duly executed[4]; (2) the prescribed statement of the first directors, the secretary and the registered office[5]; (3) the prescribed fee of £20[6]; (4) a 'declaration of compliance' by a solicitor engaged in the company's formation or a director or secretary named in the statement[7].

If satisfied that these documents are in order the Registrar issues his certificate that the company is duly incorporated and, where applicable, that it is a 'limited' or 'public limited' company[8]. Where the company is to be incorporated as a 'plc' the minimum capital requirements must also be met[9]. Prior to the date of incorporation a company has no legal existence[10]. From the date of incorporation, including the date of issue of the certificate, the company is a body corporate entitled to exercise all the consequent functions and powers, although a 'plc' requires a further certificate of entitlement from the Registrar to commence business. The company's certificate also gives the official number allocated to the company[11]. This number remains attached to the legal person whatever the subsequent change of name or status unless altered by the Registrar in exercise of his statutory powers[12].

A company is a legal personality distinct from its shareholders. Upon issue of the certificate of incorporation the subscribers of the memorandum and all subsequent members of the company are constituted as a 'body corporate' which, subject to sections 13(3) and (4) of the 1985 Act[13], is capable of exercising all the functions of an incorporated company. The corporate identity is retained even upon the company changing its corpo-

---

1 1985 Act, s 7(1).
2 1985 Act, s 8(1); Companies (Tables A to F) Regulations 1985, SI 1985/805 (amended by SI 1985/1052).
3 1985 Act, ss 2(6) and 7(3)(c) for memorandum and articles respectively.
4 1985 Act, s 10 (1).
5 1985 Act, ss 10(2) and (6), Sch I (amended by the Companies Act 1989, s 145, Sch 19, para 7).
6 Companies (Fees) (Amendment) Regulations 1994, SI 1994/2217.
7 1985 Act, s 12(3).
8 1985 Act, s 13(1) and (2).
9 1985 Act, s 11.
10 *F J Neale (Glasgow) Ltd v Vickery* 1973 SLT (Sh Ct) 88.
11 1985 Act, s 705(1) (substituted by the Companies Act 1989, s 145, Sch 19, para 14).
12 See 1985 Act, ss 705 (3) and (4).
13 1985 Act, s 13(3), (4) (amended by the Insolvency Act 1986, s 439(1), Sch 13, Pt I).

rate name[1] or its members or its directors. The company's legal existence only terminates when it is formally dissolved and this may occur either on the completion of winding up[2] or if the Registrar of Companies, after due inquiry, is satisfied that it is appropriate that it be struck from the Register[3]. The court has power to declare void any dissolution following the winding up provided that the application is made within two years or later, if the purpose is to enable proceedings to be brought against the company in order to constitute a claim for damages arising from personal injury or death[4]. Where the company has been struck off the register an application may be made to the court to have it restored within a period of twenty years[5].

A company can enter into contracts and acquire property, rights and obligations on the same basis as natural persons except in instances where the physical presence of a natural person is an essential element. The contractual power of a company is limited by the objects of the company as contained in the memorandum but despite this limitation a company can assume capacity to perform any legal act. A company may enter into a partnership, be a member of another company, hold office as director or secretary of another company and be appointed auditor of another company[6]. There are certain statutory restrictions on companies — for example, only a natural legal person may be an insolvency practitioner in terms of section 390 of the Insolvency Act 1986[7] — but they generally have wide powers due to the practice of companies drafting objects clauses as widely as possible.

A company has a business reputation which it may protect against defamation[8] although it cannot appear personally in court proceedings and must be represented by counsel or some other duly recognised representative of the court[9]. The difficulties in attributing the characteristics of a natural person to the artificial legal personality of a company are most apparent when questions of intention arise:

> 'A company may in many ways be likened to a human body. They have a brain and a nerve centre which controls what they do. They also have hands which hold the tools and act in accordance with directions from the centre. Some of the people in the company are mere servants and agents who are nothing more than hands to do the work and cannot be said to represent the mind or will. Others are directors and managers who represent the directing mind and will of the company, and control what they do. The state of mind of these managers is the state of mind of the company and is treated by the law as such. So you will find that in cases where the law requires personal

1 *Vic Spence Associates v Balchin* 1990 SLT 10, OH.
2 Insolvency Act 1986, ss 201, 204, 205.
3 1985 Act, s 652.
4 Companies Act 1985, s 651 (amended by the Insolvency Act 1986, s 109(1), Sch 6, para 45 and the Companies Act 1989 ss 141, 212, Sch 24).
5 1985 Act, s 653.
6 This power was granted by the Companies Act 1989, s 25(2). See also s 53(1).
7 See also eg the Employment Protection (Consolidation) Act 1978, s 153 (1).
8 Eg *Bognor Regis Urban District Council v Campion* [1972] 2 QB 169, [1972] 2 All ER 61.
9 *Equity and Law Life Assurance Society v Tritonia Ltd* 1943 SC (HL) 88, 1944 SLT 24.

fault as a condition of liability in tort, the fault of the manager will be the personal fault of the company'[1].

The 'state of mind' of a company is not restricted to what is formally discussed and decided at directors' meetings. If a manager has taken a deliberate and conscious decision not to perform a particular act, the company's failure cannot be treated as 'unintentional'[2]. Where the officers or employees of the company have acted negligently in a matter which is within the capacity of the company as defined by the objects clause, there is generally no doubt that the company incurs vicarious liability[3]. The company will also be liable for the deliberate wrongful acts of its officers and employees in matters which are within the legal capacity of the company, such as defamation[4] or fraud[5].

A confusion may arise where the act of the agent of the company is outwith the company's legal capacity. In general, a third party is entitled to assume that the agent is acting with authority, and need not make inquiries as to his authority in relation to a contract with the company[6]. It should be noted that this does not apply in delictual obligations and although opinion has been expressed that the company will be liable for ultra vires delictual acts of the agents or employees[7], the point is not settled. What is clear is that a company cannot defend itself by arguing that a delictual act is, by definition, unauthorised and ultra vires: In particular cases the company's liability depends upon whether ultra vires or otherwise, the act was authorised or within the implied authority of the officer or employee concerned[8].

A fundamental principle of company law is that a company is a legal person as distinct from the members and directors. The 'veil of incorporation' principle was established in the well-known case of *Salomon*[9] and has been developed ever since. Where the company is incorporated with limited liability its creditors may only proceed against the company. Almost a century after the *Salomon* case, controversial cases on 'piercing' the veil of incorporation still arise. The traditional authorities[10] have been followed by equally problematic modern cases. A recent example is *Woolfson v Strathclyde Regional Council*[11] where the strict legality of the veil

1 *HL Bolton (Engineering) Co Ltd v T J Graham & Sons Ltd* [1956] 3 All ER 624 at 630, CA, per Denning LJ.
2 *Witton Engineering Co Ltd's Patent* [1959] RPC 53.
3 *Mersey Docks and Harbour Board Trustees v Gibbs* (1866) LR 1 HL 93; *Gordon v British and Foreign Metaline Co* (1886) 14 R 75.
4 *Finburgh v Moss Empires Ltd* 1908 SC 928, 16 SLT 116.
5 *Houldsworth v City of Glasgow Bank* (1880) 7 R (HL) 53.
6 1985 Act, ss 35–35B. See also *Royal British Bank v Turquand* (1856) 6 E & B 327 on authority and constructive notice.
7 Palmer's *Company Law* (24th edn) para 18-31; Walker *The Law of Contracts and Related Obligations in Scotland* (2nd edn, 1985) para 78.
8 See *Houldsworth v City of Glasgow Bank* (1880) 7 R (HL) 53.
9 *Salomon v A Salomon & Co Ltd* [1897] AC 22, HL.
10 *Macaura v Northern Assurance Co Ltd* [1925] AC 619, HL; *Re Butt, Butt v Kelson* [1952] Ch 197, [1952] 1 All ER 167, CA; *Lee v Lee's Air Farming Ltd* [1961] AC 12, [1960] 3 All ER 420, PC.
11 1978 SC (HL) 90, 1978 SLT 59.

of incorporation principle was preferred to the more flexible approach of
the Court of Appeal in *D H N Foods Distributors Limited v Tower Hamlets
London Borough Council*[1]. The court was unable to identify special circumstances such as to justify a departure from the *Salomon* principle. In *City of
Glasgow District Council v Hamlet Textiles Ltd*[2] the court did go so far as to
allow inquiry regarding the true ownership of property in Glasgow where
the formal title was held by an English wholly-owned subsidiary of a
Scottish company whose sole function was the holding of that formal title.
However, it is more consistent with authority that only special circumstances justify departing from the *Salomon* principle[3].

The principles of separate personality apply equally to groups of companies where the members of the company are themselves incorporated
companies or, in the case of a wholly owned subsidiary, a single company
and its nominees. Creditors, including their banks, of a subsidiary cannot
claim against the parent even if the subsidiary is wholly owned[4]. Where,
however, the parent has guaranteed the subsidiary's obligation the creditors can claim against the parent. Great care must be taken with regard to
the enforceability of letters of comfort issued by a parent for its subsidiary[5]. The Cork Committee gave consideration to making a parent company liable for the activities of its subsidiaries but such a liability has
never been introduced into company law[6].

Attempts have been made to use the law of agency to circumvent the
Salomon rule by arguing that as principal to a subsidiary agent, the parent
company is liable for its subsidiary's activities. For such an argument to
succeed it is necessary for an agency relationship to be established independently of the parent/subsidiary relationship[7]. The House of Lords'
decision in the *International Tin Council*[8] case declared that the member
states of the ITC were protected from liability for the debts of that organisation because it was deemed to enjoy separate personality in the eyes of
English law and it could not be said to be acting merely as the agent of its
members.

(2)   CERTIFICATE OF INCORPORATION

The certificate issued by the Registrar of Companies is conclusive evidence that the statutory requirements in connection with the incorporation have been complied with[9]. As regards a private company, once the

1 [1976] 3 All ER 462, [1976] 1 WLR 852, CA.
2 1986 SLT 415.
3 See eg *National Dock Labour Board v Pinn and Wheeler Ltd* [1989] BCLC 647.
4 *Charterbridge Corpn Ltd v Lloyds Bank Ltd* [1970] Ch 62, [1969] 2 All ER 1185; *Re Southard &
  Co Ltd* [1979] 3 All ER 556, [1979] 1 WLR 1198, CA; *Ford and Carter Ltd v Midland Bank Ltd*
  (1979) 129 NLJ 543, HL.
5 *Kleinwort Benson Ltd v Malaysia Mining Corpn Bhd* [1989] 1 All ER 785, [1989] 1 WLR 379,
  CA; see ch 9, pp 325, 326 below.
6 *Insolvency Law and Practice* (the Cork Report) (Cmnd 8558) (1982).
7 *Smith Stone and Knight Ltd v Birmingham Corpn* [1939] 4 All ER 116; *Ford and Carter Ltd v
  Midland Bank Ltd* (1979) 129 NLJ 543, HL.
8 *J H Rayner (Mincing Lane) Ltd v Department of Trade and Industry* [1990] 2 AC 418, [1989] 3
  All ER 523, HL (the *International Tin Council* case).
9 1985 Act, s 13 (7).

original certificate has been exhibited to the bank the operations upon its bank account, including borrowing, may commence. With public companies the bankers must also have sight of the certificate from the Registrar entitling the company to commence business[1] before it can allow operation of the bank account. Prior to this juncture the banker should only permit payments into the company's account and should not allow withdrawals, with the exception of allotment money repaid to applicants.

What of contracts which are concluded prior to incorporation? The effect of a pre-incorporation contract is threefold. Firstly, if before formation of the company a contract is made by an agent, purporting to act on behalf of his principal, then the company lacks the capacity to enter that contract. The law of agency dictates that an agent cannot contract on behalf of a principal who does not exist. Even where the company has benefited in some way from the contract it is unenforceable against the company and even an equitable recovery under English law, from the company is incompetent[2]. Secondly, the company is not entitled to enforce a pre-incorporation contract after incorporation or sue for damages for breach[3]. Thirdly, the company may not ratify a pre-incorporation contract, on grounds of having no capacity at formation, although it may, however, novate the contract[4]. One of the recommendations of the Jenkins Committee was that 'a company should be enabled unilaterally to adopt contracts which purport to be made on its behalf or in its name prior to incorporation'[5]. The effect of the Companies Act 1985 is to impose personal liability on the person entering the contract[6]. It is clear, however, that there is only liability where the company was not in existence at the date of conclusion of the contract. In *Vic Spence Associates v Balchin*[7], F Ltd passed a special resolution to change its name to K P Ltd. Another firm accepted instructions from the individuals who represented themselves as acting for the company called K P Ltd and rendered services in terms of the contract. Later the certificate of incorporation on change of name was issued. The supplier company sought damages for breach of contract from the individuals as personally liable in respect of the contracts on the basis that at the date of contracting the company did not exist. Lord Prosser held that it was not necessary that the company be named correctly in order to constitute a contract, as it was possible to have sufficient disclosure of the agent's principal by use of a trading name[8]. Regardless of a change in the company name the company retains its corporate identity[9].

---

1 1985 Act, s 117.
2 *Re English and Colonial Produce Co Ltd* [1906] 2 Ch 435 at 442, CA, per Vaughan Williams LJ.
3 *Tinnevelly Sugar Refining Co Ltd v Mirrlees, Watson and Yaryan Co Ltd* (1894) 21 R 1009.
4 *Kelner v Baxter* (1866) LR 2 CP 174.
5 *Report of the Company Law Committee* (the Jenkins Report) (Cmnd 1749) (1962), para 54(b) but that possibility was ruled out by virtue of s 36 of the Companies Act 1985. See also *Reform of the Ultra Vires Rule* (the Prentice Report) (DTI consultative document 24 July 1986).
6 1985 Act, s 36C (added by the Companies Act 1989, s 130(4)).
7 1990 SLT 10, OH.
8 See also *Lin Pac Containers (Scotland) Ltd v Kelly* 1982 SC 50 at 51, 1983 SLT 422 at 423, per Lord Stott.
9 See generally Hardcastle 'Preliminary Agreements' (1992) 142 NLJ 721; *Badgerhill Properties Ltd v Cottrell* [1991] BCLC 805; *Cotronic (UK) Ltd v Dezonie* [1991] BCLC 721, CA.

(3) BORROWING POWERS OF A COMPANY

The general information concerning the powers and objects of a company is contained in the memorandum of association. Every registered company must have a memorandum of association, which is the registered company's charter[1]. The memorandum of every company must state its name, its registered office (whether in England, Wales or Scotland) and its objects[2]. A company limited by shares or guarantee must also state that its liability is limited[3]. A company is entitled by special resolution to alter its memorandum with respect to its objects, so far as may be required to enable it: to carry on its business more economically or more efficiently; to attain its main purpose by new or improved means; to enlarge or change the local area of its operations; to carry on some business which under existing circumstances may conveniently or advantageously be combined with the business of the company; to restrict or abandon any of the objects specified in the memorandum; to sell or dispose of the whole or any part of the undertaking of the company; and to amalgamate with any other company or body of persons[4]. Where, however, an application is made under section 5 of the Companies Act 1985 for objection to the alteration, the alteration will not have effect except in so far as it is confirmed by the court[5].

The arrangements for the internal management of a company are contained in its articles of association. The articles deal with issues including the transfer of shares; alteration of share capital; general meetings; voting rights; directors, their appointment and powers; managing directors; secretary; dividends; accounts; audit procedure and winding up. Articles may, in the case of a company limited by shares, and must in the case of a company limited by guarantee, or an unlimited company, be registered with the memorandum[6]. The articles may be altered or amended by special resolution without restriction[7]. The articles may adopt, according to the rules of the company, in whole or in part, the regulations contained in Table A[8]. It is therefore usually necessary, when reference is made to the company's articles, to read them in conjunction with Table A in order to ascertain powers of internal management. Companies incorporated prior to the 1985 Act are regulated by the provisions contained in the statute under which they were incorporated, although such companies have the option of passing a special resolution to adopt Table A as now prescribed.

It is generally accepted on the basis of English authority that members cannot enforce the terms of the articles against one another as there is no implied contract between individual members[9]. Rather, members should

1 *Ashbury Railway Carriage and Iron Co Ltd v Riche* (1875) LR 7 HL 653 at 667, 668, per Lord Cairns LC.
2 1985 Act, s 2(1).
3 1985 Act, s 2(3).
4 1985 Act, s 4 (substituted by the 1989 Act, s 110(2)).
5 1985 Act, s 5.
6 1985 Act, s 7.
7 1985 Act, s 9.
8 1985 Act, s 8(1); Companies (Tables A to F) Regulations 1985, SI 1985/805 (amended by SI 1985/1052).
9 *Welton v Saffery* [1897] AC 299, HL.

look to the company to enforce their rights against other members[1]. Exceptionally, however, the articles may give rise to an obligation owed by a member and enforceable by another as a contract existing independently of the articles[2]. The articles only bind members of the company so that a solicitor was not entitled to damages for breach of contract because the articles did not constitute a contract between the company and the solicitor in his capacity as solicitor to the company[3]. It is possible for the articles to be used as a basis for a contract between the company and a member in some capacity other than that of member[4]. However, the general rule is that the provisions of the articles, and the memorandum, do not constitute a contract binding the company or any member to an outsider[5].

The objects clause, contained in the company's memorandum, defines the capacity of the company to act as a legal person. To ascertain whether a company has powers to borrow, reference is made to the objects and powers specified in the memorandum, and if the objects clause contains an express power to borrow, the banker need look no further, as long as the borrowing is exercised in relation to one of the authorised objects of the company[6].

An objects clause which authorises a company to carry on any business it likes, or which it thinks might be profitable to the shareholders, is meaningless[7]. A clause may be included empowering the company to carry on any business which in the opinion of the directors may be carried on advantageously in connection with or ancillary to its stated objects, but the directors must in this situation act honestly[8]. A transaction which is ultra vires the company is void and incapable of ratification even by the unanimous consent of all the shareholders[9]. Reference must be made to the objects clause in order to ascertain whether the express or implied power to enter the particular transaction exists. A transaction exercisable 'for the purposes of the company' is ordinarily construed as imposing a limit on the director's authority rather than his capacity. Unless he is put on notice to the contrary, where a person deals in good faith with a company which is carrying on an intra vires business he is entitled to assume that its directors are probably exercising such powers for the purposes of the company as laid out in the memorandum[10].

1 1985 Act, s 14; *Hickman v Kent Sheepbreeders' Association* [1915] 1 Ch 881.
2 *Rayfield v Hands* [1960] Ch 1, [1958] 2 All ER 194.
3 *Eley v Positive Government Security Life Assurance Co Ltd* (1876) 1 Ex D 88, CA. See also *Salmon v Quin and Axtens Ltd* (1909) 1 Ch 311.
4 *Re New British Iron Co, ex parte Beckwith* [1898] 1 Ch 324.
5 *Hickman v Kent Sheepbreeders' Association* [1915] 1 Ch 881 at 900, per Astbury J; *Williams v MacPherson* 1990 SLT 279 at 281, 282, OH; *Parke v Daily News Ltd* [1962] 1 Ch 927, [1962] 2 All ER 929.
6 *Re Introductions Ltd, Introductions Ltd v National Provincial Bank Ltd* [1970] Ch 199 at 210, [1969] 1 All ER 887 at 889, CA, per Harman LJ. See also *Ashbury Railway Carriage and Iron Co Ltd v Riche* (1875) LR 7 HL 653; *Trevor v Whitworth* (1887) 12 App Cas 409, HL.
7 *Newstead (Inspector of Taxes) v Frost* [1980] 1 All ER 363, [1980] 1 WLR 135, HL.
8 *Bell Houses Ltd v City Wall Properties Ltd* [1966] 2 QB 656, 2 All ER 674, CA.
9 *Thompson v J Barke & Co (Caterers) Ltd* 1975 SLT 67 at 71, OH.
10 See *Rolled Steel Products (Holdings) Ltd v British Steel Corpn* [1986] Ch 246 at 295, CA, per Slade LJ.

The ultra vires rule has been modified by section 108 of the Companies Act 1989. Section 35 as originally enacted in the 1985 Act was criticised for failing adequately to protect shareholders and persons dealing with a company and recommendations to reform the law were tabled[1]. The original section 35 was replaced by new sections 35 to 35B. The new section 35 ensures that the validity of an act done by a company is not called into question on the grounds of lack of capacity by reason of anything in the company's memorandum[2]. A member of a company may bring proceedings to restrain an act which but for subsection (1) would be beyond the company's capacity[3]. It still remains the duty of directors to observe any limitations on their powers flowing from the company's memorandum and any action by the directors which, but for subsection (1) would be beyond the company's capacity may only be ratified by special resolution[4]. A restricting provision[5] is, however, inserted by section 109 of the 1989 Act. This provides that where a company enters into a transaction involving directors, and the board of directors, in connection with the transaction, exceed any limitation on their powers under the company's constitution, the transaction is voidable at the instance of the company.

In a consideration of a company's power to borrow it is important to remember that it is now open to all companies, no matter the date of incorporation, to include an objects clause which states simply that the object of the company is to carry on business as a 'general commercial company'[6]. The object of the company is thus to carry on any trade or business whatsoever[7] and the company has power to do all such things incidental or conducive to the carrying on of a trade or business by it[8]. It is, however, prudent for, any person involved with a company wishing to carry out a specific act, such as borrowing money, to insist instead upon the company having an express and specific capacity to do so[9].

(4)   EXERCISE OF BORROWING POWERS

Where a company has power to borrow or where it is incidental to the conduct of its business, the articles of association will usually authorise the directors to exercise the company's borrowing powers. It is common for the articles to provide that, without the sanction of the company in general meeting, the directors shall not borrow more than a specified amount. However, if a bank genuinely believes and acts upon the information furnished to it by the company or its recognised officials, it will be protected[10].

---

1   *Reform of the Ultra Vires Rule* (the Prentice Report) published by the Department of Trade and Industry as a consultative document on 24 July 1986.
2   1985 Act, s 35(1) (substituted by the 1989 Act, s 108(1)).
3   1985 Act, s 35(2) (as so substituted).
4   1985 Act, s 35(3) (as so substituted).
5   1985 Act, s 322A (added by the 1989 Act, s 109(1)).
6   1985 Act, s 3A (added by the 1989 Act, s 110(1)).
7   1985 Act, s 3A(a) (as so added).
8   1985 Act, s 3A(b) (as so added).
9   See Ferran 'The Reform of the Law on Corporate Capacity and Directors' and Officers' Authority : Part 2' (1992) 13 Co Law 177 at 182–183.
10   *Mahoney v East Holyford Mining Co* (1875) LR 7 HL 869, per Lord Hatherley.

If, however, the bank dealing with the company is on notice that the directors are exercising their powers for purposes other than the purposes of the company, the bank cannot rely on the ostensible authority of the directors and the transaction is open to challenge[1].

The new section 35A of the 1985 Act deals with the power of directors to bind the company[2]. In relation to a person dealing with a company in good faith, the power of the board of directors to bind the company or authorise others to do so is deemed to be free of any limitation under the company's constitution[3]. For this purpose a person is not regarded as acting in bad faith by reason only of his knowing that an act is beyond the powers of the directors under the company's constitution and he is presumed to have acted in good faith unless the contrary is proved[4]. A member of a company is given the right to bring proceedings to restrain the directors from doing an act which is beyond their powers[5] and the operation of the section is restricted by section 322A. It is further provided that subsection (1) of section 35A does not affect any liability incurred by the directors, or any other person, by reason of the directors exceeding their powers[6]. A party to a transaction with a company has no duty of inquiry as to whether it is permitted by the company's memorandum or as to any limitation on the powers of the directors to bind the company or authorise others to do so[7]. The effect of section 35B on a company's contractual capacity is wide. It is more than a restatement of the protection offered by case law whereby outsiders dealing with the company are generally entitled to assume that internal procedures have been complied with. Section 35B exists separately from the rule in *Royal British Bank v Turquand*[8] and indeed goes further : the internal management rule in *Turquand* does not protect a person who knows of the irregularity or who is put on inquiry[9]. Furthermore, it has been suggested that by the nature of a transaction itself persons dealing with the company could put the company on inquiry[10].

In situations where a loan is ultra vires the company and the banker cannot avail himself of the protection of section 35, he may nevertheless have certain rights against the company in respect of the money which he has lent to it. He may stand in the position of creditor of the company whose debt has been paid by the company out of money which the directors have purported to borrow in excess of their powers[11].

1 *Rolled Steel Products (Holdings) Ltd v British Steel Corpn* [1986] Ch 246 at 295, per Slade LJ.
2 1985 Act, s 35A (added by the 1989 Act, s 108).
3 s 35A(1) (as so added).
4 s 35A(2)(c) (as so added).
5 s 35A(4) (as so added).
6 s 35A(5) (as so added).
7 s 35B (as so added).
8 (1856) 6 E & B 327.
9 *Morris v Kanssen* [1946] AC 459 at 474, [1946] 1 All ER 586 at 592, HL, per Lord Simonds.
10 Ferran 'The Reform of the Law on Corporate Capacity and Directors' and Officers' Authority : Part 2' (1992) 13 Co Law 177 at 178; *Northside Developments Pty Ltd v Registrar General* (1990) 64 ALTR 427. See also *Rolled Steel Products (Holdings) Ltd v British Steel Corpn* [1986] Ch 246 at 285, per Slade LJ.
11 *Brooks & Co v Blackburn Benefit Society* (1884) 9 App Cas 857.

(5)   LIABILITY OF DIRECTORS TO BANKS

Directors carry on the business of the company as agents for the company. As such the director, acting on behalf of a disclosed principal, incurs no personal liability where the company fails to fulfil the contract. In such instances the company is liable[1]. The contrary is true, however, where the director exceeds his power, whereupon the director incurs liability on the principle that as an agent he impliedly warrants that he has the authority of his principal[2]. It makes no difference to the liability of the director in such a situation that he did not know he was exceeding his powers[3]. A director may incur personal liability, along with the company, where relevant, for delicts or negligence for which he is personally responsible[4]; and on misrepresenting the extent of his authority to contract in the name of the company the director will be liable in damages to a third party for breach of warranty of authority[5]. Signing a cheque for ultra vires expenditure constitutes personal liability on the part of the director, even where the director only signs as a matter of form[6].

(6)   INCIDENTAL MATTERS OF IMPORTANCE

Section 349(4) of the Companies Act 1985 provides that where an officer of the company signs on behalf of the company, a bill of exchange, cheque, promissory note or order for money or goods in which the company's name is not mentioned, the officer is personally liable to the holder of the cheque for the amount thereof unless it is paid by the company. The name should be absolutely correct, but in modern cases trivial variations have been allowed, though only if the name is unambiguously that of the company despite the flaw[7]. Liability is incurred even if the third party has not been misled, but not if the third party himself was responsible for the misdescription[8]. The Scottish decision to the opposite effect is regarded by many and the writer as wrongly decided[9].

A second important provision of note is section 112(6) of the Companies Act 1989, which provides that if the company is a charity and its name does not include the word 'charity' or 'charitable' it must state on cheques and other instruments that it is a charity. Failure to do so results in personal liability for the person concerned if the company defaults[10], although the rule is confined to the situations referred to in the Act. In

---

1   *Ferguson v Wilson* (1866) 2 Ch App 77.
2   *Beattie v Lord Ebury* (1872) LR 7 HL 102.
3   *Weeks v Propert* (1873) LR 8 CP 427.
4   *Cullen v Thomson's Trustees* (1862) 4 Macq 424, HL.
5   *Re Britannia Fire Association, Coventry's Case* [1891] 1 Ch 202, CA.
6   *Joint Stock Discount Co v Brown* (1869) LR 8 Eq 381.
7   *John Wilkes (Footwear) Ltd v Lee International (Footwear) Ltd* [1985] JBL 356; *Bondina Ltd v Rollaway Shower Blinds Ltd* [1986] 1 All ER 564, [1986] 1 WLR 517, CA.
8   *Durham Fancy Goods Ltd v Michael Jackson (Fancy Goods) Ltd* [1968] 2 QB 839, [1968] 2 All ER 987.
9   *Scottish and Newcastle Breweries Ltd v Blair* 1967 SLT 72, OH.
10   1989 Act, s 112(8) which applies the penalties contained in ss 349(2)–(4) of the 1985 Act.

other circumstances the failure of a director to use the correct name of the company should not result in personal liability unless the third party has been misled.

(7) POWER TO GRANT GUARANTEES

A limited company is capable of granting a guarantee provided power to do so is clearly expressed in the objects clause of the memorandum. In the absence of a specific grant of authority, any such transaction is ultra vires and unenforceable against the company. It is incumbent upon the bank to make careful study of the memorandum of the company before accepting the company's guarantee. It is clear that an objective view is taken of the guarantee in relation to whether an independent board of directors would have decided to proceed[1] While the analysis is based upon the guarantee having been necessarily granted for the purposes and objects of the company in strict terms of the objects clause, in addition wider commercial interests are relevant.

Practical guidelines exist for banks in relation to company guarantees. The main concern for the banker should be to ensure that the guarantee deed is properly executed. While not strictly necessary, it is advisable to obtain a certified excerpt minute of the directors authorising the grant of the guarantee. The bank should also forward the terms of the guarantee to the directors for their perusal before the contract is concluded. Where an overdraft is secured by a guarantee from directors personally and subsequently security from the company itself is offered in support, or in substitution of the guarantee, or in addition to it, the bank should obtain from the company a certified copy of the relevant resolution of the general meeting. As the case of *Victors Ltd v Lingard*[2] shows, if the granting of the security is an issue in which the directors are personally interested and one upon which they can vote as directors, the security will only be of value if the articles of the company so permit. In such an instance, without the express authority of the articles, the resolution of the directors is void and the security rendered ineffective. In *Bank Negara Indonesia v Taylor*[3], the Court of Appeal refused to rectify a bank guarantee signed by the managing director of a company where the guarantee covered not merely the liability of his company but also that of another company[4].

(8) FINANCIAL ASSISTANCE BY A COMPANY FOR PURCHASE OF ITS OWN SHARES

Until 1981 it was unlawful for a company to give any person financial assistance for the purchase of, or subscription for, its own shares or those

1 See *Rolled Steel Products (Holdings) Ltd v British Steel Corpn* [1986] Ch 478, [1985] 3 All ER 52, CA.
2 [1927] 1 Ch 323.
3 [1995] CLC 255 noted in Palmer's *Company Law*, Issue 4, 21 April 1995.
4 A good general guide is contained in Gordon and Mitchell *Scottish Banking Practice Handbook No 10* ch 5, pp 46–48.

of its holding company[1]. Accordingly, transactions were prohibited even if the financial assistance was only an incidental element of a larger scheme[2]. Deriving from the 1981 Act[3], sections 151 to 158 of the 1985 Act restate the general prohibition but introduce specified conditional exceptions to the rule.

The prohibition does not operate if:

(1) either the company's principal purpose in giving the assistance is not to give it for the purpose of such an acquisition as mentioned in section 151, or the giving of the assistance for that purpose but is an incidental part of some larger purpose of the company; and

(2) the assistance is given in good faith in the interests of the company[4].

The three main transactions which are not treated as unlawful financial assistance are: distributions by way of lawful dividend or distributions in the course of winding up[5]; loans made by a company in the ordinary course of business[6]; and the provision of money for the acquisition of fully-paid shares in accordance with an employees' share scheme[7]. The dividends exception protects a common form of indirect assistance where the company being acquired has accumulated substantial 'distributable profits'. A loan is made to the purchaser by a financial institution with the intention that, when the purchase is completed and the target company has become a subsidiary, repayment is funded by a dividend paid by the subsidiary to its parent. This provision has to be read alongside the rules relating to amounts of dividends payable[8]. The other exceptions have been amended to include former employees and their families, and also extend to other connected companies within the same group[9].

A private company may give financial assistance in the purchase of its own shares, in circumstances outwith the generally permitted exceptions, subject to certain conditions, namely: the assistance must either not reduce its net assets, or be given out of profits available for distribution; unless the company is a wholly owned subsidiary, the assistance must be sanctioned by a special resolution; the directors must make a statutory declaration of solvency in the prescribed form before the assistance is given, supported by an auditor's report, which must be filed with the Registrar of Companies along with a copy of the resolution[10]. In terms of section 157, the special resolution must be passed at a meeting held on or within a week after the directors' declaration of solvency and is ineffective unless the declaration and relative auditors report are available for inspec-

---

1 Companies Act 1948, s 54.
2 *Belmont Finance Corpn v Williams Furniture Ltd (No 2)* [1980] 1 All ER 383, CA; though cf *Charterhouse Investment Trust Ltd v Tempest Diesels Ltd* [1986] BCLC 1.
3 Ie Companies Act 1981, ss 42–44.
4 1985 Act, ss 153(1) and (2).
5 1985 Act, s 153(3)(a).
6 1985 Act, s 153(4)(a).
7 1985 Act, s 153(4)(b).
8 1985 Act, s 263–281.
9 1985 Act, ss 153(4), (5) (amended by the Financial Services Act 1986, ss 196 (2), (3) and the Companies Act 1989, ss 132, 144(4), Sch 18, paras 33(2), (3)).
10 1985 Act, ss 155–156 (amended by the Insolvency Act 1986, Sch 13, Pt I); Companies (Forms) Regulations 1985, SI 1985/854, reg 4(1), Sch 3, Forms 155(6)a, 155(6)b.

tion at the meeting. This provision does not apply if the company is using the 'written resolution procedure', but the documents must be given to each member on or before he signs the resolution[1].

The law is balanced between protecting creditors and shareholders and allowing companies to engage in independent profitable transactions. The important recent case of *Brady v Brady*[2] tilts the balance in favour of the former. Throughout the legislation it is indicated that the purpose of the whole transaction, rather than the form and effect of its constituent parts, determines whether it is lawful or permitted[3]. However, it is accepted that a transaction or a step in a series of transactions whose purpose, considered in isolation, is to give financial assistance should be prohibited, regardless of the other motives and purposes of the company. As a consequence, implicit in the *Brady* decision is the need to protect creditors, including banks, although opinion has been expressed that the decision is justifiably disappointing to the business and commercial world[4].

In 1990 the company law committee of the Law Society of England and Wales put forward proposed amendments to sections 151 to 158 of the Companies Act 1985. Amongst other proposals, they recommended a decriminalisation of section 151 due to problems with the standard of proof. The committee was of the view that the 'whitewash' procedure under section 155 should be extended to all cases of financial assistance not prohibited by the EEC Second Directive. Of particular relevance to banks and other third parties is recommendation 7 which reads: 'the rights of third parties should not be affected unless it is shown that they knew, or ought reasonably to have known, that the company was acting in breach of the section'[5].

(9) INTERESTS OF DIRECTORS

It is generally prohibited for a company to make loans to directors[6]. Section 330(2) of the Companies Act 1985 provides that no company (public or private) may make a loan to a director of the company or of its holding company or enter into a guarantee or provide any security in connection with a loan made by a third party to such a director. Neither a public company nor a company which is part of a group containing a public company — a 'relevant company' in terms of section 331(6) — may make a loan to a person connected with such a director or provide a guarantee or security in respect of a loan made by another person to a connected person[7]. The term 'connected persons' includes a director's spouse

1 1985 Act, Sch 15A, para 4 (added by the Companies Act 1989, s 114(1)).
2 *Brady v Brady* [1989] AC 755, [1988] 2 All ER 617, HL.
3 See especially Buckley LJ's influential judgment in *Belmont Finance Corpn v Williams Furniture Ltd (No 2)* [1980] 1 All ER 393 at 402, CA.
4 Luxton 'Financial Assistance by a Company for the Purchase of its Own Shares — the Principal or Larger Purpose Exception' (1991) 12 Co Law 18 at 20.
5 See Freedman 'Section 151: embarrassing the honest?' (1990) 87 LS Gaz 39.
6 See generally *North-West Transportation Co Ltd and Beatty v Beatty* (1887) 12 App Cas 589, PC; *Champagne Perrier-Jouet SA v H H Finch Ltd* [1982] 3 All ER 713, [1982] 1 WLR 1359; *Stephens v T Pittas Ltd* [1983] STC 576.
7 1985 Act, s 330(3).

and infant children, a company with which he is associated, a trustee of a trust in which any of the foregoing are beneficiaries and a partner of the director or of any person connected with him[1]. These prohibitions apply also to shadow-directors[2]. There are, however, exceptions to this rule and these are laid down in sections 334 to 338, namely:

(1) a loan which, together with other 'relevant amounts', does not exceed £5,000[3];
(2) a loan or guarantee for the company's holding company[4];
(3) the provision of funds to meet expenses incurred by a director in carrying out his duties, provided that the company in general meeting approves or ratifies the arrangement[5];
(4) a loan or guarantee in the normal course of business by a bank or, subject to a limit of £100,000, by a money-lending company[6];
(5) a loan not exceeding, with other 'relevant amounts' £100,000, by a bank or money-lending company on favourable terms for house purchase, if available on similar terms to other employees[7].

Particulars of loans and securities for directors must be disclosed in the annual accounts[8]. A transaction in breach of the Act is voidable at the instance of the company and both the beneficiary and any director who authorised it are liable to indemnify the company for any loss and to account for any gains[9]. Criminal penalties may also be incurred[10].

In making advances to companies, and particularly when taking securities from companies, banks usually require a certified copy of the relevant minutes of the board meeting authorising the borrowing and/or the creation of the security. Table A makes provision[11], for the regulation of proceedings, quorum for meetings and procedural requirements[12]. In particular, regulation 94 prohibits a director from voting in a matter in which he has, directly or indirectly, an interest or duty which is material and which conflicts or may conflict with the interests of the company. Hence, subject to exceptions, the director may not form part of the quorum, reflecting the equitable principle established in the case of *Victors Ltd v Lingard*[13].

A director who is in any way interested in a contract or proposed contract with the company must declare the interest at a board meeting[14]. This

1 1985 Act, s 346.
2 1985 Act, s 330(5).
3 1985 Act, s 334 (amended by the 1989 Act, s 138(b)).
4 1985 Act, s 336.
5 1985 Act, s 337(1).
6 1985 Act, s 338(1), (3)–(5) (amended by the Banking Act 1987, Sch 6, para 18(6) and the Companies Act 1989, s 138(c), Sch 10, para 10).
7 1985 Act, s 338(6) (amended by the 1989 Act, s 138(c)).
8 1985 Act, s 232(1),(2), Sch 6, Pt II (amended by the 1989 Act, s 6(3), (4), Sch 4, paras 4, 5).
9 1985 Act, s 341.
10 1985 Act, s 342.
11 See Companies (Tables A to F) Regulations 1985, SI 1985/805, Schedule, Table A, regs 88–89, 93–94.
12 Ibid, Schedule, Table A, regs 88-89, 93.
13 [1927] 1 Ch 323.
14 1985 Act, s 317.

is subject to a caveat that only the nature of the interest need be declared, and only to the board of directors, not at general meeting. However, disclosure to a meeting of a committee of directors is insufficient as illustrated by the case of *Guinness plc v Saunders*[1]. In the *Guinness* case Lord Goff of Chieveley made the following points when considering section 317:

(a) a director is not free to contract with the company of which he is a director — such contracts are voidable;
(b) a contract for services may be rescinded upon the court making a just allowance for services rendered thereunder;
(c) a director *is* free to contract with the company on obtaining the consent of the company in general meeting or if there are exempting provisions in the articles of the company and he complies therewith; and
(d) breach of section 317 attracts only criminal sanctions, as stated in the section, and does not per se entail any civil consequences[2].

For a bank providing funding to a company it must constantly be remembered that where a director has a personal and possibly conflicting interest in a guarantee or floating charge or other security which it is proposed be granted by the company, it is possible neither will be duly executed if he fails to declare his interest. For the purpose of the rule[3], a director will be so interested even if he has not yet signed a guarantee in favour of the company's bank but it is contemplated by him and the bank that he will do so in the near future[4].

15. SUBSCRIPTION OR EXECUTION OF DEEDS BY CUSTOMERS OF BANKS

(1) GENERAL

The law regulating the method of subscription or execution of documents was radically altered by the Requirements of Writing (Scotland) Act 1995[5]. The Act was based upon the 1988 report of the Scottish Law Commission on the subject[6]. Section 11(1) of the Act provides that any rule of law which requires that a contract be constituted in writing is abolished. However, section 1(2) of the Act requires that in a number of circumstances a written document is required for the constitution of the following:

(1) a contract or unilateral obligation for the creation, transfer, variation or extinction of an interest in land;

---

1 [1988] 2 All ER 940, [1988] 1 WLR 863, CA.
2 For a good general exposition of the *Guinness* case, see McCormack 'The Guinness Saga' (1991) 12 Co Law 90.
3 As enunciated in *Victors Ltd v Lingard* [1927] 1 Ch 323.
4 *Wallace and McNeil* p 72.
5 The Act came into force on 1 August 1995.
6 Ie *Report on Requirements of Writing* (Scot Law Com no.112) (1988).

(2) the creation, transfer, variation or extinction of an interest in land otherwise than by the operation of a court decree, enactment or rule of law;

(3) a gratuitous unilateral obligation, except an obligation undertaken in the course of business; and

(4) a trust whereby a person declares himself to be sole trustee of his own property or any property which he may acquire.

For the purposes of section 1(2) of the Act a written document is formally valid by virtue of section 3 if it is subscribed by the granter of it or, if there is more than one granter, by each granter. However, in such circumstances the writing need not be probative, in the sense of being witnessed, unless the document is to be recorded in the Register of Sasines or registered for execution or preservation in the Books of Council and Session or in the Sheriff Court Books, in which case section 6 demands attestation so that the document may be regarded as self-proving. Section 3 provides that for attestation, only one witness is required whereas under the previous law, two were necessary. No mention is made in this section of the Act to the Land Register as, by section 4(1) of the Land Registration (Scotland) Act 1979, the Keeper has a discretion to refuse applications for registration if he is not provided with the documents and other evidence he will require in order to issue a land certificate without indemnity[1].

Section 7 of the 1995 Act provides for subscription and signing. Where a document need not be self-proving, an individual natural person may use a nickname or an initial or mark, his full name, or an abbreviation thereof[2]. However, Schedule 2 provides special rules relating to the subscription and signing of documents by special parties including partnerships, companies, local authorities, other bodies corporate and Ministers of the Crown.

(2) EXECUTION OF DEEDS BY PARTNERSHIPS

Paragraph (2) of Schedule 2 of the Requirements of Writing (Scotland) Act 1995 provides for alternative methods of signature, namely either by any one of the partners or by a person who is authorised to sign on behalf of the partnership. In accordance with the rest of the Act, no witnesses are required for formal validity, but if appropriately attested, the document will be considered self-proving for the purposes of section 3.

(3) EXECUTION OF DEEDS BY COMPANIES

The Requirements of Writing (Scotland) Act 1995 repealed section 36B of the Companies Act 1985 as introduced by section 72 of the Law Reform

---

1 Kenneth Reid, in his general note to the annotated Act in Scottish Current Law Statutes, and Cusine and Rennie, in 'The Requirements of Writing (Scotland) Act 1995' (1995) 40 JLSS 221, presume that the Keeper will continue to require attestation. Cusine and Rennie observe that 'there will no longer be any privilege attached to writings which are holograph or adopted as holograph and likewise no similar privilege which at present attaches to documents *in re mercatoria*'.

2 1995 Act, s 7(2).

(Miscellaneous Provisions)(Scotland) Act 1990 and created what is now a third version of section 36B[1]. However, paragraph 3 of Schedule 2 of the 1995 Act permits companies to continue to execute deeds in the manner which they used immediately prior to 1 August 1995[2]. In accordance with the rest of the 1995 Act, separate procedures are required for formal validity and self-evidencing status. A document will be considered to be formally valid if is signed by a director, or by a secretary of the company or by a person bearing to have been authorised to subscribe the document on its behalf. Self-evidencing status may be achieved by two routes: (1) by subscription of a director, the secretary of the company or an authorised person as well as attestation by a single witness, or (2) by subscription of two directors, or by a director and the secretary, or by two authorised persons.

(4)   EXECUTION OF DEEDS BY LOCAL AUTHORITIES.

Local Authorities are catered for in paragraph 4 of Schedule 2 of the Requirements of Writing (Scotland) Act 1995. Until 1 April 1996 the term 'local authority' meant district, regional and islands councils. Thereafter it means the new unitary councils established by the Local Government etc (Scotland) Act 1994.

For formal validity of a document executed by a local authority, all that is required is subscription by the 'proper officer' of the authority[3]. The proper officer is an officer of the local authority appointed for the execution of deeds[4]. Contrary to the usual rule for juristic persons in Schedule 2, there is a presumption of authority to act, providing that a person purporting to sign on behalf of a local authority is presumed to be the proper officer[5]. In practice this relieves the bank, other grantee or other persons relying on a deed executed by a local authority of the need to inquire into authority to act as signing party on behalf of a local authority.

Self-evidencing (or 'probativity') is regulated by section 3 of the 1995 Act[6]. There are two possible routes to probativity. Either the document is sealed with the common seal, or the subscription of the proper officer is attested by a single witness.

(5)   EXECUTION OF DEEDS BY OTHER BODIES CORPORATE

Paragraph 5 of Schedule 2 of the 1995 Act, caters for any bodies corporate other than a company or a local authority. The provisions of the 1995 Act are subject to any enactment providing specifically for other means of

1 Companies Act 1985, s 36B (substituted by the 1995 Act, Sch 4, para 51). See also the 1995 Act, Sch 2, para 3.
2 Ie in accordance with the version of s 36B of the 1985 Act as introduced by s 72 of the Law Reform (Miscellaneous Provisions) (Scotland) Act 1990.
3 1995 Act, Sch 2, para 4(1) read together with ss 2(1) and 7(1) of the 1995 Act.
4 See the Local Government (Scotland) Act 1973, s 235(3).
5 1995 Act, Sch 2, para 4(2).
6 But with the modifications contained in the 1995 Act, Sch 2, para 5(5), (6).

execution. The requirements for formal validity are similar to those for companies and involve subscription by a member of the body's governing board or, if there is no governing board, a member of the body, or the secretary of the body by whatever name he is called or any authorised person[1].

Self-evidencing status is achieved by two possible methods. The document is either attested by a single witness, or sealed with the common seal[2].

1 1995 Act, Sch 2, para 5(2).
2 1995 Act, s 3 as modified by Sch 2, para 5(5), (6).

Chapter 4

The Relationship Between Banker and Customer

1. INTRODUCTION — A CHANGING WORLD

The relationship of banker to customer is in the general sense one of contract[1]. Paget says:

> 'It consists of a general contract, which is basic to all transactions, together with special contracts which arise only as they are brought into being in relation to specific transactions or banking services. The essential distinction is between obligations which come into existence upon the creation of the banker–customer relationship and obligations which are subsequently assumed by specific agreement; or, from the standpoint of the customer, between services which a bank is obliged to provide if asked, and services which many bankers habitually do, but are not bound to, provide'[2].

Debate has arisen as to which category particular services fall into[3], but it is clear that the latter category of services is continually expanding. It is in

---

1 *Foley v Hill* (1848) 2 HL Cas 28; *Joachimson v Swiss Bank Corpn* [1921] 3 KB 110, CA; *Space Investments Ltd v Canadian Imperial Bank of Commerce Trust Co (Bahamas) Ltd* [1986] 3 All ER 75, [1986] 1 WLR 1072.
2 Paget's *Law of Banking* (11th edn, 1996 by M Hapgood QC) p 110.
3 See *Libyan Arab Foreign Bank v Bankers Trust Co* [1989] QB 728 at 749, [1989] 3 All ER 252 at 269, per Staughton J.

this way that the special contracts arising out of the banker–customer relationship have evolved to meet the practical and market needs of banks and customers alike. As these needs have developed, so too has the relationship which governs them[1]. In a close relationship based on good faith, the banker was traditionally considered a trusted financial adviser and man of business. Modern banking relationships are, however, often different. After the 1939–45 war Britain experienced a gradual loosening of credit controls and it was during this period that the major UK clearing banks established themselves as large international lenders and became less dependent upon their domestic-based customers. Banks are now generally considered to be less personalised institutions with automation further distancing relations between banker and customer. The relationship of banker and customer is in many respects akin to that of any other business relationship — 'customers could be said to have found a new, less patient, attitude taking over from the "friendly paternalism" of the past; increasingly, they have become parties to a business relationship little different from any other'[2].

There are three principal consequences arising from the change in the fundamental nature of the banker–customer relationship since the expansion of banking services after 1945. Firstly, there has been a gradual undermining of the bank's duty of confidentiality, as bankers experience pressure to make available confidential information to other agencies[3]. The Jack Committee expressed deep concern regarding the erosion of the banks' duty of confidentiality to their customers and suggested the strengthening of the rules of *Tournier v National Provincial and Union Bank of England*[4]. A customer applying, for example, for a credit card through his bank may expect that his credit standing has been disclosed by the bank to the credit card company by way of a credit reference agency. Secondly, as the arm's length relationship between banker and customer has developed, it has resulted in more reliance being placed upon express contractual terms laid down between banker and customer[5]. For example, the use of credit cards and cheque guarantee cards is governed by express contract. The same is true of the national EFTPOS scheme (Electronic Funds Transfer at Point of Sale)[6]. An important example of this trend has been the implementation of the Jack Committee's recommendation regarding codes of practice to be issued by banks with the resultant provision by banks of full details of the operation of the accounts of customers including bank charges[7]. Thirdly, in response to these changes, a considerable consumer interest in banking practice has been developed with many more customers taking time and professional advice to ensure that their bank contracts are negotiated upon a truly fair and arm's length basis.

---

1   *Woods v Martins Bank Ltd* [1959] 1 QB 55, [1958] 3 All ER 166.
2   *Report of the Review Committee on Banking Services: Law and Practice* (the Jack Report) (Cm 622) (1989) para 2.31.
3   See pp 108 ff below.
4   [1924] 1 KB 461, CA: see pp 108, 109 below.
5   See eg *Burnett v Westminster Bank Ltd* [1966] 1 QB 742, [1965] 3 All ER 81.
6   See ch 8, pp 256 ff below.
7   See eg codes of practice in Appendix 1 below.

2. THE BANKING CONTRACT

(1) NATURE OF THE CONTRACT

The banking contract is traditionally described as a debtor–creditor relationship. In *Royal Bank of Scotland v Skinner* it was said:

> 'After some fluctuation of opinion, it is now well settled that the relationship of customer and banker is neither a relation of principal and agent nor a relation of a fiduciary nature, trust or the like, but a simple relation — it may be one-sided or it may be two-sided — of creditor–debtor. The banker is not, in the general case, the custodier of money. When money is paid in, despite the popular belief, it is simply consumed by the banker, who gives an obligation of equivalent amount'[1].

It has been suggested that the banker–customer relationship is a contractual relationship of a particular kind, an essential of the contract being that the bank is not liable to repay the customer the full amount of the balance until the customer demands payment from the branch at which the account is kept[2]. The need for a customer to make a demand in Scotland has been seriously doubted on the reasoning that regardless of demand, the general debtor–creditor relationship is sufficient to impose an obligation to repay[3]. The English position is different with demand for payment being a requirement[4].

The explanation of the banker–customer relationship in terms of simple contract is subject to one important caveat. It is more accurate and realistic to refer to and describe particular obligations which exist from time to time and are co-existent with the main incidents of the debtor–creditor relationship. It is only in this way that the true extent of the relationship and the rights and duties which flow from it may be properly understood. The relationship between banker and customer is not always understandable as a simple debtor–creditor arrangement. The banker's duty to honour his customer's cheques is an example of mandate and a banker becomes custodian of the customer's securities by agreeing to store them in safe custody. A banker becomes guarantor to the debtor customer by issuing a cheque guarantee card. Bankers are commonly investment advisers or advisers on tax or insurance matters. The nature and legal consequences of such antecedent obligations are not explainable in terms of a debtor–creditor relationship and are continually evolving[5].

(2) TERMS OF THE CONTRACT

The commonplace contract between banker and an individual customer has few express terms and conditions. Banks have traditionally relied

---

1 *Royal Bank of Scotland v Skinner* 1931 SLT 382 at 384, OH, per Lord Mackay.
2 *Joachimson v Swiss Bank Corpn* [1921] 3 KB 110 at 127, CA, per Atkin LJ; *Clare & Co v Dresdner Bank* [1915] 2 KB 576; *Bank of Scotland v Seitz* 1990 SCLR 418, 1990 SLT 584.
3 *Macdonald v North of Scotland Bank* 1942 SC 369 at 374, 375, 1942 SLT 196 at 202, 203, per Lord Justice-Clerk Cooper.
4 See *Macdonald v North of Scotland Bank* above, per Lord Justice-Clerk Cooper. See also *Foley v Hill* (1848) 2 HL Cas 28; *Prosperity Ltd v Lloyds Bank Ltd* (1923) 39 TLR 372.
5 *Woods v Martins Bank Ltd* [1959] 1 QB 55, [1958] 3 All ER 166.

upon implied rather than express terms[1]. When opening a current account, a new customer is asked to sign an account or mandate form containing a request for the opening of an account and an instruction to the banker to honour to the debit of that account all cheques or orders signed by or on behalf of the customer. Very often nothing further by way of instruction governing the operation of the account is completed by the customer. Following the recommendations of the Jack Report[2] and the government White Paper[3] banks have introduced codes of practice detailing these matters. Each situation may be different and the banker–customer relationship may be made up of a mixture of implied terms, express terms and conditions established by a course of practice between the parties.

(3)   CODES OF PRACTICE

A voluntary code of practice has been drawn up by the British Bankers' Association, the Building Societies Association and the Association for Payment Clearing Services which is to be observed by banks, building societies and card users in relation to their personal customers[4]. The code (known as the Good Banking Code) details standards of good banking with individual customers and is designed to ensure that 'Individual customers will find the Code helpful in understanding how every bank, building society or card issuer subscribing to the Code is expected to behave towards them'[5].

The full effect of the new code will only be known over time. Many banks have issued their own codes of best practice and the terms and conditions governing their customers dealings with them[6]. A restatement of implied contractual terms in express form has the effect that many consequences of the banker–customer relationship are brought explicitly to the customer's attention. It was considered by the Jack Committee that the banks' failure to promulgate express terms for the benefit of their customers was unfair and it was regarded as unsatisfactory for banks to slant contractual terms in their own favour[7] and unilaterally change terms and conditions while giving virtually no notice to the customer[8]. The code narrates the obligation of banks to provide the terms and conditions of the contract and obligations arising therefrom, such as the banker's duty of confidentiality[9]; they detail the range of services available to customers and outline complaints procedures[10].

---

1 *Joachimson v Swiss Bank Corpn* [1921] 3 KB 110 at 117, CA, per Bankes LJ.
2 *Report of the Review Committee on Banking Services: Law and Practice* (the Jack Report) (Cm 622) (1989).
3 White Paper *Banking Services: Law and Practice* (Cm 1026) (1990).
4 See Preface to the Good Banking Code and Introduction at s 1.1.
5 Preface to the Good Banking Code.
6 For examples of codes of practice, see Appendix 1 below.
7 Jack Report, para 6.24.
8 Jack Report, paras 6.25 and 17.08–17.16.
9 Good Banking Code, para 4.
10 See the Good Banking Code, para 7.

These benefits are balanced, however, against the resulting confusion over the extent to which the information and conditions published by banks and issued to customers may be relied upon by them. The terms of the code are non-mandatory and are not made under the authority of any rule of law but the Jack Committee viewed the code as having 'the general purpose of raising standards above the minimum but acceptable position of statute law'[1]. There is no statutory warrant providing that the code is admissible in evidence, nor even that the conditions of the code are relevant factors to be taken into account by courts coming to a decision in a matter of dispute arising from the banker–customer relationship. Individual codes of practice issued by banks are not necessarily legally enforceable in their own right but are persuasive only. The courts are bound to ascribe evidential value to such individually issued codes of practice only in so far as they are spoken to by witnesses who explain their content and recommendations[2].

(4) APPROPRIATION OF PAYMENTS AND *CLAYTON'S CASE*

The rules governing appropriation of payments by a customer are an important component of the banking contract. A customer has the right when paying money into the bank to appropriate (put aside the funds for a particular purpose) the moneys in any manner he thinks fit[3]. The banker who accepts such payment without objection to the manner in which it is to be applied is under an obligation to carry out the customer's instructions[4]. An unappropriated payment may be appropriated by the banker as he thinks fit[5] and such appropriation becomes irrevocable when communicated by the banker to the customer[6].

The appropriation rules are important in several situations. In practice, in instances where a customer has more than one account, banks may amalgamate accounts to bring a combined balance in the name of the customer, but the consequence of appropriation weighs heavily where one account has the effect of securing the bank as a preferential creditor towards the customer's property. In instances where a customer has a current and a loan account and declares that the two must be kept separate and distinct, the effect of the arrangement is that payments to the credit of the current account are appropriated to that account and cannot be treated as reduction of the loan account[7]. Similar difficult consequences

---

1 Jack Report, para 16.17.
2 *Kelly v Sir Frank Mears & Partners* 1983 SC 97 at 104, *sub nom Kelly v City of Edinburgh District Council* 1983 SLT 593 at 597, per Lord Justice-Clerk Wheatley; although cf *Re St Piran Ltd* [1981] 3 All ER 270 at 277, per Dillon J.
3 *Deeley v Lloyds Bank Ltd* [1912] AC 756 at 783, HL, per Lord Shaw of Dunfermline (reversing [1910] 1 Ch 648); *Siebe Gorman & Co Ltd v Barclays Bank Ltd* [1979] 2 Lloyd's Rep 142; *Devaynes v Noble, Clayton's Case* (1816) 1 Mer 529. For full description of concept of appropriation, see ch 5, pp 146 ff below.
4 See *Seymour v Pickett* [1905] 1 KB 715, CA.
5 *Jackson v Nicoll* (1870) 8 M 408; *London and Westminster Bank v Button* (1907) 51 Sol Jo 466.
6 *Simson v Ingham* (1823) 2 B & C 65; *Mills v Fowkes* (1839) 1 Bing NC 455.
7 *Bradford Old Bank Ltd v Sutcliffe* [1918] 2 KB 833, CA.

arise in instances where the moneys are applied to a secured account leaving an unsecured debt further exposed and such issues may arise with a cautioner (guarantor) of the secured account[1]. It is common for banks, failing appropriation by the customer, to exercise their right to appropriate with regard to single debts. Banks may ascribe the deposits to debts including those which have prescribed[2] or to an unsecured debt leaving a secured debt unpaid[3]. They may also apply moneys toward payment of interest which is due leaving the principal unpaid[4]. The debt to which the money is appropriated must be liquid and not contingent. In the absence of special appropriation by a single account customer or a banker, the rule in *Clayton's Case* applies[5]. This rule provides that earlier items of the account are presumed to be discharged before the latter, the appropriation itself being the act of setting one item against the other. The appropriation effectively determines which payment 'in' relates to which payment 'out'. In *Union Bank of Scotland Ltd v National Bank of Scotland Ltd*[6] a secured debt outstanding when a postponed security was intimated to the banker, was extinguished by the payment of funds into the customer's account after the date of intimation[7]. In *Royal Bank of Scotland v Christie*[8] a partner in a business partnership provided security over his own land in support of advances made to the firm. At the date of the partner's death the firm account with the bank was overdrawn but was continued without being 'ruled' or 'broken'. Further sums were paid in after death by the surviving partners which in total exceeded the sums outstanding at the time of the deceased partner's death. Thereafter the surviving partners withdrew an even larger sum leaving the account in debit beyond that outstanding at the date of death. It was held that the rule in *Clayton's Case* required payment into the account by the surviving partners to be credited first against the earlier debt in terms on the account. It followed that, the account being overdrawn, the payment into the account after the death of the partner went to pay off the debts then due at death. The rule in *Clayton's Case* is fundamental to the banker–customer relationship in determining in what manner and to what extent particular debts are extinguished. The rule will not apply to the banking contract where it appears that the intention of the customer was to reserve the right of appropriation[9]. A matter of some controversy is when and whether the bank is taken to have exercised the right of appropriation[10]. The rule in *Clayton's Case* may be seen either as a rule of evidence and subordinate to the inferred intentions of the parties, or a

1   *Anderson v North of Scotland and Town and County Bank* (1909) 2 SLT 262, OH.
2   *Good v Smith* (1779) Mor 6816, but see *Couper v Young* (1849) 12 D 190.
3   *Anderson v North of Scotland and Town and County Bank* (1909) 2 SLT 262, OH; *Mackenzie v Gordon* (1837) 16 S 311; affd (1839) Macl & R 117, HL.
4   *Scott v Sandeman* (1849) 11 D 405.
5   *Devaynes v Noble, Clayton's Case* (1816) 1 Mer 529.
6   (1886) 14 R (HL) 1. See also *Cuthill v Strachan* (1894) 21 R 549.
7   See also *Buchanan v Main* (1900) 3 F 215; *Douglass v Lloyds Bank Ltd* (1929) 34 Com Cas 263.
8   (1839) 1 D 745; affd (1841) 2 Robin 118, HL.
9   *Hay & Co v Torbet* 1908 SC 781; *Westminster Bank Ltd v Cond* (1940) 46 Com Cas 60.
10   *Jopp v Johnston's Trustee* (1904) 6 F 1028; *Hayman & Son v McLintock* (1906) 13 SLT 863; 1907 SC 936, 15 SLT 63. See also *Seymour v Pickett* [1905] 1 KB 715, CA.

rule which will not be disapplied by mere reference to the parties' conduct or actings[1]. To prevent the operation of *Clayton's Case* it is necessary for the account to be broken (suspended)[2]. If the account is not broken, any preference of the bank by way of security upon the account will be lost if the secured advances are partially or wholly repaid by subsequent credits to the account. The prudent practice to protect the secured indebtedness is that a new account is opened for future intromissions and kept in credit[3].

(5) OBLIGATION TO REPAY

The banker's obligation to repay the customer is an implied term of the contract. A customer is usually required to give notice to the bank that he requires repayment, though in Scotland an actual demand is not necessary[4]. The banker has an obligation to act strictly according to his mandate and as such must repay the proceeds received from the customer in his capacity as banker[5]. A deposit receipt issued by a bank serves as acknowledgment to the customer that the funds deposited are held by the bank and will be repaid in terms of the contract as evidenced by the deposit receipt itself[6].

The obligation to repay depends upon certain considerations.

(a) *The rules on appropriation of payments*

These rules are dealt with elsewhere[7].

(b) *Accounts in joint names*

Where the contract requires signature by both or all of the holders of the joint account[8] the banker is in breach of contract if he does not adhere to the instructions of all authorised signatories[9]. On the death of one of the parties to a joint account, the account cannot be operated if the signature of all the joint holders is required or if one of the required signatures is that of the deceased. If, on the other hand, the terms of the contract allow one party to operate the account, it follows that the death of one party does not prevent the banker being able to honour cheques signed by the survivor or survivors. It is prudent practice to cease operations upon the account if the account was in debit at the time of the death of an account holder, otherwise the rules of *Clayton's Case* will apply with the result that the bank's rights against the deceased estate, surviving parties, cautioners and other security could be prejudiced[10].

1 See *Deeley v Lloyds Bank Ltd* [1912] AC 756, HL.
2 See [1912] AC 756 at 771, HL, per Lord Atkinson.
3 Wallace and McNeil's *Banking Law* (10th edn, 1991 by D B Caskie) pp 20, 21.
4 See *Wallace and McNeil* p 9 and W M Gloag *The Law of Contract* (2nd edn, 1929) p 707.
5 *Joachimson v Swiss Bank Corpn* [1921] 3 KB 110, CA.
6 *Wood v Clydesdale Bank Ltd* 1914 SC 397, 1914 1 SLT 245.
7 See pp 103–105 and 146–150.
8 See ch 5, pp 151–157 below.
9 *Jackson v White and Midland Bank Ltd* [1967] 2 Lloyd's Rep 68; *Forrest-Hamilton's Trustee v Forrest-Hamilton* 1970 SLT 388, OH; *Catlin v Cyprus Finance Corpn (London) Ltd* [1983] 1 QB 759, [1983] 1 All ER 809.
10 See pp 153 ff below.

(c)   Combination of accounts

The banker is entitled to combine accounts[1] held by one customer to ascertain the extent, if any, of the balance due to the customer. Where, however, the accounts are of a different nature and preclude the combination of accounts the banker must give notice of the intention to combine[2]. The right to combine accounts is critical as the duty of the banker to repay is in relation to those funds at credit of the customer's account after combination of all the accounts whether in debit or credit.

(d)   Compensation or set-off

The banker may plead compensation where he has become both creditor and debtor of the customer. The right of compensation, or set-off, is founded on the Compensation Act 1592, which provides that, as a general rule, the debt must be liquid although the court does have discretion to set off an illiquid debt if it can be made liquid without delay[3]. The obligation in respect of which compensation is pleaded as a defence must be of the same nature and description as that sued on, and there must have been no specific appropriation[4]. The right extends to combine or consolidate any debit balances against any credit balances the customer maintains on all accounts even at different branches of the same bank[5]. The debt must be due to the banker at the juncture that he wishes to establish the right of set-off[6]. The parties must occupy the positions of debtor and creditor to one another in the same capacity (the principle of *concursus debiti et crediti*) at the same time and not, for example, where the debt is due to the party pleading compensation against a claim for money paid to him by his principal[7], or where a debtor attempts to set off a debt due to him as an individual by one of the partners of a firm against a claim for a debt due to the firm[8]. There can be no compensation between debts incurred by a person before his bankruptcy and liabilities incurred to the trustee as representing the creditors of the bankrupt[9], nor as regards pleas by a depository against a depositor[10]. It is also expressly prohibited for the funds of a solicitor's client account to be used for compensation or set-off against his own indebtedness to the bank[11]. If the right of set-off is pleaded by the banker

---

1   See ch 5, pp 146 ff below.
2   *James Kirkwood & Sons v Clydesdale Bank Ltd* 1908 SC 20, 15 SLT 413; *National Westminster Bank Ltd v Halesowen Presswork and Assemblies Ltd* [1972] AC 785, [1972] 1 All ER 641, HL.
3   *Ross v Ross* (1895) 22 R 461.
4   *James Kirkwood & Sons v Clydesdale Bank Ltd* 1908 SC 20, 15 SLT 413; *Middlemas v Gibson* 1910 SC 577, 1910 1 SLT 310; *Mycroft, Petitioner* 1983 SLT 342, OH.
5   *W P Greenhalgh & Sons v Union Bank of Manchester* [1924] 2 KB 153.
6   *Jeffryes v Agra and Masterman's Bank* (1866) LR 2 Eq 674; *Baker v Lloyd's Bank Ltd* [1920] 2 KB 322; *Re E J Morel (1934) Ltd* [1962] Ch 21, [1961] 1 All ER 796.
7   *Campbell v Little* (1823) 2 S 484 (NE 429); *Stuart v Stuart* (1869) 7 M 366.
8   *Morrison v Hunter* (1822) 2 S 68 (NE 62); *Thomson v Stephenson* (1855) 17 D 739; *United Rentals Ltd v Clydesdale and North of Scotland Bank Ltd* 1963 SLT (Sh Ct) 41.
9   *Asphaltic Limestone Concrete Co Ltd v Glasgow Corpn* 1907 SC 463, 14 SLT 706; *Taylor's Trustee v Paul* (1888) 15 R 313. See also *Henderson & Co Ltd v Turnbull & Co* 1909 SC 510, 1909 1 SLT 78.
10   Bell *Principles* s 574; *Mycroft, Petitioner* 1983 SLT 342, OH.
11   Solicitors (Scotland) Act 1980, s 61 (amended by the Law Reform (Miscellaneous Provisions) (Scotland) Act 1985, s 56, Sch 1, Pt I, para 31).

and it transpires that the account is a fiduciary account in trust for some third party, the bank may still exercise its right of set-off if the banker was unaware of the nature of the account. Notice of the fiduciary nature of the account is required to prevent the banker exercising the right of set-off[1]. The banker's right of set-off is traditionally extremely strong in Scotland and is often relied upon as an equivalent to the now disputed English practice of 'charge backs' over liquid assets[2].

However, caution must in particular be exercised in invoking the right of set-off if there is a dispute between the customer and the bank as to the liability of the customer to the bank. In *King v British Linen Co*[3], the bank believing that the customer owed it money, which was disputed by the customer, decided to retain the funds at the customer's credit and dishonour cheques drawn by the customer before notice was given to him of its intention to do so. The bank was held liable in damages for 'injury to its customers' credit'.

(e) Lien

The banker's obligation to repay is affected by a general lien at common law in the banker's favour over all money, bills and negotiable instruments which are in the banker's possession as banker[4]. The right is exercisable against the indebtedness of the customer to his banker[5]. While under English law the lien applies to all unappropriated securities in the hands of the banker, negotiable or not[6], in Scotland the lien merely covers all negotiable instruments which have been lodged by the customer with the banker for the purpose of collecting the proceeds and crediting the customer's account. To constitute a 'negotiable instrument' a document must be such that delivery of it will transfer to the transferee the right to the obligation contained in it and a bona fide holder for value will acquire a title valid against all the world notwithstanding any defect in the title of the transferor or prior holders[7]. Therefore, registered shares certificates are excluded from the banker's right of lien. A banker has no right of lien over bills which he knows do not belong to the customer[8], nor over bills deposited with him merely for safe custody[9], nor over bills handed to him to be discounted but which he has refused to discount[10].

1 *United Rentals Ltd v Clydesdale and North of Scotland Bank Ltd* 1963 SLT (Sh Ct) 41.
2 *Re Charge Card Services Ltd* [1988] Ch 497, [1988] 3 All ER 702, CA; *Stein v Blake* [1996] AC 243, [1995] 2 All ER 961, HL; *M S Fashions Ltd v Bank of Credit and Commerce International SA (in liquidation)* [1993] Ch 425, [1993] 3 All ER 769, CA; *Welsh Development Agency v Export Finance Co Ltd* [1992] BCLC 148, [1992] BCC 270, CA; *Re Bank of Credit and Commerce International SA (No 8)* [1996] Ch 245, [1996] 2 All ER 121, CA; see pp 307, 308 below.
3 (1899) 1 F 928, 7 SLT 58.
4 *Brandao v Barnett* (1846) 12 Cl & Fin 787, 3 CB 519, HL.
5 *National Westminster Bank Ltd v Halesowen Presswork and Assemblies Ltd* [1972] AC 785, [1972] 1 All ER 641, HL.
6 *Re London and Globe Finance Corpn* [1902] 2 Ch 416.
7 *London Joint Stock Bank Ltd v Simmons* [1891] 1 Ch 270 at 294, CA, per Bowen LJ. See ch 6, pp 173, 174 below.
8 *Dunlop's Trustees v Clydesdale Bank Ltd* (1893) 20 R (HL) 59; *National Bank of Scotland v Dickie's Trustee* (1895) 22 R 740.
9 *Leese v Martin* (1873) LT 17 Eq 224.
10 *Borthwick v Bremner* (1833) 12 S 121; *Baker v Lloyd's Bank Ltd* [1920] 2 KB 322, per Wright J; *Akrokerri (Atlantic) Mines Ltd v Economic Bank* [1904] 2 KB 465.

A valid lien is created if the customer is indebted to the bank and the banker holds the property of his customer in his capacity as banker. The property must be in the possession of the bank at the date of creation of the lien and, legitimately so[1], and remain in the possession of the holder[2]. The property must not, however, have been deposited with the banker for a specific purpose and for one unconnected with the right of lien[3]. A banker is only entitled to retain the subjects of lien, not sell them or make them over to a third party except by way of court authority[4].

(6) DUTY OF CONFIDENTIALITY

The nature of the banking contract is such that a banker has a strict duty of confidentiality to his customer. In the course of business, bankers learn intimate financial details about their customers and are accordingly expected to act with discretion[5]. The landmark case which confirmed that a duty of confidentiality, owed by a banker to his customer, comes into existence with the creation of the banker–customer relationship and examined the extent of the duty is *Tournier v National Provincial and Union Bank of England*[6]. Mr Tournier, a customer with an agreed £10 overdraft facility, gave the bank the name and address of his new employers as he had no fixed abode. After Mr Tournier defaulted on repayment of the loan the branch manager telephoned his customer's employers in an effort to search for the whereabouts of the customer. During the course of the conversation the manager disclosed the existence of the overdraft, together with Mr Tournier's default and expressed the opinion that Mr Tournier was betting heavily. After losing his employment as a result of the information disclosed in the conversation with his employers, Mr Tournier sued the bank and won on appeal. The Court of Appeal stated that:

> 'the obligation clearly goes beyond the state of the account, that is, whether there is a credit or a debit balance, and the amount of the balance. It must extend at least to all the transactions that go through the account and to the securities, if any, given in respect of the account; and in respect of such matters it must, I think, extend beyond the period when the account is closed, or ceases to be an active account ... . I further think that the obligation extends to information obtained from other sources than the customer's actual account, if the occasion upon which the information was obtained arose out of the banking relations of the bank and its customers — for example, with a view to assisting the bank in conducting the customer's business, or in coming to decisions as to its treatment of its customers ... . In this case, however, I should not extend the obligation to information as to the customer, obtained after he had ceased to be a customer ... I do not desire to express

1 *Lucas v Dorrien* (1817) 7 Taunt 278.
2 *Lloyd's Bank Ltd v Swiss Bankverein* (1913) 29 TLR 219, CA. See also *Leese v Martin* (1873) LT 17 Eq 224.
3 *Siebe Gorman & Co Ltd v Barclays Bank Ltd* [1979] 2 Lloyd's Rep 142.
4 *Robertson's Trustee v Royal Bank of Scotland* (1890) 18 R 12; and see Wallace and McNeil's *Banking Law* (10th edn, 1991 by D B Caskie) pp 21–23.
5 *Parry-Jones v Law Society* [1969] 1 Ch 1 at 9, [1968] 1 All ER 177 at 180, CA, per Diplock LJ.
6 [1924] 1 KB 461, CA.

any final opinion on the practice of bankers to give one another information as to the affairs of their respective customers except, to say it appears to me that if it is justified it must be upon the basis of an implied consent of the customer'[1].

The duty of confidentiality is not incumbent upon banks in four circumstances, namely: where disclosure is under compulsion by law; or there is a duty to the public to disclose; or the interests of the bank require disclosure; or the disclosure is made with the express or implied consent of the customer[2].

Compulsion by law

A banker is compelled by law to reveal confidential information in three general instances. Firstly, a court may order the bank to disclose confidential information, and the procedures for compliance are laid down in the Bankers' Books Evidence Act 1879[3]. Secondly, where a duly empowered official of a government agency makes a valid request, the bank may require to surrender confidential information[4]. An example is the powers of the Inland Revenue to seek information about an individual tax payer under sections 13 and 17 of the Taxes Management Act 1970. The Jack Committee detail nineteen statutes providing requirements upon banks to disclose such confidential information[5]. Particular criticism is made by the Jack Committee of the Criminal Justice Act 1988 which permits banks to disclose confidential information simply upon suspicion of a customer's involvement in any of the offences contained in a long list of offences. This directly overrides the view expressed by Bankes LJ in the course of his *Tournier* judgment, to the effect that the giving of information to the police with regard to a customer suspected of a crime would be unwarranted[6]. The third instance is where there is no direct compulsion to divulge the information but an offence may be committed by the bank for non-disclosure and banks in such instances receive specific statutory protection when divulging such information[7].

There is force in the view that the rules which govern the court's power to order a bank to disclose information in terms of the 1879 Act are outdated. Certain areas requiring attention have been identified, with the result that under the Civil Evidence (Scotland) Act 1988, sections 3 to 5 of the 1879 Act no longer apply in Scotland[8]. It is not now necessary for bankers to produce copies of the ledgers relating to the particular

---

1 [1924] 1 KB 461 at 485–486, CA, per Atkin LJ.
2 [1924] 1 KB 461 at 471–473, CA, per Bankes LJ.
3 Bankers' Books Evidence Act 1879, ss 1–10.
4 For general examples, see *R v Marlborough Street Magistrates' Court Metropolitan Stipendiary Magistrate, ex parte Simpson* (1980) 70 Cr App Rep 291, [1980] Crim LR 305, DC; *R v Nottingham City Justices, ex parte Lynn* (1984) 79 Cr App Rep 238, [1984] Crim LR 554, DC.
5 *Report of the Review Committee on Banking Services: Law and Practice* (the Jack Report) (Cm 622) (1989), and see generally ch 5, paras 5.01–5.08.
6 Jack Report, para 5.07.
7 Eg Drug Trafficking Offences Act 1986, s 27(9); *Williams v Summerfield* [1972] 2 QB 512, [1972] 2 All ER 1334; and money laundering provisions generally.
8 Bankers' Books Evidence Act 1879, ss 3–5 disapplied as to civil proceedings by the Civil Evidence (Scotland) Act 1988, s 6(3).

customer and give evidence thereon. Unless the court directs otherwise, any document in civil proceedings may be taken to form part of the records of a business if it is certified as such by an officer of the business and the document may be received in evidence without being spoken to by a witness[1]. A copy of any document purporting to be authenticated by a person responsible for the making of the copy is, unless the court directs otherwise, to be deemed a true copy and treated for evidential purposes as if it were the document itself[2].

It has been debated whether to make changes to section 7 of the 1879 Act. In terms of section 7, on application by a party to legal proceedings, a judge may authorise an inspection and the taking of copies of any entries in a banker's book. The criterion for the judge granting such an order is that there is sufficient evidence of unlawful conduct. Where there is sufficient evidence, the customer is disentitled from relying upon the strict confidential relationship with the bank to prevent the discovery[3]. The Jack Committee recommended the amendment of section 7 to permit a court to make an order if it thinks fit, whether or not legal proceedings have begun. The Jack Committee's safeguards against 'fishing expeditions' were that proceedings would have to be seriously contemplated and there would have to be grounds to support a prosecution or an action over and above what might be discovered as a result of the order[4]. The White Paper, however, treats the Jack proposals with concern and some scepticism with the consequence that the Jack Committee's views on these points have not been followed[5].

Section 9 of the Banker's Books Evidence Act 1879 provided the definition of what constituted 'bankers books'. Modern developments in banking technology led to considerable uncertainty and the section was substituted by the Banking Act 1979[6]. Bankers' books now encompass 'ledgers, daybooks, cashbooks, account books and other records used in the ordinary business of the bank, whether those records are in written form or are kept on microfilm, magnetic tape or any other form of mechanical or electronic data retrieval mechanism'[7].

Duty to the public to disclose

The exception to the duty of confidentiality owed to the customer on the grounds of duty to the public is difficult to define. In the *Tournier* case, Bankes LJ[8] cited passages from the speech of Viscount Finlay in *Weld-Blundell v Stephens*[9] who spoke of instances where the danger to the state

---

1 1988 Act, s 5.
2 1988 Act, s 6(1), (2).
3 *Bankers Trust Co v Shapira* [1980] 3 All ER 353, [1980] 1 WLR 1274, CA.
4 Jack Report, recommendation 13(7).
5 White Paper *Banking Services: Law and Practice* (Cm 1026) (1990), para 7.7
6 Banking Act 1979, s 51, Sch 6, paras 1, 13.
7 *Barker v Wilson* [1980] 2 All ER 81, [1980] 1 WLR 884, per Bridge LJ. See *Williams v Williams* [1988] QB 161, [1987] 3 All ER 257, CA; *Clinch v Inland Revenue Comrs* [1974] QB 76, [1973] 1 All ER 977; *Attorney-General v National Provincial Bank Ltd* (1928) 44 TLR 701.
8 *Tournier v National Provincial and Union Bank of England* [1924] 1 KB 461 at 473, CA.
9 *Weld-Blundell v Stephens* [1920] AC 956 at 965–966, HL.

or where public duty may supersede the duty of the agent to his principal. The application of the exception may depend on historical events such as wars, diplomatic incidents or international disagreements. An example is *Libyan Arab Foreign Bank v Bankers Trust Co*[1] where the court came to the view, tentatively, that the exception applied. The Jack Committee took the view that banks should not be released from their confidentiality obligation on the generalised ground of public interest unless by order of the court[2].

Interests of the bank require disclosure

In *Sunderland v Barclays Bank Ltd*, Mrs Sunderland telephoned the bank to complain that her cheques were being dishonoured[3]. The bank considered itself justified in dishonouring the cheques in the light of her gambling habit and the insufficient credit balance on the account. However, when her husband, Dr Sunderland joined the telephone conversation he was informed about his wife's gambling activities. The court dismissed the action for breach of the bank's duty of confidentiality to Mrs Sunderland on the grounds that it was in the bank's own interest to reveal the information and that the customer had tacitly consented to the disclosure. The conversation with the husband was deemed a continuation of the conversation with the wife[4].

There has been a growing practice of bankers to release confidential information about their customers to other companies within their own corporate group. The justification promulgated by banks is self-protection and the need to guard against bad debtors. A report by the National Consumer Council suggested that 60 per cent of the public were dissatisfied with the passing on of personal financial information, without their full knowledge and consent, to a separate subsidiary of the institution[5]. It is argued by banks that on opening an account the customer impliedly consents to such disclosures, but there has been no reported case to test the validity of this assertion. Identified particularly is the concern that banks use personal financial information for marketing purposes[6] prompting the National Consumer Council Report to recommend that the purpose of any disclosure to a third party should be made clear to the customer at the time his consent was obtained and should be adhered to.

Recent years have seen the growth of credit reference agencies and the possible disclosure to them of confidential information by banks. Modern technology is such that it is possible for large volumes of information to be collected, stored and distributed. Credit reference agencies collect from public sources, such as the records of the courts and public registers and

1 [1989] QB 728, [1989] 3 All ER 252.
2 Jack Report, para 5.30.
3 *Sunderland v Barclays Bank Ltd* (1938) 5 LDAB 163; Times, 25 November.
4 Ellinger and Lomnicka correctly doubt this point in *Modern Banking Law* (2nd edn, 1994) p 142: the dishonour was justified by the insufficiency of funds and it was not necessary to disclose that the debt related to gambling.
5 *Taking Liberties — Commercial Use of Confidential Financial Information* (National Consumer Council, 4 July 1988).
6 Jack Report, para 5.14.

from those providers of credit who are able and willing to contribute information reflecting upon the creditworthiness of individuals. The justification for banks revealing confidential information for use in the market place (the agencies sell the information to their clients) is that prospective lenders require up-to-date information about the credit standing of individuals with whom they are doing business to attempt to avoid overborrowing by customers. Banks have therefore reached agreements with the credit reference agencies to pass 'black information' about customers in default and 'white information', about individuals honouring their credit arrangements. The Data Protection Act 1984 was passed 'to regulate the use of automatically processed information relating to individuals and the provision of services in respect of such information' but as stated by the Jack Committee:

'the 1984 Act is not about confidentiality as such (the word nowhere appears in the Act); it simply regulates the use of computerised data about individuals. Thus the protection it offers the bank customer, in respect of confidential information about himself, is somewhat limited'[1].

Express or implied consent of the customer

The consent given by the customer to the bank may be express or implied. An example of implied consent is the practice of banks providing references to outside inquiries about the customer's financial standing[2]. A customer is deemed to have consented to the bank giving such information unless the customer has specifically refused the bank's permission to do so[3].

Some conclusions on confidentiality

The duty of confidentiality in *Tournier*[4] has been substantially eroded by modern banking practice. The erosion is largely due to the efforts of government to prevent and detect crime coupled with the growing risk to lenders of debtor default, which has led banks to communicate confidential information within their own corporate group. The same risk of default has increased the pressure on banks to release confidential information to credit reference agencies. The mainly statutory encroachments on the confidentiality rule place a considerable burden on a banker's confidential relationship with his customer and there is considerable public disquiet at the banks' attitude to confidentiality, especially in light of results such as those contained in the National Consumer Council poll. The Data Protection Act 1984 does not directly protect customers from a breach of the duty of confidentiality. The Act establishes a register for data users and computer bureaux under the supervision of the Data Protection Registrar[5], and establishes the Data Protection Tribunal[6]. Individuals have

---

1 Jack Report, para 5.23.
2 See pp 125 ff below.
3 See the Good Banking Code (2nd edn), paras 8.1, 8.2.
4 *Tournier v National Provincial and Union Bank of England* [1924] 1 KB 461, CA.
5 See the 1984 Act, ss 4–5.
6 See the 1984 Act, s 3(1)(b), (3)–(5).

rights of access to personal data[1], rights to compensation[2] and rights to apply to the court for rectification or erasure of inaccurate data[3]. The Act is preventative and concerned only with the misuse of information on individuals held by computers. The application of its provisions does not depend upon the confidentiality of the information in question. The result is that the provision which lists eight data protection principles applying to individuals[4] is not of assistance because there is no mechanism by which an aggrieved customer may enforce the principles on his behalf, in court, when complaining of a bank's breach of the duty of confidentiality.

The Jack Committee's views on confidentiality

The Jack Committee reviewed the erosion of the banks duty of confidentiality 'with lively concern'[5]. The Committee suggested:

(1) the rules contained in the *Tournier* case should be put into legislative form[6];
(2) the first *Tournier* exception (compulsion by law) should be restated;
(3) the second *Tournier* exception (duty to the public to disclose) should be abolished in light of the 'torrent' of miscellaneous legislation over recent years — 'cumulatively a serious inroad into customer confidentiality'[7];
(4) the third *Tournier* exception (the interests of the bank require disclosure) should be limited to situations where the bank is party to a legal action or as between members of the same banking group with safeguards, or for the purposes of, and in connection with the proposed sale of the bank itself;
(5) the fourth *Tournier* exception (implied or express consent of customer) should be limited by omitting the word 'implied' — disclosure would only be justified if given expressly, in writing, and containing a statement from the customer stating the reason for which the consent was given; and
(6) a new *Tournier* exception should be introduced justifying disclosure 'where there has been a breakdown of the banker–customer relationship arising through customer default'[8].

The case of *Robertson v Canadian Imperial Bank of Commerce*[9] considered the *Tournier* principles and in particular the duty of disclosure under 'compulsion of law'. The case observed pitfalls and concerns under this exception. In 1987 D brought an action in the High Court of St Vincent and the

1 1984 Act, s 21.
2 1984 Act, s 22–23.
3 1984 Act, s 24.
4 1984 Act, Sch 1, Pt I. See also s 2.
5 Jack Report, para 5.26
6 Jack Report, recommendation 5(1); cf the White Paper *Banking Services: Law and Practice* (Cm 1026) (1990), para 2.12.
7 Jack Report, paras 5.07, 5.08, Appendix Q; cf *Banking Services: Law and Practice* , paras 2.13–2.14.
8 See Jack Report, paras 5.38–5.48.
9 *Robertson v Canadian Imperial Bank of Commerce* [1995] 1 All ER 824, [1994] 1 WLR 1493, PC.

Grenadines seeking repayment of a loan alleged to have been made to Dr Robertson's brother for the purposes of enabling the brother to repay a debt he in turn owed Dr Robertson. The brother denied the existence of the loan, so D obtained a 'subpoena duces tecum' against the Canadian Imperial Bank of Commerce ('CIBC') requiring them to produce Dr Robertson's bank statements over a specified period, with the intention of showing that Dr Robertson had in fact received the loan proceeds. Upon receipt of the subpoena, CIBC acting through a manager, attempted to consult Dr Robertson but for unexplained reasons failed to do so. CIBC produced statements of Dr Robertson's account during the trial but without his consent. These statements were admitted in evidence and they revealed, not only that he had received the proceeds of the loan, but also a number of other transactions and in particular that by the end of the month he was overdrawn with CIBC. Afterwards, Dr Robertson was contacted by an unidentified person who revealed to him by telephone that the above information has been produced by CIBC during the trial. As a result Dr Robertson sued CIBC for negligence and for breach of contract. At first instance CIBC was held to be protected by a plea of absolute privilege, given that the disclosure was made in the witness box. A subsequent appeal to the Eastern Caribbean Court of Appeal failed. Dr Robertson took the matter to the Privy Council. The Privy Council held that Dr Robertson had failed to prove that CIBC's omission to tell the court that it was producing his bank statement without his consent, was the cause of any loss or damage to him. However, Lord Nolan in his judgment said:

> 'Their Lordships would not exclude the possibility that a particular banker–customer relationship would include some such implied term or duty of care as that for which the appellant has contended, and that damages might be recoverable as a result of its breach by the bank concerned, but this is not such a case'[1].

In proceedings where such requests are made of banks, it is prudent practice that the tenor of the judgment of Lord Nolan is taken into account and banks only disclose the relevant and specific information demanded of them.

(7)   TERMINATION OF THE CONTRACT

The relationship between banker and customer will be dissolved in accordance with the terms agreed between the parties. The relationship will be terminated in a number of different ways:

(a)   *Mutual agreement of banker and customer.*

(b)   *The closure of the account by the customer or the bank.*
In order to close an account customers must make a demand for repayment, at least in England, at the branch at which the moneys are held. No notice is required and the account is closed by the customer drawing a

---

1   [1995] 1 All ER 824 at 831, PC.

cheque for the outstanding balance due to him. It is prudent for the banker to ascertain from his customer the intention to close the account rather than merely withdrawing the credit balance. Where the account is a deposit or savings account the customer is obliged to give the required notice to the banker, unless the sum at credit is repayable at a fixed date. Customers must take care when closing their accounts that cheques which have been issued have been presented for payment. If such cheques have not been presented for payment, they will be returned marked 'account closed'[1].

The position for bankers is more complicated. Bankers may only close an account upon giving reasonable notice to the customer[2]. The notice must permit presentation of cheques which the customer has already issued[3], and allow him to arrange other matters, such as opening an account with another branch or a different bank[4]. In *National Bank of Greece SA v Pinios Shipping Co*, the Court of Appeal decided that once a bank unequivocally demanded immediate payment of outstanding sums due on account with the intention of being paid in full, thereby closing the account, the relationship of banker and customer was replaced by one of creditor and debtor[5]. The House of Lords reversed this decision upholding the bank's right to charge compound interest on the debt until repayment after the demand had been made[6]. The primary rule is that the banker is only entitled to withdraw banking facilities upon giving sufficient notice to the customer which will enable him to make other arrangements. The banker's duty of confidentiality does not cease with the closure of the account[7].

(c) The death of the customer

The death of the customer brings the banker–customer relationship to an end. Such is the personal nature of the banking contract. When the banker receives reliable notice of a customer's death his authority to honour cheques, mandates or orders is revoked[8]. The person giving the bank a valid discharge for the payment of any sum standing to the credit of the account of the deceased customer is the deceased's executor. Depending on whether the deceased left a will and expressed a clear wish to appoint a particular person, an executor nominate or executor dative is granted confirmation in the usual way[9]. When a cheque has to be returned unpaid by reason of the customer's death, the correct response on the cheque is 'drawer deceased'. In practice, banks in certain circumstances may release funds in the accounts of deceased customers to the person who appears entitled under the will or under the laws of intestacy without insisting

1 Wallace and McNeil's *Banking Law* (10th edn, 1991 by D B Caskie) p 35.
2 *Joachimson v Swiss Bank Corpn* [1921] 3 KB 110, CA.
3 *King v British Linen Co* (1899) 1 F 928, 7 SLT 58.
4 *Prosperity Ltd v Lloyds Bank Ltd* (1923) 39 TLR 372.
5 *National Bank of Greece SA v Pinios Shipping Co No 1, The Maira* [1990] 1 AC 637 at 659, [1989] 1 All ER 213 at 229, CA, per Lloyd LJ.
6 *National Bank of Greece SA v Pinios Shipping Co No 1, The Maira* [1990] 1 AC 637, [1990] 1 All ER 78, HL.
7 *Tournier v National Provincial and Union Bank of England* [1924] 1 KB 461, CA.
8 Bills of Exchange Act 1882, s 75.
9 See ch 3, pp 50 and 51 above.

that confirmation be carried out, a discharge and indemnity then being taken from the person or persons receiving the moneys[1].

(d) The mental incapacity of customers

The mental incapacity of a contracting party terminates the banker–customer relationship by making that person's contracts void. In cases of mentally incapable persons a curator bonis may be appointed to administer the incapax's estate[2]. The effect of a supervening incapacity is less clear and the effect of such incapacity on one contract at any one time depends upon the particular circumstances. The dilemma facing the banker in this situation is whether to honour cheques drawn by the customer or to refuse to honour them, on grounds of the customer's insanity, and risk damages for breach of contract[3]. The prudent practice is generally considered to be to continue to honour cheques in such a case and to notify the customer of the bank's intention to close the account.

(e) Sequestration of the customer

The main effects of sequestration have been examined[4]. Sequestration prevents the bankrupt customer from operating his bank account and terminates the bank's authority to honour a customer's cheques. By virtue of the act and warrant issued on the confirmation of the permanent trustee, the bank is obliged to surrender the funds in the account to the permanent trustee[5].

(f) Receivership of a customer

The appointment of a receiver has the effect of crystallising the floating charge over such assets of the company which are subject to the charge. The process of receivership is available to floating charge or debenture holders over such property of the company as is covered by the debenture or charge[6]. The receiver may be appointed either by an instrument in writing executed by or on behalf of the holder of the charge[7] or by the court, to whom the holder requires to apply by petition served on the company[8]. After intimation of the receiver's appointment to the Registrar of Companies[9] the floating charge attaches to the property then subject to the charge as if it were a fixed security[10]. The receiver is required within three months of his appointment or such longer period as the court may allow, to send a report to the Registrar and to the holder of the floating charge on matters relating to the receivership[11], which will be forwarded to secured and unsecured creditors. A committee of creditors may be appointed to exercise the same functions as a committee of creditors in a winding up[12].

---

1 See ch 3, pp 50 and 51 above.
2 See ch 3, pp 48 ff above.
3 See *King v British Linen Co* (1899) 1 F 928, 7 SLT 58; *Wink v Mortimer* (1849) 11 D 995.
4 See ch 3, pp 52 and 53 above.
5 See in detail ch 3, pp 52 and 53 above.
6 Insolvency Act 1986, s 51(1).
7 1986 Act, s 53.
8 1986 Act, s 54; RCS 1994, rr 74.16–74.18.
9 1986 Act, s 53(1).
10 1986 Act, ss 53(7), 54(6), and see generally *Ross v Taylor* 1985 SC 156, 1985 SLT 387.
11 1986 Act, s 67(1).
12 1986 Act, s 68. As to floating charges, see ch 9, pp 326 ff below.

The receiver may intromit with the moneys held by the bank upon production of evidence of his appointment but subject to the bank's claim to any moneys at credit by way of its right of compensation, set-off or otherwise. Evidence of the receiver's appointment should be examined prior to allowing him to intromit with moneys at credit of the account. Such evidence would be his deed of appointment (or a certified copy) and in the case of court appointment a certified copy interlocutor of his appointment.

(g) The liquidation of a company

The general effect of liquidation is to vest custody and control of the company's assets in the liquidator. The liquidation of a company is effected in one of two ways. A voluntary winding up is a resolution whereby the members of a company may conclude an arrangement with its creditors enabling the company which is nearly or actually insolvent to rationalise its affairs more speedily and with less formality than is the case normally[1]. On obtaining notice of the passing of the resolution for a winding up, the banker is entitled to regard the mandate for the operation of the company's account as determined unless the account is overdrawn, in which case the banker may refuse to honour cheques from the date on which he receives notification that a meeting with creditors is to be held. Alternatively compulsory winding up is initiated by petition to the court and is decided in terms of the Insolvency Act 1986[2].

The main two grounds for allowing a compulsory winding up are that a company is unable to pay its debts[3] or that the court is of the opinion that it is just and equitable that the company should be wound up[4]. The winding up commences at the time of presentation of the petition to the court[5], a time which is important since any disposition of the company's property after commencement of the winding up is void unless the court orders otherwise[6]. Any person who has at any time mishandled or misappropriated property belonging to the company may be compelled[7] to repay or restore or account for the money or property or to contribute such sum to the assets of the company as the court thinks fit.

As soon as the winding up order has been made by the court, the liquidator is required to effect custody and control over all the company's assets[8]. The liquidator is entitled, upon presentation of evidence of his appointment to uplift any moneys at credit of the account subject to the bank's right of compensation, set-off or otherwise.

(h) Administration of a company

The effect of an administration order on a company is to appoint an administrator who has general powers of management and specific powers similar to those of receivers and liquidators. The banker may refuse to honour the cheques of a customer who is subject to an administration

1 1986 Act, s 84.
2 1986 Act, s 122(1).
3 1986 Act, s 122(1)(f).
4 1986 Act, s 122(1)(g).
5 1986 Act, s 129.
6 1986 Act, s 127. See also *Re Gray's Inn Construction Co Ltd* [1980] 1 All ER 814, [1980] 1 WLR 711 and *Sharp v Thomson* 1995 SCLR 683, IH, 1997 GWD 9-364, (1997) Times, 26 March, HL.
7 1986 Act, s 212.
8 1986 Act, s 144.

order on receiving notice that a petition has been presented to the court. Administration is an alternative to winding up where the court considers that it is likely that the company will survive as a going concern[1]. An application to the court may be made by the petition of the company, its directors, or a creditor or creditors[2]. If a receiver has been appointed, the court is required to dismiss the petition unless it has the consent of the person by whom or on whose behalf the receiver was appointed — except in special circumstances[3]. However, after granting the administration order the receiver, if any, must vacate office, furthermore, the rights of creditors towards company property are subject to a general moratorium on proceedings against the property[4]. The administrator is entitled, upon evidence of his appointment to uplift any moneys at credit of the customer's account but subject to the bank's right of compensation or set-off. Importantly, once an order for administration has been made no steps may be taken by creditors to realise security over the company's assets nor may diligence be enforced, except by way of leave of the court[5].

3.   THE OBLIGATIONS ARISING FROM THE BANKING CONTRACT

(1)   THE BANKER'S OBLIGATIONS

The banker's primary obligation to obey his customer's mandate strictly is supplemented by more general duties of care[6]. It is clear that the ordinary relationship of banker and customer has the effect of imposing certain added obligations upon bankers in the performance of their duties[7]. A more onerous duty of care based on the constructive trust concept was imposed on banks in two English cases[8], but later questioned[9]. The constructive trust concept is underdeveloped in the law of Scotland. Of increasing importance to banks are developments in the law of negligence which impose general duties of care based on the general concept of proximity[10].

---

1 1986 Act, s 8.
2 1986 Act, s 9(1); Insolvency (Scotland) Rules 1986, SI 1986/1915, rr 2.1–2.3; RCS 1994, rr 74.10, 74.11.
3 1986 Act, s 9(3).
4 1986 Act, s 11.
5 1986 Act, s 17.
6 *Kpohraror v Woolwich Equitable Building Society* [1996] 4 All ER 119, CA.
7 *Westminster Bank Ltd v Hilton* (1926) 43 TLR 124, HL.
8 *Selangor United Rubber Estates Ltd v Cradock (No 3)* [1968] 2 All ER 1073, [1968] 1 WLR 1555; *Karak Rubber Co Ltd v Burden (No 2)* [1972] 1 All ER 1210, [1972] 1 WLR 602.
9 *Lipkin Gorman v Karpnale Ltd* [1992] 4 All ER 409, [1989] 1 WLR 1340, CA, and see p 132 below.
10 *Woods v Martins Bank Ltd* [1959] 1 QB 55, [1958] 3 All ER 166; *Hedley Byrne & Co Ltd v Heller & Partners Ltd* [1964] AC 465, [1963] 2 All ER 575, HL; *Lloyds Bank Ltd v Bundy* [1975] QB 326, [1974] 3 All ER 757, CA; *Box v Midland Bank Ltd* [1979] 2 Lloyd's Rep 391, revsd [1981] 1 Lloyd's Rep 434, CA; *Weir v National Westminster Bank plc* 1993 SC 515, 1994 SLT 1251; *Verity and Spindler v Lloyd's Bank plc* [1996] Fam Law 213, [1995] CLC 1557.

Safe custody

A banker who accepts articles for safe custody has resulting duties of care. In general terms the bank must take reasonable care to safeguard items deposited and any attempt by the bank to exclude or limit its duty of care will be subject to the provisions of the Unfair Contract Terms Act 1977[1]. A banker must exercise reasonable care as custodian of the items and in the appointment of those persons charged with the protection of property and is answerable for the dishonest acts of his employees[2], if these acts are within the scope of the employee's authority[3]. The negligence for which a banker alone becomes responsible is the want of such care as an ordinary prudent man of business would take of property of a similar description belonging to himself[4]. It follows that the accidental destruction of the items safeguarded will not involve liability. If, for example, the items are stolen by a third party no liability of the banker would follow if he could show a reasonable standard of security precautions and that the procedures for these safeguards had been adhered to. It is the failure to adhere to a reasonable standard of care by the banker which will result in liability. It should be remembered that the banker has no right of lien over items deposited with him for safe custody[5].

Advice on investments

The banker has an implied obligation to exercise reasonable skill and care in the giving of investment advice. The traditional scope of banking business did not include advice on investments[6], although it is modern practice for banks to advertise their investment services. If the bank has offered investment advice and it is part of the bank's ordinary business, there will be a sufficiently close relationship between the parties that the bank is held liable for negligent advice[7]. Where the defendant bank, however, undertook to look after the customer's business while he was absent on war leave, the court's view was that such a function was not within the scope of banking business and the bank was released from liability[8]. Ultimately, the banker is under no obligation to advise, but if he does so liability is incurred if the advice is negligent and the question may depend on whether the manager had the authority to bind the bank[9]. The extent of

---

1 Unfair Contract Terms Act 1977, ss 16, 24 (amended by the Law Reform (Miscellaneous Provisions) (Scotland) Act 1990, s 68).
2 *Morris v CW Martin & Sons Ltd* [1966] 1 QB 716, [1965] 2 All ER 725, CA.
3 *Lloyd v Grace, Smith & Co* [1912] AC 716, HL; *United Africa Co Ltd v Saka Owoade* [1955] AC 130, [1957] 3 All ER 216, PC; *Morris v CW Martin & Sons Ltd* above.
4 *Giblin v McMullen* (1868) LR 2 PC 317; *Port Swettenham Authority v TW Wu & Co (M) Sdn Bhd* [1979] AC 580, [1978] 3 All ER 337, PC. See Wallace and McNeil's *Banking Law* (10th edn, 1991 by D B Caskie) pp 77, 78; *Langtry v Union Bank of London* (1896) 1 LDAB 229.
5 See p 108 above. See also *Robertson's Trustee v Royal Bank of Scotland* (1890) 18 R 12; *Woods v Martins Bank Ltd* [1959] 1 QB 55, [1958] 3 All ER 166.
6 *Bishop v Countess of Jersey* (1854) 2 Drew 143; *Banbury v Bank of Montreal* [1918] AC 626, HL.
7 *Woods v Martins Bank Ltd* [1959] 1 QB 55, [1958] 3 All ER 166.
8 *Wilson v United Counties Bank Ltd* [1920] AC 102, HL. The bank was, however, held liable under breach of contract and damages were awarded.
9 See *Banbury v Bank of Montreal* [1918] AC 626, HL.

the duty of care of a bank to its customers has brought much debate arising from the case of *Verity and Spindler v Lloyds Bank plc*[1]. Verity and
Spindler owned two houses. They also had overdraft facilities with
Lloyds Bank as well as their mortgages. In 1988, they decided to buy a
third house as a business venture with a view to profit from renovation.
They had a copy of the Lloyds Bank brochure called 'Starting up in
Business' and approached their local Lloyds manager. The Lloyds manager viewed two houses with them. Verity and Spindler produced a business plan which not unsurprisingly showed a gain if property prices rose
by 25 per cent. Lloyds provided short-term bridging finance. Verity and
Spindler's income (including income from renting out one of their existing
houses) would be needed to service the short-term loan. The property
market subsequently collapsed and Verity and Spindler sued for losses on
the purchased property, losses on one of their existing properties which
had to be sold to fund the loss on the third property, loss of earnings arising from Verity's time working on the project and emotional distress. It
was held that the essential question was one of whether the branch manager had assumed an advisory role in relation to the purchase of the particular house on the particular assumptions made by Verity and Spindler
in their business plan. Taylor J in the Queens Bench Division was satisfied
that Verity and Spindler had specifically sought the manager's advice and
the manager had actively encouraged them in their enterprise. In his judgment Taylor said:

> 'If a bank manager undertakes to give financial advice to customers, then it
> seems to me that he must expect to be judged by the same standards as those
> applicable to other professionals who give such financial advice such as
> Verity and Spindler's expert witness [an accountant]'.

Verity and Spindler were held to be entitled to be put in the position that
they would have been in had they not embarked on the adventure,
namely the loss on the purchased property. No valid claim had been made
out for the other heads of claim. This case does not itself create new law,
but is a reminder that banks may inadvertently take on a role of adviser
with consequent standards of care which, if broken, may render them
liable to their customers[2].

Advice on securities

As a general rule, when the customer enters into a cautionary agreement
with a banker, the banker is not under a duty to explain the nature and
effect of the transaction. The banker must take care not to misstate the
position or leave the customer with a false impression. The banker is not
obliged to volunteer information which is not asked for, fulfilling his
duties by confirming his replies to what is factual and relevant[3]. The rule

---

1 [1996] Fam Law 213, [1995] CLC 1557.
2 See *Ginora Investments Ltd v James Capel & Co Ltd* (10 February 1995, unreported) in which
   the role of a financial adviser in a takeover bid was examined, and *Eagle Trust plc v SBC
   Securities Ltd* (1994) Independent, 28 September, where the importance of the distinction
   of the particular roles of a bank in its dual function as financial adviser to a company and
   underwriter of its security are discussed.
3 For specific discussion, see see ch 9, pp 332 ff below.

in the English case of *Lloyds Bank Ltd v Bundy*[1] is that the relationship of confidentiality between banker and customer imposes a fiduciary duty of care on banks where they proceed further by advising on more general matters relating to the transaction and the customer does not receive independent advice[2]. In that case, the customer, who was advanced in age and naive in business matters, had placed reliance upon the bank's advice. The bank's failure to disclose all the material facts was, it was argued, akin to the exercise of undue influence. If a customer can show that the bank has taken unfair advantage, the presumption of undue influence applies and the transaction is voidable[3]. The bank was deemed not to have faulted where it had obtained no benefit from the transaction; the misstatement was technically, not substantively, incorrect and the customer understood the legal consequences of the transaction[4].

The duties of care imposed in *Bundy's* case are open to serious criticism. There is uncertainty in Kerr LJ's suggestion, in contrast to the Scottish position, that banks are under a duty to proffer an adequate explanation as to the nature and effect of the document the person is about to sign[5]. Although this dictum has been disapproved, grey areas remain where in 'special circumstances' bankers have a duty to explain[6]. Moreover, it has been stressed that Bundy based liability promotes the policy of protecting weaker contracting parties, especially married women and the elderly. The English position was further clarified by the much celebrated case of *Barclays Bank plc v O'Brien*[7]. Mrs O'Brien signed a mortgage over the matrimonial home owned by her and Mr O'Brien to secure Mr O'Brien's indebtedness of a company in which he had an interest. Prior to the subscription of the document Mr O'Brien represented to Mrs O'Brien the duration and extent of the mortgage. Mrs O'Brien was given the impression that the mortgage was limited to £60,000 and would last for only three weeks. No advice as to the terms of the mortgage was given by the bank to Mrs O'Brien nor was she asked to seek independent legal advice. The House of Lords held that Mrs O'Brien was entitled to set aside the bank's charge as the bank had 'constructive notice' of the misrepresentations made by Mr O'Brien. Lord Browne-Wilkinson in delivering his judgment summarised the legal principles which primarily applied, as follows:

(1) A guarantor has a right against the principal debtor to set aside the guarantee where it has been procured by undue influence of misrepresentation.

(2) A guarantor will also have the right to set aside the guarantee against the creditor who has actual or constructive notice of such undue influence as misrepresentation.

---

1 [1975] QB 326, CA.
2 [1975] QB 326 at 347, CA, per Sir Eric Sachs.
3 *Cornish v Midland Bank plc (Humes, third party)* [1985] 3 All ER 513, CA.
4 *National Westminster Bank plc v Morgan* [1985] AC 686, [1985] 1 All ER 821, HL.
5 *Cornish v Midland Bank plc (Humes, third party)* [1985] 3 All ER 513 at 522, CA.
6 *Barclays Bank plc v Khaira* [1992] 1 WLR 623, per Thomas Morison QC.
7 [1994] 1 AC 180, [1993] 4 All ER 417, HL.

(3) A creditor will be fixed with constructive notice of the guarantor's rights if the circumstances are such as to put the creditor on inquiry as to the circumstances in which the guarantor had agreed to give the security. A creditor will be put on inquiry when, for example, a wife offers to stand guarantor for her husband's debts where the transaction is on its facts not to the financial advantage of the wife.

(4) A creditor should take reasonable steps to satisfy himself that the guarantor's agreement to stand guarantor has been obtained properly. Reasonable steps will have to be taken if the guarantor is worried of the potential liability and of the risks involved as well as being advised to obtain independent legal advice.

The position in Scotland presently remains as stated in *Mumford v Bank of Scotland; Smith v Bank of Scotland*[1]. Two women who were wives of partners in the same business, had signed documents at the request of their respective husbands. One had signed, together with her husband, a standard security over the matrimonial home of which they were *pro indiviso* proprietors. The other wife had signed a formal consent in terms of the Matrimonial Homes (Family Protection) Scotland Act 1981 to the granting of a standard security by her husband who was the sole proprietor of the matrimonial home. In each cases the wife was in reality acting as cautioner for her husband's business debts. Both women argued that they had been induced to sign the documents in favour of the bank by their respective husbands. They also averred that representations were false and misleading and but for which they would not have signed the documents. In neither case had they obtained independent legal advice nor had they been warned as to the implications of the documents they were signing. It was not alleged that the bank had actual knowledge of the husbands' misrepresentations. In both cases the relevant transactions were essential to the procuring of additional finance from the bank for the husbands' business. The wives did not have any financial interest in the businesses. The wives brought actions concluding for partial reduction of the standard securities in so far as affecting them. They specifically relied upon *Barclays Bank plc v O'Brien* and argued that where the relationship between co-cautioners was so close, such as a husband and wife, and where one party had no direct financial interest in the transaction but was put at a financial disadvantage because of it, the lender would be put on inquiry and was under a duty to take reasonable steps to satisfy himself that the disadvantaged party's consent to the agreement to give security had been properly obtained. Lord Johnston held that:

(1) the law of Scotland (except in the context of agency) did not infer constructive notice in the mind of the person wholly ignorant of misrepresentation simply because of surrounding circumstances — 'I can find no authority in Scotland outwith the context of agency where constructive notice can be inferred in the mind of a person wholly

---

1   1994 SCLR 856, 1994 SLT 1288, OH; 1995 SCLR 839, 1996 SLT 392, 1st Div.

ignorant of the fact that matters, namely in this case the misrepresentation by the husband, simply because of surrounding circumstances'[1]; and
(2) that in the absence of actual knowledge of undue influence or misrepresentation the lenders were not under a duty either to explain to the
wives the nature of the transactions into which they were entering
and their consequences, or require them to take independent advice[2].

The Scottish banker's position is somewhat stronger compared to his
English counterpart. In Scotland the resultant obligations to the customer
in Scotland are less onerous. Appeals of the recent Scottish cases are pending and it is conceivable that Scots law will be brought into line with
English law. In terms of 'good' banking practice in the provision of guarantees and other third party securities it is likely the Banking
Ombudsman will take cognisance of the provisions of the second edition
of the Good Banking Code[3] which states that:

> 'Banks and Building Societies will advise private individuals proposing to
> give them a guarantee or third party security for another person's liabilities
> that: (a) by giving the guarantee or third party security he or she might
> become liable instead of or as well as that other person; (b) he or she should
> seek independent legal advice before entering the guarantee or third party
> security and guarantees and other third party security forms will contain a
> prominent notice to the above effect'.

In the English jurisdiction, unlike in Scotland, bankers require to be aware
of the warning of Lord Browne-Wilkinson in *Barclays Bank plc v O'Brien* to
the effect that those who hide behind warning language may be perilled
since he regarded an independent interview as 'essential because a number of the decided cases show that written warnings are often not read and
are intercepted by the husband'[4].

Since the *O'Brien* case, English law has further refined the obligations of
a bank with regard to the advice which ought to be proffered to the guarantor of security. In *Midland Bank plc v Greene*[5] Mr and Mrs G granted a
mortgage over the matrimonial home to secure joint debts and the personal debts of Mr G. In a consideration of the security aspects of the transaction the court held that the facts created a presumption of undue
influence. In the absence of evidence to indicate that Mrs G had been
encouraged to seek independent advice, the security was invalid in so far
as it related to the personal debts of Mr G. In *TSB Bank plc v Camfield*[6] Mrs
C granted a mortgage over the matrimonial home to secure the debts of

---

1 1994 SCLR 856 at 861, 1994 SLT 1288 at 1291, OH. See also *Young v Clydesdale Bank Ltd*
   (1889) 17 R 231; *Royal Bank of Scotland v Greenshields* 1914 SC 259, 1914 1 SLT 74; *Bank of
   Scotland v Porteous* (30 July 1956, unreported), OH (Lord Strachan); and ch 9, pp 324 and
   325 below.
2 *Mumford v Bank of Scotland; Smith v Bank of Scotland* 1994 SCLR 856 at 861, 1994 SLT 1288
   at 1291, OH. See also *Rodger (Builders) Ltd v Fawdry* 1950 SC 483, 1950 SLT 345; *McCabe v
   Skipton Building Society* 1994 SCLR 501, 1994 SLT 1272.
3 Good Banking Code (2nd edn), para 14.1.
4 [1994] 1 AC 180 at 198, [1993] 4 All ER 417 at 431, HL.
5 [1993] 27 HLR 350, [1994] 2 FLR 827.
6 [1995] 1 All ER 951, [1995] 1 WLR 430, CA.

Mr C's business. Mr C had told her that the mortgage was limited to £15,000 which was untrue. No encouragement to take independent advice was given. The Court of Appeal held that the security was void. In *Massey v Midland Bank plc*[1], Mrs M had been deceived by her long-term boyfriend into providing a mortgage over her home to secure the debts of his business. Mrs M had two children by her lover but had never cohabited with him. Her lover's deception extended not only to the wealth of his business but also as to the discharge of another charge to a different bank which he had arranged for her to give in respect of a separate failed venture four years earlier. The court held that the presumption of undue influence was present but that the bank had satisfied their obligations by advising Mrs M to seek independent advice. She did, in fact, receive legal advice but only in the presence of her lover and, whilst the solicitor explained the nature of the legal charge he did not ask about or advise about the underlying business of the lover's company. It was not suggested the bank either knew or should have been an inquiry as to the procedure for interviewing clients in the solicitor's office. The bank was not responsible for the quality or absolute independence of the advice. In *Banco Exterior Internacional v Mann*[2] Mrs M granted a second charge over her matrimonial home to secure facilities being granted to her husband's company. Mrs M did receive legal advice but the giver of the advice was the solicitor to Mr M's company. The Court of Appeal held by a majority that, notwithstanding the fact that the adviser was not wholly independent, the security was enforceable. It was held to be a matter for the solicitor to determine whether he met with a conflict of interest that did not allow him to give independent advice. That position is certainly the position presently in Scotland, but English bankers require to take additional care in view of the strong dissenting opinion of Hobhouse LJ. In his view truly independent advice could not take place where it did not 'visualise that in some circumstances she may be advised not to sign a document'[3].

In *Bank of Baroda v Rayarel*[4], Mrs R signed a mortgage over her home to secure the debt of the business operated by her husband and son who also shared the same home. The mortgage contained a declaration that she has been advised of its effect and of her right to have independent legal advice. It was signed by the same solicitor who had acted for the company in the early stages of negotiations with the bank and who acted for Mrs R, her husband and son. In the Court of Appeal, Hoffman LJ said that it was unnecessary for a bank to inquire as to the adequacy of the advice given by a solicitor, particularly if the solicitor had certified the advice that was given. It was a matter for the solicitor to determine whether or not he could act in the face of a potential conflict of interest[5].

It follows that while the legal obligations for 'advice on securities' fall well below those of the English jurisdiction it is prudent to adhere to the

1 [1995] 1 All ER 929, CA.
2 [1995] 1 All ER 936, CA.
3 [1995] 1 All ER 936 at 948, CA.
4 *Bank of Baroda v Rayarel* [1995] 2 FCR 631, [1995] 27 HLR 387.
5 These purely English authorities have been included as the Banking Ombudsman may be influenced by them, and in the writer's view the Scottish courts will take note of some of the lessons to be learned from these cases. Regarding onerous liability resting on solicitors, see *Barclays Bank plc v Thomson* (1996) 146 NLJ 1778, CA.

tenor of the Good Banking Code and 'good banking practice' or otherwise risk objection and censure from the Ombudsman. Where advising on security transactions, delictual duties may be imposed on Scottish bankers by customers founding on the principle of negligent misrepresentation[1]. The nature of the *Bundy* duty is different, however, from liability established under the *Hedley Byrne* case, which depends on a banker's voluntary assumption of liability.

Bankers' references about the financial status of customers

The common practice of banks answering references from another bank about a particular customer's financial status gives rise to certain duties of care. Answering inquiries from another bank acting on behalf of its customer is within the scope of banking business and the referee bank is not bound to carry out its own investigations before supplying the information[2]. The information given in the reference is usually accompanied by a disclaimer enabling banks to minimise the risk of a successful claim against them in negligence[3]. Although the practice of banks giving references is regarded as impliedly authorised by most customers, care must be taken and banks may be held liable in two ways, either to the customer about whom the reference is made or to the person receiving the information[4].

The banker owes a duty of care to the recipient of the reference if there is fraudulent misrepresentation or negligent misrepresentation. In *Hedley Byrne & Co Ltd v Heller & Partners Ltd*[5] a group of advertising agents asked their bank to make inquiries concerning the financial status of a company for whom they had placed substantial orders. In reliance upon the bank's negligent misstatement of the company's position the agents lost considerable sums of money when they became liable for the advertising placed for the company with no right of recourse on its insolvency. Prior to the *Hedley Byrne* case, the law limited an action for negligent misrepresentation to cases where a contractual or fiduciary relationship existed between the parties[6]. The decision confirms that in some circumstances a special relationship exists and that a person possessed with special skills such as a banker owes a duty of care in the giving of information or advice. Where banks give a simple reference in the form of a brief expression of opinion the banker does not accept, and there is not expected of him, any higher duty than giving an honest answer[7]. However, where there is something

---

1 See *Hedley Byrne & Co Ltd v Heller & Partners Ltd* [1964] AC 465, [1963] 2 All ER 575, HL.
2 *Swift v Jewsbury and Goddard* (1874) LR 9 QB 301; *Parsons v Barclay & Co Ltd and Goddard* (1910) 103 LT 196, CA; *Robinson v National Bank of Scotland* 1916 SC (HL) 154, 1916 1 SLT 336.
3 *Hedley Byrne & Co Ltd v Heller & Partners Ltd* [1964] AC 465, [1963] 2 All ER 575, HL; *Mutual Life and Citizens' Assurance Co Ltd v Evatt* [1971] AC 793, [1971] 1 All ER 150, PC.
4 *Standard Investments Ltd v Canadian Imperial Bank of Commerce* (1985) 22 DLR (4th) 410, OR (2d) 473, Ontario CA.
5 [1964] AC 465, [1963] 2 All ER 575, HL.
6 *Derry v Peek* (1889) 14 App Cas 337, HL; *Le Lievre v Gould* [1893] 1 QB 491; *Candler v Crane, Christmas & Co* [1951] 2 KB 164, 1 All ER 426, CA.
7 *Hedley Byrne & Co Ltd v Heller & Partners Ltd* [1964] AC 465 at 504, per Lord Morris, and at 513, per Lord Hodson.

more, 'that is where there is an assumption of responsibility in circumstances in which but for the absence of consideration there would be a contract'[1] a duty of care will be imposed upon the banker[2].

A banker's liability is affected by the Unfair Contract Terms Act 1977. In the *Hedley Byrne* case, the bankers relied on a non-contractual disclaimer of responsibility to escape liability. Such disclaimers are now subject to the provisions of the 1977 Act, as illustrated by the English case of *Smith v Eric S Bush*[3]. A building surveyor used a disclaimer to exclude liability to a house purchaser for the accuracy of a valuation. The disclaimer did not satisfy the fair and reasonableness test under the English provisions of the Act[4]. Part II of the Act contains the Scottish provisions[5] but unlike Part I, the Scottish provisions applied only to contractual exemption clauses. The Scottish courts accepted, and sometimes with reluctance[6], that even if a disclaimer was not fair and reasonable in terms of the Act it had to be given effect if it was clear and unambiguous in its terms. Under section 68 of the Law Reform (Miscellaneous Provisions) (Scotland) Act 1990, Scots law was brought into line with English law by bringing non-contractual notices within the controls of the 1977 Act[7]. The issue for both English and Scots law is therefore whether a bank's disclaimer, when giving a reference, is likely to be struck at by the provisions of the Act, on the authority of *Smith v Eric S Bush*[8]. There is some force in Paget's view that there are no grounds for distinguishing the two cases[9] supported by the reasoning that building surveys, like references, are transactions commonly entered into every day[10]. There is one major difference between the two, however, which may be the crucial element: a building survey is an opinion which is based upon physical data while a banking reference is necessarily never more than a 'snapshot' opinion based upon the bank's past and present financial dealings with the person about whom the reference is made. The dangers of making false, misleading or negligent references is well illustrated by the House of Lords' case of *Spring v Guardian Assurance plc*[11]. The plaintiff worked for a company which sold assurance policies, and which was taken over by Guardian Assurance. Shortly after the takeover the plaintiff was dismissed. He attempted to set up business in the same locality selling the assurance policies of another company but the company

---

1   [1964] AC 465 at 529, per Lord Devlin (consideration key to requirement of contract in England).
2   See *Woods v Martins Bank Ltd* [1959] 1 QB 55, [1958] 3 All ER 166; *Box v Midland Bank Ltd* [1979] 2 Lloyd's Rep 391 (revsd [1981] 1 Lloyd's Rep 434, CA); *Lloyds Bank Ltd v Bundy* [1975] QB 326, [1974] 3 All ER 757, CA; *Commercial Banking Co of Sydney Ltd v R H Brown & Co Ltd* [1972] 2 Lloyd's Rep 360, Aust HC.
3   *Smith v Eric S Bush* [1990] 1 AC 831, [1989] 2 All ER 514, HL.
4   See the Unfair Contract Terms Act 1977, s 2(2), 11(3), 13(1).
5   The 1977 Act, Pt I, comprises ss 15–25. See particularly ss 16, 24.
6   Eg *Robbie v Graham and Sibbald* 1989 SCLR 578, 1989 SLT 870, OH.
7   But see *Melrose v Davidson and Robertson* 1993 SC 288, 1993 SCLR 365, 1993 SLT 611, affg 1992 SLT 395, OH.
8   *Smith v Eric S Bush* [1990] 1 AC 831, [1989] 2 All ER 514, HL.
9   Paget's *Law of Banking* (11th edn, 1996 by M Hapgood QC) p 128.
10 And see *Smith v Eric S Bush* [1990] 1 AC 831 at 849, 850, [1989] 2 All ER 514 at 524, 525, HL, per Lord Templeman.
11 *Spring v Guardian Assurance plc* [1995] 2 AC 296, [1994] 3 All ER 129, HL.

was obliged by the code of conduct of the insurance industry's self-regulatory body (Lautro) to obtain a reference from the plaintiff's previous employer, which was in turn required by rule 3.5(2) of the Lautro rules to give a reference which made 'full and frank disclosure of all relevant matters which are believed to be true'. The plaintiff's prospective employer received a very poor reference from Guardian Assurance stating that he kept business for himself, that he was a man of little or no integrity, he could not be regarded as honest and that he had mis-sold a policy with the aim of generating a very substantial commission for himself. The plaintiff's job application was rejected and he was unable to obtain a job elsewhere. He sued the defendants for breach of contract, malicious falsehood and negligent misstatement causing economic loss. The trial judge found that the reference was inaccurate, but that the defendants had acted negligently rather than maliciously. He allowed the action of negligence. On appeal to the Court of Appeal, however, it was held that the giver of a reference owed no duty of care in negligence to the person who was the subject of the reference either in giving or compiling the reference or in obtaining the information on which it was based. The plaintiff's only remedy lay in defamation and this could not be allowed since there would be a defence of qualified privilege, given that the defendants had to give a full, frank and truthful reference. In so deciding they allowed the appeal. The plaintiff appealed to the House of Lords. The House of Lords held that an employer can be held liable in negligence for failure to take reasonable care in providing a reference for an employee or ex-employee because (per Lords Lowry, Slynn and Woolf) there is a proximate relationship between them and it is fair, just and reasonable that the employer should be under a duty or because (per Lord Goff) the employer has assumed responsibility for the reference and the employee has relied on the employer to take reasonable care. Since an action for negligence has a different basis from an action for defamation, the fact that a defamation action for injury to reputation would be defeated by a defence of qualified privilege does not necessarily bar an action for negligence causing economic loss.

The decision is of course in relation to contracts of employment but is authority for the proposition that where there is either sufficient proximity between the parties, or where the referee assumes responsibility for the reference and there is concomitant reliance on the part of the subjects of the reference, then persons other than employers or former employers may be held liable for negligently made references. The principles enunciated in this case are relevant in a consideration of the duties of care owed by the banker in the giving of references about their customers. Banks should be careful that references are both truthful and accurate; an omission may be as damning as positive statement with consequent liability to the recipient of the reference.

What is the position of the customer about whom an inaccurate reference is made? The customer has an action based on the bank's breach of its duty to exercise reasonable care and skill. Where there is no apparent inaccuracy, an action for defamation or an action based on a breach of the bank's duty of confidentiality may be available to the customer. In the case of an action for defamation, the customer must establish generally that the information communicated was capable of lowering his esteem in the estimation of right-thinking members of society. There is authority that an answer given to a specific inquiry regarding the credit of a particular party is subject to qualified privilege[1]. As a result, the onus rests on the aggrieved party to show that the defender was acting with malice. In the case of an action for breach of confidence, a banker must bring himself within the exceptions in the *Tournier* case[2] to justify disclosing the confidential information. Criticisms have been made of the fourth *Tournier* exception which justifies disclosure made with the express or implied consent of the customer on the grounds that a customer's consent should only be given explicitly[3].

The Weir case

The case of *Weir v National Westminster Bank plc*[4] is important in extending the duty of care on banks. The First Division of the Inner House was not willing to refuse to consider a duty of care on a bank which had failed to detect forgery and bring it to the attention of the solicitor acting as sole signatory and agent by way of a power of attorney on the disclosed principal's (the customer's) account and allowed a proof before answer. The bank honoured a cheque signed by the solicitor which was allegedly forged by his cashier. As well as operating the customer's account, the solicitor had an account of his own at the same bank. The First Division held that a duty of care could be imposed on banks where there is sufficient proximity between the bank and a person relying on the bank's expertise[5]. Proximity was established in the *Weir* case through Weir's power of attorney and the fact that he was acting as sole signatory on the account. The court made it clear the appeal was decided upon its own specialist facts. It does not follow necessarily that a duty is owed to all agents of disclosed principals and the court was clear that a significantly greater burden was not imposed on bankers, who owe the same duty where the customer is sole signatory. The test is whether it is fair, just and reasonable to impose a duty of care on the banker[6]. Imposing a duty of care in cases such as *Weir* does *not* depend on the existence of a banker–customer relationship[7]. In *Weir's* case the court rejected explicitly the solicitor's argument that he was owed a duty of care with regard to that particular cashier's forgery by virtue of his own personal account with the bank.

---

1   *King v British Linen Co* (1899) 1 F 928, 7 SLT 58; *Bayne & Thomson v Stubbs Ltd* (1901) 3 F 408.
2   As to these exceptions, see pp 109 ff above.
3   See *Report of the Review Committee on Banking Services: Law and Practice* (the Jack Report) (Cmnd 622) (1989), paras 6.34, 6.36, 6.37, recommendation 6(4), and the White Paper *Banking Services: Law and Practice* (Cm 1026) (1990), para 2.15.
4   1993 SC 515, 1994 SLT 1251.
5   As in *Hedley Byrne & Co Ltd v Heller & Partners Ltd* [1964] AC 465, [1963] 2 All ER 575, HL.
6   As in *Caparo Industries plc v Dickman* [1990] 2 AC 605, [1990] 1 All ER 568, HL.
7   See also *Woods v Martins Bank Ltd* [1959] 1 QB 55, [1958] 3 All ER 166, and *Hedley Byrne & Co Ltd* above.

(2) THE CUSTOMER'S DUTIES TO THE BANKER

The leading case on a customer's duty of care is *Tai Hing Cotton Mill Ltd v Liu Chong Hing Bank Ltd*[1]. T Ltd, the plaintiff, had a current account with three different banks in Hong Kong. T Ltd had mandated one bank to pay cheques signed by the managing director. An accounts clerk, L, contrived to forge the managing director's signature and on receiving sums totalling $HK 5.5 million diverted the money into other accounts. By the time the fraud was discovered L had fled and T Ltd brought an action against the bank. In its defence the bank sought to establish that T Ltd was in breach of a customer's implied duty to take reasonable precautions in the management of his business to prevent forged cheques being presented for payment, and to take steps to check periodic bank statements, enabling him to notify the bank of any unauthorised debits. The Privy Council held that a customer has duties only to exercise reasonable care to prevent forgery and alteration when drawing cheques and to inform the bank if he knows of forgeries on his account.

Duty to prevent forgery

The duty to prevent forgery was expounded in *London Joint Stock Bank v Macmillan and Arthur*[2]. An employee of Macmillan and Arthur, A, prepared a cheque for his employers to sign. The cheque was made payable to bearer. The figure '2' was shown but the amount in words did not appear. After obtaining a partner's signature A fraudulently altered the cheque to show '120' in figures and added that amount in words. A cashed the cheque and absconded with the money. Macmillan and Arthur were left to bring an unsuccessful action for recovery against the bank. The Lord Chancellor stated:

> 'A cheque drawn by the customer is in point of law a mandate to the banker to pay the amount according to the tenor of the cheque. It is beyond dispute that the customer is bound to exercise reasonable care in drawing the cheque to prevent the banker being misled. If he draws the cheque in a manner which facilitates fraud, he is guilty of a breach of duty as between himself and the banker, and he will be responsible to the banker for any loss sustained by the banker as a natural and direct consequence of this breach of duty...'[3].

Two points should be further considered. Firstly, it is a question of degree what is negligence to constitute breach of duty. In *Slingsby v District Bank Ltd*[4] the customer was not negligent by leaving a space between the name of the payee and the words 'or order'. In *Lumsden & Co v London Trustee Savings Bank*[5] a customer's blameworthiness did have the effect of reducing damages by the proportion to which it contributed to the fraud.

---

1 [1986] AC 80, [1985] 2 All ER 947, PC.
2 [1918] AC 777, HL.
3 [1918] AC 777 at 789, HL, per Lord Finlay LC.
4 [1932] 1 KB 544, CA.
5 [1971] 1 Lloyd's Rep 114.

Secondly, the duty to prevent forgery does not extend to the customer taking reasonable care in the management of the business relating to the mandate[1]. In the *Tai Hing* case the court refused to acknowledge a wider duty of care based on implied contract[2]. However, it is worthy of note, that the Banking Ombudsman may take a different, less legislative view:

> 'As was determined in *Tai Hing Cotton Mill Ltd v Liu Chong Hing Bank Ltd*, a customer owes no general duty to his bank to check his monthly or other periodic statements to identify errors. There have been cases where in deciding that it is fair in all the particular circumstances of that case notwithstanding the decision in *Tai Hing*, I have decided that an element of contributory negligence should be attributed to the complainant'[3].

Duty to inform

The duty on a customer to inform the banker of forgery is based upon the principles enunciated in *Greenwood v Martins Bank Ltd*[4]. Greenwood had an account with Martins Bank and his wife kept his passbook and cheque book. In October 1929 he asked his wife for a cheque, indicating that he wished to withdraw £20. His wife told him that there was no money in the account because she had been funding legal proceedings in which her sister was involved. In fact, the wife had been forging her husband's cheques over a period, and Mr Greenwood adhered to his wife's urgent requests and did not advise the bank of the forgeries. Some eight months later he discovered that his wife's explanation of the forgeries was untrue whereupon he notified the bank. His wife committed suicide and he brought an action against the bank for the amount paid under the forged cheques. Scrutton LJ in the Court of Appeal stated[5]:

> '[There is] a continuing duty on either side to act with reasonable care to ensure the proper working of the account. It seems to me that the banker, if a cheque was presented to him which he rejected as forged, would be under a duty to report this to a customer to enable him to inquire into and protect himself against the circumstances of the forgery. This, I think would involve a corresponding duty on the customer if he became aware that forged cheques were being presented to his banker, to inform his banker in order that the banker might avoid loss in the future. If this is correct, there was in the present case silence, constituting a breach of duty to disclose'.

Where a customer knows or has reasonable grounds to believe that his name has been forged on a bill or cheque he is bound to disclose the forgeries to the bank to enable the bank to take steps towards recovering the money paid on the forged cheques. If the customer through neglect causes his bankers to make a payment on a forged order, it is not competent to set up against them the invalidity of a document which he has induced them to honour as genuine[6]. It was confirmed in *Tai Hing Cotton Mill Ltd v Liu*

1 *Kepitigalla Rubber Estates Ltd v National Bank of India Ltd* [1909] 2 KB 1010 at 1023, per Bray J.
2 See p 129 above.
3 Banking Ombudsman Scheme, Annual Report 1994–95, p 28.
4 [1932] 1 KB 371, CA, affd [1933] AC 51, HL.
5 [1932] 1 KB 371 at 381, CA.
6 *Orr and Barber v Union Bank of Scotland* (1854) 1 Macq 513 at 523, HL, per Lord Cranworth; *Greenwood* above; *Brown v Westminster Bank Ltd* [1964] 2 Lloyd's Rep 187.

Chong Hing Bank Ltd that the implied duty of care did not go beyond the duty specified in the *Greenwood* case[1].

Delictual duties of customers

The courts are generally unwilling to impose delictual duties of care on customers[2]. It is thought to be incorrect in principle to impose a delictual duty where the parties are free to determine their obligations to one another by contract[3], unless the events which give rise to the duty of care are outside the range of matters which realistically may be treated as within the scope of contract[4]. In the *Tai Hing* case[5], the bank submitted that the plaintiff was in breach of a tortious (delictual) duty of care under the general law of negligence. The judges in the High Court of Hong Kong penalised the plaintiff for poor accounting standards, observing in particular that operation clerks were left unattended with almost total control over receipts and payments in their division. The Privy Council's decision was that regardless of the inefficiency of the customer's system of operation, where the customer's miscreant employee secures funds on a forged cheque the bank has no claim in delict[6].

Proposals for change

The government is of the opinion that the present law is unfair to banks. View is expressed in the White Paper of 1990 that the *Tai Hing* decision[7] is balanced too favourably towards customers[8]. The White Paper[9] recommends allowing a defence of contributory negligence in actions against banks in debt or for damages arising from unauthorised payments. The government is expected to make proposals to this effect after receiving advice from the Law Commissions[10].

1 [1986] AC 80 at 106, [1985] 2 All ER 947 at 956, PC.
2 *Tai Hing Cotton Mill Ltd v Liu Chong Hing Bank Ltd* [1986] AC 80, [1985] 2 All ER 947, PC; *National Bank of Greece SA v Pinios Shipping Co No 1, The Maira* [1990] 1 AC 637, [1989] 1 All ER 213, CA; *Bank of Nova Scotia v Hellenic Mutual War Risks Association (Bermuda) Ltd* [1990] 1 QB 818, [1989] 3 All ER 628 (revsd [1992] 1 AC 233, [1991] 3 All ER 1, HL).
3 Limited exceptions exist, eg *Esso Petroleum Co Ltd v Mardon* [1976] QB 801, [1976] 2 All ER 5, CA; *Woods v Martins Bank Ltd* [1959] 1 QB 55, [1958] 3 All ER 166.
4 *Banque Financière de la Cité SA v Westgate Insurance Co Ltd* [1988] 2 Lloyd's Rep 513 at 558, 559, CA, per Slade LJ. In practice, such a liability is rare.
5 *Tai Hing Cotton Mill Ltd v Liu Chong Hing Bank Ltd* [1986] AC 80, [1985] 2 All ER 947, PC.
6 The customer's duties are those in *London Joint Stock Bank v Macmillan and Arthur* [1918] AC 777, HL and *Greenwood v Martins Bank Ltd* [1932] 1 KB 371, CA, affd [1933] AC 51, HL.
7 See *Tai Hing Cotton Mill Ltd* above.
8 Laidlaw and Roberts *Law Relating to Banking Services* (1990) p 9.
9 As does *Report of the Review Committee on Banking Services: Law and Practice* (the Jack Report) (Cm 622) (1989).
10 White Paper *Banking Services: Law and Practice* (Cm 1026) (1990) paras 7.17–7.19.

(3) THE CONSTRUCTIVE TRUST CONCEPT

A constructive trust is recognised as a trust created not by a transaction between truster and trustee but by operation of law. In English cases duties of care have been imposed on banks where although not appointed as trustees, they have been involved in the affairs of the trust and become liable to the beneficiaries in the same way as an appointed trustee[1]. In Scotland, there is authority for the general rule that where one person occupying a fiduciary position gains some personal advantage, he is a constructive trustee of the profit made[2]. The constructive trust concept has always been recognised but underused and has no tradition in the Scottish law of banking. However a similar effect may be obtained by way of recompense.

(4) UNJUST ENRICHMENT

The law of Scotland recognises that where one party becomes unjustifiably enriched, at the expense of another, he is obliged to make over a sum of money or property to the other party. The obligations arising from unjust enrichment are divided into three main categories, namely: restitution, recompense and repetition. Restitution is where a person comes into possession of moveable property without title to retain custody of the property and is obliged to restore it to the person entitled to possession[3]. Recompense is where one person has benefited from the expenditure of another and the other has lost thereby, without intention of donation, and the former is obliged to compensate the latter for and to the extent of the benefit[4]. Repetition is where money has been paid by one person to another in error, or for a consideration which has failed, and the law imposes on the payee an obligation to repay and confers on the payer a right of recovery[5]. From the simplest transactions to the most complicated, banks find themselves forwarding sums of money to individuals who are not readily identifiable. Banks may make payments authorised by the customer's mandate which it transpires are mistakenly directed to the wrong person. It follows that of the remedies available in the law of unjust enrichment, repetition and the *condictio indebiti* in particular have considerable impact upon the banker–customer relationship.

Unjust enrichment is a developing area of law affecting banks and their customers. In *Credit Lyonnais v George Stevenson & Co Ltd*[6] French bankers remitted money in error to a Scottish company. Originally the money had been paid into the bank by a third party to the credit of a firm of similar name in Glasgow. Approximately eleven months after the payment the bank discovered the error and raised the remedy of *condictio indebiti*. The

---

1 *Barnes v Addy* (1874) 9 Ch App 244; *Selangor United Rubber Estates Ltd v Cradock (No 3)* [1968] 2 All ER 1073, [1968] 1 WLR 1555; *Karak Rubber Co Ltd v Burden (No 2)* [1972] 1 All ER 1210, [1972] 1 WLR 602; though cf *Lipkin Gorman v Karpnale Ltd* [1992] 4 All ER 409, [1989] 1 WLR 1340, CA.
2 T B Smith *A Short Commentary on the Law of Scotland* (1962) p 584; *Aberdeen Rly Co v Blaikie Bros* (1854) 1 Macq 461, HL.
3 *Stair* I,7,1; *Erskine* III,1,10; *Bell Commentaries* I,281.
4 *Stair* I,8,3; *Bankton* I,9,4; *Bell Principles* s 538.
5 *Stair* I,7,9; *Erskine* III,3,54.
6 *Credit Lyonnais v George Stevenson & Co Ltd* (1901) 9 SLT 93, OH.

company's defence was that the money was received in good faith under a reasonable belief that it had been paid in by one of the company's agents in Paris. The Lord Ordinary allowed recovery on the grounds that an equitable defence to the repetition had not been established. The same result was reached in the more recent case of *Bank of Scotland v Grimm-Foxen*[1] where the recipient of a series of payments failed to establish that she had changed her position in such a way as to make repetition unjust[2].

This area of law was reviewed in *Morgan Guaranty Trust Co of New York v Lothian Regional Council*[3]. The local authority entered into a currency exchange with a merchant bank which was incorrectly believed to be valid. The transaction was invalid as it was ultra vires the powers of the local authority. It was held that the bank was entitled to recover the balance paid to the authority even although the transaction was based on mutual error as to the generally applicable law[4]. However, Lord President Hope[5] and Lord Clyde[6] emphasised that where the mistake was avoidable and the pursuer could have discovered the actual circumstances, then these factors will be weighed when considering the equities of the claim. The case yields two slightly incongruous results. Firstly the court abolished the error of law principle by founding upon the civilian tradition[7], and secondly when presented with an ideal opportunity for wholesale conceptual overhaul, stated that error is an essential component of any claim under the *condictio indebiti*, possibly under the increasingly weighty influence of English law[8]. In summary the other findings of the court were that the *condictio indebiti* was the correct basis for a claim upon the basis of the facts of this case; that the essentials of the action were that the sums which the pursuer paid were not due and had been made in error; and that it was necessary that the error had to be shown to be excusable, although the nature of the error and its avoidability may feature in the decision as to where the equities lay when raised in answer to the pursuers' claim, it being for the defender to raise the issues which might lead to a decision that the remedy be refused on the ground of equity. This case served to illustrate the abolition of the error in law rule but the area remains very difficult to navigate, although a little less so than before[9].

1 1992 GWD 37-2171, Sh Ct.
2 For the defence of change of position, see *Lipkin Gorman v Karpnale Ltd* [1991] 2 AC 548 at 577–581, [1992] 4 All ER 512 at 532–534, HL, per Lord Goff of Chieveley. For an examination of the law where bank pays money to a customer by honouring a forged cheque, see *Royal Bank of Scotland v Watt* 1991 SC 48 at 57, 58, 1991 SLT 138 at 143, 144, per Lord Justice-Clerk Ross. For comment on *Watt*, see Gretton [1992] JBL 108; Macqueen [1992] JBL 333; Stewart *The Law of Restitution in Scotland* (1992) paras 4.46 ff. See also *Bank of New York v North British Steel Group* 1992 SLT 613, OH, where money was paid in the mistaken belief that the customer had authorised the payment.
3 1995 SCLR 225, 1995 SLT 299, IH (Five Judges).
4 Thus overruling *Glasgow Corpn v Lord Advocate* 1959 SC 203; *Taylor v Wilson's Trustees* 1975 SC 146.
5 1995 SCLR 225 at 239E, 1995 SLT 299 at 316F.
6 1995 SCLR 225 at 246A–B, 1995 SLT 299 at 320I–J.
7 And in particular *Stirling v Earl of Lauderdale* (1733) Mor 2930.
8 See eg *Woolwich Equitable Building Society v Inland Revenue Comrs* [1993] AC 70, HL.
9 In particular cases attention should be paid to the informing doctrines and traditions as well as the changing climate of the law as a whole, since it is not at all unlikely that English and Scottish winds of change could at any time effect more radical changes. The concept of unjust enrichment has been dealt with very briefly in this work. See further W J Stewart *The Law of Restitution in Scotland* (1992) with supplement (1995).

4. BANKS AND SHADOW DIRECTORSHIPS

The expression 'shadow director' is defined in section 741(2) of the Companies Act 1985 and section 22(5) of the Company Directors Disqualification Act 1986 and means 'a person in accordance with whose directions or instructions the directors of a company are accustomed to act'. Professional advisers are specifically excluded by the definition from being shadow directors 'by reason only that the directors act on advice given by him in a professional capacity'[1]. The intention of the defining sections is to encompass the situation where a board is truly taking directions from an outside controller. It would, for example, include a holding company, or even the bank of the company, if the company invariably takes its instructions from the bank. Whether a person acts as a shadow director or not will depend upon whether he merely gives advice or whether he gives directions or instructions. Each determination will depend upon the circumstances of the case and the degree of intervention. Banks will frequently appoint a nominee director to a customer company in return for the provision of equity or debt finance. The purpose of the appointment from the bank's point of view is to ensure the monitoring of the company's financial position and does not per se impose liability on the bank as a shadow director. If, however, the director takes on the role of instructing the company further to directions from the bank, the bank may be liable. In general, however, banks have taken the practical view that provided they give advice only and not instructions, there is no reason for concern. If, for example, the bank indicates that unless a specific subsidiary is sold it will review its ongoing overdraft or financial support, it would be prudent to obtain a board minute indicating that 'after carefully considering the bank's advice, the directors concluded that subsidiary A should be sold'. In the case of *Re A Company (No 005009 of 1987), ex parte Copp*[2], the financial position of the company worsened when it lost a major customer in 1986. The permitted overdraft limit was reached and the bank commissioned a report into the customer's affairs and exerted pressure for the provision of security. As a result, the company granted the bank a debenture with a specific charge over the book debts from time to time due. The company also took steps to implement the recommendations of the bank's report, but after three months of the granting of the debenture a receiver was appointed by the bank and the company went into creditors voluntary liquidation. Knox J refused to strike out claims for preferences and wrongful trading against the bank which depended upon whether the bank could be construed as a shadow director. The circumstances which led to the conclusion that the bank could be found to be a shadow director were that the bank exerted pressure on the company when it discovered its financial difficulties, it obtained a debenture from

---

1 The professional exemption 'is somewhat circular'. If the professional is only giving 'advice' he is not giving 'directions or instructions' and does not need the exemption. If, however, the professional is giving 'directions or instructions' he falls outside the exemption.
2 *Re a Company (No 005009 of 1987), ex parte Copp* [1989] BCLC 13, 4 BCC 424.

the company to provide additional security for the existing overdraft and the bank obtained an independent report which contained recommendations which the directors under pressure from the bank had followed.

The principal reason for bank's concern to being considered a 'shadow director' is the potential liability of shadow directors personally to contribute to a company's assets in a company's liquidation under section 214 of the Insolvency Act 1986 (the wrongful trading provisions). The section provides that liability is triggered at the point at which a reasonable director (including a shadow director) ought to have concluded that the company has no reasonable prospect of avoiding liquidation. It must be proved that the director or shadow director 'knew or ought to have concluded that' insolvent liquidation was unavoidable[1]. The section only operates in the circumstance of the company entering liquidation and its assets are insufficient to meet its liabilities. The only defence is for the director concerned to show that 'he took every step he ought to have taken' to minimise the losses of the creditors'[2].

The case of *Re Hydrodan (Corby) Ltd*[3] does provide comfort for bankers and others as to the circumstances in which they may be held to be shadow directors. Hydrodan went into liquidation and its directors were offshore companies who were indirectly owned by the ultimate parent Eagle Trust plc. Millett J held that in order for the directors of the parent company to be liable as shadow directors there must have been established a pattern of behaviour of giving instructions or orders to the subsidiary's directors *and* equally there must be a pattern of behaviour whereby they were accustomed to act in accordance with these instructions. Millett J's view was that by merely being a director of a parent company an individual cannot become a shadow director of a subsidiary of that parent. Further, the company must be 'accustomed' to act in accordance with a shadow director's instructions with the consequence that a well established course of dealing is required and a single directive to do a particular act would fall outwith section 741 of the 1985 Act.

Perhaps most comfort may be taken from the article by the same Millett J[4] in which he concluded that in practice the whole concept of liability of banks as shadow directors was largely illusory despite the fact that most distressed or near insolvent companies had little choice but to act on the advice of the bank. He rightly concluded that so long as there was compliance with the broad rules of the legislation the banks have little to worry about in continuing to give support to financially distressed companies[5].

---

1 1986 Act, s 214(2)(b).
2 1986 Act, s 214(3). See also *Re Produce Marketing Consortium Ltd (No 2)* [1989] BCLC 520, 5 BCC 569 and *Re M C Bacon Ltd* [1990] BCLC 324, [1990] BCC 78.
3 [1994] 2 BCLC 180, [1994] BCC 161.
4 (1991) Insolvency Practitioner, p 14.
5 For inter-relation with s 212 of the Insolvency Act 1986, see *West Mercia Safety Wear Ltd v Dodd* [1988] BCLC 250, 4 BCC 30, CA.

Chapter 5

Types of Account

1. THE CURRENT ACCOUNT

(1) INTRODUCTION

The current account is the most commonly operated account held by customers of banks. It is used by customers for their personal and business transactions as well as for the withdrawal of cash on demand. For many customers it is the current account which forms the basis of the banker-customer relationship[1]. A standard form of mandate prepared by the bank is usually signed by the customer providing for the operation of the account. Typically the mandate provides that the bank will honour, to the debit of the account, all orders or cheques signed by the customer in instances where there are sufficient funds at credit of the account. The drawing of cheques is an instruction to the bank to fulfil the order which the cheque represents. Cheques or other orders payable to the customer will also be received to the credit of the account. The drawing of cheques is often supported by a cheque card which guarantees payment to the payee, provided the amount of the cheque drawn is within the limit of the amount provided for by the cheque card[2]. Crediting and debiting of the account may occur in numerous ways, for example, by operations of the Giro system, cheques, withdrawals from automated teller machines, standing orders and mandates as well as the operation of the EFTPOS system[3].

It is usual for the bank to undertake to provide the customer with periodic statements of account detailing the intromissions on the account. The second edition of the voluntary Good Banking Code drawn up by the British Banker's Association provides[4] that customers must be provided with regular statements of account. The agreement upon the benefits of the account on occasion varies from bank to bank. In some cases bank charges are not levied upon accounts which remain in credit to an agreed limit or interest accrues on balances beyond a determined financial threshold. Traditionally, however, the balance standing at credit of the account did not earn interest upon the basis that reward was provided to the customer by allowing him to draw upon funds at any time[5].

(2) SALIENT CHARACTERISTICS OF THE CURRENT ACCOUNT

There are several key features of a current account. The balance standing to the customer's credit is repayable on demand, the customer having a prime right of repayment of money deposited with the bank. It would be incorrect, however, to describe the amount standing at the credit of a customer on current account as 'cash'[6]. It is an unsecured debt, repayable on demand, but which ranks after the satisfaction of preferential claims and secured debts on the bank's insolvency[7]. Funds held in any other type of

---

1 The instruction for the account opening representing the commencement of the relationship: *Woods v Martins Bank Ltd* [1959] 1 QB 55, [1958] 3 All ER 166.
2 The amendments to the terms of reference of the Banking Ombudsman Scheme which come into effect on 1 May 1995 allowed consideration of a complaint by a retailer who is not the bank's customer and accepts a cheque drawn in his favour against a cheque guarantee card where the bank's guarantee is not met.
3 As to EFTPOS (Electronic Fund Transfer at Point of Sale), see ch 8 below.
4 Good Banking Code (2nd edn), para 4.6.
5 *Macdonald v North of Scotland Bank* 1942 SC 369, 1942 SLT 196.
6 *Joachimson v Swiss Bank Corpn* [1921] 3 KB 110, CA.
7 *Re Russian Commercial and Industrial Bank* [1955] 1 Ch 148, [1955] 1 All ER 75.

account are repayable at a fixed date or after an agreed period of notice, depending upon the nature of the agreement with the bank. It is generally accepted that repayment may be demanded by a customer only from the branch at which his account is operated and only during normal banking hours[1].

The customer may be granted an overdraft upon his current account. Overdraft facilities may be allowed either by express or implied agreement or through banking practice. Temporary advances by way of overdraft are generally repayable on demand. In the instance of more substantial advances, the value, time and repayment conditions are usually detailed formally between the bank and customer, being subject to periodic review with commensurate interest and bank charges. The case of *Crimpfil Ltd v Barclays Bank plc*[2] would, on the face of it, indicate that a bank may be liable for withdrawing an overdraft. However, the facts of that case are essentially quite special. Barclays sent Crimpfil a letter on 17 July 1989 confirming his overdraft facility for a period of twelve months, but it did not advise him that the overdraft was repayable on demand. Barclays became increasing concerned about Crimpfil's business and demanded increased collateral for the facility. When it became clear in December 1989 that Crimpfil would not and probably could not comply, Barclays withdrew the facility. The court refused to imply a term that the overdraft was repayable on demand and found that, as a matter of construction, Barclays was in breach of its contractual obligation to supply the facility for twelve months and the withdrawal of the facility had been instrumental in the downfall of Crimpfil's business. Shortly before the trial Barclays conceded liability for wrongful termination and were ordered to make an interim payment of £1.8million to Crimpfil, the full measure of damages, having, at that stage, yet to be determined. The subsequent assessment of damages was unreported. Generally, however, banks do provide that overdraft accounts are repayable on demand, except in instances where the customer negotiates otherwise at the commencement of the agreement. Where a bank employee induces a customer to believe that he will receive a favourable outcome to his application for overdraft or loan facilities, which results in the customer sustaining losses, it may be possible for the bank to be rendered liable to its customer for its employee's actings[3].

Interest on overdrafts on current accounts is usually calculated on a daily basis. The nature of interest charges is a matter for express agreement between the parties[4]. Customers usually receive periodic (normally monthly) statements of balance[5], and banks may impose commissions for banking services relating to the account or ancillary services. Typically

---

1 *Clare & Co v Dresdner Bank* [1915] 2 KB 576; but see views expressed in *Baines v National Provincial Bank Ltd* (1927) 96 LJKB 801, 137 LT 631; *Bank of Scotland v Seitz* 1990 SCLR 418, 1990 SLT 584.
2 [1995] TLR 116, (1995) Independent, 27 March, CA.
3 *Box v Midland Bank Ltd* [1979] 2 Lloyd's Rep 391, revsd [1981] 1 Lloyd's Rep 434, CA.
4 Very often rates are declared by published rates. Exceeding agreed overdraft limits will result in declared higher rates of interest.
5 See eg Clydesdale Bank Code of Practice for personal customers, para 4.6, set out in Appendix 1 below.

they are debited quarterly[1] or half-yearly. Corporate banking charges are normally individually negotiated. Current account charges are levied in accordance with pre-ordained and publicly stipulated rates and some banks impose charges in relation to the state of the account. The operation of the account may be regulated by the code of practice issued by the bank seeking to determine the conditions applying to the account[2].

Where the customer instructs the bank to pay a sum of money to a third party, the bank fulfils the instruction by paying from its own moneys, and then debits the customer's account[3]. The bank is not obliged to honour a cheque where the customer has inadequate funds to meet the demand[4] unless it is for an amount within the parameters of an agreed overdraft limit[5]. The case of *Capital and Counties Bank Ltd v Gordon*[6] provides some authority for the proposition that in the absence of an agreement to the contrary, the crediting of a sum to a customers account illustrates willingness on the part of the bank to allow the customer to draw against the credit balance as shown. It would accordingly be possible to argue that the drawing of uncleared funds is permissible. However, most banks provide against such an eventuality within the terms of their conditions for opening current accounts and in their codes of practice[7].

(3)   THE CREDITOR-DEBTOR RELATIONSHIP OF CUSTOMER AND BANKER IN CURRENT ACCOUNTS

The leading case in point is *Joachimson v Swiss Bank Corpn* in which Lord Atkin described the relationship of customer and banker[8]:

> 'The bank undertakes to receive money and to collect bills for its customer's account. The proceeds so received are not to be held in trust for the customer, but the bank borrows the proceeds and undertakes to repay them. The promise to repay is to repay at the branch of the bank where the account is kept, and during banking hours. It includes a promise to repay any part of the amount due, against the written order of the customer addressed to the bank at the branch, and as such written orders may be outstanding in the ordinary course of business for two or three days. It is a term of the contract that the bank will not cease to do business with the customer except upon reasonable notice. The customer on his part undertakes to exercise reasonable care in executing his written orders so as not to mislead the bank or to facilitate forgery. I think it is necessarily a term of such a contract that the bank is not liable to pay

---

1   Clydesdale Bank Code of Practice, para 5.4.
2   For discussion of codes of practice issued by banks, see generally pp 102, 103 above.
3   *Halesowen Presswork and Assemblies Ltd v Westminster Bank Ltd* [1971] 1 QB 1 at 33, [1970] 3 All ER 473 at 477, CA, per Lord Denning MR.
4   *Marzetti v Williams* (1830) 1 B & Ad 415; *Bank of New South Wales v Laing* [1954] AC 135 at 154, PC.
5   *Woodland v Fear* (1857) 7 E & B 519; *Arab Bank Ltd v Barclays Bank (Dominion Colonial and Overseas) Ltd* [1954] AC 495, [1954] 2 All ER 226, HL; *Barnes v Williams and Glynn's Bank Ltd* (1981) Com LR 205.
6   [1903] AC 240, HL.
7   See Clydesdale Bank Code of Practice for personal customers, para 12.1 and Glossary of Banking Terms (set out in Appendix 1 below). The clearing process is described as generally four days and moneys cannot be withdrawn until the expiry of that period.
8   [1921] 3 KB 110 at 127, CA, per Lord Atkin.

the customer the full amount of his balance until he demands payment from the bank at the branch at which the current account is kept. Whether he must demand in writing it is not necessary now to determine'.

The essential principles are also laid out in the Scottish case of *Royal Bank of Scotland v Skinner*[1]:

'... it is now well settled that the relationship of customer and banker is nei-ther a relation of principal and agent nor a relation of a fiduciary nature, trust, or the like, but a simple relation ... of creditor-debtor. The banker is not, in the general case, a custodier of money. When money is paid in, despite the popular belief, it is simply consumed by the banker, who gives an obligation of equivalent amount'[2].

The banker treats all funds in his hands to the credit of the current account as moneys lent by the customer to the bank and, despite the common mis-conception, they are co-mingled with moneys belonging to other cus-tomers of the bank. Ellinger and Lomnicka observe[3]: 'An important feature of the current account is that the role of the bank and of the cus-tomer can be reversed in given situations. If the account is overdrawn, the bank becomes the creditor and the customer the debtor'. The customer is under no implied delictual or contractual duty to check the accuracy of his periodic account statements[4]. The low standard of care is well rehearsed in the leading case[5]. The banker on the other hand, need not investigate any third party claims asserting rights to the moneys, nor need he, gener-ally, concern himself with the origin of the moneys. However, there is an important exception relating to the origin of moneys detailed in the Money Laundering Regulations 1993[6] and the Criminal Justice Act 1993. These two pieces of legislation were direct results of the EC Directive on money laundering and their effect is to impose a positive obligation on banks and other bodies or persons involved in 'relevant financial busi-ness' to report any suspicion of transactions which indicate money laun-dering to their supervisory body[7] in the case of banks being the Bank of England[8]. The Bank of England will, if it believes the report merits further attention, pass the information on to the police or other appropriate body for investigation. It is considered that where a bank or financial practi-

1 1931 SLT 382 at 384, OH, per Lord Mackay.
2 Note that in other matters of the banker–customer relationship the relationship is one of contract — a single indivisible one even if separate contracts are entered into for specific services. The nature of the relationship often means that a number of terms have to be implied into specific transactions (see eg *Lloyds Bank plc v Cobb* (18 December 1991, unreported), CA).
3 Ellinger and Lomnicka *Modern Banking Law* (2nd edn, 1994) p 167.
4 As to bank mistakes in incorrect credit entries to the customer's account, see pp 142, 143 below.
5 *Tai Hing Cotton Mill Ltd v Liu Chong Hing Bank Ltd* [1986] AC 80, [1985] 2 All ER 947, PC. See also Holden 'Pass Books and Statements' (1954) 17 MLR 41.
6 Money Laundering Regulations 1993, SI 1993/1933.
7 Money Laundering Regulations 1993, reg 5. Banks and other institutions involved in 'relevant financial business' within the meaning of reg 4 of these regulations, now have a duty to train employees involved in such business in the recognition and handling of such transactions.
8 Money Laundering Regulations 1993, reg 15.

tioner receives money in circumstances where it is put on inquiry and fails to make such inquiries as an honest and reasonable man would or, it wilfully shuts its eyes to the obvious or, it has actual knowledge of money laundering and fails to act, the bank effectively becomes a constructive trustee for the true owner of the money. This principle derived from the *Baden* case and became known as the *Baden* test[1]. The mandatory disclosure requirement is an onerous one on banks and failure to comply carries heavy penalties[2]. It is important to note that if a suspicion is reported to the Bank of England, by a bank, and permission is granted to continue the transaction, this does not sanctify subsequent transactions. The obligation to report suspicions is a continuing one and ratification of a transaction does not grant carte blanche to the bank to carry on other transactions in the same series which appear suspicious. The reasoning for this principle is that it is difficult to distinguish between different financial transactions in the same series once suspicion has been aroused, thus on-going suspicions must continue to be disclosed. Such disclosure procedures produce a dichotomy with the general rules of the banker-customer relationship since they present another exception to the confidentiality rules as propounded in *Tournier*[3].

(4) BANK STATEMENTS AS 'ACCOUNTS STATED'

An 'account stated' is an account including items of credit and debit where the figures are adjusted between the parties and a balance agreed upon[4]. It must thereafter be settled by the debtor without further reference to the specific items involved. Debate as to the existence of an account stated arises where a customer challenges items in a bank statement, usually the accuracy of an entry, or questions generally the bank's right to debit the account at all. Lord Selbourne in *Blackburn Building Society v Cunliffe, Brooks & Co*[5] believed that a statement of account could never constitute an account stated[6]. Some questioning of this proposition was raised in the important case of *Vagliano Bros v Governor & Co of Bank of England*[7] but there was no conclusive statement to the contrary[8]. It follows upon the absence of any duty upon the customer to verify and check his bank statement that the unchallenged narrative of a payment in or withdrawal from a current account narrated in a bank statement does not constitute the customer's agreement. Where such a clause is expressly incorporated into the contract between banker and customer it is properly called an express

---

1 *Baden, Delvaux and Lecuit v Société Générale pour Favoriser le Développement du Commerce et de l'Industrie en France SA* [1992] 4 All ER 161, [1993] 1 WLR 509.
2 The penalty for financial practitioners can be up to five years imprisonment.
3 *Tournier v National Provincial and Union Bank of England* [1924] 1KB 461, CA.
4 *Siqueira v Noranha* [1934] AC 332 at 337, PC, per Lord Atkin.
5 (1882) 22 Ch D 61, CA; affd (1884) 9 App Cas 857, HL.
6 Cf also *Chatterton v London and County Bank* (1891) Times, 1 January, per Lord Esher MR.
7 (1889) 23 QBD 243, CA (revsd [1891] AC 107, HL).
8 See also *Camillo Tank SS Co Ltd v Alexandria Engineering Works* (1921) 38 TLR 134, HL; *Siqueira v Noranha* [1934] AC 332, PC.

evidence clause, and is binding according to its terms[1]. It is clear from a consideration of Lord Scarman's judgment in the *Tai Hing* case[2] that the conclusive evidence clause must be drawn so as to convey to the customer the importance of the inspection he is required to make, and that it is intended to be conclusive in effect where no inquiries are made as to the bank statements. The clause must be unequivocal in its terms. Such stringent requirements of clarity are imposed upon the wording of the clause because, once effective, it operates to deny the customer rights to which he is otherwise entitled. There are, however, more persuasive arguments applying to the passbook as an account stated[3]. These arguments centre around the feature special to the passbook that it is intended to be exchanged between banker and customer as evidence of sums at credit. The looseleaf periodic statement which modern practice substitutes for the pass book is a unilateral information service with no reciprocal duties imposed upon the customer by fact of receipt[4].

(5) CREDITS TO ACCOUNT ERRONEOUSLY MADE

Disputes do arise where a bank seeks to reverse a credit entry wrongly made to a current account. However, there are two issues of particular relevance to current accounts. Firstly, the bank is ostensibly entitled to reverse and rectify a credit wrongfully made where the customer has not acted upon it to his detriment or otherwise; and secondly, the bank is not entitled to dishonour any cheque drawn in good faith and without negligence on the faith of an inaccurate entry[5]. Where an error causes the customer detrimentally to alter his position, the bank may, on limited occasions, be denied the right to rectify or reverse the entry[6]. Actings of the bank may personally bar the bank from rectifying the error where the customer is induced to misunderstand the state of his account and financial position. In *Skyring v Greenwood*[7] it was held that inaccurate entries constituted representations that the amounts stipulated stood to the credit of the customer's account[8]. Even in instances where the bank is allowed to rectify the error, it must honour cheques until the point where the

---

1 *Dobbs v National Bank of Australasia Ltd* (1935) 53 CLR 643; *Bache & Co (London) Ltd v Banque Vernes et Commerciale de Paris SA* [1973] 2 Lloyd's Rep 437, CA.
2 *Tai Hing Cotton Mill Ltd v Liu Chong Hing Bank Ltd* [1986] AC 80, [1985] 2 All ER 947, PC.
3 See *Devaynes v Noble, Clayton's Case* (1816) 1 Mer 529.
4 For discussion of this distinctive feature of the pass book, cf *Blackburn Building Society v Cunliffe, Brooks & Co* (1882) 22 Ch D 61, CA, per Lord Selbourne, and *Devaynes v Noble, Clayton's Case* (1816) 1 Mer 529 at 535–537. See generally *Bishun Chand Firm v Seth Girdhari Lal* (1934) 50 TLR 465 at 468, PC, per Lord Wright.
5 *Commercial Bank of Scotland v Rhind* (1860) 3 Macq 643 at 648, HL, per Lord Campbell LC; *Holland v Manchester and Liverpool District Banking Co Ltd* (1909) 14 Com Cas 241, 25 TLR 386.
6 Cf *Devaynes v Noble, Clayton's Case* (1816) 1 Mer 529 at 535.
7 (1825) 4 B &C 281.
8 See also *Holland v Manchester and Liverpool District Banking Co Ltd* (1909) 14 Com Cas 241, 25 TLR 386; *Holt v Markham* [1923] 1 KB 504, CA; *Lloyds Bank Ltd v Brooks* (1950) 6 LDAB 161, (1951) 72 JIB 114.

customer is informed of the corrected balance[1]. A bank is always entitled to rectify an error within a reasonable time, and there is limited, but important authority for the proposition that where a customer's statement of account is wrong, but clearly unduly high, the customer should realise the error[2].

A bank may always rectify errors which the customer induces[3] and where the customer had actual knowledge of the error, he cannot assert the error subsequent to any change in the bank's position[4]. Where the customer lacks actual knowledge but ought reasonably to have known or suspected the error, some doctrine of constructive knowledge may operate where the means of acquiring knowledge all but equate to knowledge[5] and personal bar operates where the customer's silence is deliberate to mislead the bank[6].

In instances where an account is credited with a sum smaller than that properly payable, or debited to a greater degree than a cheque drawn by the customer, the customer may question the erroneous entry, and may do so even where the customer initially returns the statement of account without adverting to an error[7].

In the United States[8] a customer is under a duty of reasonable care in checking his statement of account. He has fourteen days during which to inform the bank of any errors and thereafter loses any right of challenge. Considerably more detailed statements of account are rendered to customers in the United States than is the case in Scotland. It would be possible in Scotland (but somewhat impractical) to include such an obligation of checking the statement of account[9], but such a clause would require to be integral to the contract[10].

(6) OVERDRAFTS ON CURRENT ACCOUNTS

Harman J in *Re Hone (a Bankrupt), ex parte Trustee v Kensington Borough Council*[11] describes an overdraft as a loan: 'a payment by a bank under an arrangement by which the customer may overdraw is a lending by the bank to the customer of the money'. In an overdraft, the banker is a creditor on a loan account and the contract governing the parties depends upon its provisions. Agents, generally, have no implied authority to incur an overdraft[12]. Overdrafts generally subsist at will subject to termination by a

1 *Commercial Bank of Scotland v Rhind* (1860) 3 Macq HL 643; *British &North European Bank Ltd v Zalzstein* [1927] 2 KB 92.
2 *United Overseas Bank v Jiwani* [1977] 1 All ER 733, [1976] 1 WLR 964.
3 *Saskatchewan & Western Elevator v Bank of Hamilton* (1914) 18 DLR 411.
4 *Leach v Buchanan* (1802) 4 Esp 226; *Greenwood v Martins Bank Ltd* [1933] AC 51, HL.
5 *Morison v London County and Westminster Bank Ltd* [1914] 3 KB 356, CA; *Tina Motors Pty Ltd v Australia and New Zealand Banking Group Ltd* [1977] VR 205.
6 *Jacobs v Morris* [1902] 1 Ch 816, CA; *Brown v Westminster Bank Ltd* [1964] 2 Lloyd's Rep 187.
7 *Kepitigalla Rubber Estates Ltd v National Bank of India* [1909] 2 KB 1010.
8 See UCC s 4-406.
9 See *Columbia Graphophone Co v Union Bank of Canada* (1916) 34 DLR 743, 38 OLR 326.
10 *Tai Hing Cotton Mill Ltd v Liu Chong Hing Bank Ltd* [1986] AC 80, [1985] 2 All ER 947, PC.
11 [1951] Ch 85 at 89, [1950] 2 All ER 716 at 719.
12 *Commercial Bank of Scotland v Biggar* 1958 SLT (Notes) 46.

demand for repayment by the banker or by the customer's volitional repayment of the total amount of the loan[1]. Where the customer is requested to liquidate his debt, the banker need provide no reasons for the request and where overdrawing has been allowed against security, the banker may be liable in damages if, without reasonable notice, he later refuses to honour a cheque[2]. Only where banker and customer have reached express agreement or the obligation may be inferred from a course of dealing will the banker be compelled to extend an overdraft to the customer[3].

Demand for repayment under an overdraft facility should be exercised so as to minimise prejudice to the customer's interests[4]. While the customer must be given a reasonable time to repay the overdraft, he will not be afforded time in which to generate funds where he does not possess them at the point of calling for repayment[5]. A bank may be liable to a customer for losses sustained by withdrawing an overdraft facility established by usage over some time without giving adequate notice of repayment[6].

In the case of *Re Hone (a Bankrupt), ex parte Trustee v Kensington Borough Council*[7] a cheque was paid into the account of the council. The drawer's account was overdrawn when the cheque was drawn. On the same day, the drawer filed for petition in bankruptcy. He was declared bankrupt. The cheque was honoured by the bank shortly thereafter and was credited to the account of the council. The court held that payment was not made to the council until after the bankruptcy order was made and the moneys were an asset belonging to the drawer and was paid without the authority of the trustee in bankruptcy. Nonetheless, the money belonged to the estate of the bankrupt and it was emphasised that an overdraft is a lending by the bank to the customer of money and that the customer and not the bank makes payment. The bank pays as an agent of the customer.

Where a customer draws a cheque or accepts a bill payable at the bank in the knowledge that the credit standing to his account is inadequate to meet the demand, this act may be treated as a tacit request for overdraft facilities[8]. The customer is liable for interest on the overdraft from the moment it accrues and probably irrespective of whether the interest is compound in effect or not, providing it conforms with the bank's usual practice[9].

1 *Titford Property Co v Cannon Street Acceptances Ltd* (22 May 1975, unreported) — cited in Creswell et al *Encyclopedia of Banking Law*, vol 1, para c/183; *R A Cripps & Son Ltd v Wickenden* [1973] 2 All ER 606, [1973] 1 WLR 944.
2 *Johnston v Commercial Bank of Scotland* (1858) 20 D 790; *Ritchie v Clydesdale Bank* (1886) 13 R 866.
3 *Cumming v Shand* (1860) 5 H & N 95; *Brooks & Co v Blackburn Benefit Society* (1884) 9 App Cas 857 at 864, HL; and *Crimpfil Ltd v Barclays Bank plc* 1995 TLR 116, (1995) Independent, 27 March, CA.
4 *Johnston v Commercial Bank of Scotland* (1858) 20 D 790; *Buckingham & Co v London and Midland Bank* (1895) 12 TLR 70; *Williams and Glyn's Bank Ltd v Barnes* [1980] Com LR 205, per Gibson J.
5 *Toms v Wilson* (1863) 4 B & S 442, Ex Ch; *R A Cripps & Son Ltd v Wickenden* [1973] 2 All ER 606, [1973] 1 WLR 944; *Bank of Baroda v Panessar* [1987] Ch 335, [1986] 3 All ER 751.
6 *Smith v Hughes* (1871) LR 6 QB 597.
7 [1951] Ch 85, [1950] 2 All ER 716.
8 *Cuthbert v Robarts Lubbock & Co* [1909] 2 Ch 226 at 233, CA, per Cozens-Hardy MR.
9 *Reddie v Williamson* (1863) 1 M 228; *Gilmour v Bank of Scotland* (1880) 7 R 734.

There is no common law right in favour of the bank to charge interest on an overdraft account, but the claim so to do may be substantiated upon the basis of general banking practice and custom, or upon a course of dealing, or implied agreement[1]. The banker must debit the interest at the usual periodic date for so doing unless appropriate prior notice has been given or in a final settlement of the account. Current Scottish clearing bank practice is to debit interest to the current account quarterly together with management charges and commissions[2].

A banker is not obliged to extend overdraft facilities, but where he agrees to do so, he cannot refuse to honour a cheque in contravention of the basis of such an agreement[3]. Nor may the customer assume, even where there is a history of the extension of such facilities, that his cheques will automatically be honoured and met, beyond the amount actually standing to his account or the agreed limits of his overdraft[4].

The essentials of what should be the nature of an overdraft facility were outlined in *Joachimson v Swiss Bank Corpn*[5]:

(1) there ought to be an express term as to the repayment date for the facility;
(2) there is an implied term that repayment of the money borrowed thereunder will occur only upon reasonable notice; and
(3) the length of the notice is largely determined by the bank's knowledge of the use to which the customer will put the money.

It is normal practice to state that overdraft accounts are repayable on demand and care should be taken to ensure the documentation provides appropriately[6].

In *Williams and Glyn's Bank Ltd v Barnes*, the defendant was the chairman, founder and majority shareholder of NDH, a property development company which, since 1965 had banked primarily with Williams and Glyn's Bank[7]. In 1972, with an overdraft limit of £6.5 million, the bank lent the defendant (personally) £1 million to allow him to buy more company shares. The loan was to be repaid from funds owing to him from the company. The bank brought an action against the defendant to recover the money lent and the defendant argued that the action raised various claims and counter-claims. Gibson J held that no defence to a personal action could be based upon the bank's conduct with regard to the company and his views upon overdrafts reflect current banking practice. He said:

'There is an obligation upon the bank to honour cheques drawn within the agreed limit of an overdraft facility and presented before any demand for payment or notice to terminate a facility has been given. That obligation, however, does not by itself require any period of notice beyond simple demand'[8].

---

1 *National Bank of Greece SA v Pinios Shipping Co No 1, The Maira* [1990] 1 AC 637, [1989] 1 All ER 213, CA.
2 See eg Clydesdale Bank Code of Practice for personal customers, para 5.4, set out in Appendix 1 below.
3 *Crimpfil Ltd v Barclays Bank plc* 1995 TLR 116, (1995) Independent, 27 March, CA.
4 *Ritchie v Clydesdale Bank* (1886) 13 R 866.
5 [1921] 3 KB 110, CA.
6 *Crimpfil Ltd v Barclays Bank plc* 1995 TLR 116, (1995) Independent, 27 March, CA.
7 [1981] Com LR 205.
8 Taken from an unreported section of the judgment.

(7)   INTEREST ON CURRENT ACCOUNTS

The charging by banks of simple interest was approved by Lord Atkinson in *Yourell v Hibernian Bank Ltd*[1]. Interest charges feature in modern banking practice either as a result of the uniform custom of bankers, implied or express agreement or of a course of dealings. In *National Bank of Greece SA v Pinios Shipping Co No 1*[2] contractors built and delivered a ship. They demanded payment under a guarantee opened in their favour by the bank at the purchaser's instruction. The bank exercised its right of reimbursement against the purchaser and a third party who had executed a counter agreement in the bank's favour. The defendants contested the bank's right to charge compound interest on the outstanding amount. It was argued that the bank was entitled to simple interest only. The House of Lords held that through usage, banks were entitled to charge compound interest and considered that there was no reason to terminate the bank's right to charge interest at pre-ordained rates, simply on the basis that the bank has demanded repayment of the sum outstanding in the customer's account[3]. While the bank is entitled to charge compound interest with regard to an overdraft facility in accordance with usual practice of the bank[4] it is less certain that a similar result would arise concerning term loans not involving a revolving arrangement where the parties expect a gradually diminishing debit balance[5].

(8)   COMBINATION OF ACCOUNTS

General rules

A customer may hold a variety of types of account with one bank, and there may arise circumstances in which it is in the interests of the bank or the customer to effect a combination of these accounts. The position that the customer holds his account with the bank and not with a specific branch of the bank provides contractual support for the combination of accounts. So too, does the fact that the relationship of banker and customer is fundamentally consistent throughout, even where minor rights vary under specific accounts[6].

In the case of *National Westminster Bank Ltd v Halesowen Presswork and Assemblies Ltd*[7] Roskill J held at first instance that the bank's right of set-off

1 [1918] AC 372, 87 LJPC 1, HL.
2 [1990] 1 AC 637, CA.
3 See *Minories Finance Ltd v Daryanani* (13 April 1989, unreported): see Arora *Cases and Materials in Banking Law* (1993) p 59.
4 See Clydesdale Bank Code of Practice for personal customers, para 5.1, set out in Appendix 1 below.
5 See *National Bank of Greece SA v Pinios Shipping Co No 1, The Maira* [1990] 1 AC 637, CA, per Lord Goff of Chieveley.
6 In *Re European Bank, Agra Bank Claim* (1872) 8 Ch App 41, James LJ in the Court of Appeal in Chancery considered that even where several accounts were held there was really but one account. Cf also *James Kirkwood & Sons v Clydesdale Bank Ltd* 1908 SC 20 (for a discussion of the 'funds available' for set-off); *Re Sutcliffe & Sons Ltd, ex parte Royal Bank* (1933) 1 DLR 562.
7 [1971] 1 QB 1, [1970] 1 All ER 33.

could be conceived of as a lien. The Court of Appeal[1] reversed Roskill's judgment. It was held that the combination of accounts constituted a set-off and was not based on lien. The customer's deposits became the bank's money and the bank was unable to hold a lien over its own property[2]. The House of Lords[3] restored Roskill's initial decision, but confirmed the opinion of the Court of Appeal that the bank's right of set-off was distinct from a lien. This distinction is more than mere semantics. If the bank's right were a lien in nature, it would be exercisable over a balance standing to the credit of any of the customer's accounts. Alternatively, if it were a set-off right[4], the opposite would apply and it is arguable that a future due debt could not be set off against an immediate liability. Authority favours the latter proposition[5].

The combination of accounts is a set-off right in favour of the banker, implied at law and alterable by express provision. It is available to the bank only in instances where it is dealing with the other party as a customer in relevant transactions. The debt must be due when the plea is set up[7] and a banker cannot plead a conditional debt against one due, and cannot without prior notification set off a balance in a current account against sums conditionally due on bills[7]. A banker cannot set off an outstanding amount on a loan account unless the loan is repayable on demand and repayment has been demanded.

In *Greenwood Teale v William Williams, Brown & Co*[8] Wright J held that a bank was entitled to combine a customer's accounts in exercise of a right of set-off except in three cases: (1) where the right was superseded by express agreement; (2) where a special item of property was remitted to the bank and appropriated for a specific purpose; and (3) where the bank could not combine a customer's private account with one known to the bank to be a trust account or one used by the customer in the capacity of a trustee.

A bank can combine accounts of a customer where the accounts are held at different branches because one single contract governs the general relationship[9]. Even in instances where the bank agrees to keep the accounts separate, the agreement is generally superseded where there are changed circumstances, such as bankruptcy of the borrower[10]. In the case of *Re E J*

---

1 [1971] 1 QB 1, [1970] 1 All ER 473, CA.

2 Per Denning MR and Winn LJ — Buckley LJ dissenting.

3 [1972] AC 785, [1972] 1 All ER 641, HL.

4 The right of set-off is derived from the Compensation Act 1592 (c 61) under which any liquid debt immediately verified by the writ or oath of the party was admitted by judges as an exception or defence where proposed before the granting of decree.

5 *Jeffryes v Agra and Masterman's Bank* (1866) LR 2 Eq 674; *Bower v Foreign and Colonial Gas Co Ltd, Metropolitan Bank, Garnishees* (1874) 22 WR 740; *Business Computers Ltd v Anglo-African Leasing Ltd* [1977] 2 All ER 741, [1977] 1 WLR 578.

6 *Jeffryes v Agra and Masterman's Bank* (1866) LR 2 Eq 674; *Baker v Lloyd's Bank Ltd* [1920] 2 KB 322.

7 *Buckingham & Co v London and Midland Bank* (1895) 12 TLR 70; *Bradford Old Bank Ltd v Sutcliffe* [1918] 2 KB 833, CA; *Re E J Morel (1934) Ltd* [1962] Ch 21, [1961] 1 All ER 796.

8 *Greenwood Teale v William Williams, Brown & Co* (1894) 11 TLR 56.

9 *Garnett v McKewan* (1872) LR 8 Exch 10.

10 *British Guiana Bank v Official Receiver* (1911) 104 LT 754, 27 TLR 454, PC. But consider: *Direct Acceptance Corpn Ltd v Bank of New South Wales* (1968) 88 WN(NSW) (Pt 1) 498, in which MacFarlane J questions this decision.

Morel (1934) Ltd[1] the question of whether an account designated as other than a current account implies that its balance cannot be set off, as in the general case, was considered. Buckley LJ held that the combination of accounts applied primarily as regards different current or general accounts[2]. However, it is necessary to be vigilant in the exercise of the right of set-off as the distinct designation of the account may be evidential of the intention that the account is to be maintained wholly separately from others and the right of set-off precluded[3].

Is notice required to be made to a customer regarding the combination of accounts for set-off purposes? In *Garnett v McKewan*[4] it was unanimously considered that a bank is under no obligation to notify the customer of the combination of accounts. The opposite decision was however reached in *Buckingham & Co v London and Midland Bank*[5]. The two cases do contain significant distinguishing features. In Garnett, there was no agreement between the bank and the customer to maintain the accounts separately. In Buckingham, the right of set-off was abrogated by an agreement arising from a course of dealings between the bank and its customer. It is also possible, however, that an agreement to maintain separate accounts is superseded by a change in circumstances of the borrower – notably his bankruptcy[6]. In *National Westminster Bank Ltd v Halesowen Presswork and Assemblies Ltd*[7], it was thought that notice was probably necessary where there was no clear agreement as to the combination of accounts. Lord Cross of Chelsea took the view that the minimum to be expected of a bank would be to honour cheques drawn by the customer until he received notice of combination of accounts. It is normal and prudent practice for banks to contract with customers that no notice of set-off is required, but it is sensible to accept that in the absence of agreement to the contrary cheques drawn by the customer prior to the exercise of the right of set-off should be honoured if there were funds sufficient to meet them.

Combination of accounts in the interests of the bank

The principal instance in which this situation arises occurs in cases of bankruptcy or insolvency where the bank naturally seeks to combine accounts in order to set off debts rather than becoming an unsecured creditor in the bankrupt estate of the customer. In terms of section 323 of the Insolvency Act 1986 (replacing section 31 of the Bankruptcy Act 1914[8]),

---

1 [1962] Ch 21, [1961] 1 All ER 796.
2 Cf *Bradford Old Bank Ltd v Sutcliffe* [1918] 2 KB 833, CA, a case where the bank made no provision for the combination of accounts.
3 *Re Gross, ex parte Kingston* [1871] LR 6 Ch App 632; *Re Johnston & Co Ltd* [1902] 1 IR 43; *Bradford Old Bank Ltd v Sutcliffe* [1918] 2 KB 833, CA (a loan account is typically intended not to be combined with others). Cf also *Re E J Morel (1934) Ltd* [1962] Ch 21, [1961] 1 All ER 796, per Buckley J; and *National Westminster Bank Ltd v Halesowen Presswork and Assemblies Ltd* [1972] AC 785, [1972] 1 All ER 641, HL, per Lord Cross of Chelsea.
4 (1872) LR 8 Exch 10.
5 (1895) 12 TLR 70.
6 *British Guiana Bank v Official Receiver* (1911) 104 LT 754, 27 TLR 454, PC.
7 [1972] AC 785, [1972] 1 All ER 641, HL.
8 The Insolvency Act 1986, s 438 repealed the Companies Act 1985, s 612 which had replaced the Companies Act 1948, s 317 applying the 1914 Act, s 31 to the winding up of companies.

there is a right of set-off amongst amounts due to the creditor from the bankrupt and vice versa, provided the claims are incurred in a course of mutual dealings between the two parties. The *Halesowen* case[1] dealt with the original section 31 and held that it could apply where any dealings between the banker and the customer were mutual. Dealings would not be mutual where payments were made for specific purposes. In instances where a customer opens several bank accounts with the intention of keeping the moneys in them separate and distinct from each other, the banker may still treat them as one account further to the general nature of the debtor and creditor relationship with his customer. The debit balance on one account may be set off against the credit balances of the other accounts[2]. The banker has the fundamental right to combine his customer's accounts in whatever manner he chooses unless he has made an express or implied agreement with his customer not to do so and keep the accounts separate[3].

Combination of accounts in the interests of the customer

Where a cheque drawn on an account exceeds the balance of that account, the bank may seek to combine accounts in order to avoid the inconvenience and embarrassment which dishonouring the cheque would cause to the customer. Two issues arise: (1) whether the bank is under a duty to combine the accounts and (2) whether in the absence of such a duty there is none the less a right vesting in the bank to combine the accounts.

Since only the branch at which an account is maintained must effect any demand for repayment, the bank cannot be required to effect a combination of accounts held at different branches, where this is the case[4]. It is reasonable for a bank to combine accounts in order to honour a cheque since the customer ought to know the state of his account and it is unreasonable to require the bank to honour cheques exceeding the available balance of the account. This concept is in accordance with the principle of agency law that where an agent received an ambiguous instruction from his principal, the agent is entitled to reimbursement where he construes that instruction in accordance with what he reasonably perceives to be the principal's intention[5]. A customer paying money to a banker either expressly or by implication may appropriate it to any account he maintains with the banker, and may appropriate his payments in whatever manner he chooses[6]. The banker must then effect this instruction. Where no instruction is given, the banker may appropriate the payments to the account of

---

1   *National Westminster Bank Ltd v Halesowen Presswork and Assemblies Ltd* [1972] AC 785, [1972] 1 All ER 641, HL.
2   *James Kirkwood & Sons v Clydesdale Bank Ltd* 1908 SC 20.
3   *National Westminster Bank Ltd v Halesowen Presswork and Assemblies Ltd* [1972] AC 785, [1972] 1 All ER 641, HL.
4   Cf the *Halesowen* case above; *Garnett v McKewan* (1872) LR 8 Exch 10.
5   *Bank of New South Wales v Goulburn Valley Butter Co Pty Ltd* [1902] AC 543, PC; *Houben v Bank of Nova Scotia* (1970) 3 NBR (2d) 366. Such practices would fall under the banker's usual or customary authority as the customer's agent.
6   *Deeley v Lloyds Bank Ltd* [1912] AC 756, HL; *Siebe Gorman & Co Ltd v Barclays Bank Ltd* [1979] 2 Lloyd's Rep 142.

his choosing. Upon making this appropriation and intimating it to the customer, it becomes binding on the customer[1].

(9) CLOSING A CURRENT ACCOUNT

A customer wishing to close a current account simply requires to demand repayment of the balance due, less any bank charges and any other sums due to the bank which have accrued. The banker must ensure that the intention is to close the account and not to withdraw the remaining balance. Where the customer withdraws the exact balance of the account, it should be ascertained, after a suitable interval has elapsed, whether it is the intention to close the account. If so, he should be requested to return any unused cheque forms and the cheque guarantee card. An overdrawn current account is closed by repaying the amount of the outstanding overdraft and any interest or charges levied. The customer should provide for any cheques drawn and not yet presented for payment when the account is closed, since, if presented after closure, the bank would dishonour them. In any circumstance, the banker may only refuse to continue to give banking facilities after giving adequate notice to the customer to allow him to make further arrangements[2].

In instances where the account has become unsatisfactory[3] the banker may wish to promptly close the account. The banker must give reasonable notice of his intention to close the account, and what is reasonable notice depends upon the circumstances of each case[4]. If the account is in credit, the banker should give formal intimation that he wishes the account closed and that he will not accept further lodgements. The banker should ask the customer to write a cheque withdrawing the balance and return unused cheques and the cheque guarantee card[5].

There is an important distinction between closing an account and stopping an account in banking practice. By 'stopping an account' is meant the discontinuing of the operations on the account by reason of, for example: the death of a partner in the case of a firms overdrawn account; the laying on of an arrestment; intimation of a consignation of the balance of the account where the account is in credit; the creation of a postponed security or second mortgage or charge over security held by the bank; or on the instructions of the customer or one of the parties to a joint account. These situations do not involve the closure of the account, and if the restriction is cleared or withdrawn, operations on the account may be resumed[6].

1 For discussion of appropriation of accounts, see ch 4, pp 103 ff above.
2 *Cumming v Shand* (1860) 5 H & N 95; *Garnett v McKewan* (1872) LR 8 Exch 10; *James Kirkwood & Sons v Clydesdale Bank Ltd* 1908 SC 20.
3 Eg where the customer consistently overdraws on the account without arrangements to meet cheques or allows arrestments to be lodged on the account regularly.
4 See *Joachimson v Swiss Bank Corpn* [1921] 3 KB 110, CA, in which it was indicated that before a banker could close a customer's account he must allow two or three days to elapse in case there be cheques outstanding, for to dishonour them may leave the banker open to an action for damages.
5 In *Prosperity Ltd v Lloyds Bank Ltd* (1923) 39 TLR 372: it was held that closure of a company's account after one month's notice was not enough in the circumstances.
6 *Scottish Banking Practice* (5th edn, 1987), 'Banker and Customer' p 38.

2. JOINT ACCOUNTS

(1) INTRODUCTION

The parties to a joint account need not be related, but the most common joint account is that held by a husband and wife. Joint accounts are distinct from accounts stipulating that cheques must be signed by more than one person, in a representative capacity, since in the former the owners act jointly and severally, on behalf of themselves. An account is not joint and several on the basis solely that the mandate states that one or all of the parties may sign cheques[1].

Upon opening the account, the parties are likely to be required to answer standard inquiries on matters such as: the customer's authority[2]; the customer's identity[3]; the customer's integrity[4]; and the customer's employment[5].

(2) MANDATE FOR JOINT ACCOUNTS

Prior to opening the account, the parties complete a mandate for the joint account which incorporates the instructions of the account holders to the bank. The clauses in the mandate will not be inflexible and often consist of a series of alternatives from which the parties elect those suitable to themselves. Ideally, therefore, the specific nature and terms of the account will be tailored to the wishes and circumstances of the customers. The customers designate whether cheques must be signed by all jointly, or by more than two as a quorum, or by any one solely. Generally, customers request the bank to open or continue the account in joint names and at any later date to open such additional accounts in joint names as one or all direct. The customers further mandate the bank to debit the account with any bills, notes, cheques or orders for payment made, drawn or accepted by one or all of them and to effect any instructions regarding the account given by one or all, even in situations where this action may force the account into overdraft. Where the customers omit expressly to authorise the bank to act on one signature, any cheques and orders must be signed by all parties to the joint account[6].

---

1 *Coats v Union Bank of Scotland Ltd* 1929 SC (HL) 114, 1929 SLT 477; *McEvoy v Belfast Banking Co Ltd* [1935] AC 24, HL; *Hirschhorn v Evans* [1938] 2 KB 801, [1938] 3 All ER 491, CA.
2 *Robinson v Midland Bank Ltd* (1925) 41 TLR 170 (402, CA); *Stoney Stanton Supplies (Coventry) Ltd v Midland Bank Ltd* [1966] 2 Lloyd's Rep 373, CA.
3 *Ladbroke & Co v Todd* [1914] WN 165, 19 Com Cas 256; *Hampstead Guardians v Barclays Bank Ltd* (1923) 39 TLR 229, 67 Sol Jo 440; *Nu-Stilo Footwear Ltd v Lloyds Bank Ltd* (1956) 7 LDAB 121, 77 JIB 239; *Lumsden & Co v London Trustee Savings Bank* [1971] 1 Lloyd's Rep 114.
4 *Lloyds Bank Ltd v EB Savory & Co* [1933] AC 201, 102 LJKB 224, HL.
5 *Harding v London Joint Stock Bank Ltd* (1914) Times, 21 January.
6 *Husband v Davis* (1851) 10 CB 645. Maule J traced this principle to the Law Merchant, which prohibited payment by bankers to one of several parties jointly interested, in the absence of the others' consent.

Where the mandate stipulates that cheques must be signed jointly by more than two persons, difficulty arises in instances where the bank honours cheques bearing a forgery or where one required signature is omitted. In such an instance, the bank is not entitled to debit the account to the amount of the cheque. In *Jackson v White and Midland Bank Ltd*[1] the bank agreed with the plaintiff and the first defendant jointly to honour any cheques signed by them jointly, while agreeing with the plaintiff and the first defendant severally that it would not honour any cheques unless the plaintiff had signed them. The bank honoured cheques unsigned by the plaintiff and Park J held that the plaintiff could sue for breach of the latter agreement[2]. In the case of *Catlin v Cyprus Finance Corpn (London) Ltd*[3] the bank honoured a cheque not bearing all the necessary signatures as narrated in the agreement contained in the mandate. A husband and wife, the latter being the plaintiff, had deposited funds in a joint account with the defendant bank. A condition stated that no payment from the account would be made without the joint signature of both account holders. The bank violated the terms of the mandate by negligently transferring the funds from the account under instruction of the husband to his use and without the plaintiff's knowledge or authority. The owners of the account had given mandate to the bank jointly – but it was held the bank's duty to obey was owed to each severally. This case investigated the fundamental issue of the nature of the bank's obligation. Prior to 1982, the leading case on the matter was *Brewer v Westminster Bank Ltd*[4] when it was held that, although the debits to the account in the case were unauthorised, and the bank was in breach of its obligation under the mandate, and had obtained no discharge by paying against a forged signature, the plaintiff would succeed only if both parties were in a position to sue. The bank, it was determined, owed a single duty to the parties jointly. However, this position was questioned academically and not followed in similar factual cases in Scotland. In the case of *Catlin*, Bingham J adopted the position that although the bank in *Brewer* had made a joint agreement with the parties, it had also made a separate agreement with each party severally to dishonour any cheques which were not properly signed. Mrs Catlin received damages calculated in accordance with her half-share interest in the account.

The measure of damages in the event of wrongful payment will be reduced where the customer benefits from the wrongful payment[5]. A joint account remains so where the mandate under which it is operated provides for the bank to act upon the sole signature of either of the account holders. In the *Jackson*[6] and *Catlin* cases, one of the common features was that the funds paid into the account were the property of the plaintiffs.

---

1 [1967] 2 Lloyd's Rep 68.
2 Cf also *Twibell v London Suburban Bank* [1869] WN 127; *Welch v Bank of England* [1955] Ch 508, [1955] 1 All ER 811; *Baker v Barclays Bank Ltd* [1955] 2 All ER 571, [1955] 1 WLR 822.
3 [1983] QB 759, [1983] 1 All ER 809, per Bingham J.
4 [1952] 2 All ER 650. See also *Williams* (1953) 16 MLR 232; *Ardern v Bank of New South Wales* [1956] ALR 1210, [1956] VLR 569; *Jackson v White and Midland Bank Ltd* [1967] 2 Lloyd's Rep 68.
5 *Hirschhorn v Evans* [1938] 2 KB 801, [1938] 3 All ER 491, CA.
6 Ie *Jackson v White and Midland Bank Ltd* [1967] 2 Lloyd's Rep 68.

Thus the plaintiffs were entitled to recover the total paid out on the cheques which the bank ought to have dishonoured. The situation is different where the pursuer cannot establish ownership in the funds. It follows that the innocent joint owner of the account can recover only half of the amounts wrongfully paid against cheques he did not sign[1].

Unless it is clear that an account has been opened for a specific purpose it follows that each joint account holder may withdraw and draw upon it for personal purposes[2]. Unfortunately, there is no authority for the proposition that a bank may dishonour a cheque, if having cause for suspicion that it is drawn by one holder of the joint account in fraud of another[3].

The remaining clauses in a joint account mandate generally provide that the customers authorise the bank to effect any orders to countermand payment of bills, notes, cheques or orders where given by any one of the parties. It is generally accepted that this would be the case in any event[4], but the mandate should, however, provide expressly for this matter. Other provisions made expressly are that the customers:

(1) mandate the bank to credit the account with all amounts, including dividends, interest and capital sums arising from securities received and collected by the bank for the credit of both or all of them;
(2) instruct the bank to make secured or unsecured advances on the request of one or more of them by way of overdraft, loan or other arrangement and to discount bills and notes on the request of one or more of them; and
(3) declare that liability is incurred jointly and severally.

The customers also usually mandate the bank:

(a) to deliver up on the instruction of one or more of them, any deeds, securities, boxes and parcels and their contents and property of any description held in joint names; and
(b) to hold, on the death of any of the parties, any credit balance on any joint account and any securities, deeds, boxes and parcels and their contents and property of any description held in joint names to the order of the survivor.

The customers will also agree that the instructions given in the mandate are to remain in force until one or more of them revokes the terms in writing. Should revocation by one party occur the bank ought immediately to inform the other party or parties of termination.

(3) DEATH OF A JOINT ACCOUNT HOLDER

A survivorship clause is inserted in most modern joint account mandates and ought always to provide for the death of one of the customers of the account.

1 See also *Twibell v London Suburban Bank* [1869] WN 127; *B Liggett (Liverpool) Ltd v Barclays Bank Ltd* [1928] 1 KB 48.
2 *Re Bishop, National Provincial Bank Ltd v Bishop* [1965] Ch 450, [1965] 1 All ER 249; followed in *R E Cameron* (1967) 62 DLR (2d) 389, MPR 214 and *Feaver v Feaver* [1977] 5 WWR 271.
3 *McEvoy v Belfast Banking Co Ltd* [1935] AC 24, HL.
4 *Gaunt v Taylor* (1843) 2 Hare 413.

As between bank and customer

In the leading case of *McEvoy v Belfast Banking Co Ltd*[1], a father and son opened an account in joint names with the sums deposited of £10,000 payable to either or the survivor of them. The creation of the account and the survivorship destination was a device to attempt to avoid death duties of the father. The father died, leaving the residue of the estate to the son upon reaching the age of twenty-five. The executors of the estate obtained payment from the bank and exhausted the sum prior to the son attaining the age of twenty-five. The son claimed the sum of £10,000 from the bank, in accordance with the terms of the deposit receipt. The claim failed, but the House of Lords considered that the bank should not have acted independently to this end, having, as it did, a duty to protect the son's interests. The bank ought to have obtained instructions from the court or have initiated proceedings in which the executors and the infant (by his guardian *ad litem*) were defenders. Lord Atkin was of the opinion that even where there is no survivorship clause, a bank could obtain good discharge by meeting demands made by the survivor. Indeed, he seemed to suggest that a bank has a duty, ordinarily, to meet the demands of the surviving party to a joint account. The son in *McEvoy* would have succeeded had he been able to show that he was a party to the contract with the bank, since in that case the bank would have been shown to have broken and breached the mandate.

Where a joint account is opened without a survivorship clause, the bank gives a good discharge by paying the balance to the survivor or survivors. The transfer of money into joint names, per se, constitutes joint ownership, to which a right of survivorship attaches[2].

As between customers inter se

In determining the rights of surviving parties of the deceased's estate to the deceased's share in the balance of a joint account, there may arise difficult issues between the surviving title holder to the account and others who claim that part of the residual balance is truly due to them[3]. Legal title to the share of the deceased vests in the survivor[4]. However, the survivor may hold the balance in trust for the personal representatives of the deceased party during the trust and the balance may require to be apportioned[5]. The survivor may be beneficially entitled to the whole of the

1 [1935] AC 24, HL.
2 For rights of survivorship, see *Re Harrison, Day v Harrison* (1920) 90 LJ Ch 186. Cf also *Young v Sealey* [1949] Ch 278, [1949] 1 All ER 92. Note, however, that the presumption of survivorship can be displaced: *Husband v Davis* (1851) 10 CB 645; *Marshal v Crutwell* (1875) LR 20 Eq 328.
3 See *Forrest-Hamilton's Trustee v Forrest-Hamilton* 1970 SLT 388, OH, where the surviving spouse named in a joint account was unable to discharge the onus that the deceased intended donation. It was held that the sums belonged to the deceased and not the surviving account holder.
4 *Russell v Scott* (1936) 53 WN 178, 55 CLR 440, per Dixon J and Evatt J.
5 *Connells' Trustees v Connell's Trustee* (1886) 13 R 1175. See generally *Currie on Confirmation of Executors* (8th edn, 1995 by EM Scobbie) para 10.177.

balances[1] and in deciding these matters courts are accustomed to considering the entire history and conduct of the account[2].

If the credit standing to the account consists of sums paid in by two parties, it will be considered as having accrued to both of them. However, in instances where sums have been paid in wholly or substantially by the deceased[3], the right of the estate will depend upon the intention of the deceased in opening the joint account[4]. All of the circumstances of the case will be weighed in reaching a determination as to the beneficial owner[5]. However, existence of a bank account in joint names does not of itself prove ownership[6] but it has been suggested that even where the sum of the account was contributed solely by one party, if the account was in the name of both, this constitutes a valid nomination of one, by the other as successor to him to one half of the investment[7].

In the case of *Marshal v Crutwell*[8] a terminally-ill husband transferred the balance of his personal account into a joint account opened with his wife. The bank was mandated to honour cheques signed by either spouse. Upon the husband's death, there was a dispute between the widow and the heirs of the deceased regarding the balance of the account. Jessel MR held that the husband had no intention of effecting a gift and was motivated only by convenience. Thus the estate of the deceased had a beneficial interest to a relevant sum[9]. In *Re Harrison, Day v Harrison*[10] a husband opened a joint account in his own name and that of his wife. The wife was not initially told of the existence of the account or that she was entitled to draw upon it. Upon the husband becoming ill, the branch manager informed the wife that she was party to the account. After the husband's death, an envelope containing deposit receipts and indorsements with the wife's initials were found amongst his papers. Russell J held that the husband's motive in opening the account was that the wife would acquire it upon survival. The beneficial ownership passed to the surviving spouse. In *Russell v Scott*[11] a woman opened a joint account in her own name and that of a favoured nephew. While alive, the woman used the account for her own purposes, but had told her solicitors that the nephew was to take it as a survivor. The ownership vested in the nephew.

1 *Young v Sealey* [1949] Ch 278, [1949] 1 All ER 92.
2 *Marshal v Crutwell* (1875) LR 20 Eq 328; *Re Bishop, National Provincial Bank Ltd v Bishop* [1965] Ch 450, [1965] 1 All ER 249.
3 *Jones v Maynard* [1951] 1 Ch 572, [1951] 1 All ER 802; *Gage v King* [1961] 1 QB 188, [1960] 3 All ER 62.
4 *Young v Sealey* [1949] Ch 278, [1949] 1 All ER 92; *Forrest-Hamilton's Trustee v Forrest-Hamilton* 1970 SLT 388, OH.
5 *Husband v Davis* (1851) 10 CB 645; *Williams v Davies, Re Williams* (1864) 28 JP 664, 3 Sw & Tr 547; *Marshal v Crutwell* (1875) LR 20 Eq 328.
6 *Forrest-Hamilton's Trustee v Forrest-Hamilton* 1970 SLT 388, OH.
7 *Dennis v Aitchison* 1923 SC 819 at 825, 1923 SLT 568 at 570, per Lord President Clyde.
8 (1875) LR 20 Eq 328.
9 *Young v Sealey* [1949] Ch 278, [1949] 1 All ER 92; *Re Bishop, National Provincial Bank Ltd v Bishop* [1965] Ch 450, [1965] 1 All ER 249; *Re Figgis, Roberts v MacLaren* [1969] 1 Ch 123, [1968] 1 All ER 999. Care must be taken with these cases which partially reply upon English Chancery Court equitable principles.
10 *Re Harrison, Day v Harrison* (1920) 90 LJ Ch 186.
11 (1936) 53 WN 178, 55 CLR 440.

Presentment of a cheque for payment after the death of one party

Where a bank is notified of the death of a party to a joint account, any cheque presented for payment and signed by the deceased party should be returned with the answer 'Drawer deceased'. Where there is only one survivor a cheque signed by him will be honoured if the balance of the account vests in him. Where there is more than one survivor a new mandate should be completed and cheques should be drawn in accordance with the terms of the new mandate.

Where a joint account holder bearing joint and several liability dies while the account is in overdraft, the account should be suspended and future transactions passed through a new account. This procedure preserves the bank's rights against the estate of the deceased and prevents the operation and application of the rule in *Clayton's Case*[1]. The terms of the original mandate may also preclude this rule applying. In a typical joint account, there is a presumption that the property in its value is jointly owned and that the bank may pay the survivor who can give a good discharge of the debt[2]. If the mandate allows for payment even upon the death of one of the parties to the account, this substantiates joint ownership, entailing survivorship. (In other matters, the mandate ceases upon the death of one of the parties.)

(4)   MISCELLANEOUS MATTERS

Overdrafts on joint accounts

Where an overdraft is allowed on a joint account, the parties are jointly, but not severally liable in the absence of express stipulation to the contrary, and each may be called upon to pay a proportionate share of the indebtedness[3]. It is usual for the account-opening mandate to provide for the joint and several liability of the account holders.

Parties to an action under a joint account

Both parties to a joint account need not join in any action against a bank, since this would result in neither being able to sue if one forged a cheque resulting in the bank paying without mandate[4]. In *Jackson v White and Midland Bank Ltd*[5] the first defendant induced the plaintiff to put £2,000 into his failing business and form a partnership. A partnership account was opened with Midland Bank and cheques were to be signed by both parties. White forged the signature of Jackson upon a number of cheques. Park J held that the bank's agreement with the two customers was with

1 *Devaynes v Noble, Clayton's Case* (1816) 1 Mer 529; see pp 103 ff above.
2 *Husband v Davis* (1851) 10 CB 645; *Williams v Davies, Re Williams* (1864) 28 JP 664, 3 Sw & Tr 547; *Marshal v Crutwell* (1875) LR 20 Eq 328; *Re Bishop, National Provincial Bank Ltd v Bishop* [1965] Ch 450, [1965] 1 All ER 249; *Cullity* (1969) 85 LQR 530.
3 *Coats v Union Bank of Scotland Ltd* 1929 SC (HL) 114, 1929 SLT 477.
4 *Catlin v Cyprus Finance Corpn (London) Ltd* [1983] QB 759, [1983] 1 All ER 809.
5 [1967] 2 Lloyd's Rep 68.

them jointly to honour cheques jointly drawn and an agreement with each of them separately not to honour any cheques not drawn by him. The bank was therefore liable on the forged cheques, although it was entitled to be indemnified by the first defendant.

Bankruptcy or mental incapacity of a joint account holder

Bankruptcy or mental incapacity of a joint account customer does not trigger a survivorship clause contained in the mandate. No further drawings should be allowed against a joint account upon the bank receiving notice of the customer's bankruptcy[1]. Cheques drawn should be dishonoured with the answer 'Bankruptcy petition presented' where drawn by the bankrupt individual and an equivalent where drawn by another party to the joint account. Where the joint account is overdrawn, it is suspended in order to maintain any rights against the bankrupt's estate. The bank will not rank in the estate for the whole of the debt. Any securities deposited by the bankrupt individual will be realised for their proper value. The bank will then rank in the estate for the amount of the overdraft less the value of the security[2].

In the English case of *Midland Bank plc v Shephard*[3], the husband had an overdrawn personal account and arranged for the overdraft to be transferred to the new joint account he held with his wife. The mandate stipulated the joint and several liability of the couple for any loan or overdraft. Eventually the husband became bankrupt. The bank obtained summary judgment against the wife who argued that in agreeing to and signing the mandate, her husband acted as an agent of the bank and had placed undue influence upon her. The appeal was dismissed. The Court of Appeal too, dismissed the appeal on the basis that there was no proof of any fraudulent concealment, misrepresentation or undue influence. The result would have been identical in Scotland[4].

With regard to mental incapacity of one of the joint account holders, similar rules to the bankruptcy of a customer apply[5].

3. INTEREST-BEARING ACCOUNTS

(1) DEPOSIT AND SAVINGS ACCOUNTS

Deposit and savings accounts are intended primarily for use by small savers, as are savings accounts. The rates of interest payable upon sums at

---

1 See ch 3, pp 52 ff above.
2 *Re Dutton Massey & Co, ex parte Manchester and Liverpool District Banking Co Ltd* [1924] 2 Ch 199; *Re A Debtor (No 5 of 1967), ex parte National Westminster Bank Ltd v Official Receiver* [1972] 1 Ch 197, *sub nom Re Rushton, ex parte National Westminster Bank Ltd v Official Receiver* [1971] 2 All ER 937.
3 [1988] 3 All ER 17, CA.
4 *Mumford v Bank of Scotland; Smith v Bank of Scotland* 1994 SCLR 856, 1994 SLT 1288, OH.
5 See ch 3, pp 48 ff above.

credit in a deposit account generally exceed those applicable to savings accounts. It is the practice of some banks to allow deposit account interest rates to be applied to savings accounts in instances where the balance upon the savings account is above a specified threshold[1]. The credit balance accumulates interest and it is often provided that higher interest rates will apply where the customer agrees to give lengthier periods of notice for withdrawal of funds. In such 'fixed' deposit accounts, the customer deposits a given amount for a specified period at an agreed interest rate. If it is renewed at maturity a new interest rate will be determined. Generally such accounts provide that funds are capable of being withdrawn before the agreed maturity date and that the customer will as a result lose a portion of his interest. Other names for such accounts are 'investment accounts' and 'extra interest accounts' under which the customer deposits specified minimum amounts and withdrawal is subject to agreed periods of notice.

The moneys placed with a banker under a deposit account are repayable in terms of the contract governing the agreement and will normally be repayable on demand. The customer will usually withdraw by presenting the banker with a pass book and requesting payment. If the deposit account is subject to a condition regarding withdrawal of moneys, moneys are not withdrawable until the customer has complied with the condition[2]. The account is a continuing contract and each payment of money into the account will not establish a fresh contract[3]. The moneys paid into the account are simply a loan to the banker and are not a specific fund held in some sort of fiduciary capacity on behalf of the customer[4]. Neither deposit nor savings accounts can be overdrawn[5].

The banker must exercise care that the moneys at credit are paid to the rightful owner or his mandatory, otherwise he will be liable to pay or credit the account holder with the amount wrongly paid. If the bank pays out in breach of the terms of the agreement to, for example, an impostor or thief, the bank does so at its own risk and will not obtain a valid discharge[6]. The customer, however, requires to exercise a certain degree of skill and care by the terms of the agreement covering the amount deposited and if he does not do so he may be personally barred from denying the validity of the withdrawal[7]. On occasion supplementary terms and conditions are added to the receipt for the moneys or pass book. The effect is to incorporate these terms into the contract and these being precedent to any obligation by the bank to repay the moneys standing at credit. In the unlikely event of there being no conditions governing the customer's duties, the standard of care imposed upon him will be low in accordance with the principles of *Tai Hing Cotton Mill Ltd v Liu Chong Hing Bank Ltd*[8].

---

1 See Clydesdale Bank Code of Practice for personal customers, para 6.0, set out in Appendix 1 below.
2 *Re Dillon, Duffin v Duffin* (1890) 44 Ch D 76 at 81, CA, per Cotton J.
3 *Hart (Inspector of Taxes) v Sangster* [1957] Ch 329, [1957] 2 All ER 208, CA.
4 *Pearce v Creswick* (1843) 2 Hare 286, 12 LJ Ch 251; *Akbar Khan v Attar Singh* [1936] 2 All ER 545, PC.
5 *Barclays Bank Ltd v Okenarhe* [1966] 2 Lloyd's Rep 87.
6 *Wood v Clydesdale Bank Ltd* 1914 SC 397, 1914 1 SLT 245.
7 *Evans v National Provincial Bank of England* (1897) 13 TLR 429.
8 [1986] AC 80, [1985] 2 All ER 947, PC.

Cases which involve deposit or savings accounts which are held jointly do lead to issues regarding power to withdraw. In *Innes v Stephenson*[1] the parties to a joint saving account omitted directions as to who was entitled to withdraw funds. Lord Tenderden held that the parties were not partners or agents and therefore could not act on behalf of each other. Thus, it followed, that every withdrawal form required the signatures of both parties[2].

All of the deposits and savings accounts described have the salient feature that they are interest-bearing accounts. Such accounts are distinct from current accounts in a number of ways.

(1) Interest-bearing accounts earn a return for the customer.
(2) Current accounts may be drawn upon by cheques, which are not in modern practice generally permitted in the operation of interest-bearing accounts[3]. Where the customer holds a variety of different sorts of account, cheques may be used in regard only to the account for which they have been issued.
(3) A current account may be in credit or overdrawn – an interest-bearing account may not be overdrawn[4]. There is, however, potential for the existence of a temporary debit balance due to the withdrawal of funds reliant upon cheques later returned unpaid[5].
(4) In current accounts the customer accesses through a money transfer system where there are generally no interest payments, although some Scottish banks will grant interest on current accounts. The very name, 'interest-bearing account', indicates the certainty of payment of interest upon balances.
(5) In current accounts the bank is lent money on a short-term basis, whereas in interest-bearing accounts banks are lent money upon a longer-term basis, generally allowing for greater investment potential and therefore facilitating and explaining the payment of interest thereunder.
(6) In a current account the funds are liquid, whereas in an interest-bearing account the funds are investment deposits in the hands of the bank. The interest-bearing account renders the sums owed by the bank repayable to the customer upon pre-arranged conditions[6].

(2) DEPOSIT AND CONSIGNATION RECEIPTS

A deposit receipt is an acknowledgment by a banker of a receipt of a sum of money from a named person or persons to be placed on deposit, repayable in terms of it, normally on demand, and upon the redelivery of

---

1 (1831) 1 Mood & R 145.
2 See *Husband v Davis* (1851) 10 CB 645.
3 Although there are exceptions with some very special forms of account.
4 *Barclays Bank Ltd v Okenarhe* [1966] 2 Lloyd's Rep 87.
5 For detailed discussion of differences between current and interest bearing account, see *Re Head, Head v Head (No 2)* [1894] 2 Ch 236, CA, per Lopes LJ.
6 *Hopkins v Abbot* (1875) LR 19 Eq 222, per Malins VC; *Akbar Khan v Attar Singh* [1936] 2 All ER 545, PC.

the receipt to the banker[1]. The nature of the relationship between the bank and the depositor is one of debtor and creditor. It has been the practice of banks to treat depositors with whom they have had a course of dealing as customers[2]. The issue of banks of deposit receipts appears now to be largely confined to Scotland.

A deposit receipt is not a negotiable instrument and an indorsement is intended to signify that the named party has a right to uplift the moneys on behalf of the depositor[3]. If payment is made to a third party who is not authorised by the depositor, the bank will be liable to pay the depositor[4]. If the loss sustained by the bank is as a result of the fraud or negligence of the depositor, no repayment obligation falls upon the bank[5]. In instances where the deposit receipt is payable to either party or the survivor, the bank is obliged to follow that instruction and further if notice is received from one party to the effect that payment cannot be made without his consent the bank must comply and withhold payment.

If an arrestment is lodged in the hands of the bank against a customer who is a joint beneficiary of a deposit receipt the bank cannot pay the moneys away to the other party because the deposit receipt is not in itself evidence of true ownership. The funds may belong, in whole or in part, to the party against whom the arrestment has been made. In the event of the parties failing to agree as to the nature of true ownership of the funds the only recourse is for the bank to seek from the court a determination following an action of multiplepoinding[6].

The bank must comply strictly with the terms of the deposit receipt but has no duty to investigate the nature of the lodgement[7]. In *Dickson v National Bank of Scotland Ltd*[8] clients' moneys were lodged on deposit receipt by a firm of solicitors. The instruction for the uplift of the deposit was that the signature of one of the solicitors of the firm who was the agent for the trust funds would be sufficient. The firm was dissolved and one of the partners indorsed the deposit receipt and embezzled the moneys. In an action against the bank by the beneficiary of the trust, it was held that the bank was entitled to assume that the partner was doing an act necessary to wind up the firm's affairs and they had accordingly acted correctly in encashing the receipt[9].

When deposit receipts are presented through another bank it is the practice for the presenting banker to guarantee the indorsement. It has been said that 'this is a prudent practice but is not perhaps strictly necessary, as the presentment by the banker is a warranty of the genuineness of

---

1 See Lord Atkin's judgment in *Akbar Khan v Attar Singh* [1936] 2 All ER 545 at 548, PC. See also *Pearce v Creswick* (1843) 2 Hare 286, 12 LJ Ch 251; *Birch v Treasury Solicitor* [1951] 1 Ch 298 at 313, CA.
2 See *Scottish Banking Practice* (5th edn, 1987), 'Banker and Customer' p 39.
3 *Barstow v Inglis* (1857) 20 D 230.
4 *Wood v Clydesdale Bank Ltd* 1914 SC 397, 1914 1 SLT 245.
5 *Forbes's Executor v Western Bank* (1854) 16 D 807.
6 For discussion of arrestment, see pp 164 ff below.
7 Except in compliance with the money laundering regulations (ie the Money Laundering Regulations 1993, SI 1993/1933).
8 1917 SC (HL) 50, 1917 1 SLT 318.
9 See Wallace and McNeil's *Banking Law* (10th edn, 1991 by D B Caskie) pp 146–148.

the indorsement and of the presenting banker's authority to receive payment'[1].

On occasion moneys may be lodged with a bank on 'consignation receipt' to be held pending the outcome of a dispute, in court or otherwise between the parties[2]. It is said by Burns that:

'The repayment of such money must follow precisely the terms on which it is lodged. If the consignation is judicial, that is ordered by the court, the order or interlocutor ordering the consignation will specify the terms on which it is to be repaid and these terms must be complied with. If the moneys are lodged in the name of the Accountant of the Court or the sheriff clerk the banker may pay on the instruction of that official but taking a receipt from the recipient of the funds'[3].

Consignation receipts in sheriff court actions are issued in the name of the sheriff clerk and his successors in office and must include the name of the sheriff clerk and his successors in office together with the names of the parties on whose behalf the moneys are consigned and a reference to the action concerned.

If there is a dispute as to the ownership of the sums held on deposit the banker's only course is to raise an action of multiplepoinding.

Interest is applied to the deposit receipt at the rates advertised by the banks and is usually calculated upon a simple basis notwithstanding how long the receipt remains outstanding[4].

4. SPECIAL FORMS OF LOAN ACCOUNTS

(1) OVERDRAFTS

An overdraft is a loan granted by the bank to a customer who maintains a current account[5]. The provision of such a facility allows a customer to draw cheques to a pre-agreed level of indebtedness. As cheques are drawn on the account the available balance decreases with a corresponding increase upon lodgements being made. It is now general practice for the bank's letter authorising the overdraft to include the following: (1) the rate of interest applying to the balance outstanding; (2) the nature and total of any other charges, apart from interest, in the total credit charge; (3)

---

1 *Scottish Banking Practice* (5th edn, 1987), 'Banker and Customer' p 40.
2 For Court of Session practice, see the Court of Session Consignations (Scotland) Act 1895 and for sheriff court practice, see the Sheriff Courts Consignations (Scotland) Act 1893.
3 C Burns *The Law of Banking* (2nd edn, 1983) p 15.
4 There are statutory exceptions — under s 37 of the Judicial Factors Act 1849 every account of a deposit or lodgement by a judicial factor, tutor or curator (guardian) or under authority of the Court of Session, whether on deposit receipt or current account must at least once in every year accumulate the interest with the principal sum so that both thereafter bear interest together as principal and any bank failing to do so is liable to account as if such money had been so accumulated.
5 For full discussion of overdrafts on current accounts, see pp 143 ff above.

the limit of the overdraft; and (4) the nature and amount of any required security[1].

It is also common to state the time limit over which the overdraft will endure coupled with the provision that the facility will be repayable on demand at the bank's determination (to protect the bank against unforeseen change in circumstances of the customer)[2]. When interest is applied to the account it is capitalised to the sums outstanding and accordingly the bank earns compound interest on the amount overdrawn except in instances where the interest, when it falls due, is immediately paid by the customer.

The Consumer Credit Act 1974 will apply if the facility is made available to an individual and the amount does not exceed £15,000[3]. A bank overdraft falls within the definition of a regulated consumer credit agreement for unrestricted use running account credit[4] even if it is granted by the bank without prior arrangements with the customer[5]. However, for bank overdrafts certain stringent requirements of the Act are relaxed, the most important being the provisions relative to entering into credit agreements, their form and contents and their cancellation[6]. The Director of Fair Trading made a determination on 3 November 1984[7] that overdraft agreements under current accounts are exempt from the very detailed provisions of the Consumer Credit (Agreement) Regulations 1983 if the bank notifies (a) the Director of its intention to make overdrafts under the Determination and (b) the customer of its terms, particularly as to credit charges[8].

(2)   OTHER FORMS OF BANK LOANS

Bank loans are granted to customers for wide-ranging purposes but generally are either (1) business loans made to a company or unincorporated customer or (2) personal consumer-type loans. It is necessary in terms of the Consumer Credit Act 1974 that commercial and consumer loans are treated separately. Most forms of agreement follow a set pattern but consumer agreements require to be adapted to adhere to the statutory requirements.

---

1 These are all requirements under the Consumer Credit (Quotations) Regulations 1980, SI 1980/55, reg 6(1), Sch 1.
2 See *Crimpfil Ltd v Barclays Bank plc* 1995 TLR 116, (1995) Independent, 27 March, CA.
3 Consumer Credit Act 1974, s 8(2) (amended by the Consumer Credit (Increase of Monetary Limits) Order 1983, SI 1983/1878, art 4, Schedule, Pt II).
4 Consumer Credit Act 1974, s 10(1); and see s 9 under which credit includes a loan and any other form of financial accommodation.
5 1974 Act, Sch 2, Pt II, example 17.
6 1974 Act, Pt V (ss 54–74).
7 1974 Act, s 74 (1)(b).
8 See also the Consumer Credit (Agreements) Regulations 1983, SI 1983/1553, and the Consumer Credit (Increase of Monetary Limits) Order 1983 , SI 1983/1878.

Personal loan accounts

Personal loan accounts were first introduced by some banks in 1958 and have the key common characteristic that the bank does not require security. The loan and interest accruing are repayable by equal monthly instalments for periods generally from six months to five years. These facilities are principally intended to fund domestic expenditure and fall within the strictures of the Consumer Credit Act 1974 as the funds lent generally do not exceed £15,000.

Revolving credit schemes and budget accounts

Revolving credit schemes provide the borrower with an ability to draw sums to an agreed limit which is to be repaid by regular monthly instalments. Such facilities are distinct from ordinary loans because the borrower is not required to take up the full amount of the facility, and as the payments reduce the borrower's indebtedness, the borrower can draw the balance to the agreed financial limit. Since 1967 banks have made budget account facilities available to customers as a device to assist customers' plans for regular personal expenditure. The total cost of these items is identified at the start of the year and monthly instalments are made for that total amount. Thereafter the customer makes payment for the expenditure as it falls due from the expenditure account. There does exist the possibility of an overdraft facility within the budget account when the payment from the account is greater than the sums paid into it. Both such accounts are regulated by the Consumer Credit Act 1974[1].

5. ACCOUNTS FOR THIRD PARTIES – 'TRUST ACCOUNTS'

It is common practice for customers, and essential for solicitors, to hold money on behalf of third parties and lodge these moneys in an identified account to that effect. If in such an instance the banker is aware of the existence of the trust account held with him, he must not wrongfully deal with the funds so as to be in breach of the trust. Further, in instances where an account is headed in a distinguishing manner, but is not designated explicitly as a trust account, it may be sufficient to prove that the banker ought to have been aware of its actual nature[2]. However, in instances where the banker has absolutely no knowledge of the nature of the account he bears no fiduciary responsibilities[3].

---

1 1974 Act, s 8.
2 *Re Gross, ex parte Kingston* [1871] LR 6 Ch App 632; *United Rentals Ltd v Clydesdale and North of Scotland Bank Ltd* 1963 SLT (Sh Ct) 41; *Style Financial Services Ltd v Bank of Scotland (No 2)* 1997 GWD 7-255, OH.
3 *Union Bank of Australia Ltd v Murray-Aynsley* [1898] AC 693; *Bank of New South Wales v Goulburn Valley Butter Co Pty Ltd* [1902] AC 543, PC; *Dickson v National Bank of Scotland Ltd* 1917 SC (HL) 50, 1917 1 SLT 318; *Thomson v Clydesdale Bank Ltd* (1893) 20 R (HL) 59, [1893] AC 282.

Where the customer who holds the account occupies a position or post which involves holding moneys on behalf of third parties, (for example a solicitor, an accountant, a stockbroker) this does not of itself necessarily place the banker upon inquiry[1]. A banker cannot refuse to pay out on a cheque simply because he believes the funds are held in trust on behalf of a third party and some degree of certainty would be required to enable the banker to do so[2]. It also follows that the bank could not retain the benefit of a cheque drawn upon a trust fund, known to be such and paid into an overdrawn private account[3].

6.   ARRESTMENT OF BANK ACCOUNTS

(1)   INTRODUCTION

Arrestment is the most common form of diligence[4] which affects banking practice[5]. Arrestment is 'the diligence appropriate to attach obligations to account to the debtor by a third party and corporeal moveables belonging to the debtor which are in the hands of a third party'[6]. The creditor using the arrestment is called 'the arrester', the third party upon whom the schedule of arrestment is laid is known as 'the arrestee', and the arrester's debtor whose funds or other moveables are attached is called 'the common debtor'. The arrestment attaches the incorporeal or corporeal moveable property and prevents the arrestee from paying the arrested funds, or delivering the arrested moveables, to the common debtor and creates a preference in favour of the arrester in competition with other diligence or rights in favour of third parties[7]. Arrestment is competent against a variety of subjects including a contingent debt (where there is an obligation to account); outstanding arrears of alimentary funds[8]; interest owed by a debtor in an assurance policy which pays out upon his death even in instances where premiums must be paid before they fall due[9]. Additional subjects liable to arrestment include the debtor's interest in a deceased's

---

1 *Greenwood Teale v William Williams, Brown & Co* (1894) 11 TLR 56.
2 *Ireland v North of Scotland Banking Co* (1880) 8 R 215; *Struthers Patent Diamond Rock Pulveriser Co Ltd v Clydesdale Bank Ltd* (1886) 13 R 434.
3 *Foxton v Manchester and Liverpool District Banking Co* (1881) 44 LT 406, per Fry J (approved in *Attorney-General v De Winton* [1906] 2 Ch 106). See also *Gray v Johnston* (1868) LR 3 HL 1.
4 Diligence means 'the term used in Scotland for the body of law relating to the enforcement of obligations': W J Stewart and R Burgess *Dictionary of Law* (1996) p 130.
5 By early 1991 the number of arrestments served on the four Scottish clearing banks had increased to almost 44,000 arrestments per annum: *Statutory Fees for Arrestees* (Scot Law Com Discussion Paper no. 87) (1990) para 2.20 and *Report on Statutory Fees for Arrestees* (Scot Law Com no. 133) (1992).
6 W A Wilson *The Scottish Law of Debt* (2nd edn, 1991) p 191. See also Bell *Commentaries* II, 63; *Agnew v Norwest Construction Co Ltd* 1935 SC 771, 1935 SLT 517.
7 *Boland v White Cross Insurance Association Ltd* 1926 SC 1066, 1926 SLT 716; *Park, Dobson & Co Ltd v William Taylor & Son (Glasgow) Ltd* 1929 SC 571, 1929 SLT 415.
8 *Muirhead v Miller* (1877) 4 R 1139.
9 *Bankhardt's Trustees v Scottish Amicable Life Assurance Society* (1871) 9 M 443, OH.

estate; shares in a company holding its registered office in Scotland; the subject matter of a court action which is pending; and any sums held at credit by an individual on a current or deposit account or on deposit receipt.

In instances where a bank customer pledges securities to the bank, an arrestment in its hands will attach any reversion due to the debtor. The reversion will be calculated after allowing for the debt and interest thereon at the date the arrestment is served[1].

Arrestment is not competent against a number of subjects: debts due on bills of exchange[2]; the earnings of active members of the armed forces[3]; property over which the bank has no right of lien including items held for safe custody[4]; alimentary funds (save if excessive); the reversion of a standard security or other heritable security granted in the bank's favour; funds electronically transferred by a bank to a customer's account from that of a common debtor at any point prior to the serving of the arrestment where both accounts are held at the same branch[5]; contingent debts where there is no obligation to pay or to account, unless on the basis that the debtor is *vergens ad inopiam*[6]. Arrestment will also fail where it is lodged in the hands of the common debtor, his servant, factor or custodier[7] or where the arrestment relates to a debt which cannot be recovered in Scotland[8]. Arrestment does not apply to the attachment of earnings or pensions which are attachable by a form of statutory diligence called earnings arrestments, current maintenance arrestments, and conjoined arrestment orders[9].

An arrestment may be used on the dependence of an action for payment of a principal sum; or in execution of a decree for payment of a principal sum or judicial expenses; or in execution of an extract document of debt which has been registered in the Books of Council and Session or Sheriff Court Books or a document of debt enforceable as if so registered; or in pursuance of a summary warrant for the recovery of arrears of rates, taxes or community charge.

In order to complete the diligence of arrestment the arrester requires to raise an action of furthcoming which cites both the arrestee and common debtor as defenders[10]. Further to the action of furthcoming, the arrester obtains decree which requires the common debtor to pay to the arrester the sums or assets arrested so far as is necessary to satisfy the arrested debt, or as the case may be, for the sale of that portion of the moveable property belonging to the common debtor which, in the arrestee's hands

1 To avoid the application of the *Clayton's Case* principles (*Devaynes v Noble, Clayton's Case* (1816) 1 Mer 529), an overdrawn account should be closed and a new account opened for future transactions.
2 Bell *Commentaries* II, 68.
3 But see exceptions: Armed Forces Act 1971, ss 59, 61.
4 J Graham Stewart *The Law of Diligence* (1898) p 107.
5 *Momm v Barclay's Bank International Ltd* [1977] QB 790, [1976] 3 All ER 588; distinguishing *Rekstin v Severo Sibirsko etc* [1933] 1 KB 47, CA.
6 *Symington v Symington* (1875) 3 R 205; *Smith v Cameron* (1879) 6 R 1107.
7 *Trowsdale's Trustee v Forcett Rly Co* (1870) 9 M 88.
8 *J Verrico & Co Ltd v Australian Mutual Provident Society* 1972 SLT (Sh Ct) 57.
9 Debtors (Scotland) Act 1987, Pt III (ss 46–73).
10 *Graham Stewart* p 255.

at the time of execution of the arrestment, is necessary to satisfy the arrester's debt. The alternative is to obtain as from the common debtor, a letter mandating satisfaction of the arrester's claim from the assets arrested. The procedure is completed only when the arrestee receives the letter from the common debtor or an extract decree of furthcoming.

An action of furthcoming serves two fundamental objectives when served upon the bank:

> '(1) to ascertain the amount due by the bank to the common debtor, or, where other subjects, such as the reversionary right of the common debtor to an insurance policy or shares, have been attached, the present extent of those subjects; and (2) to have the bank as arrestee decerned to pay the attached funds or so much of them as will pay the common debtor's debt to the arrester, or, where other subjects have been arrested, to authorise a sale and payment out of the proceeds'[1].

The bank will formally make appearance in the action of furthcoming in instances only where the sum sued for is greater than the sums held by the bank[2]. Only when the bank receives the extract decree for payment may it safely pay over the funds arrested. The action of furthcoming provides the only forum in which it is competent to answer questions as to the validity of the arrestment[3].

If the common debtor can show that he is not the debtor of the arrester, the action will be dismissed. The arrestee may also seek to prove that he is not the debtor of the common debtor; that he has a lien over the property arrested; that the arrestment is informal or that there are competing claims for the moneys[4]. In such a case of competition for moneys, the arrestee should raise an action of multiplepoinding by which the court will distribute the subjects of arrestment amongst the parties in accordance with their own respective rights.

(2) EXTENT OF PROPERTY ATTACHED BY ARRESTMENT

An arrestment is executed by the service of a schedule of arrestment upon the arrestee. The schedule is normally in general terms attaching the principal sum (and the expenses) due by the arrestee to the common debtor and 'all goods, gear, debts, sums of money or any other effects whatsoever' lying in the arrestee's hands belonging to the debtor or defender. The sum to which the arrestment attaches may exceed that stated in the schedule of arrestment where the usual words 'more or less' are employed. The sum attached thereby is not limited to the specified sum[5].

---

1 Wallace and McNeil's *Banking Law* (10th edn, 1991 by D B Caskie) pp 211, 212. Cf *Lucas's Trustees v Campbell and Scott* (1894) 21 R 1096; *Stenhouse London Ltd v Allwright* 1972 SC 209, 1972 SLT 255.
2 In such instances, the practice is for the pursuer's solicitor to restrict the claim appropriately to avoid the need for appearance.
3 *Vincent v Chalmers & Co's Trustee* (1877) 5 R 43; *Barclay Curle & Co Ltd v Sir James Laing & Sons Ltd* 1908 SC 82, 15 SLT 482.
4 *Wallace and McNeil* p 212.
5 *Ritchie v McLachlan* (1870) 8 M 815.

The 'more or less' phrase is generally used in arrestments proceeding from Court of Session or sheriff court ordinary cause warrants[1].

There is no requirement that the schedule should specify the particular property or funds arrested. It follows therefore, that where the arrestee is a bank with a network of branches, the arrestment will normally attach all funds and moveable goods held by the arrestee at its head office *and* all of its branches. Accordingly, it is not necessary for the schedule of arrestment to specify the particular branches of the arrestee bank at which funds or property of the debtor are located. It is common that the arrester will not know, or have no means of knowing, whether the arrestee holds funds or goods of the debtor or at which branch of the arrestee's network the funds or goods are held. The arrestee is not under an obligation to disclose to the arrester whether or not he holds funds or goods belonging to the debtor[2].

The bank owes a duty of confidentiality to its customer and it accordingly follows that disclosure to the arrester whether or not an arrestment has attached anything would be a breach of that duty. However, the practice of Scottish banks is not to disclose whether anything has been attached by an arrestment on the dependence[3] but they will disclose the sums attached by an arrestment in execution, or its equivalent[4]. A creditor may enforce payment by an arrestee by an action of furthcoming in instances where he holds an arrestment in execution. He may not do so where he merely holds an arrestment on the dependence. Wallace and McNeil say that:

> 'It is the usual practice for a bank if it has any funds in its hands belonging or owing to the common debtor to disclose the amount of these to the arrester to enable a proper action of furthcoming to be raised. It should be noted that the bank's duty of confidentiality prevents it from disclosing details of its customer's affairs where the arrestment is on the dependence of an action since the customer's liability to the arrester has not been judicially determined'[5].

However, this statement is not supported by authority and is in conflict with the banker's duty of confidentiality regarding his customer's affairs. Further, one of the objects of an action of furthcoming is to establish the extent of the debt due by the arrestee to the common debtor[6]. It follows that it is difficult to found the duty of a bank arrestee to disclose funds arrested in execution upon the basis that it enables a proper action of furthcoming to be raised by the arrester[7]. However, two of the *Tournier* exceptions[8] are of relevance to this matter. Firstly, disclosure is competent under 'compulsion of law' and while an arrestment in execution does not

1 For historical reasons arrestments proceeding upon sheriff court summary cause warrants often arrest a maximum sum, omitting the words 'more or less'.
2 *Graham Stewart* p 229. See also *Veitch v Finlay and Wilson* (1894) 10 Sh Ct Rep 13 at 14.
3 W A Wilson *The Scottish Law of Debt* (2nd edn, 1991) p 160.
4 *Wilson* p 225.
5 *Wallace and McNeil* p 211.
6 *Graham Stewart* p 226.
7 See *Tournier v National Provincial and Union Bank of England* [1924] 1 KB 461, CA; *W v Egdell* [1989] 1 All ER 1089, [1989] 2 WLR 689.
8 See pp 108 ff above.

involve compulsion, disclosure is imminent since it will be compelled in an action of furthcoming. Such imminence has been agreed to be sufficient to bring disclosure within the exception. Secondly, disclosure is competent where it is in 'the interests of the bank'. Arguably, the bank holding arrested funds has an interest avoiding being sued in an action of furthcoming, but whether the arrestee's interest is sufficiently substantial to entitle a bank to disclose to an arrester the amount arrested in execution is still a matter for debate. However, the present practice of the Scottish banks is both sensible and practical[1]. In the majority of instances the common debtor does authorise the arrestee bank to disclose the required information in respect of the funds arrested and usually provides a mandate enabling the payment of the funds to the arrester thus avoiding further liability for the expenses of the action of furthcoming. Unarguably, the present practice is based upon practical experience and good sense. The interests of the bank should be 'treated by law as sufficient to override any duty of confidentiality which a bank or other arrestee may owe to a common debtor'[2].

(3) SERVING OF THE ARRESTMENT

There is a conflict of view as to the proper practice in serving arrestments upon banks in an effort to attach moneys due by them to a customer. Wallace and McNeil suggest that an arrestment on a bank should be made at its registered office or its head office and another schedule should be served on the branch where the common debtor's account is kept[3]. Maher and Cusine state, however:

'the exact position of service on a bank is not clear, at least as a matter of strict law. Service on a particular branch of the bank certainly operates to attach the account of the defender held there but may not be effective as regards accounts held at other branches. Practice is to serve the schedule at the head office and on branches where the defender is thought to have an account but probably service on the head office alone is sufficient to attach all accounts at the bank in Scotland, as the bank will circulate details of the arrestment to all its branches'[4].

It is difficult, however, to argue against the view that banking corporations are the same as other corporations and that the correct procedure to follow for sheriff court ordinary cause warrants is as provided in the Ordinary Cause Rules[5]. Under these rules an arrestment on a corporation may be executed by leaving a schedule of arrestment in the hands of an employee of the corporation at 'a place of business of the corporation'. The place of business includes the registered office, head office, principal place

1 See conclusions of the Scottish Law Commission in *Statutory Fees for Arrestees* (Scot Law Com Discussion Paper no. 87) (1990) para 3.70.
2 *Statutory Fees for Arrestees* para 3.71. In para 3.72 it was proposed that there should be statutory provision so that disclosure as to whether or not funds have been arrested and the value of funds would not be a breach of the duty of confidentiality.
3 *Wallace and McNeil* p 209. This is in conflict with *Graham Stewart* p 22.
4 Maher and Cusine *The Law and Practice of Diligence* (1990) para 4.24.
5 OCR rr 5.4(1) and 6.1 (substituted by SI 1993/1956).

of business or a branch place of business. If the arrestment is not executed by service at the arrestee's principal place of business a postal copy must be sent to the arrestee's principal place of business[1]. In the case of other arrestments including Court of Session warrants and warrants in extract registered writs, execution at any place of business will be sufficient as there is no enactment or rule of law which makes different provision for banks[2]. No postal copy need be served at the principal place of business. It follows that an arrestment seeking to attach all debts and moveable property due by an arrestee bank to a defender or common debtor, served at a local branch will attach all those debts and moveable property located in the head office and branch network[3]. In the case of National Girobank which holds accounts at a central office outside Scotland, the arrestment is served at its office in Edinburgh[4].

(4) THE EFFECT OF AN ARRESTMENT

The arrestment prevents the arrestee from voluntarily intromitting with the arrested funds or goods to the prejudice of the arrester. It seems accepted that if an arrestment seeks to attach a sum held on deposit with a Scottish bank but the funds are outside the Scottish jurisdiction, the arrestment will fail because the debts cannot be recovered in Scotland[5]. However, if the arrestment is seeking to attach all moneys due, the sums are attached by way of the bank's obligations to repay the deposit[6]. The arrestee could not, for example, pay the arrested sum to the common debtor. If, however, the arrestee does voluntarily part with the arrested funds, he will be liable in damages for breach of the arrestment[7]. The extent of damages will be the actual loss sustained by the arrester as a result of the breach and will generally be the amount of the debt due by the arrestee to the common debtor which has been wrongfully paid away and not exceeding the principal sum and all expenses due by the common debtor to the arrester[8].

However, if the arrestee parts with the arrested funds, or goods, in good faith and in justifiable ignorance of the arrestment, he will not be liable for breach of the arrestment[9]. Lord Moncreiff said:

---

1 OCR r 6.1 (as so substituted).
2 *Statutory Fees for Arrestees* para 2.10 and p 18.
3 *Statutory Fees for Arrestees* p 18; *R v Grossman* (1981) 73 Cr App Rep 302, [1981] Crim LR 396, CA; *Libyan Arab Foreign Bank v Bankers Trust Co* [1989] QB 728 at 748, per Saughton J.
4 Macphail *Sheriff Court Practice* (1988) p 356.
5 See *Wallace and McNeil* p 207; *J Verrico & Co Ltd v Australian Mutual Provident Society* 1972 SLT (Sh Ct) 57.
6 It is sensible to adopt the view of Lord Kyllachy in *Dunn's Executor v Canada Investment and Agency Co Ltd* (February 1898, unreported), OH, who decided that an arrestment at the head office of a Scottish bank attached funds held at its London branch. Cf also *Graham Stewart* p 125.
7 *Graham Stewart* p 220.
8 *Grant v Hill* (1792) Mor 786; *McEwan v Blair and Morrison* (1822) 1 S 313 (NE 289).
9 *Laidlaw v Smith* (1841) 2 Robin 490, HL.

'That the *mere fact* of the debtor having no personal notice or knowledge of the arrestment will not liberate him from the civil consequences of paying in the face of it, if, before he paid, he was in such circumstances that he *ought* to have known of it, and so must be *presumed* to have known it. Any other rule would certainly give occasion to pretences for evacuating the diligence of creditors'[1].

Branch based institutions accordingly have to take care to ensure prompt procedures are evoked to give notice of the arrestment to all parts of the business which might pay or deliver goods in ignorance of the arrestment[2]. In practice the Scottish clearing banks advise their branch networks daily of the arrestments that have been served. For those banks without centralised systems it is necessary for each branch to check its current account and deposit account records, deposit receipt records, safe custody records and its security records.

(5)   LOOSING AND TERMINATION OF AN ARRESTMENT

Loosing of the arrestment will be granted by the court where caution is found that the relevant sums will, if required, be made available to the arrester. Where the arrestment is shown to have been employed oppressively caution will be recalled and the common debtor may have an action of damages against the arrester[3]. General arrestments are renewable. Should questions of preference arise, the relevant date is that of renewal, and not the original date of arrestment. An arrestment in execution prescribes in three years from its date. Arrestments on a future or contingent debt, or on the dependence of an action, prescribe in three years from the date the debt becomes due, the contingency is purified or decree is pronounced[4].

Prescription may, however, be interrupted by actions of multiplepoinding or furthcoming or by appearance in such an action as raised by another[5].

(6)   COMPARISON WITH ENGLISH LAW

The English Mareva injunction is broadly equivalent to arrestment on the dependence and a garnishee order or similar equivalent to arrestments in execution. A Mareva injunction is granted on the dependence of court proceedings prior to final judgment but it is a personal order binding the defendant and third parties personally and does not create a preference for the plaintiff (as an arrestment does)[6].

---

1 *Laidlaw v Smith* (1838) 16 S 367 at 369, per Lord Moncreiff.
2 Technically a breach of an arrestment is contempt of court but penalties are rarely evoked — *Graham Stewart* pp 222–223; *Meron v Umland* (1896) 3 SLT 286.
3 *Ritchie v McLachlan* (1870) 8 M 815.
4 Debtors Scotland Act 1838, s 22.
5 *Jameson v Sharp* (1887) 14 R 64.
6 See operations of Mareva in *Z Ltd v A-Z and AA-LL* [1982] QB 558, [1982] 1 All ER 556, CA, and *Searose Ltd v Seatrain UK Ltd* [1981] 1 All ER 806, [1981] 1 WLR 894.

However, in many respects a garnishee order bears a closer resemblance to arrestments. Both are not restricted to the funds held in particular branches of the garnishee's or arrestee's business. The principal difference is however that warrants for arrestment both in execution and dependence may be obtained by a pursuer as a matter of ordinary process and may be used against any person whether or not the pursuer had reasonable cause to believe that he holds funds or goods belonging to the common debtor. In England, a preliminary application to the court must be supported by an affidavit as part of the garnishee order process[1].

7. ASSIGNATION AND ATTACHMENT OF FUNDS

The Bills of Exchange Act 1882 provides: 'In Scotland, where the drawee of a bill has in his hands funds available for the payment thereof, the bill operates as an assignation of the sum for which it is drawn in favour of the holder from the time the bill is presented to the drawee'[2]. The provision when enacted in 1882 did not create new law, but codified a principle of the common law of Scotland which covered any order to pay[3]. The law has been amended where payment upon a cheque has been countermanded by the drawer so that the stopped cheque no longer acts as an intimated assignation of money in the hands of the paying banker since he is treated as having no funds available for payment[4].

However, if a cheque is drawn on the bank and there are insufficient funds to cover the cheque or cheques presented together, and the drawee is not prepared to allow an overdraft, it follows that the bank is required to attach the available funds (pro rata if more than one cheque) by transferring the available balance to a suspense account until the cheque is represented and met, or the drawer has sufficient funds, attached or otherwise; or the holder returns the cheque to the drawer who may then demonstrate to the drawee bank that the holder has relinquished his claim to the attached funds; or five years has prescribed or a judicial settlement is reached.

It is a justifiable criticism that without greatly enhancing the protection afforded to payees the 'funds attached' principle is complex and expensive to administer for Scottish banks, is damaging to the banker-customer relationship and often causes distress and hardship to drawers who fall victim to it. It has been said that for the business customer 'the effect on his creditworthiness can be devastating, since, in a case for a large amount,

---

1 *Statutory Fees for Arrestees* (Scot Law Com Discussion Paper no. 87) (1990) p 50: the number of garnishee orders made in England (4,000 in 1988 in county courts) is small compared with the number of arrestments served on clearing banks in Scotland (29,500 to year ending 30 June 1989). 80 per cent of garnishee orders are successful in attaining funds but in Scotland only 690 of arrestments served on clearing banks attached funds.
2 Bills of Exchange Act 1882, s 53(2).
3 *British Linen Co v Carruthers and Fergusson* (1883) 10 R 923.
4 Bills of Exchange Act 1882, s 75A (added by the Law Reform (Miscellaneous Provisions)(Scotland) Act 1985, s 11).

not only would that cheque have to be returned but so also would any others for however small an amount, if they were presented at the same time'[1].

The Jack Committee[2] recommended the abolition of the 'funds attached' principle in relation to all orders to pay, except bills of exchange (other than cheques) where abolition was generally thought to be unnecessary. If such proposed abolition is given effect, the Scottish bank manager would be placed in the same position as his English counterpart and permitted to pay one cheque and return another which is an option presently not available to him.

1 *Report of the Review Committee on Banking Services: Law and Practice* (the Jack Report) (Cm 622) (1989) p 59. The Jack Committee also took the view that the 'funds attached' principle could also apply to EFTPOS.
2 Jack Report, para 7.57.

Chapter 6

Negotiable Instruments and Other Orders for Payment

1. NEGOTIABLE INSTRUMENTS AND OTHER ORDERS FOR PAYMENT

(1) CONCEPT OF NEGOTIABILITY

Financial instruments may be either negotiable or non-negotiable. A negotiable instrument is one which, by statute or mercantile usage[1], may be transferred by delivery and indorsement to a bona fide purchaser for

---

1 *Goodwin v Robarts* (1876) 1 App Cas 476, HL.

value, in such circumstances that he takes it free from defects in the title of prior parties. A non-negotiable instrument, however, is one which, though capable of transfer by delivery (with any necessary indorsement) in the same way as a negotiable instrument, may never confer upon the holder a better right than was vested upon the transferor[2]. This non-negotiable status is in accordance with the *'nemo dat quod non habet'* rule — that you cannot pass on a better title than you yourself had. Certain instruments are non-negotiable due to an absence of certain characteristics of negotiability, for example share certificates may not be transferred by simple delivery as transfer in some specific form must evidence the change of ownership (while notification to the registrar of the relevant company is required for registration). The crucial element of negotiability is what is called 'a holder in due course' who has the position of a bona fide purchaser acquiring an overriding title to the instrument.

There are many classes of negotiable and non-negotiable instrument but in all cases they fall into one of two categories: (1) an undertaking to pay a sum of money or (2) an order to pay a sum of money, whether to the person giving the order or to a third party.

Instruments taking the form of an express or implied undertaking to pay include promissory notes, bank notes, treasury bills, bearer bonds, share warrants and negotiable certificates of deposit, all of which are negotiable instruments, and non-negotiable letters of allotment. On the other hand, instruments taking the form of an order to pay are cheques and other bills of exchange, dividend and interest warrants, and bankers drafts, all of which are negotiable, and postal orders, money orders, pension warrants and child benefit orders which are non-negotiable. Fundamentally, 'orders to pay' do not as such create an obligation between the payee (the person to whom the instrument is payable) and the person directed to make the payment (the drawee). If the order is to pay on demand, the drawee either pays or refuses to pay. In the latter case, the payee's remedy is not against the drawee but the party ordering the payment (the drawer). If the order is to pay at some future date, the drawee is asked to 'accept' the instrument – that is to say add his signature by way of an undertaking to pay the instrument at maturity. If the drawee refuses, the instrument is dishonoured, but the payee's remedy is against the drawer alone. Instruments payable on demand are not accepted. It would be pointless for a drawee to undertake a payment obligation which is due for immediate performance. He either pays or declines to pay.

(2)   CHARACTERISTICS OF NEGOTIABLE INSTRUMENTS

Negotiable instruments are documents of title, the ownership of which entails possession of rights and represents financial obligations. The term 'negotiable' connotes the transfer of an indefeasible title free from existing defects to a bona fide transferee for value. The term is not to be confused with 'transferable'. As Byles illustrates[3], the loose and erroneous inter-

---

1 *Bovill v Dixon* (1856) 3 Macq 1, HL.
2 Byles *Bills of Exchange* (25th edn) p 79.

changeability of the two terms in the governing statute, the Bills of Exchange Act 1882, has led to the belief that the terms are synonymous. However, an instrument is transferable simply where all existing rights and obligations of the transferor may be passed by delivery or by indorsement and delivery. Transferability and negotiable instruments are therefore distinguished by the nature and quality of title which each conveys.

The principal characteristics of negotiability are as follows.

Firstly, simple delivery or delivery and indorsement transfers title to the instrument. A negotiable instrument stating that title belongs to the 'bearer' of the instrument (that is to say drawn in favour of the bearer and/or a specified individual) will always be in a deliverable state. This facet illustrates the potential for such instruments to be almost equivalent to money. Certain circumstances require that indorsement accompany delivery. A negotiable instrument may specify an individual to whom order of payment is made, for example a cheque payable to 'A or order'. In such a case, A may transfer the cheque to B by means of indorsement. Such indorsement may take the form of either simple signature ('indorsement in blank'), or a signature accompanied by instruction to 'pay B' ('special indorsement'). Indorsement in blank may render an instrument payable to bearer which was not previously so. Generally, indorsement places an instrument in a deliverable state, facilitating delivery and thereby, transfer of legal title. Indorsement may pre-date or post-date or be contemporaneous with delivery.

Secondly, a bona fide purchaser for value takes title free from prior defects in title, becoming a 'holder in due course'. This is the very essence of negotiability and several matters require clarification.

When is a *purchaser* bona fide? Whether purchase occurs bona fides is essentially a question of fact. A thing is deemed to be done in good faith within the meaning of the Bills of Exchange Act 1882 where it is in fact done honestly, whether it is done negligently or not[1]. It follows that objective standards of reasonable knowledge or suspicion as to defective title are irrelevant.

What does '*for value*' mean? Value is constituted by goods, money, services or other forms of consideration. Equally, it may be constituted by a promise of future payment required by the transferee[2]. There is no necessity of payment of adequate value. If a negotiable instrument is transferred gratuitously by way of gift, the transferee's title is burdened by any and all defects relevant to the transferor's title.

What does '*title free from prior defects*' mean? Possession of title, free from defects constitutes an exception to the principal of '*nemo dat quod non habet*'. It is a measure to accommodate the exigencies and realities of commercial life and constitutes the fundamental element of negotiability that the transferee may acquire a better title to the instrument than the transferor.

What is a '*holder in due course*'? The transferee becomes a holder in due course within the terms of section 29(1) of the 1882 Act, which provides that:

---

1 Bills of Exchange Act 1882, s 90.
2 1882 Act, s 27.

'A holder in due course is a holder who has taken a bill, complete and regular on the face of it, under the following conditions, namely

(a) That he became the holder of it before it was overdue, and without
   notice that it had previously been dishonoured, if such was the fact;
(b) That he took the bill in good faith and for value, and that at the time the
   bill was negotiated to him he had no notice of any defect in the title of
   the person who negotiated it'.

By section 29(2) the title of the person who negotiates a bill is defective
when he obtains the bill, or its acceptance, by fraud, duress, or force and
fear, or for an illegal consideration, or when he negotiates it in breach of
faith or under such circumstances as to amount to fraud. In terms of section 29(3) a holder in due course may give a valid discharge of the bill to
anyone paying him and can confer on any person, who is not a party to
any fraud or illegality affecting the bill, all rights entailed by his status as
holder in due course.

The third principal characteristic of a negotiable instrument is that there
is no necessity to give notice to the person primarily liable on the instrument. The final characteristic is that the holder of the instrument may sue
on it in his own name, which is incidental to the transferee's possession of
the full complement of rights following transfer of full and legal title.

The negotiable status of all the instruments encompassed within the
terms of the 1882 Act[1] rests upon the 'custom of merchants'[2]. Certain
requirements are basic to this class of instrument. Negotiable instruments
should be in writing, signed by the drawer or maker, unconditionally
promising or directing payment or performance of a right or obligation
certain or ordinarily determinable[3], to a specified payee or bearer[4], on
demand or at a fixed or determinable future time[5]. The right or obligation
in question must be assignable in its nature and the instrument itself must
permit transfer, even if certain persons or classes are excluded from being
potential transferees.

Documents may only be negotiable which constitute an obligation or
undertaking to pay money (or deliver securities for money). Only documents which constitute an obligation or undertaking to pay money (or
deliver securities for money) may be negotiable. Documents pertaining to
goods are not negotiable[6]. Negotiability depends also upon the satisfaction of objective characteristics and not the subjective beliefs of parties,
even when shared by all of them. A negotiable instrument bearing evidence of intention to negative this quality, for example, a cheque marked
'not negotiable' clearly forfeits negotiability although remaining transfer-

---

1 With the exception of the Port of London warrants.
2 See generally *Stair* I,12,1; *Erskine* III,2,25; Bell *Commentaries* I,411; *Crouch v Credit Foncier of
   England* (1873) LR 8 QB 374; *Rumball v Metropolitan Bank* (1877) 2 QBD 194; *Edelstein v
   Schuler & Co* [1902] 2 KB 144; *Lawson's Executors v Watson* 1907 SC 1353, 15 SLT 245.
3 *Martin v Brash* (1833) 11 S 782; *Bovill v Dixon* (1854) 16 D 619 (affd (1856) 3 Macq 1, HL).
4 *Fraser v Bannerman* (1853) 15 D 756.
5 *Haddin v McEwan* (1838) 16 S 331; *Morgan v Morgan* (1866) 4 M 321.
6 Bills of lading are not negotiable instruments in a strict sense and the transferor's title to
   the bill and his competency to dispose of the goods are important factors in the validity
   of the transaction: see ch 9, pp 278 ff below.

able. The cheque would remain freely transferable though burdened by prior defects on title. Documents may acquire negotiability for the purpose of, and during, a specific transaction, arising from the operation of personal bar against one of the parties[1].

(3) NEGOTIABLE INSTRUMENTS AND THE CONSUMER CREDIT ACT 1974

The Consumer Credit Act 1974 introduced provisions to prevent companies from wrongly capitalising upon their position as a holder in due course of negotiable instruments in consumer transactions such as hire arrangements. (A trend had developed of finance companies enforcing rights irrespective of legitimate claims raised by hirers against dealers with regard to goods covered.) The Act governs and restricts the use of negotiable instruments in 'regulated' consumer credit agreements and in consumer hire agreements[2]. A prohibition exists upon the taking of negotiable instruments, other than cheques, in discharge of amounts payable by the debtor, hirer or cautioner[3]. The creditor or owner must not negotiate a cheque taken in discharge of any sum payable under a regulated agreement by the debtor or hirer or by any person as cautioner, except to a banker[4].

Under section 123(5), the provisions of the Act do not apply if the regulated agreement is a non-commercial agreement[5]. A non-commercial agreement is essentially a consumer credit or hire agreement not made by the creditor or owner in the course of business carried on by him.

Agreements in contravention of the 1974 Act are enforceable only by the order of the court[6] and if an application for the enforcement of any security is dismissed, the security is treated as ineffective[7] unless dismissed only on technical grounds. An individual contravening the provisions of the Act is not 'a holder in due course'. If the individual negotiates the instrument when not permitted to do so, it constitutes a defect in title within the meaning of section 125(2) of the Bills of Exchange Act 1882. The person to whom it is negotiated (where not notified of the defect) does become a holder in due course and nothing in the 1974 Act affects the right of a holder in due course of any negotiable instrument[8]. The provisions of the 1974 Act effectively preclude the use of bills of exchange (except cheques) and promissory notes in regulated agreements. Cheques only may be used for purposes of payment.

---

1 Cf *Edelstein v Schuler & Co* [1902] 2 KB 144.
2 Consumer Credit Act 1974, s 123.
3 1974 Act, s 123(1).
4 1974 Act, s 123(2).
5 1974 Act, s 189(1).
6 1974 Act, s 124.
7 1974 Act, s 106.
8 1974 Act, s 125(4).

(4)   THE JACK COMMITTEE'S PROPOSALS FOR NEGOTIABLE INSTRUMENTS

The Jack Committee proposed broad revision of the present law[1]. In terms of its proposed scheme an instrument would be classified as negotiable[2] where it was:

(1) a bill of exchange or promissory note as defined within the proposed new legislation ('The Negotiable Instruments Act'[3]);

(2) an instrument complying substantially with the basic requirements of negotiability[4] which ex facie exhibited the clear intention of the drawer or maker that it be negotiable;

(3) a close approximation in form and effect to other negotiable instruments (though not within head (2));

(4) an instrument recognised by custom or market practice as negotiable; and

(5) in all the circumstances, in accordance with established market practice and custom for the instrument to be treated as negotiable.

Existing instruments would remain unaffected, with the classifications serving as a measure against which to test negotiability.

As regards bills of exchange and promissory notes the view of the Jack Committee was that extraneous and collateral references necessary to effect such instruments were incompatible with the 'stand alone' principle, whereby negotiable instruments should be self-contained[5]. Therefore, while section 83(3) of the 1882 Act, allowing a pledge on a promissory note, would be retained, no other collateral references would be validly contained within bills or notes[6]. The Jack Committee suggested, however, that it would not be appropriate to impose such a prohibition with regard to instruments other than bills or notes, and their formulation was intended to accord, in a limited way, the status of negotiability to instruments which contain extraneous material that would be inadmissible were it to relate to bills or notes. One of the examples used by the Jack Committee was bearer share certificates which have traditionally been considered negotiable despite two characteristics. Firstly, they carry voting rights and other rights (such as dividends) which are not likely to be set out in the certificate itself, and secondly, some of these rights attaching to the instrument may be changed during the life of the instrument. It was the dilemma of the Jack Committee that such instruments retain negotiable status as they 'offend against the "stand alone" principle which is often said to be a mark of negotiability'[7]. Present law would be unaltered as regards there being no necessity for stating the date; or stating that

---

1 *Report of the Review Committee on Banking Services: Law and Practice* (the Jack Report) (Cm 622) (1989), ch 8.

2 Jack Report, recommendation 8(3).

3 Jack Report, paras 8.05–8.06 and recommendation 8(1).

4 Set out in the Jack Report at para 8.10.

5 Eg bearer share certificates which carry voting rights and other rights (such as a right to dividends) which will probably not be contained on the certificate itself.

6 Jack Report, para 8.12.

7 Jack Report, para 8.07.

value has been received; or stating the place where the bill was drawn or performed upon the actual bill or note[1].

Recommendation 8(5)[2] proposes a changed definition of 'sums certain' within section 3(1) of the 1882 Act. Under the present law such may comprise: a sum payable with interest; or a sum payable by instalments (with or without provision that upon default in payment of one instalment, the whole sum will become due); or a sum according to a certain rate of exchange[3]. The Jack Committee suggested that the new Act should make provisions so that the revised terminology would be: 'a certain or ordinarily determinable sum including instruments expressed in a monetary unit of account established by an inter-governmental institution'[4]. This alteration accommodates ECUs and Floating Rates Notes (FRNs) presently precluded. The Committee reasoned that instruments could be classified as negotiable where the source of uncertainty was a rate of interest or currency[4].

Presently, the governing law of a negotiable instrument is that of the place where the contract is made[5]. Consequently, there exists the possibility of obligations arising on an instrument governed by different laws where the bill is issued, indorsed and accepted in different jurisdictions. Equally, there exists no scope for the operation of the choice of the parties. The Committee sought to reconcile the provision of such choice and the necessity of maximum certainty once such a choice has been made. In modification of Professor Shea's (then Dr Shea) proposal[6] it was suggested that the drawer choose the law to govern the instrument, with any later modifications ignored[7]. Where no such choice is made, the instrument would be governed by the law of the place in which the party who is, or is intended to be, primarily liable on the instrument has an obligation to pay (where place is specified by the drawer or maker). If place of payment is not specified, it is the place where the drawer or maker has his principal place of residence or business. If this cannot be determined it would be the place where the instrument was signed[8].

2. PROMISSORY NOTES

A promissory note is an established credit instrument whereby A promises to pay a sum of money to B. The creditor may appoint an agent

1 Jack Report, para 8.13.
2 Jack Report, paras 8.17–8.19.
3 1882 Act, s 9(1). Cf *Carlon v Kenealy* (1843) 12 M & W 139.
4 Jack Report, para 8.19.
5 1882 Act, s 72.
6 Jack Report, Appendix A, para 8. Professor Shea's proposals are modified and adopted at recommendation 8(7) and paras 8.24–8.30 dealing with forged signatures. For present law and proposed alterations in respect of forgeries upon instruments, see pp 189 ff below.
7 Jack Report, para 8.21. See also recommendation 8(8) and para 8.31 which suggests the abolition of mandatory noting and protest; and recommendation 8(9) and paras 8.34–8.37 regarding the law relating to screen-based transfers.
8 Jack Report, paras 8.22–8.23.

for the purposes of collection, which may necessitate the presentation of formal authorisation where the note provides only for direct payment from A to B. No such difficulty arises where A provides in the note for payment to B or his nominee as A cannot contest his own instruction or provision. However, the promissory note's scope has expanded over time and may be employed as a monetary equivalent, being a means by which B can discharge his indebtedness to C (his creditor) by transferring to C a note payable to B or his nominee. C thereby collects for himself, not merely as an agent for B.

A promissory note is defined by section 83(1) of the Bills of Exchange Act 1882 as: 'an unconditional promise in writing made by one person to another[1] signed by the maker, engaging to pay, on demand[2] or at a fixed or determinable future time, a sum certain in money[3], to, or to the order of, a specified person or to bearer'. Part IV of the 1882 Act details the provisions applicable to promissory notes. A promissory note cannot be tied to any act other than the payment of money. In *Dickie v Singh*[4] it was held that a document which, in addition to an agreement to pay a sum of money, included a promise to employ and pay the staff of a business, was not a promissory note. In *Williamson v Rider*[5] the Court of Appeal held an instrument promising payment of money 'on or before Dec 31, 1956', was not a promissory note because it did not evidence payment at a fixed or determinable future time.

Section 83(2) of the 1882 Act provides that an instrument in the form of a note payable to the maker's order is not a note within the meaning of the section unless or until indorsed by the maker[6] and a note remains valid where containing a pledge of collateral security with authority to sell or dispose or it[7]. This provision permits of greater flexibility in the use of promissory notes. However, a document containing a pledge of collateral security expressed as being in the nature of a bond (or similar obligation) with security, will not be regarded as promissory note[8] but remains valid as an agreement between the parties[9].

In the case of *McTaggart v MacEachern's Judicial Factor*[10] it was said that a document is a promissory note where it fulfils the following qualifications: (a) it contains a promise to pay with no prescribed terminology; (b) a definite sum is payable thereunder; (c) the writing need not extend far beyond a bare promise of payment; and (d) the writing is entirely unilateral.

1 *Macfarlane v Johnston* (1864) 2 M 1210; *Duncan's Trustees v Shand* (1872) 10 M 984; *Thomson v Bell* (1894) 22 R 16.
2 *McCraw v McCraw's Trustees* (1906) 13 SLT 757, OH; *McAllister v McGallagley* 1911 SC 112, 1910 2 SLT 243; *McTaggart v MacEachern's Judicial Factor* 1949 SC 503, 1949 SLT 363, OH.
3 *Lamberton v Aiken* (1899) 2 F 189.
4 1974 SLT (Notes) 3. See also *Watson v Duncan* (1896) 4 SLT 75, OH; *Dickenson v Bower* (1897) 14 TLR 146.
5 [1963] 1 QB 89, [1962] 2 All ER 268, CA.
6 Cf s 61 of the 1882 Act for the provision for bills of exchange.
7 1882 Act, s 83(3).
8 *Kirkwood v Smith* (1896) 1 QB 582.
9 Section 83(4) of the 1882 Act distinguishes foreign and inland bills. See s 4 for the provision for bills of exchange.
10 1949 SC 503 at 507, 1949 SLT 363 at 365, OH.

The promise to pay has only two parties : the maker (liable to pay on the note) and the payee (or holder in the case of a bearer note) entitled to the money which the note represents. Bank notes are not simply promissory notes, but are rather part of the currency of the realm, resting upon a special statutory basis[1]. The notes remain inchoate and incomplete until delivery to payee or bearer[2] and therefore the liability of the maker is dependent upon delivery[3]. A note may be drawn by more than two makers, who may incur joint and several liability for it[4]. This provision is in contrast to the position as regards bills of exchange because in a bill of exchange, where there is acceptance by more than one person, they are liable jointly but not jointly and severally. A note in terms 'we promise to pay' or 'I promise to pay' signed by two or more obligants is, in Scotland, the joint and several obligation of all who sign it[5]. This provision constitutes an exception to the general proposition that a joint obligation is pro rata[6]. A note signed 'jointly' by two or more obligants will render each signatory liable only for his own share. In a joint note, as distinct from a joint and several note, the death of the maker extinguishes his liability as far as he is concerned, and the holder of the note will have no recourse against the deceased maker's personal representatives. The holder of a joint and several note has power to initiate several actions against each maker of a promissory note, a power denied to the holder of a 'joint' note. The holder should, in the latter instance, always sue all the makers of the note in the single action available to him.

A note may be payable on demand[7]. 'Payable on demand' means the same as with regard to bills of exchange[8]. A bill is payable on demand[9] where expressed to be payable as such, or at sight, or on presentation, or if no future time for payment is specified. A note may also be payable at a 'fixed or a determinable future time'[10].

Bills payable on demand cease to be negotiable once overdue (the intention being for immediate payment)[11]. Notes, however, are often essentially a continuing security and different rules apply[12]. Consequently, the holder of a note in circulation for an unreasonable time may still acquire good title as against the maker, even although any indorsers may already be discharged by operation of section 86(1) of the 1882 Act. This section, unlike section 45, dismisses only the indorsers and not the maker or makers of a note. Section 86(3) extends greater powers to the holders of demand notes than those enjoyed by holders of demand bills. The former may acquire the position of a holder in due course even where, ostensibly,

---

1 *Suffell v Bank of England* (1882) 9 QBD 555, CA.
2 1882 Act, s 84.
3 1882 Act, s 84; *Martini & Co v Steel and Craig* (1878) 6 R 342.
4 1882 Act, s 85.
5 1882 Act, s 85(2); *Smith's Executors v Johnston* (1901) 9 SLT 240, OH.
6 *Coats v Union Bank of Scotland Ltd* 1929 SC (HL) 114, 1929 SLT 477. See also Bell *Commentaries* I, 363.
7 1882 Act, s 86.
8 1882 Act, ss 10 and 89. Cf also s 45(2).
9 1882 Act, s 10.
10 1882 Act, s 11: some future date or after a specified event which is certain to occur.
11 1882 Act, s 36(2) and (3); *Smith's Executors v Johnston* (1901) 9 SLT 240, OH.
12 1882 Act, s 86(3).

the note is overdue at time of negotiation. Where a note is in the nature of a continuing security, delay in presentation is generally more acceptable[1].

Where the note is in the body of it made payable at a particular place, it must be presented for payment at that place in order to render the maker liable. Presentment is not necessary in any other case to render the maker liable[2]. Presentment for payment is necessary in order to render the indorser of a note liable[3]. Where the note is in the body of the instrument payable at a particular place, presentment at that place is necessary to render the indorser liable but where the place of payment is indicated by memorandum only, presentment at that place is sufficient to render the indorser liable; but a presentment to the maker elsewhere, if sufficient in other respects, will also suffice[4]. Presentment for payment must be clearly made before the indorser will be liable for payment. The holder must attempt primarily to obtain payment from the maker[5].

The 1882 Act imposes no time limit for presentment for payment, a position supported by the common law. In *Gordon v Kerr*[6] where a note specified the due date and the specific place of payment, presentment on a subsequent day was held to be sufficient.

By virtue of section 88 of the 1882 Act, the maker of a note engages that he will pay it according to its tenor[7] and he is precluded from denying to a holder in due course the existence of the payee and his then capacity to indorse the instrument[8]. This provision attempts to preclude unnecessary opportunities for fraud.

3.   BILLS OF EXCHANGE

(1)   HISTORICAL ORIGINS

For centuries, merchants transacted business outwith their own nations. Naturally, each merchant selling wished to be paid in his own currency. However, the physical transportation of money being inconvenient and hazardous, a system devised over time allowed the use of correspondents in the creditor's country. This localised payment and avoided transportation. The Bills of Exchange Act 1882 substantially codified the then existing common laws of Scotland and England on the subject[9].

For example:

> B in Paris desires to pay S in London for goods bought by B from S. B approaches X, a Paris money changer, and puts him in funds, in France, for

---

1 *Chartered Mercantile Bank of India, London and China v Dickson* (1871) LR 3 PC 574, PC.
2 1882 Act, s 87 (1).
3 1882 Act, s 87(2).
4 1882 Act, s 87(3).
5 See 1882 Act, s 45 for analogous bills of exchange provision.
6 (1898) 25 R 570.
7 1882 Act, s 88(1).
8 1882 Act, s 88(2).
9 *McLean v Clydesdale Bank Ltd* (1883) 11 R (HL) 1.

the price plus X's own charge. X draws a bill — a written request or instruction — upon Y, his foreign correspondent in London, requiring Y to pay the sum named to S. X then sends the bill to S. S presents the bill to Y, who pays in sterling. Later, X and Y, who have numerous dealings with each other, strike a balance upon their account and settle up.

The result is that: the risk of transporting gold between nations is avoided; if B was also being given credit, the inclusion of an obligation in the bill would provide S with an investment which he could sell before maturity; and if X knew B and Y knew S, each would be able to extend credit to his own national in respect of the bill.

In the inter-war years of 1918–1939, the importance of the bill dramatically declined as other forms of payment became more convenient. It does, however, retain some importance as a means of financing international trade although it is seldom encountered in inland transactions. The primary importance of the law relating to bills of exchange, at least in inland transactions, is that it includes the law relating to cheques. The Jack Committee outlined the nature and functions of the bill as[1]: (1) a means of settling a debt; (2) a form of currency; (3) a method of providing short-term finance; and (4) a means of guaranteeing another's obligations.

(2) DEFINITION OF BILL OF EXCHANGE

General

Section 3(1) of the Bills of Exchange Act 1882 defines a bill of exchange as:

> 'an unconditional order in writing addressed by one person to another, signed by the person giving it, requiring the person to whom it is addressed to pay on demand or at a fixed or determinable future time a sum certain in money to or to the order of a specified person, or to bearer'[2].

A bill therefore evidences a debt due and is also a negotiable instrument. It follows that valid transfer vests in the transferee the right to the obligation contained within the bill, without the necessity of intimation of transfer to the drawer of it. The transferee normally obtains absolute title to the bill free of any defects of title from which prior title holders suffered and a negotiated bill assigns, without intimation, the right it evidences. As a result, it operates as an assignation of funds[3].

In the modern market bills of exchange are a means by which to raise credit for the drawer's business operations in regard to bills drawn under acceptance credits. There also exists the possibility of 'bills drawn for accommodation'. In this situation a company or other enterprise allows another to draw on it in order to facilitate the discount of the bills involved. The accommodation party does not therefore stand to make

---

1 Jack Report, para 8.04.
2 The components of the definition of bill of exchange are considered in detail below.
3 1882 Act, s 53(2) (amended by the Law Reform (Miscellaneous Provisions) (Scotland) Act 1985, s 11).

direct profit from the acceptance of the bills and usually arises from a course of dealing between the parties. In the area of international obligations, a seller drawing a bill for the price of goods transported by land or sea, on the buyer, enables the bill to be discounted by the seller's own bank. It is in this way that the seller obtains the necessary funds before delivery of goods at their destination. Bills are fundamentally instruments of credit, and for a merchant holding a bill payable at a future date it is a saleable asset, acknowledgment of a debt due and immediately enforceable, if dishonoured. Bills are self-proving and are proof of their date without the need of witnesses and designations of the drawer and acceptor are not essential[1].

'An unconditional order in writing'

Meaning of 'unconditional'

'Unconditional' means that the bill is not subject to any conditions such as specification of the account from which payment must be made. An order may indicate an account from which the sums are to be paid[2], but payment cannot rest upon the realisation of a contingency. In the case of *Carlos v Fancourt*[3], Kenyan LJ explained the manner in which the possibility of conditional orders would 'unduly perplex the commercial transactions of mankind'. Instructions at the foot of the bill need not render them to be conditional[4]. In *Nathan v Ogdens Ltd*[5] the document stated that 'the receipt on the back must be signed'. The words were addressed to the payee and not the drawee and accordingly it was held that the order on the drawee remained unconditional. A bill must order unconditional payment to be valid, but it may be accepted or indorsed conditionally and remain valid.

Meaning of 'order'

A bill is an 'order', not a request for payment. This prerequisite does not preclude polite language but bills must clearly constitute orders[6]. In *Hamilton v Spottiswoode*[7] a document reading 'we hereby authorise you to pay on our account to the order of G, £6,000', was not a bill of exchange. An order requires imperative language and accordingly in *Little v Slackford*[8], 'please to let the bearer have £7 and to place on my account and

---

1 The Requirements of Writing (Scotland) Act 1995 abolished the status of privileged writings such as documents *in re mercatoria*.
2 *Re Boyse* (1886) 33 Ch D 612; *Bavins, Junior and Sims v London and South Western Bank* [1900] 1 QB 270, CA; *Chiene v Western Bank of Scotland* (1848) 10 D 1523; *Macfarlane v Johnston* (1864) 2 M 1210.
3 (1874) 5 Term Rep 482 at 485, CA; 1882 Act, s 11(3).
4 *Nathan v Ogdens Ltd* (1905) 94 LT 126, 22 TLR 57, CA; *Thairlwall v Great Northern Rly Co* [1910] 2 KB 509.
5 (1905) 94 LT 126, 22 TLR 57, CA.
6 *Airdrie Provost v French* (1915) 31 Sh Ct Rep 189.
7 (1849) 4 Exch 200, 18 LJ 393.
8 (1828) 173 ER 1120.

you will oblige your humble servant' was held not to constitute 'an order'. There is no necessity for the use of English language[1], nor is there any prescribed form, simply the requirement of the valid expression of an order[2].

The parties to a bill are the 'drawer' who orders payment of the sum; the 'drawee' who is the person on whom the bill is drawn, that is to say, recipient of the order (and who becomes the acceptor upon acknowledgment of the liability to the drawer by his signature[3]); the 'payee' who is the person to whom payment is made, that is to say the drawer himself, or a person specified in the bill, or the bearer[4]; the 'indorser' who is a holder of a bill payable to order who signs on the bill's reverse in order to render the bill in a deliverable state for transfer; and the 'indorsee' who is the person to whom the bill is assigned by the indorser's indorsement.

The order contained in a bill must be addressed to another entailing that the drawee need be named[5] or designated by means of reasonable certainty. A bill may be addressed to more than one drawee whether they are partners or not but not alternatively or in succession[6]. In the case of a bill not payable to bearer, the payee must be named or otherwise designated with sufficient clarity[7].

In instances where the payee is fictitious or non-existent the bill is treated as payable to bearer, enabling realisation and payment of the bill[8]. The strength and scope of this provision is that it entails that the mere fact of a bill being payable to a fictitious person will not affect the rights of a person subsequently receiving the bill and paying it in good faith[9].

Signed by the person giving the order

Signature may be by the drawer, or for him by an authorised individual. The method of signature is irrelevant so long as it is made with the intention of being the drawer's signature. No one is liable on a bill, in any capacity, unless he has signed it[10]. An agent may sign on behalf of the drawer, indorser or acceptor without the necessity of indicating his agency on the instrument[11]. An agent signing in his own name and then adding further words indicating his agency capacity would be sufficient[12]. The principal will be bound only if in accordance with the ordinary rules of the law of agency the agent is performing duties within the scope of his mandate[13].

---

1 *Re Marseilles Extension Railway and Land Co, Smallpage's and Brandon's Cases* (1885) 30 Ch D 598, DC.
2 *Ellison v Collingridge* (1850) 9 CB 570.
3 1882 Act, s 17(1).
4 Ie the person in possession of a bill or note payable to bearer: 1882 Act, s 2.
5 1882 Act, s 6(1); *Chamberlain v Young and Tower* [1893] 2 QB 206, CA.
6 1882 Act, s 6(2).
7 1882 Act, s 7(1). As to which see *McCubbin v Stephen* (1856) 18 D 1224; *Erskine* III,2,26.
8 1882 Act, s 7(3).
9 For analysis of the salient cases on s 7(3) of the 1882 Act, see pp 188, 189 below.
10 1882 Act, s 23.
11 1882 Act, s 91(1); *Union Bank of Scotland v Makin & Sons* (1873) 11 M 499.
12 1882 Act, s 25.
13 *Midland Bank Ltd v Reckitt* [1933] AC 1 at 16, HL, per Lord Atkin who rejected the reasoning of *Morison v London County and Westminster Bank Ltd* [1914] 3 KB 356, CA, that s 25 of the 1882 Act operated only prior to the honouring of the instrument; ie it does not, in Lord Atkin's view, demarcate a definite time period in which it operates.

Section 26 of the 1882 Act is declaratory of signatures by representatives in their capacity as agents. Signature on behalf of a principal does not incur personal liability of the agent but the mere addition to a signature of words indicating a qualified capacity does not, of itself, exclude an individual from the possibility of personal liability as evidenced in the case of *Rolfe Lubell & Co v Keith*[1]. In that case, the plaintiffs agreed to supply goods to a company on the basis that the bills drawn in payment would be personally indorsed by two of the officers of the company. The bills were accepted by the defenders. The managing director and the secretary of the company also signed the backs of the bills with a rubber stamp composed of the words 'for and on behalf of' the company and the designations 'Director' and 'Secretary'. Upon the putting of the company into receivership, the bills were dishonoured. The plaintiffs successfully sued the defenders claiming they were personally liable on the bills. In determining whether the signature on a bill is that of the principal or of the agent by whose hand it is written, the construction most favourable to the validity of the instrument is adopted. In *Chapman v Smethurst*[2] a promissory note by the defender, as managing director of a company, named above his signature was held to be the company's note[3]. In *Elliott v Bax-Ironside*[4], two directors of a company indorsed the back of a bill of exchange 'to guarantee the liability of the company' and it was held that the directors were treated as having indorsed the bill in a personal capacity. The courts will always look to the document as a whole in order to discover the capacity in which the signatory acts. It is impossible to be unequivocal in the stipulation of the words necessary to negative personal liability and great care must be taken.

A company as drawer of the instrument

It is possible to establish personal liability of a signatory for a company under section 349(4) of the Companies Act 1985[5]. If the officer of a company or a person on his behalf signs or authorises to be signed on behalf of the company, any bill of exchange, promissory note, indorsement, cheque or order for money or goods in which the company's name is not mentioned, he is liable to a fine[6]. He is also personally liable to the holder of the bill for the amount of it unless duly paid by the company. Personal liability attaches not only to the person signing the document, but also to the person authorising its signature. (The latter is personally liable only if he expressly authorises the signature by another of a document known to be irregular.) In *Durham Fancy Goods Ltd v Michael Jackson (Fancy Goods) Ltd*[7] the plaintiffs drew a bill on the defenders wrongly naming them 'M Jackson (Fancy Goods) Ltd' and prepared a form of acceptance in the

1 [1979] 1 All ER 860, [1979] 2 Lloyd's Rep 75.
2 [1909] 1 KB 927, 14 Com Cas 94, CA.
3 See also *Parker v Winlow* (1857) 7 E & B 942.
4 [1925] 2 KB 301, CA.
5 Previously s 108(4) of the Companies Act 1948.
6 1985 Act, s 349(1).
7 *Durham Fancy Goods Ltd v Michael Jackson (Fancy Goods) Ltd* [1968] 2 QB 839, [1968] 2 All ER 987.

same way. The company director and the company signed the acceptance unaware of the misdescription. The bill was dishonoured. It was held that the director was personally liable on the bill but the plaintiffs were personally barred from enforcing his liability since they were responsible for the error in the drawing up of the bill. In *Maxform SpA v Mariani and Goodville Ltd*[1] a company director of Goodville Ltd was held personally liable on bills drawn in the registered business name (Haldesign) without mention on the bills of Goodville Ltd. Mocatta J held that section 26(2) of the 1882 Act intended that the bill be seen holistically. It was plain the defender clearly purported to sign on behalf of the drawers. In *Banque de l'Indochine et de Suez SA v Euroseas Group Finance Co Ltd*[2] it was held that the company director was not liable personally simply due to the abbreviation of 'Company' to 'Co' since such was well established and understood. Similarly in *Barber and Nicholls v R and G Associates (London) Ltd*[3] the court would not impose personal liability on several dishonoured cheques where the bank had omitted 'London' from the company's printed name on the cheque forms. The omission was the fault of the bank and not the director upon whom the bank was trying to place personal liability[4].

Meaning of 'to pay on demand or at a fixed or determinable future time'

A 'bill payable on demand' is a bill expressed to be payable as such, or at sight, or on presentation, or, if no future time for payment is specified, a determinable future time[5]. A 'determinable future time', is some future date or after some specified event which is certain to occur[6].

In *Korea Exchange Bank v Debenhams (Central Buying) Ltd*[7] it was held that to state '90 days after acceptance' was not a determinable future time, since acceptance is never a certainty. Payment upon a contingency is prohibited even where the eventuality is realised and the happening of the specified event does not cure the defect. However, in *Creative Press Ltd v Harman and Harman*[8] a promissory note payable 'on or before' 1 November 1970 was held to be a valid promissory note, as it was payable at a determinable future time. A 'determinable future time' may include 'one year after my death'[9] and 'two months after demand in writing'[10].

---

1 [1979] 2 Lloyd's Rep 385.
2 [1981] 3 All ER 198.
3 [1985] CLY 129, CAT 81/455.
4 See also *Scottish and Newcastle Breweries Ltd v Blair* 1967 SLT 72, OH; *Gader v Flower* (1979) 129 NLJ 1266; *British Airways Board v Parish* [1979] 2 Lloyd's Rep 361, CA; *Calzafaturificio Fiorella SpA v Walton* (unreported) [1979] CLY 23, CLB 8.
5 1882 Act, s 10.
6 1882 Act, s 11; *Haddin v McEwan* (1838) 16 S 331; *Macfarlane v Johnston* (1864) 2 M 1210; *Morgan v Morgan* (1866) 4 M 321.
7 [1979] 1 Lloyd's Rep 100, revsd [1979] 1 Lloyd's Rep 548, CA.
8 [1973] IR 313.
9 *Roffey v Greenwell* (1839) 10 Ad & El 222, 8 LJQB 336.
10 *Price v Taylor* (1860) 5 H & N 540.

A sum certain in money

A sum certain in money may comprise: a sum payable with interest; a sum payable by instalments (with or without provision that upon default in payment of an instalment the whole of the sum becomes due); or a sum according to a certain rate of exchange.

In the event of a discrepancy between the expression of the sum in words and the sum in figures, words prevail[1]. Where such an error occurs upon a cheque, the banker upon whom the cheque is drawn in practice returns the cheque unpaid and marked: 'words and figures differ'. Where the collecting bank[2] notices the error and the payee is content to take the smaller of the two sums, the cheque is marked: 'we claim smaller amount' by the collecting bank.

Where a bill is expressed to be payable with interest, it will run from the date of the bill unless the contrary is expressly stated[3]; and where the bill is not dated, interest runs from the date of issue[4]. The interest payable must be certain or ascertainable by calculation on the basis of information contained within the bill itself[5]. A drawer leaving a blank for the words while filling in the figures, may, in negligence, be liable to the holder for the amount inserted in the vacant space[6]. Generally the drawer will have the opportunity to prove that the bill as issued did not contain the words subsequently added. If he is able to prove that the addition of the words were unauthorised the words will constitute an 'unauthorised alteration' upon which liability may not be founded.

'To or to the order of a specified person or to bearer'

A bill not payable to the bearer of it must name or otherwise indicate the payee with reasonable certainty[7]. In *Orbit Mining and Trading Co Ltd v Westminster Bank Ltd*[8] the plaintiff company had two directors authorised to sign cheques jointly on the company's account. One of the directors, Epstein, some time prior to joining the company, opened the account with the defendant bank. The bank was not informed of his new employment upon his joining Orbit. The company's other director, when going abroad, left crossed cheques signed in blank, with Epstein. Over a period of one year, Epstein paid in three cheques, completed with his own signature and made payable to 'cash or order' for the credit of his private account. Upon discovery of the fraud, the company brought an action against the bank for recovery of the value of the cheques totalling £1,800. MacKenna J held that the three instruments were not cheques within section 73 of the 1882 Act. Rather, they were documents intended to enable a person to

1   1882 Act, s 9(2); *Vallance v Forbes* (1879) 6 R 1099; *Garrard v Lewis* (1882) 10 QBD 30, 47 LT 408; *Bartsch v Poole & Co* (1895) 23 R 328; *Gordon v Kerr* (1898) 25 R 570.
2   *Sanderson v Piper* (1839) 5 Bing NC 425.
3   *Doman v Dibdin* (1826) Ry & M 381.
4   1882 Act, s 9(3).
5   *Morgan v Morgan* (1866) 4 M 321; *Tennent v Crawford* (1878) 5 R 433; *Vallance v Forbes* (1879) 6 R 1099; *Lamberton v Aiken* (1899) 2 F 189.
6   *London Joint Stock Bank v Macmillan and Arthur* [1918] AC 777, HL.
7   1882 Act, s 7(1); *Fraser v Bannerman* (1853) 15 D 756.
8   [1963] 1 QB 794, [1962] 3 All ER 565, CA.

obtain payment from a banker within section 17 of the Revenue Act 1883 and section 4(2)(b) of the Cheques Act 1957. Harman LJ in the Court of Appeal upheld this ruling and held that 'cash' is not a specified person, and therefore a document addressed to 'cash' could not be a bill, or by implication, a cheque. Further, any mandate to pay the bearer would require to be express and not implied. The bank had lost the protection of section 4 of the Cheques Act 1957 by its negligence.

(3) BILLS OF EXCHANGE AND PRESCRIPTION

In terms of the Prescription and Limitation (Scotland) Act 1973[1] any obligation under a bill of exchange[2] is extinguished by the short negative prescription of five years. The result is that the bill is extinguished as a document of debt but the debt itself is not[3]. Payment of interest upon a prescribed bill or debt after the period of prescription has expired, is valuable proof of the existence of the debt[4]. However, a bill of exchange which has prescribed cannot be used to establish the existence of the debt or part of it[5].

(4) FORGED OR UNAUTHORISED SIGNATURES

Generally, a signature which is forged, or which is unauthorised by the person whose signature it purports to be, is inoperative and no right to retain the bill or to give valid discharge or to enforce payment against any party to it can be acquired under that signature[6]. This rule does not operate where the party against whom it is sought to retain or enforce payment of the bill is precluded from setting up the forgery for want of authority. It does not affect the ratification of unauthorised signatures which are not forgeries[7] and indeed a forged signature may be adopted[8]. Where an individual asserts that a signature was neither adhibited by him nor with his authority, the person seeking to enforce payment under the bill bears the onus of proof of the validity of the signature[9]. The party denying the validity of the signature may however be prevented from so doing on account of his conduct or by his negligence or delay in taking action once aware of the forgery[10]. It is fundamental that no one deriving title through

1 Prescription and Limitation (Scotland) Act 1973, s 6, Sch 1, para 1(e).
2 The prescriptive period runs from the date of maturity of the bill, fixed date in case of a time bill or from expiry of the period allowed if payable at a certain period after sight or demand.
3 See also *Easton v Hinshaw* (1873) 1 R 23; *MacBain v MacBain* 1930 SC (HL) 72; *Russland v Allan* [1976] 1 Lloyd's Rep 48.
4 *Campbell's Trustees v Hudson's Executor* (1895) 22 R 943.
5 *Russland v Allan* [1976] 1 Lloyd's Rep 48.
6 1882 Act, s 24.
7 *British Linen Co v Cowan* (1906) 8 F 704.
8 *MacKenzie v British Linen Co* (1881) 8 R (HL) 8.
9 *British Linen Co v Cowan* (1906) 8 F 704; *McIntyre v National Bank of Scotland Ltd* 1910 SC 150, 1910 1 SLT 63.
10 *Brook v Hook* (1871) LR 6 Exch 89; *MacKenzie v British Linen Co* (1881) 8 R (HL) 8; *British Linen Co v Cowan* (1906) 8 F 704; *Greenwood v Martins Bank Ltd* [1933] AC 51, HL.

a forged indorsement may become a holder in due course. In *Williams v Williams*[1] it was held that if A induces B to draw a bill in favour of C under false pretences and C takes it in good faith and for value, the innocent third party C, being the original payee, is not a holder in due course and cannot enforce payment. The Jack Committee[2], in considering the necessary extent of protective rules in favour of other parties against forged signatures (indorsers, drawers or acceptors) weighed the relative vulnerability of the layman dealing with cheques against the commercial experience of those dealing in the specialised area of bills or notes. It was felt legitimate to distinguish the two situations for that reason. The Committee made the following proposals.

Generally:

(1) Retention of the existing law that:
   (a) a bank is able to recover from a person wrongly paid unless personally barred; and
   (b) a bank is not normally entitled to indemnity from its customer for wrongful payment.
(2) New provisions whereby:
   (a) a bank would be entitled to indemnity if the customer were negligent thereby contributing to the loss;
   (b) if the bank were also negligent, the loss would be apportioned between the parties according to their degrees of negligence; and
   (c) if the customer had indemnified the bank in whole or in part he would be able to recover from the payee unless personally barred.

With regard to forged or unauthorised indorsement:

(1) Retention of the law that:
   (a) the true owner claims compensation from the bank paying the wrong person, and the bill is discharged upon compensation;
   (b) the paying bank has the right to recover from the person wrongly paid (unless personally barred). The collecting bank would similarly recover from its customer.
(2) New provisions whereby:
   (a) the paying bank would be entitled to indemnity from its customer, the drawer or acceptor (if accepting a bill or note payable at the bank);
   (b) the bank could not place any reliance on indemnity where it is negligent, unless the customer were also negligent, in which case losses would be apportioned according to relative degrees of negligence;
   (c) if the customer indemnified the bank or is required to contribute to the loss, he should be able to assert whatever right the bank had to recover from the payee.

1 1980 SLT (Sh Ct) 25.
2 Jack Report, paras 8.24–8.30, recommendation 8(7).

The parties would be able to vary the rule by contractual agreement without such agreement being subject to any modifications under the Unfair Contract Terms Act 1977[1].

(5) GIVING OF VALUE TO ACQUIRE STATUS OF 'HOLDER IN DUE COURSE'

It is generally considered that for an individual to acquire the status of holder in due course under section 29(1) of the 1882 Act, such person should have given value personally. It follows that section 27(2) protection, whereby a holder is deemed to be a holder for value where value is at any time given for the bill, does not apply[2]. The Court of Appeal in *Clifford Chance v Silver*[3] decided the point contrary to the established academic position. It was held that a party who has not personally given value may rely on section 27(2) in order to become a holder in due course. The facts of the case were that Clifford Chance (CC) were indorsees of a cheque drawn by a solicitor, Silver, payable to a firm of solicitors, Frederick, Hass and Stone (FHS). CC received the cheque as a result of various property transactions including the sale of land by a client of CC to FHS's client, Mr Abili. The deposit under the first sale was £100,000. Silver sent FHS a cheque for this sum on 12 December 1990 which, along with another cheque represented the deposit agreed for the subsequent land sale. The cheque was indorsed 'sans recours' by FHS and was delivered to CC to be held to the order of FHS pending exchange of the contracts. On 10 January 1991, the contracts were exchanged. The following day CC presented the cheque for payment which was dishonoured a few days later. CC thus sought to recover the amount against Silver. At first instance it was found for CC. On appeal one of the arguments was that CC were not holders in due course of the cheque and were therefore subject to any defences possibly raised — particularly those to which the payees would have been vulnerable. In support of this contention, the appellant submitted that at the time of the negotiation of the cheque, CC were aware that the title of FHS was defective; and that CC did not themselves give value for the cheque and could not therefore satisfy the first limb of section 29(1)(b). As regards the question of value, the court deemed that consideration for the cheque had been given when the contracts were exchanged[4] and CC were holders for value pursuant to section 27(2). This was deemed sufficient to enable the holder to acquire the status of a holder in due course[5]. Neill LJ cited as authority Milmo J in *Barclays Bank Ltd v Astley Industrial Trust Ltd*[6]. This case concerned section 27(3) of the 1882 Act, deeming a person to be a holder for value where he is the holder of a bill over which he has a lien. Milmo J held that a person would be regarded as having given value for a bill pursuant to section 29(1) of the 1882 Act if he could establish qualifi-

---

1 Jack Report, para 8.30.
2 Cf Goode *Commercial Law* (1982) p 448; Chalmers and Guest *Bills of Exchange* (14th edn, 1991) p 274.
3 [1992] NPC 103, (1992) Times, 11 September, CA.
4 [1992] NPC 103, (1992) Times, 11 September, CA, per Neill LJ and Sir Christopher Slade.
5 Under the 1882 Act, s 29(1).
6 *Barclays Bank Ltd v Astley Industrial Trust Ltd* [1970] 2 QB 527 at 538.

cation under section 27(3). Thus a person deemed to be a holder for value by virtue of section 27(3) is in the same position as a person who 'took for value' within section 29(1). A person seeking status as a holder in due course may satisfy the requirement to give value by relying upon section 27(2)[1]. This position introduces some consistency with section 27(3), and section 30(2) is also relevant. Every holder is prima facie presumed to be a holder in due course but if, in an action, it is established to the contrary that acceptance, issue or subsequent negotiation of a bill is affected with fraud, duress, force and fear or illegality, the burden of proof is shifted unless and until the holder proves that, subsequent to the alleged fraud or irregularity, value in good faith has been given for the bill. Thus, where one of the circumstances in section 30(2) applies and the holder seeks to be a holder in due course, he must show that value has been given in good faith. Alternatively, the holder should demonstrate all the elements of section 29(1)[2]. Section 30(2) only requires that value be given. Following the academic position to establish the status of holder in due course under section 29(1) the holder would have to establish that he personally gave value (or had a lien pursuant to section 27(3)) and accordingly *Clifford Chance v Silver* provides some consistency in these various and complementary provisions. The Jack Committee suggested abandonment of the need for establishment of consideration as a test of negotiability[3]. This would leave two categories of holder: a holder in due course and a holder[4]. The Jack Committee also recommended clarification of section 30(2). Unfortunately, the government White Paper[5] neglected to adopt or implement either of the two suggestions.

(6) NOTICE OF DISHONOUR OF BILLS OF EXCHANGE

The drawer and each indorser of a bill is entitled to notice of non-payment by way of a notice of dishonour. Notice of dishonour is formal notification of the dishonouring of the bill and its purpose is to alert the party receiving it that he has potential to the holder of the bill while preserving the rights of the holder against the parties receiving notice. Delay in giving notice of dishonour is excused where the delay is caused by circumstances beyond the control of the person giving notice and is not due to his default, negligence or omission[6]. Where due notice is not given, and the lapse is not excused by the circumstances, the drawer and any indorser is discharged from any liability both upon the bill and the consideration for which it was given[7]. This principle applies even although the omission has

1 The same view appears to be taken by Mustill LJ in *MK International Development Co Ltd v The Housing Bank* (1992), Financial Times, 22 January, CA.
2 See *Barclays Bank Ltd v Astley Industrial Trust Ltd* [1970] 2 QB 527, [1970] 1 All ER 719. A payee of a bill cannot be a holder in due course: *Williams v Williams* 1980 SLT (Sh Ct) 25.
3 Jack Report, para 8.16.
4 Jack Report, Appendix N, technical recommendation 24: value would be retained as a test of good faith for establishing a holder in due course.
5 *Banking Services: Law and Practice* (Cm 1026) (1990).
6 1882 Act, s 50(1).
7 *Eaglehill Ltd v J Needham Builders Ltd* [1973] AC 992, [1972] 3 All ER 895, HL.

not given rise to loss and is somewhat anomalous in that the drawer is entitled to notice despite him being primarily liable upon the bill[1].

The requirement for notice of dishonour is dispensed with:

(1) where after reasonable diligence the drawer or indorser cannot be found;
(2) by express or implied waiver;
(3) as regards the drawer in the following cases, namely,
   (a) the drawer and drawee are the same person;
   (b) the drawee is fictitious or does not have capacity to contract;
   (c) the drawer is the person to whom the bill is presented for payment;
   (d) where the drawee or acceptor is as between himself and the drawer under no obligation to accept or pay the bill; and
   (e) where the drawer has countermanded payment[2];
(4) as regards indorsers of bills, in the following cases,
   (a) where the drawee is a fictitious person or a person not having capacity to contract and the indorser is aware of such fact at the time he indorsed the bill;
   (b) where the indorser is the person to whom the bill is presented for payment; and
   (c) where the bill was accepted or made for his accommodation[3].

Section 49 of the 1882 Act provides for what constitutes a valid and effectual notice of dishonour. The key ingredients are that the notice must be given by or on behalf of the holder or indorser who, at the time of giving the notice, is himself liable on the bill. Notice may also be given by an agent, appropriately authorised, in his name or in that of the party entitled to give the notice. The notice must be in writing or by any form of personal communication in terms sufficient to identify the bill and intimating the fact of dishonour by non-acceptance or non-payment. It should also be intimated that the bill has been noted or protested, as should any recourse claimed against the party to whom the notice is given. Misdescription on the face of the notice will not invalidate it unless it results in the misleading of the person to whom the notice was given[4]. The notice must be given to any person to whom it is required or to his agents. In *Crosse v Smith*[5] oral notice to a solicitor was held to be insufficient but in *Viale v Michael*[6] it was held that written or verbal notice to a 'merchant's clerk' at his place of business would be sufficient. In cases where the drawer or indorser is known to be deceased, notice requires to be given to their personal representatives where they can be found. In the case of a bankrupt drawer or indorser, notice should be given to that party as well as to his trustee.

---

1 1882 Act, s 48 ; *Caunt v Thompson* (1849) 18 LJCP 125; *McLelland v McKay* (1908) 24 Sh Ct Rep 157.
2 1882 Act, s 50(1), (2). See *Bank of Scotland v Lamont & Co* (1889) 16 R 769; *Mactavish's Judicial Factor v Michael's Trustees* 1912 SC 425, 1912 1 SLT 134.
3 1882 Act, s 50(2)(d); *McLelland v McKay* (1908) 24 Sh Ct Rep 157; *Aberdeen Town and County Bank v Davidson* (1955) 71 Sh Ct Rep 212.
4 *Mellersh v Rippen* (1852) 7 Exch 578.
5 (1813) 1 M & S 545.
6 (1874) 30 LT 453.

Where there is more than one drawer or indorser notice should be given to them all unless one of them is authorised to receive notice on behalf of them. The notice of dishonour must be given immediately upon the bill being dishonoured or within a reasonable time thereafter[1]. Where an agent is in possession of a dishonoured bill he may either notify all the parties liable upon the bill or intimate appropriately to his principal[2]. The agent must notify his principal within the same time limit as if he were the holder of the bill and thereafter the principal upon receiving the notice has the same time for notification as if he were an independent holder[3].

There are elaborate and intricate rules relating to the protesting of bills of exchange which do not apply to cheques. The crucial question in issues of dishonour notices relates to their timing[4].

Section 98 of the 1882 Act provides that the Act does not affect the law with regard to summary diligence. It remains incompetent to do summary diligence on an unpaid cheque[5].

4. CHEQUES AND ANALOGOUS INSTRUMENTS

(1) INTRODUCTION

The statutory definition of a cheque is: 'a bill of exchange drawn on a banker payable on demand'[6]. Cheques accordingly bear all the characteristics of bills of exchange and synthesis with the defining section of a bill of exchange[7] yields the following definition:

> 'an unconditional order in writing signed by the person giving it, requiring the banker to whom it is addressed to pay on demand a sum certain in money to, or to the order of, a specified person or bearer'.

The elaboration of many of the salient characteristics of this definition have been discussed with regard to bills of exchange[8]. While cheques are properly a species of the genus 'bill of exchange'[9], certain features are peculiar to cheques with specific relationships and consequences arising from the use of cheques which are absent in the treatment and use of other bills. In so far as the two species intersect, they are governed by the same provisions of the 1882 Act. The principal statutory differences are dealt with in the Cheques Act 1957, the main effect of which is largely to remove the need to indorse cheques in the transmission process.

---

1 *Hirschfield v Smith* (1866) LR 1 CP 340; *Gladwell v Turner* (1870) LR 5 Exch 59. See also *Fielding & Co v Corry* [1898] 1 QB 268, CA.
2 *Lombard Banking Ltd v Central Garage and Engineering Co Ltd* [1963] 1 QB 220, [1962] 2 All ER 949; *Yeoman Credit Ltd v Gregory* [1963] 1 All ER 245, [1963] 1 WLR 343.
3 See 1882 Act, s 49; *Westminster Bank Ltd v Zang* [1966] AC 182, [1966] 1 All ER 114, HL.
4 See Wallace and McNeil's *Banking Law* (10th edn, 1991 by D B Caskie) pp 101–103.
5 *Glickman v Linda* 1950 SC 18, 1950 SLT 19, OH.
6 1882 Act, s 73.
7 1882 Act, s 3(1).
8 See pp 182–189 above.
9 See *McLean v Clydesdale Bank Ltd* (1883) 11 R (HL) 1; *Glen v Semple* (1901) 3 F 1134; *Bank of Scotland v Rorie* (1908) 16 SLT 21, OH.

Cheques serve two basic functions. Firstly, they allow a customer maintaining a current account to obtain repayment of the funds lent by him to his bank. In this instance, the customer would draw the cheque payable to his own order and cash it at the bank counter. Secondly, they enable the payment of an amount due from the drawer to a third party. The cheque is drawn in favour of the third party payee and is passed to him. The cheque is the customer's instruction to the bank to pay a specified amount to the payee or transferee.

Apart from cash, cheques are the most common means of payment in modern transactions. Nonetheless, the rate of increase in the volume of cheque usage is declining, as it is superseded by technological advances. The number of cheques used in 1915 totalled approximately 300 million and in 1985 approximately 3,700 million. However, the relative importance of the cheque and the automated teller machines (ATMs) as a means of withdrawing cash is evidenced by the recent predominance of the latter: In 1987, ATMs were the means by which over 60 per cent of all cash withdrawals from personal accounts with banks and building societies were made[1]. It is likely that the trend has expanded with the importance of cheques for cash withdrawal declining. In August 1996 the Association for Payment Clearing Services reported that personal cheque usage declined by a further 7 per cent in 1995[2]. It does, as the Jack Committee observed, remain a legal anachronism that cheques are a sub-set of bills of exchange when cheques long ago surpassed bills as a form of payment instrument. The Jack Report and the Cheques Act 1992 both reflect growing concern as to the safety of cheques as a means of payment. Cheques are predominantly an instruction to transfer part of the balance of one bank account to another and accordingly need be neither transferable nor negotiable. However, they still bear these characteristics as they are sometimes passed on to a third party by the original payee. The present law allows the interposing of a holder or holders between the drawer of the cheque and the ultimate payee, and it is this characteristic which increased the possibility of fraud and irregularities. This weakness, coupled with the diminishing of the capacity of the collecting and paying banks to detect fraud, led to the Jack Committees's proposals[3] and the consequent Cheques Act 1992.

(2)   DISTINGUISHING CHARACTERISTICS OF A CHEQUE

The primary feature of a cheque is that it is drawn on a banker and several important consequences result. Cheques do not require acceptance by the drawee as in bills. They are intended as a payment instruction and not for commercial circulation. It follows that as cheques are intended for immediate payment they become more rapidly overdue than ordinary bills. However, the drawer of the cheque is only discharged from performance by reason of delayed presentment where such delay is unreasonable, and to the drawer's real prejudice.

---

1 See Jack Report, para 2.24 and Appendix D for relevant statistics.
2 See The Herald, 19 August 1996.
3 See pp 208–210 below.

Presentment of a cheque for payment

A cheque not presented within a reasonable time of issue, where the customer had the right at the time of presentment to have the cheque paid (as between himself and the banker) and suffers actual damage as the result of delay, is discharged to the extent of the damage, that is to say to the extent to which such drawer is the creditor of such banker to a larger amount than he would have been had the cheque been paid[1]. What is a 'reasonable time' depends upon the nature of the instrument, the usage of the trade and of bankers, and all the facts and circumstances of the case[2]. The holder of a cheque as to which such drawer is discharged is the creditor, in lieu of the drawer, of such banker to the extent of the discharge, and is entitled to recover the amount from him[3].

Under section 74 of the 1882 Act, delay in presenting a cheque for payment does not discharge the drawer of the cheque unless actual damage is sustained by the delay. As between the drawer and the payee, unless the drawer proves actual loss as a result of the delay in presentation, the holder may present it at any time up to five years from its date[4]. However, a cheque is drawn essentially as a means of payment and not so as to be negotiated in the market. It is upon the basis of general banking practice that banks in Scotland regard cheques presented six months or more after their date as 'stale' and refuse payment until they receive confirmation of the cheque from their customer. The provisions of section 74 of the 1882 Act are intended to protect the drawer of a cheque who suffers because of the holder's failure to present the cheque for payment within a reasonable time and the bank becomes insolvent.

Drawn upon a banker

A cheque must be drawn on a banker. The cheque must be addressed by name to a person or body of persons whether incorporated or not, carrying on the business of bankers. A sub-branch of a bank cannot competently draw a cheque on another branch or the head office of the same bank. The bank is treated in law as an institution, as a single entity and therefore as a single party. Cheques must be drawn by and upon distinct parties[5]. It follows that an instrument drawn by one sub-branch of a bank upon another, is treated as either a bill of exchange or a promissory note (at the option of the holder)[6].

---

1 1882 Act, s 74(1). Cheques are dealt with by Pt III (ss 73–81) of the 1882 Act.
2 1882 Act, s 74(2).
3 1882 Act, s 74(3).
4 Prescription and Limitation (Scotland) Act 1973, s 6, Sch 1, para 1(e).
5 1882 Act, s 5(2).
6 *Capital and Counties Bank Ltd v Gordon* [1903] AC 240, HL. The 1882 Act, s 5(2) reflects the decision in *Prince v Oriental Bank Corpn* (1878) 3 App Cas 325, PC. It also illustrates the error in Bailhache J's decision in *Ross v London County Westminster and Parr's Bank Ltd* [1919] 1 KB 678 that one branch could draw a cheque upon another branch; see *Slingsby v Westminster Bank Ltd* [1931] 1 KB 173, 100 LJKB 195.

The customer's mandate

A cheque is the customer's mandate but is not, strictly speaking, the instruction of a debtor to discharge, wholly or partially, a debt owing to a third party. The individual drawing the cheque (the drawer) bears primary liability to the payee by virtue of the instruction to his banker to appropriate sums of his money to the payee. The drawer of a cheque is in reality the acceptor of it as a bill of exchange. The parties to a cheque generally conform to those to a bill of exchange, that is, drawer, drawee and payee. The drawer is usually referred to as the 'customer', unless the bill is drawn in a capacity distinct from that of customer. The drawee is necessarily the banker. In general course only the drawer signs, neither the payee nor the drawee being a signatory to the cheque, only the drawer signs. Therefore, neither the payee nor the drawee is strictly a party to the cheque. However, any additional party signing a cheque acquires the status and incurs the liability of a party to the bill. Cheques are payable on demand[1].

(3) ESSENTIAL REQUIREMENTS OF A CHEQUE

An unconditional order

A cheque must be unconditional[2] and is still an unconditional order, notwithstanding that the drawer is discharged if the cheque is not presented within a reasonable time[3]. It is only the order that need be unconditional. Any instrument conditional upon a specified event — most commonly completion of a receipt form on the document by the banker — is a 'conditional order to pay' and not a cheque[4]. An order to pay money on the condition that the payee complete such a receipt form on the document, would fall within the terms of the Cheques Act 1957[5]. Where the order regarding the completion of the receipt form is addressed to the payee as opposed to the banker, the cheque is treated as unconditional[6].

Where the order to complete the receipt is addressed to the banker, the paying banker normally takes from his customers issuing such instruments an indemnity against loss. The Cheques Act 1957 places him in the same position as if he had paid on the cheque. The collecting banker may have the same protection as if the instruments were cheques[7]. However, such protection may be lost in the case of evidence of such an instrument having been transferred and the collecting banker should only, therefore, handle such instruments for the named payee. Cheques incorporating a form of receipt normally have printed upon them a bold 'R'.

---

1 For definition of 'payable on demand', see pp 187, 188 above.
2 Cf 1882 Act, ss 3(3) and 11 in respect of bills of exchange. For discussion of term 'conditional', see p 184 above.
3 1882 Act, s 74; *Thairlwall v Great Northern Rly Co* [1910] 2 KB 509 at 520, per Coleridge J.
4 *Bavins, Junior and Sims v London and South Western Bank* [1900] 1 QB 270, CA; *Capital and Counties Bank Ltd v Gordon* [1903] AC 240, HL.
5 Cheques Act 1957, ss 1(2)(a), 4(2)(b) and 5.
6 Cf *Nathan v Ogdens Ltd* (1905) 94 LT 126, 22 TLR 57, CA; *Thairlwall v Great Northern Rly Co* [1910] 2 KB 50; *Roberts & Co v Marsh* [1915] 1 KB 42, CA.
7 Cheques Act 1957, ss 1 and 4.

In writing

Cheques must be in writing. While the form and medium of any writing is not prescribed, in practice banks prefer to demand the drawing of cheques on prefabricated official forms legible by computers[1]. Generally cheques include three strips of magnetically imprinted figures on the left hand bottom margin of the cheque form representing the individual cheque number, the branch's national number (the sort code), and the drawer's account number.

Cheque books also contain a single sheet at the back for bank use only, for the purpose of recording the cashing of cheques through other banks or branches with a cheque guarantee card guaranteed to a prescribed limit. The page is stamped to indicate the date of withdrawal. Where one withdrawal is already made within any particular day, at any branch or bank, the verification and confirmation of the issuing bank is usually necessary prior to any second payment. There is no theoretical necessity that a cheque be written in ink; however, practice and the susceptibility of pencil writing to forgery and alteration, dictate the universal use of ink. Banks generally return unpaid a cheque written in pencil, requesting confirmation of the instructions in ink[2]. The signature of the drawer is required but there is no prescribed place for adhibition. In practice, signature is upon the lower right-hand corner of the cheque form. The signature must be either (1) that of the account holder or (2) that of a party authorised to sign on behalf of the account holder or authorised to sign in his own name. There is no necessity for subscription: all that is required is sufficient authentication of the drawer's instructions and consequently, a self-proving cheque as regards the drawer containing his name is adequate. The banker is required and ought only to honour cheques signed in the manner and style agreed with and familiar to the customer. Where the manner is unfamiliar to the customer, the banker is not required to honour the cheque, even upon adequate proof of authenticity. Any form of stylistic irregularity ought to result in the rejection of the cheque and loss resultant upon wrongful failure to reject such a cheque on this basis falls upon the banker.

Payable to a specified person or to bearer

Cheques must be payable to a specified person or bearer[3]. It follows that a cheque payable to bearer is negotiated by delivery without indorsement; and a cheque payable to order is payable to the order of the drawer and requires his indorsement. An instrument made payable to 'cash or order'

---

1 Cf *Burnett v Westminster Bank Ltd* [1966] 1 QB 742, [1965] 3 All ER 81.
2 Cf *Geary v Physic* (1826) 5 B & C 234.
3 For discussion of this term in relation to bills of exchange, see pp 188, 189 above.
   Chamberlain v Young and Tower [1893] 2 QB 206, CA ('to order' indicates 'to my order');
   Orbit Mining and Trading Co Ltd v Westminster Bank Ltd [1963] 1 QB 794, [1962] 3 All ER
   565, CA.

is not a cheque within the terms of the 1882 Act[1]. It may, however, constitute a valid order for the payment of money[2] and a bank paying such an instrument to an employee or agent of the drawer obtains a good discharge[3].

A cheque payable to 'AB or order' is negotiated by indorsement completed by delivery. Where there is indorsement in blank, the cheque is payable to bearer[4]. A cheque payable to more than one person ('AB and CD') or order, requires indorsement by all to be rendered negotiable. Where payable to more than one person jointly and severally it is payable to and negotiated by the indorsement of any one of them. A cheque payable in the alternative to one of two persons is negotiable by the indorsement of either of them[5]. Cheques payable to the holder of an office for the time being are payable to such an individual[5]. Where cheques are only payable to such an individual and not to the person 'or order' implying the intention that payment be non-transferable, it is not negotiable by the indorsement of the payee. Where payable to 'holder or order' it is negotiable by the indorsement of the payee. Indorsement bears the signature of the holder of the office and a designation of his position.

A cheque payable to 'pay or order' is not a bill since there is no payee[6]. It is prudent for a banker not to pay bills in such a form and it is not advisable to allow the holder to insert his own name as payee[7].

Any omission in a bill must be completed within a reasonable time and in specific conformity with the authority conferred. That the instrument is not a cheque does not preclude the court from finding that the drawer intended the banker to pay out on the instrument to the person presenting the document[8]. In *Daun and Vallentin v Sherwood*[8] Kennedy J held that a promissory note without a payee, containing neither the words 'order' nor 'bearer' was payable to the bearer because that was the natural legal effect. Such reasoning, however, is inappropriate in an instance where the use of the words 'or order' negates the concept of a cheque being payable to bearer[9]. Cheques which bear restrictive directions (for example: 'to A only'; 'for the account of B'; or 'to A or order for collection') indicate restrictive intentions and preclude the negotiation of the cheque. The banker is liable to the drawer in repetition of the amount in the case of an indorsee misapplying it. The drawer may indicate on the face of the cheque form an intention that payment be made only to a specified payee.

1 Falling within ss 1(2)(a), 4(2)(b), 5 of the Cheques Act 1957.
2 *Henderson, Sons & Co Ltd v Wallace and Pennell* (1902) 5 F 166 (it is questionable whether a cheque payable to 'to ... or order' could be valid in the absence of the completion of the blank); *North and South Insurance Corpn Ltd v National Provincial Bank Ltd* [1936] 1 KB 328.
3 1882 Act, s 34.
4 1882 Act, s 7(2).
5 *R v Randall* (1811) Russ & Ry 195, CCR; *R v Richards* (1811) Russ & Ry 193, CCR.
6 Any authority yielded by s 20 of the 1882 Act is prima facie only and may have been revoked.
7 *North and South Insurance Corpn Ltd v National Provincial Bank Ltd* [1936] 1 KB 328. As regards personal bar/estoppel, see *London Joint Stock Bank v Macmillan and Arthur* [1918] AC 777, HL: the operation of personal bar relates to the payee, the holder in due course and the paying bank.
8 (1895) 11 TLR 211 at 212.
9 *Chamberlain v Young and Tower* [1893] 2 QB 206, CA.

Such intention is indicated by the addition of 'only' after the payee's name; or by the deletion of 'or order' by the drawer; or simply by adhibiting 'not transferable' on the face of the cheque form. Such a cheque must not be honoured by a banker having any suspicion or evidence of the transfer of the cheque.

A cheque drawn in favour of fictitious or non-existent persons is treated as payable to the bearer, even where the drawer intended payment to a person believed to be existent[1]. The paying banker is protected in dealing with such cheques[2]. The collecting banker is also protected[3]. These provisions enable realisation and payment of the bill and the fact of the bill being payable to a fictitious or non-existent person will not affect the rights of any person receiving or paying for it in good faith. Included are cases where the payee is actually non-existent and also cases where the name of an existing person is inserted by the drawer without any intention that that person should receive the money or have any association with the bill.

In *Vagliano Brothers v Governors & Co of Bank of England*[4] the plaintiffs, a London firm of merchants, banked with the Bank of England. The firm corresponded regularly with Vucina and drew bills on Vagliano in favour of Petridi & Co. A clerk in Vagliano's forged a series of bills purportedly drawn on Vagliano by Vucina in favour of Petridi. The clerk also forged corresponding letters of advice. Vagliano accepted the forged bills which were subsequently misappropriated by the clerk, who indorsed them with a forgery of Petridi & Co's signature. On maturity (the time at which payment of the bill may properly be demanded by the holder) the clerk presented the bills at the Bank of England. The bank paid over the counter to the clerk upon advisement of Vagliano's acceptance and then debited Vagliano's account. Vagliano discovered the fraud and brought an action to determine whether the bank was entitled to debit their account with the amount of the misappropriated bills. Vagliano argued that the forged payee's indorsement resulted in payment being made to one unable to give good discharge and therefore in terms of section 24 of the 1882 Act the bank was not entitled to debit Vagliano's account. The bank argued that Vagliano's negligence precluded them from setting up the forgery of Petridi's indorsement and that the bank received protection[5]. In the House of Lords, Lord Halsbury LC and Lord Selbourne held that the bank was authorised in making the relevant payments. As regards the general rule relating to personal bar on the basis of negligence, it was held that the negligence relied upon must be the direct and proximate cause of the false signature being taken as genuine. The payees in the bill (Petridi) were held to be fictitious within the scope of the section. The bills were payable to bearer and the payment sufficiently discharged the bills. Both Lord Macnaghten and Lord Herschell took 'fictitious' to be synonymous with 'feigned' or 'counterfeit' as opposed to 'imaginary'. Thus 'fictitious' did not connote the absence of real existence but the pretence of purporting to

1 1882 Act, s 7(3).
2 1882 Act, s 60.
3 1882 Act, s 7(3); Cheques Act 1957, s 4.
4 (1889) 23 QBD 243, CA; *revsd sub nom Bank of England v Vagliano Bros* [1891] AC 107, HL.
5 Ie under the 1882 Act, s 7(3).

be something not truly the case. The fact of the actual existence of Petridi & Co did not alter the position that within this particular bill, Petridi & Co were utterly fictitious[1], in the sense of 'counterfeit'. Upon this interpretation the intention of the clerk is determinative of the construction of 'fictitious'. The actual subsisting status of Petridi & Co is irrelevant. Lord Bramwell and Lord Field both dissented from the majority holding that Petridi as a matter of fact existed and could not therefore be imaginary.

In *Clutton v Attenborough & Son*[2] it was held that where a drawer is induced by fraud to draw the bill in favour of a person whom he believed to exist but who was actually non-existent, it is immaterial in a question with a good faith holder for value. The cheques in question were drawn in favour of someone named B, a person whose name might hypothetically exist, nonetheless the payee of the cheque remained fictitious on the basis that the name had been provided by the person wishing to commit the fraud and the company had no acknowledgment of anyone of that name.

In *Vinden v Hughes*[3], Warrington J held that it was relevant only to look at the state of matters at the time the cheque was drawn. The payee was not a fictitious or non-existing payee because at the time the cheques were drawn the drawer intended certain identifiable persons to receive the relevant sums[4]. The particular importance of section 7(3) of the 1882 Act is that it enables any forged indorsement purporting to be that of the payee to be disregarded. It allows the paying bank to debit its customer's account correctly with the amount of the cheque.

The following guidelines may be drawn from the principles of the common law. Firstly, the intention of the drawer of a cheque where the drawer contemplates an existing and definite person, with the intention that he become the payee, will render such payee 'not fictitious' under section 7(3) of the 1882 Act. This remains the case even where, by third party inducement or fraud, such person never acquired or exercised rights in relation thereto. Secondly, where, by third party fraud, someone is induced to draw a cheque in which the name inserted as payee is that of an imaginary person (though persons of such designation may exist) such is regarded 'fictitious or non-existent' — even where the drawer contemplates or intends someone of that name to receive the money. Finally, a cheque encompassed within section 7(3) of the 1882 Act which is treated as payable to bearer applies not only to a holder for value, but to anyone else in whose interest it is so to treat it (for example, a banker who has paid such a bill on a forged indorsement).

(4) CROSSED CHEQUES

The origin of the practice of crossing cheques

The practice of crossing cheques grew out of the practice of London bankers who in 1775 set up the London Bankers' Clearing House where

---

1 Cf *Bank of England v Vagliano Bros* [1891] AC 107 at 161, HL, per Lord Macnaghten.
2 [1897] AC 90, HL.
3 [1905] 1 KB 795.
4 [1905] 1 KB 795 at 800.

cheques given to bankers for collection by their customers could be taken and passed over to the representatives of the bank upon which the cheque was drawn. As a means of identifying the cheques the bank employee wrote across them the name of the bank handing them over for payment. In this way, a bank dishonouring a cheque would know to which bank it should be returned[1]. Over time drawers of cheques adopted the practice[2] and would mark their cheques with the name of the payee's banker (a special crossing) or, if unaware of the payee's place of banking would simply add the words '& Co' (a general crossing). It was in this way that the drawer was able to ensure that his cheques were paid through a banker and bankers construed the crossing as an instruction only to pay the cheque through a banker.

Legislation on the matter originated in the Drafts on Bankers Act 1856 which made it an offence to fraudulently alter or erase crossings upon cheques and the Crossed Cheques Act 1876 rendered banks liable to compensate the true owner of a cheque when paying the cheque in contravention of the crossing. Prior to the Act the position was uncertain and the need for clarification through statute was becoming increasingly obvious[2]. The Act also gave recognition to 'not negotiable' crossings, while also laying the basis of protection afforded to bankers by section 82 of the Bills of Exchange Act 1882 and section 4 of the Cheques Act 1957.

The nature of crossings

The protection afforded to a banker and drawer on a crossed cheque is contained in section 80 of the 1882 Act. Any crossing results in the paying banker receiving protection only where he pays the cheque to another banker. With the exception of a 'not negotiable' crossing, no crossing affects the negotiability of a cheque. Crossings protect the rights of the true owner of the cheque while also protecting the rights of its drawer. In the event of the bank paying a cheque in a manner contrary to the crossing, it exceeds its authority and is not entitled to debit the drawer's account[3]. However, in an action brought by the drawer or true owner of a cheque, a drawee bank will desire the protection of section 80 where in accordance with the tenor of a crossing, it pays the cheque.

Types of crossing

There are two particular types of crossing. Firstly, general crossings which involve two transverse parallel lines, with or without the words 'and company' (or any abbreviation thereof, typically '& Co') and with or without the words 'not negotiable' — the form most frequently used is two transverse lines alone[4]. Secondly, special crossings which involve two

---

1 Early discussions of the practice are contained in *Bellamy v Marjoribanks* (1852) 7 Exch 389 at 402 and *Carlon v Ireland* (1856) 5 E & B 765, 25 LJQB 113.
2 See *Smith v Union Bank of London* (1875) 1 QBD 31, CA.
3 *Bobbett v Pinkett* (1876) 1 Ex D 368 at 372, 373.
4 1882 Act, s 76(1).

transverse parallel lines, with or without 'not negotiable' bearing also the name of a specific bank — the intended collecting bank[1].

Crossing by a holder

The holder of a cheque need not be a 'holder for value'. Section 2 of the 1882 Act defines a holder as the payee or indorsee of a bill in possession of it, or a bearer thereof. It follows that 'a holder' need not be a lawful holder of the cheque and a thief in possession of a bearer cheque is a holder. An agent for the collection of a cheque is a holder of the cheque[2], and a collecting banker may alter a general crossing in the same way as any transferee acquiring the cheque in his own right. An innocent purchaser for value of an order cheque under a forged indorsement is not a holder, except with the operation of personal bar against an indorser subsequent to the forgery[3]. Such a possessor of the cheque could not, therefore, cross or afford the paying bank protection[4].

Crossings by the collecting bank

In the case of a cheque crossed specially, the banker to whom it is crossed may cross it again, specially to another banker for collection[5]. The objective of this provision was to enable banks who were not members of the clearing house system to remit cheques payable to customers to a clearing bank for payment. Prior to the Cheques Act 1957, crossed and uncrossed cheques had very differing effects upon collecting banks; now they have much the same effect[6].

Crossings between branches of a bank

Cheques may be presented for payment crossed to two offices of the same bank, the cheque having been transmitted from one branch to the other for convenience of collection. The second of these crossings straddles sections 5, 6 and 7 of the 1882 Act, while not fitting exactly into any of them. The head office and sub-branches of a bank are treated as a single entity[7] and consistency would suggest that the crossing is not strictly a crossing to another banker.

---

1 1882 Act, s 76(2). For the execution and effect of crossings, see the 1882 Act, s 77. The drawer or holder may cross a cheque generally or specially: s 77(2). Where the cheque is crossed generally, the holder may cross it specially: s 77(3). Where the cheque is crossed generally or specially, the holder may add the words 'not negotiable': s 77(4). A cheque crossed specially to a banker may be crossed again, specially, by the banker to whom it is addressed, to another banker for collection: s 77(5). A banker receiving an uncrossed or generally crossed cheque may cross it specially to himself: s 77(6).
2 *Akrokerri (Atlantic) Mines Ltd v Economic Bank* [1904] 2 KB 465; *Sutters v Briggs* [1922] 1 AC 1, HL; *Baker v Barclays Bank Ltd* [1955] 2 All ER 571, [1955] 1 WLR 822.
3 1882 Act, s 55(2). See generally *Phillips v Italian Bank Ltd* 1934 SLT 78, OH.
4 *Akrokerri (Atlantic) Mines Ltd v Economic Bank* [1904] 2 KB 465.
5 1882 Act, s 75(5).
6 See generally *Capital and Counties Bank Ltd v Gordon* [1903] AC 240, HL, affg [1902] 1 KB 242, CA (s 55(2) of 1882 Act).
7 See p 196 above.

Alteration or erasure of crossings

A crossing is a material part of a cheque and save where an addition is authorised by the Act, it is unlawful for any person to alter or tamper with a crossing[1].

Bankers' duties with regard to crossed cheques

A bank on whom a cheque is drawn, crossed specially to more than one banker (save where a second special crossing is to a banker for collection) is bound to refuse it. Where the customer of a collecting bank has no title to the cheque, failure to refuse it will render the bank liable to the true owner of the cheque for any losses he might sustain by reason of wrongful payment. In *Smith v Union Bank of London*[2] a cheque was crossed to two bankers and was paid by the drawee bank to the holder of the cheque despite the crossings. The Court of Appeal held that the negotiability of the cheque was not affected and that the holder was the lawful owner of it. This case, interestingly, was the catalyst to recognition in the 1876 Crossed Cheques Act of the 'not negotiable' crossing.

If a drawee bank pays a cheque other than in a manner authorised by the crossing, it is liable to compensate the true owner of the instrument for any loss sustained by the latter due to the improper payment of the cheque[3]. However, where a cheque is presented for payment and does not, at that time, appear to be crossed or to have had a crossing altered or erased, the drawee bank does not incur liability to the true owner, provided the cheque is paid in good faith and without negligence by him. If a paying banker disregards a crossing, he is negligent and if he pays the cheque to a thief or finder, or upon a forged or unauthorised indorsement or in disregard of a general or special crossing, he will be liable to the true owner in instances where that owner can prove that he has suffered loss by the cheque having been paid[4]. The banker may not debit the drawer's account upon the basis of his negligence and payment is in breach of his customer's mandate.

Opening a crossing

It is possible to neutralise a crossing by writing 'pay cash' on the face of the cheque and initialling the amendment[5]. This is referred to as opening the crossing and a drawer may open a crossing only before the cheque is delivered to the payee or at the request of the payee after delivery. It is the essence of the matter that after a cheque has been issued by the drawer, he cannot retract or neutralise the mandate to the prejudice of any party

1 1882 Act, s 78. Section 64 (2) defines 'material' for the purposes of the Act.
2 (1875) 1 QBD 31, CA.
3 1882 Act, s 79(2); *Phillips v Italian Bank Ltd* 1934 SLT 78, OH.
4 *Smith v Union Bank of London* (1875) 1 QBD 31, CA; *Bobbett v Pinkett* (1876) 1 Ex D 368.
5 *Smith v Union Bank of London* above.

taking the cheque as delivered to him[1]. Paget[2] is of the view that if a cheque is a crossed cheque and notwithstanding the crossing has been opened, it is prudent that the paying bank should review paying over the counter unless completely satisfied that he is adhering to the drawer's intention. A paying banker who pays a crossed cheque which has been opened is entitled to indemnity from his customer unless the opening is a forgery, in which case it is ineffective and contrary to the customer's mandate. Any opening requires the full signature of the drawer to the alteration in order to be valid[3].

A 'not negotiable' crossing

'Not negotiable' crossings are authorised by section 76 of the 1882 Act, and in terms of section 81 of the Act 'where a person takes a crossed cheque which bears on it the words "not negotiable", he shall not have and shall not be capable of giving a better title to the cheque than that which the person from whom he took it had'. Such a crossing renders the cheque transferable but not negotiable. Accordingly, each transferee takes the cheque subject to all the defects of title affecting prior parties to the cheque, thus the transferee cannot accordingly become a holder in due course with all the resultant benefits. If a cheque is obtained from the drawer by fraud and marked 'not negotiable' the drawer is not liable to an innocent third party who gives value for the cheque. Such a provision affords protection to the original, true owner of the cheque, thereby preserving his rights against any subsequent holder. In *Great Western Railway Co v London and County Banking Co Ltd*[4] a Mr Huggins falsely pretended to the appellants that sums were due from them to him. He obtained a cheque drawn by them on the London Joint Stock Bank, payable to 'Huggins or order'. The cheques were marked '& Co' and 'not negotiable'. Huggins indorsed the cheque and presented it for payment at the respondent bank. The bank (as requested by Huggins) paid part of the amount of the cheque into a current account of one of the bank's customers and the balance was paid to Huggins in cash, with which he absconded. The respondent bank crossed the cheque to themselves and sent it to their head office for collection through the clearing system. Upon discovery of the fraud, the appellants sued the respondent bank. In the House of Lords, Lord Halsbury LC stated that 'people who take a cheque which is upon its face "not negotiable" and treat it as a negotiable security must recognise the fact that if they do so they take the risk of the person for whom they negotiate it having no title to it[5]', and Lord Lindley stated 'every one who

---

1 *Smith and Baldwin v Barclays Bank Ltd* (1944) 5 LDAB 370 at 375.
2 Paget's *Law of Banking* (11th edn, 1996 by M Hapgood QC) p 246.
3 Statement of Committee of London Clearing Bankers (7 November 1912) (but often in practice the full signature of the drawer is not a requirement).
4 [1901] AC 414, HL. Cf also *Universal Guarantee Pty Ltd v National Bank of Australasia Ltd* [1965] 1 Lloyd's Rep 525 at 531, PC; *Miller Assocs (Australia) Pty Ltd v Bennington Pty Ltd* (1975) 7 ALR 144 (Aust).
5 *Great Western Rly Co v London and County Banking Co Ltd* [1901] AC 414 at 418, HL.

takes a cheque marked "not negotiable" takes it at his own risk, and his title to the money obtained by it, is as defective as his title to the cheque itself'[1].

Location of the crossing

The 'not negotiable' crossing must be combined with either a special or general crossing[2] in order to effect the intention that the instrument become non-negotiable[3]. The words need not appear within the crossing (as '& Co' must) but require to be on the face of the cheque.

The title to the cheque — void or voidable?

In a cheque marked 'not negotiable' it is irrelevant whether any defect in title is such as to render it void or voidable. Lord Lindley in *Great Western Railway Co*[4] explained that such debate is redundant since whichever case applies the instrument is still not negotiable[5]. The situation differs from the general case, in which (in a negotiable instrument) an instrument voidable, but not void, renders to the person in possession of it, a temporary, revocable property in the instrument[6].

'Account payee' crossing prior to the Cheques Act 1992

Crossings could take the form of 'account payee' or 'account payee only'. An 'account payee' crossing does not have the authority of the 1882 Act. In *National Bank v Silke*[7] it was decided that an 'account payee' crossing should not be construed as a direction to the drawee bank[8]. In *A L Underwood Ltd v Bank of Liverpool and Martins*[9] it was held that the words had no effect upon the negotiability of the cheque although they may have some effect in restraining transfer in practice. Absence of statutory authority does not however, in some instances, prevent common law acceptance of the crossing. In *House Property Co of London Ltd*[10] the plaintiff company dealt in property. The other plaintiffs were trustees of a trust account and the plaintiff company had mortgaged a property to the trust. Norman, a solicitor to the trustees, wrote a fraudulent letter calling in the mortgage.

---

1 [1901] AC 414 at 424, HL. Cf also *Morison v London County and Westminster Bank Ltd* [1914] 3 KB 356 at 375, CA.
2 1882 Act, s 76.
3 1882 Act, s 81.
4 *Great Western Rly Co v London and County Banking Co Ltd* [1901] AC 414 at 424, HL.
5 1882 Act, s 81 and the *nemo dat quod non habet* rule.
6 Cf *Great Western Rly Co v London and County Banking Co Ltd* [1900] 2 QB 464 at 474, CA, per Vaughan Williams LJ (reversed by House of Lords on other points).
7 *National Bank v Silke* [1891] 1 QB 435 at 439, CA.
8 Were the Court of Appeal to have reached the contrary view, it would have required the drawee bank only to pay the cheque if presented for the account of the payee. It would have been impractical to impose such an obligation upon the drawee bank.
9 [1924] 1 KB 775, CA, per Scrutton LJ.
10 *House Property Co of London Ltd and Baylis and Burlacher v London County and Westminster Bank* (1915) 84 LJKB 1846.

After negotiation, the plaintiff company arranged to repay £800 of the mortgage money due and sent a cheque to the solicitor. The cheque was drawn to the trustees 'or bearer' and crossed 'account payee'. The solicitor misappropriated the cheque and payment was made to the credit of his personal account. An action was brought on the basis that the collecting banker was negligent in receiving a cheque so crossed for one other than the named payee. The bank argued that the cheque was a bearer cheque and the bank having collected it for the payee as bearer was not liable. The bank was held not to be negligent. Rowlatt J stated 'on the meaning of this document, I cannot in the least doubt that "account payee" does not mean the account of the man who in the process of negotiation is the owner of the cheque when collected'[1].

'Account payee only' as an extended crossing has been the subject of a number of cases[2]. In *Importers Co Ltd v Westminster Bank Ltd*[3] Aitken LJ expressed the view that the additional word 'only' had no effect or importance and did not impose any further obligation upon the banker. Lord Upjohn in *Universal Guarantee Property Ltd v National Bank of Australasia*[4] said of the words 'not negotiable':

'The words "not negotiable" do not prevent the cheque from being negotiated but mean that the holder of the cheque cannot have, and is not capable of giving, a better title than that of the holder from whom it is obtained'.

And of the words 'account payee only', Lord Upjohn said:

'The addition of the words "account payee only" refers to the payee named in the cheque and not the holder at the time of presentation but they do not prevent, at law, the further negotiation of the cheque. The words merely operate as a warning to the collecting bank that if it pays the proceeds of the cheque to some account it is put on inquiry and it may be in difficulty in relying on any defence ... in an action against it for conversion of the cheque'.

Crossing of analogous instruments

The provisions of crossings applying to cheques where relevant also apply to dividend warrants[5]. Further, the relevant sections are extended to 'any document issued by a customer of a bank which, though not a bill of exchange, is intended to enable a person to obtain payment from that banker of the sum mentioned in the document'[6]. The provisions also apply to 'any document issued by a public officer which is intended to enable a person to obtain payment from the Paymaster General or Queen's and Lord Treasurer's Remembrancer of the sum mentioned in the document'[7].

1 (1915) 84 LJKB 1846 at 1847. See also *Kenton v Barclay's Bank Ltd* in Chorley and Smart *Leading Cases in the Law of Banking* (6th edn, 1990) p 186.
2 Eg *Sutters v Briggs* [1922] 1 AC 1, HL; *Universal Guarantee Pty Ltd v National Bank of Australasia Ltd* [1965] 2 All ER 98, [1965] 1 Lloyd's Rep 525, PC.
3 [1927] 2 KB 297, CA.
4 [1965] 2 All ER 98, [1965] 1 Lloyd's Rep 525, PC.
5 1882 Act, s 95.
6 Cheques Act 1957, s 4(2)(b), read with s 5.
7 1957 Act, s 4(2)(c), read with s 5.

(5)   THE JACK COMMITTEE: CROSSINGS AND 'BANK PAYMENT ORDERS'

Crossings

While crossings evolved as an administrative convenience, their primary role was to enhance the security of cheques as a means of payment[1]. They were not, however, wholly effective in protection of either the drawer or the payee. The very limited and technical nature of crossings tend to confuse both drawers and drawees. In fact, many users believe themselves to be enjoying greater protection than they actually do[2]. The general misunderstanding of these statutory provisions was further hindered by the confusion of the terms 'negotiable' and 'transferable'.

The Jack Committee sought to minimise and clarify the available crossings to drawers of cheques[3]. Transverse parallel lines would, the Jack Committee suggested, be retained as a crossing upon the basis that they approximated reasonably closely to what was generally believed to be the actual legal effect. It was also suggested that such crossings imply not only payment to a bank but they would also be 'not negotiable' without the addition of these words. In this way, the Jack Committee sought to provide non-negotiable status for a greater number of cheques and thus reduce the opportunities for fraud and irregularities. However, the result would necessitate that any person wishing to make payment by way of a crossed cheque without destroying its negotiability would now require to use an uncrossed cheque with all its attendant risks. The Jack Committee took the view that the benefits of clarity and simplicity would considerably outweigh these risks.

The view was also taken that there should be no legal recognition of the terms 'account payee' or 'account payee only' as crossings, as such represent an instruction to the collecting bank with which the drawer of the cheque has no contractual relationship[4]. The view was taken that confusion was heightened by the restrictive legal force afforded to these terms in certain cases[5]. Several consultees suggested that 'account payee' be given statutory recognition as a crossing more accurately reflecting and enforcing the drawer's intention that the proceeds of the cheque be made available only to the named payee. However, the Committee considered that this view placed an unreasonable burden upon the paying bank which had generally no means of ensuring that the drawer's instruction be complied with. This would, however, not be the case if 'account payee' operated not as a crossing but as an instruction to the collecting bank in terms which removed the bank's statutory protections if the cheque were collected for other than the account of the payee. In either case, the collecting bank would be required to ensure that any cheques so annotated were not paid into the account of a third party. The view was taken that the delay

1 *Report of the Review Committee on Banking Services: Law and Practice* (the Jack Report) (Cm 622) (1989).
2 1882 Act, 76; see also ss 80–81A.
3 Jack Report, para 7.15.
4 Jack Report, para 7.17.
5 *National Bank v Silke* [1891] 1 QB 435, CA.

which this process would generate at bank counters and the resulting inconvenience to the customer (along with increased costs to the bank) would negate and outweigh any advantages of it. It was in conjunction with this proposal for the introduction of a new non-transferable instrument operating alongside the cheque[1] that the Committee took the view that there was no need to retain the 'account payee' crossing which should therefore, in their view, be denied legal effect[2]. The Jack Committee also proposed the abolition of the special crossing authorised by section 76 of the 1882 Act on the basis of its infrequent use[3]. If abolished, the banks would simply rubber stamp the name of the collecting bank across the face of the cheque as a means of identification during the clearing process. It would be in this way that there would be retained only the two transfer line crossings, making a cheque non-negotiable and requiring payment only to the banker[4]. Both the Treasury and the Department of Trade and Industry approved these proposals of the Jack Committee.

'Bank payment orders'

The Jack Committee proposed the introduction of a new instrument called the 'bank payment order'('BPO') which would lack the qualities of transferability and negotiability and thus further reducing any opportunities for fraud[5]. In the case of such an instrument the banks would be required to collect the cheque on behalf of the named payee only. It was not intended that the BPO would wholly replace the cheque as it was believed that if some of the adult population in the UK did not have bank accounts through which to collect cheques it would be unfair to prevent the possibility of obtaining payment by indorsing the cheque to a third party. Although legislation would be required to introduce the new instrument, the Jack Committee took the view that the additional transitional problems of cost, confusion and customer eduction would be justified by the certainty and simplicity that their proposals entailed. The new instrument would be distinguished from cheques by the characteristic whereby the proceeds would be paid only to the person specified as the payee in the BPO in order that it could not be transferred or negotiated. Like a crossed cheque, the BPO would be addressed by the account holder or his agent; addressed to the banker holding his account; require the banker to pay on demand, for a specified sum in writing, and only through the agency of the collecting bank (or internal transfer if the accounts of the payer or payee were held at the same bank).

The Jack Committee's views as to the legal characteristics of the BPO are as follows:

(1) The payee of the BPO would be able to sue on it in his own name.
(2) The forged or unauthorised drawer's signature would be wholly inoperative and the drawee bank would be unable to debit the customer's account.

---

1 See 'Bank payment orders' below.
2 Jack Report, para 7.20, recommendation 7(2).
3 Jack Report, para 7.21, recommendation 7(3).
4 Jack Report, para 7.22, recommendation 7(4).
5 Jack Report, paras 7.29–7.34, recommendation 7(7).

(3) The BPO would be discharged by payment in due course, or if the payee renounced rights against the drawer, or if the BPO were intentionally cancelled by the payee, or if it were fraudulently or materially altered by anyone but the drawer.

(4) A paid order or a photocopy or other reproduction of it would be evidence of receipt by the payee of the specified sum.

(5) Presentment of the BPO would not operate as an assignation of funds in the hands of the drawee bank.

(6) Rules governing the presentment for payment would still be required and these should specify that presentment be made if a demand for payment is made at a bank, and that such demand may be made by exhibiting the payment order to the drawee bank or by any other means whereby the identity of the BPO were reasonably certain and in a form intelligible to and decipherable by the drawee bank. Since instruments would only be presented by a bank to the drawee bank, it should not be necessary to be more specific as to the place of presentment.

(7) Provided the paying bank acts in good faith and without negligence it should have protection upon the same basis as is currently afforded to cheques under section 80 of the 1882 Act whereby it is protected if paying to a bank presenting the order for payment, but not otherwise.

(8) The collecting bank would be protected against claims by the true payee on the same basis as suggested in para 7.27 of the Jack Report with regard to cheques. If the bank were acting as an agent for another bank, these requirements would apply to that other bank.

(6)   THE CHEQUES ACT 1992

The government responded to the Jack Committee's report in a White Paper. A Private Member's Bill was introduced to the House by Conal Gregory MP, at the instigation of the Consumers' Association and with the aid of the British Banker's Association and the Treasury to amend the law regarding cheques. The resulting Cheques Act 1992 became effective from 16 June 1992 and introduced the following important changes.

Section 1 of the 1992 Act added a new section 81A to the 1882 Act. Section 81A(1) provides:

> 'Where a cheque is crossed and bears across its face the words 'account payee' or 'a/c payee', either with or without the word 'only', the cheque shall not be transferable, but shall only be valid as between the parties thereto'.

This clause applies the provisions of section 8(1) of the 1882 Act to cheques bearing a crossing accompanied by the words 'account payee only'. This form of cheque has the same effect as one in which the words 'non transferable' appear or one in which the word 'only' is added after the payee's name. It is in this way that under section 8(1) and section 81A of the 1882 Act, the title to an instrument bearing any of these formulae cannot be passed by way of negotiation. The original payee to whom the instrument has been issued, remains its owner notwithstanding any attempt to transfer the title to the instrument. The transferee has no enforceable title and cannot bring an action to enforce the cheque in his own name. Section 81A(2) provides:

> 'A banker is not to be treated for the purposes of section 80 as having been negligent by reason only of his failure to concern himself with any purported indorsement of a cheque which under subsection (1) above or otherwise is not transferable'.

It therefore follows that a bank collecting upon an 'account payee' crossed cheque for someone other than the named payee is not liable for any loss incurred by the true holder of the cheque or the drawer, provided the banker acts in good faith and without negligence. Banks may accordingly still safely act upon indorsement on cheques instructing the transfer of an 'account payee' cheque provided it is satisfied as to the authenticity of the indorsement. In instances where the bank is not so satisfied it would be vulnerable to claims from the person to whom the cheque ought to have been paid. It also follows that a bank is not protected by section 4 of the Cheques Act 1957 where it collects a cheque crossed 'account payee only' for an account other than that of the person named without first obtaining an adequate explanation[1]. Where a suitable explanation is given the bank continues to avoid liability[2].

Crossings which are now acceptable are[3]:

(1) a general crossing — two transverse lines across the face of the cheque;
(2) special crossing — two transverse lines between which the name of a specified bank is written, which bank alone should receive payment;
(3) account payee — crossing as detailed[4] and previously affected by the common law and legislated for in the 1992 Act; and
(4) a 'not negotiable' crossing[5].

It is a demonstrative feature of the 1992 Act that it opposes many of the objectives and suggestions of the Jack Committee whose proposals won the approval of both the Treasury and the Department of Trade and Industry. Perhaps part of the reason is that the 1992 Act received its impetus from consumers' associations which focus the Act on attempts to cure the primary difficulty of cheque forgery and minimise public concern regarding increasing theft and misappropriation of cheques with consequent lack of general consumer protection. In rejecting the Jack Committee's proposals regarding crossings they also rejected the 'bank payment order' concept[6] upon the basis that there was no need for such a non-transferable payment order in light of the developing UK giro system. Some writers including Ellinger[7] consider that the drawing of non-

---

1 *Akrokerri (Atlantic) Mines Ltd v Economic Bank* [1904] 2 KB 465; *House Property Co of London Ltd and Baylis and Burlacher v London County and Westminster Bank* (1915) 84 LJKB 1846.
2 *Souhrada v Bank of New South Wales* [1976] 2 Lloyd's Rep 444.
3 1882 Act, ss 76, 81A (s 81A added by the Cheques Act 1992, s 1).
4 See p 120 above.
5 1882 Act, s 81.
6 *Banking Services: Law and Practice* (Cm 1026) (1990), Appendix 5, para 5.6.
7 See 'Is there a need for non-transferable cheques?' (1992) 108 LQR 15.

transferable cheques places a burden on the banking system without conferring upon the customer defences significantly more effective than those provided by the crossing 'non negotiable — account payee only'.

Cancellation of designation 'account payee'

There is nothing in the Cheques Act 1992 to prevent customers of banks from cancelling the designation 'account payee' on pre-printed cheques provided by banks. Cancellation must be made by the drawer of the cheque at or before the time of issue and must be authenticated by the drawer's full signature and not merely initials. Cancellation may accordingly circumvent the 1992 Act's purpose of preventing the misappropriation of cheques. Banks receiving or collecting such cheques may decline to accept them as the validity of the cancellation may be open to challenge. Where customers of banks are aware that recipients of cheques do not have banks accounts, or where, as drawers, they are anxious to make the cheques transferable, a non-transferable cheque is not an appropriate instrument for that purpose. A better course of action for a customer is to use a completely open cheque or cheques bearing the traditional crossing of two parallel lines with or without the words '&·Co'. It is worthy of note that solicitors who handle non-transferable cheques payable to their clients incur a degree of risk. Scottish clearing banks[1] are prepared to enter into individual arrangements with legal firms regarding the practice of continuing to handle crossed cheques or indorsed cheques on behalf of solicitors and clients in circumstances whereby the solicitors have signed a form indemnifying the bank from any losses which might result from such transactions. The standard form of indemnity presently in use includes authority granted by the solicitor permitting the debiting of losses incurred by the bank against the solicitor's firm account. Solicitors should ensure that any form of indemnity they agree to sign obliges the bank to redebit such losses against the firm's account and not the client's account in contravention of the Solicitors (Scotland) Account Rules.

(7)   INDORSEMENT OF CHEQUES

Negotiation of a cheque occurs upon transfer from one party to another so as to constitute the transferee the holder of the cheque[2]. While delivery alone is sufficient as regards a bearer cheque[3], a cheque payable to order requires the indorsement of the holder prior to delivery[4]. Indorsement has, however, become increasingly infrequent since the operation of the Cheques Act 1957 and the Cheques Act 1992 but it still remains effective as a means of enabling the indorsee of a cheque to sue the indorser and any previous holder of it. Indorsement proper will involve the holder of

---

1 Statement of the Committee of Scottish Clearing Bankers on the Cheques Act 1992 (1993) 38 JLSS 33, 34.
2 1882 Act, s 31(1).
3 1882 Act, s 31(2).
4 1882 Act, s 31(3).

the cheque signing the reverse of it prior to delivery, and it is in this way that it is negotiated to the subsequent holder. Such indorsement cannot be partial, and must be entire, if it is to be effective. Nor is it possible for an indorsement to purport to transfer the title to the cheque severally to two or more indorsees[1].

Indorsement may be in blank, special[2] or restrictive[3]. A bearer cheque is either expressed as such or has as its only, or more recent indorsement, an indorsement in blank. An indorsement to be valid must be upon the cheque itself and must be signed by the indorser or his duly authorised agent[4].

Regularity of indorsement

The regularity of an indorsement is a matter quite distinct from the validity of it. In the case of *Arab Bank Ltd v Ross*[5] the partners of a firm indorsed two promissory notes omitting the word 'Company' which formed part of the firm's name. The indorsements were valid as a transfer of title to the instruments to the bank, but the omission rendered the indorsements irregular and created doubt as to whether they were indorsements of the named payee. The notes therefore were neither complete not regular on their face and thus prevented the bank from becoming holders in due course. The bank remained only holders for value of the cheques.

Payment against an irregular indorsement is not covered by the statutory protections of sections 60 and 80 of the 1882 Act. However, section 1 of the Cheques Act 1957 does afford protection with the result of the diminishing relevance of the regularity of an indorsement. But this protection is extended only where payment upon a cheque occurs within the ordinary course of business. To be a regular indorsement it must be written on the bill itself and signed by the indorser[6]. Simple signature of the indorser alone suffices but it should reproduce as exactly as possible the name typed and shown upon the cheque[7]. It follows that irregularity is evidenced where the payee's indorsement differs materially from the drawer's description of the payee. Payment against an absent or irregular indorsement is outwith the ordinary course of business and, therefore, irregular and does not receive the statutory protection of section 1 of the 1957 Act. Prior to the 1957 Act any cheque irregularly indorsed was, in the proper course, dishonoured by the paying bank. Where a cheque was presented through the clearing system the same principle would apply since the collecting bank was expected to require the payee's indorsement even where the cheque was not negotiated to a third party. As Ellinger and Lomnicka observe, such indorsement is truly no more than a receipt

---

1 1882 Act, s 32(2).
2 1882 Act, s 34.
3 1882 Act, s 35.
4 1882 Act, ss 32(1) and 91(1).
5 [1952] 2 QB 216, [1952] 1 All ER 709, CA.
6 1882 Act, s 32(1). See generally *Alderson v Langdale* (1832) 2 B & Ad 660; *Macdonald v Union Bank of Scotland* (1864) 2 M 963.
7 *Slingsby v District Bank Ltd* [1931] 2 KB 588 at 597, per Wright J; [1932] 1 KB 544, CA.

rather than for the proper function of an indorsement, namely for the negotiation of the instrument[1]. However, any irregularity would place payment upon the cheque outwith the ordinary course of business and would require to be rejected. Consequently, banks were required to reject large numbers of cheques and the Mocatta Committee on cheque indorsement proposed reform of a situation which was no longer acceptable to the banks[2]. The Committee recommended that indorsement be unnecessary as a prerequisite of the payment of cheques except where they were presented over the counter and this proposal became the extended section 1(1) of the 1957 Act.

Section 1 of the Cheques Act 1957 provides:

'(1) Where a banker in good faith and in the ordinary course of business pays a cheque drawn on him which is not indorsed or is irregularly indorsed, he does not, in doing so, incur any liability by reason only of the absence of, or irregularity in, indorsement, and he is deemed to have paid it in due course;

(2) Where a banker in good faith and in the ordinary course of business pays any such instrument as the following, namely:

   (a) a document issued by a customer of his which, though not a bill of exchange, is intended to enable a person to obtain payment from him of the sum mentioned in the document;

   (b) a draft payable on demand drawn by him upon himself, whether payable at the head office, or some other office of his bank; he does not, in doing so, incur any liability by reason only of the absence of, or irregularity in, indorsement and the payment discharges the instrument'.

Forged indorsements

A bill is discharged by payment in due course by or on behalf of the drawee or the acceptor of it. Payment in due course means payment made at or after the maturity of the bill to the holder of it in good faith and without notice that his title to the bill is defective[3]. Payment to a person claiming under a forged indorsement does not obtain this protection because a forged indorsement is wholly inoperative and the person claiming under such an indorsement is not an indorsee of the bill[4]. A person claiming under a forgery has no title and importantly cannot give title to it. Further, where a bill payable to order on demand is drawn on the banker, and the banker on whom it is drawn pays the bill in good faith and in the ordinary course of business, it is not incumbent upon the banker to show that the indorsement was made by or under the authority of the person whose indorsement it purports to be, and the banker is deemed to have paid the bill in due course, even although such indorsement has been forged or made without his authority[5].

---

1 Ellinger and Lomnicka *Modern Banking Law* (2nd edn, 1994) p 383.
2 *Report of the Committee on Cheque Indorsement* (Cmd 3) (1956).
3 1882 Act, s 59.
4 1882 Act, s 24; *Macdonald v Union Bank of Scotland* (1864) 2 M 963.
5 1882 Act, s 60.

It follows that payment by the drawee banker in good faith and in the ordinary course of business, of a cheque bearing a forged indorsement, discharges the instrument and entitles the banker to debit his customer. It is in this way that section 60 of the 1882 Act extends the protection unavailable under section 59 of the 1882 Act.

'Good faith' in terms of the declaratory section is an act which is in fact done honestly, whether it is done negligently or not[1]. It follows that even considerable negligence will not be construed as equivalent to want of good faith[2]. With regards to words or indorsements in foreign characters, unless the banker has personal knowledge of the language used, it is doubtful that the mere placing on the cheque of such language conveying nothing to the banker's understanding brings the case within section 60 of the 1882 Act[3]. It is not within the ordinary course of business to pay upon a partially incomprehensible document[4]. This view is compounded by the opinion of Denning LJ in *Arab Bank Ltd v Ross*[5] that for an indorsement to be regular it must be in the same lettering as that of the name of payee.

The objective of the Cheques Act 1957 was to eliminate the necessity of an indorsement of a cheque as a precondition to the bank's protection under sections 60 and 80 of the 1882 Act. However, this aim has not been wholly achieved as a circular of the Committee of London Clearing Bankers of 23 September 1957 indicated that an indorsement on cheques and instruments would be required where it was: (a) cashed at the counter, including those cashed under open credit; or (b) cashed on combined cheque and receipt forms marked 'R'; or (c) cashed on cheques payable to joint payees where offered for credit to an account to which all are not party. Arguably these guidelines may modify and redefine some of the parameters of the terming of 'ordinary course of business' as understood in decisions under the 1882 Act, and Ellinger and Lomnicka submit that the usefulness of the practice established under the 1957 circular is somewhat dubious[6]. They consider that where Y steals X's cheque payable to X's order, and presents the cheque over the counter, Y may forge X's indorsement before going to the bank then adding an indorsement in his own name. They further contend that the bank would in that situation be protected under section 60 of the 1882 Act where the forged indorsement is regular. The signature forged would be that of X and not of Y and would accordingly not deprive the bank of its protection[7]. It is contrary to this view that Paget considers that where a forged signature is presented subsequent to a request for indorsement, there is no valid payment, no discharge and therefore no statutory protection[8].

---

1 1882 Act, s 90.
2 *Woods v Martins Bank Ltd* [1959] 1 QB 55, [1958] 3 All ER 166, per Salmon J.
3 Paget's *Law of Banking* (11th edn, 1996 by M Hapgood QC) p 385.
4 See *Carlisle and Cumberland Banking Co v Bragg* [1911] 1 KB 489 at 496, per Buckley LJ: 'I should for the purposes of the document be both blind and illiterate'. (*Carlisle* overruled by *Saunders v Anglia Building Society* [1971] AC 1004, [1970] 3 All ER 961, but not on the subject of indorsement.)
5 *Arab Bank Ltd v Ross* [1952] 2 QB 216 at 228, [1952] 1 All ER 709 at 716, CA.
6 Ellinger and Lomnicka *Modern Banking Law* (2nd edn, 1994) p 384.
7 As occurred in *Smith v Commercial Banking Co of Sydney* (1910) 11 CLR 667.
8 Paget's *Law of Banking* (11th edn, 1996 by M Hapgood QC) p 390.

Indorsement 'per pro', 'for' and 'on behalf of'

A signature by procuration operates as notice that the agent has a restricted authority to sign and that the principal is only bound by the signature if the agent signs while acting within the limits of his authority[1]. Indorsement is regular only if the representative capacity stated is adequately compatible with the authority given to him to indorse the bill. There has been some debate as to distinctions existing between 'per pro', 'for' and 'on behalf of' indorsement appearing on bills[2].

Indorsement on behalf of companies and partnerships

Where a cheque is payable to the order of two or more payees, or indorsees who are not partners, all must indorse, unless the person indorsing has authority to indorse for all the others[3]. With regard to partners, every partner is an agent of the firm and his partners for the purposes of the business of the partnership[4]. One partner may indorse cheques payable to the partnership. Where a cheque is payable to order and the payee or indorsee is wrongly designated, or his name misspelt, he may indorse the cheque in the manner in which he had been described adding if he wishes his proper signature[5].

In the case of a company, a negotiable instrument is deemed to be made, accepted or indorsed in the company's name where it is signed in the name of, or by or on behalf of, or on account of the company, by any person acting under its authority[6]. A company's indorsement is regular where its name is written out or impressed with a rubber stamp upon the cheque. It is common practice, however, for a bank to require that the person executing the indorsement identifies his capacity and name. Where a director signs a cheque or accepts a bill which describes the company incorrectly he is personally liable upon the instrument[7].

(8)   DATING OF CHEQUES

A cheque does not require to be dated[8] and can be post-dated, ante-dated or dated on a Sunday[9]. However, the date is considered to be material and

1   1882 Act, s 25; *North of Scotland Banking Co v Behn, Möller & Co* (1881) 8 R 423; *Midland Bank Ltd v Reckitt* [1933] AC 1, HL.
2   *Gerald McDonald & Co v Nash & Co* [1922] WN 272 (revsd on a different point [1924] AC 625, HL) expressed the opinion that 'for' was distinct from 'per pro' or 'under power of attorney', with only the latter cases putting the bank upon inquiry. This was adopted from the reasoning of Chief Baron Pigott in *O'Reilly v Richardson* (1865) 17 ICLR 74. Also approved per Rowlett J in *Alexander Stewart & Son of Dundee Ltd v Westminster Bank Ltd* [1926] WN 126, revsd [1926] WN 271, CA.
3   1882 Act, s 32(3).
4   Partnership Act 1890, s 5.
5   1882 Act, s 32(4); *Arab Bank Ltd v Ross* [1952] 2 QB 216 at 226, CA.
6   Companies Act 1985, s 32.
7   Companies Act 1985, s 349(4); Chitty *Contracts* (27th edn 1994, by Guest) vol 2, para 33-031); *Scottish and Newcastle Breweries Ltd v Blair* 1967 SLT 72, OH. See also pp 90, 91 above.
8   1882 Act, s 3(4)(a).
9   1882 Act, s 13(2).

thus any unauthorised alteration of it invalidates the cheque[1] and any individual receiving such a cheque, even in good faith and without negligence, cannot recover from the drawer[2].

An undated cheque is valid and any person in lawful possession of it may date it if it is within the limits of his authority to do so. In *Griffiths v Dalton*[3] the insertion of a date eighteen months after receipt was considered to be invalid as occurring after the lapse of a reasonable period of time. A banker may insert the date on a cheque with the authority of the drawer, but he may be open to a claim by the drawer that the cheque had not, in fact, been issued[4]. It is common and prudent practice for bankers not to honour undated cheques upon the basis of exposure to risk[5]. Post-dated cheques are valid for the purposes of negotiation between the date of issue and their maturity and for a reasonable time thereafter[6]. A banker must not cash a cheque prior to the date on which it purports to be drawn. It is only valid to credit the customer's account with the relevant amount on the stated date of the cheque and premature honouring by the banker followed by any event precluding the honouring of the cheque by the drawer at its date (for example death, bankruptcy or countermanding) would result in loss to the banker who has no mandate to debit his customer's account.

Overdue (stale) cheques

A cheque is deemed to be overdue when it appears on the face of it to have been in circulation for an unreasonable period of time[7]. An unreasonable period of time is a question of fact[8] and may be such a period as might give rise to suspicion in the mind of 'an ordinary careful holder'[9]. The primary purpose of a cheque is as a payment instrument and it follows that it is unacceptable to negotiate the cheque for an unreasonable period of time. In the case of a cheque presented for payment unduly late, the banker should consult the drawer before paying upon it. In Scotland, the prevailing bank custom is to treat as 'stale' any cheque presented for payment more than six months after the due date. In the event of the customer failing to confirm that such a stale cheque should be paid, payment should be refused.

The Jack Committee[10] proposed that for the convenience of the drawer and the certainty of the payee, a standard of best practice should be established to the effect that a bank should not return, within six months from the date of issue, a cheque upon the basis that it was out of date.

---

1 1882 Act, ss 64(1) and (2).
2 *Vance v Lowther* (1876) 1 Ex D 176.
3 *Griffiths v Dalton* [1940] 2 KB 264.
4 1882 Act, s 20.
5 This practice was approved in *Griffiths v Dalton* [1940] 2 KB 264.
6 *Hitchcock v Edwards* (1889) 60 LT 636; *Carpenter v Street* (1890) 6 TLR 410; *Royal Bank of Scotland v Tottenham* [1894] 2 QB 715, CA; *Robinson v Benkel* (1913) 29 TLR 475; *Hodgson & Lee Pty Ltd v Mardonious Pty Ltd* (1986) 5 NSWLR 496.
7 1882 Act, s 36(3); *Russland v Allan* [1976] 1 Lloyd's Rep 48.
8 1882 Act, s 36(3).
9 *Serrell v Derbyshire Rly Co* (1850) 9 CB 811; *London and County Banking Co v Groome* (1881) 8 QBD 288; *Griffiths v Dalton* [1940] 2 KB 264.
10 Jack Report, para 7.51, recommendation 7(15).

(9)   LOST CHEQUES

Where the holder of a cheque loses it, he does not forfeit his right to it either against the drawer or any third party who holds it. In instances where a cheque is lost before it is overdue the holder may apply to the drawer to provide him with an identical replacement but only if he is prepared to indemnify the drawer against any claim which may arise following the finding of the original cheque[1].

The finder of a lost cheque may be compelled to deliver it up to the true owner or if he has transferred it to a third party for value, pay over the moneys he received for it. If the cheque falls into the hands of a holder in due course, he would have a valid claim against the drawer and any other party.

(10)   CHEQUES AS A MEANS OF PAYMENT

The delivery of a cheque to the payee operates as payment of the debt for which it was provided[2]. However, if on encashment of the cheque it is dishonoured[3] or the drawer countermands payment, the original debt revives[4]. If the payee loses or has the cheque stolen from him and it is subsequently encashed, he loses his right to seek payment from the drawer and the debt is extinguished[5], except in instances where personal bar operates against the drawer. The fact that a person has drawn a cheque does not prevent him from challenging it[6].

It does not fall upon a creditor to accept payment of a debt due by the tendering of a cheque by his debtor[7]. If the creditor does accept a cheque in payment of the debt due, he does so upon the implied basis that the cheque will be honoured upon presentation. It is for that reason that the validity of the original debt is not impugned[8]. There is argument for the view that even upon acceptance of a cheque in payment of a debt due, the creditor may sue for the debt until the cheque is presented and paid[9]. The cheque is finally discharged by payment in due course to the holder of the cheque who has taken it in good faith and without notice that his title to the cheque is defective[10].

The banker upon whom a lost cheque is drawn is unaffected and, where valid, a cheque must be given effect. In the absence of a countermand for

---

1   1882 Act, s 69.
2   *Beevers v Mason* (1978) 37 P & CR 452, 122 SJ 610, CA. See *Glasgow Pavilion Ltd v Motherwell* (1903) 6 F 116.
3   *Caine v Coulson* (1863) 1 H & C 764.
4   *Cohen v Hale* (1878) 3 QBD 371; *Walker and Watson v Sturrock* (1897) 35 SLR 26, OH; *McLaren's Trustee v Argylls Ltd* 1915 2 SLT 241; *Sutherland v Royal Bank of Scotland plc* 1996 GWD 6-290, OH.
5   *Charles v Blackwell* (1877) 2 CPD 151, 25 WR 472, CA; *Robb v Gow Bros and Gemmell* 1905 8 F 90; *Coats v Glasgow Corpn Gas Department* (1912) 28 Sh Ct Rep 38.
6   *Thompson v Jolly Carters Inn Ltd* 1972 SC 215, OH.
7   See *Wood v Bruce* (1907) 24 Sh Ct Rep 24.
8   *Leggat Bros v Gray* 1908 SC 67.
9   *Stuart v Cawse* (1859) 5 CBNS 737, 28 LJCP 193; *Macdougall v McNab* (1893) 21 R 144.
10   1882 Act, s 59 (1); *Smith v Union Bank of London* (1875) 1 QBD 31, CA; *Bobbett v Pinkett* (1876) 1 Ex D 368.

payment by the drawer, the banker will honour the cheque in the ordinary way. It follows that a banker collecting payment upon such a cheque does not incur liability to the true owner simply by virtue of having received payment for it[1].

(11) PAID CHEQUES

Once a cheque is paid it is incumbent upon the holder who receives payment to deliver it up to the banker making payment[2]. After payment, the cheque reverts to the ownership of the customer who drew it and is evidence for the banker and his customer that the sums due have been paid. The banker is entitled to retain the cheque from the customer until his account with the customer is settled or agreement to pay on an overdrawn account accepted. A cheque which has been paid by the banker upon whom it is drawn is prima facie evidence of receipt by the payee of the sum payable by the cheque[3].

1 Cheques Act 1957, s 4; consider *Mintons v Hawley & Co* (1882) 20 SLR 126; *Holt v National Bank of Scotland* 1927 SLT 484, OH.
2 1882 Act, s 52(4).
3 Cheques Act 1957, s 3; *Charles v Blackwell* (1877) 2 CPD 151, 25 WR 472, CA; *Westminster Bank Ltd v Zang* [1966] AC 182, [1966] 1 All ER 114, HL.

Chapter 7

The Collecting Banker and the Paying Banker

1. THE COLLECTING BANKER

(1) INTRODUCTION AND METHODS OF CHEQUE PRESENTATION

The banker is under a duty to his customer to ensure that all cheques paid in for collection are presented for payment promptly. Cheques must be presented for payment within a reasonable time after issue in the case of a drawer, or within a reasonable time of indorsement in the case of an indorser[1]. Previously under the common law a cheque drawn upon a bank located in the same town as the collecting banker required to be presented upon the day of receipt[2].

There are three basic methods of cheque presentation. Firstly, through the clearing house system. Such presentation is in accordance with the current practice of bankers which is the determining factor as to whether or not a cheque has been presented within a 'reasonable time'[3]. The presenting bank's responsibility to its customer in the collection of a cheque is discharged when the cheque is physically delivered to the branch of the bank on which it is drawn for a decision as to whether it should be paid or not[4]. The second method of presentation is by one bank to another. Physical delivery by one bank to another for payment is a competent method of presentation, but is normally only utilised for a special purpose. Practice suggests that the paying bank may hold the cheque until the day after receipt. If not paid immediately it must be paid the day after receipt[5]. Thirdly, cheque presentation may be by post but such presentation is only competent in accordance with agreement or usage[6]. Generally, bankers only authorise presentation by post of cheques where they have been presented by a bank. In instances where a cheque is drawn by one customer of a bank and is received by another customer of the same branch it will be a question of fact whether it is paid in for collection or presented for payment[7].

Special presentation occurs in instances where the payee is anxious to determine whether or not the cheque will be honoured and involves the collecting bank delivering the cheque to the bank office where it is payable with a request for immediate clearance. This process usually involves the cheque being 'cleared for payment' a day earlier than if it had been despatched into the standard clearing process[8].

1 Bills of Exchange Act 1882, s 45(2); *Alexander v Burchfield* (1842) 7 Man & G 1061 (where a recipient of a cheque was held bound to present it the day after receipt); *Hare v Henty* (1861) 25 JP 678, 10 CBNS 65. In determining what is a reasonable time, regard should be had to the nature of the bill, the usage of trade with regard to similar bills, and the facts of the particular case: 1882 Act, s 45(2).
2 *Rickford v Ridge* (1810) 2 Camp 537; *Alexander v Burchfield* above; *Forman v Bank of England* (1902) 18 TLR 339; *Hamilton Finance Co Ltd v Coverley Westray Walbaum and Tosetti Ltd and Portland Finance Co Ltd* [1969] 1 Lloyd's Rep 53.
3 1882 Act, ss 45 and 74.
4 Wallace and McNeil's *Banking Law* (10th edn, 1991 by D B Caskie) p 125.
5 *Bailey v Bodenham* (1846) 16 CBNS 288 at 296. Cf also Paget's *Law of Banking* (11th edn, 1996 by M Hapgood QC) p 409 and *Barclays Bank plc v Bank of England* [1985] 1 All ER 385 at 394, per Bingham J: 'If it is to be said that the drawer loses that right [ie to have the cheque duly presented] as the result of a private agreement made between the banks for their own convenience, the very strongest proof of his knowledge and assent would be needed, not only because of the general rule that an individual's rights are not to be cut down by agreement made between others but also because, in this particular case, the rights of additional parties (such as indorsers) could be affected'.
6 1882 Act, s 45(8).
7 *Carpenters' Co v British Mutual Banking Co Ltd* [1938] 1 KB 511, [1937] 3 All ER 811, CA. As illustrated by the case of *Boyd v Emmerson* (1834) 2 Ad & El 184, where the cheque is paid in for collection, the bank has the usual time of an agent for returning it and for giving notice of dishonour.
8 *Ringham v Hackett* (1980) 124 Sol Jo 201, CA.

If the collecting banker fails to present the cheque within a reasonable time, he may be liable to his customer for any losses which result. A delay of three weeks before presentation was held to be inconsistent with established banking custom and practice[1].

(2)   NOTICE OF DISHONOUR

The collecting banker has a duty to give prompt notice of dishonour[2] to his customer with regard to any cheques referred to him after presentation for payment[3]. The notice should be in writing and should be on the same day as the unpaid item is received by the bank[4]. Lord Lindley in *London City and Midland Bank Ltd v Gordon*[5] recognised the right of the collecting bank to debit the customer with the value of the returned cheque and immediately return the cheque to him[6]. On instruction from the customer, the collecting bank may re-present the cheque at a future time in the hope that the drawer has sufficient funds to make payment. Where the account for which the cheque is collected is already in debit at the time of dishonour, the banker may elect either to increase the overdraft facility or to debit a suspense account in order to reserve his rights against other parties as if he were a holder for value of the cheque[7]. It is not necessary to intimate notice of dishonour to the drawer of the cheque[8] and if the bank returns the cheque to its customer its claim to be 'a holder for value' of the cheque will be extinguished[9].

The terms 'value' and 'holder for value' are determined by section 27 of the Bills of Exhange Act 1882 and for a bank to be a holder for value it must have given valuable consideration which is usually evidenced by the bank allowing its customer to draw the uncleared moneys of the cheque, decreasing the sums at credit of the account or increasing the customer's indebtedness[10]. In *A L Underwood v Barclays Bank Ltd* Scrutton LJ said: 'The cases where an agent for collection becomes a holder for value, must turn

---

1   *Lubbock v Tribe* (1838) 7 LJ Ex 158, 3 M & W 607. See also *Yeoman Credit Ltd v Gregory* [1963] 1 All ER 245, [1963] 1 WLR 343.

2   For full discussion, see pp 192 ff above.

3   1882 Act, s 49.

4   *Godwin v Francis* (1870) LR 5 CP 295 at 303, per Willes J; *Lombard Banking Ltd v Central Garage and Engineering Co Ltd* [1963] 1 QB 220, [1962] 2 All ER 949. In *London Provincial and South-Western Bank Ltd v Buszard* (1918) 35 TLR 142, it was held that an order to stop a cheque addressed to the wrong branch was ineffective.

5   [1903] AC 240, HL.

6   Even though it has been credited as cash. Cf also *Re Mills Bawtree & Co, ex parte Stannard* (1893) 10 Morr 193; *Lombard Banking Ltd v Central Garage and Engineering Co Ltd* [1963] 1 QB 220, [1962] 2 All ER 949.

7   Debiting the customer's account may result in the banker relinquishing his lien. Cf *Westminster Bank Ltd v Zang* [1966] AC 182, [1966] 1 All ER 114, HL. Taking back the cheque would not enable the banker to refresh his lien — he would not have received the cheque as banker.

8   1882 Act, s 50(2)(c).

9   Cheques Act 1957, s 2.

10   See *Midland Bank Ltd v R V Harris Ltd* [1963] 2 All ER 685, [1963] 1 WLR 1021.

on an express or implied agreement between the bank and the customer that the latter may draw against the cheques before they are cleared'[1].

Where a banker has a lien over the cheque, arising from contract or by implication of law, 'he is deemed to be a holder for value to the extent of the sum for which he has a lien'[2]. In instances where the customer is indebted to the bank, a lien in its favour operates over any cheques delivered to it for collection. If the bank releases the cheque back to its customer, the right of lien is lost. In *Westminster Bank Ltd v Zang*[3] a cheque was delivered back to the customer in order that he might sue the drawer. The action did not proceed and the bank took back the cheque in order that it might sue. Denning MR and Salmon LJ held that the bank had lost its lien and it could not be recovered by the indorsement of the cheque in its favour by the customer. The bank could not be 'a holder in due course' because it knew of the dishonouring of the cheque and could only be a holder for value (on the assumption that the bank had given value to the customer).

The bank's title, as a holder for value of the cheque, will be defeated if its customer has a defective title to the cheque and by the more personal defences available to prior parties among themselves[4]. If, however, the bank can demonstrate that it is a 'holder in due course' of the dishonoured cheque, its claim cannot be defeated. In most instances the bank is a holder in due course in compliance with the requirements of section 29 of the 1882 Act and does not normally have to rely upon the holder for value provisions. In *Barclays Bank Ltd v Astley Industrial Trust Ltd*[5], the bank sued in respect of cheques drawn by the defendants, which had enabled the bank upon receiving them, to authorise the payment of cheques of their customer which they would otherwise have dishonoured. Milmo J held that the bank was a holder for value upon the basis that it had given value for the cheques and had taken them in good faith and without knowledge of any existing defects. In this way, the bank held a lien over the cheques, was deemed to be a holder for value in terms of section 27(3) of the 1882 Act and, upon satisfying the requirements of section 29(1) of the Act, was also deemed a holder in due course.

(3) STATUTORY PROTECTION OF COLLECTING BANKER

It is practically impossible for banks to check that their customers have good title to every cheque which is delivered to them for credit of their accounts, and the true owner of a cheque may have a claim against the bank which collected the proceeds of the cheque as well as against the person who stole the cheque or perpetrated the fraud[6]. Protection was

---

1 [1924] 1 KB 775 at 804, CA. Cf also *Alexander Stewart & Son of Dundee Ltd v Westminster Bank Ltd* [1926] WN 126 (revsd [1926] WN 271, CA).
2 1882 Act, s 27(3).
3 [1966] AC 182, [1966] 1 All ER 114, HL.
4 1882 Act, ss 38(2) and 29(2).
5 [1970] 2 QB 527, [1970] 1 All ER 719.
6 At common law the collecting banker who acts only as agent does not incur liability merely because the transaction is tainted with fraud, or the signature of the drawer or indorser is forged: *Clydesdale Bank v Royal Bank of Scotland* (1876) 3 R 586.

originally afforded to banks by way of the Crossed Cheques Act 1876[1] which was reproduced in section 82 of the 1882 Act. There were, however, two qualifying provisions to this section. Firstly, the protection only applied to crossed cheques and secondly, the payment involved must have been 'received by the customer'. In *Capital and Counties Bank Ltd v Gordon*[2], the House of Lords held that the protection of section 82 was not available because the bank had credited the customer's account before clearance and accordingly received payment for itself rather than the customer. Further protection was made available to collecting bankers by the Bills of Exchange (Crossed Cheques) Act 1906 and finally by the bulwark protection of section 4 of the Cheques Act 1957.

It is important to remember that in England the action by the true owner of a cheque against the collecting bank was based upon the strict tort of conversion[3] which is unknown to Scots law. This English tort is one of strict liability and it is against this liability that statute evolved protection. It is prudent that English Authorities should be treated carefully but it is the practice to consider and refer to them relative to claims against a collecting banker in Scotland[4].

If a claim is pursued by the true owner of a cheque against the collecting bank upon the basis that it has collected the cheque for a non-owner, the bank has a statutory defence if it complies with the provisions of section 4 of the Cheques Act 1957, subsections (1) and (2) of which provide that:

'(1) Where a banker, in *good faith* and *without negligence*[5],
   (a) receives payment for a customer of an instrument to which this section applies; or
   (b) having credited a customer's account with the amount of such an instrument, receives payment thereof for himself;
and the customer has no title, or a defective title, to the instrument, the banker does not incur any liability to the true owner of the instrument by reason only of having received payment thereof.
(2) This section applies to the following instruments, namely,
   (a) cheques;
   (b) any document issued by a customer of a banker which, though not a bill of exchange, is intended to enable a person to obtain payment from that banker of the sum mentioned in the document;
   (c) any document issued by a public officer which is intended to enable a person to obtain payment from the Paymaster General or the Queen's and Lord Treasurer's Remembrancer of the sum mentioned in the document but is not a bill of exchange;
   (d) any draft payable on demand drawn by a banker upon himself, whether payable at the head office or some other office of his bank'.

The crucial aspect of section 4 is subsection (3) which provides the essence of the protection of the collecting banker:

1 See pp 201, 202 above.
2 [1903] AC 240, HL.
3 See *Hollins v Fowler* (1875) LR 7 HL 757.
4 D J Cusine 'The Collecting Banker's Protection in Scots Law' 1978 JR 233.
5 Emphasis added.

'A banker is not to be treated for the purposes of [section 4] as having been negligent by reason only of his failure to concern himself with absence of, or irregularity in, indorsement of an instrument'.

To derive protection under the ambit of section 4 of the 1957 Act the banker *must* have acted 'in good faith' and 'without negligence'.

Good faith

'Good faith' is synonymous with the concept of honesty and it is irrelevant whether or not the banker has acted negligently[1]. 'The whole transaction from the taking of the cheque to the receipt and disposition of the money must be in good faith and without negligence and even transactions with the customer prior to collection'[2]. In Scotland there is no equivalent remedy based upon the English tort of conversion and under common law there is a defence to the bank, save in the presence of actual bad faith[3].

Without negligence

Neither the 1882 Act nor the 1957 Act provisions define the precondition 'without negligence'. The 1957 Act[4] harmonises the interpretation of the two Acts by providing that similar, if not necessarily identical, considerations will apply in their interpretation. Evolving banking practice and trends will alter the perceptions of what facts ought to be known to the banker, as will the facts and circumstances which should place him upon inquiry[5].

Sankey LJ in *Lloyds Bank Ltd v Chartered Bank of India, Australia and China*[6] said the banker must 'exercise the same care and forethought with regard to the cheque paid in by the customer, as a reasonable man would bring to bear on similar business of his own'. Bankes LJ in *AL Underwood Ltd v Bank of Liverpool and Martins*[7] approved the test put forward in *Taxation Comrs v English, Scottish and Australian Bank Ltd*[8], that the bank's actions must comply with the ordinary practice of bankers, but that this duty did not extend to 'microscopic examination'. Sankey LJ in the *Lloyds Bank* case[9] adopted the view of Bailhache J in *Ross v London County Westminster and Parr's Bank Ltd*[10] that there must be attributed to the cashiers and clerks of banks, the degree of intelligence and knowledge typically required of individuals in their positions to enable them to discharge their duties. It follows that the exigencies of banking practice mean that too detailed an inquiry would be excessive[11]. Lord Warrington in the *Lloyds Bank* case took the view that:

---

1 1882 Act, s 90 and p 175 above.
2 Paget's *Law of Banking* (11th edn, 1996 by M Hapgood QC) p 441.
3 See 'Jack Committee recommendations' at p 231 below.
4 1957 Act, s 6(1).
5 *Lloyds Bank Ltd v EB Savory & Co* [1933] AC 201, 102 LJKB 224, HL.
6 [1929] 1 KB 40 at 69, CA.
7 [1924] 1 KB 775, CA.
8 [1920] AC 683 at 689, PC.
9 *Lloyds Bank Ltd v EB Savory & Co* [1933] AC 201, 102 LJKB 224, HL.
10 [1919] 1 KB 678.
11 Cf also *Orbit Mining and Trading Co Ltd v Westminster Bank Ltd* [1962] 3 All ER 565 at 574, per Sellers LJ and at 579, per Harman LJ, CA.

'the standard by which the absence, or otherwise, of negligence is to be determined must in my opinion be ascertained by reference to the practice of reasonable men carrying on the business of bankers, and endeavouring to do so in such a manner as may be calculated to protect themselves and others against fraud'[1].

A more relaxed perspective was advocated by Harman LJ in *Orbit Mining and Trading Co Ltd v Westminster Bank Ltd*[2]: 'it is never possible to lay down a rule as to what constitutes negligence and what avoids it. Each case depends on its own facts'. The most acceptable formula, if one need be adopted, would be considered to be the ordinary practice of bankers and not individuals. The authorities were reviewed in *Marfani & Co Ltd v Midland Bank Ltd*[3] and the conclusions which may safely be drawn from it are:

(a) The onus of showing that reasonable care has been taken lies upon the collecting banker.
(b) Current banking practice determines what is, or is not, proper conduct on the part of bankers. Older authorities will lose some of their weight as practice and custom evolve.
(c) The duty of care owed by the banker to the true owner of the cheque only arises upon delivery of the cheque to him by the customer. It is only at this juncture that inquiry requires to be made and any inquiries already made are only relevant in so far as they have provided information that the banker ought to know about his customer.

Examples of section 4 negligence

The following are examples of 'negligence' on the part of bankers in terms of section 4 of the Cheques Act 1957.

(1)   Failure to comply with the bank's internal rules or practices

Negligence on the basis of failure to comply with the bank's internal rules or practices was pled in both *Lloyds Bank Ltd v EB Savory & Co*[4] and in *Motor Traders Guarantee Corporation Ltd v Midland Bank Ltd*[5]. In the latter case Goddard J concluded:

> 'The question in every case is not whether the bank require a particular standard of conduct, but whether the particular acts which are done are enough to discharge the onus which is upon the bank either in respect of their own customer or in respect of some other customer'[6].

Sellers LJ in *Orbit Mining and Trading Co Ltd v Westminster Bank Ltd* approved this attitude since 'although they have no statutory effect, such instructions are a helpful guideline'[7]. It will be for the court in every case

1   *Lloyds Bank Ltd v EB Savory & Co* [1933] AC 201 at 221, HL.
2   [1962] 1 QB 794 at 822, [1962] 3 All ER 565 at 578, CA.
3   [1968] 2 All ER 573, [1968] 1 WLR 956, CA.
4   [1933] AC 201, HL.
5   [1937] 4 All ER 90.
6   [1937] 4 All ER 90 at 96.
7   [1963] 1 QB 794, [1962] 3 All ER 565 at 574, CA. See also *Lumsden & Co v London Trustee Savings Bank* [1971] 1 Lloyd's Rep 114, per Donaldson J.

to examine current practice and upon deliberation conclude whether or not the banker has complied with a standard of care a prudent banker should have adopted.

(2) Sudden fluctuations in account balances

In *Crumplin v London Joint Stock Bank Ltd*[1], some weight was attached to the suggestion that in a typically steady and small balance, the paying in for collection of a large sum might place the banker on inquiry. However, generally bankers will not regard sudden fluctuations as sources of immediate suspicion[2], but the opening of an account with a nominal sum followed by the paying in of a considerable sum will not generally be ignored[3].

(3) Failure to inquire upon opening an account

A group of older cases illustrate that where a bank fails to make inquiries as to the prospective customer's standing or fails to take up references in the opening of an account, where this is standard practice amongst other banks, such will be germane to the proof of negligence[4]. However, the traditional practice of obtaining references is generally considered to be outdated and failure to do so is unlikely to lead to the presumption of negligence. Banks are now able to establish identity, standing and creditworthiness using other more modern sources of information[5].

(4) Request for special collection

In *Turner v London and Provincial Bank Ltd*[6] a fraudulent customer requested a special collection of a cheque. Such collection serves the purpose of allowing speedy discovery of whether the cheque will or will not be paid. Special presentation without further inquiry or explanation was held incapable of rendering a bank liable as 'negligent.' In *Marfani & Co Ltd v Midland Bank Ltd*[7], Diplock J in the Court of Appeal held that special collection and its significance would depend upon the judge's assessment of 'the credibility of the bank officials who gave evidence'. It was held that special collection did not indicate that the bank's suspicions had been aroused, but rather that the speed of collection of what was a large sum would be to the customer's benefit.

1 (1911) 19 Com Cas 69, 109 LT 856.
2 *Thomson v Clydesdale Bank Ltd* [1893] AC 282; *Taxation Comrs v English, Scottish and Australian Bank Ltd* [1920] AC 683, 89 LJPC 181, PC; *Morison v London County and Westminster Bank Ltd* [1914] 3 KB 356, CA.
3 *Slingsby v District Bank Ltd* [1932] 1 KB 544 at 556, CA, per Scrutton LJ.
4 *Turner v London and Provincial Bank Ltd* (1903) 2 LDAB 33; *Ladbroke & Co v Todd* [1914] WN 165, 19 Com Cas 256; *Harding v London Joint Stock Bank Ltd* (1914) 3 LDAB 81.
5 Wallace and McNeil's *Banking Law* (10th edn, 1991 by D B Caskie) p 128.
6 (1903) LDAB 33.
7 [1968] 2 All ER 573, [1968] 1 WLR 956, CA.

(5)   Failure to verify an indorsement

Prior to the Cheques Act 1957, failure to ensure the apparent regularity of an indorsement would establish the negligence of the collecting banker[1]. This position has been greatly relaxed by the Cheques Act 1957[2]. Some banks still adopt a practice in which cheques presented over the counter for payment must still be indorsed by the payee. Cheques paid in for collection for an account other than that of the payee, must be indorsed. In the former case, the signature is clearly a receipt as opposed to an indorsement. Section 4(3) of the 1957 Act states that a banker is not to be treated as having been negligent by reason only of his failure to concern himself with the absence or irregularity of an indorsement and therefore it follows that where a banker requests an indorsement, it must then be regular. Where the instrument in question requires a receipt as a condition of payment, the collecting banker should ensure that the receipt is completed and that the signature is regular. Since the introduction of the Cheques Act 1992 indorsement difficulties are less problematic.

(6)   Exigencies of business

Bankers are not generally able to plead the exigencies of business as a defence to negligence. Pickford J in *Crumplin v London Joint Stock Bank Ltd*[3] stated: 'It is no defence for a bank to say that they were so busy and had such a small staff that they could not make inquiries when necessary; they must take the consequences'.

(7)   Cheques paid by fiduciaries into private accounts

Collecting banks in practice refuse to collect for a private account, a cheque appearing to be the property of, or intended for the benefit of a company, firm or other person, and which is presented for collection by a person holding or purporting to hold a fiduciary position in relation to it. This rule applies whether the cheque is indorsed or crossed by the fiduciary, or not[4]. Where the cheque is paid in and also drawn by a fiduciary for his private account, precautions by the collecting bank are all the more important[5].

(A)   CHEQUES PAYABLE TO A COMPANY

Generally banks do not accept for the credit of private accounts, cheques drawn in favour of limited companies[6]. In *United Australia Ltd v Barclays*

1 *Bissell & Co v Fox Bros & Co* (1884) 51 LT 663, varied (1885) 53 LT 193, CA; *Bavins, Junior and Sims v London and South Western Bank* [1900] 1 QB 270, CA.
2 See pp 212 ff above ('Indorsements upon cheques').
3 (1911) 19 Com Cas 69, 109 LT 856. See Paget's *Law of Banking* (11th edn, 1996 by M Hapgood QC) p 449.
4 *Hannan's Lake View Central Ltd v Armstrong & Co* (1900) 5 Com Cas 188, 16 TLR 236; *Souchette Ltd v London County, Westminster and Parr's Bank Ltd* (1920) 36 TLR 195; *Slingsby v Westminster Bank Ltd* [1931] 1 KB 173; *Baker v Barclays Bank Ltd* [1955] 2 All ER 571, [1955] 1 WLR 822; *Orbit Mining and Trading Co Ltd v Westminster Bank Ltd* [1963] 1 QB 794, [1962] 3 All ER 565, CA.
5 *Midland Bank Ltd v Reckitt* [1933] AC 1, HL. See *Paget* pp 449 ff.
6 *Motor Traders Guarantee Corpn Ltd v Midland Bank Ltd* [1937] 4 All ER 90.

Bank Ltd[1], Lord Atkin expressed the opinion that: 'In these days every bank clerk sees the red light when a company's cheque is indorsed by a company's official into an account which is not the company's'.

The gravity of the rule was laid down in *Nu-Stilo Footwear Ltd v Lloyds Bank Ltd*[2]. The tenor of the decision implied that the bank must at all times be aware, through all of its officers, present and future, of the information gained when the account was opened and this they should hold for all time, lest the customer transpire to be fraudulent. This test is, however, probably too harsh and would not be applied[3].

(B) CHEQUES PAYABLE TO A PARTNERSHIP

Upon the same basis as companies it is prudent practice to make inquiries prior to taking a cheque payable to a partnership, for the private account of one of the partners[4].

(C) CHEQUES PAYABLE TO OFFICIALS

In *Ross v London County, Westminster and Parr's Bank Ltd*[5], it was held to be negligent to collect for a person's personal account cheques payable to the individual in an official capacity — unless the banker was quite certain that the person had the authority of his superiors so to deal with the cheque.

(D) FAILURE TO MAKE INQUIRIES OF PRINCIPAL OR EMPLOYER

Negligence founded upon failure to inquire of the customer's employers upon the opening of an account was introduced in *Lloyds Bank Ltd v EB Savory & Co*[6]. Lord Wright states that the banker must ensure that his opening inquiries disclose the nature of the person's employment and further that his information is verified and updated from time to time. Lord Blanesburgh and Lord Russell both dissented from this opinion, a view, as Paget[7] observes which is to be much preferred. Lord Wright's declaration places an unreasonable burden upon the collecting bank, and seeks no parity of responsibility between the banker and the true owner of the instrument.

1 *United Australia Ltd v Barclays Bank Ltd* [1941] AC 1 at 23–24, [1940] 4 All ER 20 at 33, HL; Paget's *Law of Banking* (11th edn, 1996 by M Hapgood QC) p 450.
2 (1956) 7 LDAB 121, 77 JIB 239.
3 Harman LJ in *Orbit Mining and Trading Co Ltd v Westminster Bank Ltd* [1963] 1 QB 794, [1962] 3 All ER 565, CA, and Diplock LJ in *Marfani & Co Ltd v Midland Bank Ltd* [1968] 2 All ER 573, [1968] 1 WLR 956, CA, clearly regard such a position as being too severe
4 *Bevan v National Bank Ltd* (1906) 23 TLR 65. Cf also *Smith and Baldwin v Barclays Bank Ltd* (1944) 5 LDAB 370, 65 JIB 171; *Baker v Barclays Bank Ltd* [1955] 2 All ER 571, [1955] 1 WLR 822.
5 [1919] 1 KB 678.
6 [1933] AC 201, 102 LJKB 224, HL.
7 Paget's *Law of Banking* (11th edn, 1996 by M Hapgood QC) p 453; *Maltissen v London & County Bank* (1879) 5 CPD 7.

(E)   PROCURATION INDORSEMENTS

In terms of section 25 of the 1882 Act 'a signature by procuration operates as notice that the agent has but a limited authority to sign'[1]. In this context, it is probably wiser to treat as a procuration signature, any signature which purports to be placed by delegated authority. The collecting banker is probably required to advert to a signature by procuration only in instances where the cheque otherwise puts him on inquiry. Where the collecting banker takes as a holder for value, the signature by procuration takes on more significance[2].

(8)   BANKER EMPLOYING ANOTHER BANK AS AGENT FOR COLLECTION

One banker may employ another as an agent for collection[3]. In *Akrokerri (Atlantic) Mines Ltd v Economic Bank*[4], Bingham J held that the use by a non-clearing bank of a clearing bank, was an ordinary incident of the general process of collection and in no way diminished or affected the protection[5].

(9)   FORGED INDORSEMENT AND SECTION 4 PROTECTION

The protection afforded for collecting banks with regard to stolen or defective title cheques of their customers also extends to forged indorsement under section 4 of the Cheques Act 1957. Paget[6] expresses such a view and is supported in two important cases[7]. In one of these cases, *Souchette Ltd v London County, Westminster and Parr's Bank Ltd*, an employee obtained from his company cheques which were payable to customers of the company for amounts larger than were actually due. He forged indorsements on the cheques and paid them into his own personal account at the same time discharging the actual debt with his own cheques drawn on the collecting bankers. It was held that the bank was only liable to the company for the difference of the amounts due to the company creditors and those sums paid to the fraudulent employee.

(10)   CONTRIBUTORY NEGLIGENCE

In circumstances where the collecting banker cannot rely upon the protection of section 4 of the 1957 Act because he has not collected the cheque

---

1   See p 216 above.
2   *Midland Bank Ltd v Reckitt* [1933] AC 1, HL; *Great Western Rly Co v London and County Banking Co Ltd* [1901] AC 414 at 422, HL, per Lord Brampton. In *Morison v London County and Westminster Bank Ltd* [1914] 3 KB 356 at 373, CA, Lord Reading also speaks of negligence based upon a failure to be put upon inquiry upon receipt of a cheque marked 'not negotiable' for anyone but the payee: although he regards such as only 'some evidence of negligence' as opposed to conclusive per se. See also *Capital and Counties Bank Ltd v Gordon* [1903] AC 240 at 244, HL.
3   1882 Act, s 77(5).
4   [1904] 2 KB 465.
5   *Importer's Co Ltd v Westminster Bank Ltd* [1927] 1 KB 869 (affd [1927] 2 KB 297, CA).
6   Paget's *Law of Banking* (11th edn, 1996 by M Hapgood QC) p 458.
7   *Lloyds Bank Ltd v Chartered Bank of India, Australia and China* [1929] 1 KB 40 at 61, CA, per Scrutton LJ; and *Souchette Ltd v London County, Westminster and Parr's Bank Ltd* (1920) 36 TLR 195.

'without negligence' he may plead contributory negligence on the part of the drawer which would amount to a breach of the banker–customer relationship[1].

(4) JACK COMMITTEE RECOMMENDATIONS: COLLECTING BANKER

The Jack Committee[2] complained that the protection of section 4 of the Cheques Act 1957 was too extensive in the respect that the intended payee may have no remedy against the bank which collects the proceeds for another party without the true payee's knowledge or consent. It is accordingly relatively simple for a thief to open an account and abscond with the proceeds a few days later. The protection afforded in that situation to the collecting bank is generous and in the Committee's view, even more generous in Scotland because there is no such equivalent remedy based upon the English tort of conversion. It follows that under Scottish common law there is a defence to the bank, save in the presence of actual bad faith.

The Committee concluded that banks should take reasonable steps to satisfy themselves as to the identity of new customers prior to transactions but such practice should incorporate the test propounded in the *Marfani* case[3]. Current banking practice should be taken into account when deciding what duty a careful banker owes, in order that he acts 'without negligence' and thus, in compliance with the provisions of section 4 of the 1957 Act. Considering the more privileged position of Scottish bankers the Committee recommended a statutory enactment to restrict the bank's protection to a level equivalent to that in the rest of the UK[4].

2. THE PAYING BANKER

(1) GENERAL DUTIES

The general duties regarding a paying banker have already been discussed in some detail[5]. The primary duty resting upon the paying banker when he receives a cheque to pay on behalf of one of his customers is to examine and satisfy himself that the signature or signatures on the cheque are genuine. The banker has no authority (mandate) to debit his customer's account with any sums if the signature on the cheque is a forgery.

---

1 Banking Act 1979, s 47; Law Reform (Contributory Negligence) Act 1945. And generally see Wallace and McNeil's *Banking Law* (10th edn, 1991 by D B Caskie) p 130; *Carpenters' Co v British Mutual Banking Co Ltd* [1938] 1 KB 511, [1937] 3 All ER 811, CA.
2 As to the recommendations of the Committee relative to the collecting banker, see *Report of the Review Committee on Banking Services: Law and Practice* (the Jack Report) (Cm 622) (1989) paras 7.27 and 7.28.
3 See p 226 above.
4 Jack Report, recommendation 7(6).
5 See generally ch 6 above.

This rule emanates from the principle that the banker is deemed to know his customer's signature[1]. Further, if the cheque contains an unauthorised alteration, the paying banker cannot debit his customer's account as he does not have the mandate to do so[2].

(2)   STATUTORY PROTECTION

What statutory protection is afforded to a bank which incorrectly pays the cheque to someone whose title to it is flawed? In terms of section 59(1) of the 1882 Act, a cheque or other bill is discharged by payment in due course, by or on behalf of the drawee or acceptor. Payment in due course in terms of the section means payment made after the date of the cheque, or maturity of any other bill, to the holder in good faith and who does not have notice that title to the bill is defective[3]. 'Payment' is widely interpreted and may be by actual delivery of the money to the presenter of the cheque or other instrument, or transfer of the sums to the account of the payee or through the operation of the clearing bank system[4]. A cheque drawn on one branch of a bank and paid in at another, appearing as an item on balancing the accounts between the two branches, was held to have been paid by the bank on which it was drawn[5]. A payment between two international banks was completed when the paying bank initiated the computer processes by which transfer was effected[6].

A holder means the payee or indorsee of the cheque or other bill or the bearer of it[7]. But section 59 does not protect the paying banker who makes payment under a forged indorsement. However, the terms of section 60 of the 1882 Act provide that when a banker pays a cheque in good faith and in the ordinary course of business he is not required to show that the indorsement of the payee, or indeed any subsequent indorsement was made with the authority of the person it purports to be. In such an instance the banker will be deemed to have paid the cheque in due course even although the indorsement has been forged or made without authority. 'Good faith' in terms of section 60 does not (unlike section 80) make the absence of negligence a condition for the protection. 'Good faith' in terms of the 1882 Act, means an act done honestly, whether it is negligent or not[8]. In the 'ordinary course of business' is a matter determined by ref-

---

1   For discussion of customers' responsibilities in drawing cheque, see pp 129 ff above. See also *Tai Hing Cotton Mill Ltd v Liu Chong Hing Bank Ltd* [1986] AC 80, [1985] 2 All ER 947, PC.

2   *London Joint Stock Bank v Macmillan and Arthur* [1918] AC 777, HL.

3   1882 Act, s 59(1).

4   *Meyer & Co Ltd v Sze Hai Tong Banking and Insurance Co Ltd* [1913] AC 847, PC, held that a bank paying a crossed cheque across the counter by giving its own cheque on another bank constituted payment.

5   *Ogden v Benas* (1874) LR 9 CP 513 at 516; *Gordon v London City and Midland Bank* [1902] 1 KB 242, CA; affd [1903] AC 240, HL.

6   *Momm v Barclays Bank International Ltd* [1977] QB 790, [1976] 3 All ER 588.

7   1882 Act, s 2.

8   1882 Act, s 90; *Woods v Martins Bank Ltd* [1959] 1 QB 55, [1958] 3 All ER 166, per Salmon J.

erence to the general custom of banking[1]. It therefore follows that the drawee banker who complies with the requirements of section 60 and pays in good faith and in the ordinary course of business, a cheque bearing a forged indorsement will discharge the instrument and be allowed to debit his customer[2].

In addition to these provisions, section 80 of the 1882 Act (in conjunction with section 79) provides that a banker who pays upon a crossed cheque drawn upon him, acting without negligence and in good faith and 'if crossed generally, to a banker, and if crossed specially, to the banker to whom it is crossed, or his agent for collection being a banker, the banker paying the cheque, and, if the cheque has come into the hands of the payee, the drawer, shall respectively be entitled to the same rights and be placed in the same position as if payment of the cheque had been made to the true owner thereof'[3].

The protection afforded by section 19 of the Stamp Act 1853 and sections 60 and 80 of the 1882 Act was supplemented by section 1 of the Cheques Act 1957 which provides:

'(1) Where a banker in good faith and in the ordinary course of business pays a cheque drawn on him which is not indorsed or is irregularly indorsed, he does not, in doing so, incur any liability by reason only of the absence of, or irregularity in, indorsement, and he is deemed to have paid it in due course.
(2) Where a banker in good faith and in the ordinary course of business pays any such instrument as the following, namely:
(a) a document issued by a customer of his which, though not a bill of exchange, is intended to enable a person to obtain payment from him of the sum mentioned in the document;
(b) a draft payable on demand drawn by him upon himself, whether payable at the head office or some other office of his bank; he does not, in doing so, incur any liability by reason only of the absence of, or irregularity in, indorsement, and the payment discharges the instrument'.

All of these foregoing protective sections attempt to protect the banker paying cheques which are subject to forgery but do not protect against risks apparent from an examination of the cheque. An important result of the 1957 Act, and one of its principal objectives, was that paying bankers no longer required cheques to be indorsed except cheques cashed over the bank counter[4]. Section 82 of the 1882 Act was repealed by the 1957 Act, but it is in effect re-enacted in section 4 of the 1957 Act which extended it as to the protection of the collecting banker and clarified the ambit of protection. By contrast, however, section 1 of the 1957 Act adds to the protection of the paying banker as being supplementary to previous enactments. It

1 *Arab Bank Ltd v Ross* [1952] 2 QB 216 at 227, CA; *Bank of England v Vagliano Bros* [1891] AC 107, HL; *Auchteroni & Co v Midland Bank Ltd* [1928] 2 KB 294; *Phillips v Italian Bank Ltd* 1934 SLT 78, OH; *United Dominions Trust Ltd v Kirkwood*[1966] 2 QB 431, [1966] 1 All ER 968, CA.
2 A protection not afforded by s 59 of the 1882 Act.
3 1882 Act, s 80; and for general discussion and views of term 'without negligence', see pp 225 ff above.
4 See pp 223, 224 above.

remains the case that the paying banker must remain more wary of indorsements than a collecting banker.

(3)   WHERE THE COLLECTING BANK IS ALSO THE PAYING BANK

The situation that the collecting bank is also the paying bank arises in two instances. Firstly, where one branch of a bank acts as the collecting agent of the payee and the cheque is drawn upon another branch of the same bank; and secondly, where both the drawer and the payee hold accounts with the same branch of the bank.

Each situation generates difficulties arising from the fact that a bank has a single legal personality, covering all of its branches, although not sub-sidiary companies, such as affiliated merchant banks. The owner of the cheque requires to demand payment at the branch at which the account is held and each branch of the same bank is not treated as a separate legal personality for clearing purposes. It therefore follows that the bank acts as both paying and collecting banker where two of its branches act as collecting agent and paying station. This situation blurs the clear legislative demarcation between paying and collecting banker protections[1].

Ellinger and Lomnicka submit that there are three solutions to the situation arising where the collecting bank is also the paying bank[2]. Firstly, there is the option to confer upon the banker a right to allow it to act as both paying and collecting banker. In such an instance, a bank which was sued for wrongful payment of a cheque could plead the defence of section 4 of the 1957 Act, provided that it could establish an absence of negligence from its actions. The second option is to expect the bank to carry out *all* the duties imposed upon it as regards both the collection and payment of cheques; or finally, one could expect the bank to meet the standard prescribed in respect of the function or functions consciously performed by it in respect of any particular given cheque.

Accordingly, if a cheque is collected and paid through two separate branches, the bank knowingly performs the roles of both collecting and paying bank. Therefore, if the bank is expected to demonstrate the duty of care expected of a bank in both capacities, it would thereby be allowed to plead the defences available to it in both of these roles. If a cheque is paid to the credit of a customer whose account is maintained with the branch on which it is drawn, the cheque is paid rather than collected. In this way, the bank would be regarded as a paying rather than collecting bank and its liability should not exceed that to which it is subjected when a cheque is presented for payment over the counter.

There does not appear to be any Scottish authority on this point and it is sensible to assume that the English authorities, which tend to prefer the

---

1   As Ellinger and Lomnicka note in *Modern Banking Law* (2nd edn, 1994) p 536 this separation of protection arises from the nineteenth-century predominance of small independent banks, often with only one office. While the modern structure in a major trading bank has led to a different practical environment, the Cheque Acts of 1957 and 1992 both reflect the past order.
2   *Ellinger and Lomnicka* pp 536–541.

third solution proposed by Ellinger and Lomnicka, are satisfactory. The courts have, on occasion, also preferred this solution. In *Bissell & Co v Fox Bros & Co*[1] a firm had a salesman whose personal account was maintained with the same single office bank as was his employers' account. The salesman indorsed a number of cheques payable to the firm by subscribing the 'per pro' indorsement and arranged for their payment to the credit of his own personal account. One of the cheques was actually drawn by the customer on the bank with which the salesman and the firm both kept their accounts. Denman J held, as did the Court of Appeal, that the bank should be treated as having paid rather than collected the cheque drawn, on itself and was thereby entitled to the protection of section 60 of the 1882 Act. A similar approach was adopted in *Gordon v London City and Midland Bank*[2] in which it was held that where the bank was able to satisfy the requirements of section 60 of the 1882 Act it was not liable as a collecting bank.

However, Ellinger and Lomnicka[3] support the views of Greer LJ in the Court of Appeal decision in *Carpenters' Co v British Mutual Banking Co Ltd*[4] who indicated that the bank ought to be in a more onerous position than where it paid the cheques over the counter. He took the view that where the bank was sued as collecting bank it could seek the protection of section 82 of the 1882 Act, and section 60 where sued as a paying bank. If, however, the bank was sued in both capacities, it would require to succeed under both sections to escape liability. The underlying principle of the decision is that the bank is required to exercise the standard of professional skill expected of it in respect of *each* of its roles as paying and collecting bank.

3. REVOCATION OF BANKER'S AUTHORITY TO PAY A CHEQUE

Section 75 of the 1882 Act provides: 'The duty and authority of a banker to pay a cheque drawn on him by his customer are determined by (1) countermand of payment; (2) notice of the customer's death'.

(1) COUNTERMAND OF PAYMENT

Countermand is an instruction by the customer not to pay on a cheque. Countermand may be made in any manner, written or oral, but in the interests of certainty, bankers should require confirmation of the instruction in writing. It is the customer who carries the burden of ensuring that the banker is informed of the intention to countermand and it is only when the countermand comes to the 'conscious knowledge' of the banker

1 (1885) 53 LT 193, CA.
2 [1902] 1 KB 242 at 274–275, CA.
3 *Ellinger and Lomnicka* pp 540 and 541.
4 [1938] 1 KB 511, [1937] 3 All ER 811, CA.

that it becomes effective[1]. Constructive countermand will never suffice[2]. The customer must take care to ensure that the cheque is specifically identified. In *Westminster Bank Ltd v Hilton*[3], a cheque was drawn on 31 July 1924, being cheque number 117285. It was postdated to 2 August 1924 and on 1 August 1924 the customer sent a cable to the bank ordering that cheque number 117283 be stopped. While giving the wrong number, he gave the correct amount and the payee's name. Cheque number 117285 was presented and paid on 6 August 1924. The customer failed in his action as the instructions to the bank were insufficiently clear and it was reasonable for the bank to assume the number of the cheque as stated.

In instances where the customer telephones the bank to countermand payment of a cheque which is presented before written confirmation is received, the practice is to postpone payment by returning the cheque marked 'payment countermanded by telephone and postponed pending confirmation'[4]. It is important to remember that branches of banks are considered independently of each other and an instruction of countermand delivered to one branch is not necessarily effective against another[5].

The drawer's right to countermand his instruction sustains until the banker pays or dishonours the cheque. The critical time is usually the close of the business day when the cheque is presented but if the bank has indicated to the presenter that the cheque has been paid and met, the countermand is ineffective. Difficulties do arise as to when payment has been completed and therefore denies countermand. In *Royal Products Ltd v Midland Bank Ltd and Bank of Valletta Ltd*[6], the plaintiffs maintained an account in the UK with Midland Bank. They held two Maltese accounts — one with bank N and the other with bank B. The plaintiffs wished to transfer £13,000 from their account with Midland Bank to the credit of their account with bank N. Bank N, however, had prohibitively high banking charges so the plaintiffs instructed the defendant bank to remit the amount involved to the credit of their account with bank B, with the intention of remitting the account from bank B to bank N. Webster J held that in order for payment to be complete three events must have occurred:

(1) bank B must have been put in a position where it was entitled to draw on the funds made available for transmission to the plaintiff's account;
(2) bank B must have been informed that the funds were to be made available to the plaintiff; and
(3) the transfer must have been complete even before the payees, the plaintiffs, were notified that the funds had been credited to their account.

Bank B had received definite notice that the funds were available to it for drawing when it obtained the payment order which completed the transfer. The plaintiff's order to reverse payment was issued after the transfer of funds had been completed.

---

1 *Curtice v London City and Midland Bank Ltd* [1909] 1 KB 293, CA.
2 *Commonwealth Trading Bank v Reno Auto Sales Pty Ltd* [1967] VR 790; *Giordano v Royal Bank* (1973) 38 DLR (3d) 191.
3 (1926) 43 TLR 124, HL.
4 Wallace and McNeil's *Banking Law* (10th edn, 1991 by D B Caskie) p 136.
5 *London Provincial and South-Western Bank Ltd v Buszard* (1918) 35 TLR 142.
6 [1981] 2 Lloyd's Rep 194.

A cheque issued upon a joint account may be countermanded by any of the account holders. Any one of several partners[1] or any trustees or executors has the power to stop a cheque given by any or all[2]. A countermand order upon a company account may be given by any director, the secretary or other authorised official[3].

A cheque which has been issued in exchange for value cannot, in a question with a holder for value, be countermanded by the drawer unless the condition upon which it was drawn does not happen (for example where the cheque is in payment of a contract of sale and the goods are not delivered)[4].

Section 75A of the 1882 Act, which applies to Scotland only and was inserted by section 11 of the Law Reform (Miscellaneous Provisions) (Scotland) Act 1985, provides that when payment has been countermanded, the subsequent presentment of the cheque no longer operates as an intended assignation of money in the hands of the paying banker as he is treated as having no funds for payment. Formerly the Scottish banks required to place the moneys contained within the countermanded cheque upon a suspense account and await the confirmation of the payee that the moneys could be released to the drawer, which was an extremely cumbersome procedure[5].

(2) DEATH OF THE CUSTOMER

The duty and the authority of the banker to pay cheques drawn upon him are determined by notice of the customer's death[6]. Payment of a cheque subsequent to the customer's death, but before the banker has had sufficient and reasonable time to be informed of the death will be valid and that upon the basis that it is not the death, but rather notice of it, that operates as the revocation of the banker's mandate[7].

It accordingly follows that if a cheque is effectively countermanded either by specific instruction or by death and the banker thereafter pays upon the cheque, the liability falls upon the banker, who cannot then debit the customer's account, nor look to the person receiving the money for repayment where the recipient has acted in good faith[8].

1 *Grant v Taylor* (1843) 2 Hare 413.
2 *Twibell v London Suburban Bank* [1869] WN 127; *Curtice v London City and Midland Bank Ltd* [1909] 1 KB 293, CA; *Reade v Royal Bank of Ireland* [1922] 136 LT 315, HL; *Burnett v Westminster Bank Ltd* [1966] 1 QB 742, [1965] 3 All ER 81.
3 See generally *Wallace and McNeil* pp 135–136.
4 *Agra and Masterman's Bank v Leighton* (1866) LR 2 Exch 56, 4 H & C 656; *Watt's Trustees v Pinkney* (1853) 16 D 279; *McLean v Clydesdale Bank Ltd* (1883) 11 R (HL) 1; *Webster & Co Ltd v Hutchin* (1922) 39 Sh Ct Rep 231; *Williams v Williams* 1980 SLT (Sh Ct) 25.
5 See ch 5, pp 171, 172 above.
6 *Tate v Hilbert* (1793) 2 Ves 111; 1882 Act, s 75(2). See also pp 50, 51, 156 above.
7 Sequestration or mental illness may similarly effect the banker's duties: see pp 48–50, 52, 53 above.
8 *Bank of Scotland v Reid* (1886) 2 Sh Ct Rep 376. See also *Credit Lyonnais v George Stevenson & Co Ltd* (1901) 9 SLT 93, OH; *Stewart's Trustees* 1953 SLT (Notes) 25.

(3)   CHEQUE CARDS AND COUNTERMAND

Cheque guarantee cards are typically issued by banks to their customers for use in conjunction with their cheques. In *Re Charge Card Services Ltd*[1] Millet J said that the obligation undertaken by a bank to the supplier, which it enters into through the agency of the customer when he uses the card, is not to dishonour the cheque upon presentation, for want of funds in the account. Typical conditions attaching to the use of the card and the guarantee of payment include: the cheque is signed in the presence of the payee; the payee writes the card number on the reverse of the cheque; the amount of the cheque is not greater than a specified amount (usually £100); no other cheque is used to settle the same transaction; and the cheque is dated before the date that the cheque guarantee card expires.

Further, the customer generally agrees not to countermand payment of any cheque which has been accompanied by a cheque guarantee card. Any such countermand is probably invalid or, at least, entitles the bank to damages from the customer equal to the amount of any payment under its guarantee to the supplier. It is probably safe to assume, however, that the presumption that the giving of a cheque operates as condition of payment only, is not displaced simply by the fact that the cheque was accompanied by a bank card[2].

(4)   THE JACK COMMITTEE ON COUNTERMAND: MODERN TRANSMISSIONS SYSTEMS/COMPLETION OF PAYMENT

Two basic questions were addressed by the Jack Committee[3]. Firstly up to what stage of the payment process does the initiator of a payment instruction have the right to countermand or revoke it and secondly, at what stage in the payment process does a payment by one bank customer to another bank customer become complete or final, in the sense that the bank making the payment cannot unilaterally reverse it? The Jack Committee observed that these problems and questions are becoming much more acute with the advent of the proliferation of modern payment systems (for example EFTPOS[4]) and the growing globalisation of banking systems.

Part of the difficulty arises in that countermand is fundamentally a matter of interest to the customer whereas completion of payment is a matter of primary concern to the banker. The present law offers no clear definition as to the point at which a payment becomes irrecoverable. Under the law of agency, the bank acts upon the customer's mandate when effecting a payment instruction on his behalf. It follows that if the mandate is withdrawn, the bank could be considered to be under an obligation to stop the

---

1 [1987] Ch 150 at 166, [1986] 3 All ER 289 at 301.
2 See obiter comments of Miller J in *Re Charge Card Services Ltd* [1987] Ch 150 at 166, [1986] 3 All ER 289 at 301.
3 *Report of the Review Committee on Banking Services: Law and Practice* (the Jack Report) (Cm 622) (1989), paras 12.6–12.13.
4 See pp 256 ff below.

payment process, if still practicable. In the case of payment by cheque, the clearing process usually allows a certain lapse of time within which the payment can in practice be stopped, and the bank is therefore legally obliged to stop a cheque on notice from its customer. It is, however, largely left to banking practice to define the point at which a payment by cheque becomes irrevocable. It is clear that under dated common law provisions, a customer who instructs his bank to pay a third party is committed to his bank from the moment the bank incurs a commitment to the third party[1].

In modern payment systems countermand usually falls within the provision of express contract. Payment by credit card is revocable by the card holder up until the point at which the process of authorisation of the debiting of the transaction from his account is complete. Under the rules of EFTPOS UK Limited, EFTPOS transactions based on both debit and credit cards are to be guaranteed and thus irrevocable, once accepted into the system[2]. CHAPS payments[3], however, which are normally credited to the payee in advance of settlement of the clearing process, are guaranteed and irrevocable once there has been a 'logical acknowledgement' by the payee bank. Under the rules of BACS[4] the drawer may countermand any item during the processing. BACS allows a customer to reverse a payment if he considers that it should not have been made, and from the customer's point of view this process has the effect of providing him with an extended right of countermand.

The situation is less clear as regards SWIFT[5], where instructions are sent with a specified date by which value has to be given to the beneficiary (which is usually two days ahead). The rules do, however, imply that a forward value dated payment might in some cases be countermanded by the payer before the value date. In home and banking systems countermand rules may vary contractually from one system to another[6].

The Jack Committee was not persuaded of a need for reform or uniform rules for countermand in modern payment systems. The principle underlying the banking practice of countermand of cheques was considered applicable to more modern payment systems and the customer should be allowed a reasonable period of time for countermand, in so far as this right may be reconciled with the efficient operation of the payment system. The Committee therefore proposed that a standard of banking practice should require banks, when establishing countermand rules for individual payment systems, 'to allow customers a period of time for countermand wherever possible, only eliminating it where that is necessary for the efficient working of the system'[7]. The Committee also recommended that banks should takes steps to make customers aware of the different countermand rules applying to different payment systems[8].

---

1 *Warlow v Harrison* (1859) 1 E & E 309; *Astro Amo Compania Naviera SA v Elf Union SA and First National City Bank, The Zographia M* [1976] 2 Lloyd's Rep 382.
2 For discussion, see ch 8 below.
3 Ie Clearing House Automated Payments System. See p 250 below.
4 Ie Bankers' Automated Clearing Services. For discussion, see pp 251, 252 below.
5 Ie Society for Worldwide Interbank Financial Telecommuniction. See p 251 below.
6 See generally ch 8 below.
7 Jack Report, para 12.13, recommendation 12(1).
8 Jack Report, recommendation 12(1).

With regard to the timing of completion of payment, the Committee recognised that there was an absence of satisfactory definition in the existing law. While section 59 of the 1882 Act provides that a cheque or negotiable instrument is discharged by payment in due course, it does not, however, elaborate upon what constitutes payment. Common law does not generally draw a line between the concepts of completion of payment and discharge of the underlying obligation[1].

Completion of payment is sometimes governed by the contract and the rules of the clearing house, where applicable. In the main, however, payments may be reversed by agreement between banks and with the authority of the initiating customer, up until the point of settlement as between the customers' respective accounts. The Jack Committee explained, however, that there was some doubt as to the legal effect of these rules as regards banks which are not clearing house settlement members. The view was also expressed that the desirability for specific definition of payment was increased by the risk of sudden failure of non-clearing bank members involved in transactions so large as to have repercussive effects upon the clearing banks themselves. The view was taken that this risk had been significantly increased by the ever-increasing number of international banking transactions which themselves are linked to the rules on electronic fund transfers[2]. Specific definition would not forestall, but could mitigate any such crisis by the provision of a sound basis of legal principle. It was for that particular reason that the Committee proposed that rules to define completion of payment should be enacted in primary legislation and they should provide as follows:

'(a) that payment is to be regarded as complete at the point where the payee's bank (or its agent in the clearing), having actual or ostensible authority to accept payment on behalf of the payee, accepts a transfer of funds from the paying bank (or its agent in the clearing process) for the payee's account — provided that the transfer is or has become unconditional; and

(b) that, where the transfer is between two accounts at the same bank, payment should be regarded as complete when the bank has taken the decision to treat the instructions for transfer as irrevocable.

The rules should be subject to modification by contractual agreement, among parties to a contract governing a payment system'[3].

Finally, the Committee recommended that the Bank of England should convene a working group of interested parties to consider and report upon the operational implications of the rules which are recommended, before they are enacted[4].

---

1 *Re Farrow's Bank Ltd* [1923] 1 Ch 41, CA; *W J Alan & Co v El Nasr Export and Import Co* [1971] 1 Lloyd's Rep 401, revsd [1972] 2 QB 189, [1972] 2 All ER 127, CA; *Momm v Barclays Bank International Ltd* [1977] QB 790, [1976] 3 All ER 588; *Royal Products Ltd v Midland Bank Ltd and Bank of Valletta Ltd* [1981] 2 Lloyd's Rep 194.
2 Eg collapse of Herstatt Bank of West Germany in 1977.
3 Jack Report, recommendation 12(2), paras 12.27, 12.29.
4 Jack Report, recommendation 12(3), para 12.30.

4. ANALOGOUS INSTRUMENTS TO CHEQUES AND THEIR PROTECTION

(1) INTRODUCTION

The Cheques Act 1957 extends statutory protection to certain instruments which, though not cheques, are analogous to cheques[1]. Several important instruments fall generally within these categories.

(2) DIVIDEND WARRANTS

Dividend warrants are often cheques in a style form. They would, however, cease to be so, should they be conditional. Section 95 of the 1882 Act provides that the provisions as to crossed cheques apply to 'a warrant for payment of dividend'. In addition section 97(3)(d) of the Act provides that nothing in the Act affects the validity of any usage relating to dividend warrants, or their indorsement. A dividend warrant which is not a cheque is usually a document intended to enable a person to obtain payment from a banker within section 1(2)(a) or section 4(2)(b) of the 1957 Act.

The Jack Committee observed that section 95 of the 1882 Act makes no mention of interest warrants or those used for repayment of capital, but took the view that there was no longer any need of separate provision as most of these payments are now made by cheque[2]. Nonetheless, the Committee's view was that the definition of a cheque and a bank payment order[3] ought to be wide enough to include instruments used for payments of interest, capital or dividends.

(3) INTEREST WARRANTS

It is debatable as to whether sections 95 and 97(3)(d) of the 1882 Act extend to warrants for the payment of fixed interest, or apply only to dividend warrants strictly so termed. Of particular concern is whether a banker is entitled to pay an interest warrant, payable to two payees or order, on the indorsement of one of them. This is permitted in relation to dividend warrants by section 97(3)(d) of the Act and general practice of bankers does extend such treatment to interest warrants[4]. An interest warrant which is not a cheque normally falls within section 1(2)(a) or section 4(2)(b) of the 1957 Act.

(4) CONDITIONAL ORDERS FOR PAYMENT

These are instruments issued by a customer of a bank, addressed to that bank, imposing a condition of payment, such as the signing by a payee of

---

1 1957 Act, ss 1(2) and 4(2).
2 Jack Report, para 7.67 and recommendation 7(11).
3 Cf at pp 209, 210 above.
4 *Slingsby v Westminster Bank Ltd* [1931] 1 KB 173, per Finlay J.

a form of receipt placed on an instrument or annexed to it. Any conditional instrument ceases to be a bill of exchange and by implication, ceases to be a cheque[1].

Section 6(2) of the 1957 Act provides that the Act's provisions do not make negotiable any instrument not independently negotiable. *Gordon v London City and Midland Bank*[2] illustrates that while conditional orders for payment are often made payable to order or bearer, this renders them neither negotiable nor transferable. Were such to be possible, in a purported transfer, A (transferee) would only accept the instrument upon signature of the receipt by the payee, B. Otherwise A would be unable to tender the document in the proper form. However, as a result, when the instrument was paid, the bank would be paying money to A which B had already recognised as having been paid to him in compliance with the order[3].

A conditional order is a document within sections 1(2)(a) and 4(2)(b) of the 1957 Act. The protection which these provisions afford may, however, often be restricted. Section 1(2) only relieves the paying banker in respect of any absence or irregularity in indorsements and only where the payment is in good faith and in the ordinary course of business. Where the banker violates the mandate and pays a transferee from the payee or indorsee, he treats the instrument as negotiable and may be unable to debit the drawer's account.

With regard to the collecting banker, statutory protection is contingent upon receiving payment for a customer in good faith and without negligence. Section 4(3) of the 1957 Act protects the collecting banker where he fails to advert the absence of or irregularity in indorsement.

(5)   CHEQUES REQUIRING RECEIPT

Some cheques bear an instruction addressed to the payee that there is a receipt which requires completion[4]. Such cheques are regarded either strictly as cheques or as instruments within sections 1(2)(a) and 4(2)(b) of the 1957 Act. The protection enjoyed by the paying banker by virtue of these sections depends largely upon whether the payee's receipt constitutes an indorsement. Where it represents an indorsement the banker has the protection of section 1(2), relieving him of any liability incurred by reason only of the absence of, or irregularity in the indorsement. A signature by way of receipt only, would not afford protection to the banker under section 60 of the 1882 Act where it transpired to be a forgery. However, if circumstances dictate, a signature may constitute both a receipt and an indorsement[5].

---

1   *Bavins, Junior and Sims v London and South Western Bank* [1900] 1 QB 270, CA; *London City and Midland Bank Ltd v Gordon* [1903] AC 240, HL.
2   [1902] 1 KB 242 at 275, CA.
3   Example used in Paget's *Law of Banking* (11th edn, 1996 by M Hapgood QC) at p 254.
4   *London and Montrose Shipbuilding and Repairing Co Ltd v Barclays Bank Ltd* (1925) 31 Com Cas 67 (reversed on appeal without affecting this point (1962) 31 Com Cas 182, CA).
5   Paget's *Law of Banking* (11th edn, 1996 by M Hapgood QC) p 390.

(6) BANKER'S DRAFTS

A banker's draft is an instrument drawn by the banker on himself in favour of a payee of the customer's nomination. Drafts drawn by one branch upon another or on the head office of the same bank (or vice versa) are not cheques or bills, there being no definite drawer and drawee. In *London City and Midland Bank Ltd v Gordon*[1], it was considered that drafts fell within the protection of section 19 of the Stamp Act 1853. The House of Lords held that the drafts in question were not cheques or bills within section 3 of the 1882 Act on the basis that there was no distinct drawer and drawee as required by that section. The power given by section 5(2) of the 1882 Act to treat as a bill a document in which drawer and drawee were the same person, is also confined to the benefit of the holder of it. While section 19 of the 1853 Act applied to the drafts, section 60 of the 1882 Act did not. However, since the enactment of the Bills of Exchange Act (1882) Amendment Act 1932, the crossed cheques sections of the 1882 Act have been applied to banker's drafts as if they were cheques. The Cheques Act 1957 repeals the 1932 Act, and re-enacts its provisions in sections 1 and 4.

The advantage to the payee of a banker's draft is that it guarantees him that the bank is liable to pay on the draft. Drafts have largely supplanted certified cheques in the usage of bankers, and drafts are generally acceptable as an equivalent to cash. Section 5 of the 1957 Act states that the crossed cheque provisions of the 1882 Act apply equally to drafts and cheques. The Jack Committee considered that it remained at the discretion and choice of bankers as to whether to continue the present system or issue instead bank payment orders[2]. Indeed, they may prefer to offer customers a choice. The definitions clause in the proposed Cheques and Bank Payment Orders Act would have to clarify which was which on the basis of the form in which they were drawn.

If a customer loses a banker's draft, the branch from whom it has been issued should be immediately advised so that payment may be postponed pending investigation of the title of the holder who presents it for payment. If a duplicate draft is issued to the customer, the bank should obtain an indemnity against the liability of the bank in the event of the draft being presented and paid by the bank to someone who has obtained a good title to it[3].

(7) FOREIGN BANKER'S DRAFTS

Paget[4] argues that despite the authority of the *Gordon* case[5] and *Brown, Brough & Co v National Bank of India Ltd*[6], any relevant statutory provisions would apply equally to inland and foreign drafts or orders[7].

---

1 [1903] AC 240, HL.
2 Jack Report, para 7.71, recommendation 7(11).
3 Wallace and McNeil's *Banking Law* (10th edn, 1991 by D B Caskie) p 146.
4 *Paget* pp 255–256.
5 *London City and Midland Bank Ltd v Gordon* [1903] AC 240, HL.
6 (1902) 18 TLR 669.
7 *Attorney-General v Edison Telephone Co of London* (1880) 6 QBD 244.

(8)   TRAVELLERS' CHEQUES

Travellers' cheques generally resemble cheques but lack the essential characteristics. The categorisation of a travellers' cheque depends upon its form and content, and the conditions upon which it is issued. Most are drawn in such a manner as to leave the place for the name of the payee blank, in which case they are not cheques at the time of issue. In the case of a travellers' cheque, the issuer undertakes to pay the specified amount of money to the order of the original holder (the purchaser) of the instrument or to a transferee, so long as the signature of the original holder when he purchased the instrument accords with the counter signature signed by him at the time he cashes it. The promise or order that appears in the travellers' cheques is usually conditional, with the issuer agreeing to pay the instrument only where there is correspondence between the two signatures signed by the original holder.

Ellinger and Lomnicka[1] consider that travellers' cheques are a new species of negotiable instrument established by a general mercantile usage[2].

(9)   POSTAL AND MONEY ORDERS

The Post Office Act 1969 governs postal and money orders. The money order is largely obsolete but those which remain, when paid into a bank are paid by the Post Office without examination, and where payment ought not to have been made, the Post Office may deduct the amount from later collections by that bank in regard to money orders[3]. The bank then debits the customer for whom they collected the impugned money order. As witnessed in *Fine Art Society Ltd v Union Bank of London Ltd*[4], neither money orders nor postal orders are negotiable. Where they are crossed they will be paid only to another bank[5].

(10)   PAYABLE ORDERS

Payable orders or warrants are issued mainly, but not exclusively, by government departments. They are not cheques within the terms of the 1957 Act, but section 5 of the 1957 Act does apply the 1882 Act provisions on crossed cheques to those drawn on the Paymaster's General office. Others are not so included but are, for clearing purposes, treated in a similar manner. For the purposes of the 1882 Act outwith crossings, the rules of negotiability do not apply.

The Jack Committee took the view that any new legislation ought to grasp the opportunity to harmonise and equate as closely as possible the

1   Ellinger and Lomnicka *Modern Banking Law* (2nd edn, 1994) p 263.
2   Chitty *Contracts* (27th edn 1994, by Guest) paras 33-147, 33-158.
3   Post Office Act 1969, s 71(1); *London & Provincial Bank v Golding* (1918) 39 JIB 136.
4   (1886) 17 QBD 705, CA.
5   See Paget's *Law of Banking* (11th edn, 1996 by M Hapgood QC) p 258.

rules applying to orders and cheques. The Committee did not perceive any reason why the bodies concerned ought not to be able to issue, if so wishing, non-transferable orders under the provisions relating to bank payment orders, including a suitable annotation on the lines of 'document equivalent to a bank payment order'[1].

The Committee suggested a definition of the payable order in the following terms[2]:

> 'any document issued by a government department and drawn on the same or another government department or issued by and drawn on one of the persons or bodies specified in [a schedule] which, not being a cheque or bank payment order, is intended to enable a person to obtain payment from the department or body on which it is drawn of the sum mentioned in the document'.

1 Jack Report, para 7.69.
2 Jack Report, para 7.70.

Chapter 8

Modern Methods of Money Transfer

1. INTRODUCTION

(1) GENERAL

In its original form, credit transfer occurred by way of individual letters whereby customers directed banks to pay given amounts of money to the credit of designated payees. However, the origin of the system in its modern format, rests upon the widening of banking activity following the end of the credit squeeze regime that existed until August 1958. The study by several banks of the operation of the foreign giro systems had generated considerable interest in the UK for the provision of an analogous system. The Radcliffe Committee Report[1] provided further impetus to the move-

---

1 *Report of the Committee on the Working of the Monetary System* (Cmnd 827) (1959) (the Radcliffe Report).

ment towards a giro system. The Committee stated that in the absence of an early move on the part of existing institutions to provide the services of a giro system, there would be a case for investigating the possibility of instituting a giro system to be operated by the Post Office[1]. The Payment of Wages Act 1960 for the first time authorised the payment of wages by credit transfer, cheque, or money or postal order, provided that the employee had made a written request that this be done and the employer had agreed. Previous legislation had prevented many employers and employees from making agreements whereby wages could be paid otherwise than in legal tender.

The modern integrated banking giro system has been fully operational since the beginning of the 1960s in the wake of the originating Post Office Giro System. The banks and National Giro Bank[2] are currently linked, and sums are transferable from an account held with a clearing bank to an account maintained by the National Giro Bank[3].

There are four basic giro transactions, namely: individual money transaction forms; standing orders; trader's credits; and direct debits. The method of transfer is, fundamentally, consistent throughout the variant forms of transfer. The payor (effecting transfer) instructs his bank (transferring bank) to pay a specified amount to the credit of a designated account, usually that of a third party (the payee). The recipient bank is that to which the amount is remitted by the transferring bank. The payor completes a standard form, stating the name of the transmitting bank and the recipient bank. Details also given include the date of instruction; the number of the payor's account; the name of the payee; details regarding the recipient bank (the name and number of account to be credited); the amount; and (sometimes) the object of the payment, for example, rent or insurance.

The payor signs the document, which ideally should be delivered to the branch which handles his account although it may be delivered to another branch or indeed any bank within the giro system. Such instructions may take several forms, some examples of which are: bank giro credits, standing orders, trader's credits and direct debits.

(2) BANK GIRO CREDITS

Bank giro credits are basic instruments of money transfer operation. Bank giro credits bear blanks for the insertion of details regarding the transfer including, for example, the name of the payee's account and the amount involved. The payor signs the form which is the basis of the payor's mandate to the bank regarding the remittance of the funds. The bank giro credit does not confer upon the bank authority to reimburse itself. The payor remits to the bank the cash required, a personal cheque, or cheques from a third party payable to himself.

---

1 Radcliffe Report, para 964.
2 See ch 2, p 23 above.
3 Under the Post Office (Banking Services) Act 1976, the Post Office has the power to provide full banking services for its customers.

(3)   STANDING ORDERS

Standing orders are a means by which periodic payments of fixed amounts may be made to third parties. The payor authorises the bank to debit his account with the amount of each payment to be made. The order is not accompanied by cheque or cash and is usable only by the customer maintaining an account with the transferring bank.

(4)   TRADER'S CREDITS

Trader's credits are a mechanism for simplifying the payment of accounts rendered to a trader regarding goods and services supplied to him for his ongoing business. It enables accounts to be settled periodically. The system operates by the trader listing all of the amounts to be paid by him in a standard form of payment from his bank. He details the identity of each payee and the account to be credited with each amount and then fills out a credit for each item. In such a way this notifies the recipient bank of the details of the credit and a copy of the voucher is then forwarded by the bank to the payee. The payor posts the trader's credits and vouchers with a single cheque, drawn on his account with his bank covering the total amount paid out. The cheque authorises the payor's bank (transferring) to debit his account with the amounts transferred. Trader's credits encoded on tapes are cleared through the Bank's Automated Clearing Services ('BACS'). BACS is the transferring bank's agent and the instructions transmitted by the customer are transmitted for his bank.

(5)   DIRECT DEBITS

The direct debits system was introduced in 1967 and enables the prompt payment of amounts due under commercial and consumer contracts by allowing the supplier, dealer or creditor to obtain payment of the amount due by issuing direct demands for payment to the debtor's bank. The debtor signs a standard form for the creditor, such form being lodged with the debtor's (transferring) bank. The form authorises the bank to pay the amounts demanded by the creditor. There is no need to require, on each occasion, confirmation of the fact of indebtedness by the debtor. Often, however, creditors send accounts to the debtor before claiming payment from the bank. Generally, creditors remit direct debit forms to the recipient bank, which makes arrangement for clearance (instead of first sending the form direct to the transferring bank). Direct debit is a mechanism usually operated for the payment of varying amounts falling due at regular or irregular intervals and in practice banks demand an indemnity from each customer using this method. The indemnity is addressed to all banks within the transfer system and covers each of them against any losses and expenses incurred directly or indirectly due to the direct debit and authorises the banks to compromise any claim on the creditor's behalf[1].

1   *Mercedes-Benz Finance Ltd v Clydesdale Bank plc* 1996 GWD 27-1563, OH.

2. DIFFERENCES BETWEEN CHEQUE USAGE AND THE GIRO SYSTEM

There are essentially three principal differences between cheques and the giro system. Firstly, in the case of a cheque, the payor's account is debited after the payee's account has been credited. In the case of a giro transfer, the payor's account is debited first and thereafter the payee's account is credited. In this respect the giro procedure is simpler than the cheque payment process. An 'uncovered' giro will not be carried out and does not affect the accounting of the payor's bank, the payee's bank or the payee. An uncovered cheque, however, affects all three such parties. Secondly, when payment is made by cheque, the payor sends the cheque direct to the payee, who hands it to his bank for the credit of his account. Apart from a statement of account, the collecting bank does not send any further credit advice to the payee, nor does the paying bank send a debit advice to the payor, other than the usual statement of account, accompanied in some cases by the paid cheque. In this way, one single document is used for the entire cheque procedure. In the case of a giro transfer, however, the payor sends an order to his bank and in due course, the payee's bank sends to the payee specific advice that the payor's order has been carried out. In this respect the giro procedure is less simple than that followed for payment by cheque. Thirdly, with cheque payment, the sorting of cheques requires to be carried out by reference to the payor's bank. It is a simple matter to identify this bank by means of a code printed on the cheque in advance. With giro payments, the sorting requires to be carried out by reference to the payee's bank. This information cannot be indicated by a code number printed in advance on the general giro order form. In this respect also the giro procedure is less simple than that followed for payment by cheque.

It follows that it was generally accepted that cheque payments were an easier method of payment for banks to handle than giro transfers. However, the latter were simpler for the customer, at least in cases where no cash payments were required. The case of *HMV Fields Properties Ltd v Bracken Self-Selection Fabrics Ltd*[1] illustrates that outwith the general contract framework, there is lack of specific regulation of the giro system and that the system facilitates the making of payments without the consent or knowledge of the payee or recipient. In that case a landlord served a notice to irritate a lease upon his defaulting tenants. The tenants refused to vacate the premises and proceeded to arbitration, meanwhile continuing to make payments of rent by way of the giro system. The landlord, for several weeks, was not aware of these payments and when he noticed that they were being applied to his account, wished to pay the rent back, while the tenants remained unwilling to receive them. The landlord in turn, paid the moneys back to the defaulting tenants through the giro system to which the tenants again responded by making payment by giro, a process which continued for some time. The landlord instructed his bank to refuse further giro payments but it transpired that there was no mechanism

1 1990 SCLR 677, 1991 SLT 31.

through which such refusal could be effected. The only process that the bank could employ was to return any payments after receipt but, unfortunately, the bank could not guarantee to be able to identify all of the giro payments. The issue in point was whether the landlord was barred from insisting upon the irritancy by reason of having accepted the rent. The court upheld the decision of the arbiter to the effect that to constitute 'acceptance' of rents, is a question of the facts and circumstances of each particular case and that upon these facts, there had been no acceptance by the landlord, despite the delay of several weeks prior to the landlord realising that payments were continuing[1].

3. CLEARING SYSTEMS

(1) INTRODUCTION

All giro transactions rely upon adequate and suitable clearing systems. Most transfers between accounts with financial institutions in the UK are processed by way of the clearing systems established under the auspices of the Association of Payment Clearing Services (APACS). APACS is an unincorporated association which was set up by its members in 1985 to oversee payment clearing services and money transmission generally. The principal clearing systems are divided and owned by four separate trading companies[2] these being: the Cheque and Credit Clearing Company Ltd, which operates bulk paper clearings; the CHAPS and Town Clearing Company Ltd, which operates same day, high value transactions; BACS Ltd, which provides bulk electronic clearing services; and EFTPOS UK Ltd covering electronic fund transfer at point of sale.

The principal systems in operation are BACS, CHAPS and SWIFT.

BACS

The first clearing system in the UK was set up in 1968 by the Inter-Bank Computer Bureau which was transferred to a separate company, Bankers Automated Clearing Services Ltd in 1971 and became part of the APACS structure in 1985, when its name changed to BACS Ltd .

CHAPS

The Clearing House Automated Payment System is an electronic sterling credit transfer service within APACS providing same day settlement of single high value payments. It was introduced in 1984 and operates by way of 'gates' using a network of British Telecommunications. There also

1 See Gretton 'The Bank Giro System—A Possible Problem' (1992) JBL 335.
2 Membership of a clearing company is given to an institution able to meet a minimum set of criteria which includes trading of 0.5 per cent of the volume of a given clearing: *Report of the Review Committee on Banking Services: Law and Practice* (the Jack Report) (Cm 622) (1989), Appendix E.

exist two alternative systems, the first of which is used for bank giro credits and is similar to the clearing of cheques and the second of which relates to amounts transferred from an account held within a branch operating within the City of London to another within the same system. Transfer is effected in the same day of payment by 'banker's payments'.

SWIFT

Swift is the Society for Worldwide Interbank Financial Telecommunications. This system provides an international message switching service for payment instructions, statements and other messages associated with international finance transactions between banks. Such transfer is also possible by telex or mail transfer. The transferring bank communicates to the recipient bank (directly or through an intermediary), the details of the account to be credited, and the method by which the recipient bank is to reimburse itself. Transfer is effected by debiting the payor's account and crediting the payee's account without there being any physical handling of moneys. However, it is not a method of undertaking the payments themselves. These must still be settled across accounts, typically in the major financial centre of the country of the relevant currency.

(2) CLEARING OF MONEYS THROUGH BACS

BACS is primarily used for periodic payment, certain trader's credits, direct debiting and similar transfers. The main difference between manual and electronic clearance is the methodology, but the duration of clearance is generally the same — three days[1]. BACS uses electronic transfers with commensurately fewer documents and less physical transmission of documents. As regards payments directly between banks, the transferring bank prepares a form of magnetic media, diskette or tapes which sets out the relevant data, such data being generally the same as the data contained within a bank giro credit. The tape is delivered to BACS' premises in Edgeware, London by the close of the first day of the three day clearance cycle. It is processed immediately, with the computer connecting the tape into other tapes classified by reference to the recipient banks and payees. BACS' tapes are expected to be available by 3 am the following morning and are despatched to the head offices of the recipient banks on the same day. On the second day of the clearance cycle, the BACS' tapes are processed at the recipient banks' computer centres. The relevant amounts are credited to the account of the customers. The information contained within the tapes becomes available to the branches of the banks on the third day of the cycle. All necessary notification is generally despatched to customers by the branch on the third day. There is some scope for the rectification of errors within the system. Where a reversal of an entry is requested after the third day of the clearing cycle, a 're-debit request' must be issued, explaining the error. The error is rectified when all parties have reached agreement.

---

1 See Crerar 'Making Money Work for You and Your Clients' (1995) 40 JLSS 108–111.

Where payment is directed by one of BACS' 'sponsored clients' (approximately 50,000 in 1994), there are some repetitions in the process. The initial tape is prepared by the client's computer centre and delivered direct to BACS. The sponsoring bank is the transferring bank in the tape. The total of the amount covered by the tape is debited to the client's account with his bank. Otherwise the process follows as that for tapes emanating from a bank.

Direct debits are dealt with differently within the BACS system. In the case of a direct debit, where demand is made by a trading firm authorised by its client, through BACS, the transferring bank (the creditor's bank) issues a demand for payment[1]. The difference between this procedure and a payment instruction is that the recipient bank must pay, not receive the payment. The request may be refused (with no necessary provision of reasons) before the third day of the clearing cycle. The main disadvantage of the BACS system is that its use is confined to the transfer of periodic or regular payments by large enterprises[2].

(3)   CLEARING OF MONEYS THROUGH CHAPS

CHAPS was initiated as an attempt to provide a more efficient and effective system than BACS. The intention is that CHAPS covers all same day settlements by British clearing banks and all other banks within the UK jurisdiction. There are two principal distinctions between CHAPS and BACS. Firstly, BACS operations are conducted through one main centre in Edgeware, London, with its own computer system. CHAPS, however, operates through 'gateway' terminals maintained individually by major settlement banks or jointly by smaller banks. Secondly, BACS operations involve the compilation of tapes delivered by participating banks manually to centres and vice versa. CHAPS is entirely automated and is effected by direct electronic messages.

In the case of CHAPS, the transferring bank of the customer transmits the relevant message to a gateway. The message is then sent by cypher through 'British Telecom Switching Service' to the recipient bank's gateway. The message received at the recipient bank's gateway is then transmitted to the relevant branch or head office and the payee's account is credited with the amount involved. In the case of participating banks who do not possess gateways, they use those of 'settlement banks' as their agents. The settlement banks treat the participating banks as though they were branches of their own bank.

(4)   REGULATION OF RIGHTS OF THIRD PARTIES

The governing principles are based upon the law of agency. The payor mandates the transferring bank, which issues a specified order to the

---

1 This is not an order to transfer or pay.
2 BACS is a nationwide service and cleared 1059 million items to year-end November 1987: Jack Report, Appendix E, para 2, p 324.

recipient bank and directly in the case of bank giro credits. In other cases, an intermediary bank will be used (where a bank giro credit form is issued to a bank outwith the clearing house system). Issues central to electronic fund transfer are the status of the recipient bank and the method of determining the time of payment of the amount transferred, particularly where the payor wishes to countermand the order to transfer. The status of the recipient bank depends upon whether the bank is operating as an agent effecting the transferring bank's instruction or as an agent acquiring the relevant credit on behalf of the payee. In the 'Golden Memo' of 1967, the pertinence of agency law was clear[1]. The participating banks agreed to give one another notice that each was authorised to act on behalf of all the others in giro transactions. Customers of any participating bank could use all other participating banks in the system. In the case of a customer without a current account, he could still use the giro to pay cash to the credit of any account maintained with a participating bank. It seems generally accepted that it is a question of debate as to whether someone using a bank with which he does not have an account to carry out giro operations, is in the relationship of principal and agent with the bank, or whether the bank is the agent of the payor's bank.

4. COMPARISON OF BANK GIRO CREDITS AND CHEQUES

In the case of cheques there is a danger that the payee, obtaining possession of the cheque, may alter it by raising the amount. In the case of giros this risk of fraud is almost totally eliminated. There is a residual danger, but a fraud in the case of a bank giro credit would require to be perpetrated by the payor's clerk or agent. The posting and delivery to the transferring bank of the bank giro credit and not to the payee, considerably reduces the dangers of fraud. Further, in the case of cheques, presentment for payment through a bank entails that they may be dishonoured by virtue of non-payment. The payee's account is credited prior to the cheque being sent into transmission for presentment to the drawee bank. Where the cheque is dishonoured by the latter bank, due to an irregularity on the face of the cheque or inadequate funds in the drawer's account, the cheque is returned to the collecting bank and thereafter returned to the payee. The credit entry in the account of the payee is reversed. In the case of bank giro credits the transferring bank initially processes the form. The bank must be satisfied that the form is regular and the payment in order. The recipient bank, only at this juncture becomes involved in the transaction. The transferor's account is debited before the crediting of the payee's account. Ledger entries are reversed only where the amount that is credited is to an incorrect account which is due, usually, to a decoding error, or the insertion of an inaccurate detail in the bank giro credit.

---

1 Later abandoned due to its possible violation of the Restrictive Trade Practices Act 1956.

Bank giro credits do, however, involve much more laborious filling out of forms which are avoided in dealings with cheques. They also generate additional effort for the transferring bank and the recipient bank in the process method. The transferring bank delivers the credit voucher to the recipient bank in the clearing house system and some of the leading banks undertake the burden of advising the transferor about the execution of the instruction. The recipient bank then notifies the payee. Cheques, on the other hand, serve in themselves the function of notice and, except where dishonoured, clearance involves the minimum of paperwork.

5.   LEGAL CHARACTERISTICS OF MONEY TRANSFER ORDERS

This area of banking law is made difficult by the absence of any guiding case law and the distinction which exists between different types of transfer orders. This position contrasts with that regarding cheques where the foundations are consistent and widely interpreted by common law. Ellinger and Lomnicka suggest that there are, however, some areas of certainty with regard to money transfer orders namely: (1) money transfer documents are not negotiable instruments; (2) the law of assignment is probably inapplicable; and (3) agency law governs most of the relationships of parties to such orders[1].

Difficulties are sometimes, however, compounded by the uncertainty of determining upon whose behalf a bank is acting at any given time, particularly with regard to the validity of countermand[2].

(1)   MONEY TRANSFER ORDERS ARE NOT NEGOTIABLE INSTRUMENTS

The money transfer order is not negotiable because it fails to satisfy the criterion stipulated in the enabling section 3 of the Bills of Exchange Act 1882, to the effect that is must be an unconditional order in writing addressed by one person to another, instructing the addressee to pay on demand or at a fixed or determinable future time a certain sum of money to the order of a specified person or to bearer. Money transfer orders are not negotiable because they are not payable at a determinable future time or on demand. They are payable as soon as the transferring bank (the drawee) can make payment. An instrument may only be regarded as payable on demand where the payee has the opportunity or the right to claim payment. Neither are they payable to the order of a specified person or to bearer. To satisfy this requirement, it must be clear from the nature of each instrument paid, that the payee can transfer the document to

---

1   Ellinger and Lomnicka *Modern Banking Law* (2nd edn, 1994) pp 443–457.
2   See ch 7, pp 238–240 above.

another, if he so desires. In money transfer orders, the payee cannot determine to whose order they are to be paid. In such instruments there are no words which are open to interpretation as an instruction formally given by the payor to the transferring bank. It therefore follows that, where a money transfer order is fraudulently altered or issued, the parties rights are determined by the principles of contract and agency.

(2)   MONEY TRANSFER ORDERS AS NON-ASSIGNMENTS

A money transfer order is an authorisation and instruction from the customer to his bank to transfer an amount standing to the credit of that customer with that bank to the credit of its account with another bank. That other bank is then impliedly authorised by the customer to accept that credit by virtue of the fact that the customer has a current account with it and there is no expectation or indeed necessity that the other bank provide its consent to the receipt of the credit[1].

(3)   AGENCY LAW GOVERNS MOST OF THE RELATIONSHIPS

The transferring bank

The transferring bank acts in a representative capacity in bank giro transactions. It is generally instructed by the payor who orders the transfer of a given amount of money, usually to a third party but occasionally to the credit of the payor's own account with an overseas bank. It therefore follows that any instruction received by the transferring bank must be executed with reasonable care and skill[2]. Most writers consider that the obligations constituted within the duty of reasonable care by the transferring bank involve that the transfer must be timeous and any stipulated deadline must be complied with where reasonable and that the bank must employ a reasonable correspondent in the payee's country. That latter obligation is of immediate concern to the bank since the transferring bank is vicariously responsible for the default or negligence of its correspondent[3]. Where a bank uses one of its own overseas branches it would of course be liable for its actings, as the bank is considered as a single legal entity. The bank's obligation is owed only to a payor or transferor who is also a customer.

Ellinger and Lomnicka take the view that where the payor is an unrelated member of the public there exists no contractual relationship whatsoever and that the bank operates for the individual within the spirit of the 'Golden Memo'[4]. Under this memorandum the banks act as agents for

1 See *Royal Products Ltd v Midland Bank Ltd and Bank of Valletta Ltd* [1981] 2 Lloyd's Rep 194 at 198, per Webster J.
2 See *Royal Products Ltd v Midland Bank Ltd and Bank of Valletta Ltd* above and *Midland Bank Ltd v Seymour* [1955] 2 Lloyd's Rep 147.
3 *Equitable Trust Co of New York v Dawson Partners Ltd* (1927) 27 Ll L Rep 49, HL; *Calico Printers' Association Ltd v Barclays Bank Ltd* (1930) 36 Com Cas 71.
4 Ellinger and Lomnicka *Modern Banking Law* (2nd edn, 1994) p 450.

each other and not therefore as agents of strangers. Others disagree with this view[1]. Such debate, however, may be superfluous as a result of the expanding liability in delict in which the underlying relationships evolve further from contract[2].

The correspondent bank

The correspondent bank is employed by the transferring bank and it follows that there is no contractual relationship between the correspondent and the payor[3].

The recipient bank

The role of the recipient bank is largely dependent upon the nature of the transaction taking place. In the case of a direct debit transaction the recipient bank is the payee's agent. The payee in designating the receiving bank provides that the receiving bank acts in a representative capacity, but also proposes to accept the payment involved in his own right. The recipient bank, therefore, becomes the payee's agent for that purpose. Where the payor transfers funds to the credit of an account chosen by the payee, the recipient bank acts as a recipient of the funds on behalf of the payee. Where the transfer is initiated by the payor without the prior and express consent of the payee the law differs and the recipient bank acts at the request of the payor or his agent (the transferring bank). The payee may, in certain circumstances, refuse the transfer or the method of it.

It appears an arguable point as to whether the recipient bank owes a duty of care to the payor. In the United States case of *Securities Fund Services Inc v American National Bank & Trust Co*[4] it was held that the loss of the transferred funds was the reasonably foreseeable result of a deposit made where the name on the transfer instructions differed from that on the account in which the funds were deposited and the court therefore found in favour of the transferor.

6.   ELECTRONIC FUND TRANSFER

Electronic Fund Transfer (EFT) describes the generality of transmission systems which involve 'a transfer of funds effected through the banking system by electronic techniques, with input and output methods being largely or completely in electronic form'[5].

---

1 Chorley and Smart *Leading Cases in the Law of Banking* (6th edn, 1990) pp 277 ff.
2 *Marc Rich & Co AG v Bishop Rock Marine Co Ltd, The Nicholas H* [1994] 3 All ER 686, [1994] 1 WLR 1071, CA; *Henderson v Merrett Syndicates* [1995] 2 AC 145, [1994] 3 All ER 506, HL.
3 *Calico Printers' Association Ltd v Barclays Bank Ltd* (1930) 36 Com Cas 71, per Wright J; but see *Securities Fund Services Inc v American National Bank & Trust Co* 542 F Supp 323 (1982).
4 542 F Supp 323 (1982).
5 Jack Report, Glossary of Terms Interpretation, p x.

(1) EVERYDAY APPLICATIONS OF EFT

ATMs

The manifestation of EFT which is best known to the retail consumer is the cash dispenser or automated telling machine (ATM). The first ever cash dispensing machines were introduced in the UK in 1967. The customer inserts a plastic card into the machine, accompanied by a personal identification number (PIN number). The account is debited immediately upon the ATM reading the data encoded on the card and by doing so, authorising the transaction. ATMs generally dispense cash, but most now have been developed to provide balance statements and the provision of receipts for the value of the cash withdrawn. Most of the banks, and in some cases building societies, have linked their ATM networks allowing withdrawal from each other's ATMs. Such reciprocal use of the ATM networks has mutual benefit to the institutions (who may spread their costs) and their customers (who have access to a greater number of machines)[1].

EFTPOS

More recently, however, banks have introduced EFTPOS which is an acronym for electronic funds transfer at point of sale. Such a system allows retail payments to be made by transferring funds electronically from customers to retail accounts without any need for cash or cheques. Typically the customer inserts his card into a reader terminal at the retailer's sale desk and information relating to the transaction is sent to a central processing point where the validity of the card is authenticated. The customer proceeds to authorise the transaction by keying in his PIN or signing a receipt produced by the terminal. At the central processor, the retailer's account is credited with the value of the transaction and the customer's account debited[2]. The most favoured system is the Switch system which was originally operated by the Royal Bank of Scotland, the National Westminster, Midland, Clydesdale, Yorkshire and Bank of Scotland together with the Halifax Building Society. EFTPOS UK Limited is a clearing company within the structure of APACS and has the objective of the management of investigation, specification development and implementation of the EFTPOS schemes[3].

Home and office banking systems

Home and office banking systems were originally introduced by the Bank of Scotland (in conjunction with the Nottingham Building Society) in 1982 and are now operated by all the major UK clearing banks. These systems connect the bank's central computer directly to the home or office by way of television or telephone and are operated by a key pad or personal computer. They presently comprise functions such as the provision of balance

---

1 See the Jack Report, Appendix E(4).
2 Jack Report, para 9.09
3 See p 250 above.

inquiries and other account information; funds transfer between accounts; and bill payments from the customers to agreed third party accounts (which usually require a written mandate from the customer)[1].

(2)   RELATIONSHIP BETWEEN THE PARTIES IN AN EFT TRANSACTION

There are a considerable number of parties to an EFT transaction with a consequent number of legal relationships. The participants may include the following[2]: the customer who holds the account (the cardholder); the bank or institution which issues the card (the card issuer); the bank receiving the transfer ordered by another bank according to the cardholder's instructions; the bank responsible for the ATM terminals through which transactions are made by cardholders, many of whom are not clients of that bank; the company providing the equipment and software for the installation of an ATM or EFTPOS facility; the organisation managing the ATM, EFTPOS or home/office banking network; the organisation providing the physical means of communication to transport signals between terminals, bank computers and central system computers; the bank or institution acting as the clearer between the banks and business enterprises linked to the system; and the retailers receiving payment for goods and services by means of an EFT transaction.

The bulk of these relationships are governed by express contract but some may only have an implied contractual link arising from course of conduct or none at all. In an EFTPOS transaction the contractual relationships which are likely to be express include: (1) the contract between the card issuer and the organisation managing the EFTPOS network; (2) the contract between the card-issuing bank and its account holder (the cardholder); (3) the contract between the retailer accepting the EFT payments and the organisation managing the network. Ancillary to these express contracts is the contract between the cardholder and the retailer, most frequently a contract of sale.

In the case of contracts between the card-issuing bank and the account holder, most involve the provision of standard conditions which are designed to limit or exclude the liability of the card issuer arising from EFT transactions. In all cases the cardholder is required to agree to memorise his PIN and destroy immediately the number notification slip. Most card issuers provide that they have a general authority to debit the cardholders account at the card issuer's discretion with the result that cardholders have little protection, although generally the customer does not incur liability for unauthorised use of the card after notification to the card issuer (usually in writing). The Unfair Contract Terms Act 1977 does provide some protection to cardholders and provisions in standard form conditions are enforceable only so long as they are 'reasonable in the circumstances'[3].

---

1 Jack Report, para 9.10.
2 R Robertson 'Limitation of liability in EFT transactions' (1990) Computer Law and Practice, September/October.
3 Unfair Contract Terms Act 1977, s 16(1).

(3) THE JACK COMMITTEE'S VIEW ON EFT LAW AND PRACTICE

The Jack Committee identified four main areas of difficulty: (1) authentication of instructions; (2) operational security on existing systems; (3) liability of loss in the event of fraud or technical failure; and (4) countermand or reversal of instructions.

Authentication of instructions

Authentication of the instructions by way of electronic key as opposed to the customer's signature introduces new problems in the area of fraudulent transactions which require consideration of the security measures necessary at the design stage of EFT systems activated by customers. Complex issues relating to the question of the burden of proof do arise in situations of customer activated EFT, where there is a dispute as to whether the transaction recorded by the bank, and reflected in the periodic statement of account provided to the customer was in fact authorised[1]. The Consumer Credit Act 1974 presently places the burden on the consumer. The Jack Report recommended[2] that a provision of statute law should apply, notwithstanding the terms of any express contract to the contrary, as to the apportionment of loss arising from a transaction carried out through a customer activated EFT system. This would take into account such factors as: the steps taken by the customer to protect his PIN number; the extent to which the system provided by the bank protects the customer against unauthorised transactions on his account; and the relative weight of the contentions of the parties in support of their respective arguments that the transaction was or was not authorised.

Operational security on existing systems

The principal concern relates to the standard of care appropriate to the safeguarding of cards and PIN numbers. Matters arise from the generation of personal information into the terminals which are capable of being read by other parties. Security issues also arise from the ease by which magnetically stored messages may be altered or erased.

Liability of loss in the event of fraud or technical failure

The Jack Committee expressed some disquiet over the difficulties arising from questions as to where the burden of proof should rest in instances where the authority for a transaction is disputed by a cardholder. In the instances of liability in cases arising from fraudulent use of an operative card under an EFT system, banks presently set their own terms and conditions on the matter, binding the customer. In terms of the Consumer Credit Act 1974 a customer's liability ceases immediately upon notification of the loss to the bank[3]. Usually this rule is fixed by express contract

---

1 See *First Sport Ltd v Barclays Bank plc* [1993] 3 All ER 789, [1993] 1 WLR 1229, CA.
2 Jack Report, recommendation 10(12).
3 Consumer Credit Act 1974, ss 83 and 84.

providing a pre-ordained limit to the customer's potential liability except in circumstances where the customer has consented to the use of the card by someone else, in which case liability is unlimited[1].

Countermand or reversal of instructions

The view was expressed that the difficulties already present in paper-based transactions have been exacerbated by the electronic era (for example, problems of insolvency and practical inconvenience to the customer). The Jack Committee[2] was of the view that the very one-sided contractual relationships between card issuers and cardholders was no longer sustainable and that there was a pressing need for EFT regulation which should be in such a fashion so as not to hamper the development and design of continually evolving systems. It was principally for that reason that the Committee suggested a 'two tier' system with statute law confined to a few central issues common to all EFT systems[3]. Detailed issues bearing upon specific technologies should be governed by 'standards of best practice'[4]. In particular, a standard of best practice should cover consumer activated EFT systems upon the basic principle that the bank's principal and general duty is to maintain its customer's mandate. The Committee's view[5] was that banks should adopt the principle that an EFT system must meet minimum standards of security in its authorisation procedures, so as to provide an acceptable degree of protection for the customers against the consequences of unauthorised instructions with the ongoing obligation to upgrade systems by the introduction, so far as practicable, of new technology based upon the recognition of a signature or other personal characteristic[6].

1 See *First Sport Ltd v Barclays Bank plc* [1993] 3 All ER 789, [1993] 1 WLR 1229, CA.
2 Jack Report, paras 9.13 ff.
3 Jack Report, para 9.30.
4 See R Robertson 'Limitation of liability in EFT transactions'; H Rowe 'Legal Issues between Banks Sharing Networks'; O Longe 'Electronic Fund Transfers at Point of Sale in U S'; J Lambert 'The Challenge of Organisations outside the Banking System' — all in (1990) Computer Law and Practice, September/October. For the European dimension, see the Jack Report, ch 3.
5 Jack Report, recommendation 10(1).
6 This proposal foresees that banks would, in the future, be liable for any losses incurred as a result of security shortcomings in existing technology.

Chapter 9

Security for Advances made by Bankers

1. INTRODUCTION

(1) THE CONCEPT OF SECURITY

The broadest, and most often quoted definition of the concept of security is:

'... any right which a creditor may hold for ensuring the payment or satisfaction of his debt, distinct from, and in addition to, his right of action and
execution against the debtor under the latter's personal obligation. A creditor, in other words, who holds a right in security, has at his disposal some
means of realising payment or exacting performance of the obligation due to
him, distinct from, and in addition to the means which are at the disposal of

the debtor's personal credit. Whatever the special form of the right in security may be, its effect is in all cases to put the party entitled to it in a position of advantage, and to render his power of realising payment of his debt more sure'[1].

The definition clearly covers any accessory right, the essential purpose of which is to provide the favoured creditor with a safeguard against the personal failure of the debtor, notably in the event of his insolvency[2].

It follows therefore that, in order to have a means of realising payment or exacting performance of the obligation due to him, distinct from and in addition to the means which are at the disposal of the debtor's general (unsecured) creditors, the creditor must also either hold some right to realise payment out of particular assets, this right being indefeasible by the rights of other creditors who have claims on the debtor's estate, or be creditor in a personal obligation granted to him by a third party whereby the third party undertakes to perform the principal debtor's obligation on the latter's default.

The concept of security, in its broadest sense, can therefore be broken down into two separate areas: security rights over property, and cautionary security, whereby, in addition to his personal right against the principal debtor the creditor obtains a personal right against a third party (the cautioner) enforceable in the event of the principal debtor's default.

Without such 'security', the creditor will merely possess, in common with all other creditors of the debtor, a right to claim a share in the debtor's estate on his insolvency. On the debtor's sequestration or liquidation, this estate, less any assets secured by particular creditors and after deduction of preferential debts, will be distributed pro rata ('rateably') as far as it will go, in satisfaction or part satisfaction of such claims[3].

(2)   SECURITY RIGHTS OVER PROPERTY

To understand security rights over property it is necessary to consider the importance of the requirements for the creation of real rights, and the categories of security devices appropriate to different categories of property.

Need for more than personal obligation of debt

The personal obligation of debt itself cannot constitute a real right:

'Since the main characteristic of a right in security over property lies in its conferring on the creditor, who is entitled to it, the right to vindicate a par-

---

1 W M Gloag and J M Irvine *The Law of Rights in Security and Cautionary Obligations* (1897) pp 1, 2. 'The concept of security is far more slippery than at least some legislators (and judges) seen to suppose': G L Gretton 'The Concept of Security' in *A Scots Conveyancing Miscellany: Essays in Honour of Professor J M Halliday* (1987) p 140.
2 *Bowe v Spankie* 1 June 1811 FC: 'Where nothing more is granted than the personal obligation of the debtor, it can never be understood that a security is given. Every creditor has a personal claim against the debtor who does not deny the debt, but he has no security in legal language, unless he holds some other person or some special subject bound for a debt'.
3 Bankruptcy (Scotland) Acts 1985 and 1993; Insolvency Act 1986.

ticular subject, and, consequently, a preference over that subject on the bankruptcy of the debtor, it is clear at the outset that a merely personal pecuniary obligation by the debtor himself is not in any sense a right in security'[1].

Nor can an obligation to pay the debt in a particular manner or out of a particular fund create any preferential right in favour of the creditor. Thus an undertaking by a company to repay a debt by fixed annual instalments 'out of profits' did not give the creditor a *jus in re* (real right) over the profits as they accrued so as to entitle him to a preference upon the profits over the general creditors of the company. Lord McLaren said: ' ... it is perfectly clear that a mere pecuniary obligation is not a security, and that it does not become one by reason of a fund being designated out of which payments shall be made'[2].

Need for more than a mere agreement to create security

Like the personal obligation of debt itself, a mere agreement to give security in general does not create a real right, although various attempts have been made to avoid this principle. For example:

> 'The theory was put forward that if the debtor had agreed to transfer some specific thing to a particular creditor by way of security, the debtor then held the thing in trust for that creditor, the result being that if the debtor became bankrupt the specific thing would not be counted part of the bankrupt's estate but would be made available to the creditor for whom it was supposed to be held in trust'[3].

This theory was rejected by the House of Lords in *Bank of Scotland v Hutchison, Main & Co Ltd Liquidators*[4]. A company indebted to the bank entered into an agreement whereby the bank would surrender £2,000 worth of golf balls which belonged to the company and which the bank held in security. In exchange, the company was to procure and assign in security to the bank a debenture over property belonging to one of its own debtors. After the bank had surrendered the golf balls and the debenture had been obtained by the company, but before the company had assigned the debenture to the bank, the company went into liquidation. The bank claimed the debenture on the ground that the company held it as trustee for the bank. It was held that, at most, the company was under a contractual obligation to assign the debenture. The bank had no real right but only a personal right to compel the company to assign the debenture to it. Since the assignation had not been obtained by the date of liquidation, the debenture formed part of the company's assets to be distributed pro rata amongst all of the company's general creditors[5].

---

1 *Gloag and Irvine* p 5.
2 *Graham & Co v Raeburn & Verel* (1895) 23 R 84 at 89, per Lord McLaren.
3 E A Marshall *Scots Mercantile Law* (2nd edn, 1992) p 446.
4 1914 SC (HL) 1, 1914 1 SLT 111.
5 For the requirements for creation of a valid trust in favour of the creditor, see *Clark Taylor & Co Ltd v Quality Site Development (Edinburgh) Ltd* 1981 SC 111, 1981 SLT 308; *Tay Valley Joinery Ltd v C F Financial Services* 1987 SCLR 117, 1987 SLT 207; *Balfour Beatty Ltd v Britannia Life Ltd* 1997 SLT 10, OH.

The 'overt act' requirement

Gloag and Irvine state:

> 'Apart from ... special instances in which rights in security created by simple contract or arising by implication of law are recognised, all rights in security by the law of Scotland require for their constitution not only an agreement between the parties, but some overt act'[1].

Historically, the required overt act was some form of delivery of the security subjects to the creditor. 'Delivery', however, has taken on various forms according to the type of property concerned. In general it is one of the following:

(1) actual, constructive or symbolic delivery of possession (corporeal moveables other than ships or aircraft and secured otherwise than by way of floating charge);
(2) intimation of assignation of the security subjects (incorporeal moveables, intimation being to the person liable to pay the debt evidenced by the incorporeal moveable property); or
(3) registration of the security agreement or transfer in some public register (heritably property, ships, aircraft, certain agricultural property, company shares and property secured by way of floating charge).

However, there are certain 'special instances' where a real right in security may arise either without any overt act of possession, intimation or registration or without any express agreement, namely conventional hypothecs, tacit or legal hypothecs or liens.

Conventional hypothecs

'Hypothec' is defined as 'a real right in security in favour of a creditor over subjects which are allowed to remain in the possession of the debtor'[2]. A conventional hypothec over moveable property is therefore a real right created by mere agreement without delivery of possession to the creditor. While conventional hypothecs enjoyed liberal recognition in Roman law, they have not found favour in modern legal systems, even in countries where the influence of Roman law was strong[3]. Only two such securities are recognised in Scots law but even these are now virtually obsolete[4]. They are bonds of bottomry over a ship and bonds of respondentia over a ship's cargo. Either can be granted by the owner or master of a ship, only at a foreign port and only where money which is indispensable for the prosecution of the voyage or for the benefit and safety of the cargo cannot be obtained in any other manner[5].

---

1 *Gloag and Irvine* vol II, p 8.
2 *Gloag and Irvine* p 406.
3 Bell *Commentaries* II,25.
4 20 *Stair Memorial Encyclopaedia* para 6.
5 20 *Stair Memorial Encyclopaedia* para 6; *Gloag and Irvine* pp 297–302.

Tacit or legal hypothecs

Tacit or legal hypothecs are securities arising without the need for either possession by the creditor or any express agreement. The recognised tacit hypothecs are: a solicitor's hypothec for the expenses of an action; a landlord's hypothec for rent (on urban subjects); and a superior's hypothec for his feu duties[1].

Liens

Liens are security rights arising, like tacit hypothecs, by implication of law. the basis of a lien is usually 'a collateral or ancillary condition implied by law in a contract whose main preoccupation will be something other than the creation of security'[2]. Thus, for example, the banker's lien is an ancillary or collateral condition implied by law in the contract between banker and customer[3]. Liens are distinguished from tacit hypothecs in that they demand possession by the creditor[4].

With the exception of these 'special instances', all rights in security over property for their constitution require both agreement to create the right and some overt act of possession, intimation or registration by which the right is, in law, completed and rendered 'real'.

Function of the overt act

The requirement for some overt act in addition to a mere exchange of consent applies whether the real right to be granted to the creditor is a real right in security or a real right of ownership intended to operate as security. The ostensible function of this overt act is to make other parties, such as potential creditors of the debtor or purchasers of the property, aware of the secured creditor's prior interest in the property, 'that commerces may be the more sure, and that every one may more easily know his condition with whom he contracts'[5]. Thus, Bell states: '... it is against the principle and spirit of the law of Scotland to admit a real right or security which is not attended with some badge manifest and palpable'[6]. The theory is that the overt acts of possession, intimation and registration are necessary for third party protection, demonstrating the existence of the right in security held by a particular creditor.

1 E A Marshall *Scots Mercantile Law* (2nd edn, 1992) paras 7-43 to 7-72; *Gloag and Irvine* pp 406–439.
2 20 *Stair Memorial Encyclopaedia* para 67.
3 See 20 *Stair Memorial Encyclopaedia* paras 66–100; *Gloag and Irvine* pp 303–405.
4 Bell *Principles* s 1415. Note that consensual or express liens (where property is subjected to a lien by express provision in a contract) are common in certain standard form contracts of haulage, storage or repair. In such cases, the express provisions supplement or vary the rules of common law (*Anderson & Co's Trustee v Fleming* 1871 9 M 718). For problems arising in relation to the status of consensual liens (eg their ranking in relation to floating charges), see G L Gretton 'The Concept of Security' p 142.
5 *Stair* I,13,14.
6 Bell *Principles* s 1385.

The contrast with English law

The need for some overt act to demonstrate the existence of a right in security is the essential feature that distinguishes the Scottish from the English law of security.

> 'The systematic body of rules developed by the Court of Chancery to temper the injustices of the English common law and known generally as the rules of equity attached great importance to the intention and the agreement of the contracting parties. Accordingly, the equitable assignment and the equitable mortgage, which rely for their efficacy on agreement alone, give far-reaching protection to the equitable assignee and the equitable mortgagee. The protection afforded by an equitable security is not complete and unassailable in all circumstances, but it is usually effective for all practical purposes or can readily be made so'[1].

So, for example, an equitable assignment of a debt is complete and effective in the bankruptcy or liquidation of the assignor without notification to the debtor. Thus, the mere deposit of a life assurance policy constitutes an equitable mortgage and gives the banker the rights of an equitable mortgagee[2].

(3)   CATEGORIES OF SECURITY

The principal category of security devices used in relation to property is the express, or conventional, security arising by the voluntary grant of the debtor and, with the exception of the conventional hypothecs, requiring some overt act to complete the real right of the creditor over the property. Secondly, certain tacit, or legal, securities over property may arise automatically under certain circumstances, independently of the consent of the debtor. Some of these require the overt act of possession (for example liens) while others do not (for example tacit hypothecs). A third class of security over property can also be created by diligence, granted by the court on the application of the unpaid creditor.

2.   SECURITY OVER CORPOREAL MOVEABLES

(1)   COMMON LAW EMPHASIS ON DELIVERY OF POSSESSION TO THE CREDITOR

At common law, with the exception of hypothecs, there can be no security over corporeal moveable property without delivery of possession by the

---

1   20 *Stair Memorial Encyclopaedia* para 5.
2   *Spencer v Clarke* (1878) 9 Ch D 137. Hence the recent problems with English lenders operating in Scotland believing they held security by mere deposit or assignation of life assurance policies without intimation to the relevant debtors. Note also the possibility of non-possessory securities over moveables in English law by 'hypothecation' provided the security is registered as a bill of sale (Ellinger and Lomnicka *Modern Banking Law* (2nd edn, 1994) pp 662–665). Registration replaces possession as the overt act required to complete the security.

debtor to the creditor[1]. This general principle is said to be expressed in the maxim *traditionibus, non nudis pactis, transferentur rerum dominia* ('by delivery, not by mere agreement, are real rights in property transferred'). This principle is a cornerstone of Scottish property law.

There being no public register of interests in moveable property, possession was seen, in Scots law, as '... the badge of real right'[2]. Consequently, delivery of possession became the overt act required at common law to vest a real right in a creditor. The general rule with regard to moveables is that possession presumes property (ownership). A mere instrument of possession is not sufficient to transfer moveables assigned or disponed in security[3]. At common law, delivery of possession is required to create a real right in security, being still considered as a means of third-party protection, albeit a primitive one. If the debtor retains possession, no security exists: 'A mere assignation of corporeal moveables *retenta possessione* is nothing whatever but a personal obligation, and creates no preference of any kind'[4]. It has been said: 'There is no principle more deeply rooted in the law than this, that in order to create a good security over subjects delivery must be given. If possession be retained no effectual security can be granted'[5].

Fictitious sales to creditor

There have been various unsuccessful attempts to create security over moveables by ex facie absolute transfer in the form of sale to the creditor (the 'buyer') without delivery, the debtor (the 'seller') remaining at all times in possession of the moveables and repaying the debt in the guise of some buy-back, lease-back with option to repurchase or hire-purchase-back agreement[6].

Under section 17(1) of the Sale of Goods Act 1979[7], on a sale of goods, ownership passes when the parties intend it to pass, whether or not possession of the goods has passed to the buyer. The buyer may therefore have ownership without possession. Attempts have been made to rely on this concept to create security without possession by transactions of the sale and buy-back type, the 'price' ostensibly paid by the creditor (the 'buyer') being reflected in the amount advanced to or due by the debtor. The debt is gradually amortised by instalments paid under the buy-back, lease or hire-purchase agreement. However, such transactions have generally fallen foul of section 62(4) of the 1979 Act[8] which disapplies the pro-

---

1 Bell *Commentaries* II,21; *Clark v West Calder Oil Co Liquidators* (1882) 9 R 1017.
2 *Moore v Gledden* (1869) 7 M 1016 at 1022, per Lord Neaves.
3 Bell *Commentaries* II,11.
4 *Clark v West Calder Oil Co Liquidators* (1882) 9 R 1017 at 1024, per Lord President Inglis.
5 *Clark v West Calder Oil Co Liquidators* (1882) 9 R 1017 at 1033, per Lord Shand; *Pattison's Trustee v Liston* (1893) 20 R 806; and *Gavin's Trustee v Fraser* 1920 SC 674 at 683, per Lord President Clyde.
6 See eg *Jones & Co's Trustee v Allan* (1901) 4 F 374; *Hepburn v Law* 1914 SC 918; *Newbigging v Ritchie's Trustee* 1930 SC 273, 1930 SLT 333; *Scottish Transit Trust Ltd v Scottish Land Cultivators Ltd* 1955 SC 254, 1955 SLT 417; *G and C Finance Corpn v Brown* 1961 SLT 408; *Ladbroke Leasing (South West) Ltd v Reekie Plant Ltd* 1983 SLT 155, OH.
7 Restating s 17(1) of the Sale of Goods Act 1893.
8 Restating s 61(4) of the 1893 Act.

visions of the Act to any transaction 'in the form of a contract of sale which is intended to operate by way of mortgage, pledge, charge, or other security'. If the Act, and in particular, section 17(1), is disapplied, then an ex facie absolute transfer of ownership to the creditor, even if intended to operate as security, would nonetheless be valid provided the sale is in accordance with the common law. But to be so there must at some point have been actual delivery of possession of the goods to the creditor. Once a valid common law sale is completed in this way, the creditor can part with possession to the debtor under some buy-back transaction while validly retaining title to the goods, just as any owner under a hire-purchase agreement may do. Thus, in *McBain v John Wallace & Co*[1] sale and buy-back transactions were held effectual provided that the initial sale was validly carried through in accordance with the general law[2].

However, since in none of the above-mentioned cases did the creditor (the 'buyer') receive even temporary possession of the goods, the common law of sale could not apply and the validity of each transaction was examined solely in terms of the Sale of Goods Act. While the courts have not provided any clear criteria for distinguishing sale from security for the purposes of deciding whether a transaction is struck at by section 62(4) of the 1979 Act, it would appear that, if, from the nature of the transaction, the court considers that the 'seller' has not intended absolute cession of ownership to the 'buyer' but has intended solely to raise finance using the goods as security, then it will hold the 'sale' to be a security transaction, and section 17(1) will therefore be disapplied. Nor, of course, can there be valid security at common law since the creditor has neither received nor retained possession[3].

Statutory exceptions to the requirement of possession

The common law rule by which delivery of possession is required to create an express real right in security over moveables has been altered by statute in particular instances to replace the overt act of delivery of possession with that of registration of the security interest in a specified public register. These instances are: securities over ships[4]; aircraft[5]; agricultural charges created by certain bodies in favour of banks over agricultural merchandise and produce[6]; and floating charges over a company's moveable and heritable property[7]. The statutory facilities do not

---

1 (1881) 8 R 360, affd 8 R (HL) 106.
2 In *Jones & Co's Trustee v Allan* (1901) 4 F 374 at 389, Lord Moncreiff stated: 'I do not dispute that a good security can be effected by means of a sale; but then the sale must be completed by delivery or by what the law considers equivalent to delivery'.
3 See, however, *Armour v Thyssen Edelstahlwerke AG* 1991 SCLR 139, 1990 SLT 891, HL, reversing 1989 SCLR 26, 1989 SLT 182, 2nd Div, with regard to retention of title clauses for unpaid debts due to creditor (bearing in mind that a security was not actually created).
4 Merchant Shipping Act 1995, Sch 1, paras 7–13.
5 Civil Aviation Act 1982, s 86; Mortgaging of Aircraft Order 1972, SI 1972/1268 (amended by SI 1981/611 and SI 1986/2001).
6 Agricultural Credits (Scotland) Act 1929, ss 5–10 and the Agricultural Marketing Act 1958, s 15.
7 Companies Act 1985, ss 462–466 and ss 410–420 (ss 410–420 substituted by the Companies Act 1989, ss 100–104) (see pp 326 ff below).

supersede the common law but offer what will usually be a more convenient method of creating a security right. However, where no such statutory facilities are available, then, at common law, the creditor may obtain a real right in moveables only by ex facie absolute transfer of ownership completed by delivery (accompanied, where security only is intended, by a personal agreement to that effect), or by delivery in security proper under an agreement of pledge.

(2) PLEDGE OF MOVEABLES AND TRANSFER OF DOCUMENTS OF TITLE IN SECURITY

Definition and description of the contract of pledge

Pledge is an express security over moveable property, the real right of the creditor (the pledgee) being constituted by both the voluntary grant of the debtor (the pledgor) and the overt act of delivery of the property to the pledgee. The nature of the contract is defined as:

> 'a kind of mandate whereby the debtor for his creditor's security gives him the pawn, or thing impignorated, to detain or keep it for his own security, or in case of non-payment of the debt, to sell the pledge, and pay himself out of the price, and restore the rest, or restore the pledge itself upon payment of the debt'[1].

Pledge is a true security in that it creates a real right in the property of another (the pledgor). Two real rights therefore coincide in the same property, the pledgee's right being the lesser: 'The right conferred is merely to retain in security, and to resist all attempts by the owner, or those in his right, to recover possession till the debt be satisfied'[2]. The real right in security entitles the holder to retain the object in security of the debt for which it has been pledged. It would also empower him to have it sold judicially for payment[3]. However, 'the special subject pledged continues to be the debtor's property[4]', and since the real right of ownership, subject to the burden of the security interest, remains with the debtor, 'so the risk is with him'[5]. Upon performance of the obligation to which the pledge relates, the pledgor has a right to the return of the property[6], together with any benefit accruing to it. In the absence of agreement to the contrary, it is the actual property pledged which must be returned and not some equivalent article[7]. The property must be returned in the condition it was in when pledged, and the creditor must have bestowed 'ordinary care in the custody of the subject while in his possession'[8]. The pledgor will therefore incur liability for loss or damage resulting from his own negligence or that

1 *Stair* I,13,11; cf also Bell *Principles* s 207.
2 Bell *Principles* s 1364. Cf also 11 *Encyclopaedia of the Laws of Scotland* (ed Lord Dunedin and J Wark, 1931) para 754, and 20 *Stair Memorial Encyclopaedia* para 20.
3 Bell *Principles* s 206.
4 *Erskine* III,1,33.
5 Bell *Principles* s 206.
6 *Stair* I,13,11; Bell *Principles* ss 203, 206.
7 *Crerar v Bank of Scotland* 1921 SC 735, 1921 2 SLT 112; affd 1922 SC (HL) 137, 1922 SLT 335.
8 Bell *Principles* s 206.

of his servants[1], but the risk of accidental loss or damage remains with the pledgor[2].

There are other important consequences which follow from the fact that the pledgee's real right under a contract of pledge is less than that of ownership. Firstly, a contract of pledge can confer no implied power to sell the property on the debtor's default, only a mandate to seek judicial authority to do so and thereby realise payment of the debt[3]. The contract of pledge may, however, confer an express power of sale, by 'special agreement[4]', and such an express power is frequently conferred[5]. Secondly, on sale of the property, the pledgee must account for any surplus to the pledgor after satisfying the obligations due him. On the pledgor's insolvency, any such surplus or reversionary interest forms part of the debtor's estate and may be attached by the pledgor's other creditors[6]. Thirdly, since a pledgee's real right is less than that of ownership, the common law would raise a presumption that the subject of a pledge (as opposed to the subject of an ex facie absolute transfer of ownership) cannot be retained for payment of debts other than the particular debt for which it was expressly pledged[7]. Where a moveable has been pledged without limitation of the security, 'the universal right presumed from possession will effectually cover further advances, which cannot be supposed to be made but on that footing[8]'. If there is any proof to limit the pledge to a specific advance made at the time of its constitution there would be no ground on which, as against the pledgor's other creditors, the original security could be held to be extended[8]. Where the original pledge expressly secures a particular debt, but additional advances are later made to the debtor, then 'the security may be expressly extended to cover a further advance, but not after diligence by third parties to attach the subject, or after sequestration[8]'. It is clear in principle, however, that the pledgee's right is to retain the pledged property until repayment of the whole debt for which it was pledged[9], 'and is not weakened by payment of a part of the debt, but remains as complete for the last shilling as for the whole[10]'. Fourthly, the creditor has no right to use the pledged goods during his possession of them[11] and if he does so he may be liable to pay the pledgor for their hire[12]. However, use

1 *Dominion Bank v Bank of Scotland* (1889) 16 R 1081; affd (1891) 1 R (HL) 21.
2 Bell *Principles* s 206.
3 'Our custom allows not the creditor to sell the pledge', this right being exercisable only through the court: *Stair* I,13,11. Cf also Bell *Principles* s 207.
4 Bell *Principles* s 1364.
5 *Gloag and Irvine* p 213, and see eg *North-Western Bank Ltd v Poynter, Son and Macdonalds* (1894) 22 R (HL) 1.
6 *Stair* I,13,11; Bell *Commentaries* II,19.
7 'There is indeed no decisive authority to that effect, but the point is presupposed in a number of cases, and certainly the contrary view has never been advanced': G L Gretton 'Pledge, Bills of Lading, Trusts and Property Law' 1990 JR 23 at 25. And see eg *Hamilton v Western Bank of Scotland* (1856) 19 D 152 at 166, per Lord Deas; *Rintoul, Alexander & Co v Bannatyne* (1862) 1 M 137; *Alston's Trustee v Royal Bank of Scotland* (1893) 20 R 887.
8 Bell *Principles* s 1367.
9 *Erskine* II,12,67.
10 Bell *Principles* s 1365.
11 Bell *Principles* s 206.
12 Hume *Lectures* vol IV (Stair Soc vol 17, 1955 ed GCH Paton) p 8.

of the goods is not a material breach justifying recision of the contract and return of the goods to the pledgor[1].

Subjects which may be pledged

Bell states:

> 'The subject of pledge must be capable of delivery; such as corporeal moveables, goods, wares and merchandise. Debts also may be pledged when identified with the document as in bills and notes. And so may title-deeds, as corporeal moveables, but not carrying an interest in the land'[2].

Later commentators stress, however, that the only debts which fall within this category are those represented by negotiable instruments, and that a pledge of title deeds is not only ineffectual in conveying any interest in the land, but, except in the case of a solicitor, gives no right of retention of the deeds themselves[3].

In general, incorporeal property cannot be pledged by mere delivery of the document evidencing the existence of the right which constitutes the incorporeal property. Assignation of the right and intimation of the assignation to the debtor in the corresponding obligation is generally required. Thus:

> '... documents such as share certificates, personal bonds and receipts for sums advanced on loan cannot be pledged to any useful purpose. The title to the debt or other incorporeal property which is the subject of any such document is separable from the document and is ... transmitted by assignation and not by pledge of the document (which merely evidences the existence of the property). Accordingly, the pledge of a document such as a share certificate will not vest any right of property or retention in the pledgee, and he will be obliged to surrender the document to any person to whom the pledgor may assign the right to the property represented by the document'[4].

However, negotiable instruments differ from other incorporeal property in respect that the obligation of payment is said to be contained in the instrument itself. As a result, the obligation can be transferred by delivery of the instrument, so that such instruments can effectively be pledged in the same way as corporeal moveables[5].

Constitution and retention of the real right

The real right is effected by delivery and possession, delivery being competently given only by a party enjoying rights of ownership or disposal.

1 *Wolifson v Harrison* 1977 SC 384, 1978 SLT 95.
2 Bell *Principles* s 205.
3 Cf 11 *Encyclopaedia of the Laws of Scotland* (ed Lord Dunedin and J Wark, 1931) para 757; *Christie v Ruxton* (1862) 24 D 1182; *Robertson v British Linen Co* 1890 18 R 1225, OH; Bell *Principles* s 1442; 20 *Stair Memorial Encyclopaedia* para 15.
4 20 *Stair Memorial Encyclopaedia* para 57.
5 Note, however, ss 123–125 of the Consumer Credit Act 1974 (discussed fully at p 177 above) which prohibit the taking of a negotiable instrument in security or in payment in relation to a regulated agreement as defined by that Act.

The right is completed by the continued possession of the object pledged. This statement gives rise to two separate issues, namely; the question of who may confer a real right on the pledgee and what constitutes delivery and possession for the purposes of creating a real right in security by pledge?

Who may confer a real right?

'A person in lawful possession of goods with the owner's consent may pledge them'[1]. 'Owner', in this context, includes a buyer who has possession on 'sale or return' even although he becomes owner only at the moment of pledging, instead of returning, the goods[2]. The Sale of Goods Act 1979, allows a valid sale or pledge to be made to a third party acting in good faith by either the seller of goods or his mercantile agent who, having sold the goods, remains in possession of the goods or of the documents of title to them[3] or the buyer of goods or his mercantile agent where the person who has bought or agreed to buy the goods has obtained, with the consent of the seller, possession of the goods or of the documents of title to them[4]. However, a person holding under a conditional sale agreement to which the Consumer Credit Act 1974 applies cannot confer any title to the goods by sale or pledge[5]. Nor, in general, could a person having possession under a hire-purchase agreement do so[6]. However, it would appear that a pledgee of such goods could retain them in a question with the owner if he pays the outstanding instalments under the hire-purchase agreement[7]. As in the case of sale of goods[8], a person who has only a voidable title to goods (for example under a contract induced by fraud) could, until such time as his title is avoided by reduction of contract, confer a real right in security over the goods in favour of a third party who acted in good faith and without notice of the defect in title[9]. In such circumstances the true owner bears the loss.

With regard to agents in lawful possession of the goods with the owner's consent, only an agent falling within the definition of 'mercantile agent' in the Factors Act 1889[10] can confer a valid security. The mere fact that the pledgee may have given value and acted in good faith will not of

1 Walker *Principles of Scottish Private Law* (4th edn, 1989) vol III, p 394, note 3.
2 *Brown v Marr* (1880) 7 R 427; *Bryce v Ehrmann* (1904) 7 F 5. Both were cases of fraud by retail jewellers receiving goods from wholesalers on sale or return, then, without paying the wholesalers, pledging the jewels to raise loans. The pledgees in each case, being unaware of the fraud at the time of the pledge, were entitled to retain the jewels until their advances were repaid, the loss falling on the wholesalers.
3 Sale of Goods Act 1979, s 24.
4 1979 Act, s 25(1); Factors Act 1889, s 9.
5 1979 Act, s 25(2); Consumer Credit Act 1974, s 192(3), Sch 4, para 2.
6 But see the Hire Purchase Act 1964, ss 27, 29.
7 *Whiteley Ltd v Hild* [1918] 2 KB 808, CA.
8 1979 Act, s 23; *MacLeod v Kerr* 1965 SC 253, 1965 SLT 358; *Morrisson v Robertson* 1908 SC 332.
9 See eg *Brown v Marr* (1880) 7 R 427 discussed above, and *Price and Pierce Ltd v Bank of Scotland* 1910 SC 1095, affd 1912 SC (HL) 19.
10 Extended to Scotland by the Factors (Scotland) Act 1890, s 1.

itself suffice, if the agent who purports to pledge the goods does not fall within the statutory definition[1].

In addition to the circumstances mentioned in which such an agent may confer a valid title under the Sale of Goods Act 1979, the Factors Act provides that where a mercantile agent is, with the consent of the owner, in possession of goods or of the documents of title to goods, then, any sale, pledge, or other disposition of the goods, made by him when acting in the ordinary course of business of a mercantile agent, is

> 'as valid as if he were expressly authorised by the owner of the goods to make the same; provided that the person taking under the disposition acts in good faith, and has not at the time of the disposition notice that the person making the disposition has not authority to make the same[2]'.

The general rule 'is perfectly well settled, that the possessor of corporeal moveables can give no better title to the purchaser or pledgee than he has himself acquired from the owner'[3]. This general rule may be modified, however, where the true owner is, at common law, personally barred from denying the validity of the pledge because he has acted in a way calculated to allow the pledgee to be misled into thinking that the pledgor is the owner of the security subjects or has authority to pledge them[4].

What constitutes delivery and possession?

'The law on the subject of security rights over moveables is beset with difficulties'[5]. The main area of complexity, as regards delivery, is (unfortunately) precisely the area likely to be of most importance to banks, being taking of security by means of transfer of documents of title (which term is used here to include warehousekeepers' warrants, delivery orders and bills of lading.) The complexities arise from both an imprecise use of terminology and a discrepancy between strict legal theory and legal practice[6].

Pledge: actual delivery of the goods

Actual or constructive delivery will transfer a real right in a corporeal moveable[7]. Actual delivery will be constituted by transfer of the subject

1 *Martinez y Gomez v Allison* (1890) 17 R 332. A 'mercantile agent' is an agent who may confer a valid title on sale or in security is defined as one 'having in the customary course of his business as such agent authority either to sell goods, or to consign goods for the purpose of sale, or to buy goods, or to raise money on the security of goods': Factors Act 1889, s 1(1).
2 1889 Act, s 2 (1).
3 *Mitchell v Heys & Son* (1894) 21 R 600 at 610, per Lord Kinnear.
4 However, in 20 *Stair Memorial Encyclopaedia* para 23, note 1, A J Sim states that a plea of personal bar is 'more likely to be successful where the pledge consists not of actual corporeal moveable property but of a document of title to such property', and refers to *Pochin & Co v Robinows and Marjoribanks* (1869) 7 M 622, and, for contrast, *Mitchell v Heys & Sons* (1894) 21 R 600.
5 *Gloag and Irvine* p 187.
6 For a full examination of the issues, see A Rodger 'Pledge of Bills of Lading in Scots Law' 1971 JR 193 at 202 and G L Gretton 'Pledge, Bills of Lading, Trusts and Property Law' 1990 JR 23 at 27.
7 But note that 'constructive' delivery will apparently serve to transfer a real right of ownership only and cannot create a lesser real right in security: see *Hamilton v Western Bank of Scotland* (1856) 19 D 152; *Hayman & Son v McLintock* 1907 SC 936.

and by delivery to a carrier prior to transmission to the transferee. This will not apply where, by the contract of carriage, the sender reserves control over the subject. Actual delivery therefore includes: delivery of goods into a ship chartered by the purchaser[1] provided the bill of lading has been indorsed by the transferor to the transferee; delivery of goods to a warehouse to be held in the name of ,and subject to the order of, the transferee[2]; and where goods are situated in a house, cellar or store and the key is given to the transferee with the intention of giving him full control over them[3]. There is no delivery where goods are sent to a warehouse to be stored in the name of the transferee but under a contract by which the transferor retains a right to remove the whole or part of the goods[4]. Nor is there delivery where goods are merely marked or labelled to bear the name of the transferee. In *Smith v Allan and Poynter*[5], A sent whisky in casks to a bonded warehouse. The casks bore labels addressed to the warehousekeeper, but containing in the corner the name of B (to whom they had been sold). It was held that this was not delivery to B and the warehousekeeper was liable in damages to A for delivering the whisky to B's order without A's instruction[6].

However, if the goods are merely set aside on the seller/pledger's property but the creditor is also given complete control over them, then delivery will have occurred. In *West Lothian Oil Co Liquidator v Mair*[7] barrels sold to a purchaser were retained on the debtor's premises but were separately enclosed within a locked fence, the keys to which were given to the purchaser. It was held, in a question between the purchaser and the liquidator, that delivery had occurred and ownership had therefore passed to the purchaser[8].

Civil Possession

'The creditor, being owner of the premises on which the goods are situated, may have possession of them although the debtor, as contractor or lessee, has the use of them'[9]. Where a person who has sold a subject remains in possession of it under a contract which makes him the servant or lessor of the purchaser, and where, therefore, his continued possession may be ascribed to a subordinate contract, and not to his original ownership then it may be held that the actual possession of the seller/pledgor has become the civil possession of the purchaser/pledgee, and delivery of the goods may thus be held to have occurred[10]. Whether this is described

1 Bell *Commentries* I,183.
2 Bell *Commentries* I,185.
3 *Maxwell & Co v Thomas Stevenson & Co* (1830) 8 S 618; revsd (1831) 5 W & S 269, HL.
4 *Mackinnon v Max Nanson & Co* (1868) 6 M 974.
5 1859 22 D 208.
6 See also *Gibson v Forbes* (1833) 11 S 916; *Boak and Greig v Megget and Symington* (1844) 6 D 662; *Orr's Trustee v Tullis* 1870 8 M 936; *Stiven v Scott and Simpson* (1871) 9 M 923.
7 (1892) 20 R 64.
8 Contrast, however, *Pattison's Trustees v Liston* (1893) 20 R 806: A creditor who had been given keys to the debtor's house for the purpose of letting it was held not to have received delivery of the debtor's household furniture and effects for the purposes of constituting security, despite a written assignation of the furniture to him in security.
9 W A Wilson *The Scottish Law of Debt* (2nd edn, 1991) para 7.3.
10 See *Gloag and Irvine* p 194.

as 'actual' or 'constructive' delivery appears of little relevance. The important issue is that this form of delivery by change in the nature of the seller/pledgor's possession is regarded as delivery of the goods themselves and can complete either a transfer of ownership in the goods or the creation of a real right in security by pledge of the goods[1].

Pledge: ex facie absolute transfer in security

Constructive delivery by transfer of documents of title, delivery orders and transfer of ownership

'Constructive delivery' is a term normally reserved for delivery by an order on a custodier 'where the ownership of goods is transferred by an order on a third party in whose custody the goods happen to be'[2].

Lord President Inglis in *Pochin & Co* puts it thus:

> 'Constructive delivery may take place, and generally does take place, where specific goods or other moveables being in the custody of some person other than the owner, the owner gives to a purchaser of these goods a delivery order addressed to the custodier, ordering him to deliver to the purchaser these specific goods. When this delivery order is intimated to the custodier constructive delivery is effected, because the custodier from that time becomes in law holder for the purchaser, just as before he was holder for the seller. But to the completion of such constructive delivery two things are indispensable — that the custodier shall hold an independent position, and be neither the owner nor in any way identified with the owner of the goods; and that the goods themselves shall be specific in this sense, that they be capable of identification, either as one total undivided quantity stored in a particular place, or at least a specific quantity, forming part of an identified whole'[3].

The goods must be in the possession of an independent custodier and the delivery order must be drawn on and intimated to him[4]. In *Rhind's Trustee v Robertson and Baxter*[5] a spirit merchant, the tenant of a general bonded warehouse (which could not be opened except by using two keys, one of which was kept by the tenant and the other by an officer of excise) obtained advances on the security of certain casks of wines and spirits belonging to him in the warehouse, for which he granted to the lender delivery orders addressed to the excise officer who made entries of the transfer in his books. In a question between the trustee on the tenant's sequestrated estate and the lender it was held that there had been no

---

1 *Orr's Trustee v Tullis* 1870 8 M 936; *Moore v Gledden* (1869) 7 M 1016. For treatment of same area by other texts, cf: Wallace and McNeil's *Banking Law* (10th edn, 1991 by D B Caskie) p 163; Walker *Principles of Scottish Private Law* (4th edn, 1989) vol III, p 295; 20 *Stair Memorial Encyclopaedia* para 10; Carey Miller *Corporeal Moveables in Scots Law* (1991) para 11-06.
2 *Gloag and Irvine* p 191; 11 *Encyclopaedia of the Laws of Scotland* (ed Lord Dunedin and J Wark, 1931) para 762; *Hamilton v Western Bank of Scotland* (1856) 19 D 152 at 164, per Lord Deas; A Rodger 'Pledge of Bills of Lading in Scots Law' 1971 JR 193 at 197: 'this is a difficult and complex area of law'.
3 *Pochin & Co v Robinows and Marjoribanks* (1869) 7 M 622 at 628, per Lord President Inglis.
4 *Anderson v McCall* (1866) 4 M 765 at 770, per Lord Cowan.
5 (1891) 18 R 623.

constructive delivery of the goods to the lender. The goods had remained in the tenant's warehouse and the excise officer was not custodier of the goods, even although he held one of the keys[1].

Goods must be ascertained

In *Hayman & Son v McLintock*[2] a flour merchant sold to purchasers a certain number of sacks of flour and received payment for them. He had at the time a large number of sacks in a neutral store, and in implement of the sale he handed to the purchasers delivery orders addressed to the storekeeper for the specified number of sacks. These orders were duly intimated to the storekeeper, who gave the purchasers transfer notes acknowledging that he had transferred the specified number of sacks to their accounts and that he now held them subject to their instructions. He also transferred them in his books to the purchasers' accounts. The individual sacks of flour were not separately marked or identified in any way, and nothing was done to separate them from the other sacks of flour in the store. The flour merchant's estate was subsequently sequestrated and his trustee claimed the whole flour in the store. It was held, that as the goods sold were unascertained, no property in them had passed to the purchasers. Section 16 of the Sale of Goods Act 1893, which specially provided that where there was a sale of unascertained goods the property did not pass until the goods had been ascertained, applied[3].

Obligation or order to deliver goods must be unqualified

The obligation or order to deliver the goods which the document of title contains must be unqualified. In *Mackinnon v Max Nanson & Co*[4] A gave to B in security of an advance, a delivery order on a warehouse keeper with whom A had deposited goods. The order was framed to the effect that the warehouse keeper held a quantity of the goods at B's disposal subject to special agreement that A might remove any of them which he might require in the course of his business. It was held that B had no right to the goods in a question with A's trustees in bankruptcy.

Delivery order must be intimated to the custodier

Delivery orders, warehousekeepers' warrants and bills of lading all fall within the statutory definition of 'documents of title' given in the Factors Act 1889[5], section 1(4), (5) of which provides:

---

1 See also *Dobell, Becket & Co v Neilson* (1904) 7 F 281, 12 SLT 543.
2 1907 SC 936.
3 1907 SC 936 at 952, per Lord McLaren. On the need for ascertainment and identification of the goods to which the delivery order refers, see also Lord President Inglis in *Pochin & Co v Robinows and Marjoribanks* (1869) 7 M 622. See now the Sale of Goods Act 1979, ss 16, 20A (amended and added respectively by the Sale of Goods (Amendment) Act 1995, s 1(1), (3)).
4 (1868) 6 M 974.
5 The 1889 Act was extended to Scotland by the Factors (Scotland) Act 1890.

'For the purposes of this Act—

(4) The expression "document of title" shall include any bill of lading, dock warrant, warehouse-keeper's certificate, and warrant or order for the delivery of goods, and any other document used in the ordinary course of business as proof of the possession or control of goods, or authorising or purporting to authorise, either by endorsement or by delivery, the possessor of the document to transfer or receive goods thereby represented:

(5) The expression "pledge" shall include any contract pledging, or giving a lien or security on, goods, whether in consideration of an original advance or of any further or continuing advance or of any pecuniary liability'.

Section 3 of the Act provides that 'a pledge of the documents of title to goods shall be deemed to be a pledge of the goods' and section 11 provides that the transfer of such documents 'may be by endorsement, or, where the document is by custom or by express terms transferable by delivery, or makes the goods deliverable to the bearer, then by delivery'.

The argument could therefore be put forward that, whether transferred by the owner of the goods or his mercantile agents, a transfer of documents of title with the intention to pledge the goods so represented does not transfer ownership in the goods but creates only a security right in pledge, and under the Factors Act 1889, as in the case of bills of lading, intimation of a delivery order or warrant to the custodier of the goods is not required to complete a real right in the goods. Mere indorsement and delivery suffice. However, such arguments encounter considerable difficulty[1].

The need for intimation of a delivery order is stated by most commentators[2]. The suggestion in the judgments of the Court of Session in *Inglis v Robertson and Baxter* was that the purpose of this section was 'to validate contracts [that is personal obligations] of agents as binding upon the true owners'[3]. It did not affect the general law of completion of title in sales or in securities — 'on the contrary, the rights constituted are throughout personal rights as distinguished from real rights'[4]. They were 'rights taking effect not by any assumed completion of title, but by being declared good as against true owners'[4].

---

1 *Inglis v Robertson and Baxter* (1897) 24 R 758, affd (1898) 25 R (HL) 70; *Hamilton v Western Bank of Scotland* (1856) 19 D 152.
2 Eg C Burns *The Law of Banking* (2nd edn, 1983) p 226; *Wallace and McNeil* p 165; Walker *Principles of Scottish Private Law* (4th edn, 1989) vol III, p 395. In *Wallace and McNeil*, however, it is also mentioned (at p 165), under 'Pledge by factor or agent' that a mercantile agent 'may effectively pledge the property of his principal. This he may do by the transfer of the documents to a party making bona fide advances on the goods'. This is clearly a reference to section 2 of the Factors Act 1889 (powers of a mercantile agent with respect to dispositions of goods).
3 *Inglis v Robertson and Baxter* (1897) 24 R 758 at 779, per Lord Kinnear.
4 (1897) 24 R 758 at 781, per Lord Kyllachy.

Delivery by transfer of bills of lading

Gloag and Irvine state the position as follows:

> 'In addition to being a receipt for the goods and an expression of the contract on which they were put on board, the bill of lading is also a symbol of the goods. As it is assignable, by indorsement and delivery, it forms a means of transferring the property in the goods at a time when, being in transit, they are incapable of actual delivery. When the bill of lading is indorsed and delivered with the intention to pass the property, the property and the possession of the goods are thereby transferred, without any intimation to the shipowner or shipmaster, who is the actual custodier'[1].

No intimation is accordingly required.

In *Sewell v Burdick*[2] the House of Lords provided that transfer of a bill of lading did not necessarily pass property in the goods. The nature of a transferee's title depended on the nature of the transaction under which the bill was delivered. In Scotland, however, *Hamilton v Western Bank of Scotland*[3] remained seen as authority for the proposition that transfer of any document of title (including a bill of lading) which was absolute in its terms, always transferred ownership, regardless of whether the parties intended pledge[4]. This rule appears to have been altered, if only for bills of lading, in *North-Western Bank Ltd v Poynter, Son and Macdonalds*[5]. Lord Justice-Clerk Macdonald in the Court of Session said:

> 'The bank did not become owners of the goods, but only pledgees, stipulating that they should have power of sale, and that Page & Company should in selling sell for them and pay them the proceeds. The bank's case is that they were in ownership of the goods and that Page & Company in selling were only their agents ... But this can only be maintained if the written contract is ignored. Its express words indicate that the bank receive the bill of lading as security only for an advance. The property therefore remained with the pledger, and was only burdened with the bank's right under their contract'[6].

Ascertainment of goods (bills of lading)

Bills of lading often represent unsegregated shares of bulk goods. In *Hayman & Son v McLintock*[7] a distinction was clearly drawn between delivery orders and bills of lading. In the case of an order for delivery of goods held in a warehouse, section 16 of the Sale of Goods Act 1893 applied. Property in the goods could not therefore pass until the goods were ascertained. Lord McLaren said:

---

1 *Gloag and Irvine* pp 274–275.
2 *Sewell v Burdick* (1884) 10 App Cas 74, HL. See *Sanders v Maclean* (1883) 11 QBD 327, CA, per Bowen LJ.
3 (1856) 19 D 152.
4 See *Mackinnon v Max Nanson & Co* (1868) 6 M 974.
5 (1894) 21 R 513; (1894) 22 R (HL) 1.
6 (1894) 21 R 513 at 518, per Lord Justice-Clerk Macdonald.
7 1907 SC 936.

'It is perfectly true that a delivery-order is worthless as passing specific property until the goods have been ascertained, but that is exactly the distinction between the effect of a delivery-order for goods on shore and a bill of lading. Bills of lading have been long in use, and as far back as we have any knowledge of their use they were held to be negotiable. Such bills, expressed to be for so many bags of flour or quarters of grain on board a particular ship, would pass by blank indorsation from hand to hand while the ship was at sea. How is it possible, consistently with such a state of the law, that the goods could be specifically ascertained, or that the various persons who took such bills of lading could examine and verify the goods while the ship was in mid-ocean? We know that the bills of lading are granted for portions of cargo in bulk which cannot, of course, be ascertained; and where bills of lading are granted in these circumstances they must operate as a transfer of an unascertained quantity of goods on board the ship, until delivery is made in terms of the obligation. Delivery had not been made here, and therefore Mr Stevenson's right to these undelivered goods was as effectual as if they were identified by marks and numbers'[1].

Releasing the security

If the goods are held on a warehouse warrant, the bank should indorse and deliver it back to the customer, as in the case of bills of lading[2]. If the goods are held by the bank on a warehouse receipt, the bank must issue a delivery order on the warehousekeeper in favour of the customer and this must be intimated. Where the bank wishes to sell the goods and apply the proceeds to repayment of the advances it has made, and wishes to use the services of the customer as agent or broker for the purposes of selling the goods on its behalf, it appears established by the House of Lords decision in *North-Western Bank Ltd v Poynter, Son and Macdonalds*[3] that by releasing the goods or a document of title to the customer subject to a trust letter or trust receipt, the bank retains its security over the goods and over the proceeds of their sale. The trust letter must clearly state that the customer is to hold possession of the goods and of the proceeds of their sale as agent or trustee for the bank, so that the actual possession of the goods or document of title by the customer is civil possession by the bank. Trust receipts are widely used by banks. This apparently protects the bank in the event of the customer's insolvency during the period in which the customer has possession of the goods or of the proceeds of their sale. However, there is English authority that the bank will have no protection against any fraud-

---

1 1907 SC 936 at 952, per Lord McLaren. The Sale of Goods (Amendment) Act 1995 implements *Report on the sale of goods forming part of a bulk* (Scot Law Com no. 145; Law Com no. 215 (1993)). The 1995 Act amends the Sale of Goods Act 1979 so that notwithstanding s 16, an undivided proprietary share in bulk goods will pass to the buyer upon payment of all or part of the price. There is no ownership of the particular objects, but the buyer does acquire an immediate undivided share which will prevail in insolvency. See in particular ss 20A, 20B of the 1979 Act (added by s 1(3) of the 1995 Act).
2 Note, however, that, following *Inglis v Robertson and Baxter* (1898) 25 R (HL) 70, in the case of a warehouse warrant, unless the initial transfer to the bank was not recorded in the books of the warehouse, the customer will have to intimate the re-assignation of the warrant to him by the bank in order to complete his real right to the goods.
3 (1894) 22 R (HL) 1 (decided under Scots law but also given in English texts as authority on this point).

ulent dealings during this period whereby the customer confers title to or real right in security over the goods on a bona fide third party[1].

Pawn and the Consumer Credit Act 1974

The general law of pledge is common law, but a form of pledge known as 'pawn' has long been regulated by statute[2]. The Consumer Credit Act 1974 does not aim specifically at regulating the activities of banks. Indeed, transacting with corporate customers and transactions for amounts exceeding £15,000 — which constitute an important cross-section of banking business — are largely unaffected by it. However, where a transaction does come within the ambit of the Act, compliance with the Act is required for the bank involved. An essential question in any credit and security transaction which a bank enters into with a customer must therefore be whether there are consumer credit implications. The Act extends protection to consumers who enter 'regulated agreements'. These are defined as 'a consumer credit agreement or consumer hire agreement, other than an exempt agreement'[3]. A 'consumer credit agreement' is defined as 'a personal credit agreement by which the creditor provides the debtor with credit not exceeding £15,000'[4]. The 'debtor' must be a 'consumer', that is 'a person other than a body corporate (or an entity consisting entirely of bodies corporate)'. The financier or credit provider may be 'any other person'[5].

'Pawns' or pledges taken under a regulated agreement are governed by sections 114 to 122 of the Act. However, non-commercial agreements and pledges of documents of title and of bearer bonds are excluded from such regulations[6]. Ellinger and Lomnicka explain:

> 'Many of the pledges obtained by banks fall within the ambit of these exclusions. This is so despite the fact that the exclusions involved are narrower than may appear at first glance. To start with, as "document of title" is not defined, the phrase is confined to documents of title in the strict (or common law) sense of the word. Accordingly, whilst a pledge of a bill of lading is unaffected by the 1974 Act, a pledge of documents such as delivery orders and non negotiable warehouse receipts is regulated by the Act. Similarly, whilst a pledge of bearer bonds is excluded, a pledge of share warrants requires a pawn receipt'[7].

In relation to pledges or pawns which do come within the ambit of the Act the provisions applicable are not cumbersome for banks. 'Pawn' is defined as 'any article subject to a pledge'[8]. The person who pledges the

---

1 *Lloyds Bank Ltd v Bank of America National Trust and Savings Association* [1938] 2 KB 147, [1938] 2 All ER 63, CA. However, see the very persuasive views of A Rodger in 'Pledge of Bills of Lading in Scots Law' 1971 JR 193.
2 The Pawnbrokers Acts 1872 and 1960 and the Moneylenders Act 1927 now replaced by parts of the Consumer Credit Art 1974, particularly ss 114– 122.
3 Consumer Credit Act 1974, s 189 (1).
4 1974 Act, s 8(2).
5 1974 Act, s 189(1).
6 1974 Act, s 114(3)(a).
7 Ellinger and Lomnicka *Modern Banking Law* (2nd edn, 1994) p 689.
8 1974 Act, s 189(1).

article is referred to as the 'pawnor' and the person who receives it the 'pawnee'. The person taking any article in pawn under a regulated agreement must give a 'pawn receipt' in the prescribed form at the time of receiving it[1]. This receipt may be incorporated in the regulated agreement but, if separate, must follow the requirements of the Consumer Credit (Pawn Receipts) Regulations[2]. Where an article is taken in pawn from a person whom the recipient knows to be, or who appears to be and is, minor, the recipient commits an offence[3]. It is an offence to fail to deliver any copy agreement, notice of cancellation rights or pawn receipt as required by the Act[4].

A pawn is redeemable at any time within six months after it is taken or within such longer period as has been fixed for the duration of the credit secured by the pawn or as has been agreed by the parties[5]. Where the pawn is not redeemed within the redemption period, it may still be redeemed at any time before the pawn is realised or becomes the property of the pawnee[6]. The pawnee may charge for the safekeeping of the pawn during such extended redemption period, but the charge must not be at a higher rate than any applicable before the end of the redemption period. No special charge may be made for redemption of the pawn after the end of the redemption period. On surrender of the pawn receipt and payment of the sum owing by the pawnor, the pawnee must deliver the pawn to the bearer of the pawn receipt unless he knows or has reasonable cause to suspect that the bearer of the pawn receipt is neither the owner of the pawn nor authorised by the owner to redeem it[7].

Provision is made for redemption of the pawn where the pawn receipt has been lost[8]. The person entitled to redeem the pawn must tender to the pawnee a prescribed form of statutory declaration or, in the case of credit not exceeding £25, a prescribed form of written statement[9]. It is an offence for a pawnee to refuse, without reasonable cause, to allow the pawn to be redeemed[10]. Where a pawnee does so refuse, or where the article pawned is a stolen article or one which has been obtained by fraud and a person has been convicted of an offence in relation to such theft or fraud, the court has power to order delivery of the pawn to the owner or person otherwise entitled thereto. In making such an order, the court may impose such conditions as to payment of the debt secured by the pawn as it thinks fit[11]. If, at the end of the redemption period, the pawn has not been redeemed, then[12] the pawn becomes realisable by the pawnee. If,

1 1974 Act, s 114(1).
2 Consumer Credit (Pawn Receipts) Regulations 1983, SI 1983/1566.
3 1974 Act, s 114(9).
4 1974 Act, s 115.
5 1974 Act, ss 116(1) and (2).
6 1974 Act, s 116(3).
7 1974 Act, s 117.
8 1974 Act, s 119.
9 Consumer Credit (Pawn Receipts) Regulations 1983, SI 1983/1566, and Consumer Credit (Increase of Monetary Amounts) Order 1983, SI 1983/1571.
10 1974 Act, s 119.
11 1974 Act, s 122.
12 1974 Act, s 120.

however, the redemption period was six months and the credit did not exceed £25 ownership of the article pawned passes to the pawnee[1].

Once a pawn becomes realisable, the pawnee may sell only after giving to the pawnor notice of his intention to sell in accordance with the prescribed period of notice. The asking price must be indicated in the notice. Once sale has taken place, the pawnee must give the pawnor information as to proceeds and expenses. If the net proceeds of sale discharge the debt, any surplus must be paid to the pawnor. Where the net proceeds are less than the debt secured, the debt is reduced to the amount by which the net proceeds fall short of full payment. If the pawnor claims that the true market value of the article was not obtained, the onus is on the pawnee to show that he or his agent used reasonable care to ensure that the true market value was obtained. If the pawnor alleges that the expenses of the sale were unreasonable, the pawnee has the onus of showing that they were reasonable. The regulations are not onerous and where the amount of the agreement involved exceeds £15,000 or where the pledgee is a company, the transaction is not a regulated agreement under the Act.

Pledge of negotiable instruments

A negotiable instrument may be pledged by simple delivery to the creditor with the intention of giving security. The pledgee in such a transaction is in a favourable position since, provided he has taken the instrument for value and in good faith, without knowledge of any defect in the pledgor's title, he is a holder in due course of the instrument. The pledgee of a negotiable instrument therefore takes good title to it even where it is pledged by a person who has stolen it or obtained it by fraud from the true owner. However, where the underlying loan in security of which such a pledge is made is a regulated agreement within the meaning of the Consumer Credit Act 1974, such a pledge is prohibited. Section 123 of the Act expressly prohibits a creditor in a regulated agreement from taking a negotiable instrument as security for any sum payable by the debtor or hirer under the agreement or as surety in relation to it. Nor may a creditor accept a negotiable instrument other than a bank note or cheque in discharge of any sum payable under a regulated agreement. Under sections 124 and 125 of the Act contravention of the prohibition has the result that the regulated agreement or, where the contravention occurs in relation to a sum payable by any surety, the security, will be enforceable only by court order[2]. Where an application for such a court order is dismissed the security may become ineffective. A holder in due course of the instrument (a subsequent transferee who has taken the instrument in good faith and for value) will have the normal rights of such a holder. However, the creditor who originally took the instrument in contravention of section 124 must indemnify the debtor, hirer or surety (the 'protected person') from whom the instrument was taken in respect of any liability to a holder in due course[3].

---

1 1974 Act, s 121 and the Consumer Credit (Realisation of Pawn) Regulations 1983, SI 1983/1568 prescribe the formalities of sale of the pawn.
2 1974 Act, s 189(1): 'court' means sheriff court.
3 See p 177 above.

(3) PROPOSALS FOR REFORM

The 1994 DTI Consultation Paper

In the three decades prior to the 1994 publication of the Department of Trade and Industry Consultation Paper *Security over moveable property in Scotland*, three reports were published which included recommendations for the reform of securities law as regards moveable property in Scotland. The 1971 Crowther Report on consumer credit made recommendations for the reform of law where the secured credit was to be provided for business or consumer transactions[1]. Professor Halliday's *Report of the Working Party on Security over Moveable Property* (Scottish Law Commission, March 1986), addressed the particular needs of the Scottish legal system — previous reports having the wider ambit of Great Britain. The purpose of the third report, Professor Diamond's *A Review of Security Interests in Property* submitted to the DTI in 1989, was to review existing law while the proposals of the Crowther Committee remained neglected. The scheme suggested by the Diamond Committee was also very similar to that under article 9 of the American Uniform Commercial Code. The proposals covered the whole of the UK but made certain recommendations particular to Scotland.

Post-Diamond Report responses in England and Wales have been hostile to substantial reform. On the contrary, Scottish consultees have responded in favour of reform. The law in this area is largely underdeveloped in Scotland — a fact which places Scottish businesses at great disadvantage when seeking financing (as compared with their English and Welsh counterparts). English law offers a wider ranges of securities, workable in commercial practice. It was for this principal reason the DTI were asked to consider the matter and to prepare a draft Bill for public consultation, with the attendant appointment of an advisory panel.

In examining the extent of necessary reform, two salient problems emerged. Firstly, it is not presently possible to create a non-possessory, fixed security over corporeal moveable property (apart from certain categories of property where special statutory provision has been made, as in the case of ships and aircraft), and secondly, there are practical difficulties associated with the granting of securities over incorporeal moveable property. The creation of a fixed security over book debts requires not only the assignation of the rights to the book debts to the creditor in the security agreement but also the intimation of that assignation to the common debtors under those debts. This is both practically inconvenient and makes it impossible to create a fixed security over future book debts, as intimation cannot be made to as yet unascertained common debtors.

Various approaches to reform were considered. Crowther, Halliday and Diamond, as mentioned above, had all to varying extent, gravitated towards a model of reform similar to that in article 9 of the Uniform Commercial Code. An article 9 security shares some characteristics of the current Scottish floating charge in that it is capable of applying to all present and future corporeal and incorporeal moveable property of a

---

[1] *Report of the Committee on Consumer Credit* (the Crowther Report) (1971) (Cmnd 4596), Pt V, based largely upon art 9 of the American Uniform Commercial Code.

business; the grantee of the security is able to retain possession of the secured property and may dispose of it in the ordinary course of business; and the security may continue in the proceeds of the disposed property.

However, the article 9 security operates as a fixed security from the time of its creation — 'fixed' indicating a security which is fully effective in respect of the property subject to it. A floating charge, in contrast, has effect as if it were a fixed security on the attachment or crystallisation of the charge. Attachment will occur only when the company which granted the charge goes into liquidation, or where a receiver is appointed. The property remains free of an effective security and may be subject to the diligence of unsecured creditors. It became apparent that the article 9 model, while evidencing certain important strengths would result in too comprehensive a security operating to the prejudice of unsecured creditors. Such a model would also have called for wholesale reform of the substance and structure of law in this area. A system of notice filing was also considered unsuitable.

The approach finally adopted in the 1994 Consultation Paper[1] was one which concentrated on building upon existing law, while eradicating specific existing weaknesses. The law on floating charges would be extended to enable persons other than companies to grant such securities over moveable property (since at present, partnerships, individual businessmen and most bodies corporate (not companies) cannot create floating charges). The floating charge is particularly employed by companies as a means of obtaining finance. Such an approach would not introduce upheaval into the law and would retain familiar concepts. This in itself would not, however, suffice to supply the defect of existing law. Thus it was considered necessary to introduce a new, fixed security over moveable property — the 'moveable security'.

The moveable security

The draft Bill attached to the 1994 DTI consultation paper made detailed provision for the creation of the new 'moveable security'. Clause 9 of the Bill proposes that it be possible to create a new form of fixed security over moveable property — in addition to those securities which may be granted under the present law. The security, which could be granted by any person (incorporated or otherwise), would be capable of being given over all or any part of the moveable property of the granter. Clause 9(3) defines 'moveable property' as any right or interest in corporeal or incorporeal moveable property of the granter at the time when the moveable security is granted. The term 'moveable property' is also to include industrial growing crops (otherwise regarded as heritable property until severed from the land) which are property of the granter and are in existence when the security is granted, and any right or interest in 'receivables' which is property of the granter at the time the security is granted, or thereafter. Clause 30 defines 'receivables' as any amounts due or to become due to the granter of a moveable security in respect of goods sup-

1 Cf *Security over Moveable Property in Scotland* (DTI Consultation Paper) (1994), para 2.9.

plied or services tendered or to be rendered by a person (whether or not the granter of the security) in the course of that person's business. Clause 12 provides the moveable security would not be capable of extending to any consumer goods, goods exempted from poinding or property held on trust (as in the case of the floating charge). Nor would the moveable security extend to the proceeds of a sale or other disposal of property subject to the security. Clause 22 provides for the creation through registration of both the floating charge and the moveable security and provides that a new register of security interests should be established. The register would be divided into two parts, one for the floating charge and one for the moveable security. The Registrar of Companies would also keep the register of security interests, recording the name of the grantees of floating charges and moveable securities. Members of the public would then be entitled to make searches against these records. A registration fee would be necessary to cover the costs of running the register[1]. As yet these proposals have not received legislative approval.

3. SECURITY OVER INCORPOREAL MOVEABLES

(1) USE OF INCORPOREAL PROPERTY AS SECURITY

What is incorporeal property?

Gloag and Henderson categorise incorporeal property as follows:

> 'Within the category of incorporeal moveable property are included subjects so diverse as rights to debts (*nomina debitorum*) or obligations, claims *ex contractu* and *ex delicto*, rights to shares in companies, goodwill, patents, copyright and trade marks and names'[2].

Rights which can be classed as incorporeal property, however, may be either personal, such as a right to a debt or a right in contract or of delict, or they may be real, such as a right in security or in lease.

Transfer of incorporeal property

Kenneth Reid says of the transfer of incorporeal property:

> 'In principle all personal rights are capable of transfer. Real rights are also capable of transfer except that real conditions, such as servitudes, cannot be separated from the dominant tenement to which they are attached and pass automatically with that tenement as a pertinent thereof. Where a contract confers a number of separate rights, the rights may be transferred separately and to different people. A right is not, however, transferable if it involves *delectus personae* or if, as commonly happens in the case of leases, assignation is expressly prohibited, or again if and to the extent that the right is alimentary in nature. Statute may also prohibit transfer, as for example in the case

---

1 Suggested as £25.
2 Gloag and Henderson *The Law of Scotland* (10th edn, 1995) p 609.

of certain social security benefits[1]. In all the cases mentioned a purported transfer would be void'[2].

Express statutory provision would be required to prohibit assignation of a right not involving *delectus personae* and not of an alimentary nature. The fact that no statutory provision for registration of an assignation of a floating charge had been made does not preclude assignation of such a charge[3]:

> 'The law of Scotland allows incorporeal rights to be assigned except those of a personal nature as, for example, an alimentary liferent. The [Companies Floating Charges (Scotland) Act 1961] does not expressly declare a floating charge to be unassignable by the holder, and the fact that no means were prescribed in the statute for registering any assignation did not in my view necessarily create a prohibition against assignation'[4].

Future or contingent rights may be assigned, although such assignation raises particular difficulties of intimation which may render its security value nugatory. Difficult questions arise concerning the assignation of future rights, such as a *spes successionis* (an expectation of succeeding to property) or rights to payment under contracts which have yet to be entered into. Thus:

> 'It appears that while some future rights may be transferred, others may not, and the reported cases give little indication of underlying principle. To some extent, of course, the issue turns on the principle of whether there is in existence a debtor to whom intimation may be made'[5].

However, it is not only personal rights which may be assigned in security. Securities over rights in leases are common and with increased trading in debt assets the practice of assigning heritable securities is reviving[6].

The main forms of personal rights accepted by banks as security are: life policies, stock exchange securities, interests in trust estates and debts due under contracts. Before examining these in detail, it is necessary that the general principles of assignation of incorporeal property be considered.

(2) GENERAL PRINCIPLES OF ASSIGNATION

Nature of the rights involved

George Gretton, dealing with the transfer of incorporeal moveable property in security as a typical functional security, says:

> 'A good example of a right of retention which is functionally a security is an assignation in security of a incorporeal moveable asset, such as a policy of

---

1 Social Security Act 1975, s 87.
2 18 *Stair Memorial Encyclopaedia* para 652.
3 *Libertas-Kommerz GmbH* 1977 SC 191, 1978 SLT 222, OH.
4 1977 SC 191 at 203, 1978 SLT 222 at 224, OH.
5 18 *Stair Memorial Encyclopaedia* para 652. See also G L Gretton 'The assignation of contingent rights' 1993 JR 23.
6 See G L Gretton 'The assignation of contingent rights' 1993 JR 23. The definition of 'interest in land' in s 9(8)(b) of the Conveyancing and Feudal Reform (Scotland) Act 1970 is such that it is possible to create a standard security over a standard security.

life assurance, or, to take a commercial example, a receivable. In such an assignation, dominium is transferred to the creditor. Thus the life policy or the receivable become payable to the assignee instead of to the cedent, though of course there will exist an obligation to account for the proceeds. What right remains in the cedent? Merely a personal right. The main content of this personal right is the right to a retrocession on payment of the debt, or, if the subject assigned has matured in the hands of the assignee the right to be paid the free proceeds, if any. An assignation in security is thus a right of retention functioning as a security, rather than a security in the narrow sense'[1].

An intimated assignation of incorporeal property, even if only in security, has the effect that from the moment of intimation (or, in the case of real rights, from the moment of registration or possession) the cedent no longer 'owns' the right represented by the incorporeal property. At most, he will 'own' a reversionary right — a personal right against the assignee to have the rights which constitute the incorporeal property restored to him on performance of the obligation he owes to the assignee. He cannot, however, be described as the 'owner' of the property of the right assigned. This follows from the fact that intimation (or, in the case of real rights, registration or possession) of the assignation to the debtor in the obligation which constitutes the property divests the cedent of his right as creditor in that obligation and vests it in the assignee. Consequently, after intimation of an assignation of a personal right, any unintimated assignation of the same property by the same cedent is ineffectual. After intimation, the cedent has no right which he may assign (other than any right he may have to a reversionary interest in the property)[2].

Form of assignation

Except in those cases where writing is made obligatory by statute[3], it is uncertain whether writing is required for the assignation of incorporeal property[4]. The universal practice, however, is for assignation to be in formal writing. With regard to form 'an assignation doth necessarily require the clear expressing of the cedent, assignee, and thing assigned' and 'in terms that may express the transmission of the right assigned from cedent to the assignee'[5].

Simple forms of assignation of personal bonds were introduced by the Transmission of Moveable Property (Scotland) Act 1862. The word 'bond' in this context includes:

'personal bonds for payment or performance, bonds of caution, bonds of guarantee, bonds of relief, bonds and assignations in security of every kind, decrees of any court, policies of assurance of any assurance company or association in Scotland'[6].

1 G L Gretton 'The Concept of Security' in *A Scots Conveyancing Miscellany: Essays in Honour of Professor J M Halliday* (1987) p 130.
2 See *Stair* III,1,6.
3 Eg Registration of Leases (Scotland) Act 1857, s 3(1), Sch (A); Conveyancing and Feudal Reform (Scotland) Act 1970, s 14, Sch 4, Forms A, B.
4 See 18 *Stair Memorial Encyclopaedia* para 655 and *Report on Requirements of Writing* (Scot Law Com no. 112 (1988)) paras 2.51–2.52.
5 *Stair* III,1,4.
6 Transmission of Moveable Property (Scotland) Act 1862, s 4.

The assignation may be either separate from, or indorsed on, the bond. However, the Act expressly preserves existing methods of assignation and intimation[1]. The result is that it is unnecessary that any particular form or that any particular words of conveyance be used in the assignation[2].

Lord Justice-Clerk Inglis in *Carter v McIntosh* said:

> 'if anything is settled in the law of Scotland, it is that no words directly importing conveyance are necessary to constitute an assignation, but that any words giving authority or directions, which if fairly carried out will operate a transference, are sufficient to make an assignation'[3].

Some forms of assignation for certain specific subjects are prescribed by statute[4].

Proof that assignation is in security

Assignation in security is effected by the same means as outright assignation of ownership, but is subject to an obligation expressed either in the assignation or in a separate agreement to retrocess or reassign to the cedent the rights assigned on repayment of the debt or performance of the obligation secured by the assignation. Where the assignation in security is ex facie absolute, proof that it was effected in security will be required in any dispute as to the cedent's right to reassignation. Once the ex facie absolute transfer of ownership has occurred, such proof will be provided only by the writ or oath of the assignee[5].

Mere agreement to assign will be insufficient to constitute assignation. In *Bank of Scotland v Hutchison, Main & Co Ltd Liquidators*[6] a company entered an arrangement with the bank to which it was indebted whereby it was agreed that, on the bank surrendering certain moveable property held in security (golf balls), the company should assign to the bank a debenture to be obtained over the assets of one of the company's own debtors. After the moveable property had been surrendered by the bank and the debenture obtained by the company, but before assignation of the debenture to the bank had been effected, the company became insolvent. It was held that at best the arrangement constituted a contractual agreement to assign the debenture.

1 1862 Act, s 3.
2 'All that is required is the expression of an irrevocable intention by the creditor in a debt that his debtor should make payment to another person': 20 *Stair Memorial Encyclopaedia* para 46.
3 (1862) 24 D 925 at 933. See also *McCutcheon v McWilliam* (1876) 3 R 565 at 571, per Lord Justice-Clerk Moncreiff: 'Any words which express a present intention to transfer are sufficient as an assignation apart altogether from forms of style or the schedules of the recent statute'; *Ritchie v Maclachlan* 1870 8 M 815 where an order in these terms, 'Pay the above account to C,' written on an account and signed over a penny stamp an delivered to C, was held to be a mandate in *rem suam* and to be effectual as a valid assignation of the sum in the account when duly intimated to the debtor or holder of the fund; and *Brownlee v Robb* 1907 SC 1302.
4 Eg Registration of Leases (Scotland) Act 1857, s 3(1) (amended by the Law Reform (Miscellaneous Provisions) (Scotland) Act 1985, s 3); Policies of Assurance Act 1867, s 5, Schedule (life assurance policies); Conveyancing and Feudal Reform (Scotland) Act 1970, s 14, Sch 4, Forms A, B (standard securities).
5 *Purnell v Shannon* (1894) 22 R 74; *Walker v Buchanan, Kennedy & Co* (1857) 20 D 259.
6 1914 SC (HL) 1, 1914 1 SLT 111.

Effect of delivery without assignation

Mere delivery and possession of the document evidencing the existence of the incorporeal property cannot constitute an assignation. This is in contrast to English law, under which an equitable security over, for example, life assurance policy, may be created by mere delivery and possession of the policy. In *Wylie's Executrix v McJannet*[1] a solicitor, to cover advances he had made to his client, persuaded him to insure his life. The solicitor paid all the premiums and the policy remained in his hands. No formal assignation (or intimation) was effected. The client died insolvent and the solicitor claimed preferential ranking to the extent of the premiums paid by him and interest thereon on the grounds that he had custody of the policy and that his expenditure had preserved it in force. Alternatively, he claimed a lien to the extent of that expenditure over the proceeds of the policy. The payments of the premiums by the solicitor, it was held, were cash advances on behalf of the assured. They created only an unsecured debt against the assured and gave no preferential right over any other creditor to the fund produced by the policy. Nor could the solicitor use his hypothec to maintain a right to hold the policy. The hypothec which a law agent has over his client's papers can be exercised only for the amount of a professional account and not for cash advances[2].

Intimation of the assignation

Assignation without intimation binds only the cedent and therefore his personal representatives[3]. However, as in the case of other unilateral deeds, even the cedent will not be bound unless the assignation is delivered to the assignee[4]. Once the personal obligation has been granted by the cedent coupled with delivery of an assignation, it is enforceable also against his personal representatives. There are two points in the doctrine of intimation; the interruption of bona fides on the part of the debtor, and the completion of the transference. Intimation is necessary for both purposes, not merely to give preference in competition, but as step of diligence to complete the assignee's right. Assignation is completed by intimation, even though the deed of assignation should not itself be delivered. Even an unintimated assignation, if delivered, is valid against the granter, who cannot dispute his own deed, and against his personal representatives[5].

In the case of executors, the estate of the deceased vests in them by virtue of their confirmation[6]. If, before his death, a person delivers an assignation of his incorporeal property to another but this assignation is not intimated prior to confirmation of executors in his estate on death,

---

1 (1901) 4 F 195.
2 *Christie v Ruxton* (1862) 24 D 1182.
3 'Though ... intimation be a necessary solemnity to assignations, yet the assignation alone will be sufficient against the cedent, he should quarrel it, because he is author thereof, and can do no deed contrary thereto': *Stair* III,1,15.
4 *Erskine* III,5,4.
5 *Erskine* III,5,3; *Grant v Gray* (1828) 6 S 489.
6 Succession (Scotland) Act 1964, s 14(1).

then the property remains part of the deceased's estate at the date of confirmation. This is because it is intimation of an assignation, and not the assignation itself, which divests the cedent of the property assigned and vests it in the assignee. As personal representatives of the deceased, however, the executors (provided the estate is solvent) are bound to implement obligations entered into by the deceased prior to death. They are effectively bound, therefore, to allow the assignee to complete title to the property assigned[1]. However, if the estate of the cedent of an unintimated assignation were insolvent, the assignee would merely rank with other unsecured creditors for a pro rata share in the estate of the cedent to the extent of the personal right created by the unintimated assignation or by any debts which the assignation was intended to secure. Where a cedent's estate is sequestrated, as of the date of sequestration it becomes vested in the permanent trustee by virtue of the act and warrant of sequestration[2]. Any incorporeal property forming part of the estate is deemed to be assigned and the assignation intimated at that date. An award of sequestration therefore defeats any unintimated assignation in existence at the date of sequestration.

Intimation in the case of an incorporeal moveable is equivalent to delivery or change in the nature of possession of a corporeal moveable. In other words, it is the overt act required to complete the transference of the right which constitutes the property[3]. Until the assignation is intimated to the debtor in the obligation assigned, ownership of the right as creditor in that obligation remains vested in the cedent, and the assignee has only a personal right to complete title to that right on intimation[4].

In a competition between two assignees of the same debt, A and B, whichever intimates first has the preferential right to payment of the debt by the debtor. If B intimates first, he will thus acquire a real right to the property even although the assignation to him was subsequent to the assignation to A. B's protected status as the first assignee to intimate can be explained in two ways. Firstly B's preferential right derives from the fact that it is intimation of an assignation and not the assignation itself which divests the cedent of his right to the property (the debt) and vests it in the assignee. As soon as B's assignation is intimated, therefore, then as far as B, the debtor or any other third party is concerned, the prior unintimated assignation to A effectively falls, since the cedent no longer owns the property which the assignation purports to transfer. But in a question between A and the cedent, A retains personal right of action against the cedent for breach of contract. Secondly, B's protected status follows from the fundamental rule of property law that, 'on acquiring the real right of

1 *Brownlee v Robb* 1907 SC 1302: the assignation of a life policy by the assured to his daughter was held preferable to the rights of the executrix of the assured, although the assignation had not been intimated to the assurance company prior to the death of the cedent or to grant of confirmation to the executors. See also similar approach in *Grant v Gray* (1828) 6 S 489.
2 Bankruptcy (Scotland) Act 1985, s 31.
3 Bankton *Institute* III,1,6; *Gallemos Ltd v Barratt Falkirk Ltd* 1990 SLT 98 at 101, per Lord Dunpark: 'Intimation of an assignation to a debtor is the equivalent of delivery of a corporeal moveable and is necessary to complete the title of the assignee'.
4 *Stair* III,1,6–10; *Campbell's Trustees v Whyte* (1884) 11 R 1078; *Allan v Urquhart* (1887) 15 R 56; *Wyllie's Trustees v Boyd* (1891) 18 R 1121 at 1126, per Lord Kincairney (OH).

ownership in the course of voluntary transfer, a transferee has no concern with any personal rights which may be prestable against his author'[1]. B's ownership of the incorporeal property (the debt) is therefore unaffected by the prior personal obligation the cedent owes to A under the prior unintimated assignation to him. However, there is scope to argue that where B takes an assignation of debt or other property from the cedent in the knowledge that the latter has already assigned the debt to A, then B's right, even if intimated prior to that of A, is defeasible at the instance of A. This would follow from the so-called rule against offside goals which creates an exception to the general rule that a grantee is not affected by personal obligations of his author which are, in Reid's terminology, 'extrinsic' to the property transferred[2].

Where A is the holder of an unintimated voluntary assignation of incorporeal property, his right to complete title to the property will be defeated by any one of the following:

- intimation to the debtor of another assignation of the same property, where the assignee was unaware of the assignation to A and has given value (and regardless of the respective dates of the assignations themselves; payment in good faith by the debtor to the cedent[3];
- diligence by the cedent's creditors[4];
- confirmation to the debt by an executor-creditor in the cedent' estate[5];
- confirmation of a permanent trustee on the cedent's sequestrated estates[6];
- the attachment of a floating charge[7] at the date of attachment of a floating charge being the date of appointment of receiver over the whole property, heritable and moveable, of a company. The floating charge has effect 'as if it is a fixed security' and is accordingly an effective security over the property concerned[8].

Any book debts included in that property are therefore to be deemed to be assigned to the charge holder and intimated to the debtors concerned at

1 18 *Stair Memorial Encyclopaedia* para 688. See also *Erskine* II,3,48; Hume *Lectures* vol IV (Stair Soc vol 17, 1955 ed GCH Paton) pp 311–318; Bell *Commentaries* I,307–308.
2 18 *Stair Memorial Encyclopaedia* paras 690 and 695. 'The rule against offside goals is of some antiquity in Scots law and was already well established by the time of Stair [I,14,5]. The paradigm example of its operation is in cases of double sale'; and reference is made to Lord Kinloch in *Morrison v Somerville* 1860 22 D 1082 at 1089, OH (affd 1860 22 D 1082, IH) (para 695).
3 Since such payment discharges the debtor's liability: *Drummond v Muschet* (1492) Mor 843; *McDowal v Fullerton* (1714) Mor 576; *Allan v Urquhart* (1887) 15 R 56.
4 *Erskine* III,6,19; *Strachan v McDougle* (1835) 13 S 954: an arrestment was held preferable to an unintimated assignation of a life policy — an attempt to argue that, title to such a policy, like title to a negotiable instrument, was completed be delivery alone was unsuccessful.
5 *Sinclair v Sinclair* (1726) Mor 2793.
6 Bankruptcy (Scotland) Act 1985, s 31(4). Note, however, that the estate of the bankrupt does not vest in the interim trustee in the same way as it does in the permanent trustee. The interim trustee may deal with certain assets but does not do so as 'owner'. Subject to the rules on unfair preferences, an assignation could therefore be completed by intimation even after appointment of interim trustee in the cedent's estate.
7 *Forth and Clyde Construction Co Ltd v Trinity Timber and Plywood Co Ltd* 1984 SC 1, 1984 SLT 94.
8 Companies (Floating Charges and Receivers) (Scotland) Act 1972, s 31(1).

that date. It follows that any prior assignations of the debts which have not been intimated at the date of attachment of the floating charge are defeated by such attachment[1] and the appointment of a liquidator of an incorporated company where intimation has not been made prior to the liquidator's vesting order under section 145 of the Insolvency Act 1986[2].

Bankruptcy (Scotland) Act 1985, section 36

There is a possibility that, under section 36 of the Bankruptcy (Scotland) Act 1985 an intimated assignation could be reduced as an unfair preference, where the assignation has been delivered outwith the six month or other relevant period mentioned in section 36 but the intimation is made within this period. The Act of 1696[3], declared that 'voluntary dispositions, assignations or other deeds' made or granted by a debtor within a set period (sixty days, later six months) of bankruptcy were voidable as unfair preferences to creditors where they created security for a prior debt. Similar provision was contained in section 110 of the Bankruptcy (Scotland) Act 1856 in relation to the bankrupt estate of a deceased debtor. Likewise, under the common law on fraudulent preferences the security was struck at only if it was the 'voluntary' deed of the debtor[4]. Where an assignation of incorporeal property had been granted prior to the relevant period but the assignee did not intimate until later, during the relevant period, the question arose as to whether the intimated assignation could be reduced as security for a prior debt creating an unfair preference. In *Scottish Provident Institution v W H Cohen & Co*[5] it was held that the 1856 Act struck at securities 'created by some act or deed of the bankrupt or deceased debtor'. In this instance intimation of life assurance policy was the act of the creditor, who thereby rendered effectual a security which was validly constituted by assignation by the assured before his death and not for a prior debt. The date at which the assignee completed his title by intimation was therefore not relevant[6].

What constitutes intimation?

At common law, intimation could be effected by delivery of a copy of the assignation and a schedule of intimation to the debtor by a procurator for the assignee, in the presence of a notary and two witnesses. The notary then expeded an instrument of intimation signed by him and the two witnesses. Alternatively, the assignee could produce the assignation and a copy of it to the debtor and obtain an attested or holograph acknowledgment of intimation[7].

These older methods of intimation are still competent but have been superseded in practice by the procedures prescribed by section 2 of the

1 Cf also K Reid 'Unintimated Assignations' 1989 SLT (News) 267.
2 W A Wilson *The Scottish Law of Debt* (2nd edn, 1991) para 25-7.
3 Act of 1696 (c 5).
4 See E A Marshall *Scots Mercantile Law* (2nd edn, 1992), para 9-37.
5 *Scottish Provident Institution v W H Cohen & Co* (1888) 16 R 112.
6 See *Caledonian Insurance Co v Beattie* (1898) 5 SLT 349, OH.
7 A Montgomery Bell *Lectures on Conveyancing* I,312.

Transmission of Moveable Property (Scotland) Act 1862. Under these procedures, a notary delivers a copy of the assignation (or if the deed of assignation contains other provisions a copy of the part which effects the assignation), certified as correct, to the debtor in the presence of two witnesses. The intimation must then be certified in the form set out in Schedule C to the 1862 Act, the certificate being executed by the notary and the two witnesses. If intimation cannot be made personally to the debtor the copy may be left at his house and the person to whom it was delivered must then be named in the certificate. Alternatively and much more practically, section 2 of the Act authorises postal intimation whereby the assignee or his agent transmits a certified copy of the assignation (or of such part of the deed containing the assignation as concerns the assignation) by post to the debtor and obtains a written acknowledgment of receipt of the copy from him. Where the debtor is located outside Scotland, intimation may be made by post in conformity with the 1862 Act[1]. If the address of the debtor is unknown, intimation can only be made edictally[2].

In the ordinary case, intimation is made to the person who is the debtor in the obligation assigned. However, where the debtor is not a natural person, or where there is some speciality as to legal capacity, or where more than one debtor, or a cautioner, is involved, special rules may apply.

Formal intimation

Intimation to several debtors, whether bound jointly and severally or not should be made to all of them[3]. Where an interest in a trust has been assigned or the fund from which payment of the assigned debt is to be made is held by trustees or executors, intimation should, in prudence, be made to each trustee or executor[3]. However, intimation to one of a body of trustees has been held sufficient[4]. An assignee who has given intimation to all the trustees holding office at the time is not bound to renew the notice on any change in the trustees. For the purpose of intimation to trustees, it appears that intimation to their law agents is sufficient[5].

Prior to the Age of Legal Capacity (Scotland) Act 1991, where the debtor was a pupil intimation had to be made to the pupil and his tutor, and if a minor to the minor and his curators (if any)[6]. By analogy, it would appear that where the debtor is under the age of sixteen, intimation should now be made to the debtor and his guardian.

Intimation to a company should be made to the company at its registered office[7]. However, an assignation of uncalled share capital of a company requires to be intimated to all its shareholders[8].

1 'Registrar of Companies: assignations in security' 1983 SLT (News) 173.
2 A Montgomery Bell *Lectures on Conveyancing* I,314–315.
3 *Erskine* III,5,5.
4 *Jameson v Sharp* (1887) 14 R 64. Note, however, that this appears to have been a special case, in which, of two trustees, only one was acting. The other was in ill health and had left the entire administration of the trust in the hands of his co-trustee.
5 *Browne's Trustee v Anderson* (1901) 4 F 305.
6 A Montgomery Bell *Lectures on Conveyancing* I,314.
7 Companies Act 1985, s 725.
8 *Union Club Liquidator v Edinburgh Life Assurance Co* (1906) 8 F 1143; *Ballachulish Slate Quarries Co Ltd Liquidator v Malcolm* (1908) 15 SLT 963, OH; *Ballachulish Slate Quarries Co Ltd v Bruce* (1908) 16 SLT 48.

Intimation to a firm should be made to the firm and to all its partners. If there is an appointed managing partner, intimation to him will be sufficient[1]. In the case of a bank, intimation should be made to the bank at its head office and, if expedient, to the branch office at which the fund assigned is lying. Intimation of a debt due by a principal debtor and a cautioner may be made to the principal debtor without being made also to the cautioner[2], but intimation only to the cautioner is not sufficient to prevent bona fide payment by the principal debtor to the cedent, which also liberates the cautioner[3].

Where property which has not yet come into existence, such as a future interest in a trust or estate, is assigned outright or in security, intimation can only be made once a debtor exists. Thus, a prospective legatee may assign in security his legacy before the death of the testator, but intimation can be given only to the executor of the testator and must therefore be deferred until after the testator's death[4].

Constructive intimation

Certain conduct on the part of the debtor may be regarded as equivalent to intimation. The following is a list of examples, but may not be an exhaustive list of circumstances which the courts would hold akin to intimation:

- The assignee's taking possession of the right by entering into possession of the rents or interest, which implies the debtor's knowledge of and compliance with the assignation[5].
- Actual payment by the debtor of part of the principal, or payment of interest, to the assignee[6].
- Court action or diligence against the debtor by the assignee and founded on the assignation[7].
- Written promise by the debtor to pay to the assignee[8].
- Participation of the debtor as a party to the assignation[9].
- Production of the assignation in a multiplepoinding or other court action to which the debtor is also a party[10].

---

1   Intimation to one who is merely a de facto managing partner will be insufficient: *Hill v Lindsay* (1846) 8 D 472.
2   *Mosman v Bells* (1670) 2 Brown's Supp 457.
3   *Lyon v Law* (1610) Mor 1786.
4   *Bedwells and Yates v Tod* 2 Dec 1819 FC.
5   *Erskine* III,5,3.
6   *Erskine* III,5,5: 'Payment of interest made by the debtor to the assignee is equivalent to intimation; for the assignee, by his receiving interest, is truly in the actual possession of the debt in virtue of his conveyance; and all rights not feudal may be completed by the acquirer's entering into the natural possession'. And see *Livingston v Lindsay* (1626) Mor 860.
7   *Erskine* III,5,4; *Whyte v Neish* (1622) Mor 854; *Dougal v Gordon* (1795) Mor 851; *Carter v McIntosh* (1862) 24 D 925.
8   *Home and Elphinstone v Murray* (1674) Mor 863.
9   *Turnbull v Stewart* (1751) Mor 868. But not mere presence of the debtor as a witness: *Murray v Durham and Lady Winton* (1622) Mor 855.
10   *Dougal v Gordon* (1795) Mor 851.

- Intimation in correspondence to the debtor or his agent, replied to by either of them[1]. Where only part of a right is assigned, the communication must specify clearly which part[2]. The communications must be acknowledged by the debtor in order to demonstrate that, despite its informality, he understands and accepts its terms, and, intimation does not take effect until acknowledgment is made[3].
- Intimation to a factor or agent for the debtor and corresponding entry made in the debtor's books[4].
- Attendance and voting at a meeting of partners by an assignee of a share in the firm[5].
- Registration of the deed containing the assignation in the Register of Sasines[6], but not in the Books of Council and Session, will also be construed as 'constructive intimation'[7].

The debtor's private knowledge of an assignation is sufficient to prevent him from paying the cedent[8] and since any such payment will be deemed to be payment in bad faith, he may be liable to pay again to the assignee[9].

Circumstances in which intimation is unnecessary

Where the assignation is granted by one who is the debtor himself intimation is unnecessary[10]. Likewise, where the assignee is himself the person to whom intimation would appropriately be made intimation is unnecessary[11]. Intimation is also unnecessary where the assignation is effected by act and warrant of a trustee on a sequestrated estate[12]. Any involuntary transfer of the debtor's estate through arrestment, the grant of confirmation of an executor-creditor, the attachment of a floating charge, an award of sequestration or, possibly, an order for the winding up of an incorporated company, will have effect as if an assignation of any incorporeal property involved had been delivered and intimated. It is for this reason that such involuntary transfers defeat the right of any assignee who has not intimated his assignation at the date of the involuntary transfer.

Obligations of cedent and assignee

Cedent/debtor

In assignations of incorporeal moveables, the law implies that the cedent confers on his assignee all powers necessary to make the assignation

---

1 *Libertas-Kommerz GmbH* 1977 SC 191 at 205, 1978 SLT 222 at 226, OH.
2 *Gallemos Ltd v Barratt Falkirk Ltd* 1990 SLT 98.
3 *Wallace v Davies* (1853) 15 D 688.
4 *Earl of Aberdeen v Earl of March* (1730) 1 Pat 44, HL.
5 *Hill v Lindsay* (1846) 8 D 472.
6 *Rodger v Crawfords* (1867) 6 M 24.
7 *Tod's Trustees v Wilson* (1869) 7 M 1100.
8 *Leith v Garden* (1703) Mor 865.
9 *Macpherson's Judicial Factor v Mackay* 1915 SC 1011, 1915 2 SLT 110.
10 *Browne's Trustee v Anderson* (1901) 4 F 305.
11 As where eg the assignee is a trustee of the fund from which the assigned debt is to be paid: *Earl of Argyle v Lord McDonald* (1676) Mor 842; *Russell v Earl of Breadalbane* (1831) 5 W & S 256, HL; *Miller v Learmonth* (1870) 42 SJ 418; *Ayton v Romanes* (1895) 3 SLT 203, OH; *Mounsey* (1896) 4 SLT 46, OH.
12 Bankruptcy (Scotland) Act 1985, ss 31–33; *Tod's Trustees v Wilson* (1869) 7 M 1100.

effectual, by intimation or otherwise[1]. It is implied that the debt is subsisting. This warrants that the bond, decree or other deed assigned is such as cannot be reduced, that the cedent has undoubted right to the debt and that the debtor and any cautioner bound by a collateral obligation are bound to make payment of the debt[2]. There is, however, no implied warranty of the solvency of the debtor[3].

Assignee/creditor

DUTY OF REASONABLE CARE

The assignee under an assignation in security (as in any security) is bound to exercise reasonable care in his management of the security subjects. He may be obliged to account to the cedent for any profit drawn on the subjects[4] and may be obliged to take any action appropriate to safeguard the interest of the cedent in the subjects[5]. These are merely personal obligations undertaken or implied in the security agreement which accompanies the assignation. Breach by the assignee would therefore be actionable as breach of an implied term of the loan and security agreement, but would not necessarily release the cedent from his own obligations to the assignee/creditor. In *Waddell v Hutton*[6] the pursuer assigned shares in security to the defender. The defender became duly registered as owner in the company's books. During the currency of the security agreement, the defender was offered additional shares in proportion to his holdings. Without communicating with the pursuer he declined to take up this 'rights issue'. The shares being at a premium, a large profit was thereby lost to the pursuer. The pursuer brought an action in damages against the defender for breach of his duty as security holder. It was held that:

> 'Shares in public companies are often made the subject of securities with banks and others who advance the money to enable their clients to purchase the same, and obtain themselves registered as shareholders so as to complete the security title. The contract so constituted is, in fact, just a form of pledge; but the peculiarity of it consists in the pledgee having the only property title in the subject of the pledge, and being, accordingly, the only person recognised by the company as having right to the shares. It follows that notices with regard to a fresh issue of shares offered to existing shareholders, or as to payment of calls where the shares are not fully paid up, or the like, may never reach the true owner's knowledge, as they fall to be sent by the company to the person who, ex facie of the register, appears to be the owner. It would be a strong thing to hold that, in such circumstances, there is no duty on the creditor to inform the true owner of the shares of a valuable right which he possesses in respect of them, or of an obligation which he must meet under penalty of the forfeiture of his property'[7].

1 *Miller v Muirhead* (1894) 21 R 658.
2 *Barclay v Liddel* (1671) Mor 16591; *Reid v Barclay* (1879) 6 R 1007.
3 *Erskine* II,3,25.
4 *Marquess of Queensbury's Trustees v Scottish Union Insurance Co* (1839) 1 D 1203.
5 *Waddell v Hutton* 1911 SC 575, 1911 1 SLT 223.
6 1911 SC 575, 1911 1 SLT 223.
7 1911 SC 575 at 578, 579, 1911 1 SLT 223 at 224, per Lord Salvesen.

CONSEQUENCES OF ACCIDENTAL LOSS OF SUBJECTS

A creditor is not liable for the accidental loss or destruction of the subjects he holds in security, nor is his right to recover his debt affected. Accidental loss only affects the creditor if the debtor becomes insolvent after the security subjects are lost and before repayment of the advance which was until then secured. If the debtor becomes insolvent once the security subjects are accidentally lost, the creditor will rank along with general (unsecured) creditors in respect of the advances he has made. If, on the other hand, the debtor remains solvent, then effectively, it is the debtor who bears the losses: he loses any right to a reconveyance of the security subjects (since these no longer exist) and so loses this right to the debt which they comprise. He remains liable, however, to repay the creditor the advance in security of which he had assigned the debt. But once the debtor has tendered repayment of any amount owed, then if the creditor wrongfully refuses to release the security subjects to him, the creditor will thereafter be liable to the debtor for their value should they be lost or destroyed, even accidentally[1].

THE EXACT SUBJECTS MUST BE RESTORED ON PAYMENT

On payment of the debt, it is the duty of the creditor to restore the exact subjects given in security, unless there was agreement to the contrary. In *Crerar v Bank of Scotland*[2] the bank made advances to customers by means of 'secured loan accounts'. The practice in relation to these accounts was that shares were transferred in security by the customer to the bank's nominees and were registered in their names. No evidence of the identity of the particular shares so transferred was preserved. The customer was then credited in the bank's books with a certain quantity of shares in the aggregate block of shares of that particular denomination held by the bank. When shares were retransferred to the customer, a quantity corresponding to the quantity originally transferred was retransferred, but not the identical shares. A customer opened such an account in 1902 and, between then and 1918, transferred various shares and received various retransfers in accordance with the practice described above. In 1918, however, she brought an action against the bank for an accounting relative to its intromissions with her shares. It was held that the course of dealing since 1902 showed that the customer must have known and acquiesced in the practice of the bank whereby she surrendered her right to specific shares in return for a right to a corresponding quantity of shares of the same denomination in the block of such shares held by the bank. Consequently she failed in her action against the bank[3].

1 *North Albion Property Investment Co Ltd v MacBean's Curator Bonis* (1893) 21 R 90; *Mackirdy v Webster's Trustees* (1895) 22 R 340; *Fraser v Smith* (1899) 1 F 487; *Ellis & Co's Trustee v Dixon-Johnston* [1925] AC 489, HL; *Nelson v National Bank of Scotland Ltd* 1936 SC 570.
2 1921 SC 735, 1921 2 SLT 112; affd 1922 SC (HL) 137, 1922 SLT 335.
3 Opinions were expressed, however, that, apart from express or implied authority to act otherwise, the bank would have been bound, so far as specific shares were transferred in security, to retain and account for the individual shares so transferred (see eg 1921 SC 735 at 751, 1921 2 SLT 112 at 118, per Lord President Clyde).

Distinction between assignations ex facie absolute and those bearing to be in security

An assignation of incorporeal property may appear on the face of the document of assignation to be an absolute transfer of ownership. In such a case, any agreement that the transfer was in security and that the property is to be reassigned to the transferor on payment of the debt secured by the assignation requires to be proved by the writ or oath of the assignee[1]. Where such an ex facie absolute assignation is intended to be in security, it is usual to set out the terms of the security agreement in separate back letter or 'back bond'. Alternatively, and nowadays more usually, the security agreement may be contained in the assignation itself, in which case it is said that the assignation bears to be in security. In either case, however, the legal effect of intimation of the assignation will be to divest the cedent of ownership of the right assigned (his real right to the personal right which constitutes the property) and to vest it in the assignee. The terms of the security agreement, whether set out in a separate deed or in the assignation itself, create only a personal, or contractual, right to a reassignation or retrocession of the property on repayment of the debt secured, or a right to any surplus proceeds on sale of the property by the assignee after satisfaction of the debt secured.

Assignations which bear to be in security are treated, in the case law, as good security for whatever present and/or future debts are stated in the security agreement to be covered by the security. On satisfaction of those specified debts, the assignee must grant a retrocession, or account for any surplus proceeds of sale (if sale had been agreed) to the cedent or his estate. The onus will be on the assignee to prove that any additional advances not mentioned in the security agreement have been made in reliance on an agreement that they are covered by the security. In *National Bank of Scotland v Forbes*[2] A assigned to B, in security of a debt of £500, a life assurance policy on his own life for £1,000, with power, in case of his death and the debt being then unpaid, to uplift and recover the contents, but making B bound to account for any surplus after extinction of the £500 debt, principal and interest.The security agreement was contained in the assignation and expressly stated that A was entitled to redeem the policy at any time on a payment of the £500 debt. A subsequently obtained an additional advance of £700 from B and granted a personal bond for that amount. The bond bore no reference to the prior transaction or to the insurance policy. A died insolvent, and a competition ensued between B and the trustee on A's sequestrated estate as to the entitlement to the balance due on the policy after payment to B of the original £500 debt plus interest thereon. It was held that B's title to the security was limited to a security of the £500 debt and interest. He had no right to retain the policy or the balance of its contents in security or extinction of the subsequent advance of £700.

---

1 See *Purnell v Shannon* (1894) 22 R 74 and *Walker v Buchanan, Kennedy & Co* (1857) 20 D 259.
2 (1858) 21 D 79.

(3)   SPECIAL FEATURES IN THE TRANSFER OF PARTICULAR INCORPOREAL PROPERTY

Most of the above comments on the general principles of assignation of incorporeal property apply equally to the assignation of life policies, stock exchange securities, trust or contingent interests and book debts. Certain special features in the transfer of such property in security are, however, mentioned below.

Life assurance policies

Assignation of existing policies in security

Where an existing life policy is taken in security by the bank, there is the risk that third parties may already have acquired rights over it or that the insurance company itself may have claims against the cedent which reduce the value of the policy as security or render it susceptible to reduction. Verification of the validity of the policy, the effectiveness of an assignation, and of the existence of any claims against the cedent by the insurance company is therefore advisable. In a question between the assignee and the insurance company (the debtor in the obligation assigned), the assignee will enjoy the same rights as the cedent. The assignee may therefore recover under the policy to the extent of the insurable interest of the cedent. However, the assignee's rights under the policy will be no greater than those which the original assured would have enjoyed[1]. Thus, for example, if the assured's right under the policy was defeasible at the instance of the debtor, an assignee of the policy takes no higher right. Even where the assignee has acquired the right in good faith and for value, in a question with the debtor in the right assigned he may be defeated[2].

If the insurance company has already advanced moneys to the assured on the policy, or some irregularity in payment of the premiums has occurred, the value of the policy as security may be substantially diminished by the company's right to set off these sums (so long as they remain unpaid) once the policy becomes due. In *Borthwick v Scottish Widows' Fund*[3] at the date of sequestration of the assured, three life policies were in force, effected with an insurance company to whom the assured was indebted. Two of the policies had been deposited with the company in security of a specific loan. Further sums were owed by the assured to the company in respect of a debit balance arising out of his intromissions with the premiums. The trustee in sequestration claimed right to all the policies on payment of the specific loan for which two of the policies had been deposited with the company in security, but free of all other claims on the

1   *Christie v Armstrong* 1996 SCLR 745, 1996 SLT 948.
2   *Buist v Scottish Equitable Life Assurance Society* (1876) 3 R 1078; affd (1878) 5 R (HL) 64.
    Buist was the onerous assignee to a policy of life assurance effected by the deceased on his own life. The House of Lords affirmed the decision of the First Division that the policy be reduced on the ground that it had been obtained by false statements by the deceased in the proposal for insurance.
3   (1864) 2 M 595.

part of the company on the proceeds when these should fall due. It was held on payment of the specific loan, the trustee was entitled to delivery of the two policies. But the insurance company, so long as the bankrupt remained indebted to it in respect of either the loan or the intromissions with premiums, would be entitled to withhold payment of the proceeds of the policies when such payment became due.

In a case where Scots law applies, however, mere delivery and possession of the document evidencing the existence of the incorporeal property cannot constitute an assignation, and intimation of such delivery to the debtor (in the case of life policies, the insurance company) will create no preference[1]. Policies of life assurance are assignable only by the assured, the party to whom the benefits of the policy are payable. It is immaterial in this respect, who pays the premium[2].

The form of the assignation may be as prescribed by the Policies of Assurance Act 1867[3], or in one of the forms authorised by the Transmission of Moveable Property (Scotland) Act 1862. In the case of an assignation in accordance with the 1867 Act, this may be effected either by indorsement on the policy or by separate instrument. Both Acts appear to be permissive rather than mandatory, so that methods sufficient to assign incorporeal property at common law will be equally valid. At common law any words conveying an intention to assign will suffice[4].

A policy may specifically state that it is not assignable, and in certain circumstances, assignation may be precluded by law. Thus a policy of assurance effected by a married man on his own life for the benefit of his wife or children[5] is not assignable by him, since it does not form part of his estate but creates a trust on behalf of the beneficiaries. Under the Married Women's Policies of Assurance (Scotland) (Amendment) Act 1980[6], such policies constitute trusts within the meaning of the Trusts (Scotland) Act 1921, and the trustee therefore has all of the powers listed in section 4 of the 1921 Act in relation to the policy. Nevertheless, since these powers may not be exercised if at variance with trust purposes, and since the purpose of such a policy is to benefit the spouse or children of the person who effected the policy, it is unlikely that the trustee could sell or assign such a policy without first obtaining express power to do so under section 5 of the 1921 Act. In contrast, the beneficiaries under the policy may assign their interest in it.

Where bonuses arise in regard to a policy assigned in security[7], and if the matter is not otherwise regulated by special agreement, no creditor is entitled to make a profit on the security granted to him. Provision as to liability for future payments of premiums and observance of other conditions of the policy by the debtor should be made in the security agreement. The creditor should nonetheless take all powers necessary to

1 *Wylie's Executrix v McJannet* (1901) 4 F 195.
2 *Thomson's Trustees v Thomson* (1879) 6 R 1227.
3 Policies of Assurance Act 1867, s 5, Schedule.
4 *Brownlee v Robb* 1907 SC 1302; *Scottish Provident Institution v W H Cohen & Co* (1888) 16 R 112.
5 Under the Married Women's Policies of Assurance (Scotland) Act 1880, s 2.
6 Married Women's Policies of Assurance (Scotland) (Amendment) Act 1980, s 2.
7 The general proposition settled by the case of *Shand v Blaikie* (1859) 21 D 878 applies.

maintain the policy in force by advancing premiums on the debtor's default or sequestration, and to recover such sums from the proceeds of the policy. Where a policy is assigned in security, the cedent will have a contractual right to retrocession of the policy on payment of the debt which is secured by the assignation. No power enabling the assignee to assign further to a third party in sale or to surrender it will be implied. Express powers to deal with the policy by sale or surrender, to receive the policy moneys on surrender or maturity, and to grant a discharge of it should therefore be included if desired.

New policies effected by the bank on the life of its debtor

Section 1 of the Life Assurance Act 1774 provides that:

> 'no insurance shall be made by any person or persons, bodies politic or corporate, on the life or lives of any person or persons, or on any other event or events whatsoever, wherein the person or persons for whose use, benefit, or on whose account such policy or policies shall be made, shall have no interest, or by way of gaming or wagering'.

A policy effected in breach of this prohibition will be null and void[1].

Section 3 provides that 'no greater sum shall be recovered or received from the insurer or insurers than the amount or value of that interest'. It follows that the interest assured must be pecuniary or at least capable of valuation in money[2]. Accordingly, a creditor will have an insurable interest over the life of his debtor to the extent of the debt. The combined effect of sections 1 and 2 of the 1774 Act is that the creditor will be unable to assure the life of his debtor for more than the amount of the debt, since that is the limit of his insurable interest. Thus, if the assured has received the full amount of his insurable interest from one insurer, he cannot recover again from any other insurer[3]. The insurable interest must have existed when the policy was effected but the policy remains valid although the interest has ceased before the policy matures. Therefore, where the principal security subjects are a contingent right assigned by the debtor, such as a right to property to which the debtor will succeed only if he survives a certain occurrence, and the creditor takes out a policy on the life of the debtor as additional security for the debt, the fact that the debtor survives to succeed to the property and that the debt is then satisfied from the proceeds of realisation of that property will not affect the validity of the policy and the creditor's entitlement to its proceeds on the debtor's demise. In any case in which the creditor has taken out such a policy, questions may, however, arise as to ownership of the policy. If the creditor has paid the premiums from his own funds, his ownership will be beyond dispute[4]. In *North British Insurance Co v Lindsay and Barmcotte*[5] two brothers received a joint loan of £500 from an insurance company to allow the younger brother to start up a business. In security, a policy on the life

---

1 Life Assurance Act 1774, s 1.
2 See Bell *Principles* s 520.
3 *Simcock v Scottish Imperial Insurance Co Ltd* (1902) 10 SLT 286, OH.
4 *Stevenson v Cotton* (1846) 8 D 872.
5 (1851) 13 D 718.

of the younger brother was effected with the same company, but in the name of the elder brother, for the sum of £1,000. The premiums and regular interest payments to reduce the loan were paid by the elder brother but from funds remitted to him by the younger brother for this purpose. On the death of the younger brother, the elder claimed the balance of the proceeds after satisfaction of the remaining balance of the debt owed to the company. It was held that the loan had been for the benefit of the younger brother and that the premiums and interest had been paid from his funds. Although the elder brother was named as the assured, he had acted merely as agent for his younger brother in this transaction. The younger brother therefore had the interest in the policy and the balance of the proceeds were payable to his estate.

Stock exchange securities

Many of the relevant cases concerning transfer of shares, in security are discussed above in the general section on assignation of incorporeal property. The following cases relate to special features of transfers.

Many of the banking law texts refer to the 'pledge' of shares in security. As with other forms of incorporeal property, however, when a transfer of shares in security is duly completed, ownership of the shares becomes wholly vested in the transferee, the security agreement creating mere contractual rights and obligations in relation to the transaction. But in pledge properly so called, the real right of ownership would remain with the debtor (the pledgor), and a lesser real right — a right in security — would be conferred on the creditor (the pledgee). The term 'pledge', where used to describe the transfer of shares in security, is therefore being used in a somewhat colloquial sense[1].

Completion of transfer

Mere agreement to transfer shares in security will *not* create security and gives rise only to a personal claim against the debtor or an ordinary ranking in his estate[2]. Neither will delivery of the shares with an agreement to execute a transfer at a later date effect a transfer capable of completion by registration. In the case of the transfer of shares in a company, an executed form of transfer takes the place of a written assignation. In *Gourlay v Mackie*[3], shortly before bankruptcy, a firm obtained a loan from another firm to which it granted a promissory note and delivered shares with a letter stating that the shares were handed over in security with an undertaking to execute a transfer of them whenever the creditor so desired. It was held that the letter was merely an agreement to transfer the shares and, as such, was an undertaking to give security at a later date for a prior debt. It therefore constituted an illegal preference. It is acceptable practice in England to deposit the share certificates with the transferee accompanied

---

1 See eg the judgment of Lord Salvesen in *Waddell v Hutton* 1911 SC 575 at 578–579, 1911 1 SLT 223 at 224.
2 *Bank of Scotland v Hutchison, Main & Co Ltd Liquidators* 1914 SC (HL) 1, 1914 1 SLT 111.
3 (1887) 14 R 403.

by blank transfers (transfers executed by the transferor but without insertion of the name of the transferee). This enables the transferee in turn to transfer the shares to a third party without first registering as owner in the register of the company's shares[1]. 'Assignation' is therefore effected, in the case of shares, by delivery of both the share certificates and an executed transfer. This enables transfers to be made to a nominee company and the transfers to be recorded in the registers of the company.

'Intimation' in the case of the transfer of stock or shares in registered companies is effected by registration of the transfer in the company's register. This divests the transferor of ownership and vests it in the transferee, who is issued a new share certificate in his name. Registration therefore completes the security, rendering the transferee's title to the shares good against the claims of other creditors of the transferor.

The act and warrant of confirmation of a trustee in sequestration is, by statue, deemed to be intimation of assignation of incorporeal moveable property in a bankrupt's estate[2]. It will therefore defeat the right of an assignee holding an assignation of such property which is unintimated at the date of sequestration. However, in the case of shares in a company, without registration of the transfer of the shares to the trustee in the company books, the act and warrant of his confirmation will not defeat the right of a transferee who obtains registration of his transfer after the date of sequestration but before the trustee registers his title to the shares. In *Morrison v Harrison*[3] a shareholder executed a transfer of his shares but the transfer was not registered until after his sequestration. Several years later, the trustee in sequestration, who had not taken steps to complete his title to the shares, raised an action for reduction on the ground that, in virtue of his act and warrant of confirmation (which statute declared equivalent to an intimated assignation of the bankrupt's incorporeal property), the shares vested in him at the date of sequestration. It was held that completion of title to shares was not by bare intimation to the company but by the reception of the trustee as a member of the company according to the forms prescribed by statute. Although the trustee had been in position to complete title at the date of sequestration, as he had not done so, he could not now displace the party who had since been duly entered in the company register as holder of the shares.

The articles of the company may provide that the directors have power to refuse to register transfers. The agreement to transfer and the transfer itself do not imply a guarantee that the shares will be registered[4] but only that the transferor will do nothing to prevent registration[5]. In the absence of an express guarantee that the shares will be registered, the transferee has no remedy against the transferor[6]. The power of directors to refuse registration will be exercisable only for the benefit of the company. Where

1 *Colonial Bank v Cady and Williams* (1890) 15 App Cas 267, HL. It is probably now a more acceptable practice since the Requirements of Writing (Scotland) Act 1995, but see *Shaw v Caledonian Rly Co* (1890) 17 R 466 at 478. It is a practice best avoided.
2 Bankruptcy (Scotland) Act 1985, s 31.
3 (1876) 3 R 406.
4 *Marr v Buchanan, Younger & Co* (1852) 14 D 467.
5 *Hooper v Herts* [1906] 1 Ch 549, CA.
6 *London Founders Association Ltd and Palmer v Clarke* (1888) 20 QBD 576, CA.

a valid refusal occurs, the transferor may avoid the contract on repayment of the price or other consideration, which, in the case of a transfer in security of a loan, will be the loan itself. Where the company validly refuses to register the transfer and the transferor does not choose to avoid the contract, he is deemed to hold the shares and to receive any dividends as trustee for the transferee[1].

The holding of the shares by the transferor as trustee for the transferee occurs only in these limited circumstances. It is not the case[2] that once the agreement to transfer is concluded the transferor holds the shares as trustee for the transferee. Such a claim was expressly rejected in *Bank of Scotland v Hutchison, Main & Co Ltd Liquidators*[3]. Indeed, if such a trust arose from mere agreement to transfer property, there would no need for a transferee to take any further steps to complete title, since all property subject to such agreement would be unattachable by the transferor's personal creditors.

Nature of the transferee's rights

In any question between the transferee and the company as to the rights attaching to the shares the transferee is in no better position than the transferor. Where the shares are only partly paid, the transferee will, as far as the company is concerned, be liable for any calls for payment. A creditor taking such shares in security would therefore make the debtor personally bound for such calls. Where the creditor is a bank, it may wish to obtain a lodgement from the debtor for the unpaid amount. Where the shares were held by the transferor in trust for a third party, or for the company itself, it will not be evident from the share certificates or the company register. The title of a transferee who has acquired the shares for value and in good faith, unaware of the latent trust, will be unassailable by third party claims, including claims by creditors of the company[4].

Obligations of transferee

Where the transfer is in security, the contractual obligations of the transferee in relation to retransfer or sale of the shares will be contained in the security agreement. Certain obligations will also be implied by law. The following cases are particularly relevant to banking practice. In *Waddell v Hutton*[5] where shares are transferred in security the creditor will become registered as the shareholder to complete his security. He must nonetheless have some regard to the interests of his debtor and exercise reasonable care in relation to the security subjects. He is under no obligation to take steps to enhance their value, but he is not entitled deliberately and wilfully so to act or abstain from acting as to bring about any loss or damage to his debtor merely because he has at the moment an exclusive title to the shares. He is under an implied duty, therefore, to inform the debtor of

1 *Stevenson v Wilson* 1907 SC 445, 14 SLT 743.
2 As stated in 4 *Stair Memorial Encyclopaedia* para 373.
3 1914 SC (HL) 1, 1914 1 SLT 111.
4 *Redfearn v Somervail* (1813) 5 Pat 707, *sub nom Readfern v Ferrrier* (1813) 1 Dow 50, HL.
5 1911 SC 575, 1911 1 SLT 223.

any rights issues offered by the company to existing shareholders. As in *Ellis & Co's Trustee v Dixon-Johnston*[1] a creditor may not demand payment of a loan unless he is in a position to return the subjects over which the loan was secured intact against payment of the loan. If the creditor sells shares transferred to him in security without the agreement of the debtor he will be unable to demand payment of the loan in security of which the shares were transferred to him. Unless the sale (the release of part of the security subjects) was with the debtor's consent, the creditor may not even recover the balance of the debt after giving credit for the proceeds of sale. He is therefore completely disabled from recovering the debt. In *Nelson v National Bank of Scotland Ltd*[2] it was shown that where a power of sale of a sufficient number of the transferred shares to satisfy the transferor's debt is conferred, in arranging for the sale, there is an implied duty on the transferee to protect the ultimate reversionary interest of the transferor. If, in such circumstances, there is an oversale of the shares, the transferee will be bound to restore or secure the transfer of the oversold shares to the transferor. In *Crerar v Bank of Scotland*[3] where the transferor had a right to have the shares retransferred to her on payment of the debt in security of which they were transferred, then, apart from express or implied authority to act otherwise, the transferee was bound to retain and account for the specific shares which were originally transferred[4].

Trust interests and other contingent rights

Interests in trust estates and contingent rights such as rights to payment of moneys to become due at a later date are frequently offered to banks as security for advances. While a creditor has the option of taking out, or taking an assignation, of a policy on the life of the debtor as additional security in such circumstances, the pitfalls involved in taking security by assignation of trust interests and other contingent rights are nonetheless worth examining. Quite apart from the need to ascertain whether the value of the obligation to be assigned is affected by any advances already made to the assignee by the debtor in the obligation, or by any other claims which this debtor may set off against the cedent's right, various difficulties arise. The main points of difficulty in relation to acquiring effective security by assignation of such interests is ascertainment of whether the potential cedent is actually vested in the right he proposes to assign, and of whether the right itself is certain or is merely contingent or subject to suspensive or resolutive conditions. Both the validity of the assignation in any contest with third parties (such as the cedent's other creditors) and, where the assignation is valid the value of the security obtained hinges upon these issues[5].

1 [1925] AC 489, HL.
2 1936 SC 570.
3 1921 SC 735, 1921 2 SLT 112; affd 1922 SC (HL) 137, 1922 SLT 335.
4 For registered securities other than shares in companies, see *Scottish Banking Practice* (6th edn, 1989) vol 10, pp 21–22.
5 *Scottish Banking Practice* vol 10, pp 75–78; G L Gretton 'The assignation of contingent rights' 1993 JR 23; R Rennie 'Mandate, Assignations and Arrestments' (1993) 38 JLSS 185.

The rules as to whether a conveyance of a personal right having an element of futurity or contingency is possible and will be valid against third parties are as follows. Firstly, a debt which exists but which is not payable until some future date or until the occurrence of some event which is bound to happen can be conveyed, to give an indefeasible title, by intimated assignation before that date or event. Secondly, a debt which exists but whose amount (or, for example, whose date of payment) is subject to contingencies may be conveyed by intimated assignation to give an indefeasible title. Thirdly, where the right is merely to a debt which does not yet exist and whose future existence is subject to contingencies (for example a right to a legacy in an estate), a contract to convey the debt if or when it exists will be binding as between the parties to the contract. However, conveyance of the debt will only be possible, once it exists. It follows between contract and conveyance, the 'assignee's' right to a conveyance will be defeated if the 'cedent' becomes insolvent. The same should, in principle, apply whether the future or contingent right 'assigned' is an interest in a living testator's estate, a non-vested interest in fee or an interest in contract moneys which will not become due until performance by the 'cedent' of his own obligations under the contract.

It seems clear that Scottish banking practice with regard to trust interests is to accept in security only a vested interest in an estate and that it is recognised that assignation of a non-vested interest does not give security. If a bank were taking an assignation of an interest which would not vest in the cedent unless the cedent survived some occurrence, it would insist on collateral security in the form of a policy of assurance on the life of the cedent.

Mandates authorising payment to the bank

General banking practice operates on the basis that an irrevocable mandate granted by someone to his debtor in an obligation, instructing the latter to pay the sum, when it becomes due, directly to the granter's bank, is effective as an intimated assignation of the debt to the bank[1]. But, where the debt is not yet due, doubt might arise as to the effectiveness of such a mandate as security for any advance the bank has made to the granter. Arguably, however, although the debt itself may not yet exist, so that no intimation of its assignation is possible, the obligation to pay the debt, if and when it becomes due exists and it is this obligation which is assigned by the irrevocable mandate. The case of *City of Glasgow Executive Council v T Sutherland Henderson Ltd*[2], is commonly cited as authority that such an irrevocable mandate to a debtor to pay directly to an assignee sums due and to become due to the cedent operates as a transference indefeasible by subsequent arrestment of the sums in the hands of the debtor[3].

---

1 *Scottish Banking Practice* vol 10, pp 75–78.
2 1955 SLT (Sh Ct) 33.
3 However, in the case of *Hernandez-Cimorra v Hernandez-Cimorra* 1992 SCLR 611, Sh Ct, it was held that the equation of such mandates with intimated assignations falls where a seller of property grants an mandate to the solicitor who is acting for him in the sale to receive the proceeds of sale and to pay these directly to the seller's creditors in satisfaction of debts owed to them by the seller. See R Rennie 'Mandate, Assignations and Arrestments' (1993) 38 JLSS 185.

Cash deposits and charge back

The only method by which a customer, in Scotland, may create a security in favour of a third party, over a credit balance in a bank account, is by assignation followed by intimation to the bank as debtor. If it is an incorporated company which grants the assignation, it will be necessary to register the assignation as a charge with the Register of Companies[1].

It is not uncommon for a customer with sums at credit with his bank to seek to use it as security for another facility or obligation he owes to the same bank. The customer may, for example, wish to mitigate interest on a loan by lodging a cash sum at credit with the bank to be set off against the indebtedness in the event of default. Such a position was, until recently in England, secured by a formal charge over the credit balance (known as charge back). However, the case of *Re Charge Card Services*[2] put such practices into serious doubt. The Court of Appeal held that there is no general principle in law that whenever a method of payment is adopted involving risk of non-payment by third parties that acceptance of payment by that method is conditional upon that third party actually making payment. In this case, Charge Card Services operated a scheme (the fuel card scheme) for the purchase of petrol from approved garages with the use of charge cards issued by the company. In 1985, Charge Card Services went into liquidation owing substantial sums to garages. The court held that in view of the nature of the scheme the retailers acceptance of the card was an acceptance of that payment in substitution for cash. It was therefore an absolute payment and the garages could not recover the sums outstanding from the individual purchasers of fuel. However, the case is more important to English banking practice for other reasons[3]. The view was expressed by Millett J that it was conceptually impossible for a creditor to grant a security over a debt, owed by the debtor, back to that debtor (conveniently called a charge back). The remark giving rise to this view was probably obiter but has caused banks operating in England considerable consternation. This concern arises because there are numerous situations where a creditor is reciprocally indebted to his debtor and is a major feature of not just banking relationships (for example the charge bank of a deposit in security of a loan) but for most markets where trade between counterparties gives rise to mutual indebtedness. If, for example, an individual takes out an endowment policy from an insurance company, then the insured individual is the creditor and the insurance company the debtor on the policy. If the individual insured wishes to raise money on the security of the policy he could ask the insurance company to provide him with a facility. The insurance company makes the loan to the insured who in turn assigns the policy back to the insurance company by formal assignation. In this transaction, therefore, the creditor (the individual insured) has created a 'charge' in favour of the debtor (the insurance company) over a claim which the debtor owes the creditor (the policy). If the judgment of Millett J is correct, such a charge

---

1 Companies Act 1985, s 395: *Siebe Gorman & Co Ltd v Barclays Bank Ltd* [1979] 2 Lloyd's Rep 142; *Re Brightlife Ltd* [1987] Ch 200, [1986] 3 All ER 673.
2 [1987] Ch 150, [1986] 3 All ER 289; on appeal [1988] Ch 497, [1988] 3 All ER 702, CA.
3 See [1987] Ch 150, [1986] 3 All ER 289, per Millett J.

back is conceptually impossible. This judgment has been criticised[1] but remains the leading case in England and thus discourages the former practice of a customer assigning or charging back the benefit of a deposit in security of a loan from the same bank[2].

In Scotland such instruments have never had validity, and in supplement of the banks right of compensation or set off and its right to combine accounts[3] the customer is required to undertake not to withdraw the deposit until such time as his indebtedness is cleared. It is also usual to state that the bank may without notice to the customer apply the sum at credit in reduction or extinction of the indebtedness at any time.

4.   CAUTIONARY OBLIGATIONS

(1)   NATURE, CONSTITUTION AND DISTINGUISHING FEATURES

A cautionary obligation is:

> 'an accessory engagement, as surety for another, that the principal obligant shall pay the debt or perform the act for which he has engaged, otherwise the cautioner shall pay the debt or fulfil the obligation'[4].

The principal objective of a cautionary obligation (more commonly known as a guarantee obligation) is to protect a creditor from loss if his principal debtor or obligant fails to make payment or perform some sort of obligation. The guarantee obligation thereafter provides the creditor with the right to recover his loss from a person other than his principal debtor or obligant and it is that person who is referred to as a cautioner or guarantor. The English law of surety and the Scottish law of caution are similar in many respects but care must be taken in absolute reliance upon English authorities[5].

There are three parties involved in a contract of caution: the creditor, the principal debtor and the cautioner or guarantor. The creditor is the person to whom some sort of obligation must be performed or a debt paid; the principal debtor is the person who has either undertaken to perform the service or has incurred the debt liability; and the cautioner or guarantor is the person that guarantees that if the principal debtor fails to perform or pay the debt, then he, the guarantor, will be liable to the creditor.

---

1 See *Welsh Development Agency v Export Finance Co Ltd* [1991] BCLC 936 (revsd [1992] BCLC 148, CA); *Re Bank of Credit and Commerce International SA (No 8)* [1996] Ch 245, [1996] 2 All ER 121, CA.
2 The English law has been briefly explained as security over cash deposits in England were so prevalent for Scottish customers and English based banks have much difficulty in comprehending that charges over cash or book debts in Scotland is incompetent. Other jurisdictions have quickly reacted to provide a valid practice of charge-back of cash deposits, eg Isle of Man (the Isle of Man (Miscellaneous Provisions) Act 1996).
3 See ch 5, pp 146 ff above.
4 See Bell *Principles* s 245.
5 See *Aitken's Trustees v Bank of Scotland* 1944 SC 270, 1945 SLT 84; *Standard Chartered Bank Ltd v Walker* [1982] 3 All ER 938, [1982] 1 WLR 1410, CA; *Yorkshire Railway Wagon Co v Maclure* (1881) 19 Ch D 478.

The nature of undertaking

Cautionary obligations are fundamentally accessory obligations and require the existence of a principal debt or obligation. If the principal debt or obligation is unenforceable or a fundamental nullity, the cautioner is not liable. Therefore, where an obligation is granted by a person with no power to contract or if the contract is *pactum illicitum*, the cautioner will not be liable[1]. If, however, the cautioner was aware that the principal obligation was invalid, the doctrine of personal bar may preclude the cautioner pleading the invalidity of the principal obligation[2]. However, a guarantee for a debt or other obligation to be contracted for in the future is binding[3]. When the principal obligation is at an end or the debt is repaid the liability of the cautioner automatically ceases[4].

Constitution of cautionary obligation

A cautionary obligation may arise from an offer, addressed to a particular creditor and offering to guarantee a particular debt, or the conduct of a third party. It is then a question of construction, of which no definite rule can be given, whether express acceptance is required, or whether the cautioner's liability is established when credit is given to the third party whose actings or dealing he has offered to guarantee. In *Wallace v Gibson*[5] two businesses granted a guarantee to a Mr A for payment of £7,000 which Mr A had lent to a third party in return for a mortgage over a property in Ceylon. He called up his loan and an agent for both of the businesses offered an investment to Gibson. The letter said 'it is therefore an excellent security apart from our guarantee of principal and interest'. Gibson advanced the moneys and obtained the mortgage over the property. When both businesses became bankrupt, Mr Gibson raised an action against the respective trustees in bankruptcy for payments of the sums due while founding on a guarantee obligation which he claimed was contained in the letter he had received. It was held that the trustees were liable as the letter did constitute a guarantee obligation[6].

A cautionary obligation may also:

'arise from an undertaking to guarantee the debt or dealings of another, given to the party who is to be guaranteed, and not addressed to any particular creditor. In that case, anyone who has given credit on the faith of the guarantee is entitled to enforce it, unless from its terms it appears that it was limited to some particular class of prospective creditors'[7].

---

1 *Garrard v James* [1925] Ch 616.
2 *Stevenson v Adair* (1872) 10 M 919; *Yorkshire Railway Wagon Co v Maclure* (1881) 19 Ch D 478.
3 *Fortune v Young* 1918 SC 1.
4 *Commercial Bank of Tasmania v Jones* [1893] AC 313, PC; *Aitken's Trustees v Bank of Scotland* 1944 SC 270, 1945 SLT 84. See also *Carlisle and Cumberland Banking Co v Bragg* [1911] 1 KB 489; *Royal Bank of Scotland plc v Purvis* 1989 SCLR 710, 1990 SLT 262, OH.
5 (1895) 22 R (HL) 56, [1895] AC 354.
6 See (1895) 22 R (HL) 56, [1895] AC 354, per Lord Chancellor Herschell.
7 Gloag and Henderson *The Law of Scotland* (10th edn, 1995) para 20.3.

In *Fortune v Young*[1], Young was a partner in a business and had signed a letter in his firm's name guaranteeing the financial covenant of a person who was applying for a lease of a farm. The letter was not specifically addressed to anyone, but it was shown that Young knew the letter might be shown to the farm owner or his factor. Relying on the letter, the farm was leased to the applicant who subsequently became bankrupt. In an action by the farm proprietor against Young for his losses, it was held that the letter was a guarantee which could be relied upon[2]. In the case of guarantees provided to banks, they are likely to be in the bank's standard form whereby the cautioner addresses his obligation to the bank without need for the bank acceptance. It is in essence the cautioner's unilateral promise addressed to the bank. The law providing for writing to constitute or prove certain types of obligation and also the requirements which certain writings must meet were radically altered by the Requirements of Writing (Scotland) Act 1995 which came into force on 1 August 1995[3]. It is of particular importance with regard to cautionary obligations as the position of constitution of the obligation was formerly governed by section 6 of the Mercantile Law Amendment (Scotland) Act 1856. In terms of that section:

'all guarantees, securities or cautionary obligations made or granted by any person for any other person ... shall be in writing and subscribed by the person undertaking such guarantee, security or cautionary obligation'.

This much criticised section[4] has been repealed and in terms of section 1(2) of the 1995 Act a written document will be required complying with section 2 of the Act[5] where it is a gratuitous unilateral obligation except an obligation undertaken in the course of business. It follows that it is necessary to distinguish between guarantees granted gratuitously and those granted for reward. Most guarantees are granted gratuitously and accordingly should be constituted in writing, signed by the granter and without need for further solemnity[6]. Gratuitous obligations undertaken in the 'course of business' do not require to be constituted in writing[7]. It would follow that a commercial customer granting an undertaking on behalf of an associated company to the bank need not do so in writing in order to be valid and enforceable[8].

---

1 1918 SC 1.
2 See in contrast *Williams v Lake* (1859) 2 E & E 349, 29 LJQB 1.
3 Requirements of Writing (Scotland) Act 1995, s 15(2).
4 See *Report on Requirements of Writing* (Scot Law Com no. 112 (1988)), paras 2.7 and 2.12.
5 See the 1995 Act, s 1(2)(a)(ii).
6 Eg *Wallace v Gibson* (1895) 22 R (HL) 56, [1895] AC 354; *Clydesdale Bank Ltd v Paton* (1896) 23 R (HL) 22. See also *Kirklands Garage (Kinross) Ltd v Clark* 1967 SLT (Sh Ct) 60 where an oral undertaking to become a cautioner was held not to be enforceable.
7 1995 Act, s 1(2)(a)(ii).
8 Thus conferring relaxation upon a category of obligation formerly evidenced by writs '*in re mercatoria*' whose privileged status has also been abolished (1995 Act, s 11(3)(d)). See cases under the former law: *William Beardmore & Co Ltd v Barry* 1928 SC 101, 1928 SLT 143; *Union Bank of Scotland Ltd v Taylor* 1925 SC 835, 1925 SLT 583.

Distinguishing caution from similar obligations

Caution as opposed to an independent obligation

There are many situations where it may be difficult to ascertain whether a cautionary obligation as opposed to an independent obligation has been undertaken by a purported cautioner. If, for example, A orders goods to be supplied to B, and undertakes to be responsible for payment, this arrangement, may according to circumstances be an independent obligation by A, or a cautionary obligation for a debt primarily undertaken by B.

Contracts of indemnity as opposed to contracts of caution

A contract of indemnity is a contract by which one party undertakes to relieve another of loss incurred by that person in certain circumstances[1]. Such a 'guarantee' against loss from a contract does not involve any obligation or performance by the principal debtor. In *Milne v Kidd*[2] an obligation was given to take over shares if they did not reach a certain price and was held to be a contract of indemnity and not one of caution. Guarantee policies, which are issued by insurance companies are contracts of indemnity but bear many similarities of a contract of caution. In effect, the insurance company agrees to pay any loss which may be incurred by the insured as a result of default of the insured's debtor. It is this fact that may be crucially important, as a contract of caution unlike a contract of insurance/indemnity is not a contract *uberrimae fidei* (of utmost good faith) and so it follows that a contract of insurance will be voidable if full disclosure of the material facts are not given at the time of the creation of the policy[3].

Delegation as opposed to a contract of caution

Delegation describes the situation where a new debtor is substituted for an old debtor with the creditor's consent. In the case of caution, there is an additional obligant, the cautioner, who may be resorted to by the creditor in the event of the default by the debtor. In situations of delegation the liability of the original debtor is extinguished and a new one substituted[4].

Proper and improper caution

A cautionary obligation may in form be either proper or improper. In proper caution the relationships of the parties, the creditor, principal debtor and cautioner are made clear by the document creating the relationships. In improper caution, the principal debtor and cautioner are bound as if they are co-obligants, jointly and severally liable for the obligations. Whether the caution is proper or improper has important consequences for the cautioner. If it is proper caution, he is entitled to all of the

1 *Fortune v Young* 1918 SC 1; *Union Bank of Scotland Ltd v Taylor* 1925 SC 835, 1925 SLT 583.
2 *Milne v Kidd* (1869) 8 M 250.
3 *Falconer v North of Scotland Banking Co* (1863) 1 M 704; *Young v Clydesdale Bank Ltd* (1889) 17 R 231; *Royal Bank of Scotland v Greenshields* 1914 SC 259, 1914 1 SLT 74.
4 *Morrison v Harkness* (1870) 9 M 35; *Jackson v MacDiarmid* (1892) 19 R 528.

privileges of a cautioner. In the case of improper caution, however, these privileges are only open to the cautioner if he is able to prove that the creditor was a party to the arrangement and new that he was truly a cautioner and not a joint debtor. Bell puts it thus:

> 'Cautionary is proper or improper: Proper where the engagement is avowedly as cautioner; Improper where both cautioner and principal are bound as principals, in which case the rights of the cautioner are renounced as to the creditor, but reserved as to the principal debtor'[1].

There are instances where the cautionary obligation may arise as a result of implication of law. The most common examples are those arising from partnership and bills of exchange. In partnership, the individual partners may be fairly said to be cautioners for the debts of the firm on the basis that failure by the firm to make payment renders the partners liable, jointly and severally[2]. In the case of bills of exchange, once the bill has been accepted by the drawee, the acceptor is in the same position as the principal debtor, and the drawer and indorsers are in the position of cautioners and are accordingly liable to the holder of the bill if the acceptor fails to make payment[3].

(2) CAUTIONER'S OBLIGATION: CONSTRUCTION AND INTERPRETATION

The obligation of the cautioner will be construed in the narrowest sense which the words will reasonably bear[4]. In *Ayr County Council v Wyllie*[5], Wyllie was a sheriff officer and was held not to be liable for sums embezzled by another sheriff officer when that officer was not acting in his official capacity as sheriff officer but as a debt collector for the county council. It is similarly fundamental that unless the contrary is clearly stated, the cautioner will not be liable for more than the principal debtor. In *Aitken's Trustees v Bank of Scotland*[6], Aitken guaranteed an overdraft with the Bank of Scotland but the guarantee stated that his liability would not exceed £500. When the overdraft stood in excess of £2,000 the bank asked the debtor to lodge sums in reduction of the indebtedness. The debtor paid the sum of £1,500 and the bank concurred to the debtor's motion in court that he be granted decree of absolvitor. Thereafter, the bank applied £500 of the cautioner's funds to extinguish the residual sums due by the debtor. The cautioner raised an action against the bank who claimed that they had been given authority 'to compound' with the debtor without affecting the cautioner's liability. It was held that authority to 'compound' did not per-

---

1 Bell *Principles* s 247.
2 Partnership Act 1890, s 9; see ch 3, pp 61 ff above.
3 See ch 6, pp 183 ff above, and *Duncan, Fox & Co v North and South Wales Bank* (1880) 6 App Cas 1, HL.
4 *North of Scotland Banking Co v Fleming* (1882) 10 R 217; *Veitch v National Bank of Scotland* 1907 SC 554, 14 SLT 800.
5 1935 SC 836, 1935 SLT 544.
6 1944 SC 270, 1945 SLT 84.

mit the bank to discharge a solvent debtor in whole or in part and there-after resort to the cautioner[1].

Construing guarantees strictly

In *Bank of Scotland v Wright*[2], Mr Wright who had recently been made redundant decided to invest his redundancy money in a freezer and butchery business called Dinewell Holdings Limited and its subsidiary, Dinewell Frozen Foods Limited. The capital base proved too small for the enterprise although the Bank of Scotland was willing to provide further capital but required a personal guarantee from the directors and second charges (mortgages) over their homes. The facility was thereafter extended by the bank but the group collapsed. Mr Wright denied personal liability for the overdraft (£200,000) of the subsidiary freezer company, claiming liability was only for the holding company's ultimate debit balance. The guarantee, as is common, provided that Mr Wright guaranteed full and final payment of the sums 'due to the bank by its customer whether solely or jointly with any other obligant or by any other firm or in any manner whatsoever'. The holding company had guaranteed the subsidiary's liability and Mr Wright had guaranteed the holding company's liability. It was held that guarantees must be construed strictly but where capable of more than one meaning, the surrounding circumstances may be taken into account. Mr Wright was held liable for the group debt under the guarantee and importantly it was shown that he was aware that it was an inter-linked guarantee and the facility extended to the holding company included the grant of a facility upon which the parent and subsidiary company could draw.

The extent of the cautioner's liability can never be more than the principal debtor with that liability being the sum outstanding, interest and the expenses reasonably incurred in enforcing the debt against the principal debtor. Therefore, in *Jackson v McIver*[3] where the cautioner was bankrupt and had granted a blank promissory note to the creditor, it was held that the creditor could not fill up the note with a greater sum than the advance to the principal debtor in the expectation that his dividend on the cautioner's estate would produce the actual advance which was provided to the debtor.

In instances where the cautioner limits the amount for which he undertakes his obligation, it is a question of construction whether in the event of the time being reached and exceeded, he remains liable for the sum or whether payments made by the debtor to reduce his indebtedness are applied in reduction of the lesser guaranteed sum[4]. Most standard bank guarantees will provide against such circumstances benefitting the cautioner and thereby avoiding the problems of *Clayton's Case*. It is possible for the cautioner to limit his obligations as to time and is accordingly

1 See *Harvie's Trustees v Bank of Scotland* (1885) 12 R 1141; *F W Harmer & Co v Gibb* 1911 SC 1341, 1911 2 SLT 211.
2 *Bank of Scotland v Wright* [1991] BCLC 244.
3 (1875) 2 R 882.
4 *Devaynes v Noble, Clayton's Case* (1816) 1 Mer 529; see pp 103–105 above for full discussion of this case.

released at expiry of the defined period. It is natural that a cautionary obligation with regard to a current account of a debtor at a bank should be a continuing one, and not limited in time and not restricted to a particular advance only[1]. In the case of such a continuing guarantee, the cautioner may withdraw his undertaking as regards future transactions by giving reasonable notice to the creditor[2]. At any time, a cautioner who has not committed for a specific period may upon reasonable notice call upon the debtor to relieve him of his liabilities and deliver a discharge from the creditor[3].

Obligations by more than one cautioner

Where there are two or more cautioners each is bound only on the understanding that the other or others are also validly bound to the creditors. It is the duty of the creditor to ensure that all co-cautioners become bound to the obligation and failure to do so releases from liability any cautioner who has signed. Each cautioner who signs does so upon the strict implied condition that the others are to be bound with him and he will accordingly not be liable if that condition is not fulfilled. In *Scottish Provincial Insurance Co v Pringle*[4] an insurance company lent money on condition that four other persons were to become jointly and severally liable with the borrower for repayment. Three of the four obligants signed and the borrower forged the signature of the fourth. It was held that the creditor had failed to secure that all four had been bound and accordingly was unable to enforce the bond against the other three[5]. This fundamental principle does not apply in the case of judicial cautionary where a Bond of Caution is lodged further to a court order[6]. In such instances, the creditor is not under an obligation to ensure that all of the signatures are obtained[7].

(3)   RIGHTS OF THE CAUTIONER

Right of relief against the principal debtor

The cautioner upon payment of the debt or part of it, is entitled to relief against the principal debtor for the amount he had paid and any necessary expenses he had incurred[8]. The cautioner is considered to have an implied mandate to pay the debt and can pay any sums due to end his liability and thereafter look to the principal debtor for reimbursement. He may also pay if the debtor is, or is about to become, insolvent[9]. In any case in which

1 See *Caledonian Banking Co v Kennedy's Trustees* (1870) 8 M 862.
2 *Willison v Ferguson* (1901) 9 SLT 169, OH; *Clydebank and District Water Trustees v Fidelity and Deposit Co of Maryland* 1916 SC (HL) 69, 1915 2 SLT 359.
3 *Nicolsons v Burt* (1882) 10 R 121; *Doig v Lawrie* (1903) 5 F 295, 10 SLT 523.
4 (1858) 20 D 465.
5 See *Ellesmere Brewery Co v Cooper* [1896] 1 QB 75; *James Graham & Co (Timber) Ltd v Southgate Sands* [1986] QB 80, [1985] 2 All ER 344, CA.
6 Eg in respect of interim interdict.
7 *Simpson v Fleming* (1860) 22 D 679.
8 Bell *Principles* s 245; *Doig v Lawrie* (1903) 5 F 295, 10 SLT 523.
9 *Kinloch v McIntosh* (1822) 1 S 491 (NE 457); *Brodie v Wilson* (1837) 15 S 1195; *McPherson v Wright* (1885) 12 R 942.

he has paid, he may exercise the full rights of a creditor against a debtor. In the case of improper caution, the cautioner must firstly prove the cautioner relationship in order to claim his right of relief. If he could not show the existence of the relationship, he is simply a co-debtor with a pro rata right of relief against his fellow co-debtors[1].

Right of relief against co-cautioners

Amongst each other, co-cautioners are only liable for their pro rata share of the principal debt and it follows that if he has paid more than his pro rata share he is entitled to relief from each of his co-cautioners to the extent of his excess[2]. Co-cautioners who are insolvent are excluded from the formula of computing the sums due by each of them to their fellow co-cautioners. In *Buchanan v Main*[3] of the five co-cautioners, two were insolvent. The liability fell to be shared equally between the remaining three solvent co-cautioners. If, however, co-cautioners enter into a separate contract whereby each cautioner engages to pay a specific sum, there is no right of relief[4].

Benefit of discussion

In proper caution the cautioner had at common law the right that he could not be called upon to pay the debt until the creditor had first discussed (pursued and done diligence against) the principal debtor[5]. However, since the Mercantile Law Amendment (Scotland) Act 1856[6] it is no longer necessary to proceed against the principal debtor, and in the absence of express stipulation to the contrary, the creditor may take direct action against the cautioner without primary recourse against the debtor[7]. Although the 1856 Act abolished the implied right of discussion, at common law the principle never applied to improper caution[8]. In situations where the caution is in respect of an act to be performed by the principal obligant, the cautioner is liable only to make up the loss proved to have been caused by the failure of the debtor[9].

Benefit of securities held by the creditor

The cautioner who pays the debt of the principal debtor is entitled to demand from the creditor an assignation of the debt due, any security held for it, and any diligence done upon it, so as to as enable him to

---

1 *Hamilton & Co v Freeth* (1889) 16 R 1022; *Buchanan v Main* (1900) 3 F 215; *Marshall & Co v Pennycook* 1908 SC 276, 15 SLT 581.
2 *Marshall & Co v Pennycook* 1908 SC 276, 15 SLT 581.
3 (1900) 3 F 215.
4 *Morgan v Smart* (1872) 10 M 610.
5 *Macfarlane v Anstruther* (1870) 9 M 117.
6 Mercantile Law Amendment (Scotland) Act 1856, s 8.
7 *Ewart v Latta* (1865) 3 M (HL) 36, 4 Macq 983; *Sheldon and Ackhoff v Milligan* (1907) 14 SLT 703, OH.
8 *Johannesburg Municipal Council v D Stewart & Co (1902) Ltd* 1909 SC (HL) 53, 1909 2 SLT 313.
9 *Blackwood v Forbes* (1848) 10 D 920.

enforce his primary right of relief against the debtor, or against co-cautioners. The cautioner is also entitled to:

> 'the benefit of assessory securities held by the creditor, whether the surety knew of them or not and any act of the creditor by which he voluntarily does away or even impairs such security, directly or indirectly, *pro tanto* liberates the cautioner. It is held that this rule applies to securities received by the creditor after the contract of cautionary'[1].

For the right to the benefit of security to be available, the relationship must be one of caution and not joint and several liability. The cautioner's right to assignation of securities rests upon the principle that cautioners are entitled to a right of relief from the estate of the principal debtor, but that right does not extent to securities which are granted by third parties[2]. The right to the assignation of the security held by the creditor from the principal debtor extends even to those securities of which the cautioner was unaware at the time he granted caution[3]. The right may not, however, be enforced to the prejudice of the creditor. It follows that the creditor need not grant the assignation of his rights of security until he has been paid in full[4]. The cautioner may only enforce securities over the estate of the debtor and it therefore follows that if securities had been granted by third parties, the cautioner has no right to them[5]. The cautioner who has paid the creditor is also entitled to obtain from the creditor an assignation of the debt as well as the securities held by him[6].

Right to share in securities held by co-cautioner

A cautioner is entitled to share in the benefit of any securities which any of his co-cautioners may have obtained over the estate of the principal debtor upon the basis that the debtor's estate is a 'fund' in which the cautioners are entitled to share equally. But,

> 'where the cautioners being originally equal, one gets an advantage over the rest on the demand being likely to arise or where the security to one is secret, the principle which rules the case is, that the co-cautioners are bound to act, or held to have acted, for the general benefit; so that what is given for the relief of one is to be communicated for the benefit of all'[7].

In *Scott v Young*[8], however, both Scott and Young were co-cautioners for an account of a Mr M with the Bank of Scotland. Upon breach by Mr M,

1 Bell *Principles* s 255; *Sligo v Menzies* (1840) 2 D 1478.
2 *Scott v Young* 1909 1 SLT 47, OH.
3 *Duncan, Fox & Co v North and South Wales Bank* (1880) 6 App Cas 1, HL; *Forbes v Jackson* (1882) 19 Ch D 615 at 621, per Hall V-C: 'the surety is entitled to have all the securities preserved for him, which were taken at the time of the suretyship or, as I think it has now been settled, subsequently'.
4 *Ewart v Latta* (1865) 3 M (HL) 36, 4 Macq 983, in which it was held that a cautioner who has not made full payment is not entitled to an assignation of securities and that payment of a dividend in a bankruptcy did not amount to full payment.
5 *Thow's Trustee v Young* 1910 SC 588, 1910 1 SLT 134.
6 *Ewart v Latta* (1865) 3 M (HL) 36, 4 Macq 983.
7 Bell *Commentaries* I,367.
8 1909 1 SLT 47, OH.

Scott and Young paid the debt equally. Scot discovered that Young had acquired an assignation by Mrs M of her right in her father's estate. It was held that the right to share in security does not extend to securities granted to a co-cautioner by a third party and so Scott was not entitled to one-half of the benefit of the security made over by Mrs M[1].

Ranking in bankruptcy

Gloag and Henderson state:

'On the bankruptcy of the principal debtor, if the creditor ranks for the debt, receives a dividend, and obtains payment of the balance from the cautioner, the latter is not entitled to a ranking for what he has paid, because to allow it would conflict with the principle that no debt can be ranked twice on a sequestrated estate'[2].

However, if the cautioner's liability is limited to a fixed amount and is exceeded by the principal debt, then the cautioner's obligation may be construed as a guarantee of only part of the debt. In that event, if the cautioner pays the guaranteed amount, he is entitled to rank in the creditor's place. If the creditor ranks, the cautioner is liable for the balance of the guaranteed amount after payment of the dividend. In *Veitch v National Bank of Scotland*[3], individuals R, V and H, granted a bond in favour of the Bank of Scotland. The bond provided that the bank had agreed to allow the three individuals credit to the extent of £1,500 on an account to be opened in the name of R. R subsequently became bankrupt and, at the time, the amount due to the bank was £5,855. The bank received a dividend on the bankrupt estate of R but was left with balance due of £1,951. The bank claimed the balance to the extent of £1,500 from V on the grounds that he had guaranteed repayment to that extent. It was held that the construction of the bond provided that V's guarantee was limited to £1,500 and that, as the bank had already received £1,000 of the advance, V's liability was restricted to £500.

If, however, the guarantee is construed as one for the full debt, subject to a limit, the general rule is that the creditor is entitled to rank for the whole debt and recover the balance from the cautioner, so long as that amount does not exceed the cautioner's guaranteed amount. In *Harvie's Trustees v Bank of Scotland*[4], M had a current account with the Bank of Scotland, which was considerably overdrawn, and in support of further advances to be granted to him, the bank obtained a guarantee which Mr Harvie had agreed to provide. The guarantee was for all sums for which M might become liable but the total amount of liability was restricted to £15,000. M became bankrupt and the bank sought recovery of the sums due to them of £44,000. Mr Harvie adhered to his guarantee and paid the sum of £15,000. The bank lodged a claim in M's sequestration for the full amount of the debt. Mr Harvie had since died and his trustees claimed a

1 See, however, *Hamilton & Co v Freeth* (1889) 16 R 1022.
2 Gloag and Henderson *The Law of Scotland* (10th edn, 1995) para 20.17; *Anderson v Mackinnon* (1876) 3 R 608; *Mackinnon v Monkhouse* (1881) 9 R 393.
3 1907 SC 554, 14 SLT 800.
4 (1885) 12 R 1141.

ranking upon the sequestrated estate for the proportion of the amount which they had paid. It was held on a proper construction of the guarantee, that Mr Harvie's trustees were not entitled to interfere with the bank's ranking for the full amount[1]. In the event of the principal debtor and some, but not all, of the cautioners being insolvent, the creditor may elect to rank for the whole debt on each of the insolvent estates and then demand from the solvent cautioners any balance remaining after deduction of any dividends[2].

(4)   TERMINATION OF CAUTIONARY OBLIGATIONS

Discharge of the principal debtor

As caution is essentially an accessory obligation, the extinguishing of the principal obligation necessarily implies the extinguishing of the cautionary obligation. If the principal debtor is released by some act or omission of the creditor, or otherwise by the creditor without the consent of the cautioner, then the cautioner is discharged[3]. If the principal obligation is terminated by performance or by some other method or the principal debtor is discharged by the creditor without the cautioner's consent, the cautioner's liability is at an end. However, if the principal obligation is discharged by operation of law, such as the bankruptcy of the principal debtor, then the cautioner is not discharged[4]. The Bankruptcy (Scotland) Act 1985[5] provides that where a creditor has a co-obligant bound to him along with the debtor for the whole or part of the debt, then that co-obligant is not released or discharged from his liability for the debt by reason of the discharge of the debtor or by virtue of the creditor's voting or drawing a dividend or assenting to, or not opposing, the discharge of the debtor or any composition. The term 'co-obligant' includes cautioners[6]. In *Aitken's Trustees v Bank of Scotland*[7], a father guaranteed his son's overdraft with the bank to the extent of £500 of the total indebtedness of £2,000. The first £1,500 was repaid by the son by way of a loan from another bank and the balance of £500 was claimed from the father under the guarantee. It was held that the bank having discharged the son by allowing an unqualified decree of absolvitor being pronounced in an action against him and that without the consent of the guarantor, the guarantor was discharged[8].

---

1 See also *Mackinnon's Trustee v Bank of Scotland* 1915 SC 411, 1915 1 SLT 182, where it was held that when a cautioner had paid the sums due under his obligations prior to the sequestration of the principal debtor, the bank was only entitled to rank for the balance of the principal debt.
2 *Morton's Trustees v Robertson's Judicial Factor* (1892) 20 R 72. For operation of ranking, see the example provided by Cusine and Forte in *Scottish Cases and Materials in Commercial Law* (1987) p 194; and see 3 *Stair Memorial Encyclopaedia* paras 948–957.
3 Bell *Principles* s 260; *Halyburtons v Graham* (1735) Mor 2073; *Wallace v Donald* (1825) 3 S 433 (NE 304); *National Westminster Bank plc v Riley* [1986] FLR 213, CA.
4 Bell *Commentaries* I, 364 ff.
5 Bankruptcy (Scotland) Act 1985, s 60(1).
6 1985 Act, s 60(4).
7 1944 SC 270, 1945 SLT 84.
8 See also *Muir v Crawford* (1875) 2 R (HL) 148.

Death of one of the parties

The death of the cautioner has no effect upon his existing liability, which may be enforced against his representatives. Further, if the cautionary obligation is a continuing guarantee, the representatives of the deceased cautioner will remain liable for any debts subsequently incurred unless they specifically intimate that the guarantee is withdrawn. It is irrelevant that the representatives are unaware of the cautionary obligation and no duty exists upon the creditor to intimate to the representatives, the cautionary obligation granted by the deceased[1].

Novation of the principal debt

The cautioner's liability is extinguished where the principal debt is novated — that is, where the original debt is discharged and a new debt substituted. For novation to operate there must be a substitution of the debt and not merely an addition to it[2].

Compensation of the principal debt

If the principal debt is extinguished by compensation, the cautionary obligation comes to an end. This would occur in a situation where the creditor sues the principal debtor and the defence succeeds: a debt due by the creditor to the debtor must be set off against the creditor's claim against the principal debtor[3]. The termination of the cautioner's liability may also arise as a result of the rule in *Clayton's Case*[4]. This case is one of banking laws most fundamental cornerstones and provides that in instances where there exists a continuing account, such as a current account at a bank, payments into that account extinguish debt items on the account in ascending order of dates. Therefore it will follow that if such an account is guaranteed by a cautioner, and that obligation is terminated for example by notice or sequestration of the cautioner, the guarantee crystallises at that time and any subsequent payments into the account go towards reducing the amount for which the cautioner is liable. It further follows that the cautioner's liability could be extinguished, even although the account shows a greater debit balance than it did at the time when the guarantee crystallised[5].

Revocation and discharge of cautionary obligation

Where the cautioner is expressly discharged by the creditor, he is freed from liability. If the caution is limited in time, the cautioner's liability will be at an end once the period of guarantee has expired. However, revocation of the guarantee obligation may occur where the period of guarantee

1 *British Linen Co v Monteith* (1858) 20 D 557.
2 *Hay and Kidd v Powrie* (1886) 13 R 777.
3 *Hannay & Sons' Trustee v Armstrong Bros & Co* (1875) 2 R 399; affd (1877) 4 R (HL) 43.
4 *Devaynes v Noble, Clayton's Case* (1816) 1 Mer 529; see pp 103–105 for full discussion of this case.
5 *Hay & Co v Torbet* 1908 SC 781, 15 SLT 627; *Cory Bros & Co Ltd v Turkish SS Mecca (Owners), The Mecca* [1897] AC 286, HL.

has yet to expire or where the guarantee is a continuing one. The rules catering for such revocation are different depending upon whether the obligation of caution is for a payment of debt or in respect of a fidelity guarantee. The effect of valid revocation is to release the cautioner for liability for future transactions. If liability has already been incurred, the cautioner must indemnify the creditor for that amount[1]. In the instance of a guarantee for a fixed period of time, the cautioner is not entitled to withdraw before the expiry of that period unless he pays the debt to the creditor and the cautioner thereby becomes the creditor of the principal debtor. If, however, the guarantee is for an indefinite period (a continuing guarantee) the cautioner must give notice to the debtor to relieve him of liability incurred. The principal debtor must deliver to the cautioner a discharge of the cautioner's liability from the creditor[2]. A fidelity guarantee is provided by a cautioner as to trustworthiness of someone else. If the fidelity guarantee relates to a fixed period the cautioner is not entitled to withdraw before the expiry of that period. However, if there is misconduct on the part of the employee and the employer fails to notify the cautioner promptly, he looses his right to hold the cautioner liable[3].

The conduct of the creditors

Actings of the creditor may substantially affect the cautioner's liability or the rights of relief he has against the principal debtor, and if done without the cautioner's consent, may lead to a discharge of the cautioner's liability. There are no absolute rules, but the general principle is that it is a question of fact whether in any particular case the acts or omissions of the creditor are sufficiently prejudicial to lead to the discharge of the cautioner[4]. If the creditor, without the consent of the cautioner, postpones the time of payment, that act will discharge the cautioner because it has long been established that given time, whether or not it is truly prejudicial to the cautioner, discharges him unless the creditor is able to show that he has reserved his rights against the cautioner or the cautioner has himself agreed to the giving of time[5]. In *C and A Johnstone v Duthie* it was held that giving accommodation to the principal debtor by allowing him to grant bills of exchange payable three or six months ahead freed the cautioner from liability[6]. The alteration of the contract between the creditor and the principal debtor may affect the cautioner's position adversely and so, if done without the cautioner's consent, may terminate the cautionary obligation[7]. A cautioner is entitled to rely upon the whole circumstances as he knows them at the commencement of his cautionary undertaking. It follows that if the creditor materially alters the contract between him and the principal debtor without the cautioner's consent, the cautioner may be

1 *Reid v Royal Bank of Scotland* (1899) 6 SLT 380.
2 *Doig v Lawrie* (1903) 5 F 295, 10 SLT 523.
3 *Snaddon v London, Edinburgh and Glasgow Assurance Co Ltd* (1902) 5 F 182, 10 SLT 410.
4 *Lord Advocate v Maritime Fruit Carriers Ltd* 1983 SLT 357, OH.
5 *Richardson v Harvey* (1852) 15 D 628; *Rouse v Bradford Banking Co* [1894] AC 586, HL.
6 (1892) 19 R 624. See also *Calder & Co v Cruikshank's Trustee* (1889) 17 R 74.
7 Bell *Principles* s 259; *N G Napier Ltd v Crosbie* 1964 SC 129, 1964 SLT 185.

discharged[1]. The alteration of the agreement with one cautioner will discharge the others[2]. Where there are several cautioners, the discharge of one of them without the consent of the others has the effect, under statute, of discharging them all[3]. Therefore, where co-cautioners are bound jointly and severally and the creditor, without the consent of the other cautioners, releases one he releases them all. The rule would not apply, however, where each cautioner is bound for a separate sum and not jointly and severally for the whole debt[4]. If a creditor holds securities in addition to the cautionary obligation for due performance by the principal debtor, the cautioner has a right to the assignation of the securities if he is called upon to pay[5]. It follows therefore that if, without the cautioners consent, the creditor voluntarily gives up the securities he holds from the principal debtor, the cautioner's rights are impaired and he is released to the extent that he is prejudiced which will be the value of the surrendered security[6].

The prescription of the cautionary obligation

In terms of the Prescription and Limitation (Scotland) Act 1973[7], a cautionary obligation is extinguished on the lapse of five years after 'the appropriate date,' providing that no relevant claim nor acknowledgment of the existence of the obligation has been made during that period. There has been debate as to what is 'the appropriate date' in relation to bank guarantees. Schedule 2 of the Act provides for the 'appropriate date' for specific kinds of obligations[8], but cautionary obligations are not expressly stated to be covered. Further the schedule provides 'the appropriate date' for 'any obligation to repay the whole, or any part of, a sum of money lent to .... the debtor under a contract of loan ...'[9]. However, in *Royal Bank of Scotland Ltd v Brown* it was held that this statutory category does not cover caution, 'debtor' meaning the principal debtor[10]. The Act provides that, where the obligation is not covered by the auspices of Schedule 2, 'the appropriate date' is the date upon which the obligation became 'enforceable'[11]. Most commonly, bank guarantees provide that the cautioner is required to make payment on demand, and such demand by the bank is a condition precedent to the obligation becoming enforceable. In such instances, time does not begin to run upon the obligation until the

---

1 *N G Napier Ltd v Crosbie* 1964 SC 129, 1964 SLT 185; *Lord Advocate v Maritime Fruit Carriers Ltd* 1983 SLT 357, OH; *Royal Bank of Scotland plc v Welsh* 1985 SLT 439.
2 *Royal Bank of Scotland plc v Welsh* 1985 SLT 439.
3 Mercantile Law Amendment (Scotland) Act 1856, s 9.
4 *Morgan v Smart* (1872) 10 M 610.
5 *Sligo v Menzies* (1840) 2 D 1478.
6 *Wright's Trustees v Hamilton's Trustees* (1835) 13 S 380.
7 Prescription and Limitation (Scotland) Act 1973, s 6(1), (2), Sch 1, para 1(g).
8 1973 Act, s 6(3), Sch 2.
9 1973 Act, Sch 2, para 2.
10 *Royal Bank of Scotland Ltd v Brown* 1982 SC 89, 1983 SLT 122.
11 1973 Act, s 6(3).

demand is made[1]. Otherwise, cautionary obligations are in general enforceable immediately upon default of the principal debtor and accordingly time would run from the date of default by the principal debtor or more likely from the date of the bank's claim against the principal debtor[1]. The creditor must take care when notifying the cautioner of the default of the principal debtor that he does not make any demand or request for payment unless he is unconcerned that the five-year prescriptive period will begin to run[2].

(5) MISREPRESENTATION AND CONCEALMENT

By the creditor

Good faith between the bank and the cautioner is a prerequisite of entering into a cautionary obligation, but it is not a contract *uberrimae fidei* (of utmost good faith). The cautioner will be able to escape liability if he is able to show materiality and inducement by the misstatement made by the creditor. It matters not that the misstatement is innocent, and it is the misrepresentation rather than the motives of the bank as creditor which is relevant[3]. However, the misrepresentation must have materially misled the customer so inducing him to enter into the contract. It is a question of fact, to be judged upon the circumstances of each case[4]. If the cautioner is not affected by the misrepresentation and would have entered into the obligation in any event, the inaccuracy will be of no effect. In *Royal Bank of Scotland v Ranken*[5] the relevant binding deed contained a material misrepresentation which was known to one cautioner and not the other. The cautioner who was aware of the true position was held bound but his unknowing co-cautioner was released from liability.

Any creditor, including a bank, is not under a general duty to disclose to a prospective cautioner the affairs of its customers or the state of his account[6]. It is the customer's own responsibility to make such inquiries as to the debtor's circumstances as he believes necessary. It follows that there is no duty incumbent on a bank to advise a cautioner of the debtor's indebtedness to them[7]. In *Royal Bank of Scotland v Greenshields*, H had an overdraft facility with the Royal Bank of Scotland for £300 and owed them a further £1,100[8]. H asked Greenshields to guarantee the overdraft and he subsequently did so, without any knowledge of H's financial position or the extent of the overdraft. H defaulted upon his payments to the bank who resorted to Greenshields under the guarantee. It was held that there was no duty upon the bank to disclose the nature and extent of the indebt-

1 *Royal Bank of Scotland Ltd v Brown* 1982 SC 89, 1983 SLT 122.
2 J M Halliday *Conveyancing Law and Practice in Scotland* vol I (1985) para 6-30 at p 198.
3 *Smith v Bank of Scotland* (1829) 7 S 244.
4 *Royal Bank of Scotland v Ranken* (1844) 6 D 1418 at 1437, per Lord Jeffrey.
5 (1844) 6 D 1418.
6 *Young v Clydesdale Bank Ltd* (1889) 17 R 231; *Royal Bank of Scotland v Greenshields* 1914 SC 259, 1914 1 SLT 74; *Cooper v National Provincial Bank Ltd* [1946] KB 1, [1945] 2 All ER 641.
7 *Young v Clydesdale Bank Ltd* (1889) 17 R 231. Nor is there a duty if the debtor is insolvent: *Hamilton v Watson* (1845) 4 Bell App 67, HL.
8 1914 SC 259, 1914 1 SLT 74.

edness of H to the bank. However, silence on the bank's part may in special circumstances amount to misrepresentation. If the cautioner inquires of the bank, or the bank chooses to disclose any matters, then it must take care to disclose the whole circumstances material to the undertaking of the cautionary obligation. Lord Jeffrey in *Royal Bank of Scotland v Ranken* said:

> 'It is no doubt quite true, that a creditor who requires a cautioner along with his principal debtor, or to whom such a security is offered, is no way bound to make any representation to such proposed cautioner, or to give him any warning or information as to the extent of the risk he is undertaking. But then, if he does make any such representation, he must take care that it is a fair and full one; and if he either conceals any facts which obviously and materially affect the risk, and still more, if he in any way so misrepresents those facts, whether intentionally, or from mere blunder or carelessness, as necessarily to mislead the cautioner as to the hazards of his undertaking, then certainly the cautioner must be liberated, and can never be held to an obligation substantially different from that held out to him'[1].

The creditor is not under any duty to disclose subsequent adverse knowledge which is brought to his attention after the granting of the guarantee[2].

By the debtor

It is not unusual for the debtor to make misrepresentations concerning his financial standing to the proposed cautioner. However, misrepresentations of the debtor whether fraudulent or innocent do not effect the validity of the contract of caution. The duty rests upon the cautioner to satisfy himself as to the financial standing of the debtor[3].

Undue influence and cautionary obligations

A matter of considerable concern to banks has been whether they could have guarantee obligations set aside as voidable upon the basis that undue influence had been exerted upon the guarantor to enter into the guarantee obligation[4]. The principle arises from the grounds of public policy that a contract should be voidable and therefore capable of reduction if one party has taken advantage of a dominant relationship to gain benefit at the expense of the weaker party[5]. The person exerting the undue influence must be the creditor and not the debtor. In *North of Scotland Bank Ltd v Mackenzie*, a guarantor claimed that misrepresentations made by the principal debtor 'acting as agent for and in the interest of the bank' had

---

1 *Royal Bank of Scotland v Ranken* (1844) 6 D 1418 at 1434.
2 *Bank of Scotland v Morrison* 1911 SC 593, 1911 1 SLT 153; but see obiter dicta of Lord Low in *Britannia Steamship Insurance Association Ltd v Duff* 1909 SC 1261 at 1270.
3 *Falconer v North of Scotland Banking Co* (1863) 1 M 704; *Young v Clydesdale Bank Ltd* (1889) 17 R 231; *North of Scotland Bank Ltd v Mackenzie* 1925 SLT 236, OH; but see 3 *Stair Memorial Encyclopaedia* para 896 and the consideration of *Clydesdale Bank v Paul* (1877) 4 R 626 and *Sutherland v W M Low & Co* (1901) 3 F 972.
4 This concern emanates from the English case of *Lloyds Bank Ltd v Bundy* [1975] QB 326, [1974] 3 All ER 757, CA.
5 *Gray v Binny* (1879) 7 R 332.

induced him to grant the guarantee[1]. It was held insufficient, however, to justify a conclusion that the guarantor signed the guarantee under essential error due to the fault of the bank. In England, a bank which was shown to have knowledge that undue influence was being exerted was under a duty to ensure that the obligation was being entered into freely and in full knowledge of the facts[2].

In *Lloyds Bank Ltd v Bundy* it was held that there was undue influence by a bank in relation to a customer[3]. The undue influence arose from the nature of the relationship between the bank and its elderly customer who had guaranteed his son's overdraft with the bank and gave a charge over his farm. The bank manager had not disclosed to the father, who was advanced in age and naive in business matters, the extent of the financial problems his son faced nor had he suggested that the father seek independent legal advice. The Court of Appeal set aside the guarantee, as the bank had not discharged its fiduciary duty of care to its customer. It was conceded that such a fiduciary duty of care did not usually exist when a customer agrees to guarantee the debt of a third party to a bank, but in this case the crucial factor was that the guarantor, a customer of long standing, had relied upon the advice given by the bank manager. In Scotland, however, there is no doubt that there is no presumption of a fiduciary relationship between a bank and its customers[4]. It does serve as a reminder, however, that exceptional circumstances may arise where the degree of trust and reliance placed on the bank by a cautioner/customer may give rise to an enhanced duty on the bank's behalf.

A conclusion on bank guarantees

Most standard form bank guarantees seek to enhance the bank's position and remove the benefits which would otherwise accrue to cautioners under common law. The Good Banking Code[5] (2nd edition) at clause 14 states:

> '14.1   Banks and Building Societies will advise private individuals proposing to give them a guarantee or other security for another person's liabilities:
>
> (i)   that by giving the guarantee or third party security he or she might become liable instead of or as well as that other person;
>
> (ii)   whether the guarantee or third party security will be unlimited as to amount or, if this is not the case, what the limit of liability will be;
>
> (iii)   that he or she should seek independent legal advice before entering into the guarantee or third party security.
>
> 14.2   Guarantees and other third party security documentation will contain clear and prominent notice to the above effect'.

---

1   *North of Scotland Bank Ltd v Mackenzie* 1925 SLT 236, OH.
2   See ch 4, pp 120–125 above; *Barclays Bank plc v O'Brien* [1994] 1 AC 180, [1993] 4 All ER 417, HL.
3   *Lloyds Bank Ltd v Bundy* [1975] QB 326, [1974] 3 All ER 757, CA.
4   *Royal Bank of Scotland v Greenshields* 1914 SC 259, 1914 1 SLT 74; *Honeyman's Executors v Sharp* 1978 SC 223, 1979 SLT 177, OH.
5   See ch 3, pp 102, 103 above.

The Good Banking Code is recited almost verbatim in the Clydesdale Bank Code[1]. However, the Bank of Scotland Code goes somewhat further in the declaration of protection to its customers[2] and provides:

> '14.3   In regard to guarantee, joint security and third party security transactions entered into by private individuals after 1st June 1994, the Bank will voluntarily adopt a procedure which is intended to offer protection to parties to guarantees and/or third party security who may be subjected to the undue influence of another.

> 14.4.   In addition, the Bank will no longer seek nor accept guarantees or third party security for unlimited amounts from parties who may be subjected to undue influence'.

It is perhaps inevitable that Scots law in this area will move more into line with the more privileged position afforded to customers of Scottish and English banks who are located in England. Pressure from the Banking Ombudsman will also have its effect but it should be remembered that it is very unlikely that the plea of undue influence would be sustained where the cautioner is advised to seek and in fact receives independent legal advice[3].

(6)   LETTERS OF COMFORT

In circumstances where no security is provided for a loan or a contract of guarantee is not considered to be appropriate, a letter of comfort (sometimes known as a letter of respectability) may be provided which is designed to give confidence to a person who is dealing with a third party. Such letters are usually given by a parent company in relation to debts incurred by one of its subsidiary companies or by a government agency which is otherwise unable to provide guarantees. The intention is that the giver of the letter of comfort will provide an undertaking to support the subsidiary's business ventures and confirm that the latter will be in a position to meet its liabilities to the lenders. It may seem logical to assume that the use of such a letter of comfort, rather than a guarantee, is such that the granter would necessarily wish to ensure that the letter of comfort does not of itself constitute a legally binding commitment. However, the courts have on occasion treated such letters as constituting a legal enforceable contract. In *Chemco Leasing SpA v Rediffusion plc*, it was held that a parent company was liable as guarantor of the liabilities of the subsidiary company upon the basis of the letter of comfort which said inter alia that if the parent was considering disposing of its subsidiary, and if it did dispose of its subsidiary it would undertake its liabilities[4]. In *Kleinwort Benson v Malaysian Mining Corpn Bhd* a claim arose as a result of the collapse of the tin market in 1985 and related to the obligations of the Malaysian Mining

---

1   See Clydesdale Bank's Code of practice for personal customers, para 14, set out in Appendix 1, below.
2   See Bank of Scotland Code of Banking Practice, para 14, set out in Appendix 1, below.
3   *Gray v Binny* (1879) 7 R 332; *Sutherland v W M Low & Co* (1901) 3 F 972; *Barclays Bank plc v Thomson* (1996) 146 NLJ 1778, CA.
4   [1987] FTLR 201, CA.

Corporation which had formed a wholly owned subsidiary to trade upon the London metal exchange[1]. The letter by the Malaysian parent company to the bank said: 'It is our policy to ensure that the business of our subsidiary company is at all times in a position to meet its obligations to you under the above arrangements'[2]. Hirst J held that the bank could claim damages equal to the whole amount of the loan because the wording of the letter was not ambiguous and constituted a commercial undertaking which could be relied upon by the plaintiffs; it did not follow that once the guarantee had been rejected by the parent company there was no further scope for a contractually binding agreement; the bank had acted in reliance of the letter and made advances to the subsidiary; it was paramount to the bank that the parent company would ensure the subsidiary was in a position to meet its liabilities and the bank should have an ability to resort to the parent company should the subsidiary default; and the letter of comfort was a matter of importance to the parent company as it was evidenced by a formal board resolution being given to allow the execution of the letter of comfort. However, the decision was overturned by the Court of Appeal, who treated the letter as a mere statement of the parent company's present policy. The words did not constitute a promise but were a mere representation of fact and only a moral obligation on the part of the parent company. On appeal it was considered of particular relevance that the parent company had refused throughout the course of the negotiations to assume legal liability for repayment of the loan to the subsidiary. Great care has to be taken by banks to ensure that the words used in the letter of comfort must be such as to amount to a legally binding promise to indemnify the bank for the obligations of the subsidiary[3].

5.   FLOATING CHARGES

At Scottish common law it was not competent to grant a floating charge, even with regard to assets situated in England where a floating charge was recognised[4]. The floating charge was only introduced to Scotland in 1961[5], and it was the Companies (Floating Charges and Receivers) (Scotland) Act 1972 which introduced the office of 'receiver' who under a floating charge could seek appointment of the court for control of the assets subject to the charge. The law of floating charges is now principally found in Part III, Chapter II of the Insolvency Act 1986 which came into force on 29 December 1986. The 1986 Act consolidates the provisions on receivers contained in the Companies Act 1985 and Insolvency Act 1985.

---

1 [1988] 1 All ER 714, [1988] 1 WLR 799.
2 [1989] 1 All ER 785, [1989] 1 WLR 379, CA.
3 If the statement regarding the financial status of the subsidiary or other party was not true at the time it was made, it is possible that there may be grounds for a claim under negligent misstatement.
4 *Carse v Coppen* 1951 SC 233, 1951 SLT 145.
5 By the Companies (Floating Charges) (Scotland) Act 1961.

Specific procedural regulations are laid down in the Receivers (Scotland) Regulations 1986[1]. Where a receiver is appointed by a holder of a floating charge over the whole or a substantial part of the company's undertaking, he is called an administrative receiver[2] and in any other case he is known as a receiver[3].

(1) NATURE OF FLOATING CHARGE AND APPOINTMENT OF RECEIVER

A floating charge is an instrument created by an incorporated company which the Court of Session has jurisdiction to wind up[4] and gives the holder of the floating charge a security or charge over the assets to the extent described in the charge[5].

A floating charge may cover all or any part of the property (including uncalled capital) of the company which may from time to time be comprised in its property and undertaking[6]. Most standard form bank floating charges provide that it is granted over the whole property and assets of the company, 'present and future' and accordingly assets acquired after crystallisation of the charge are included[7].

A floating charge is not immediately effective over any particular asset of the company, unlike a fixed security granted in the bank's favour over land or other particular assets. The charge 'floats' over the company's assets leaving the company free to intromit and deal with its assets at it wishes. The floating charge becomes effective over the assets of the company (called crystallisation) upon the liquidation of the company or on appointment of a receiver[8]. Upon the occurrence of either of these events, the floating charge attaches to the property comprised within the terms of the floating charge, as if it were a fixed security[9]. Lord President Emslie in *Forth and Clyde Construction Co Ltd* said:

> 'The intention appears to me to be that the holder of the floating charge shall, on the appointment of a receiver, enjoy all the protection in relation to any item of attached property that the holder of a fixed security over that item thereof would enjoy under the general law'[10].

1 SI 1986/1917.
2 Insolvency Act 1986, s 251.
3 This distinction is of importance with regard to administration orders and some ancillary matters but generally the distinction is not of substantial consequence.
4 Companies Act 1985, s 462(1) (subsection (2) repealed by the Law Reform (Miscellaneous Provisions) (Scotland) Act 1990, s 74, Sch 8, para 33(1), (6), Sch 9).
5 A floating charge is recognised where granted by a foreign company over Scottish assets so long as it has a separate legal status in its local jurisdiction and the charge is in a general sense a 'floating charge'.
6 Companies Act 1985, s 462(1).
7 See *Ross v Taylor* 1985 SC 156, 1985 SLT 387.
8 Companies Act 1985, s 463(1); Insolvency Act 1986, s 53(7). See *Sharp v Thomson* 1995 SCLR 683, IH, 1997 GWD 9-364, (1997) Times, 26 March, HL. The issue of what is comprised in assets has been the subject of much debate: see R Rennie 'Sharp v Thomson: The Final Act' (1997) 42 JLSS 130–134.
9 Companies Act 1985, s 463(1), (2); see *Re Yorkshire Woolcombers Association Ltd* [1903] 2 Ch 284, CA, particularly judgment of Romer LJ at 295 for a description of the characteristics of a floating charge.
10 *Forth and Clyde Construction Co Ltd v Trinity Timber and Plywood Co Ltd* 1984 SC 1 at 10, 1984 SLT 94 at 96, per Lord President Emslie.

The crystallisation of the floating charge secures not merely the principal obligation or debt due to the company but also interest due both before and after the receiver's appointment until payment of the sum due[1].

Upon crystallisation of the floating charge, it attaches to the property of the company, and the primary duty of the receiver is to pay moneys he receives to the holder of the floating charge but he must firstly satisfy[2]:

(1) the holder of any fixed security which has property subject to the floating charge and which ranks prior to or *pari passu* with it;
(2) all persons who have effectually executed diligence on any part of the property which is subject to the charge by virtue of which the receiver is appointed;
(3) creditors in respect of all liabilities, charges and expenses incurred by or on behalf of the receiver;
(4) the receiver in respect of his liabilities, expenses and remuneration, and any indemnity to which he is entitled out of the property of the company; and
(5) the preferential creditors entitled to payment.

(2) RANKING OF FLOATING CHARGES

Section 464 of the Companies Act 1985 lays down detailed rules regarding the ranking of floating charges with other instruments granted by the company. In instances where any part of the company's property is subject to a fixed charge, created before the floating charge, then the fixed charge has priority[3]. The Act further provides[4] that the instrument creating the floating charge may contain provisions (1) prohibiting or restricting the creation of any fixed security or any other floating charge having priority over, or ranking pari passu with the floating charge, or (2) regulating, with the consent of the holder of any subsisting floating charge or fixed security which would be adversely affected, the order in which the floating charge shall rank with other subsisting or future floating charges or fixed securities. If the floating charge does contain such a provision it will confer upon it priority over any fixed or floating charge created after it[5]. In terms of section 464(4)(b) and (c), floating charges rank with one another according to their time of registration with the Registrar of Charges and charges received by the Registrar for registration by the same postal delivery rank equally with one another.

Where a holder of a floating charge over all or any part of the company's property has received intimation in writing of the subsequent reg-

1 Companies Act 1985, s 463(4); *National Commercial Bank of Scotland Ltd v Liquidators of Telford Grier Mackay & Co Ltd* 1969 SC 181, 1969 SLT 306.
2 In terms of the Insolvency Act 1986, s 60(1).
3 Companies Act 1985, s 464(2).
4 1985 Act, s 464(1)(a), (b).
5 See *AIB Finance Ltd v Bank of Scotland* 1993 SC 588, 1993 SCLR 851, 1995 SLT 2, and discussion of ranking at pp 363, 364 below. See generally G L Gretton 'Floating charges in Scots law: the saga continues' [1995] JBL 212–214.

istration of another floating charge over the same property, or part of it, the preference in ranking of the first floating charge holder will be restricted to:

(a) the holders present advances;
(b) future advances which he may be required to make under the instrument creating the floating charge or under any ancillary document;
(c) interest due or to become due on all such advances;
(d) any expenses or outlays which may reasonably be incurred by the holder; and
(e) in the case of a floating charge to secure a contingent liability other than a liability arising under any further advances made from time to time, the maximum sum to which that contingent liability is capable of amounting whether or not it is contractually limited[1].

It would therefore follow that upon intimation being received by the bank of the creation of a further floating charge, the account of the customer should be stopped (suspended) to avoid the adverse affects of *Clayton's Case*[2].

Alteration of floating charges are dealt with by section 466 of the 1985 Act. Any instrument of alteration of the floating charge must be executed by the company, the holder of the charge and the holder of any other charge (including a fixed security) which would be adversely affected by the alteration[3].

(3)   REGISTRATION OF CHARGES

Sections 410 to 424 of the Companies Act 1985 provide for the registration in Scotland of charges created by companies. Registration of a charge granted by a company registered in Scotland, no matter where the property is situated is made with the Registrar of Companies in Edinburgh[4]. Charges requiring registration are:

(1) a charge upon land or any interest in land;
(2) a security over the uncalled share capital of the company;
(3) a security over incorporeal moveable property of any of the following categories: the book debts of the company, calls made but not paid, goodwill, patent or licence under patent, a trade mark, a copyright or a licence under a copyright, a registered design or a licence in respect of such a design, a design right or a licence under a design right;
(4) a security over a ship or aircraft or any share in a ship; and
(5) a floating charge.

Registration in Scotland is necessary wherever the property charged is situated[5]. It is fundamental that every charge created by a company is

---

1 1985 Act, s 464(5).
2 For operation of the rule of *Clayton's Case*, see pp 103–105 above.
3 1985 Act, s 466(1).
4 1985 Act, s 410(2).
5 1985 Act, s 411.

'so far as any security on the company's property or any part of it is conferred by the charge, void against the liquidator [or administrator] and any creditor of the company unless the prescribed particulars of the charge, together with a copy (certified in the prescribed manner to be a correct copy) of the instrument (if any) by which the charge is created or evidenced, are delivered to or received by the Registrar of Companies for registration in the manner required by [Chapter II of Part XII], within twenty-one days after the date of the creation of the charge'[1].

The time limit for registration is within twenty-one days after the date of the creation of the charge. In the case of the floating charge, the date of creation is the date of execution by the company and in the case of a fixed security (for example a standard security) it is the date on which the right of the person entitled to the benefit of the security was constituted in a real right. In the case of a standard security, it is the date of recording or registration of the instrument in the Sasine Register or Land Register respectively. In the instance of a security being granted over incorporeal moveable property, the date of creation of the right is the effective date of intimation.

In *Cusine and Forte* it is said:

'The relatively short experience of floating charges in Scotland has not been an especially happy one. Much of the literature on the subject is both critical of the legislation and the decisions under it. Indeed, the judiciary has also found reason to criticise the often obscure wording of the statutes'[2].

The writer can but agree[3].

---

1 1985 Act, s 410(2).
2 Cusine and Forte *Scottish Cases and Materials in Commercial Law* (1987) p 363.
3 Floating charges, receivers and the registration of charges have been dealt with briefly in this work. See further Greene and Fletcher *The Law and Practice of Receivership in Scotland* (2nd edn, 1992) and St Clair and Drummond Young *The Law of Corporate Insolvency in Scotland* (2nd edn, 1992).

Chapter 10

Security over Land, Buildings and Attachments to Land: Heritable Securities

1. INTRODUCTION

In terms of the Conveyancing and Feudal Reform (Scotland) Act 1970, from 29 November 1970 the standard security became the only competent method of creating a heritable security for debt over an estate in land (with the exception of entailed estates and any interest therein)[1]. Heritable securities created by other methods and duly recorded before enforcement of the 1970 Act nonetheless remain valid[2].

Three principal methods were used before 29 November 1970 (and are still appropriate to create security over entailed estates): the bond and disposition in security; the cash credit bond and disposition in security; and the ex facie absolute disposition qualified by backletter. Given that heritable properties continue to be burdened by such securities the law relating to them remains relevant and a brief description of them appropriate.

(1) BONDS AND DISPOSITIONS IN SECURITY

Bonds and dispositions in security, as the name suggests, consist of a personal bond granted by the debtor, in security of which land or other heritable property is conveyed (disponed) to the creditor by the debtor or a third party. They were used to secure obligations to pay a definite sum advanced before infeftment (registration of title) was given to the creditor. This sum could include interest, provided that the rate was specified in the deed so that the total sum secured was clear on the face of the deed[3]. Other obligations (for example, to pay insurance premiums) could be covered by the security, provided the obligation was specified and quantified, appearing as a definite sum in the deed. The debtor (or third party) retains possession of the security subjects, the creditor's real right in security having been completed by recording of the bond and disposition (bearing to be in security) in the Register of Sasines. A statutory form of bond and disposition in security was provided by the Titles to Land Consolidation (Scotland) Act 1868[4].

The debtor in possession of the subjects can perform all ordinary acts of administration and management, including the granting of leases of ordi-

---

1 Conveyancing and Feudal Reform (Scotland) Act 1970, ss 9(8)(b), 54(2)(a).
2 1970 Act, s 31.
3 *Alston v Nellfield Manure and Chemical Co Ltd* 1915 SC 912.
4 Titles to Land Consolidation (Scotland) Act 1868, s 118, Sch FF.

nary duration for a fair rent. But his is acts must not prejudice the creditor[1], nor cause depreciation of the security subjects[2].

The creditor has a corresponding right to object to any act which diminishes his security including a disposal of any part of the security subjects, or sale of fixtures[3]. However, it is only on taking possession of the subjects under his powers to enforce the security, that the creditor acquires powers of ordinary management of the subjects. Although under the Conveyancing (Scotland) Act 1924[4], the creditor does have statutory power to insure all buildings against loss by fire to the extent of the creditor's interest and to recover the premium from the borrower. This power arises without the need of prior entry into possession[5].

(2) CASH CREDIT BOND AND DISPOSITION IN SECURITY

The Debts Securities (Scotland) Act 1856 introduced the cash credit bond and disposition in security method of creating a heritable security to allow security to be held for a fluctuating sum, including advances made after infeftment of the creditor in the bond and disposition. This superseded the provision of the Bankruptcy Act 1696 (now repealed) which precluded creation of security for future debts over heritable property. But while the amount due at any time under a cash credit bond and disposition may vary, the maximum sum secured must be definite and specified in the deed as the principal sum with three years' interest at 5 per centum per annum. Any advance in excess of that sum would be recoverable under the personal obligation contained in the bond, but would not be secured[6].

The provisions in relation to bonds and dispositions in security generally apply also in the case of cash credit bonds and dispositions. However, given that the latter may cover sums advanced after completion of the security, certain specialities arise in relation to ranking. Section 7 of the 1856 Act expressly introduced the fiction that sums advanced after completion of the bond (but within the limit specified) were deemed to have been advanced prior to the date of completion of the security:

> 'the sasines or infeftments taken upon such heritable securities shall be equally valid and effectual as if the whole sums advanced upon such cash account or credit had been paid prior to the date of the sasine or infeftment taken thereon, and ... any such heritable security shall remain and subsist to the extent of the sum limited or any lesser sum, until the cash account or credit is finally closed, and the balance paid up and discharged, and the sasine or infeftment renounced'.

Where a debtor's heritable estate became subject to an inhibition after completion of a bond of cash credit, the question could arise as to whether

1 *Smith v Smith* (1879) 6 R 794.
2 *Reid v McGill* 1912 2 SLT 246, OH; *Edinburgh Entertainments Ltd v Stevenson* 1926 SC 363, 1926 SLT 286.
3 *Edinburgh and Leith Gas Comrs v Smart* 1918 1 SLT 80, OH.
4 Conveyancing (Scotland) Act 1924, s 25(1)(a).
5 For full discussion, see J M Halliday *Conveyancing Law and Practice in Scotland* vol III (1985) para 33–67, and J J Gordon and W A Mitchell 'Securities for Advances' in *Scottish Banking Practice* (6th edn, 1989) vol 10, paras 20–28 to 20–33.
6 See *Halliday* vol III, paras 33–72 to 33–76 and *Gordon and Mitchell* para 20–84.

the creditor under the bond retained preference for post-inhibition advances to the debtor. Given the fiction provided for by section 7 of the 1856 Act, the inevitable conclusion reached in *Campbell's Trustee v De Lisle's Executors*[1] was that in such circumstances post-inhibition advances were to be considered as if they were pre-inhibition advances. Consequently, the use of an inhibition against the debtor did not destroy the effect of a cash credit bond and disposition in security recorded prior to the date of the inhibition as a security to a bank for advances made after the date of the inhibition, or render the bank liable for the loss sustained by the inhibiting creditor[2].

(3)   EX FACIE ABSOLUTE DISPOSITION QUALIFIED BY BACKLETTER

Creating a heritable security by ex facie absolute disposition qualified by backletter avoided both the rule that the security could cover only sums advanced before the creditor's infeftment and the rule that the sum secured must be definite and specified in the deed. Given this flexibility, it was, until the commencement of the 1970 Act the most commonly used form of heritable security. The borrower granted an ex facie absolute conveyance of the property to the creditor (a disposition stating that the grant was made heritably and irredeemably) which, on recording in the Register of Sasines, vested ownership of the subjects in the creditor. But it was qualified by an unrecorded bilateral agreement or unilateral backletter granted by the creditor which specified that the disposition was granted in security only and which set out the terms of the loan and the terms on which ownership of the security subjects was held by the creditor. The debtor's right was reduced to a personal right against the creditor to have the subjects of the disposition reconveyed to him on payment of his debt, or to have the proceeds of sale of the subjects paid to him after deduction of his debt. It follows that, in principle, the creditor may retain the subjects in security of any obligation, present or future, which the debtor may owe him, subject to the terms of the contractual agreement contained in the backletter. In addition, since the creditor was, on the face of the record, absolute owner of the subjects, he could sell or burden the subjects and give valid title to purchasers for value or lenders who transact with him on the faith of the record and in ignorance of any contractual agreement between him and the debtor which precludes such transactions. As between debtor and creditor, however, as Gordon comments[3] the rules affecting such arrangements 'are something of an uneasy compromise between the fiction that the creditor is owner and the reality that he is a security holder'.

---

1   (1870) 9 M 252.
2   However, no such statutory fiction as that applicable under s 7 of the Debts Securities (Scotland) Act 1856 to cash credit bonds exists in the case of either ex facie absolute dispositions in security or standard securities. Sums advanced after completion of such securities are not deemed by statute to have been advanced before completion of the security.
3   *Gordon and Mitchell* para 20–86.

2. STANDARD SECURITIES

(1) GENERAL

The older forms of security are now virtually obsolete, being appropriate methods of creation of security only in the case of entailed estates[1]. The provisions relating to the older securities, particularly those regarding their redemption and enforcement, nevertheless remain relevant, since such securities constituted before 1970 may still be held by banks. For all other purposes, it is the statutory provisions relating to the standard security, as interpreted by case law, which are relevant to the modern day banker.

The older forms of heritable security had certain disadvantages. The Bankruptcy Act 1696 rendered ineffective heritable securities in respect of future debts (debts contracted after recording of the security) and required that in any real burden for a sum of money the sum secured must be specified in the deed creating it. The bond and disposition in security was subject to both of these rules. The cash credit bond and disposition was constrained by the latter. The disadvantage of the ex facie absolute disposition which had evolved in order to avoid the 1696 Act constraints, was that such arrangements were heavily weighted in favour of the creditor (who appeared on the record as absolute owner and open to abuse by him). The 1970 Act sought to introduce a method which avoided such problems of inflexibility and abuse. The rules of the Bankruptcy Act 1696 are therefore specifically disapplied in the case of standard securities[2]. A standard security may be used to secure a debt whether it is fixed or fluctuating, due at the date of recording or registration of the security or to become due at a future date. No predetermined amount need be specified. Any other pre-existing statutory provisions relating to heritable securities are also made inapplicable, so far as they are inconsistent with the provisions on standard securities[3]. Any provisions not inconsistent continue to apply[4].

(2) DEFINITIONS

Section 9(3) of the 1970 Act provides that a grant of any right over an interest in land for the purposes of securing any debt by way of a heritable security is competent only if it is embodied in a standard security. Section 9(8)(b) defines 'interest in land' to mean

> 'any estate or interest in land, other than an entailed estate or any interest therein, which is capable of being owned or held as a separate interest and to which title may be recorded in the Register of Sasines'.

---

1 1970 Act, s 9(8)(b). However, since the creation of entails has been incompetent since 1914, the need to use these methods will arise rarely, if at all.
2 1970 Act, s 9(6).
3 1970 Act, s 32, Sch 8.
4 1970 Act, s 32.

This can now be read to include interests capable of registration in the Land Register[1]. The interest requires to be capable of recording or registration but need not in fact have been so. The definition therefore includes: the ownership of land held on feudal tenure, whether superiority or dominium utile, and any more limited interest therein (for example, salmon fishings or a proper liferent) to which a title as a separate interest may be recorded; registrable leases (whether recorded, registered or not); and the creditor's interest in a standard security itself. It is also commonly assumed that servitude rights created by deed (whether recorded, registered or not) come within the section 9(8)(b) definition of 'interest in land' since the deed is capable of being recorded or registered[2]. Interests which are outwith the statutory definition are: a right to shootings or fishings (other than salmon fishings), since these are not deemed to be separate from the interest in the land itself; leases for a period of less than twenty years, since these cannot be recorded or registered; liferents or annuities protected by trusts, since the liferenter or annuitant does not have a separate title capable of recording or registration; and entailed estates or interests in such estates.

Section 9(8)(c) defines 'debt' to mean:

> 'any obligation due, or which will or may become due, to repay or pay money, including any such obligation arising from a transaction or part of a transaction in the course of any trade, business or profession, and any obligation to pay an annuity or *ad factum praestandum*, but does not include an obligation to pay any feuduty, ground annual, rent or other periodical sum payable in respect of land, and "creditor" and "debtor", in relation to a standard security, shall be construed accordingly'.

This wide definition covers present or future advances of money of fixed or fluctuating amounts, an obligation to pay interest on a loan (since these are periodical sums payable, not in respect of land, but in respect of the loan) and cautionary (guarantee) obligations under which money may become due on a principal debtor's default. Only periodical payments in respect of land are excluded.

The words 'obligation arising from a transaction or any part of transaction in the course of any trade' comprehend fluctuating sums in a trading account. A standard security can therefore be granted to cover any future overdraft which may arise and can be phrased in such a way that the security is not extinguished if at any time the account is in credit (although at such times, it will be a security which secures nothing other than an overdraft which may arise again in future).

Throughout the 1970 Act, the terms 'granter' and 'grantee' are used to denote the original parties to a standard security. There is no requirement that the 'debt' secured be that of the granter of the security. The section 9(8)(c) definition of 'debtor' and 'creditor' by reference to the definition of 'debt', however, means that these terms include not only the original parties but their successors in title, assignees or representatives[3]. The Act also

---

1 See the Land Registration (Scotland) Act 1979.
2 See eg *Halliday* vol III, para 36-04 and D J Cusine *Standard Securities* (1991) para 4.03.
3 This is confirmed in the interpretation section of the 1970 Act (s 30(1)).

uses the term 'proprietor' in relation to the security subjects and this term may include successors to the original granter of the security.

(3) CONSTITUTION OF THE SECURITY

Section 9(2) of the 1970 Act requires that the standard security 'be expressed in conformity with one of the forms prescribed in Schedule 2'. Form A of Schedule 2 includes the personal obligation and the security agreement, and Form B may be used where the personal obligation is constituted separately. Section 53(1) provides that sufficient compliance is achieved if the deed 'so conforms as closely as may be' to either form. Where Form A is used, the import of the personal obligation contained within it is defined in section 10.

Where the security is for a fixed amount advanced at or prior to delivery of the deed, the personal obligation undertaking to repay the creditor imports: an acknowledgement of receipt by the debtor of the principal sum advanced; a personal obligation to repay that sum with interest at the stated rate on written demand of the creditor; an obligation to pay all expenses for which the debtor is liable under the security or the Act[1].

Where the security is for a fluctuating amount, whether limited to a maximum sum or not and whether advanced partly or wholly before or after delivery of the deed, the personal obligation imports an obligation to repay the creditor on demand in writing: the amount, subject to any maximum specified , advanced or due and outstanding at the date of demand; interest on each advance from the date it was made until repayment, or on each sum payable from the date it became due until payment, at the rate and on the dates specified; all expenses for which the debtor is liable under the standard security or the Act[2].

The provision that the debtor is liable to pay on demand means that personal action is always available against him in addition to the remedies available under the standard security itself. Form A contains a clause of consent to registration for execution allowing enforcement of the personal obligation by summary diligence[3]. Where Form B is used, a similar clause may be contained in the separate personal obligation or minute of agreement allowing the document to be registered for execution.

Details of the rates of interest, how interest is to be calculated and how payments of interest are to be applied should be specified in the personal obligation. Failing specification to the contrary, simple interest will be implied[4]. Similarly, while Form A imports an obligation to repay[5], the creditor will wish to specify details of the repayments to be made

---

1 1970 Act, s 10(1)(a).
2 1970 Act, s 10(1)(b).
3 Summary diligence is a procedure whereby certain constituted obligations can be enforced without the need to apply to a court. To be able to exercise this right it is necessary that the deed contains a clause containing the debtor's consent to registration for execution. Once registered the debt can be enforced in much the same way as a court decree: W J Stewart and R Burgess *Dictionary of Law* (1996) p 376.
4 See *Halliday* vol III, para 36-10.
5 1970 Act, s 10.

(whether monthly, whether of principal sum, interest or both) and any arrangements whereby the repayments may be varied.

Both Forms A and B contain clauses providing for: grant of a standard security over the subjects described in conformity with Note I of Schedule 2 of the Act[1]; a statement that the standard conditions in Schedule 3 of the Act, together with any lawful variation of them operative for the time being, will apply[2]; and a clause of warrandice.

Section 10(2) provides that the warrandice clause, unless specially qualified, imports absolute warrandice as regards the security subjects and title deeds thereof, and warrandice from fact and deed as regards rents. Prior securities over the subjects should therefore be specifically excepted from warrandice, since, if this is not done, the granter will be liable to indemnify the bank as grantee against them[3]. In such circumstances[4], a clause should be inserted immediately before the warrandice clause expressing the security and warrandice as subject to any prior securities specified. Where the standard security is to rank prior or postponed to, or *pari passu* with, any existing security, a ranking clause may be inserted immediately prior to the warrandice clause[5]. Section 10(4) imports an assignation to the creditor of the title deeds, searches and all conveyances affecting the security subjects, with power to the creditor, in the event of sale under the powers conferred by the standard security, to deliver such title deeds, to the purchaser and to assign to him any right the creditor may have to such deeds. No assignation of rents clause is needed, since power to enter into possession on the debtor's default and to uplift rents is conferred on the grantee[6].

(4)   COMPLETION OF TITLE

The right of the creditor is created (made real) by recording the standard security in the Register of Sasines with a warrant of registration on behalf of the creditor or by registration of the creditor's interest in the Land Register. The legal effect of such recording or registration is to give a real right in security ancillary to the personal obligation in respect of which the right is granted[7]. Where the principal obligation (the debt) is an advance of a fixed amount, full repayment will extinguish the security automatically, although a formal discharge will be required to clear the security from the record. In the case of a security granted by a company incorporated under the Companies Acts, the security will be void as against the liquidator, administrator and creditors of the company unless, within

1 For specialities in relation to descriptions valid in standard securities, see *Cusine* para 4-19 and works referred to therein.
2 For discussion of standard conditions, see pp 344–346 below.
3 *Horsbrugh's Trustees v Welch* (1886) 14 R 67.
4 1970 Act, Sch 2, note 5.
5 For ranking, see pp 339–343 below.
6 By standard condition 10(3) of Sch 3 of the 1970 Act it follows that the provisions of s 25(1) of the Conveyancing (Scotland) Act 1924 and the action of maills and duties in relation to bonds and dispositions in security have no application in enforcement of a standard security.
7 1970 Act, s 11(1).

twenty-one days of the date of recording in the Register of Sasines or registration in the Land Register, it is also registered in the Register of Charges kept by the Registrar of Companies in terms of Part XII of the Companies Act 1985[1]. The Companies Act 1989 has now made it possible to register the charge outwith the twenty-one-day period, but does not alter the rule that, in the case of late registration, the charge will be void against anyone who has acquired an interest in or a right over the charged property prior to the date of registration as a company charge[2].

3.   RANKING OF STANDARD SECURITIES

(1)   SECURITIES FOR FIXED SUMS: EXPRESS RANKING

Where two or more securities are granted over the same property, preference, in the absence of express agreement, will be determined according to the date of their recording or registration. The parties may, however, enter an express agreement as to ranking[3]. If the loans are made at the same time, reciprocal ranking clauses may be included to establish any *pari passu* or postponed ranking of the securities between themselves. If one security is already recorded or registered, any alteration in its ranking is competent only with the consent of the holder of the first recorded security. In such circumstances, the creditor in the first security may be included as a party to the deed constituting the second security, consenting to the change to his position. Alternatively a ranking agreement between the security holders and the borrower may be entered into. In the absence of express agreement, where two standard securities are received by the Keeper on the same day, they are deemed to rank *pari passu*[4].

(2)   SECURITIES FOR FLUCTUATING OR UNCERTAIN AMOUNTS

Section 13(1) of the 1970 Act provides that where the creditor in a standard security duly recorded has received notice of the creation of a subsequent security over the same interest in land or any part thereof, or of the subsequent assignation or conveyance of that interest in whole or in part, being a security, assignation or conveyance so recorded, the preference in ranking of the security of that creditor is to be restricted to security for:

---

1 Companies Act 1985, s 410 (amended by the Insolvency Act 1986, s 109(1), Sch 6). Pt XII of the 1985 Act comprises ss 395–424
2 For further details of conveyancing law and practice in relation to deduction of title in standard securities, see the 1970 Act, s 12 and *Halliday* vol III, paras 36-21 to 36-30 and Halliday *Conveyancing and Feudal Reform (Scotland) Act 1970* (2nd edn, 1977) paras 6-24 to 6-33.
3 1970 Act, s 13(3)(b).
4 *Pari passu* denotes an entitlement to payment of their debts in shares proportionate to their respective advances.

(1) his present advances;
(2) future advances which he may be required to make under the contract to which the security relates;
(3) present and future interest due or to become due on these advances; and
(4) any expenses or outlays (including interest thereon) which may be, or may have been, reasonably incurred in the exercise of any power conferred on the creditor by the deed expressing the existing security.

The provision clearly affects creditors in securities for uncertain amounts, but is also relevant to creditors in securities for fixed sums, since it alters the previous common law rule that in such circumstances, the first creditor's security was limited from the date of intimation not only to the advances then outstanding but also to the interest then due[1]. It would seem therefore that the 'freeze' on preference begins only on intimation of the existence of a recorded security[2].

Mere recording of the subsequent security does not by itself constitute notice to the creditor in the existing recorded security[3]. However, assignation or conveyance to any other person of the interest of the debtor in the security subjects or in any part of it resulting from any judicial decree, or otherwise by operation of law, constitutes notification to the creditor[4]. Therefore in the absence of a ranking agreement, crystallisation of a floating charge over the security subjects, operating to vest the interest in the charge holder by operation of law, will have the effect of restricting the preference in ranking of a prior standard security holder without notice to him[5].

(3)   CATHOLIC AND SECONDARY SECURITIES

Where A and B each have security over the same subjects, and B's security is postponed to that of A, and if A also has security over other subjects belonging to the debtor, the normal rule (that in the absence of express ranking agreement the securities rank according to date of recording or registration) is qualified. A, who is known as the catholic creditor, may not take payment for his debt from the subjects over which B, the secondary creditor, also has security until A has exhausted the subjects over which he alone has security. If he does realise the subjects over which B has postponed security, he must assign to B his interest in the other

1 *Union Bank of Scotland Ltd v National Bank of Scotland Ltd* (1886) 14 R (HL) 1; *Campbell's Judicial Factor v National Bank of Scotland* 1944 SC 495, 1944 SLT 309, OH.
2 *AIB Finance Ltd v Bank of Scotland* 1993 SC 588, 1993 SCLR 851, 1995 SLT 2.
3 1970 Act, s 13(2)(a).
4 1970 Act, s 13(2)(b).
5 Halliday *1970 Act* para 5-36. For debate upon s 13 of the 1970 Act and ranking provisions, see G L Gretton 'Ranking of Heritable Creditors' (1980) 25 JLSS 275, (1981) 26 JLSS 275 and 280; and J M Halliday (1981) 26 JLSS 26. See also *Trade Development Bank v Warriner and Mason (Scotland) Ltd* 1980 SC 74, 1980 SLT 49 and 223; and generally G L Gretton *The Law of Inhibition and Adjudication* (2nd edn, 1996) chs 7 and 9.

subjects. Where both subjects are realised, B has preference over any balance remaining after A's debt has been satisfied. The general rule is that in exercising his rights, A must have regard to the secondary creditor's interests[1].

(4) HERITABLE SECURITIES IN COMPETITION WITH OTHER RIGHTS

Competition with floating charges

When a floating charge created by a company attaches to the property, it does so subject, to the rights of any person holding fixed (standard) security over the property or any part of it ranking in priority to the floating charge[2]. The floating charge may contain provision regulating its ranking with subsisting or future fixed securities[3]. In the absence of such provision, a fixed security will rank in priority to the floating charge if it has been 'constituted as a real right' before crystallisation of the floating charge[4].

The term 'constituted as a real right' refers to recording in the Register of Sasines or registration in the Land Register rather than to registration as a company charge, although the latter registration will be required within twenty-one days of the former if the real right obtained is to be enforceable against other creditors of the company[5]. A standard security will have priority if recorded in the Register of Sasines or registered in the Land Register before crystallisation of the floating charge provided that the standard security is then registered as a company charge within twenty-one days of its recording in the Register of Sasines or registration in the Land Register. Priority would be retained if registration of the standard security as a company charge occurred after crystallisation of the floating charge, but within twenty-one days of recording in the Register of Sasines or registration in the Land Register where such recording or registration occurred before crystallisation of the floating charge.

Section 464(1)(a) of the 1985 Act allows inclusion in a floating charge of a prohibition or restriction on 'creation' of a fixed security or other floating charge with priority over it or ranking *pari passu* with it. It has been held[6] that in this context the date of 'creation' of a standard security is as specified in section 410(5)(b) — 'the date on which the right of the person entitled to the benefit of the charge was constituted as a real right'. In accordance with section 410(5)(a), however, the date of creation of a floating charge is the date of its execution and not of its registration. Accordingly, a floating charge containing prohibition on the creation of subsequent securities having priority over or ranking *pari passu* with it (a

---

1 Bell *Commentaries* II,417.
2 Companies Act 1985, s 463(1)(b).
3 1985 Act, s 464(1)(b).
4 1985 Act, s 464(3), (4)(b).
5 1985 Act, s 410(2), (5).
6 By the Second Division in *AIB Finance Ltd v Bank of Scotland* 1993 SC 588, 1993 SCLR 851, 1995 SLT 2.

'negative pledge') and which is executed on the same day as execution of a standard security over the same subjects, will have priority over the standard security, irrespective of the dates of registration or recording of the two charges.

Competition with rights acquired by diligence

Adjudication

An adjudger is the holder of a judicial heritable security and, as against other heritable securities, his ranking is determined by date of infeftment. Infeftment occurs on the extracted decree of adjudication being recorded in the Register of Sasines or registered in the Land Register. However, registration under the name of the debtor of a notice of summons of adjudication (notice on the dependence of an action of adjudication) in the Register of Inhibitions and Adjudications renders the subjects of the action litigious and has the effect of an inhibition against the debtor. If decree is subsequently granted and recorded or registered, no infeftment taken by another creditor over the same subjects (for example, under a standard security) after registration of the notice of litigiosity, may rank before the adjudger's right.

The rule that adjudications rank amongst themselves according to date of infeftment is subject to a statutory exception under the Diligence Act 1661. Where there is more than one recorded or registered adjudication over the same subjects, then any of these for which decree of adjudication was granted within one year and one day of the granting of decree in relation to the first adjudication to be registered will rank *pari passu* with the first adjudication. In the unlikely event that a standard security is taken after the first adjudication, the ranking of the standard security will be unaffected by the 'equalisation' of subsequent adjudications. The prior adjudger will be ranked for his whole debt in preference to the standard security holder who is then ranked in preference to the subsequent adjudgers. The latter are then entitled to draw back from the first adjudger the amount by which his ranking exceeded that which it would have been had the question been between the adjudgers alone[1].

In the more likely event of adjudication registered or recorded after the infeftment of a standard security holder, the adjudger will rank as a heritable creditor *secundo loco* with the proceeds of sale by the standard security holder being applied in accordance with section 27 of the 1970 Act. However, since recording or registration of an adjudication creates heritable security over an interest in land, notice of such a recorded adjudication to an existing standard security holder would mean that section 13 of the 1970 Act applied, and wouldprevent the preference in ranking of the standard security holder for any post-notice advances which he is not contractually bound to make[2].

---

1 Bell *Commentaries* II,404.
2 See further *Gretton* ch 13; 20 *Stair Memorial Encyclopaedia* para 251.

Inhibition

An inhibition takes effect on recording of notice in the Register of Inhibitions and Adjudications. Section 18 of the Court of Session Act 1868 provides that at the moment of recording the inhibition 'shall be held to be duly intimated and published to all concerned'.

Inhibition strikes at such 'debts and deeds' voluntarily granted by the debtor after the date of inhibition as affect his existing heritable estate in Scotland to the prejudice of the inhibitor. It confers no real right on the inhibitor, but operates as a 'freeze' on the debtor's heritable property, preventing future voluntary dealings with it. Bell puts it thus:

> 'It is an injunction ... forbidding the debtor to grant any conveyance, or to execute any deed, or to incur any other debt, by which the [inhibiting] creditor may be disappointed in obtaining payment or performance of the obligation whereupon the letters proceed, and prohibiting the public from giving the debtor credit, or receiving from him conveyances out of which such effect may arise'[1].

The effect is that debts contracted by the debtor after the date of the inhibition are postponed to the claim of the inhibitor in any process of realisation and distribution of the debtor's heritable estate and any future voluntary security granted over the property in violation of the inhibition will be voidable at the instance of the inhibitor[2]. It does not create preference in respect of the proceeds of realisation of heritage acquired by the debtor after the inhibition and does not render securities granted over such property voidable. Since an inhibition strikes only at future voluntary acts, it cannot prevent subscription of securities which the debtor was already contractually bound to grant. Nor can it prevent completion of security which the debtor had granted before the inhibition. The power of sale and the priority ranking on sale of a pre-inhibition standard security holder will be unaffected. However, where a pre-inhibition heritable security is an ex facie absolute disposition in security or a standard security for a fluctuating amount, the holder's preference for advances which he was not contractually bound to make and which he makes after an inhibition has been recorded will be postponed to the claims of the inhibitor[3]. As a result of section 18 of the Court of Session Act 1868, actual notification of the inhibition to the existing standard security holder would seem unnecessary to create this 'freeze' on preference[4].

---

1 Bell *Commentaries* II,134.
2 See further *Gretton* pp 73–74.
3 See further *Gretton* pp 111–116.
4 Where the pre-inhibition security is in the form of a cash credit bond and disposition, the Debts Securities (Scotland) Act 1856, s 7, creates a statutory fiction that all advances made under the security are deemed to have been made at the date of its completion. It would seem therefore that post-inhibition advances made under a pre-inhibition cash credit bond and disposition remain not only secured, but retain preference in ranking: *Campbell's Trustee v De Lisle's Executors* (1870) 9 M 252. See further G L Gretton *The Law of Inhibition and Adjudication* (2nd edn, 1996), especially chs 6 and 9, and 20 *Stair Memorial Encyclopaedia* para 252.

4.   THE STANDARD CONDITIONS

(1)   INTRODUCTION

The standard conditions are set out in Schedule 3 of the 1970 Act, together with any variations as have been agreed by the parties under the powers conferred by the Act, and regulate every standard security[1]. These standard conditions express the respective rights and duties of the parties in relation to the security subjects and to the redemption or enforcement of the standard security. Section 11(3) permits variation of any standard conditions other than standard condition 11 (redemption) and the provisions of Schedule 3 relating to the powers of sale, foreclosure and the exercise of those powers. It further provides that no variable standard condition may be varied in a manner inconsistent with any conditions which may not be varied. In this context, the term 'variation' includes the insertion of additional conditions or the exclusion of a standard condition[2]. Any purported variation which contravenes section 11(3) will be void and unenforceable[3]. The main object of these restrictions on variation is to protect the debtor who is generally in the weaker bargaining position in negotiating the terms of the security. However, he can at least be assured that the statutory terms relating to redemption, sale and foreclosure cannot be varied to his prejudice.

(2)   THE VARIABLE STANDARD CONDITIONS

The variable standard conditions are:

- standard condition 1 which regulates the debtor's obligations of maintenance and repair of the security subjects;
- standard condition 2 which regulates the debtor's obligation to complete unfinished buildings and not to demolish, alter or add to any buildings forming part of the security subjects without the consent of the creditor;
- standard condition 3 which regulates the debtor's obligation to observe conditions of title and other obligations affecting the standard security;
- standard condition 4 which regulates the debtor's obligation to comply with any planning or similar notices;
- standard condition 5 which regulates the debtor's obligation to insure or permit the creditor to insure the security subjects;
- standard condition 6 which regulates the debtor's obligation not to let or sub-let, or agree to let or sub-let, the security subjects or any part of them without the prior written consent of the creditor;

---

1   1970 Act, s 11(2), Sch 3.
2   1970 Act, s 11(4)(a).
3   1970 Act, s 11(4)(b).

- standard condition 7 which regulates the creditor's power to perform at the debtor's expense any obligations imposed by the standard conditions on the debtor which the debtor has failed to perform;
- standard condition 9 which regulates the definition of 'default';
- standard condition 10 which regulates the creditor's rights on the debtor's default other than his right of sale and or foreclosure, including the right to enter into possession to uplift of rents (10(3)), or to let the subjects (10(4)), and manage and maintain them (10(5)), and the right to enter on the subjects to effect such repairs or improvements as would be expected of a prudent manager (10(6)); and
- standard condition 12 which regulates the debtor's liability for expenses incurred by the creditor.

Any of these conditions may be varied at the option of the contracting parties, so long as the variation is made in due form[1].

Section 16(1) and (2) of the Act provide that where the standard conditions were originally imported in a personal obligation contained in the recorded standard security, future variation should be similarly recorded (either by indorsement on the standard security in conformity with Form E of Schedule 4 or by separate recorded deed). Where the standard conditions were initially imported or contained in an unrecorded personal obligation or minute of agreement, however, any future deed containing variations need not be recorded. Where the standard conditions or variations are contained in an unrecorded instrument, third parties will be unable to tell from the public record whether all of the variable standard conditions apply, or whether some have been varied or excluded. The effect of unrecorded standard conditions and variations on the rights of third parties has been questioned before the courts, namely in relation to leases or subleases granted by the debtor in breach of standard condition 6[2].

(3) THE NON-VARIABLE STANDARD CONDITIONS

The non-variable standard conditions are as follows.

- Standard condition 11 which regulates redemption. The debtor's previously unfettered right of redemption under the 1970 Act was qualified to allow restriction on the right of redemption[3] but prohibiting variation of standard condition 11 which regulates the procedure for redemption[4].

1 Note 4 to Sch 2 of the 1970 Act allows such variations to be effected either by an instrument other than the standard security (which instrument need not be recorded or registered) or by inserting particulars of the variations in the standard security itself.
2 *Trade Development Bank v Warriner and Mason (Scotland) Ltd* 1980 SC 74, 1980 SLT 223; *Trade Development Bank v Crittall Windows Ltd* 1983 SLT 510; *Trade Development Bank v David W Haig (Bellshill) Ltd* 1983 SLT 510.
3 1970 Act, s 18(1A) (added by the Redemption of Standard Securities (Scotland) Act 1971, s 1(c), and amended by the Land Tenure Reform (Scotland) Act 1974, s 11(6)).
4 1970 Act, s 11(3) (amended by the Redemption of Standard Securities (Scotland) Act 1971, s 1). Note, however, that s 18(1A) of the 1970 Act is subject to s 11 of the Land Tenure Reform (Scotland) Act 1974, which restricts to 20 years the maximum period during which a standard security over a private dwelling house may be made irredeemable. This prevents evasion of the prohibition on long leases of such dwelling houses contained in Part II of the 1974 Act.

- Standard conditions 8, 9 and 10 which regulate sale and foreclosure. The scope of the prohibition on variation of the provisions relating to the powers of sale and foreclosure and to the exercise of these powers cannot be altered.

5. ENFORCEMENT OF THE STANDARD SECURITY

(1) THE PERSONAL OBLIGATION

Form A and Form B

If Form A of Schedule 2 of the 1970 Act is used, the undertaking contained within it imports liability to pay the amount borrowed, interest thereon and all expenses for which the debtor is liable on demand in writing at any time after delivery of the standard security[1]. If the security is for a fluctuating amount, provision for ascertaining the amount due at any time should be inserted immediately prior to the clause granting security[2]. It is therefore common to state in the standard security that the amount due by the debtor at any time shall be that certified as being due by an official of the lender. Form A contains a clause of consent to registration for execution allowing the creditor to enforce the personal obligation by summary diligence. If summary diligence is to be competent, however, provision must have been made for ascertaining the amount due at any time[3]. As in the case of an ordinary action for payment of a debt or for implement of an obligation, summary diligence will be incompetent if the debt or obligation is not precise. In *Hendry v Marshall*[4], a lease required a tenant 'to cultivate the lands let' according to approved methods of husbandry, in addition to payment of rent. The lease was registered for execution with the tenant's consent. The proprietor charged him by warrant 'to implement the whole obligations of the lease'. It was held that if the contract contains vague or indefinite obligations, these cannot be enforced by order against the defender. It must be clear what he should have done before the court can order him to do it. Thus implement of a continuing obligation to 'cultivate lands' could not be ordered.

If Form B is used, there is no statutory provision that the personal obligation contained in the separate instrument imports liability on demand.

---

1 1970 Act, s 10(1).
2 1970 Act, Sch 2, Note 6.
3 *Gordon and Mitchell* para 20-173. Such provision will also be necessary for enforcement of the security. Thus Cusine notes (at para 4-30 of *Standard Securities*) that if no such provision is made, 'the lender would either have to state in any calling-up notice the exact sum due, or provide that it is subject to adjustment. If the latter course is chosen, the debtor may call upon the creditor to state the correct amount "within ...one month from the date of service of the calling-up notice". A shrewd debtor who wishes to "buy time" might request this information the day before the month expired and if the creditor did not comply, he would have to recommence the calling-up procedure [1970 Act, s 19(9)]'.
4 (1878) 5 R 687.

This must therefore be expressly stated in the instrument and a clause of consent to registration for execution incorporated if summary diligence is to be competent.

In the case of either Form A or Form B, summary diligence by the original creditor against a successor to the original debtor will be competent only if an agreement to that effect has been executed by the successor in accordance with section 15 of the Conveyancing (Scotland) Act 1924 and if diligence proceeds in accordance with section 47 of the Conveyancing (Scotland) Act 1874.

Where the standard security is assigned to another creditor[1], using one of the statutory forms[2], in the case of a Form A standard security containing the personal obligation, the assignation of the security transfers both the debt and the security together with all rights competent to the grantor of the assignation. Enforcement of the obligation to repay the debt by summary diligence will therefore remain competent[3].

The effect of assignation of a Form B standard security by means of one of the statutory forms[4] is unclear[5], and it is uncertain whether the debt is transferred with the security. Halliday suggests that where the personal obligation is contained in a separate instrument, the debt must be specifically assigned. In any case in which enforcement of the personal obligation by summary diligence is not competent, the obligation to repay the sum lent may be enforced by ordinary action for payment. Since the creditor's remedies against the security subjects are independent of his rights of enforcement of the personal obligation, both may be enforced concurrently. In practice, however, it is generally only necessary to enforce the personal obligation where the full amount due cannot be obtained by realisation of the security subjects.

The security

Common law

Standard condition 10(1) provides that exercise by the creditor of the statutory rights against the security subjects is without prejudice to any other remedies arising out of the contract to which the security relates. In addition to his remedies against the heritable subjects, the creditor may exercise the common law remedy of poinding of the ground to attach any moveables on the subjects. Where the creditor has not taken power in the standard conditions to deal with such moveables, and where the value of the heritable subjects has declined, poinding of any plant, stock or other moveable property of value remains a useful remedy[6].

1 In terms of s 14 of the 1970 Act.
2 Set out in Sch 4 of the 1970 Act.
3 Although further complications arise where the security was for an uncertain or fluctuating amount: see Halliday *1970 Act* paras 9-01 to 9-07.
4 Set out in Sch 4 of the 1970 Act.
5 See Halliday *1970 Act* para 9-02.
6 For details, see G L Gretton *The Law of Inhibition and Adjudication* (2nd edn, 1996) ch 13.

Under the 1970 Act

On the debtor's default, the creditor may acquire power to sell the subjects, the right to enter into possession to uplift rents or to let the subjects, the right to enter the subjects to repair and maintain them and, power to apply to the court for decree of foreclosure. To exercise these or other rights arising under the security, he can proceed by various means: service of a calling-up notice under section 19; service of notice of default under section 21, or application to the court under section 24 for warrant to exercise his rights.

(2)   DEFAULT

In terms of standard condition 9(1), the debtor will be in default where a calling-up notice has been served and not complied with; where there has been a failure to comply with any other requirement of the security; or where the proprietor of the security subjects has become insolvent. Standard condition 9(2) defines the circumstances in which the proprietor will be taken to be insolvent. This definition of default is frequently expanded to include other circumstances, such as a failure to pay a specified number of monthly instalments.

(3)   CALLING UP

Subject to the terms of the security, where the creditor requires the debt discharged, he may at any time call up the security in the manner prescribed[1]. If an agreed period for repayment was set, however, it will only be competent to demand earlier repayment where the debtor has defaulted in some other requirement. Failing discharge of the debt in terms of any calling-up notice, the debtor will be in default within the meaning of standard condition 9(1)(a). Where this occurs, the creditor then becomes entitled under section 20 to exercise such of his rights under the security as he may consider appropriate (in addition to any other remedy arising under the contract to which the security relates). If standard condition 10 has been adopted unchanged, these rights include all of the powers listed in standard condition 10 (sale, entry into possession, repair and maintenance, and application to the court for decree of foreclosure). Given the extensive powers available to the creditor on the debtor's failure to comply with a calling-up notice, the form of notice and procedure for its service must be strictly adhered to.

Section 19(1) requires that the calling-up notice be in conformity with Form A of Schedule 6. It may relate only to the amount secured by the standard security, since the power of sale may be exercised only in relation to the debt secured. If there is doubt as to the amount secured, the sum stated in the notice may be qualified as subject to adjustment.

---

1 Ie the manner prescribed by s 19 of the 1970 Act: Sch 3, standard condition 8.

However, if this is stated, then section 19 (5) permits the debtor to request statement of the amount as finally determined within one month of the date of service of the notice and a failure by the creditor to comply with this requirement will render the notice without effect.

If the standard security or the separate instrument creating the personal obligation contains provision that a certificate by a named official of the creditor shall be conclusive of the amount due at any time, then it must be annexed to the calling-up notice. Provided that the amount specified in the notice is correct as at the date of service, the notice will not be invalidated by subsequent repayments or advances[1].

Notice is served on the person last infeft and appearing on the record as the proprietor of the security subjects[2]. If the proprietor and debtor are not one and the same person, notice must also be served on the debtor[3]. In addition, notice should be served on any person against whom the creditor wishes to preserve recourse, such as co-obligants and guarantors[4]. Notice should also be served on other creditors who may be affected (postponed or *pari passu* security holders) and on any non-entitled spouse, because the consent of such parties to any waiver or reduction of the period specified in the notice will be required[5]. The procedure for service is set out in subsections (2) to (8) of section 19 of the Act[6].

The period of notice is normally two months[7]; but, subject to the requirement of consent of postponed or *pari passu* security holders and of any non-entitled spouse, the person on whom the notice is served may agree to a shorter period of notice[8]. For the purposes of conferring on the creditor a power of sale, the calling-up notice prescribes on expiry of a period of five years from the date of the notice or, if offer or exposure for sale occurs, from the date of the last offer or exposure[9].

(4) NOTICE OF DEFAULT

General

Under section 21 of the 1970 Act, where the debtor is in default within the meaning of standard condition 9(1)(b) and the default is remediable, the creditor may, without prejudice to any other powers he may have by virtue of the Act or otherwise, issue a notice calling on the debtor and (if the debtor is not the proprietor) the proprietor, to 'purge the default'[10]. Default within the meaning of standard condition 9(1)(b) means failure to comply with any requirement arising out of the security other than failure

---

1 For further details, see Halliday *1970 Act* paras 10-03 to 10-05.
2 1970 Act, s 19(2).
3 See Halliday *1970 Act* para 10-09.
4 1970 Act, s 19(5).
5 1970 Act, s 19(10).
6 And fully discussed in Halliday *1970 Act* paras 10-02 to 10-09.
7 1970 Act, Sch 6, Form A.
8 1970 Act, s 19(10).
9 1970 Act, s 19(11).
10 1970 Act, s 21(1).

350 Security over Land, Buildings and Attachments to Land

to comply with a calling-up notice. It therefore has an extremely wide meaning and overlaps with circumstances in which the creditor might wish to serve a calling-up notice, such as a failure to pay instalments of the debt or interest thereon. The form of notice prescribed is Form B contained in Schedule 6, and the procedure for service is the same as that required in the case of a calling-up notice[1]. The period for compliance with the notice is one month[2]. However, the provisions of section 19(10) in relation to the dispensing with or shortening of the period of notice in the case of a calling-up notice apply also in the case of a notice of default[3]. For the purposes of conferring any powers on the creditor, the notice prescribes on expiry of a period of five years from the date of the notice[4]. The person on whom a notice of default is served may, within fourteen days of service of the notice, object to the notice by way of application to the court, and must serve a copy of any such application on the creditor and any other party on whom the notice of default was served[5]. On such application, the court may, after hearing the parties, order the notice to be set aside in whole or in part, or to be varied or upheld[6]. Where an objection to the notice of default is lodged,the respondent may make a counter-application requesting any of the remedies conferred by the Act and the court may grant any such remedy as it may think proper[7]. In the context of such a counter-application, a certificate[8] stating the nature of the default is prima facie evidence of the default stated[9]. The onus will fall upon the applicant who disputes that default has occurred to prove that he is not in default.

Where a person fails to 'purge the default' within the one-month period of notice, the creditor may proceed to exercise such of his rights on default under standard condition 10(2)[10] as he may consider appropriate[11]. In contrast to the calling-up procedure, the creditor cannot use the notice of default procedure to obtain the power to enter into possession to uplift rents or to let the subjects.

A further distinction between the notice of default and calling-up procedures lies in the fact that at any time after expiry of the period stated in a notice of default but before conclusion by the creditor of an enforceable contract to sell the security subjects, the debtor or proprietor may, subject to any agreement to the contrary, redeem the security without the necessity of observance of any requirement as to notice[12]. In any other circumstance, two months' notice of the intention to redeem the security must be given to the creditor[13].

1 1970 Act, s 21(2).
2 1970 Act, Sch 6, Form B.
3 1970 Act, s 21(3).
4 1970 Act, s 21(4); see Halliday *1970 Act* paras 10.19 to 10.23.
5 1970 Act, s 22(1).
6 1970 Act, s 22(2).
7 1970 Act, s 22(3); see Halliday *1970 Act* para 10.28.
8 In conformity with Sch 7 of the 1970 Act.
9 1970 Act, s 22(4).
10 Ie sale of the subjects; entry at all reasonable times to repair or maintain the subjects; and application to the court for a decree of foreclosure.
11 1970 Act, s 23(2).
12 1970 Act, s 23(3).
13 1970 Act, s 18. See also *Forbes v Armstrong* 1993 SCLR 204, 1994 SLT 199, OH.

Application under section 24 of the 1970 Act

Without prejudice to the creditor's right to proceed by way of notice of default in respect of a default within the meaning of standard condition 9(1)(b), where the debtor is in default within the meaning of either standard condition 9(1)(b) or standard condition 9(i)(c) (on the proprietor's insolvency), the creditor may apply to the sheriff court for a warrant to exercise any of the remedies arising under standard condition 10 or other provision of the security[1]. The remedies sought to be exercised must be specified in the application. For the purposes of such an application, a certificate stating the nature of the default in accordance with Schedule 7 will be prima facie evidence of the facts stated therein[2].

Cusine notes[3] that the creditor may use a 'belt and braces' approach of serving a calling-up notice or a notice of default as well as applying to the court under section 24. In such circumstances, if decree is granted under section 24, any defects in the calling-up or default procedure may be ignored. This safety net would seem useful, given that strict interpretation of section 19(1) and section 21(2) would lead to the conclusion that any departure from the statutory forms of calling-up and default notices will invalidate the notice however trivial the error involved.

(5) SALE OF SECURITY SUBJECTS

The right of sale arises: where a calling-up notice is not complied with[4]; if a notice of default is not complied with[5]; and if warrant is obtained from the court under section 24.

A creditor having the right to sell the subjects may exercise that right either by private bargain or by exposure to sale (public roup) and in either case has a duty 'to advertise the sale and to take all reasonable steps to ensure that the price at which all or any of the subjects are sold is the best that can be reasonably obtained'[6].

The duty to advertise

There are no specific requirements relating to the procedure for advertisement in the case of sale under a standard security and the adequacy of the advertising used would appear to depend on the nature and location of the property and other circumstances of the case. The set requirements for advertising subjects for sale under a bond and disposition in security, set out in the Conveyancing (Scotland) Act 1924[7], are not specifically required to be followed in the case of sale under a standard security. Halliday[8] and

1 1970 Act, s 24(1).
2 1970 Act, s 24(2).
3 *Cusine* para 8-20.
4 1970 Act, ss 20(1), (2) and 10(2).
5 1970 Act, s 23(2).
6 1970 Act, s 25. Note also that s 35 extends the right to sell by private bargain to creditors holding bonds and dispositions in security.
7 See the 1924 Act, s 3.
8 Halliday *1970 Act* para 10-38; *Halliday* vol III, paras 33-27 to 33-28.

Gordon[1] both suggest, however, that the safest course would be to adhere, in general, to the requirements of the 1924 Act. Certificates of advertisement should be obtained from the publishers and preserved in case of future challenge by the debtor.

The duty to obtain the best price

The statutory requirement that a creditor selling under a standard security (or bond and disposition in security) must obtain the best price that can reasonably be obtained is a broad restatement of 'the existing principle that a heritable creditor in exercising his power of sale is in the position of a quasi-trustee of the debtor'[2].

Both at common law and by statute the creditor is bound to act in the debtor's best interest in accepting a particular purchase price. Halliday[3] comments, however, that the phrase 'best price' will not be construed 'with undue literalism'. For example, in a situation where two offers of different amounts are received but the higher offer is subject to a condition of obtaining loan finance or planning permission, which may not be purified, acceptance of the lower offer may be justifiable if in all the circumstances the court considers that it was reasonable, to do so[4].

The onus of proving that the price accepted or which the creditor intends to accept is less than the best price which could reasonably be obtained will lie with the debtor or other creditor challenging the sale. If the sale has proceeded and the debtor can show that a better price could have been obtained at that time, damages may be available. The debtor's case will be strengthened if a relationship of interest between the debtor and purchaser can also be shown. In *Rimmer v Thomas Usher & Son Ltd*[5] it was held that a creditor has an overriding common law obligation to the debtor to exercise the power of sale with regard to the interest of the debtor and to obtain a full and fair market price for the subjects. A hotel and goodwill had been conveyed by ex facie absolute disposition in security for a loan. On the debtor's bankruptcy and failure to repay the loan, the defenders did not advertise the subjects for sale but accepted an offer to purchase for £8,000. The purchaser in fact borrowed the purchase price from the selling creditor and this loan was granted on condition that the purchaser thereafter buy all hotel supplies from the creditor, his associates or nominees so long as the loan remained unpaid. It was averred that had the subjects been advertised, they could reasonably have been sold for at least £12,000. The debtor sued the creditor for the £4,000 difference. It was held that a creditor in realising by sale the security subjects, acts as quasi-trustee for the debtor to whom he is bound to account for the difference between the price obtained and the amount of the loan still due. The defenders were relying on a minute of agreement which provided that on

---

1 *Gordon and Mitchell* para 20-196.
2 Halliday *1970 Act* paras 5-11 and 10-39.
3 Halliday *1970 Act* para 5-11.
4 See also Gloag and Irvine *The Law of Rights in Security and Cautionary Obligations* (1897) pp 120, 121, on the common law duty to act in the debtor's interest in relation to obtaining the best price.
5 1967 SLT 7, OH.

the debtor's default, they could sell 'by public roup or private bargain with or without advertising and on such terms and conditions and at such price as they think proper'. This contractual agreement did not, however, relieve the creditor of his common law duty to act fairly and with due regard for the debtor's interest. He was not, therefore, entitled to accept an offer when he knew that the property was worth more[1].

Provided the debtor can prove that a better price could reasonably have been obtained at the time of the sale, there appears to be no bar to his obtaining damages for breach of the common law or statutory duty by the creditor after the breach has occurred. But greater difficulty appears to arise where the debtor or another of his creditors attempts to prevent such a breach before it occurs[2].

More recently, the question of whether the debtor himself can interdict a particular sale which would breach the creditor's common law or statutory duties has attracted attention. In *Associated Displays Ltd v Turnbeam Ltd*[3] a standard security was granted to secure a debt of £15,820 and was later assigned to T Ltd. On the debtor's failure to comply with a calling-up notice, T Ltd advertised the subjects and received a single offer of £20,000. The pursuers had had the subjects valued at £180,000 if sold in separate lots and at £125,000 if sold as a whole. Missives of sale were drawn up and exchanged. Three days before the purchaser's entry, the liquidator of Associated Displays Ltd obtained interim interdict preventing T Ltd from selling the subjects before satisfying the court that they had complied with section 25 of the 1970 Act by obtaining the best price that could reasonably be obtained. On appeal to the sheriff principal, the interim interdict was held incompetent on two principal grounds. Firstly, section 25 confers no right upon the debtor to call upon the creditor to demonstrate that he has fulfilled his duties under section 25. The onus is on the debtor to prove that he has not. The debtor sought to invert this onus and interim interdict was held incompetent on that ground alone. Secondly, even if the debtor had shown that the creditor had not fulfilled his section 25 duty, interim interdict is never competent against a completed wrong. An enforceable contract of sale had already been completed and could not therefore be interdicted[4].

Provided the debtor satisfies the onus of proof of breach of section 25, and does not seek to invert that onus, a petition for interdict or interim interdict should therefore be competent. In *Gordaviran Ltd v Clydesdale Bank plc*[5] the pursuer raised an action for interdict and interim interdict against conclusion of missives of sale by the creditor, thus avoiding the stumbling block of ground two of the decision in *Associated Displays*. However, the pursuer's crave sought to invert the onus in section 25 by seeking interdict from conclusion of missives:

---

1 *Royal Bank of Scotland plc v A and M Johnson* 1987 GWD 1-5, OH.
2 *Beveridge v Wilson* (1829) 7 S 279; *Kerr v McArthur's Trustees* (1848) 11 D 301.
3 1988 SCLR 220, Sh Ct.
4 See T Guthrie 'Controlling Creditors' Rights under Standard Securities' 1994 SLT 93 at 94.
5 1994 SCLR 248, Sh Ct.

'until such time as the defenders can satisfy the court that all reasonable steps have been taken under [section 25 of the 1970 Act] to ensure that the price at which the subjects are sold is the best that could reasonably be obtained'.

Their complaint was that, given that planning permission for use of the security subjects as a golf course had been granted, the creditor should have advertised the subjects in national newspapers and in golfing magazines, and not merely, as they had done, in a local paper and in a farming magazine because the value of the subjects with the planning permission as a golf course was far higher than its value as agricultural land. The sheriff principal, however, following the first ground of the decision in *Associated Displays*, held on appeal that the 1970 Act confers no right on a debtor to call upon a creditor to demonstrate that he has fulfilled the duties incumbent on him under the section and that the crave for interdict and interim interdict was accordingly incompetent. Certain additional observations made by the sheriff principal would appear to suggest that, even if the debtor's crave had not sought to invert the onus in section 25, such an action for interdict would nonetheless be incompetent. He said:

'I am particularly impressed by the consideration that, if a debtor can obtain interdict in a situation such as this, the creditor is effectively prevented from exercising the right to sell, granted to him by the court, except with the consent of the debtor. That is surely not the intention of the 1970 Act. If a creditor, in breach of his duty under section 25, does sell security subjects at a throwaway price, there are remedies other than interdict available to the debtor after the event. The onus would, however, be on the debtor to show that the creditor had been in breach of duty and that the debtor had suffered some prejudice thereby'[1].

To obtain damages after the event, the debtor cannot rely merely on proof that the price obtained was less than the value of the land, but must show that the price was not the best which could reasonably have been obtained at that time. In *Dick v Clydesdale Bank plc*[2] the debtor had granted a standard security over land, part of which was used for commercial purposes and part for agricultural purposes. The bank, in exercise of its power of sale, advertised the subjects on the open market and accepted an offer. The pursuers claimed damages on the basis that the land was sold below its true value, since the whole estate had been advertised and sold as agricultural land only, without regard to its commercial value. Lord President Hope[3] affirmed that 'the creditor in a heritable security must pay due regard to the interests of the debtor when he comes to sell the security subjects' and cited with approval[4] Halliday's view that a creditor is in the position of quasi-trustee for the debtor. However, in the present case there was no suggestion that the creditor had failed to accept the best offer made. The criticism, rather, was of the manner in which the property had been marketed. While the pursuer had averred that the land had 'hope value', he had not averred that sale at a higher price had been capable of being achieved at the time of the sale.

1 1994 SCLR 248 at 251, Sh Ct.
2 1991 SLT 678.
3 1991 SLT 678 at 681A.
4 1991 SLT 678 at 681B.

The issue of whether the creditor can be prevented from selling where sale, even at the best price reasonably obtainable, would not fully discharge the debt or produce a surplus, was recently examined in *Halifax Building Society v Gupta*[1]. The debtor in a standard security had fallen into arrears and the creditors raised an action seeking warrant to enter into possession of the subjects and sell them. They also sought the common law remedy of ejection. The action was defended on the basis that the right to possession was a discretionary one and that it was not, equitable to insist upon it. The debtor had sought to have his debts rescheduled but this had not been accepted by the creditor. The defender's defences were rejected.

The court has no discretion, to prevent the creditor from enforcing his security by exercise of one or other of the remedies available to him merely on grounds that some arrangement other than enforcement of the security by these means would be less prejudicial to the debtor's interest. In granting security, the debtor has consented to the exercise of the creditor's powers of enforcement should he later default. Even if sale of the subjects would not generate a surplus, it cannot be prevented unless the debtor shows that another remedy available under the security would serve the creditor's interest equally well but would prejudice the debtor's interest less. Since sale, even if not generating a surplus, will recoup some of the outstanding debt, and since this is in the creditor's and the debtor's interest, it is unlikely that in such circumstances the debtor will be able to show that a different remedy available under the security should be pursued. The position in England and Wales is considerably different where the courts have some discretion as to how to act where a creditor seeks possession of a dwelling house because of mortgage arrears and the debtor offers to pay the amount of the arrears[2]. The court, in such circumstances, may stay or suspend execution of an order for possession if satisfied that the debtor is likely to be able to repay the arrears within a reasonable time. Scottish consumers find themselves in a less favourable position than those south of the border.

(6) EFFECT OF SALE ON OTHER CREDITORS

The effect of recording of a disposition which bears to be in implement of a sale by a creditor in a standard security is to disburden the subjects of all heritable securities or diligences ranking *pari passu* with or postponed to the security of the selling creditor[3]. Under section 27, the holders of *pari passu* or postponed securities or diligence nonetheless have a right to a due share of the proceeds of sale. The subjects are not disburdened of any heritable securities prior in ranking to that of the selling creditor, but the selling creditor has the right to redeem them[4], and must apply the proceeds of sale in payment of the whole amount due under any prior

---

1 1994 SLT 339.
2 Administration of Justice Act 1970, s 36; Administration of Justice Act 1973, s 8.
3 1970 Act, s 26(1).
4 Under s 26(2) of the 1970 Act (in order to give the purchaser an unencumbered title).

security to which the sale is not made subject, before deducting payment of the amount due under his own security[1].

Application of proceeds

Section 27(1) of the 1970 Act provides that the proceeds of sale are held in trust by the selling creditor to be applied in accordance with the following order of priority:

(a) first, in payment of all expenses properly incurred by him in connection with the sale, or any attempted sale;

(b) secondly, in payment of the whole amount due under any prior security to which the sale is not made subject;

(c) thirdly, in payment of the whole amount due under the standard security, and in payment, in due proportion, of the whole amount due under a security, if any, ranking *pari passu* with his own security, which has been duly recorded; and

(d) fourthly, in payment of any amounts due under any securities with a ranking postponed to that of his own security, according to their ranking.

Any residue is then paid 'to the person entitled to the security subjects at the time of sale, or to any person authorised to give receipts for the proceeds of the sale thereof'[2]. If the selling creditor is for any reason unable to obtain a receipt or discharge for a payment which he is required to make under section 27(1), he may consign the amount due in the sheriff court for the person appearing to have the best right thereto and lodge in court a statement of the amount consigned[3]. Consignation thus made will discharge the payment of the amount due and a certificate under the hand of the sheriff clerk will be sufficient evidence[4].

Section 41 of the Conveyancing (Scotland) Act 1924[5] is applied by section 32 of the 1970 Act in relation to standard securities. This ensures that the title of a purchaser from a creditor in a standard security is protected against challenge on grounds of legal incapacity of the persons on whom a calling-up notice or default notice was served. The purchaser's title cannot be challenged on grounds of irregularities in procedure or the debt having ceased to exist, provided the exercise of the power of sale by the creditor has been regular and the sale was to a bona fide purchaser for value.

---

1 1970 Act, s 27(1).
2 1970 Act, s 27(1). The area of law with regard to the rights of inhibiting creditors competing for the proceeds of sale is complex: see G L Gretton *The Law of Inhibition and Adjudication* (2nd edn, 1996) pp 108–124, 140–156. See also *George M Allan Ltd Waugh's Trustee* 1966 SLT (Sh Ct) 17; *Bank of Scotland v Lord Advocate* 1977 SLT 24, OH; *McGowan v A Middlemas & Sons Ltd* 1977 SLT (Sh Ct) 41; *Abbey National Building Society v Shaik Aziz* 1981 SLT (Sh Ct) 29; *Ferguson and Forster v Dalbeattie Finance Co* 1981 SLT (Sh Ct) 53; *Halifax Building Society v Smith* 1985 SLT (Sh Ct) 25; *Abbey National Building Society v Barclays Bank plc* 1990 SCLR 639, Sh Ct.
3 1970 Act, s 27(2).
4 1970 Act, s 27(3). For further discussion, see *Halliday* vol III, para 39-52 and Halliday *1970 Act* paras 10-49, 10-50.
5 Conveyancing (Scotland) Act 1924, s 41 (amended by the 1970 Act, s 38).

6.   ENTRY INTO POSSESSION

(1)   GENERAL

The right to enter into possession is available whatever the nature of the interest in land over which the debt is secured[1]. Unlike a bond and disposition in security, a standard security contains no clause of assignation of rents on which to base an action of maills and duties. Instead, the legal basis of a creditor's right under a standard security to enter into possession and uplift rents on the debtor's default is statutory[2]. The statutory right to enter into possession arises automatically, without application to the court, only where the debtor's default is default within the meaning of standard condition 9(1)(a)[3]. In all other cases of default[4], an application to the court under section 24 for warrant to enter into possession will be necessary. However, it is open to the parties at the time of granting the security to vary or extend the circumstances in which creditor may be entitled to enter into possession and the powers available to him when he does so. Section 11(3) prohibits alteration of the provisions relating to exercise of powers of sale and foreclosure, but does not restrict variation of the powers of entry into possession. Where the subjects are let or comprise a superiority interest or confer a right to recover ground annual, even where the creditor has the right to enter into possession without a court warrant, he may prefer to obtain a declarator of his right of possession in order to satisfy tenants and others that he has authority to collect the income from the subjects[5].

Where the proprietor of the security subjects is in personal occupation, an action of ejection under section 5 of the Heritable Securities (Scotland) Act 1894 will be competent provided the debtor has failed to pay an instalment of interest or some part of capital which has been requisitioned[6]. Where there has been default by non-compliance with a calling-up notice, an action of ejection[7] will be possible. In all other cases, unless the right of ejection by summary action has been agreed, an ordinary action of ejection must be brought at the time of seeking warrant to exercise the remedy of entry into possession.

There was previously some confusion as to whether, since an application under section 24 to exercise standard condition 10 remedies had to be made by way of summary action[8], a crave for ejection could competently be included in a section 24 application or had to be by separate ordinary action but this matter has now been resolved[9]. The present rule is that

1 *Halliday* vol III, para 39-60; Halliday *1970 Act* para 10-59.
2 1970 Act, Sch 3, standard condition 10(3).
3 Failure to comply with a calling-up notice: 1970 Act, s 20(1).
4 Whether within the meaning of standard condition 9(1)(b) or 9(1)(c).
5 Halliday suggests (vol III, para 39-55) that tenants and others would themselves still be entitled to require a decision of court to authorise payment of rents etc to a person other than the proprietor. See *Tamroui v Clydesdale Bank plc* 1997 SLT (Sh Ct) 20.
6 *Halliday* vol III, para 39-62; *Gordon and Mitchell* para 20-201; *Cusine* para 8-36.
7 Under s 5 of the Heritable Securities (Scotland) Act 1894.
8 1970 Act, s 29(2).
9 1970 Act, s 29(2) repealed by Act of Sederunt (Amendment of Sheriff Court Ordinary Cause, Summary Cause and Small Claims Rules) 1990, SI 1990/661.

where the creditor applies to court for any remedies under standard condition 10 and no other remedy, he must proceed by summary application. If, in addition to standard condition 10 remedies, he craves ejection or another remedy, the whole application must be by way of ordinary action[1]. A prior creditor is entitled to take over possession from a creditor in possession with a right postponed to his and may object to an attempt by a postponed creditor to take possession[2].

(2)   POWERS ON ENTRY INTO POSSESSION

If possession has been taken by agreement with the debtor or proprietor, the powers of the creditor will be regulated by the agreement. If possession has been taken under the rights conferred on the creditor[3] on the debtor's failure to comply with a calling-up notice, the creditor will have all powers conferred by standard condition 10 being the right to recover or receive feuduties, ground annuals or rent[4]; the right to let the security subjects[5]; and the right to manage and maintain the subjects[6]. If possession is acquired by warrant issued by the court on default within the meaning of standard condition 9(1)(b) or (c) and application by the creditor under section 24, the creditor may exercise those powers which the warrant authorises him to exercise[7].

The extent to which the proprietor's obligations become incumbent upon the creditor on entry into possession was examined by the House of Lords in *David Watson Property Management v Woolwich Equitable Building Society*[8]. A firm of property managers sought recovery of arrears of common charges relating to a house which the owner had failed to pay. The sums were due before the heritable creditors had taken possession following the debtor's default. The sheriff and, on appeal, the sheriff principal held that section 20(5)(b) rendered the heritable creditor liable. The defenders appealed on the basis that section 20(5)(b) concerned only future obligations. The Inner House held that debts personal to the proprietor before the creditor's entry into possession did not transmit to the heritable creditor. To hold otherwise would mean that where the debtor and the proprietor were not the same person, a heritable creditor would have to pay debts personal to the proprietor which the creditor would then be unable to recover from the proceeds of sale. The House of Lords held that an obligation to maintain heritable property carried with it an obligation to pay for that maintenance. However, where the obligation to pay a particular sum for maintenance arose, that was a debt due by the

---

1 Note that *Halliday* vol III, para 39-63; Halliday *1970 Act* para 10-61; *Gordon and Mitchell* para 20-201; and 20 *Stair Memorial Encyclopaedia* para 216, all pre-date SI 1990/661 and therefore state the law prior to the repeal of s 29(2) of the 1970 Act.
2 *Skipton Building Society v Wain* 1986 SLT 96, OH.
3 1970 Act, s 20(1).
4 1970 Act, Sch 3, standard condition 10(3).
5 Standard condition 10(4), (5) and s 20(3), (4).
6 Standard condition 10(5) and s 20(5).
7 *Budge v Brown's Trustees* (1872) 10 M 958.
8 *David Watson Property Management v Woolwich Equitable Building Society* 1992 SC (HL) 21, 1992 SCLR 357, 1992 SLT 430, HL.

owner who was so at the time the work was carried out. The obligation to pay the unpaid debt of that owner was not transmitted[1] and indeed was not transmissible. To hold otherwise would be contrary to the doctrine that an obligation to pay an indefinite sum of money cannot be constituted a real burden or condition of the title binding singular successors to it[2].

(3) REPAIR, RECONSTRUCTION AND IMPROVEMENT

Standard condition 10(6) confers on the creditor, on default, the right to enter on the subjects at all reasonable times, without notice, to effect such repairs, alterations and improvement on the subjects as may be necessary to maintain their market value. This right may be exercised: on non-compliance with a calling-up notice[3]; on non-compliance with a default notice[4]; and on obtaining a warrant to exercise this remedy on application to the court under section 24. This remedy contemplates the situation in which the creditor does not intend to enter into possession but wishes, for example, to repair or alter the subjects in preparation for sale.

(4) FORECLOSURE

The right to apply for a decree of foreclosure[5] arises where the debtor has failed to comply with a calling-up notice[6] or where a person on whom notice of default has been served has failed to purge the default[7]. Since warrant to exercise any of the remedies which the creditor is entitled to exercise on the debtor's failure to comply with a calling-up notice can also be applied for under section 24[8], it would appear that the right to apply for a decree of foreclosure may also be acquired on application to the court under section 24. However, all of these provisions must be considered in conjunction with section 28(1). Section 28(1) provides that where a creditor in a standard security has exposed the security subjects for sale (at a public roup) at a price not exceeding the amount due under the security and under any security ranking prior to, or *pari passu* with, the security, and has failed to find a purchaser, or where, having so failed, he has succeeded in selling only a part of the subjects at a price which is less than the amount due, he may on the expiration of a period of two months from the date of the first exposure for sale, apply to the court for a decree of foreclosure[9].

---

1 Under s 20(5)(b) of the 1970 Act.
2 *Northern Rock Building Society v Wood* 1990 SLT (Sh Ct) 109; *Bank of Scotland v Community Charges Registration Officer for Central Region* 1991 SCLR 394.
3 1970 Act, s 20(1).
4 1970 Act, s 23(2).
5 To exercise the remedy provided in standard condition 10(7).
6 1970 Act, s 20(1).
7 1970 Act, s 23(2).
8 Where the debtor is in default within the meaning of standard condition 9(1)(b) or (c).
9 For full discussion, see *Halliday* vol III, paras 39-70 to 39-85; *Halliday 1970 Act* paras 10-71 to 10-86; *Gordon and Mitchell* paras 20-207 to 20-213; and *Cusine* paras 8.42 to 8.45.

7.   ASSIGNATION OF A STANDARD SECURITY

(1)   GENERAL

The creditor's right in the standard security may be transferred in whole or in part by assignation in conformity with either of the forms contained in Schedule 4 to the 1970 Act[1]. Form A is an assignation by separate instrument, and Form B an assignation by indorsement on the standard security. Recording of the assignation vests the security or that part assigned in the assignee 'as effectually as if the security or that part had been granted in his favour'[1]. An assignation therefore preserves the benefit of ranking. Unless otherwise stated in the instrument, an assignation conveys all rights competent to the grantor and vests in the assignee: the full benefit of all related corroborative or substituted obligations for the debt; the right to recover payment from the debtor of all expenses properly incurred by the creditor in connection with the security; and the benefit of all notices served and procedures instituted in respect of the security[2].

Nothing is said in the 1970 Act about assignation of the personal obligation. Where the personal obligation is contained in the standard security, it will be carried by assignation of the security. Where the personal obligation is separately constituted, it would appear that it must be separately assigned and the assignation intimated to the debtor to complete the assignee's right[3]. Where a loan has been re-arranged, the new creditor will have to decide whether to take an assignation or a new standard security. The benefits of an assignation are the retention of the ranking of the original creditor and that assignation is a less expensive process than creation of a new security. The disadvantages are noted by Halliday[4] as follows:

(1) the liability upon the assignor of warranting the validity of the security and existence of the debt[5];
(2) the risk that the debt has been wholly or partially repaid — such repayments will not appear on the record and if the debt has been wholly repaid then the assignation will be void[6]; and
(3) a bond of corroboration by the owner of the security subjects will be necessary if the owner was not the grantor of the security and the personal obligation has not transmitted against him.

(2)   AMOUNT SECURED BY THE ASSIGNED SECURITY

Where the standard security has been granted for a maximum or uncertain amount, it can only be assigned to the extent of the sum outstanding

---

1 1970 Act, s 14(1).
2 1970 Act, s 14(2).
3 *Halliday* vol III, paras 40-14; Halliday *1970 Act* para 9-02; *Gordon and Mitchell* para 10-153.
4 *Halliday* vol III, paras 40-17.
5 *Reid v Barclay* (1879) 6 R 1007; J Burns *Conveyancing Practice* (4th edn, 1957 by F MacRitchie) pp 556–557.
6 *Jackson v Nicoll* (1870) 8 M 408.

at the time of the assignation. The amount outstanding should be stated in the assignation[1]. Where the standard security is for a fluctuating amount, Halliday suggests that an assignation is undesirable since it will not cover future advances:

> 'The personal obligation of the debtor will have been created in favour of the original creditor and will have covered sums due to him by the debtor: after assignation of the standard security there will normally be no further course of dealing between these parties. So if any further advances are to be made by the assignee and are to be covered by the security, then (a) if the personal obligation was contained in the original standard security either a recorded variation or a new standard security will be necessary to secure the further advance or (b) if the personal obligation was contained in a separate instrument or an unrecorded instrument it will be necessary to constitute the new personal obligation for the further advances or a new standard security may be granted in respect of them. In practice it will probably be simpler and clearer to discharge the existing standard security and have a new comprehensive standard security'[2].

8. TRANSMISSION OF THE RIGHTS AND OBLIGATIONS OF A STANDARD SECURITY

(1) CREDITOR'S SUCCESSION

A standard security is moveable in the creditor's succession but remains heritable for purposes of legal rights[3]. Completion of title by an executor or beneficiary is regulated by the provisions of the conveyancing statutes applicable to bonds and dispositions in security and which are made applicable to standard securities by virtue of section 32 of the 1970 Act[4].

(2) DEBTOR'S SUCCESSION

A standard security is a heritable debt which must be satisfied from the debtor's general estate (or, more usually, from the proceeds of any insurance policy assigned to the creditor). The debtor's successors will be personally liable only to the extent of any estate received.

Where a successor has become liable for the debt, summary diligence will be competent against him only if an agreement to that effect has been executed by him[5].

---

1 1970 Act, Sch 4, Note 2; *Halliday* vol III, para 40-15.
2 *Halliday* vol III, para 40-19. The same passage appears at Halliday *1970 Act* para 9-07.
3 Titles to Land Consolidation (Scotland) Act 1868, s 117 (amended by the Succession (Scotland) Act 1964, s 34(2), Sch 3).
4 For details of completion of title, see *Halliday* vol III, paras 40-36 to 40-40; Halliday *1970 Act* paras 9-23 to 9-48; *Cusine* para 6.20.
5 Conveyancing (Scotland) Act 1924, s 15(2).

(3)   SALE BY DEBTOR

Where the debtor transfers property in sale under burden of the security, the personal obligation, even if contained in the security, will not transmit against the new owner unless there is an agreement to that effect in the disposition[1]. A form of agreement for transmission of the obligation is provided at Form 2 of Schedule A to the Conveyancing (Scotland) Act 1924. A new personal obligation may, alternatively, be created by bond of corroboration granted by the new owner[2].

(4)   SEQUESTRATION OF DEBTOR

Under section 31(1) of the Bankruptcy (Scotland) Act 1985, subject to section 33 of the Act, the whole estate of the debtor vests at the date sequestration in the permanent trustee for the benefit of the creditors by virtue of the act and warrant issued on confirmation of the permanent trustee's appointment. The act and warrant has, in respect of the heritable estate in Scotland of the debtor, the same effect as if a decree of adjudication in implement of sale, as well as a decree of adjudication for payment and in security of debt, subject to no legal reversion, had been pronounced in favour of the permanent trustee[3]. This provision simply means that the trustee acquires title to the debtor' heritable property and that the debtor loses his right of redemption.

If, at the date of sequestration, the debtor had not completed title to the heritable property, completion of title in the name of the debtor does not validate by accretion any unperfected right in favour of any person other than the permanent trustee[4]. Any property which the debtor held on trust for any other person will not vest in the trustee in sequestration[5].

The vesting of the debtor's property in the permanent trustee is without prejudice to the right of any secured creditor preferential to the right of the trustee[6]. Standard securities completed by recording or registration before sequestration will therefore retain their preference in ranking. Subject to the conditions stated in section 39(4), the trustee in sequestration is given power to sell property forming part of the debtor's personal estate by public roup or by private bargain[7]. Where the permanent trustee wishes to sell heritable estate over which any creditor has a duly recorded prior heritable security[8]:

---

1 In accordance with the Conveyancing (Scotland) Act 1874, s 47 (amended by the Conveyancing (Scotland) Act 1924, s 15(1) and the Succession (Scotland) Act 1964, s 34(2), Sch 3).
2 Halliday recommends (although without explaining why) that where the security is for an uncertain or fluctuating amount, the standard security be discharged and a new one granted: *Halliday* vol III, para 40-42; Halliday *1970 Act* para 9-29.
3 Bankruptcy (Scotland) Act 1985, s 31(1)(b).
4 1985 Act, s 31(3).
5 Under s 33(1)(b) of the 1985 Act.
6 1985 Act, s 33(3).
7 1985 Act, s 39(3).
8 1985 Act, s 39(4).

(1) the permanent trustee may sell only with the concurrence of every such creditor unless he obtains a sufficiently high price to discharge every such security;

(2) (a) the creditor may not take steps to enforce his security after the permanent trustee has intimated to him that he intends to sell the property which is subject to that security;

    (b) the permanent trustee may not commence procedure for sale after the creditor has intimated to him that he intends to commence the procedure for its sale;

(3) where either the trustee or the creditor has intimated that he intends to sell the property but has unduly delayed in proceeding with the sale, then the party to whom intimation has been given may proceed to sell the property or, if he is the creditor, enforce his security over it.

The validity of the purchaser's title is not challengeable on grounds of failure to comply with these provisions[1].

(5) LIQUIDATION OF DEBTOR

On the winding up of a company, the court may, on application of the liquidator, direct that all or part of the property belonging to the company or held by trustees on its behalf is to vest in the liquidator[2]. The liquidator therefore requires a vesting order before the company property is vested in him. On commencement of winding up, the liquidator's powers of realisation of company property are the same as those conferred on a trustee in sequestration and are subject to the same provisions in relation to the rights of prior heritable creditors[3].

(6) RECEIVERSHIP

On the appointment of a receiver, the floating charge by virtue of which he is appointed attaches to the property then subject to the charge as if the charge was a fixed security over the property to which it has attached[4]. It does so, however, subject, inter alia, to the rights of any person holding a fixed (standard) security over the property or any part of it ranking in priority to the floating charge[5]. In the absence of an express ranking agreement, a standard security will rank in priority to the floating charge if it has been 'constituted as a real right' (by recording in the Register of Sasines or registration in the Land Register) before creation of the floating charge[6].

---

1 1985 Act, s 39.
2 Insolvency Act 1986, s 145(1).
3 1986 Act, s 185.
4 1986 Act, s 53(7).
5 Companies Act 1985, s 463(1)(b).
6 Companies Act 1985, ss 464(3), (4)(b); *AIB Finance Ltd v Bank of Scotland* 1993 SC 588, 1993 SCLR 851, 1995 SLT 2; see pp 341, 342.

A receiver has, in relation to such part of the property of the company as is attached by the floating charge by virtue of which he was appointed, the power, if any, given to him in the instrument creating the floating charge[1]. The receiver also has in relation to the property attached the powers listed in Schedule 2 to the Act in so far as these are not inconsistent with the provisions of the charge[2]. These powers include the power to sell or otherwise dispose of the property by public roup or private bargain with or without advertisement[3].

The exercise of these powers is, however, subject to the rights of any person who holds over all or any part of the property of the company fixed security or a floating charge having priority over, or ranking *pari passu* with, the floating charge by virtue of which the receiver was appointed[4]. Where a receiver wishes to sell or dispose of any of the attached property which is subject to any security which ranks prior to, or *pari passu* with, or is postponed to the floating charge, and the receiver is unable to obtain the consent of the prior, *pari passu* or postponed creditor the receiver may apply to the court for authority to sell or dispose of the property free of the creditor's security[5]. The court has discretion whether to authorise such sale free of the security and may impose on the sale such terms and conditions as it thinks fit[6]. In the case of an application where a fixed security over the property or interest in question which ranks prior to the floating charge has not been met or provided for in full, the court shall not authorise the sale or disposal unless it is satisfied that the sale would be likely to provide a more advantageous realisation of the company's assets than would otherwise be effected[7]. Such authorisation may only be given on condition that the net proceeds of the disposal be applied towards discharging the sums secured by the fixed security[8]. Recording of the conveyance granted by the receiver in implement of sale authorised by the court[9] has the effect of disburdening the property of the security affecting it[10].

(7)   ADMINISTRATION ORDERS

Where an application to the court for an administration order in relation to a company has been made under section 9 of the Insolvency Act 1986, during the period beginning with the presentation of the application and ending with the making of such an order or the dismissal of the application, a creditor having security over property of the company may take no steps to enforce his security without leave of the court[11]. On appointment,

1 Under s 55(1) of the Insolvency Act 1986.
2 Under s 55(2) of the 1986 Act.
3 1986 Act, Sch 2, para 2.
4 1986 Act, s 55(3)(b).
5 1986 Act, s 61(1).
6 1986 Act, s 61(2).
7 1986 Act, s 61(3).
8 1986 Act, s 61(4).
9 1986 Act, s 61(2).
10 1986 Act, s 61(8).
11 1986 Act, s 10.

the administrator may dispose of or otherwise exercise his powers in relation to any property of the company which is subject to a floating charge as if the property were not subject to the security[1]. Where the property is subject to a fixed charge, however, the administrator requires the authority of the court to dispose of the property free of the security[2]. The net proceeds of such sale must be applied towards discharge of the sums secured by the fixed security[3]. Recording of a disposition granted by an administrator[4] disburdens the property of the security[5].

9. RESTRICTION OF A STANDARD SECURITY

A recorded standard security may subsequently be restricted to part of the interest in land over which the debt was originally secured. The form of deed of restriction is prescribed by section 15 of the 1970 Act and Forms C and D of Schedule 4. Form D is used where a partial discharge of the debt is to be combined with the deed of restriction. Upon recording of the deed of restriction, the interest in land is disburdened of the security to the extent specified in the deed[6]. The deed of restriction may be included in a disposition of the subjects thereby disburdened[7].

10. VARIATION OF STANDARD SECURITY

Section 16 of the 1970 Act introduced a method of varying the terms of a recorded standard security (including any variable standard condition). However, this method may not be used to effect any variation which may appropriately be effected by an assignation, discharge or restriction of the standard security or which involves an addition to or an extension of the interest in land mentioned in the security[8]. In the case of addition to or extension of the interest in land, a new security will be required[9]. A variation effected[10] may be indorsed on the standard security in conformity with Form E of Schedule 4 or may be contained in separate deed 'in a form appropriate for that purpose'. Where the variation is to a provision included in the recorded security, the variation must likewise be recorded. Where the variation is to an unrecorded personal obligation or other pro-

---

1 1986 Act, s 15(1), (3).
2 1986 Act, s 15(2), (3).
3 1986 Act, s 15(5).
4 Under the powers in s 15 of the 1986 Act.
5 1986 Act, s 16.
6 1970 Act, s 15(1).
7 For further details, see *Halliday* vol III, paras 40-44 to 40-49; Halliday *1970 Act* paras 9-32 to 9-37.
8 1970 Act, s 16(1).
9 Halliday *1970 Act* para 9-38.
10 Under s 16 of the 1970 Act.

vision (including any variable standard condition) which has not been recorded, the variation may be effected by any deed appropriate for that purpose and need not be recorded[1].

11.   REDEMPTION

Section 18 of the 1970 Act[2] provides that the debtor in a standard security or, where the debtor is not the proprietor, the proprietor of the security subjects, is entitled to redeem the security on giving two months' notice of his intention so to do in conformity with the terms of standard condition 11 and the appropriate forms in Schedule 5[3]. Here, as elsewhere in the Act, the term 'debtor' includes successors in title, assignees or representatives of the debtor[4]. The existence of a right of redemption is subject to any agreement to the contrary, although any such agreement is, in turn, subject to section 11 of the Land Tenure Reform (Scotland) Act 1974 which limits to twenty years the period during which a standard security over private dwelling house may be irredeemable[5]. Once a standard security becomes redeemable, however, it is then exercisable in conformity with standard condition 11 and the forms in Schedule 5. Standard condition 11 is, by virtue of section 11(3), a non-variable condition, but standard condition 11(2) states that nothing in the Act precludes the creditor from waiving the necessity for a notice of redemption or from agreeing to a period of notice of less than the two months to which he is entitled under section 18(1). Furthermore[6], a debtor who has failed to comply with notice of default may, at any time before completion of sale of the subjects by the creditor, redeem the security without giving notice[7].

The procedure for serving notice of redemption on the creditor is set out in standard condition 11(3). Standard condition 11(5) provides that where the debtor exercises this right and has paid the whole amount due under the contract to which the security relates, the creditor must grant a discharge in the terms prescribed in section 17 of the Act. Where the debtor is unable to obtain discharge by this procedure, provision is made[8] for

1   1970 Act, s 16(2). For further details, see *Halliday* vol III, paras 40-01 to 40-12; Halliday *1970 Act* paras 9-38 to 9-49; *Gordon and Mitchell* paras 20-161 to 20-163.
2   1970 Act, s 18 (amended by the Redemption of Standard Securities (Scotland) Act 1971, s 1, and the Land Tenure Reform (Scotland) Act 1974, s 11(6)).
3   1970 Act, s 18(1).
4   1970 Act, s 30(1).
5   1970 Act, s 18(1A) (added by the 1971 Act, s 1(c), and amended by the 1974 Act, s 11(6)).
6   Under s 23(3) of the 1970 Act.
7   Note, in this context, the decision in *Forbes v Armstrong* 1993 SCLR 204, 1994 SLT 199, OH. Although s 23(3) of the 1970 Act expressly confers a right to redeem on the debtor who has failed to comply with a notice of default, but is silent as to whether a similar right exists where a calling-up notice has not been complied with, the general right of redemption under s 18 is not fettered by service of a calling-up notice. A debtor may therefore give the requisite 2 months' notice of his intention to redeem, even though the creditor is proceeding to sell the subjects.
8   See 1970 Act, s 18(2)–(4).

redemption of the security by consignation of the whole amount due in any bank in Scotland. The debtor may then obtain declarator from the court that the obligations under the contract to which the security relates have been performed and may record an appropriate form[1] to disburden the security subjects[2].

Section 26(2) confers on the creditor who has effected a sale of the property subject to a prior security the like right as the debtor to redeem the security. The postponed creditor who sells the subjects is therefore entitled, on redemption of the prior security, to a discharge in accordance with standard condition 11(5) and in the terms prescribed in section 17 of the Act. In relation to a bond and disposition in security, by general law a postponed bondholder is entitled to redeem a prior security and the prior creditor must accept payment and grant discharge[3]. In *Reis v Mackay*[4], it was held that even where the postponed bondholder was not selling the subjects, he had a right to redeem the prior security and a right to demand either a discharge or an assignation of the prior security[5].

12. DISCHARGE

Section 17 of the 1970 Act provides that a duly recorded standard security may be discharged and the interest in land disburdened of the security in whole or in part by a discharge in conformity with Form F in Schedule 4[6] duly recorded or followed by the appropriate entry in the Land Register. Form F allows the discharge to be by separate deed or by indorsement on the standard security. Any ancillary or cautionary obligations for payment of the amount due under the security and any collateral security given for the obligations of the debtor will fall when the principal obligation of the debtor is extinguished by payment or discharge[7].

1 1970 Act, Sch 5, Form D.
2 1970 Act, s 18(3).
3 *Adair's Trustee v Rankin* (1895) 22 R 975.
4 (1899) 6 SLT 331, OH.
5 *Gordon and Mitchell* suggest (at para 20-164) that the same rules would apply in a standard security. For further details, see *Halliday* vol III, paras 40-50 to 40-62; Halliday *1970 Act* paras 9-60 to 9-72.
6 1970 Act, s 17 (amended by the Land Registration (Scotland) Act 1979, s 29(2)).
7 See *Halliday* vol III, paras 40-63 to 40-72; Halliday *1970 Act* paras 9-50 to 9-59.

Appendix 1

Bank of Scotland Code of Banking Practice (Second Edition, June 1994)

PREFACE TO THE SECOND EDITION

Bank of Scotland's Code sets out the standards of good banking practice to be observed by the Bank in the United Kingdom.

This is the Second Edition of the Bank's Code which has been prepared following a review of submissions from Government Departments, consumer and other organisations, the Banking Ombudsman and members of the public.

It is effective from 1st June 1994 and another revision will be completed by March 1997. [*Note:* at the time of going to press, the 1997 revision was not available.]

The Bank's Code meets with the standards required by the British Bankers' Association.

TABLE OF CONTENTS

Introduction

PART A – GOVERNING PRINCIPLES

PART B – BANKING SERVICES

PART C – CARD SERVICES

15.   Opening an Account
16.   Terms and Conditions
17.   Issue of Cards
18.   Security of Cards
19.   Lost or Stolen Cards
20.   Liability for Loss
21.   Records
22.   Handling Customers' Complaints

INTRODUCTION

The Bank's slogans **'A Friend for Life'** and **'Partners in Business'** are intended to convey its desire to establish with its customers a long term, constructive relationship.

To make clear its intent, the Bank decided to issue its own Code in 1992. This adopted concepts of good banking practice beyond those required by *'Good Banking'*, the Code which was issued by the British Bankers' Association.

The publication of a Second Edition has again provided the Bank with the opportunity to adopt additional new standards of good banking practice.

Unless it is stated otherwise, **the Bank's Code will apply to dealings with all personal, business and corporate customers in the United Kingdom.**

The Bank's Code does not apply to the Bank's subsidiaries which will comply with the Codes of Practice applicable to their respective businesses.

For clarification of any of the terms used in the Bank's Code customers might wish to refer to the Glossary, which is available on request at any of the Bank's branches.

The Bank's Code is in three parts:

PART A – GOVERNING PRINCIPLES

PART B – BANKING SERVICES

This applies to banking services provided by the Bank such as cheque accounts, savings accounts, overdrafts, loans and various other services.

PART C – CARD SERVICES

This applies to financial services provided by the Bank by means of Credit Cards, Charge Cards and Debit Cards.

PART A – GOVERNING PRINCIPLES

1. Governing Principles

1.1 The governing principles of the Bank's Code are:

- to set out the standards of good banking practice which the Bank will follow in its dealings with its customers;
- to emphasise that the Bank will act fairly and reasonably in all its dealings with its customers;
- to help customers understand banking services and how their accounts operate; and
- to maintain confidence in the security and integrity of the banking and card payment systems – the Bank recognises that its systems and technology need to be reliable.

1.2 Although, in legal terms, the Bank's Code is not a contract, in most instances the Bank is prepared to operate as if it is.

1.3 The Bank will comply with all relevant legislation, judicial decisions and codes of conduct or similar documents which are observed by members of the British Bankers' Association.

1.4 Throughout the Bank, there are management officials who have been specifically trained for different categories of business – and are so identified by their titles. The Bank is committed to the principle of permitting only appropriately trained and clearly identified officials to provide customers with selected types of advice.

PART B – BANKING SERVICES

2. Relationship with Customers

2.1 In serving customers' needs:

- the Bank considers it to be of the utmost importance to 'know its customer' – for a sound banking relationship to exist, customers must help the Bank to help them;
- the Bank recognises that certain customers have special needs – for example, disabled customers. Details of the Bank's initiatives to assist such customers are available at any branch of the Bank.

2.2 In working closer with customers:

- the Bank is committed to providing customers with as easy access to accounts as is possible. Many services function on a 24-hour, 7-days-a-week basis. To obtain such access, customers can subscribe to *'Phoneline'* or to *'HOBS'*, the Bank's Home and Office Banking Service or to Centrebank division's *'Telephone Banking'* – details of which are available in all of the Bank's branches;
- the Bank wants to help customers to understand technical or legal terminology. As a step towards this, the Bank has published an extensive Glossary explaining some common banking terms and practices;
- the Bank will provide information and guidance to customers about any specific banking product or service at any time on request and at the time when an account is opened. This information will also be available to customers in all of the Bank's branches.

3.   Opening an Account and Customer Identification

3.1   The Bank is required by law to satisfy itself about the identity of a person seeking to open an account. This is to assist in protecting its customers, members of the public and itself against fraud and other misuse of the banking system.

A good form of verification of identity is by way of personal introduction from a known and respected customer of the Bank.

As a result of national and international concerns about 'money laundering', the Bank may not allow funds paid into an account to be taken out until a customer's identity has been established to the Bank's satisfaction. However, this happens only in exceptional situations.

Customers will be required to complete the Bank's account opening forms. The Bank reserves the right to decline an application to open an account.

3.2   Personal Customers

Where appropriate, personal customers may be requested to establish their identity by providing at least one of:

- a current Passport
- a full UK Driving Licence
- an Employer's Identity Card.

If a customer is unable to produce any of the above items, a combination of alternative identification documents may be acceptable, for example:

- a Birth Certificate
- a Credit Card
- a National Health Card
- a Provisional Driving Licence
- a Student Union Card.

Customers may also be required to verify their address.

3.3   Corporate and business customers

In addition to providing copies of requested constitutional documents, these customers may be required to provide proof of identity of directors or office bearers of their organisations, as if they were personal customers.

4.   Terms and Conditions

4.1   The Bank will:

- ensure that all written terms and conditions of a banking service are expressed in plain language and provide a fair and balanced description of the relationship between the customer and the Bank;
- tell its customers how any variation of the terms and conditions will be notified and give its customers reasonable notice before any variation takes effect;
- issue to customers, if there are sufficient changes in a twelve month period to warrant it, a single document providing a consolidation of the variations made to the terms and conditions over that period;
- provide new customers with a written summary or explanation of the key features of the more common services that it provides. This will include an explanation, when accounts are held in the names of more than one customer, of the rights and responsibilities of each customer;
- not close customers' accounts without first giving reasonable notice; and
- help customers manage their accounts and check entries by providing them with regular statements of account. Except where this would be inappropriate to the nature of the account (eg passbooks are issued) this should be at no less

than 12 month intervals, but customers will be encouraged to order statements at shorter intervals.

4.2 If loan facilities are agreed by the Bank it will be made clear when these may become repayable.

4.3 If a customer requires to overdraw the balance available in an account **the Bank's agreement must be obtained**. If an overdraft facility is made available, it will be in accordance with 'normal banking practice'. This means that:

- all overdrafts are **repayable on demand**. However, where the Bank says that an overdraft is to be reviewed on a certain date, it will not change the terms or demand repayment of the facility before that date **unless** the Bank considers that:
  a) the terms of the facility have been breached; or
  b) the financial condition of its customer or of a guarantor has altered in any material way; or
  c) the facility was agreed on the basis of materially incorrect or incomplete information from the customer or a guarantor; or
  d) the basis upon which the facility was agreed by the Bank has altered in any material way;

- the Bank is not obliged to pay any cheque or meet any other payment which takes an overdraft beyond an agreed limit or creates an unauthorised overdraft. If it does so, that does not mean that a limit has been increased or agreed, nor that the Bank will agree to pay any other cheque or meet any other payment which would have the effect of exceeding the credit limit again.

5. Bank Charges and Debit Interest

5.1 The Bank will provide customers with details of the basis of charges, if any, payable in connection with the operation of their accounts. For basic account services, these will be in the form of published price lists which will be given or sent to customers using the particular services:

- when accounts are opened;
- at any time on request; and
- before new prices take effect.

New price lists will usually be sent with statements and at least one month's notice will be given before the new prices take effect.

Published price lists will be available in all branches of the Bank.

5.2 Charges for services not included in the published price lists will be advised on request or at the time the service is offered.

5.3 The Bank will tell customers the interest rates applicable to their accounts, the basis on which interest is calculated and when it will be charged to their accounts.

The Bank will specifically warn customers about the interest rates which may be charged when accounts are overdrawn (or exceed an agreed borrowing limit) without prior arrangement between the customer and the Bank.

5.4 The Bank was one of the first of the United Kingdom clearing banks to give advance notice to customers of the charges to be applied for the normal operation of their accounts (and how these are calculated).

The Bank is committed to extending its practice of pre-notification and will give 14 days advance notice of an interest payment which will be deducted from a current or savings account. This new practice will be implemented as soon as possible, but before 31st December 1996.

5.5   When the Bank changes its interest rates with immediate effect, it will publicise these changes by notices in its branches (if applicable), or in the press, or on statements.

6.   Credit Interest

6.1   The Bank will make freely available information about the rates of interest payable on interest-bearing accounts which it offers (whether or not these are open to new customers). This will be done by one or more of the following means:

- notices and/or leaflets in branches;
- press advertisements;
- personal notice;
- a telephone service.

6.2   The Bank will tell customers the interest rates applicable to their accounts, the basis on which interest is calculated and when it will be paid to their accounts. The Bank will explain also the basis on which it may vary interest rates.

6.3   When the Bank changes interest rates with immediate effect, it will publicise those changes by notices in its branches (if applicable), or in the press, or on statements.

7.   Complaints Procedure

7.1   In trying to provide the highest possible standard of service and facilities to its customers, the Bank realises that there may be occasions when it does not succeed.

An important part of the Bank's customer service policy is that all complaints which customers have about any banking service are thoroughly investigated.

For some services, which are specifically identified as having a guaranteed response time, where the Bank does not meet the publicised standard it will make a payment for inconvenience which may have been caused.

7.2   The Bank's procedures for handling customers' complaints are as follows:

i)   For a complaint relating to a service provided by one of the Bank's branches, there are three stages in the formal complaints procedure. These are:

- first, the customer should take up the grievance by letter, by telephone or in person, with the Senior Manager of the branch where the complaint arose;
- secondly, if a satisfactory response is not received, then the customer should write to the Regional Manager responsible for that branch; and
- failing satisfaction at Regional Manager level, the matter should then be referred to the General Manager with ultimate responsibility for the particular branch.

The name and address of the Senior Manager, Regional Manager and General Manager responsible for a particular branch of the Bank will be displayed in that branch.

ii)   For a complaint relating to a service provided by a department of the Bank, there are two stages in the formal complaints procedure. These are:

- first, the customer should contact the Senior Manager of the department where the complaint arose; and

- secondly, if the complaint has not been resolved satisfactorily, the matter should be referred to the General Manager with ultimate responsibility for the particular department.

At every stage, immediate action will be taken to investigate the complaint and to respond as soon as possible.

7.3 Banking Ombudsman Scheme – Personal and Small Business Customers only

In the event that a personal or small business customer is still not satisfied after following this procedure, he or she then may be able to apply to the Banking Ombudsman to assist.

The Bank is a member of the Banking Ombudsman Scheme and is bound by any decision which the Banking Ombudsman, acting within his or her powers, may make. In specified circumstances where a decision by the Banking Ombudsman involves a point of law, the Banks may submit the matter to a Court to be decided, in accordance with the terms of the Scheme.

Customers are not bound by the Ombudsman's decision and may submit the matter to a Court to be decided.

The Banking Ombudsman is not empowered to consider all disputes. For example, the Banking Ombudsman cannot deal with a dispute concerning a situation where the Bank has exercised its commercial judgement about lending or security; nor any complaint relating to the Bank's interest rate policies.

Details on how to make an application and leaflets explaining the procedures and who may refer to the Ombudsman are available at all branches of the Bank.

The Banking Ombudsman's address is:

70 Gray's Inn Road,
London WC1X 8NB
Telephone Number: 0171-404 9944
Fax Number 0171-405 5052

8. Confidentiality of Customer Information

8.1 The Bank observes a strict duty of confidentiality about its customers' (and former customers') financial affairs. The Bank will not disclose details of customers' accounts or their names and addresses to any third party (including the Bank's subsidiaries) except in the four exceptional cases permitted by law; namely where:

- the Bank is legally compelled to do so;
- there is a duty to the public to disclose;
- the interests of the Bank require disclosure; or
- disclosure is made at the request, or with the consent, of the customer.

8.2 The Bank will not say that its own interests justify passing details of customers' account or their names and addresses to any third party (including any of the Bank's subsidiaries) for marketing purposes.

8.3 The Bank will give customers 28 days notice if it intends to disclose to Credit Reference Agencies information on undisputed personal debts which are in default and where no satisfactory proposals have been received following formal demand.

The Bank will inform customers that, where it has acquired the legal right to sell mortgaged or charged property, this information may be disclosed to Credit Reference Agencies.

Any other disclosure to Credit Reference Agencies shall be with the customer's consent.

8.4   The Bank will comply at all times with the terms of the Data Protection Act when obtaining and processing data relating to personal customers.

8.5   The Bank's personal customers have the right of access under the Data Protection Act 1984 to their personal records held on the Bank's computer files.

9.   Status Enquiries (Bankers' References)

9.1   The Bank will provide a status enquiry, or banker's reference, on a customer only if that customer consents in writing. A copy of the reply will be available at request.

9.2   Once a customer has consented, a reply will be sent to an enquirer *direct* – not to the enquirer's bank. The Bank is committed to using plain language in the replies which are issued.

9.3   By arrangement, the Bank will assist customers in seeking status enquiries on third parties with whom a customer may deal.

10.   Marketing of Services

10.1   The Bank will:

- advise new customers at the time they open their accounts that they may choose not to receive marketing material; and
- remind customers, from time to time and at least once every 3 years, of their right to say that they do not wish to receive marketing material.

If so instructed by a customer, the Bank will not send marketing material to that customer.

10.2   The Bank will not:

- pass customers' names and addresses to any subsidiaries of the Bank for marketing purposes:
  - a) without express written consent held at the time or obtained immediately after; or
  - b) unless in response to a customer's specific request;
- make the provision of basic banking services conditional on customers giving such written consent. For this purpose 'basic banking services' includes the opening and the maintenance of accounts for money transmission by way of cheques and other debit instruments;
- use direct mail indiscriminately and, in particular, will exercise restraint and be selective:
  - a) where customers are minors; and
  - b) when marketing loans and overdrafts.

10.3   Where the Bank wishes to obtain the customer's agreement to disclosure of confidential information for marketing purposes, the reason will be disclosed and no pressure will be applied.

11.   Marketing and Provision of Credit

11.1   All lending is subject to appraisal by the Bank of the applicant's financial standing. This requirement is also stated in advertising and promotional material.

11.2 The Bank acts responsibly and prudently in marketing. All advertising complies with The British Code of Advertising Practice, The British Code of Sales Promotion Practice and other relevant Codes of Practice of similar standing. In particular, the Bank ensures that all advertising and promotional literature is fair and reasonable, does not contain misleading information and complies with all relevant legislation.

11.3 In considering whether or not to lend, the Bank will take account of information from various sources which may include:

- prior knowledge of the applicant's financial affairs gained from the Bank's past dealings;
- information obtained from Credit Reference Agencies;
- information supplied by the applicant;
- Credit Scoring;
- the applicant's age; and
- the applicant's ability to repay, with the aim of avoiding over-commitment.

11.4 Customers in financial difficulty should contact the Bank's branch or department concerned immediately a problem becomes likely or apparent. The Bank's officials will use their best endeavours to give practical information and advice and, subject to normal commercial judgement, will try to help.

12. Availability of Funds

12.1 Methods of paying in or withdrawing funds
Funds can be paid into or withdrawn from an account in many ways. The most frequent methods are by:

- paying in or withdrawing cash;
- issuing a cheque;
- a Standing Order arrangement;
- a Direct Debit instruction;
- a Debit Card (eg by using a '*Switch*' card to pay for goods or services);
- an electronic banking service (eg by '*HOBS*').

With the exception of cash, all these methods are not actually payments – they are payment instructions – and it takes time for the instruction to be carried out. So, a cheque is a payment instruction – it is not equivalent to cash until the cheque is 'cleared'.

12.2 Clearing Cheques
In order to 'clear' Sterling cheques amongst themselves, some of the UK banks operate 'clearing' systems in London and Edinburgh. Where both the paying and recipient banks' branches are in the same clearing system, the cheque is a 'single clearing' cheque. Where the branch of the paying bank is in Scotland and the branch of the recipient bank is in England or Wales (or vice versa) the cheque is a 'cross border' cheque.

There are banking systems and rules to achieve this clearing process. By these rules, if a cheque is not going to be paid by a bank's branch, then that branch must say so without delay. This system lets banks determine the normal timescale in which a cheque might be returned unpaid.

12.3 Effect of a cheque 'bouncing'
Very few cheques 'bounce' (ie are not paid). It is practice amongst the banks to assume that *all* cheques are paid when presented and the proceeds will be shown on the recipient's account as being credited at the close of the Business Day on

which the cheque is presented to the recipient's branch. So, if a cheque does 'bounce', this entry has to be reversed by debiting the recipient's account. In such a case the money has never actually been available, even although the bank had assumed that it would be.

Consequently, an account can be made overdrawn retrospectively. This occurs only if a payment is not completed in the normal way.

12.4   Withdrawing Funds
The terms and conditions applicable to some accounts may require notice for withdrawals or may set maximum or minimum limits for withdrawals. Normally the maximum amount which can be withdrawn from an account is the credit balance on the account, to the extent that the balance consists of 'cleared funds'.

However, the amount which can be withdrawn will be affected by:

● whether the Bank has agreed an overdraft;
● cheques 'bouncing' etc; and
● the Bank exercising its right of Offset.

Any funds paid into an account in cash count immediately towards the balance available for withdrawal.

Normally, the Bank will treat a cheque paid in as having 'cleared' and will allow the funds to be counted towards the balance available for withdrawal three Business Days after lodgement of a 'single clearing' cheque and four Business Days after lodgement of a 'cross border' cheque. However, cheques drawn and paid on the same branch of a bank are usually cleared overnight.

In special circumstances, by prior arrangement, funds may be counted towards the balance to be withdrawn before the cheque has cleared, or conversely a bank may decide not to allow funds to be withdrawn for a longer time until satisfied that the cheque has actually cleared (eg where the issuer's bank is located outside the United Kingdom).

12.5   Other Factors
There are a number of variable factors beyond a bank's control which affect how long it takes for a cheque which a customer has issued to be debited to his or her account. These factors include the time it takes the recipient of the cheque to pay it into a bank, whether presentation of a cheque for payment is to the same branch of a bank where the issuer's account is kept and postal delays.

12.6   Interest
The proceeds of a 'single clearing' cheque credited to a recipient's account are included for interest calculations after two Business Days and if it is a 'cross border' cheque after three Business Days.

12.7   Payment Date of a Standing Order/Direct Debit
Where a Standing Order or Direct Debit payment is due out of an account on a day that is not a Business Day, then the payment will be made on the *next* Business Day.

12.8   Other Methods of Payment
Payments may be effected by the service known as 'CHAPS'. This service – details of which are available on request – enables payments over a specific amount to be sent or be received by a bank, with the funds transferred by this method counting immediately in ascertaining the amount that can be withdrawn.

12.9   Stopping Payment or Countermand
If a customer wants to stop a payment instruction (which technically is known as 'Countermanding a payment') the following rules apply:

- payment made by a Direct Card, Credit Card or by using a 'same day' instruction on the Bank's electronic banking service (ie *'HOBS'*) **cannot be stopped**;
- a cheque can only be stopped by an instruction received by the Bank **prior to payment** by the Bank. Customers wishing to stop cheques should write to the Bank with detailed instructions. The Bank may accept verbal instructions but, to avoid misunderstanding, will request that these are also given in writing. Under the rules of the Cheque Guarantee Card Scheme, an instruction to stop a cheque which has been supported by a Cheque Guarantee Card can neither be given nor accepted by the Bank;
- Standing Orders and Direct Debits can be stopped by writing to the Bank before the next payment is due to be made. The cancellation of a Direct Debit or standing Order payment will be treated as an instruction to stop all future payments on that mandate, unless the Bank is otherwise instructed.

12.10   Arrestment and Attachments of Funds
Legally, in Scotland, a customer's right to withdraw funds from an account may be limited by an Arrestment or an Attachment of Funds. The Glossary explains what happens in such circumstances.

12.11   Injunctions and Garnishee Orders
Similarly, in England, a customer's right to withdraw funds from an account may be limited by a court Injunction or by Garnishee Order. The Glossary explains these terms.

12.12   Other Statutory Provisions
A customer's right to withdraw funds from an account may also be restricted by law (eg on Sequestration).

12.13   Out of Date Cheques
A bank may refuse to pay a cheque which is dated more than six months earlier than the date upon which it is presented for payment. In that case, the cheque should be returned to the issuer with the request to issue another cheque or redate it and initial the alteration.

13.   Foreign Exchange Services and Cross Border Payments

13.1   The Bank will provide customers with details of the exchange rate and the commission charges which will apply to foreign exchange transactions. When this is not possible at the time of the transaction, the basis on which they will be calculated will be provided.

13.2   The Bank will provide customers wishing to effect cross border payments with details of the services it offers. In doing so it will provide, as a minimum:

- a basic description of the appropriate services available and the manner in which they can be used;
- an indication of when money sent abroad on customers' instructions will usually arrive or, when an exact date cannot be given, the latest date by which the money might be expected to arrive; and
- the details of any commission or charges payable by customers to the Bank, including a warning where agents' charges may also be incurred.

14.   Guarantees and other types of Third Party Security

14.1   The Bank will advise private individuals proposing to give it a guarantee or any other security for another person's liabilities that:

- as a consequence of giving the guarantee or third party security, he or she might become liable instead of or as well as that other person; and
- he or she should seek independent legal advice before entering into the guarantee or third party security.

The guarantee and other third party security forms to be signed by private individuals will contain a clear and prominent notice to this effect.

14.2   Where a guarantee or third party security form to be signed by a private individual is intended to be relief upon by the Bank for an unlimited amount, the form will contain a clear and prominent notice to that effect and will include a statement as to how liability may be terminated as regards further borrowing.

14.3   In regard to guarantee, joint security and third party security transactions entered into by private individuals after 1st June 1994, the Bank will voluntarily adopt a procedure which is intended to offer protection to parties to guarantees and/or third party security who may be subjected to the undue influence of another.

14.4   In addition, the Bank will no longer seek nor accept guarantees or third party security for unlimited amounts from parties who may be subjected to such undue influence.

In all other cases, the Bank will clearly make known whether a guarantee or third party security is unlimited as to amount or, if this is not the case, what the limit of liability will be.

PART C – CARD SERVICES

15.   Opening an Account

15.1   Customers will be required to complete the Bank's applicable account opening forms.

15.2   The Bank is required by law to satisfy itself about the identity of a person seeking to open an account or to obtain a card, so as to assist in protecting customers, members of the public and itself against fraud and other misuse of the banking and card processing systems. The Bank will provide to prospective customers details of the identification needed.

15.3   The Bank reserves the right to decline an application to open an account.

16.   Terms and Conditions

16.1   The Bank will express the written terms and conditions of its card services in plain language and these terms and conditions will provide a fair and balanced description of its relationship with its customers.

16.2   Variation of the terms and conditions for use of cards will be notified to customers in accordance with applicable law and the terms and conditions pertaining to the cards concerned. Except for interest rate changes (which are dealt with in Section 16.4 below) customers will always be given reasonable notice before any variation takes effect – usually such notice will be sent with statements and changes will come into effect after one month's notice.

16.3   The Bank will issue to customers, if there are sufficient changes in a twelve month period to warrant it, a single document providing a consolidation of the variations made to the terms and conditions over that period, of a service used by that customer.

16.4 The Bank will publish changes to its Credit Card interest rates in its branches or in the press or in statements of account sent to Credit Cardholders or by all those methods when such changes are made with immediate effect.

16.5 The Bank will tell Credit Cardholders how frequently they will receive a statement of account for payment and the period within which payment should be made.

17. Issue of Cards

17.1 The Bank will issue cards to Cardholders only when it has been requested to do so in writing or to replace or renew cards that have already been issued.

17.2 The Bank will tell Cardholders if a card has more than one function. Details of the functions available on the Bank's cards are given in the Glossary. The Bank will comply with requests from customers not to issue a Personal Identification Number ('PIN') where they do not wish to use those functions operated by a PIN.

18. Security of Cards

18.1 The Bank will always issue PINs separately from cards and will advise PINs only to the applicable Cardholders. When requested, the Bank will retain a Debit Card at the customer's branch for collection.

18.2 It is the customer's responsibility to take care of his or her card and PIN in order to prevent fraud. Specifically, a Cardholder should:

- never allow anyone else to use his or her card and PIN;
- take all reasonable steps to keep his or her card safe and PIN secret at all times;
- never write a PIN down without making a reasonable attempt to disguise it;
- never write a PIN down in a way which can be deciphered by a 3rd party;
- never write a PIN down on a card or anything usually kept with it (even if the PIN is disguised);
- destroy all PIN advices promptly on receipt; and
- take reasonable care to shield from other persons' vision the keying of a PIN on Automated Telling Machines.

18.3 In the case of Debit Cards, the Bank will require Cardholders to acknowledge receipt of their PIN before the card is available for use for transactions where a PIN is required.

18.4 The Bank has systems which help identify unusual patterns of Payment Card use and is committed to finding more effective ways of identifying incidence of possible card misuse.

18.5 As part of its commitment to reduce unauthorised card use, the Bank has installed video cameras in selected branches to record transactions which take place. Customers are encouraged to contact the Bank for assistance if they think that an unauthorised transaction has occurred.

19. Lost or Stolen Cards

19.1 Cardholders must tell the Bank as soon as reasonably practicable should they find that:

- their card has been lost or stolen;
- someone else knows their PIN;
- their account includes an item which seems to be wrong.

19.2 The Bank's telephone contact number, to be used when a card is lost or stolen, is included in telephone directories. This contact will be available at any time of the day or night. The Bank will remind customers of this at regular intervals on their statements or by other means.

19.3 The Bank will act on telephone notification of a card being lost, stolen or possibly misused and may ask Cardholders to confirm in writing any details given by telephone.

19.4 The Bank accepts notification of loss or theft of a card from Card Notification Organisations.

19.5 On being advised of loss, theft or possible misuse of a card or that the PIN has become known to someone else, the Bank will take action to prevent further use of the card.

20.   Liability for Loss

20.1 The Bank will bear the full losses incurred:

- in the event of misuse of a card which has not been received by the Cardholder to whom it has been issued;
- for all transactions not authorised by the Cardholder of the relevant card, after the Bank has been told that the card has been lost or stolen or that someone else knows or may know the PIN (subject to Sections 20.4 and 20.5 below); or
- if faults have occurred in the machines, or other systems used, which cause customers to suffer direct loss.

20.2 The Bank's liability will be limited to those amounts wrongly charged to customers' accounts and any interest and charges on those amounts.

20.3 Customers' liability for transactions not authorised by a Cardholder will be limited to a maximum of £50 Sterling in the event of misuse before the Bank has been notified that the relevant card has been lost or stolen or that someone else knows the PIN (subject to Sections 20.4 and 20.5 below).

20.4 Customers may be held liable for *all* losses in cases of gross negligence.
   'Gross negligence' may be construed as including failure to comply with any of the requirements of Section 18.2, if such failures have caused those losses.
   Customers should always ensure that they and any other Cardholders follow the guidance above and contained in leaflets issued by the Bank from time to time which describe ways in which cards should be kept secure. In particular, Cardholders should never give their cards to anyone else or enable anyone else to gain possession of their cards.

20.5 If Cardholders act fraudulently, then they will be responsible for *all* losses.

20.6 In cases of disputed transactions, the burden of proving fraud or gross negligence or that a card has been received by a Cardholder, will lie with the Bank. In such cases, the Bank will except Cardholders to co-operate with any investigation by it or the Police.

21. Records

21.1 The Bank will provide customers with a written record, on their statement of account, of all payments and withdrawals made. In addition, in many cases, customers will be provided with an immediate written record.

21.2 Customers will also be informed that they should tell the Bank, as soon as reasonably practicable, if they receive a statement of account which includes an item that seems to be wrong.

22. Handling Customers' Complaints

22.1 The Bank has its own internal procedures for handling customers' complaints fairly and expeditiously.

22.2 The Bank's complaints procedure is set out in Section 7 of this Code.

22.3 The Bank will ensure that all its staff who deal directly with customers are aware of its internal complaints procedures and are able to help customers by giving correct information about them.

BANK OF SCOTLAND

Code of Practice to be observed by Clydesdale Bank in their relations with Personal Customers

CONTENTS

FOREWORD

One of the goals which Clydesdale Bank has set itself is to provide customer service of the highest quality on the way to becoming the pre-eminent Scottish Bank. In order to succeed, we must at all times recognise and respond to the individual needs of our customers and, with this in mind, I am pleased to present this Customer Charter.

We believe the information it contains and the commitments it makes will strengthen and develop a long and successful partnership between the Bank and our customers.

To ensure its continuing relevance as our customers' needs evolve, the Charter will be subject to regular review.

Any query which you may have will be dealt with promptly by the Bank's well trained, friendly and helpful staff. I am proud of our record for customer service and we are determined to build on the high standards staff have already achieved.

Sir David Nickson KBE DL
Chairman

1.0 INTRODUCTION

1.1 This Code sets out the standards of good banking practice to be observed by the Clydesdale Bank in our relations with personal customers in the United Kingdom. Individual customers will find the Code helpful in understanding how we are expected to behave in our relations with them. We will ensure that our staff are aware of the Code.

The Code first came into effect on 16 March 1992 and it was stated then that it would be reviewed from time to time. This second edition is issued in the light of the first review and it will be effective from 28 March 1994, except for paragraph 5.5.

The Code will continue to be reviewed from time to time and another revision will be completed by March 1997. [*Note:* At the time of going to press, the 1997 revision was not available.]

There is a glossary of banking terms at the end of the Code.

1.2 The Code has been written to promote good banking practice and meets the standards required by the second edition of the Code of Banking Practice of the British Bankers' Association (BBA). Specific services may have their own terms and conditions which will comply with the principles contained in the Code.

1.3 The Code is in three parts.

Part A – Governing Principles.

Part B – Banking Services. We offer personal customers banking services such as current accounts, deposits and other savings accounts, overdrafts and loans, and various other services.

Part C – Card Services. We provide financial services by means of cards.

PART A – GOVERNING PRINCIPLES

2.0 GOVERNING PRINCIPLES

2.1 The governing principles of the Code are:

(a) to set out the standards of good banking practice which we will follow in our dealings with you;

(b) that we will act fairly and reasonably in all our dealings with you;
(c) that we will help you to understand how your account(s) operate(s) and will seek to give you a good understanding of banking services;
(d) to maintain confidence in the security and integrity of banking and card payment systems. We recognise that our systems and technology need to be reliable to protect you and ourselves.

2.2 We will comply with all relevant legislation, judicial decisions and codes of conduct or similar documents which are observed by members of the BBA.

2.3 Under the Code we undertake to provide certain information to you. This will usually be at the time when an account is opened. Information will also be available to you from any of our Branches. We will provide additional information and guidance about specific services at any time on request.

2.4 In the event of an error made by us being identified it will be corrected immediately and any charges applied by us as a result of our error will be refunded in full without hesitation.

PART B – BANKING SERVICES

3.0   OPENING AN ACCOUNT

3.1 As required by law we will satisfy ourselves about the identity of a person seeking to open an account to assist in protecting you, members of the public and ourselves against fraud and other misuse of the banking system.

3.2 We will provide to prospective customers details of the identification needed. The main examples of recognised forms of identification are:

(a) current valid full passport;
(b) signed Employer Identity Card bearing a photograph and signature:
(c) Armed Forces Identity Card;
(d) Student Matriculation/Identity Card;
(e) full UK driving licence.

4.0   TERMS AND CONDITIONS

4.1 Written terms and conditions of a banking service will be expressed in plain language and will provide a fair and balanced description of the relationship between you and ourselves.

4.2 We will tell you how any variation of the terms and conditions will be notified. We will give you reasonable notice before any variation takes effect.

4.3 We will issue to you, if there are sufficient changes in a 12 month period to warrant it, a single document to provide a consolidation of the variations made to our terms and conditions over that period.

4.4 We will provide you with a written summary or explanation of the key features of the more common services we provide. This will include an explanation of the rights and responsibilities of each customer when accounts are held in the names of more than one customer.

4.5 We will not close your account without first giving reasonable notice.

4.6 To help you manage your accounts and check entries, we will provide you with regular statements of account. Except where this would be inappropriate to the nature of the account (eg where passbooks are issued) this will be at no less than 12 monthly intervals but you will be encouraged to request statements at shorter intervals.

5.0   CHARGES AND DEBIT INTEREST (PAYABLE BY CUSTOMERS)

5.1 We will provide you with details of the basis of charges, if any, payable in connection with the operation of your account(s). These will be in the form of published tariffs covering basic account services which will be given or sent to customers:

(a) when accounts are opened;
(b) at any time on request,

and be available in Branches.
   Details of any changes will also be given or sent to customers and be available in Branches before the changes are implemented.

5.2 Charges for services outside the tariff will be advised on request or at the time the service is offered.

5.3 We will give you 14 days' advance notice of the amount due to be deducted from your account in respect of charges for account activity that have accumulated during the charging period in accordance with our published tariffs.

5.4 The quarterly dates on which these charges will be passed against your accounts will be advised to you around August/September each year for the succeeding year.

5.5 We will introduce systems to come into effect by 31 December 1996 to ensure that we will give you no less than 14 days' notice of the amount to be deducted from your current account in respect of interest. In the interval we will disregard the charge to be applied to your account for any charging period if those were incurred solely as a result of the application of interest.

5.6 We will tell you the interest rate(s) applicable to your account(s), the basis on which interest is calculated and when it will be charged to your account(s). These will include the rates applicable when accounts are overdrawn without prior agreement or exceed the agreed borrowing limit. We will explain also the basis on which we may vary interest rates.

5.7 When we change interest rates with immediate effect we will effectively publicise the changes, for example by notices in our Branches, or in the press, or both.

6.0   CREDIT INTEREST (PAYABLE TO CUSTOMERS)

6.1 We will make information about the rates on interest bearing acounts which we offer (whether or not these are open to new customers) freely available and accessible to you by one or more effective means, for example:

(a) notices and/or leaflets in branches;
(b) press advertisements;

(c) personal notice;
(d) a branch/central telephone service.

6.2   We will tell you the interest rate(s) applicable to your account(s), the basis on which interest is calculated and when it will be paid to your account(s). We will explain also the basis on which we may vary interest rates.

6.3   When we change interest rates with immediate effect we will effectively publicise the changes, for example by notices in our Branches, or in the press, or both.

7.0   HANDLING CUSTOMERS' COMPLAINTS

7.1   We have procedures for the fair and expeditious handling of customers' complaints and our staff who deal directly with customers are aware of these procedures. If you wish to make a complaint a leaflet is available in our Branches explaining to you how to do so and what further steps are available if you believe that the complaint has not been dealt with satisfactorily either at Branch or more senior level within the Bank.

7.2   We belong to the Banking Ombudsman Scheme as stated in notices in our Branches where a leaflet is available giving details of the Scheme including how to apply to the Ombudsman to arbitrate on any matter in dispute.

8.0   CONFIDENTIALITY OF CUSTOMER INFORMATION

8.1   We will observe a strict duty of confidentiality about your affairs (both while you are a customer and after you cease to be a customer). We will not disclose details of your account(s) on your name and address to any third party, including other companies in the Clydesdale Bank Group, other than in the four exceptional cases permitted by law, namely:

(a) where we are legally compelled to do so;
(b) where there is a duty to the public to disclose;
(c) where our interests require disclosure;
(d) where disclosure is made at your request, or with your consent.

8.2   We will not use exception (c) above to justify the disclosure for marketing purposes of details of your account(s) or your name and address to any third party, including other companies within the Clydesdale Bank Group.

8.3   We will give customers at least 28 days' notice if we intend to disclose to Credit Reference Agencies information on undisputed personal debts which are in default and where no satisfactory proposals for repayment have been received following formal demand.

We will inform customers if we intend to disclose to Credit Reference Agencies that we have acquired the legal right to sell mortgaged or charged property.

Any other disclosure to Credit Reference Agencies shall be with your consent.

8.4   We will at all times comply with the Data Protection Act when obtaining and processing your data. You have the right of access under the Data Protection Act 1984 to your personal records held on computer files. Information on how to obtain this is available on request.

9.0 STATUS ENQUIRIES (BANKERS' REFERENCES)

9.1 (a) We provide bankers' references or bankers' opinions in reply to status enquiries made about our customers, provided we have their express consent.

(b) An explanation of how the system of status enquiries (bankers' references) works appears in the glossary at the end of the Code.

(c) Should you wish to know to whom references or opinions have been given we will be happy to let you have details.

10.0 MARKETING OF SERVICES

10.1 Except in response to your specific request we will not pass your name and address to other companies in the Clydesdale Bank Group for marketing purposes in the absence of your express written consent. We will not make the provision of basic banking services conditional on customers giving such written consent. For this purpose 'basic banking services' include the opening and the maintenance of accounts for money transmission by means of cheques and other debit instruments.

10.2 We will give you at the time you open your account(s) the opportunity to give instructions that you do not wish to receive marketing material.

10.3 We will remind you from time to time, and at least once every three years, of your right to give instructions at any time that you do not wish to receive marketing material.

10.4 We will not use direct mail indiscriminately and in particular will exercise restraint and be selective:

(a) where customers are minors; and
(b) when marketing loans and overdrafts.

11.0 MARKETING AND PROVISION OF CREDIT

11.1 In our advertising and promotional material we will tell you and potential customers that all lending will be subject to our appraisal of your financial standing.

11.2 We will act responsibly and prudently in marketing. All advertising will comply with the British Code of Advertising Practice. The British Code of Sales Promotion Practice, and other relevant Codes of Practice of similar standing.

In particular we will ensure that all advertising and promotional literature is fair and reasonable, does not contain misleading information and complies with all relevant legislation.

11.3 In considering whether or not to lend, we take account of information which may include:

- prior knowledge of your financial affairs gained from past dealings;
- information obtained from Credit Reference Agencies;
- information supplied by you;
- credit-scoring;
- your age; and,
- your ability to repay, with the aim of avoiding over-commitment.

11.4   We encourage you to let us know as soon as possible if you are in financial difficulty so that we can use our best endeavours to give you practical information and, subject to normal commercial judgement, try to help you.

12.0   AVAILABILITY OF FUNDS

12.1   We will provide you with details of how your account(s) operate(s). In the glossary at the end of the Code there is information about:

– how and when you may stop a cheque or countermand other types of payments;
– when funds can be withdrawn after a cheque or other payment has been credited to the account;
– out of date cheques.

13.0   FOREIGN EXCHANGE SERVICES

13.1   We will provide you with details of the exchange rate and the charges which will apply to foreign exchange transactions or, when this is not possible, the basis on which they will be calculated.

13.2   We will provide you with details of the services we offer to effect cross-border payments. In doing so, we will provide, as a minimum:

(a) a basic description of the appropriate services available and the manner in which they can be used;
(b) information as to when money sent abroad on your instructions will usually reach its destination or, when an exact date cannot be given, the latest date by which the money might be expected to arrive;
(c) the details of any commission or charges payable by you to us including a warning where agents' charges may also be incurred.

14.0   GUARANTEES AND OTHER TYPES OF THIRD PARTY SECURITY

14.1   If you propose to give us a guarantee or other security for another person's liabilities we will advise you:

(a) that by giving the guarantee or third party security you might become liable instead of or as well as that other person;
(b) whether the guarantee or third party security will be unlimited as to amount or, if this is not the case, what the limit of the liability will be;
(c) that you should seek independent legal advice before entering into the guarantee or third party security.

14.2   Guarantees and other third party security documentation will contain clear and prominent notice to the above effect.

PART C – CARD SERVICES

15.0   OPENING AN ACCOUNT

15.1   As required by law we will satisfy ourselves about the identity of a person seeking to open an account or to obtain a card to assist in protecting you, members of the public and ourselves against fraud and other misuse of the banking and card processing systems.

15.2 We will provide to prospective customers details of the identification needed eg bankers' references.

16.0 TERMS AND CONDITIONS

16.1 The written terms and conditions of a card service will be expressed in plain language and will provide a fair and balanced description of the relationship between you and us.

16.2 We will tell you how any variation of the terms and conditions will be notified. We will give you reasonable notice before any variation takes effect.

16.3 We will issue to you, if there are sufficient changes in a 12 month period to warrant it, a single document providing a consolidation of the variations made to our terms and conditions over that period.

16.4 We will publish changes to our credit card interest rates in our Branches or in the press or on the statement of account sent to you, or by all those methods when such changes are made with immediate effect.

16.5 We will tell you how frequently you will receive a demand for payment of sums due on your credit card account and the period within which payment should be made.

17.0 ISSUE OF CARDS

17.1 We will issue cards to you only when they have been requested in writing or to replace or renew cards that have already been issued.

17.2 We will tell you if a card issued by us has more than one function. We will comply with your request not to issue a Personal Identification Number (PIN) where you do not wish to use the functions operated by a PIN.

18.0 SECURITY OF CARDS

18.1 We will issue PINs separately from cards and will advise the PIN to you only.

18.2 We will tell you of your responsibility to take care of your card(s) and PINs in order to prevent fraud. We will emphasise to you that:

(a) you should not allow anyone else to use your card and PIN;
(b) you should take reasonable steps to keep the card safe and the PIN secret at all times;
(c) you should destroy any PIN advice promptly on receipt;
(d) you should never write the PIN on the card or on anything usually kept with it;
(e) you should never write the PIN down without making a reasonable attempt to disguise it;
(f) you should take reasonable care to shield the keying of your PIN on an ATM

(Automated Teller Machine/Cash Machine) or terminal at a bank counter from other people by use of your other hand or your body.

19.0   LOST CARDS

19.1   You should let us know as soon as reasonably practicable after you find that:

(a) your card has been lost or stolen;
(b) someone else knows your PIN.

19.2   We will tell you, and will remind you at regular intervals on your statement or by other means of the place and the telephone number where you can give the details of a lost or stolen card at any time of the day or night. We will arrange for that telephone number to be included in British Telecom phone books.

19.3   We will act on telephone notification but may also ask you to confirm in writing any details given by telephone.

19.4   We accept notification of loss or theft of a card from card notification organisations approved by us.

19.5   On being advised of a loss, theft or possible misuse of a card or that the PIN has or may have become known to someone else we will take action to prevent further use of the card.

20.0   LIABILITY FOR LOSS

20.1   We will bear the full losses incurred:

(a) in the event of misuse when you have not received the card;
(b) for all transactions not authorised by you after we have been told that the card has been lost or stolen or that someone else knows or may know the PIN (subject to 20.4 below);
(c) if faults have occurred in the machines, or other systems used, which cause you to suffer direct loss unless the fault was obvious or advised by a message or notice on display.

20.2   Our liability will be limited to those amounts wrongly charged to your account and any interest and/or service charge arising on those amounts.

20.3   Your liability for transactions not authorised by you will be limited to a maximum of £50 in the event of misuse before we have been notified that a card has been lost or stolen or that someone else knows or may know the PIN (subject to 20.4 below).

20.4   You will be held liable for all losses if you have acted fraudulently. You may be held liable for all losses if you have acted with gross negligence. Gross negligence may be construed as including failures to comply with any of the requirements of paragraphs 18.2 if such failures have caused those losses.

20.5   In cases of disputed transactions the burden of proving fraud or gross negligence or that a card has been received by you will lie with us. In such cases we will expect you to co-operate with us in our investigations.

21.0   RECORDS

21.1   To help you manage your account and check entries we will provide you with a written record on your statement of account of all payments and withdrawals made.

21.2 You should let us know as soon as reasonably practicable if you receive a statement of account that includes an item which seems to be wrong.

22.0 HANDLING CUSTOMERS' COMPLAINTS

22.1 We have procedures for the fair and expeditious handling of customers complaints and our staff who deal directly with customers are aware of these procedures. If you wish to make a complaint a leaflet is available in our Branches explaining to you how to do so and what further steps are available to you if you believe that the complaint has not been dealt with satisfactorily by us.

22.2 As a card issuer we belong to the Banking Ombudsman Scheme as stated in notices in our Branches where a leaflet is available giving details of the Scheme including how to apply to the Ombudsman to arbitrate on any matter in dispute.

GLOSSARY OF BANKING TERMS

This glossary explains the meaning of words and phrases. They are not precise legal or technical definitions.

Availability of Funds/Calculation of Interest

Cheques paid into an account are initially 'uncleared' and they may be returned unpaid by the bank on which they are drawn.
(a) If you pay cash into your account your statement will show the cash being credited to your account on the day of receipt by your branch and these funds will be available to draw on that day.

For interest purposes, value will be given to you on the day your account is credited.
(b) If you pay into your account cheques drawn on a branch of Clydesdale Bank or another UK bank your statement will show the funds being credited to your account on the day of receipt by your branch. However these funds may not be available for you to draw until the fourth business day after day of lodgment (eg cheques paid in on a Monday may not be available to draw until the Friday, except where there are any intervening Bank Holidays when availability will be delayed accordingly). This holding period is to allow time for, firstly, the cheques to be cleared (ie for your branch, or any other branch accepting your lodgment, to receive value from the branches on which the cheques are drawn) and, secondly, for any cheques being returned unpaid (ie bounced) to be received by your branch.

For interest purposes value for these cheques will normally be given to you on the third business day after day of lodgment. Where your lodgment contains 'single clearing' cheques only, value can be given after two business days. (A cheque is known as a 'single clearing' cheque where both the bank branch on which the cheque is drawn and the bank branch where it is paid in are in the same clearing system. Within the UK, Scotland has a separate clearing system from England and Wales.)

Any cheques which you have paid into your account and which are subsequently returned to your branch unpaid will be debited to your account and you will be advised accordingly.
(c) When you use another branch or bank to make a pay-in to your account by means of a Bank Giro Credit it may take two or three business days for the pay-in to reach your branch.

Bank Draft

A voucher similar to a cheque which is drawn by a bank on itself. These vouchers are issued as a service to customers who do not have a cheque book and/or require a bank-backed instrument to pay for goods and services.

Bank Giro Credit

A form available at branches of banks to enable payments of cash and/or cheques to be transferred to an account at another branch or bank. The transfer is made through the bank giro system which is a nationwide system for the remittance of credits.

Banking Ombudsman Scheme

The Ombudsman acts as an arbiter in respect of complaints made by customers against a bank when customers have been unable to resolve such complaints themselves with their bank.
Details are:
Office of the Banking Ombudsman
70 Gray's Inn Road
London WC1X 8NB
Tel. No. 0171-404 9944

Card Notification Organisations

Companies which will, at the request of a card holder, maintain a record of all the cards held by the card holder and notify card issuers of the loss or theft of those cards when so advised by the card holder.

Cards

A general term for any plastic card which may be used to pay for goods and services or to withdraw cash. A card may be used for more than one function.
Common examples are:
CREDIT CARD – a card which allows customers to buy on credit and to obtain cash advances. Customers receive regular statements and may pay the balance in full, or in part usually subject to a certain minimum, interest is payable on outstanding balances.
CHARGE CARD – similar to a Credit Card. It enables customers to pay for purchases, and in some cases to obtain cash advances. When the monthly statement is received the balance must be paid in full.
DEBIT CARD – a card, operating as a substitute for a cheque, that can be used to obtain cash or make a payment at a point of sale. The customer's account is normally debited for such a transaction two or three business days later.
BUDGET CARD – similar to a Credit Card but customers agree to pay a fixed amount into their card account each month.
CASH CARD – a card used to obtain cash and other services from an ATM (Automated Teller Machine/Cash Machine) or a terminal at a bank counter.
CHEQUE GUARANTEE CARD – a card issued by a bank which guarantees the payment of a cheque up to the amount shown on the card provided its conditions of use are followed.
EUROCHEQUE CARD – a specific cheque guarantee card which can be used either with special eurocheques to pay for goods or services, or by itself to withdraw cash from machines, in the UK and other countries.
MULTI-FUNCTION CARD – a card which combines two or more functions, for example, Debit Card, Cheque Guarantee Card and Cash Card (see separate definitions).

CHAPS-Clearing House Automated Payments System

An electronic payment transfer system which links banks in the UK. Funds are guaranteed for delivery to another bank on the same day.

Countermand (Stopped Payment)

An instruction from a customer to a bank to cancel or override a previous instruction to make a payment or transfer of funds. This is effected as follows:
(a) Cheques
You may stop payment of a cheque by giving your branch an instruction in writing, or by telephone followed promptly by written confirmation. Your branch will act on your instruction provided the cheque has not been paid before the instruction is received. You can not stop payment of a cheque which has been backed by a cheque guarantee card and which is within the guarantee limit of the card.
(b) Direct Debits
If you wish to cancel an authority for your branch to pay direct debits you must give your branch an instruction in writing, or by telephone followed promptly by written confirmation, and it would be prudent for you also to advise the originator of the direct debits. Your instruction will be implemented by your branch and any direct debit received by it after receipt of your instruction will not be paid. You can not place a stop on an individual direct debit except where you dispute the amount and/or date of a payment advised to you in an Advanced Notice issued under the terms of a variable direct debit authority; otherwise the whole direct debit authority must be cancelled.
(c) Standing Orders
You may cancel a standing order authority or stop the making of an individual payment by giving your branch an instruction in writing, or by telephone followed promptly by written confirmation. Your branch will act on your instruction in respect of any payment due to be debited to your account after receipt of your instruction.
(d) Bank Giro Credits
It may be possible to withdraw a payment made by you by a Bank Giro Credit during the course of the day in which it was lodged provided the branch is still in possession of the voucher.
(e) Payments by Card
Transactions instigated by use of your card at an ATM (Automated Teller Machine/Cash Machine) or at a point of sale terminal in a retail outlet can not be countermanded.
(f) Payments by Electronic Means
An instruction by you to effect a payment by electronic means eg by CHAPS (Clearing House Automated Payments System) can not be countermanded.

Credit Reference Agencies

Organisations licensed under the Consumer Credit Act 1974 to hold information about individuals. Banks may refer to these agencies to assist with various decisions, eg whether or not to open an account or to provide loans or grant credit.

Credit Scoring

A method of assessing risk, based on statistical analysis of previous lending experience and other factors: used, for example, to help in deciding whether a loan should be granted.

Cross-Border Payments

A payment in sterling or a foreign currency between the UK and another country.

Direct Debits

An arrangement by which, with a customer's authority, a company or other organisation (known as an originator) can claim regular payments direct from a customer's account. The amount can be fixed or variable and if variable the originator must advise the customer of any variation in advance – normally at least 14 days before the payment date.

Guarantee

An undertaking given by a person (the guarantor) promising to pay the debts of another person if that person fails to do so.

Personal Customers

A private individual who maintains an account (including a joint account with another private individual or an account held as an executor or trustee, but excluding the accounts of sole traders, clubs and societies) or who takes other services from a bank.

PIN-Personal Identification Number

A confidential number provided on a strictly confidential basis by a card issuer to a card holder. Use of this number by the customer will allow the card to be used either to withdraw cash from an ATM (Automated Teller Machine/Cash Machine) and a terminal at a bank counter or to authorise payment for goods or services in retail or other outlets, by means of a special terminal.

Published Tariff

A list of prices for basic account services provided by a bank.

Security

A word used to describe items of value such as houses, stocks and shares, life policies etc, pledged to lenders in support of borrowing. Under a secured loan the lender has the right to sell the security if the loan is not repaid.

A guarantee is also a form of security – see separate definition.

Standing Orders

An arrangement by which customers instruct their bank to make regular payments from their account to another account at a bank or building society.

Status Enquiries (Bankers' References)

An opinion as to a customer's ability to support or undertake a financial tranaction or commitment. It is given to the enquirer by a bank, on request, and subject to the express consent of the customer concerned.

These requests are normally received only where a customer has business dealings with another party who then seeks a reference. Replies are given only in general terms to the other party stating that the information is given in confidence for their private use only.

Third Party Security

Security provided by a person who is not the borrower.

Travellers Cheques

Specially printed cheques ordered by customers, mainly for use abroad, to obtain cash and pay for goods and services. These special cheques are available in fixed amounts in sterling and other currencies.

Unpaid Cheques

A cheque which is not paid, for one of a number of reasons, the most common of which are:
REFER TO DRAWER – this frequently means that there is not sufficient money in the drawer's account. The recipient of the cheque (the payee) should ask the person issuing the cheque (the drawer) why it has not been paid.
REFER TO DRAWER, PLEASE REPRESENT – similar to above but used when the bank expects money to be available to pay the cheque in the near future and therefore suggests it is presented again for payment.
POST-DATED – the cheque cannot be paid because its date is some time in the future.
OUT OF DATE – the cheque has not been paid because its date is too old, normally meaning more than six months ago.
EFFECTS NOT CLEARED – there is money in the account of the drawer of the cheque but not available as cleared balances, because it is not yet certain that cheques recently credited to the account will be paid.
WORDS AND FIGURES DIFFER – the amount of the cheque written in words is different from the amount written in numbers.
ORDERS NOT TO PAY/PAYMENT STOPPED – the issuer (drawer) of the cheque has instructed his or her bank not to pay the cheque, ie to stop payment.
SIGNATURE DIFFERS/SIGNATURE DOES NOT CONFORM TO SPECIMEN HELD – the signature on the cheque is different from that recorded by the bank.

Written Terms and Conditions

Those provisions governing a banking sevice which are produced in written form. They will be expressed in clear and straightforward language but the precise wording of some contracts must, of necessity, be in technical or legal language.

Clydesdale Bank PLC
30 St Vincent Place
Glasgow G1 2HL
March 1994

Appendix 2

The Ombudsman Scheme – Terms of Reference

These Terms of Reference have been adopted by the Board of the Office of the Banking Ombudsman in accordance with its Articles of Association. They include a number of amendments, some made with effect from 29 April 1988, and others with effect from 12 July 1989, 26 January 1993, 1 June 1993 and 10 May 1995. The exact terms of reference applicable to a particular complaint depend on the date of the events complained about.

Certain expressions used in this document are defined in paragraph 29 below.

THE OMBUDSMAN'S PRINCIPAL POWERS AND DUTIES

1. The Ombudsman's principal powers and duties will be:
   - to receive complaints relating to the provision within the United Kingdom of banking services by any Bank (ie a Member of the Office or a Designated Associate) to any individual;
   - subject to paragraphs 16, 17, 18 and 19, to consider such complaints and facilitate their satisfaction, settlement or withdrawal whether by agreement, by his making recommendations or awards, or by such other means as seem expedient.
2. The Ombudsman may give advice on the procedure for making a complaint to him. He shall not provide general information about Banks or banking services.

PROCEDURE

3. Subject to the other provisions of these Terms of Reference, the Ombudsman shall in his own discretion decide the procedure to be adopted by him in considering complaints. He shall also decide whether or not a complaint falls within the Terms of Reference, and in reaching this decision shall consider representations from the complainant and from the Bank named in the complaint. When requested, he shall give the reasons for his decision in writing.
4. The Ombudsman may reject and cease to consider a complaint without fully investigating it if it does not appear to him that there may have been both a breach of duty by the Bank named in the complaint and some loss, damage or inconvenience suffered by the complainant.
5. The Ombudsman
   (a) shall promptly produce to the Bank named in the complaint any waivers of the kind referred to in paragraph 19(h) received by the Ombudsman;
   (b) may require a Bank named in the complaint to provide any information relating to the subject matter of the complaint which is, or is alleged to be, in its possession. If the Bank possesses such information, it shall as soon as is reasonably practicable disclose it to the Ombudsman (unless the Bank certified to the Ombudsman that the disclosure of such information would

place the Bank in breach of its duty of confidentiality to a third party whose consent it had used its best endeavours to obtain).

6. If any party to a complaint supplies information to the Ombudsman and requests that he treat it as confidential, the Ombudsman shall not disclose that information to any other party to the complaint or any other person, except with the consent of the first-mentioned party.

7. The Ombudsman may take account of a Bank's security measures of which he has knowledge notwithstanding that no disclosure of those measures has been or will be made to the complainant.

8. Notwithstanding paragraph 14 the Ombudsman shall not be bound by any legal rule of evidence.

SETTLEMENTS, RECOMMENDATIONS AND AWARDS

9. At any time that a complaint is under consideration by him the Ombudsman may seek to promote a settlement or withdrawal of the complaint by agreement between the complainant and the Bank named in the complaint.

10. If there is no such agreement, the Ombudsman, at the request of the complainant or the Bank named in the complaint, may make a recommendation for settlement or withdrawal of the complaint. However, he shall first give the complainant and the Bank at least one month's notice of his intention to make a recommendation; and during the period of that notice (or such longer period as the Ombudsman may agree) the complainant and the Bank may make further representations to the Ombudsman in respect of the complaint. A recommendation shall be in writing and shall include a summary of the Ombudsman's reasons for making his recommendation.

11. If :
    (a) the Ombudsman is minded to (i) propose that a complaint be settled or withdrawn on terms which appear to him to be acceptable to both the complainant and the Bank named in the complaint, or (ii) make a recommendation for the settlement or withdrawal of a complaint; and
    (b) that settlement or withdrawal would involve the provision by the Bank of valuable consideration (whether in the form of a money payment or otherwise);
    then, unless the Bank has otherwise requested or agreed, the Ombudsman's proposal or recommendation shall state that it is only open for acceptance by the complainant if he accepts it in full and final settlement of the subject matter of the complaint.

12. If the Ombudsman has made a recommendation which, within one month after it is made, has been accepted by the complainant but not by the Bank named in the complaint, the Ombudsman may make an award against any Bank named in the complaint. An award shall comprise a money sum not exceeding £100,000[1]. No award shall be of a greater amount than that which in the opinion of the Ombudsman is appropriate to compensate the complainant for loss or damage or inconvenience suffered by him by reason of the acts or omissions of the Bank against which the award is made.

13. An award shall be in writing and shall state the amount awarded and a summary of the Ombudsman's reasons for making the award. The award shall state that, if within one month after its issue the complainant agrees to accept it in full and final settlement of the subject matter of the complaint, the award shall be binding on the complainant and (in accordance with its undertaking to the Office) the Bank against which it is made. The Ombudsman shall issue a copy of the award to the complainant and the Bank against which it is made and shall issue to the complainant a form (addressed to the Ombudsman and the Bank) to be completed by the com-

plainant whereby he may accept the award in full and final settlement of the subjects matter of the complaint.

14. In making any recommendation or award under these Terms of Reference the Ombudsman shall do so by reference to what is, in his opinion, fair in all the circumstances, and:

    (a) shall observe any applicable rule of law or relevant judicial authority (including but not limited to any such rule or authority concerning the legal effect of the express or implied terms of any contract between the complainant and any Bank named in the complaint); and

    (b) shall have regard to general principles of good banking practice and any relevant code of practice applicable to the subject matter of the complaint; and

    (c) may deem in relation to a complainant any maladministration or other inequitable treatment by a Bank as being in breach of the obligation or duty owed to him by the Bank.

    The Ombudsman shall not be bound by any previous decision made by him or by any predecessor in his office. In determining what are the principles of good banking practice he shall, where he considers it appropriate, consult with the industry or elsewhere.

15. The Ombudsman shall not make a recommendation or award except in accordance with the provisions of paragraphs 10 to 14.

LIMITS ON THE OMBUDSMAN'S POWERS

16. The Ombudsman shall have power to consider a complaint made to him except:

    (a) to the extent that the complaint relates to a Bank's commercial judgment in decisions about lending or security (as defined in paragraph 29), but this shall not preclude the Ombudsman from considering complaints about maladministration in lending matters;

    (b) to the extent that the complaint relates to a Bank's general interest rate policies;

    (c) to the extent that the complaint relates to (i) any decision taken by a Bank in accordance with a discretion exercisable by it under any will or trust or (ii) any lack of consultation of beneficiaries by a Bank before exercising any such discretion (except where it is under a legal obligation to consult); but this shall not exclude complaints about maladministration in dealing with wills or trusts;

    (d) to the extent that the complaint relates to the provision by a Designated Associate by banking services of a kind excluded from the Ombudsman's consideration by a notice given by the nominating Member of that Designated Associate in accordance with the Office's Articles of Association;

    (e) if at any time it appears to the Ombudsman that it is more appropriate that the complaint be dealt with by a court, under another independent complaints or conciliation procedure or under an arbitration procedure;

    (f) if the subject matter of the complaint falls within the jurisdiction of any complaints, conciliation or arbitration procedure established by the Securities and Investments Board or by any Recognised Self-Regulatory Organisation;

    (g) if at any time it appears to the Ombudsman that (i) the amount which the complainant claims or could claim in respect of the subjects matter of the complaint exceeds £100,000[2]; or (ii) the claim comprised in the complaint is part of a larger claim which the complainant is making or could make, or is related to another claim which the complainant is making or could make, and the aggregate amount of all such claims exceeds £100,000[3];

(h) if any Bank named in the complaint duly gives the Ombudsman a notice of the kind described in paragraph 20.

17. The Ombudsman shall have no power to make a recommendation or award in respect of a complaint to the extent that the complaint relates to a practice or policy of a Bank which does not itself give rise to a breach of any obligation or duty owed by the Bank to the complainant.

18. Subject to the other provisions of these Terms of Reference the Ombudsman may consider a complaint which relates to charges made by a Bank for banking services but, in doing so, he shall have regard to any scale of charges published by that Bank and, in the case of Executor and Trustee business, to any authorisation for charging made by the testator or settlor.

19. The Ombudsman shall only consider (or, continue to consider) a complaint made to him if he is satisfied that:

(a) the complaint is made to him by or on behalf of the individual to whom or for whom the banking services in question were provided, or the personal representatives of that individual;

(b) the complaint is made to him by or on behalf of all the living persons collectively who are or may be entitled to make (whether or not to the Ombudsman) the claim comprised in the complaint, and all such persons are (or were) individuals: but so that personal representatives of any person so entitled may stand in his place after his death; but the Ombudsman may waive the participation of any person if he sees just cause to do so;

(c) the senior management of the Bank named in the complaint (at the management level notified to the Ombudsman) have had the opportunity to consider the complaint, but the applicant has not accepted any observations made or conditions of settlement or satisfaction offered by the Bank and deadlock has been reached;

(d) the complaint is made to him not later than six months after the Bank has informed the complainant that deadlock has been reached, and informed him at the same time of the existence of the Ombudsman and of the six months limit;

(e)(i) the act or omission giving rise to the complaint occurred on a date within six years of the complaint first being made to the Ombudsman or on a date after the Bank joined the scheme (whichever is the later date), unless the complainant could not with reasonable diligence have become aware of the relevant act or omission until after the later of these dates, and

(ii) in the case of a small company, such act or omission first occurred on or after 26 January 1993;

(f) except where relevant new evidence is available, the subject matter of the complaint was not comprised in a complaint by the same complainant (or any one or more of them) previously considered by the Ombudsman;

(g) except where the Bank named in the complaint consents in writing to the Ombudsman's considering it, neither the complaint made to him nor any other complaint by the same complainant (or any one or more of them) in respect of the same subject matter has been, is or becomes to the knowledge of the Ombudsman the subject of any proceedings in or before any court, tribunal or arbitrator, or any other independent conciliation body;

(h) the complainant and any other person to whom any Bank named in the complaint owes a duty of confidence in respect of any information which the Ombudsman may request that Bank to produce to him for the purpose of his consideration of a complaint have waived in writing that duty of confidence;

(i) the complaint is being pursued reasonably by the complainant and not in a frivolous or vexatious manner.

'TEST CASES'

20. At any time before the Ombudsman has made an award a Bank named in the complaint may give to the Ombudsman a notice in writing containing:
    (a) a statement with reasons that, in the opinion of the Bank, the complaint involves or may involve (i) an issue which may have important consequences for the business of the Bank or Banks generally or (ii) an important or novel point of law; and
    (b) an undertaking that, if within six months after the Ombudsman's receipt of the notice either the complainant or the Bank institutes in any Court in the United Kingdom proceedings against the other in respect of the complaint, the Bank will (i) pay the complainant's costs and disbursements (to be taxed, if not agreed, on a solicitor and own client basis) of the proceedings at first instance and any subsequent appeal proceedings commenced by the Bank (except by way of respondent's notice, cross-appeal or other similar procedure) and (ii) make interim payments on account of such costs if and to the extent that it appears reasonable to do so.
21. Upon the Ombudsman's receiving such a notice he shall consider the reasons given by the Bank and if he finds them reasonable he shall cease to consider the complaint and he shall inform the complainant in writing of the receipt of the notice, the date of its receipt and the effect of the notice upon the complaint, and shall send the complainant a copy of the notice.

OTHER POWERS AND DUTIES

22. The Ombudsman shall have overall responsibility for the conduct of business of the Office. He may appoint any Administrator to be responsible to him for day to day matters of administration. The Ombudsman shall have power to incur expenditure on behalf of the Office in accordance with the current financial budget approved by the Board.
23. The Ombudsman shall not exercise any power which the Articles of Association of the Office expressly assign to the Board, the Council or any other person.
24. In consultation with the Chairman of the Council and subject to his approval, the Ombudsman shall have power on behalf of the Office to appoint and dismiss employees, consultant, independent contractors and agents, and to determine their terms of employment or engagement.
25. The Ombudsman shall endeavour to attend each meeting of the Council and shall give the Council any information and assistance (including general information about any reference) which they reasonably request.
26. Save as mentioned in paragraph 27 or as required by any competent authority or as properly and reasonably required in connection with any legal proceedings instituted by or against the Office or any of its officers, the Ombudsman shall not disclose to any person (including a Board Member or Council Member) any information concerning a complaint considered by him from which it would or might be possible to identify the complainant or any Bank named in the complaint or any other information of a confidential nature which he has obtained in the course of his duties.
27. Paragraph 26 shall not prohibit the disclosure of any information to the complainant and any Bank named in the complaint or to the Chairman of the Council or any authorised deputy of the Chairman; or to any employees, consultant, independent contractor or agent of or with the Office to the extent that such information is reasonably required by that person for the purpose of performing his duties to the Office. And the Ombudsman shall report to the Bank concerned any threat to Bank staff or property of which he becomes aware in the course of his duties.

28.   At least twenty eight days before the Annual Meeting of the Council, the Ombudsman shall send to Council members (and also to Board members) a report containing, in relation to the preceding financial year of the Office, a general review of his activities during that year and such other information as the Council may reasonably direct.

INTERPRETATION

29. In these Terms of Reference:
   (a) the following expressions have the following meanings:
      'United Kingdom' does not include the Channel islands or the Isle of Man;
      'The Office' means the company called The Office of the Banking Ombudsman;
      'designated associate' has the meaning ascribed by the Office's Articles of Association;
      'Bank' means a Member of the Office or a Designated Associate;
      'banking services' means all banking services provided by Banks in the ordinary course of their business to individuals, and the provision by Banks of credit card services, executor and trustee services and advice and services relating to taxation, insurance and investments;
      'individual' includes a small company and a partnership or other unincorporated body of persons not consisting entirely of bodies corporate;
      'complainant' means an individual making a complaint to the Ombudsman;
      'Bank named in the complaint' means any Bank against which a complaint is made;
      'commercial judgment' means assessments of risk, of financial or commercial criteria, or of character;
      'decisions about lending or security' include any decision (or the consequences thereof) concerning any advance or similar facility, guarantee or security, whether or not actually made, provided or taken;
      'small company' means a company having a turnover of less than £1,000,000 in its last financial year prior to the Ombudsman's receipt of its complaint, and for this purpose:
         (i)   a company shall not be treated as a small company if it is a member of a group of companies (as defined below) having a combined turnover of £1,000,000 or more in the relevant financial year;
         (ii) the turnover of any company shall be determined by reference to its annual accounts for the relevant financial year or, if such accounts are not available, by such other means as the Ombudsman shall decide;
      'a group of companies' comprises the complainant company and:
         (i)   any company which is in the same 'group' (as defined in section 262(1) of the Companies Act 1985) as the complainant company; and
         (ii) any other company which appears to the Ombudsman to be controlled and managed by the same person(s) as control and manage the complainant;
   (b) references to the provision of banking services include, where the context admits, references to their non-provision;
   (c) a Bank shall be treated as providing banking services to an individual by virtue of its;
         (i)   being an executor, administrator or trustee of the will or on the intestacy of a deceased person or under a trust if the individual is a beneficiary under that will, intestacy or trust; or
         (ii) having the benefit of a guarantee or charge given or created by the individual in favour of the Bank to guarantee or secure any monies

owing to it by another individual under any advance or analogous facility; or

(iii) being the issuer of a cheque guarantee card accepted by the individual as guaranteeing payment of a cheque drawn in his favour; or

(iv) paying or collecting payment of a cheque of which the individual is the true owner or the individual entitled to immediate possession of it; or

(d) references to the singular number (including without limitation references to 'individual', 'complainant' and 'Bank') include, where the context admits, the plural number and vice versa;

(e) references to the masculine gender include the feminine;

(f) references to paragraphs are to paragraphs of these Terms of Reference.

NOTES TO APPENDIX 2

1 £50,000 in respect of events occurring before 25 January 1988.
2 £50,000 in respect of events occurring before 25 January 1988.
3 £50,000 in respect of events occurring before 25 January 1988.

Index

Shares
security over—
    completion of, 302–304
    creditor's rights and obligations,
        304, 305
    generally, 302
    partly paid shares, 304
**Society for Worldwide Interbank
    Financial Telecommunications**
See SWIFT
Solicitors
cheques—
    handling on behalf of clients, 212
generally, 66, 67, 163, 164
Special presentation
See CHEQUES
Standard securities
adjudication, effect of, 342
administration of debtor, 364, 365
assignation—
    fluctuating sum securities, 360, 361
    generally, 360
completion of title, 338, 339
constitution of, 337, 338
death of creditor, 361
death of debtor, 361
debt, meaning, 336
debtor and creditor, meaning, 336
discharge, 367
enforcement—
    personal obligation, 346, 347
    security—
        application of proceeds, 356
        calling up notice, 348, 349
        creditors, effect on, 355, 356
        duty to advertise, 351, 352
        duty to obtain best price,
            352–355
        entry into possession, 357–359
        foreclosure, 359
        generally, 347, 348
        notice of default, 349, 350
        prevention of by debtor, 353–355
        repair and improvement powers,
            359
        s 24 application, 351, 357
        sale of subjects, 351
        summary diligence, 346, 347
floating charges and, 341, 342
forms, 337, 338, 346, 347
generally, 332, 335
granter and grantee, meaning, 336
inhibition, effect of, 343
interest in land, meaning, 335, 336
liquidation of debtor, 363
proprietor, meaning, 336, 337

Standard securities—*contd*
ranking—
    catholic and secondary securities,
        340, 341
    fixed sum securities, 339
    fluctuating sum securities, 339, 340
    generally, 338
receivership of debtor, 363, 364
redemption, 366, 367
restriction of, 365
sale by debtor, where, 362
sequestration of debtor, 362, 363
standard conditions—
    generally, 344
    non-variable, 345, 346
    variable, 344, 345
variation of, 365, 366
warrandice, 338
Standing orders
generally, 248
Stock exchange securities
See SHARES
Stockbrokers
generally, 68
Subscription of deeds
See EXECUTION OF DEEDS
Summary diligence
Bill of exchange, 194
Supervision
audited accounts, duties as to, 31, 32
authorisation, *see* AUTHORISATION
banking names, 32–34
Banking Ombudsman Scheme, *see*
        BANKING OMBUDSMAN SCHEME
controllers of institutions, 29
deposit advertisements, 29
deposit protection scheme, 32
disclosure of information, 30, 31
European Union—
    generally, 37, 38
    single licence, 38, 39
general regulatory powers, 30, 31
generally, 14, 24, 25, 35
international standards, 37
overseas banks, 34, 35
reform of, 36, 37
SWIFT
countermand and, 239
generally, 251
Switch
See EFTPOS

Trade unions
customers, as, 56, 57
Trader's credits
generally, 248